BY CLARA BINGHAM

Witness to the Revolution: Radicals, Resisters, Vets, Hippies, and the Year America Lost Its Mind and Found Its Soul

Class Action: The Landmark Case That Changed Sexual Harassment Law (with Laura Leedy Gansler)

Women on the Hill: Challenging the Culture of Congress

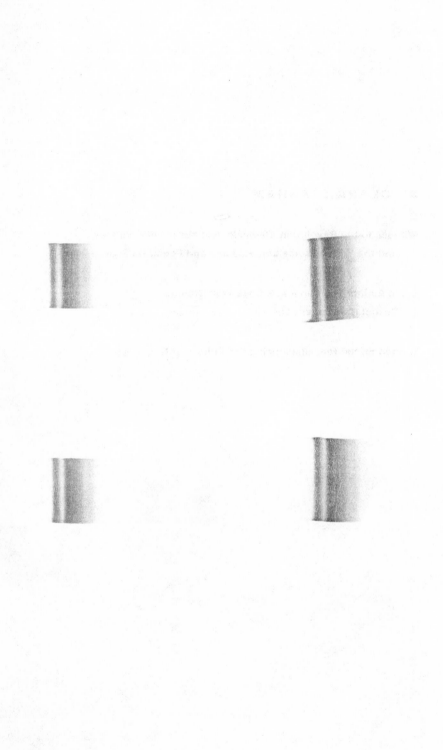

WITNESS TO
THE REVOLUTION

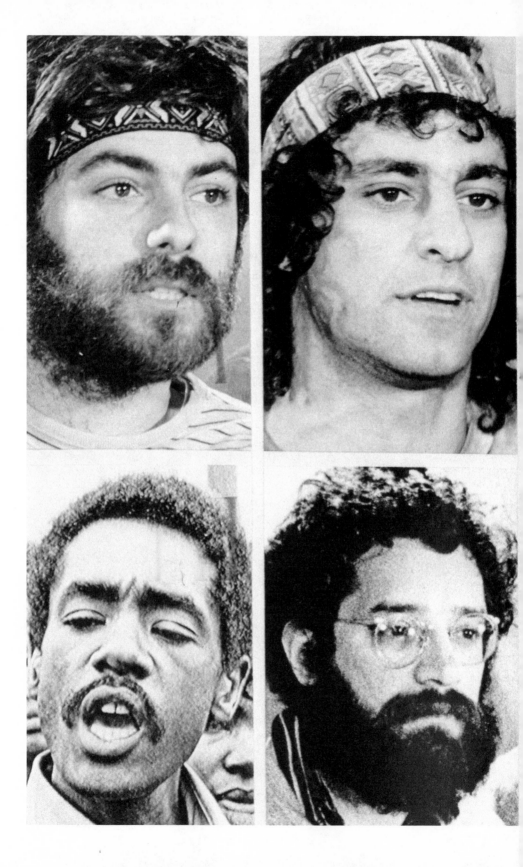

WITNESS TO
THE REVOLUTION

RADICALS,

RESISTERS,

VETS,

HIPPIES,

AND THE YEAR

AMERICA LOST

ITS MIND

AND FOUND

ITS SOUL

CLARA BINGHAM

Random House
New York

Published in the United States by Random House, an imprint and division of Penguin Random House LLC, New York.

RANDOM HOUSE and the HOUSE colophon are registered trademarks of Penguin Random House LLC.

Permission credits are located on pages 577–78.

LIBRARY OF CONGRESS CATALOGING-IN-PUBLICATION DATA
Names: Bingham, Clara, author.
Title: Witness to the revolution : radicals, resisters, vets, hippies, and the year America lost its mind and found its soul / Clara Bingham.
Description: New York : Random House, 2016. | Includes index.
Identifiers: LCCN 2015046134| ISBN 9780812993189 (hardback) | ISBN 9780679644743 (ebook)
Subjects: LCSH: United States—Social conditions—1960–1980—Interviews. | Social movements—United States—History—20th century—Interviews. | Student movements—United States—History—20th century—Interviews. | Vietnam War, 1961–1975—Protest movements—United States—Interviews. | Radicalism—United States—History—20th century—Interviews. | Nineteen sixty-nine, A.D.—Interviews. | Nineteen seventy, A.D.—Interviews. | BISAC: HISTORY / United States / 20th Century. | SOCIAL SCIENCE / Popular Culture. | HISTORY / Military / Vietnam War.
Classification: LCC HN59 .B49 2016 | DDC 303.48/40973—dc23
LC record available at http://lccn.loc.gov/2015046134

Printed in the United States of America on acid-free paper

randomhousebooks.com

987654321

First Edition

Book design by Barbara M. Bachman

FOR JOE

CONTENTS

POLITICAL TRIALS OF
THE LATE SIXTIES

Baltimore 4

Beaver 55

Boston 5

Buffalo 9

Camden 28

Catonsville 9

Chicago 8/7

D.C. 9

Fort Hood 3

Fort Hood 46

Harrisburg 7

Intrepid 4

Kansas City 4

Kent 25

Milwaukee 14

Motor City 9

New Haven 9

Oakland 7

Panther 8

Panther 21

Pittsburgh 26

Presidio 27

Seattle 8/7

Silver Spring 3

Tucson 5

TIMELINE

- August 15–18: Half a million people converge on a dairy farm in Bethel, New York, for the Woodstock Music & Art Fair, where thirty-three bands play.
- August 19: The film *Alice's Restaurant* is released, starring Arlo Guthrie. The film follows the travails of a hippie trying to avoid the draft.
- August 25–31: War Resisters' International holds its 13th Triennial Conference at Haverford College, in Pennsylvania. Pacifist Randy Kehler delivers a speech on draft resistance that inspires Daniel Ellsberg to copy and release the Pentagon Papers.
- August 26: The film *Medium Cool,* directed by Haskell Wexler, opens in theaters, and critics praise it for capturing the political unrest of the times.
- August 29: Weathermen meet in Cleveland to plan for the Days of Rage protests, scheduled for October.

- September 1: President Nixon announces the withdrawal of 35,000 U.S. troops from Vietnam, for a total of 60,000.
- September 2: Ho Chi Minh dies.
- September 3: Women from the Weathermen stage a "jailbreak" demonstration at South Hills High School in Pittsburgh.
- September 17: The movie *Bob & Carol & Ted & Alice* opens.
- September 24: Chicago Eight trial begins.
- September 26: At a news conference, President Nixon acknowledges popular opposition to the war but declares that "under no circumstances will I be affected whatever by it."
- September 29: Merle Haggard and the Strangers release the anti-

hippie single "Okie from Muskogee." By November the record reaches No. 1 on the *Billboard* Hot Country Singles chart.

OCTOBER 1969

- October 1: The Beatles release *Abbey Road* in the United States.
- October 1: Daniel Ellsberg, with the help of his former RAND Corporation colleague Anthony Russo, begins copying the Pentagon Papers in Santa Monica, California.
- October 3: *The Selling of the President 1968* by Joe McGinniss appears on the *New York Times* bestseller list.
- October 5: The Weathermen bomb the Haymarket police statue in Chicago.
- October 8: Six RAND Corporation foreign policy experts, including Daniel Ellsberg, write an open letter to *The New York Times* calling for unilateral U.S. withdrawal from Vietnam.
- October 8–11: The Weathermen stage the Days of Rage riots in Chicago. Police arrest more than 120 protesters.
- October 9: The Illinois governor calls in the National Guard to control crowds protesting outside of the Chicago Eight trial.
- October 11–16: The New York Mets defeat the Baltimore Orioles to win the World Series. "If the Mets can win the World Series, the United States can get out of Vietnam," says Mets pitcher Tom Seaver.
- October 15: The Moratorium to End the War in Vietnam takes place across the country, and 2 million people peacefully participate in what is the largest protest against the war to date.
- October 24: Twentieth Century Fox releases *Butch Cassidy and the Sundance Kid,* starring Paul Newman and Robert Redford.
- October 29: Black Panther cofounder Bobby Seale is gagged and manacled to his chair at the Chicago Eight trial.

NOVEMBER 1969

- November 1: Jefferson Airplane releases the album *Volunteers.*
- November 3: Nixon delivers his Silent Majority speech to a television audience of 70 million people. Following the speech, the president's approval ratings climb from 52 percent to 77 percent.
- November 12: Seymour Hersh breaks the My Lai massacre story.
- November 15: Half a million protesters gather for the Moratorium March on Washington.
- November: Jeremy Rifkin and Tod Ensign launch the Citizens' Commission of Inquiry to publicize American war crimes in Indochina.

- November 24: Mike Wallace interviews Private Paul Meadlo on the *CBS Evening News*. Meadlo tells the story of the My Lai massacre in graphic detail to 30 million television viewers.
- November 30: Steppenwolf releases its most controversial and antiwar album, *Monster*.

DECEMBER 1969

- December 1: The first draft lottery takes place.
- December 1 and 19: A Cook County, Illinois, grand jury indicts sixty-four Weathermen on thirty-seven counts of aggravated battery, resisting arrest, mob action, and other offenses arising from the Days of Rage in October.
- December 4: Black Panthers Fred Hampton and Mark Clark are killed in their sleep by the Chicago police.
- December 5: The Rolling Stones release *Let It Bleed*.
- December 6: The Weathermen bomb several Chicago police cars, stating in a communiqué that it is in retaliation for the Hampton and Clark shootings.
- December 6: Altamont Free Concert is held at the Altamont Speedway, near Livermore, California. Three hundred thousand people attend "Woodstock West," and four die.
- December 8: Hundreds of Los Angeles police officers wearing military gear, bearing M16 rifles, and driving armored cars raid the Black Panther office in South Central. The Panthers hold off the police in a five-hour shoot-out before surrendering.
- December 8: Charles Manson and four others are indicted for the murders of Sharon Tate and her friends. The grand jury goes on to indict the five plus Leslie Van Houten for the murders of Rosemary and Leno LaBianca.
- December 11: Thousands of Black Panther supporters rally in Los Angeles to protest the police raid on the Panther office.
- December 27: The ROTC building at the University of Wisconsin–Madison is firebombed in reaction to the My Lai massacre.
- December 27–31: The Weathermen meet in Flint, Michigan. "War Council" leaders refocus the group on covert strategies, with plans to attack institutions of the U.S. government. Taking their fight underground spurs the group to change its name to the Weather Underground Organization (WUO).
- December 31: Brothers Karl and Dwight Armstrong attempt unsuc-

cessfully to bomb the Badger Army Ammunition Plant in Baraboo, Wisconsin.

- December 31: The total U.S. death toll in the Vietnam War reaches 43,021. For the calendar year 1969 11,363 American soldiers were killed, down from a peak in 1968 of 16,899.

JANUARY 1970

- January 1: The National Environmental Policy Act becomes law, leading the way to the formation of the Environmental Protection Agency.
- January 1: Gil Scott-Heron releases his first record, *A New Black Poet: Small Talk at 125th and Lenox*. On it Scott-Heron introduces the black power song "The Revolution Will Not Be Televised."
- January 3 and 4: The New Year's Eve Gang, led by Karl and Dwight Armstrong, firebombs the University of Wisconsin–Madison Armory, Gymnasium, and Primate Lab.
- January 6: Simon & Garfunkel release the album *Bridge Over Troubled Water*.
- January 14: Felicia and Leonard Bernstein host ninety people at their Manhattan apartment to raise money for the Panther 21 defense fund.
- January 21: Timothy Leary receives a ten-year sentence for a 1968 Laguna Beach, California, arrest for possession of two marijuana "roaches." While in custody Leary gets another ten years, for a 1965 drug bust at the Texas-Mexico border.
- January 22: President Nixon devotes much of his State of the Union speech to the environment: "Clean air, clean water, open spaces—these should once again be the birthright of every American. If we act now, they can be."
- January 31: New Orleans police bust Grateful Dead soundman and legendary LSD manufacturer Augustus Owsley Stanley III, known as Bear. Stanley is charged with possession of narcotics, LSD, and barbiturates. He goes to jail for two years, where he takes up metalworking.

FEBRUARY 1970

- February 2: Pretrial hearings in the Panther 21 case begin in New York City.
- February 16: A pipe bomb explodes in the San Francisco Police Department Golden Gate Park station. Sergeant Brian McDonnell is killed by shrapnel. The case is never solved.
- February 18: Jury convicts five of the Chicago Seven for intent to riot, but acquits them of conspiracy charges. Judge Julius Hoffman sen-

tences the defendants to five years in jail and fines each five thousand dollars. Militant protests erupt in response to the convictions, which are overturned in 1972.

- February 21: The Weather Underground bombs the home of Judge John Murtagh, Sr., a New York State Supreme Court justice presiding over the Panther 21 trial. No one is injured.

MARCH 1970

- March 2: The National Book Award for Arts and Letters goes to Lillian Hellman for her memoir *An Unfinished Woman*.
- March 6: Weather Underground members Theodore Gold, Diana Oughton, and Terry Robbins die in a Greenwich Village townhouse when a bomb they were making accidentally detonates.
- March 9: Two officials of the Student Nonviolent Coordinating Committee, Ralph Featherstone and William "Che" Payne, die when a bomb on the floor of their car explodes along U.S. Route 1, south of Bel Air, Maryland.
- March 11: Crosby, Stills, Nash & Young release their debut album, *Déjà Vu*, featuring the counterculture anthems "Almost Cut My Hair" and "Teach Your Children."
- March 11–12: In Annapolis, Maryland, the Citizens' Commission of Inquiry holds its first hearing on Vietnam War atrocities. Veterans testify, giving their firsthand accounts. In April and May, CCI hosts more hearings in Boston, Los Angeles, New York City, and Buffalo.
- March 16: American Civil Liberties Union lawyer Eleanor Holmes Norton files a gender discrimination complaint on behalf of forty-six *Newsweek* women employees—the first of its kind.
- March 18: Approximately one hundred women take over the offices of the *Ladies' Home Journal,* stay for eleven hours, and demand that the magazine hire a woman editor in chief.
- March 25: Jimi Hendrix's new group, Band of Gypsys, releases the song "Machine Gun."
- March 25: Jane Fonda embarks on a two-month cross-country road trip, visiting off-base GI coffeehouses to learn the extent of antiwar sentiment growing among servicemen.
- March 26: *Woodstock,* the three-hour documentary, is released in theaters nationwide. The film wins the Academy Award for Best Documentary Feature.
- March 30: Chicago police and the FBI discover a sophisticated

Weather Underground bomb factory on Chicago's north side. No arrests are made.

- April 2: Federal indictments are leveled against twelve members of the Weather Underground for the Days of Rage demonstrations, to little avail. Eleven members are already in hiding.
- April 9: Brothers Philip and Daniel Berrigan, both Catholic priests, refuse to surrender to authorities to serve a three-year jail sentence for destroying draft files at the Catonsville, Maryland, Selective Service office. The brothers become fugitives.
- April 10: The Beatles break up.
- April 13: Nine women, including editor Robin Morgan, are arrested after a five-hour sit-in at Grove Press, protesting pay inequity.
- April 15: Linda Evans and Dianne Donghi of the Weather Underground are arrested in New York City for Days of Rage indictments.
- April 20: Nixon announces the withdrawal of 150,000 U.S. troops from Vietnam.
- April 21: Fugitive priest Philip Berrigan is arrested by the FBI at Riverside Church in New York City and sent to jail.
- April 22: The first Earth Day—20 million people take to the streets all over the world in peaceful demonstrations urging environmental reform. It is the largest protest in history.
- April 22: Yale students strike for the first time in the university's 268-year history, in support of the Black Panthers who are on trial in New Haven, Connecticut.

- May 1: President Nixon announces a joint U.S. and Army of the Republic of Vietnam invasion of Cambodia combining ground forces and airpower. The invasion surprises the nation and sparks intense opposition.
- May 1: Fifteen thousand students and activists protest in a May Day rally at Yale to support Black Panthers Bobby Seale and Ericka Huggins, who are on trial in New Haven. President Nixon dispatches National Guard troops as jury selection begins.
- May 4: Thirteen students are shot and four killed by the Ohio National Guard at Kent State University. Across the country, seven hundred university campuses shut down and more than two and a half million students strike.

- May 5: David Harris, Joan Baez, and their infant son, Gabriel, appear on the cover of *Look* magazine.
- May 6: The Grateful Dead play a free concert at Kresge Plaza on the campus of the Massachusetts Institute of Technology to protest the Kent State killings.
- May 7: Lieutenant John Kerry is a guest on *The Dick Cavett Show*. Kerry speaks out in opposition to U.S. involvement in Vietnam.
- May 8: The Hard Hat Riot takes place in lower Manhattan—200 construction workers attack 1,000 people protesting the Kent State shootings and the Cambodian invasion. More than seventy people are injured.
- May 9: President Nixon talks to protesters at the Lincoln Memorial at dawn before one hundred thousand people rally on the Ellipse.
- May 10: In response to the Kent State shootings, the Weather Underground bombs the National Guard headquarters in Washington, D.C.
- May 10: The Boston Bruins win the Stanley Cup, defeating the St. Louis Blues. Bobby Orr scores the winning goal and is named most valuable player.
- May 11: Jimi Hendrix plays at a benefit to raise money for Timothy Leary's defense fund at the Village Gate in Greenwich Village.
- May 12: Six black men are shot dead by police in Augusta, Georgia, during a protest over the killing of a mentally handicapped black teenage prisoner.
- May 13: Columbia Pictures debuts the film *Getting Straight,* with Elliott Gould and Candice Bergen.
- May 14: Police shoot and kill two black students and injure twelve during a demonstration at Jackson State College in Mississippi.
- May 21: The Weather Underground issues its first communiqué, announcing a "Declaration of a State of War" against the U.S. government and expressing allegiance with the counterculture.

JUNE 1970

- June: John Kerry joins Vietnam Veterans Against the War. The organization expands rapidly as tens of thousands of soldiers return home in 1969 and 1970.
- June 9: The Weather Underground bombs the New York City police headquarters in response to "police repression."
- June 27: The Festival Express: Janis Joplin, the Grateful Dead, the Band, and other performers travel across Canada on a train for five days giving concerts.

- June 28: Gay pride marches take place on the first anniversary of the Stonewall riots, in New York, San Francisco, Los Angeles, and Chicago.

JULY 1970

- July 1: New York becomes the first state in America to legalize abortion.
- July 26: The Weather Underground bombs the Presidio army base in San Francisco on the eleventh anniversary of the Cuban Revolution.

AUGUST 1970

- August 2: Fugitive and former Cornell University chaplain Daniel Berrigan gives a surprise sermon at a Methodist church in Germantown, Pennsylvania: "I come in the name of all those who have said no to this war—from prison, from the underground, from exile, from death itself."
- August 5: Black Panther Huey Newton is released from jail and five thousand celebrate him outside the Alameda County Courthouse in Oakland, California.
- August 7: Armed seventeen-year-old Jonathan Jackson holds a judge, a prosecutor, and three jurors hostage in San Rafael, California, hoping to force the release of his imprisoned brother, revolutionary George Jackson. Four die in the ensuing gunfire, including the judge and Jackson.
- August 12: Fugitive Daniel Berrigan is seized by undercover FBI agents posing as bird watchers on Block Island, Rhode Island.
- August 18: J. Edgar Hoover puts fugitive and former UCLA assistant professor Angela Davis on the FBI's Most Wanted Fugitive list.
- August 24: The Madison, Wisconsin, bombing of Sterling Hall math center kills thirty-three-year-old physics graduate student Robert Fassnacht.
- August 26: Women's Strike for Equality (fiftieth anniversary of the adoption of the Nineteenth Amendment). Twenty-five thousand people in New York City march down Fifth Avenue, demanding equal pay for equal work and free abortion on demand.

SEPTEMBER 1970

- September 1: The Senate rejects, by a vote of 55–39, the McGovern-Hatfield Amendment to set a December 31, 1971, date for U.S. withdrawal from Vietnam.

- September 4–7: Operation "Rapid American Withdrawal" takes place and 200 Vietnam veterans march from Morristown, New Jersey, to Valley Forge State Park in Pennsylvania.
- September 12: Timothy Leary escapes from jail in San Luis Obispo, California, with the help of the Weather Underground, and becomes a fugitive in Algeria.
- September 18: Jimi Hendrix dies from a drug overdose in London.
- September 26: *The New Yorker* publishes "The Greening of America" by Charles A. Reich. The nearly seventy-page article describes the revolution of a new generation and the coming change of consciousness.

Witness to the Revolution is an oral history. The core of this book comes from one hundred interviews I conducted between 2012 and 2015 with members of the Vietnam antiwar movement of the late sixties. I began the process of writing *Witness* by editing tens of thousands of pages of transcripts and shaping them into a tightly woven chronological narrative. Occasionally, I used secondary sources when they fit among the first-person voices in the book—usually from memoirs or diaries of witnesses to that historical time. To provide context, I relied on the substantial body of published sixties scholarship in writing chapter introductions, footnotes, and biographical sketches of each "voice" in the book.

THE AWAKENED GENERATION

We were a whole generation that, for the first time, said No to a war that the country had found itself mired in, and then began saying No to other things, and did so awkwardly at times and with bombast and rhetoric and prick waving but at least was questioning the death grip of the 1950s, which was a stultification of passion and sanity and the genius of the human spirit. . . . And this burst through all of that with Day-Glo colors like in *The Wizard of Oz* when it goes from black-and-white to color. Everything suddenly was Technicolor and there was hope.

—ROBIN MORGAN

IN AUGUST 1969, HALF A MILLION STONED AND SCRUFFY PILGRIMS descended on Max Yasgur's farm near Bethel, New York, and Woodstock Nation was born. One week later, a RAND Corporation defense analyst had an epiphany. Daniel Ellsberg vowed to do everything within his power to stop the Vietnam War, even if it meant going to jail for treason. Two months later, Ellsberg began photocopying seven thousand pages of top-secret Vietnam War documents that he planned to leak to the press. That October a record two million people participated in the nationwide Moratorium protest to end the war—a figure so high that the antiwar movement could no longer be written off as radical fringe. A month later journalist Seymour Hersh broke the story of the massacre of hundreds of civilian women and children by American soldiers in the Vietnamese village of My Lai.

It is almost impossible to imagine the apocalyptic atmosphere of America in those months. From the start of the academic year in 1969 until the beginning of classes in September 1970, a youth rebellion shook the nation in ways we may never see again. It was the crescendo of the sixties, when years of civil disobedience and mass resistance erupted into anarchic violence. Hundreds of thousands of young Americans took to the streets in 1969 and 1970. They were fueled by marijuana, LSD, and rock and roll; inspired by the third-world freedom revolutions of Che Guevara in Cuba and Ho Chi Minh in Vietnam; disillusioned by the assassinations of Martin Luther King, Jr., and Robert F. Kennedy; battered by the police at Berkeley, Chicago, and Columbia; and appalled by mounting U.S. casualties and images of napalm-disfigured Vietnamese civilians.

And yet, the school year of 1969–70 has gone largely overlooked. In popular memory the sixties crested in 1968, with the assassinations of Bobby Kennedy and Dr. King, with the Tet Offensive and Nixon's victory in November. The usual mental jump from '68 to Watergate obscures a crucial historical moment—1969–70—when the sixties went wide and the nation arguably came close to civil war. This book is the story of twelve months that changed the nation forever. In early-twenty-first-century America, when political debate is often confined to shouting on cable television or posting on Twitter, it's even more valuable to revisit an era when arguments over politics and culture were palpable, urgent, even *revolutionary*.

I use that word advisedly, for the United States was then veering awfully close to just that: a rebellion that threatened the very order of society. *Witness to the Revolution* offers eyewitness accounts from people who were on the front lines of a dazzling period of change and challenge. This book explores what it *felt* like to be alive and active in this extraordinary moment. My hope is to help readers understand, through dozens of firsthand accounts, the circumstances that made such a large segment of the population become outlaws. Together the stories of the participants of what was known as the "awakened generation" create a portrait of a movement that deserves credit for having the courage to try—even if it failed in many ways—to make the nation live up to its ideals.

For three years, I traveled the country talking to the leaders and foot soldiers of the sixties peace movement. Most of the one hundred people I interviewed were early baby boomers born in the mid-1940s, and all of them played an important role in bucking the system. White, black, male, female, they were almost to a person traumatized and transformed by their experiences during that time. "I'm certainly a victim of post-traumatic stress syndrome," Tom Hayden told me. "I think everybody, whether they went to 'Nam or not, everybody had a life that was profoundly altered," said John Perry Barlow.

Grown men and women wept in many of my interviews, their wounds still fresh, their anger and frustration from that time still hot. Daniel Ellsberg, at age eighty-three, broke down when he recalled listening to draft resister Randy Kehler give a speech about going to jail. So did photographer John Filo when he described taking a Pulitzer Prize–winning photograph of a dying student at Kent State. Many were still anguished by their mistakes. Mark Rudd apologized for the Weather Underground's violent, destructive tactics; Jane Fonda wished she could rewind the fateful moment when her picture was taken in front of an anti-aircraft gun in Hanoi.

THE WAR OVERSHADOWED EVERYTHING. A Gallup poll of students conducted in the spring of 1967 revealed that 35 percent considered themselves "doves" and 49 percent "hawks." Yet the numbers had moved dramatically by 1969, with 69 percent identifying as "doves" and only 20 percent as "hawks." By January 1970, the bloodshed in Vietnam had become increasingly intolerable, and for the first time a majority of Americans believed the United States had made a mistake sending troops to fight there.

In 1969 discharged Vietnam soldiers organized in large numbers, creating a powerful new force in the antiwar movement: Vietnam Veterans Against the War. More and more GIs resisted the military from inside the military, and thousands deserted, creating a near mutiny. It was the year that Students for a Democratic Society (SDS), founded in 1960, splintered, and a group of militant radicals calling themselves the Weathermen became a media sensation and began to dominate the New Left's political landscape. That year the Chicago Eight conspiracy trial put the generation gap—the yawning disconnect between those under thirty and their parents—on the stand in Judge Julius Hoffman's courtroom. The FBI launched a covert campaign to disrupt and destroy the Black Panther Party, which in many ways was the vanguard of the revolution. In December 1969 Black Panthers Fred Hampton and Mark Clark became movement martyrs after they were gunned down in their sleep by the Chicago police.

A thousand antiwar protesters christened Richard Nixon's new presidency on January 20, 1969, by pelting his inaugural parade motorcade with rocks and bottles. In his first week in office, Nixon ordered the ramping up of secret FBI intelligence on all left-wing radicals. He never delivered on his campaign pledge to end the war but instead escalated it with massive secret bombing campaigns. In the first two years of his administration, Nixon so heightened the air war that by the end of the conflict the United States had dropped more bombs on Southeast Asia than it did worldwide during all of World War II.

By mid-1969 it was clear that four years of the peace movement's efforts to end the war were lost on the Nixon administration, and an increasing number of what Nixon called "America's youth" descended into deep despair and mounting rage. Meanwhile, the draft displaced the lives of 27 million young men as they reached the age of eighteen between 1965 and 1973, politicizing an entire generation. Author Kirkpatrick Sale, who chronicled the student movement in the sixties, called this acutely politically engaged cohort "the awakened generation."

Enraged by Nixon and Kissinger's escalation of the war and frustrated to the point of madness by the impotence of their efforts to end it, some reacted with violence while others found solace in "making the personal political." In March 1970, three Weathermen accidentally killed themselves while building a bomb in a West Village townhouse. This was also the year when women brought the revolution home, split from their male comrades in the antiwar left, and launched the "second wave" women's liberation movement.

By 1970 at least two million Americans had tried LSD, and up to three million lived in communes. Thousands of fugitives were on the run from

An anti–Vietnam War protester in San Francisco on November 16, 1969, holds a sign that sums up the point of view of millions of youth in the late sixties.
PHOTOGRAPH BY ROBERT ALTMAN.

the draft, bombing and disturbance charges, and draconian drug laws. Federal prisons held 3,250 draft resisters, and the Department of Defense reported that more than 400,000 men had deserted the armed forces, with about 100,000 fleeing to foreign countries, including Canada and Sweden. An entire generation seemed to be living outside the law. The counterculture set up shop in Haight-Ashbury, Big Sur, Laurel Canyon, Cambridge, the East Village, and Madison. These "free zones" became safe havens for draft resisters, dodgers, and military deserters. The cross-pollination of left-wing activists with hippie drifters and dropouts, who were all part of the same Great Refusal to conform, created a new brand of rebel.

Nixon announced the invasion of Cambodia May 1, 1970, and days later the National Guard, in response to student protests, killed four white students at Kent State and two African American students at Jackson State. Soon after, the largest student strike in American history erupted, and two and a half million students boycotted classes, shutting down seven hundred colleges. During that academic calendar year, nine thousand protests and eighty-four acts of arson and bombings plagued schools.

The Scranton Commission, appointed by Nixon after Kent State, warned that the student strikes had imposed a "crisis as deep as the Civil War [and] if this crisis of understanding endures, the very survival of the nation will be threatened." FBI director J. Edgar Hoover compared student unrest to the violent coal and steel strikes of 1919–22. *Life* magazine concurred when it declared, "Never in the history of this country has a small group, standing outside the pale of conventional power, made such an impact or created such havoc."*

In late August 1970, radicals at the University of Wisconsin detonated a truck bomb that destroyed an entire university building, accidentally killing a thirty-three-year-old graduate student. Two weeks later, Timothy Leary, imprisoned for marijuana possession, escaped from jail with the help of the Weather Underground, high jinks that publicly sealed the alliance between the counterculture and the political left. As Leary's lawyer Michael Kennedy said in a September 1970 press conference, "This is the year of dope and dynamite, flowers and flames."

The country was coming unhinged. By the end of 1970, American deaths in Vietnam had reached 53,849, and 52 percent of Americans reported knowing someone who had been injured or killed in Vietnam. In 1969 and 1970 alone, 13,600 American soldiers came home to Delaware's Dover Air Force Base in flag-draped coffins, their mournful ceremonies televised nationally. This was more than twice the number of casualties that would occur decades later in ten years of fighting in Iraq and Afghanistan. In total, the grueling ground war and relentless U.S. bombing attacks would take the lives of three million Vietnamese.

---

* Edward Kern, "Can It Happen Here?," *Life*, October 17, 1969, quoted in Kirkpatrick Sale, *SDS* (New York: Random House, 1973), p. 10.

———

AS OF THIS WRITING, six people I interviewed for this book (Tod Ensign, Stanley Karnow, Albert Maysles, Richard Moose, Haskell Wexler, and Michael Kennedy) have died. Most of the people I talked to were in their late sixties and early seventies, ready to reflect and analyze the impact history made on their lives and the impact their lives made on history. It felt like the right time to ask this generation to talk about an era that was so vivid, so violent, so infuriating, and, at times, so much fun.

Witness is a narrative oral history that recounts some of the events between August 1969 and September 1970 in chronological order, and also dips back in time to reveal what shaped the lives of the book's main actors. For example, the students at Kent State did not take to the streets to protest the invasion of Cambodia in a vacuum. Each person I interviewed, whether they were journalists or students shot by the National Guard, had been personally and politically shaped by the events of previous years. As much as I tried to tame the scope of this book by limiting its timeline to one year, its footprint is much larger. The movement was by definition leaderless and divided into so many, often quarreling, factions defined by race, gender, violence or nonviolence, civilian or military, communist radicals or party-line Democrats. I describe this wide scope and complex weave of movements and events through the emblematic experiences of some of its most engaged players.

THE TERM *YOUTHQUAKE* BARELY captures the destructive vibrations of this anti-establishment explosion. "If you didn't experience it back then," Nixon aide Stephen Bull told me, "you have no idea how close we were, as a country, to revolution." No matter which side of the White House fence you were on, the future looked perilous. "America was on the verge of a civil war every day," Daniel Ellsberg told me. Bill Ayers concurred: "I was convinced that we were on the verge of a revolution. I'd never been in one. I had only read about it. But I was convinced that the contradiction between the American people and its government was so great, and so profound, that it was unresolvable, and we were zooming towards some kind of cataclysmic explosion between us and them."

Charles Reich, a Yale law professor, struck a chord when he published *The Greening of America* in September 1970. Reich believed that at the heart of the revolution was a change in conscience that challenged the country's core values. "The [Vietnam] War did what almost nothing else could have," Reich wrote. "It forced a major breach in consciousness. And it made a gap in belief so large that through it people could begin to question all the other myths of the corporate state." Reich considered the hippies to be the revolution's most effective foot soldiers. "The violence with which some older people have reacted to long hair shows that they feel a threat to the whole reality that they have constructed and lived by." Reich alleged that the sixties shook the foundation of America's social structure, creating a permanent cultural revolution. "The present revolution goes beyond anything in modern history. Beside it, the French Revolution and the Russian Revolution were mere shifts in the base of power," wrote Reich. *The Greening of America* climbed to number one on the *New York Times* bestseller list, sold two million copies, and overnight Reich became a celebrated sage. His optimistic take on the social upheaval of the time gave hope to readers who were ardently trying to make sense of the sixties.

The new pursuit of self-determination posed an existential threat to America's 1950s backbone of traditions, laws, and customs. Jack Nicholson's character George in the 1969 cult film *Easy Rider* describes "straight" America's reaction to the hippie menace to Dennis Hopper's character, Billy, before George is beaten to death and Billy is shot by southern redneck characters:

> GEORGE: They're scared of what you represent to them.
> BILLY: All we represent to them is someone who needs a
>   haircut.
> GEORGE: What you represent to them is freedom.
> BILLY: What the hell is wrong with freedom? That's what it's
>   all about.

GEORGE: That's what it's all about all right. But talking about it
and being it—that's two different things. It's real hard to be
free when you are bought and sold in the marketplace. . . .
When they see a free individual, it's going to scare them. . . .
It makes them dangerous.

FORTY-FIVE YEARS LATER, REICH'S utopian vision for America can
seem naïvely idealistic, and Reich himself admits that he has spent the last
several decades watching the "ungreening of America." The political revolution never took place. The New Left didn't overthrow the government.
Nixon was reelected in a landslide in 1972, and the Vietnam War dragged
on until 1975 (with American troops withdrawing in 1973). Capitalism is
thriving, and economic inequality has reached nearly Gilded Age proportions.

From the ashes of the destruction and extremism of the sixties and
early seventies rose the victorious Reagan Revolution, and the nation took
a turn to the right. As California's law-and-order governor in the late sixties, Ronald Reagan called the Berkeley campus of the University of California "a haven for communist sympathizers, protesters, and sex deviants."
Vietnam, our most unpopular war, left a dark stain on the American
psyche, and hyperpatriotism became salve on the wounds inflicted by a
decade of self-criticism and revolt. The sixties and its excesses were a convenient scapegoat in the country's quest to shed the Vietnam syndrome.
Along the road to revisionism, hippies were mocked, New Left radicals
vilified, and the antiwar movement tarnished for being traitorous and anti-
veteran. Now, almost half a century after My Lai, Kent State, and the Moratorium to End the War, we can see with clearer eyes the genetic imprint
that the decade's denouement has left on the DNA of our country.

Generations X, Y, and Z have been raised by their baby boomer parents, many of them members of Woodstock Nation, and the conventional
conformism of the 1980s has evolved into gay marriages populating the
New York Times wedding pages, medical marijuana legalization in twenty-
four states, women permitted to serve in combat positions in every branch

of the military, and renewed diplomatic relations with Cuba. America elected our first African American president in 2008, and President Barack Obama (born in 1961) wrote in his memoir *The Audacity of Hope,* "I've always felt a curious relationship to the sixties. In a sense, I'm a pure product of that era." Obama came of age after the dust settled and, like many members of his generation, he is unscarred by the decade's political and cultural wars, yet a direct beneficiary of them.

Your opinion of the sixties today—whether you think the rebellion pushed the country toward Shangri-La or Armageddon—may depend on your political views. Former president Bill Clinton (born in 1946 and a Yale Law School student of Charles Reich) describes this divide: "If you look back on the sixties and, on balance, you think there was more good than harm, then you're probably a Democrat. If you think there was more harm than good, you're probably a Republican."

Almost everyone born before 1960 has a strong opinion about the sixties and the Vietnam War, and the debate continues. "The war to explain the war has gone on for longer than the war," former Weather Underground leader Bernardine Dohrn told me. "How can we still be fighting Vietnam? But we are. Why? Because it was a mass popular resistance, and the truth was told about it. It was subversive of the whole structure of what we value and what we do." No other antiwar movement was as widespread and threatening to the status quo as opposition to the Vietnam War. "The 1965–75 peace movement reached a scale which threatened the foundations of the American social order," said SDS founder Tom Hayden, "making it an inspirational model for future social movements and a nightmare which elites ever since have hoped to wipe from memory."

WITNESS IS A SELECTIVE HISTORY. It provides a snapshot portrait of the many movements and events of 1969–70, and it leaves readers to draw their own conclusions. I tried to understand what motivated people to act the way they did, and capture the visionary idealism and high passion of that year and decade, but I didn't shy away from revealing the excess and squalor of the times—the drug abuse, sex abuse, commune chaos, radical political irrationality, and violent extremism. *Witness* touches only lightly on the black experience, feminism, and the music scene, and doesn't delve into gay rights, Native American rights, the environmental movement, and pop art. There just wasn't room enough in one book.

Born in 1963, I approached each interview as an intergenerational exploration into a decade that I was too young to know, but which always fascinated me. I grew up in New York City in the late 1960s and early '70s; my earliest political memories are of feminist and antiwar activist Bella Abzug's election to the House of Representatives in 1970, and the first African American woman to run for president, New York congresswoman Shirley Chisholm, in 1972. Photos of these two pioneers covered the walls of my Upper West Side bedroom. They were my hometown heroines.

When I graduated from high school in 1981, at the dawn of the Reagan Revolution, former hippies like Ben Cohen and Jerry Greenfield had become ice cream entrepreneurs, and California kids who had taken LSD in high school were starting personal computer companies in the Bay Area. Some members of the New Left switched to the right, but most dropped their radical ideals and adopted more centrist liberal ones.

When I went to college, I didn't think twice about coed dorms, women's and African American studies departments, tenured female professors, and premarital sex. Wars were being fought covertly, the draft would never come back, and the streets were mostly quiet, except for those of us who protested against apartheid in South Africa. When I graduated in 1985, free to pursue the career of my choice, I still felt I had missed the party. The turmoil and passion of the 1960s was a hazy memory, and even hazier was the understanding of what could possibly have mattered so much. Why had so many people just fifteen years before taken to the streets and sacrificed their lives, their livelihoods, their comfort, even their sanity? That is the question *Witness to the Revolution* tries to answer. What follows is what they told me.

WITNESS TO
THE REVOLUTION

CHAPTER 1

THE DRAFT

(1964–1967)

We are people of this generation, bred in at least modest comfort, housed now in universities, looking uncomfortably to the world we inherit.

—PORT HURON STATEMENT,
STUDENTS FOR A DEMOCRATIC
SOCIETY, 1962

THE ROOTS OF THE VIETNAM ANTIWAR PROTEST MOVEMENT CAN BE traced to the American crusade for civil rights. In August 1964, Congress authorized the use of troops in Vietnam in response to the Gulf of Tonkin incident—the alleged North Vietnamese attack on a U.S. naval ship. That same month, civil rights workers put their lives on the line for voter registration in the Mississippi Summer Project. Seven months later, on Sunday, March 7, 1965, John Lewis and six hundred protesters were filmed being beaten as they walked across the Edmund Pettus Bridge in Selma, Alabama, at the start of their march to Montgomery for voting rights; the images of the attack on a nonviolent protest vividly dramatized the stakes of the struggle. Just one day after Bloody Sunday, the first U.S. combat troops landed in Vietnam. "I don't see how President Johnson can send troops to Vietnam and can't send troops to Selma, Alabama," Lewis, chairman of the Student Nonviolent Coordinating Committee (SNCC), remarked. The military draft exploded soon after, ultimately calling 2.2 million men to fight in Vietnam. Skills learned on the battleground for racial equality in the South—mass civil disobedience and grassroots organization—were soon employed in the new campaign against the war in Vietnam. In reaction to the disproportionate number of black soldiers being killed in Vietnam, SNCC activists organized one of the first anti-draft demonstrations, at the Atlanta induction center in 1966, and coined the slogan "Hell no, we won't go!" The war over there was soon to become a war over here.

DAVID HARRIS
(Stanford student, draft resistance organizer)

I came from Fresno, California, where I was Fresno High School "Boy of the Year" in 1963. Several weeks after I got to Stanford, there was a meeting about volunteers going to Mississippi. This was the first time that the black students in Mississippi had issued an invitation to white students to come down, and they invited students from Stanford and Yale. In the fall of '64, I started classes and was meeting my girlfriend for dinner and she said, "I was at a meeting. There's a car going down to Mississippi tomorrow." They were running a parallel election in Mississippi called the Freedom Vote, to show what would happen if black people were allowed to vote, and they needed volunteers, so I said, "I'm going." I told my brother to call my parents after I was gone, and I got a seat in the car and left that night.

Two days later, we were in Mississippi. I was worried about missing the great adventure of my time. You didn't have to have an ideology or politics to go to Mississippi in those days. You just had to have values.

That summer of '64 we had all been watching what was going on in Mississippi,* so it was a no-brainer for me. Campaigning for the right of black people not to be lynched for trying to vote was a pretty easy call. So I went. I was eighteen years old.

---

* In the summer of 1964, in what was called the Freedom Summer, or the Mississippi Summer Project, nearly 1,500 mostly white, northern college students organized by SNCC and the Congress of Racial Equality (CORE) went to Mississippi to help register black voters. At the time, Mississippi had the lowest percentage of registered African American voters in the country—a dismal 6.7 percent.

WESLEY BROWN (Black Panther, draft resister)

My family moved to East Elmhurst, right near LaGuardia Airport, in 1952. It was formerly an Italian neighborhood, but as more blacks moved in, of course, the whites made their departure. By 1955 it was nearly an all-black neighborhood. These were working-class blacks trying to move up. They saved their money like my parents, and bought a home, and tried to enter the lower middle class. My father was a machinist at a tool and die factory in the Bronx, where he worked for about forty years. Queens at that time was called God's country. If you could get out of the projects and buy a house in Queens, you were on your way. It was a very solid, tight-knit community where parents wanted to make a better life for their kids. In fact, Eric Holder, President Obama's first attorney general, lived on our block. My sister used to babysit him and his younger brother, Billy. So it was that kind of neighborhood. Everyone was trying to do the right thing, be responsible, and trying to make a way for themselves and their families. And of course, that leads to a certain amount of conservatism, a wish not to stir things up.

These were black folks who knew their history, because they were only the second generation born after emancipation. My father's grandmother was born into slavery and he knew her. She would show him her thumb, which was all splayed out and deformed, because when she did something that the overseer didn't like, he would take a razor blade and split her thumb open, and it would never heal sufficiently before he would open it up again. My father was born in North Carolina and was the tenth of twelve children. These black folks knew what this country had been through with slavery and segregation and they weren't prepared for their children being boisterous and assertive in a way that they couldn't afford to be.

DAVID HARRIS

Four of us were working together in a team trying to register people for the Freedom Vote, in the black part of a town called Lambert. After working all morning, we came back to where the car was parked, and the three guys wanted to go to the post office to mail some letters and I said, "I'll stay here by the car." I'm standing by our car, and up pulls a pickup truck with two white guys in it. They get out. One's got a shotgun; the other one's got a pistol. The guy with the shotgun sticks it right up against my nose and says, "Nigger lover, I'm giving you five minutes to get out of town before I blow your head off." I'm an eighteen-year-old Stanford student. "Well, what do you mean? Who are you?" And he just says, "Nigger, I said five minutes." At that point, the other three guys came back, took one look at the situation, and we all jumped in the car and left Lambert, Mississippi.

WESLEY BROWN

I remember vividly the photographs in *Jet* magazine of Emmett Till in his casket in 1955. His mother wanted an open casket so people could see what was done to him—his misshapen face that was bludgeoned into non-recognition.* And I remember watching those kids in Little Rock in '57 trying to go to Central High and Eisenhower finally getting the National Guard to come in, so that they could go to school without being killed. The memory of those images and the virulent hatred directed at those kids was indelible for me. And of course, there were the Freedom Rides, the lunch counter sit-ins by those students from Shaw University in North Carolina, and the 1955 Montgomery Bus Boycott. We got our first television in 1949, so all of these images were a part of my coming of age.

DAVID HARRIS

Everything that followed grew out of the Mississippi taproot. We learned how to organize by working with SNCC in Mississippi, and perhaps

---

* Emmett Till, a fourteen-year-old African American boy from Chicago, was visiting his cousins in Money, Mississippi, in August 1955 when he was accused of flirting with a white female store clerk. He was kidnapped by two white men, bludgeoned, shot to death, and dumped in a river. When his maimed body was discovered, his mother insisted that it be displayed in an open casket for two days in Chicago, and more than ten thousand people came to the viewing and the funeral. In September a panel of white male jurors found the two murderers innocent (they later confessed) despite the abundance of evidence to the contrary. Till's murder sparked large protests and served as a catalyst for the emerging civil rights movement. Jesse Jackson called Till's murder the "Big Bang" of the civil rights movement.

much more important was the spirit of Mississippi; there was a kind of inspiration in the heroism of the black people in Mississippi. It's really hard to recapture what that was like. For example, we were working in Quitman County; the county seat is called Marks. There was a seventy-five-year-old black woman there who walked into the registrar of voters office and said, "I want to register to vote." They arrested her, threw her in jail, tortured her with an electric cattle prod, and then released her from jail. She walked out of jail and down the street to the registrar of voters office and said, "I want to register to vote." These are people whose names are lost to history, but when you have that kind of encounter, somehow you get a whole new perspective on what's of value and how to behave in the face of oppression, and the strength that any single person or a group of people can bring with their own will.

The third thing that came out of Mississippi was the experience of seeing America from a different perspective. You see what was being done to black people for simply trying to exercise the rights that we supposedly won with hard-fought battles a hundred years ago. And to see not only that that was going on, but how the rest of the country had turned a blind eye to it and talked bullshit about the southern way of life, and courtly manners. Isn't it sweet? These were mean, vicious, narrow-minded people, who were standing on the backs of people who were helpless to fight back. And everybody in America let that happen. So suddenly, you come back from that, and you can't look at it the same way. It was precisely that perspective that brought the Vietnam War into focus.

WESLEY BROWN

So I was at SUNY Oswego in January 1965, on Lake Ontario, in central New York, and some SNCC workers came to speak. I was already feeling that I wanted to be a part of something that was going on that I felt would make a difference. I was about twenty years old at that point. Their visit changed my life in many ways, and I decided to go to Mississippi.

My parents couldn't believe that I would put myself in harm's way, given what had happened in Mississippi the year before. They left the

South in the thirties, as many blacks did, because of the Depression, to find work in the North as part of the Great Migration. They couldn't believe that I would return to a place that they left.

I remember taking a Port Authority bus in June of 1965 to Memphis, about a twenty-eight-hour bus ride, and then having to get another bus to

Working on the 1964 Freedom Summer campaign to register black voters in Mississippi, James Chaney (twenty-one) from Meridian, Mississippi, Andrew Goodman (twenty), and Michael Schwerner (twenty-four), both from New York City, were abducted and murdered on June 22 by members of the local Ku Klux Klan. Their bodies were discovered forty-four days later buried in an earthen dam. The murders caused a national uproar.

Holly Springs, Mississippi. So that began the four months I spent in northern Mississippi, right near the Tennessee border, working on voter registration.

DAVID HARRIS

Right after I got back from Mississippi came the first major escalations of the Vietnam War, when all of a sudden we went from advisor status to deploying full combat units there, and the rise to six hundred thousand troops began. I marched in my first antiwar march about six months after I got back from Mississippi.

My father was an officer in the Army Reserve for twenty years. My brother ended up a captain in the Eighty-second Airborne Division. I've had ancestors in every war starting with the revolution. Like all my generation, I assumed that we would have a war to fight. We grew up watching *Victory at Sea* on television. But when the war that they had for us came, it was obvious this wasn't what I thought I would be doing. This wasn't about freedom or democracy or wearing white hats or helping people. This was essentially keeping a bunch of scumbags in power and prolonging the French Empire. Coming back from Mississippi, I could believe it.

WESLEY BROWN

A few days after my arrival, I was sent to Jackson, Mississippi, for a demonstration with the intent of filling up the jails. Within minutes of getting out of the car in Jackson, I was arrested, and thrown into a field house with hundreds of protesters, because the city jails were full. Before bail was set, the lawyers were interviewing people, and they asked me, "Do you want us to get in touch with your family to let them know where you are?" It was Father's Day, and this lawyer talked to my father, and wished him happy Father's Day for me. After I got out a week later, I contacted my parents and I let them know that I was okay. It was a very emotional and not a happy time for them.

Like any parents, my father and mother did not want their children to have to go through the things they had gone through when they lived in the South. They shared my beliefs but didn't want me to have to deal with the consequences of my beliefs. My father used to say, "You can't get up in the face of the powers that be. You have to find a way to work around the system, but if you make too much noise and draw attention to yourself, you're just setting yourself up for a fall."

DAVID HARRIS

I considered myself part of the movement from the day I left for Mississippi. What we call "The Movement," capital *T*, capital *M*, was a commitment to justice and the values of democracy. They called us the New Left because it wasn't an ideology. There wasn't a specific politics attached to it. What it was, was a set of values finding ways to express themselves.

I was in marches, I was in rallies and demonstrations. But there was always the larger question of the conscription system. In that era, when any male turned eighteen, he had to go to the post office and register for the Selective Service System. When you registered for Selective Service, they gave you two cards. One was proof that you had registered, and the other indicated your classification. Because under the Selective Service, there were various classifications, starting from 1-A, which meant you were cannon fodder, to you were going to get a notice soon in the mail saying "Report to 4-F," which meant you were physically unable to perform and therefore exempt. In between that, the largest one was 2-S, which was the student deferment. Anybody in college making, quote, "reasonable progress towards a degree" had a temporary exemption until they finished their education. So that was the system that covered all of our lives—all of the male lives, anyway.

Always there was floating out there, what happens when they call your number? We—understandably—focused on that a lot. I mean there were people going to graduate school so that they wouldn't get drafted. There were people getting married so they wouldn't get drafted, because early on, being married was an exemption. They weren't going to draft family men. They thought if I want to take a year off and just go to Paris and write poetry, you're headed for the tall grass if you do that. This defined everybody's life.

WESLEY BROWN

After I left Mississippi and returned to college, I went to the school registrar with a friend and we asked that our student deferment classifications not be sent to the Selective Service, because we felt that it discriminated against blacks who didn't have the opportunity to go to college. The registrar went ballistic but honored my request, and my classification was changed to 1-A, which meant I was subject to be drafted. But because I had been arrested in Mississippi, my classification was changed to 1-Y, which meant that if you had an outstanding legal charge against you, you wouldn't be among the first who would be called.

DAVID HARRIS

What got me was a sense of moral responsibility, whether you like it or not, it's your war. This is yours. You participate in a society; you're responsible for what the society does. I had read a lot about the Indian Revolution and Gandhi and the use of satyagraha, or truth force. I, like everybody, watched what was going on with the war, in which more and more people were doing things that Americans were never supposed to do. Ultimately, we killed two million people, for Christ's sake, and left God knows how many people crippled for life, including generation after generation. Agent Orange is still working its way through the gene pool in Southeast Asia, and we're the ones who put it there. We committed massacres from thirty thousand feet. We walked into villages and burned them down. We followed a strategy of forcing people out of the countryside into the urban areas that we could control, and we did that by desecrating their culture and killing them and forcing them to run.

I got elected Stanford student body president at the end of my junior year, in '66. Nobody expected me to be student body president, including me. At that time, student politics at Stanford was fraternity row. Everyone put on their suits and ties and did whistle-stop campaigns around the campus, and I was in my movement uniform, blue work shirt, Levi's, moccasins. I had what passed for long hair in those days. It was over my ears. That was considered amazing in those days. This was at the same time

Haight-Ashbury was forming up thirty miles north in San Francisco. There was this kind of lead cultural edge. I had one big musical rally for my campaign, in which, to get a sound system for the rally, we traded a lid of marijuana with Jefferson Airplane* for the use of their system.

Fraternities at that time didn't want anything to do with someone like me, and we had a really radical platform. We were talking about student control of student justice, equal rights for women students. They hadn't gone to coed dorms. Typically, if you and your girlfriend stayed out all night, nothing happened to you and she was kicked out of school, because she was supposed to sign in at ten o'clock. They had all this in loco parentis bullshit. Part of our platform was ending cooperation with the war in Vietnam, legalizing marijuana. We threw it all in there, because I didn't care. Hey, if I lose, I lose. I'm counting on losing. At the interfraternity council the first question was "Well, what do you think of fraternities?" And I said, "I think fraternities are a pile of shit." I took 60 percent of the fraternity vote in the election. Go figure.

I won in the biggest turnout by the biggest margin in the history of Stanford student politics. So all of a sudden, Stanford has a radical student body president. If I had been at Berkeley and gotten elected, nobody would have noticed, but suddenly I was noticed. Stanford was the other end of the political spectrum from Berkeley, supposedly.

MICHAEL KAZIN

(Harvard leader of Students for a Democratic Society)

I grew up in New Jersey, and both my parents were liberal Jews. I went to teach-ins, and the first antiwar demonstration SDS [Students for a Democratic Society] sponsored in 1965. I joined the Young Democrats of America [YDA] first, and then I got recruited to join SDS.[†] I think I was

---

*   Jefferson Airplane, a band founded by Paul Kantner and Marty Balin in California in 1965, was a pioneer in the psychedelic rock genre.

†   Students for a Democratic Society (SDS) was a New Left student organization founded in Ann Arbor, Michigan, in 1960 by student activists Tom Hayden and Alan Haber. By the late sixties it became one of the leading antiwar organizations, with about one hundred thousand members, with chapters at hundreds of colleges.

the only person who was on the executive board of both SDS and the Young Democrats at the same time, but then I became so disgusted by the war that I quit the Young Democrats. The war was a great dividing line at the time. The YDA slogan in '64 was "part of the way with LBJ." Well, that was unsustainable by '65, '66, once U.S. troops took over the brunt of the fighting and we started bombing the North. So I couldn't be a Young Democrat anymore, at least in that context, because I felt like being a Young Democrat was supporting the administration, which was prosecuting the war. There were Democrats like Al Lowenstein, Eugene McCarthy, and Bobby Kennedy who could be critical of the war and still be Democrats, and people supported them. But at the time, I was nineteen, twenty years old, I saw politics as a moral pursuit, and I thought it was immoral to remain a Young Democrat.

I went to Harvard in '66 and became one of the chairs of SDS. A few years later, the Selective Service System was interested in me because I had taken the fall off to cut sugarcane in Cuba. And then they called me up—I was still a Harvard kid, and my local draft board liked that fact. They didn't have that many kids going to Harvard from my hometown. But then I burned my draft card—I actually rolled marijuana in my draft card and smoked it; you know, a little combination of counterculture and politics—at a party. I told the draft board that I'd done that, and I told them that they could take their 2-S and shove it, or words to that effect, because I didn't think that I should get a deferment when some working-class kid could not get a deferment. So they called me up for a physical.

DAVID HARRIS

I was trying to make up my mind about what to do about the draft. I had one more year, plus every year you have to renew your student deferment. Each year that became harder for me, because I didn't believe in student deferments. Why should rich people be exempted from the war? If we're going to fight wars, everybody's supposed to fight. I didn't think this war was worth fighting, but I didn't think that separating the classes, in terms of who does combat and who doesn't, was right. So that became harder, and then that year the Selective Service System amped things up. Not only was the draft call getting bigger and bigger, but they created a new system where they were going to administer a test every year so that you could prove you were making reasonable progress towards a degree.

They were going to come onto the Stanford campus, with the cooperation of the university, to give this goddamn test, which raised all kinds of questions, like whose university is this? Why is the university cooperating with this kind of thing? This is not in line with the values that are supposed to hold sway in a university. You believe in the life of the mind, and the life of the mind doesn't napalm people. That was the last straw for me. I refused to take the test.

There was a sit-in at Stanford against the test, just after I was elected student body president, which I joined. So at that point I had made up my mind that I wasn't going to do this. Right after the end of the school year, I sent a letter to my local draft board with my draft cards enclosed. It said, "I'm not carrying these ever again. And if you don't like it, you know where to find me."

MICHAEL KAZIN

I thought it was a horrible war, and resisting the draft in any way you could was fine. I think we helped get the U.S. out of Vietnam by so many people resisting the draft. Did I do it in the most moral way possible? No. I have friends who went to jail. I didn't do that. The physical was in the middle of May and some friends of mine and I were scheduled for a physical the same day. We sat around calling out answers to the questions to make sure everyone failed it. We decided we had to make it a democratic procedure, so at each stop along the way of the physical—give urine, get your lungs tested—we said, "Let's have a vote! Do we want to do this or don't we? Discussion?" We stretched it out as much as we could.

In the end I saw a psychiatrist and I told him I would shoot my officers if they drafted me, I lied and said I was a homosexual, and I pretended to stutter seriously. I remember he put his hand on my shoulder and said, "Mike, you should get some help." I guess he believed me.

DAVID HARRIS

It's fall quarter. I'm student body president. I had gotten an invitation from one of the fraternity row houses at Stanford, and I was kind of surprised. But, I thought, hey, I'll go. So I'm about twenty yards from this row house, and a guy steps out from behind a bush and he says, "Mr. Harris?" And I thought, Why is this guy in a Beta jacket and penny loafers calling me Mr. Harris? All of a sudden, the rest of them jumped out, grabbed my arms, my legs, and carried me into a vacant lot. They had some clippers, and they were going to cut my hair off, and my beard. They were all wearing Halloween masks.

I recognized some voices, a couple of guys who were in my freshman house. They weren't saying much, but I thought, Hey, I never get to talk to these people. What the hell? I recognized the voice of this one guy whose nickname was Gooey. I said, "Gooey, is that you out there?" I said, "Jesus. Are you guys working with the Ku Klux Klan or something?" I just was giving them shit.

They made it through cutting my hair off, and took a picture of me while my hair was being cut, that they gave to the *San Francisco Chronicle,* which ran it the next morning. Their thought was the student body was going to rise up, proclaim them to be their liberators, and thank God somebody did this to this hippie fuck. But instead the opposite happened, and they solidified my standing and political power on campus.

The hair-cutting incident was a manifestation of the cultural and political divide that was going on in America between the ones who wanted things to be the way they were and the ones who wanted things to be different. That's the simplest way to put it. We didn't accept the way the institutions were being run. We didn't accept the policies that were made by the government. On the other side, there were these guys who said, "Love it or leave it."

JOHN PERRY BARLOW (Grateful Dead lyricist)

I graduated from Wesleyan in 1969 and the draft board in my hometown of Pinedale, Wyoming, wanted to draft me because I was the only hippie from

Pinedale. People forget the country was divided into two extremely hostile camps. The cowboy culture in Pinedale was definitely not pro-hippie, and I was definitely a hippie. I'd come back there from Wesleyan, to have a few drinks in a bar, and this little bus would stop on its way from Jackson to Rock Springs, and if a long-haired guy got off the bus to go to the bathroom, they'd come out of the bar and nab him and take him off into the alley and shave his head. That was the kind of stuff that was going on. So I would come home with this long hair, and they'd take a run at shaving my head.

MICHAEL KAZIN

As I walked out of my physical, I saw this guy with short hair who was waiting to go in. I was a draft counselor, so I knew ways he could get out even then, and I said, "Hey, I could get some papers, you can say you are a conscientious objector, you can delay this process or get out of it completely." He was very nervous and he said, with a strong Southie accent, "What do you mean, man? If I don't pass this physical my parents are going to kill me. Every man in my family has been in the military, going back to World War I, and I got no job anyway, and I better not fail this physical." That was an important moment for me. It helped me understand that with the moral righteousness and self-righteousness of a lot of people like me in the New Left, we were missing the emotions, the needs, of a broad swath of America. The war wasn't doing them any good, but we didn't understand the problems they had. I thought we were not reaching the people. We were pissing them off—the "people" meaning primarily white working-class, lower-middle-class people.

JOHN PERRY BARLOW

I was very worried about the draft, and I had finally shaped my future expectations around it. I was just going to resist, and then at the last minute, I thought, Ah, I don't know. I don't want to do this if there's a way around it. So I went to a series of doctors' offices in Hartford, and in Middletown, Connecticut, and stole letterhead from ear, nose, and throat specialists. I studied stress-induced asthma and wrote a bunch of letters attesting to my

Young men burning draft cards in New York's Central Park in 1967.

having a fairly serious case of it, and then I showed up for my induction physical in Salt Lake with these letters. The guy at the end of the line read them, and gave me a 1-Y, which meant that I was drafted if they attacked us, which seemed pretty unlikely. I'm starting to walk away and he said, "Hey. Let me see those letters again." So I go back and I hand him the letters, and he looks at them and he says, "You put in a lot of work on these." And I said, "What makes you think I wrote them?" And he said, "If it had been me, I would have used a different typewriter for each one." And then he said, "What are you going to do if I tell you to get on the bus?" I said, "Well, you're going to have to call a federal marshal because I'm not getting on that bus." And he said, "Really?" And I said, "No, I'm not." And he looked at me for a long time and he said, "Well, you know, I get about thirty cowboys in here every week that cannot wait to kill a gook. And I can't see a good reason to make you kill one. So take your letters and take your 1-Y and get out of here." I was completely dumbfounded to be in the state of unanticipated liberty.

WESLEY BROWN

Because of my involvement in Mississippi, I found it reprehensible that I could be asked to put my life at risk in the Mekong Delta, when the rights and lives of blacks in the Mississippi Delta were not being protected. I could not, in good conscience, put myself at risk, ten thousand miles away, to fight for values that were not being honored in the country of my birth.[*] I was put in touch with Howard Moore, who was a lawyer for SNCC, and I explained my situation to him, and he said, "You might be interested in being part of a case that Rabinowitz, Boudin, and Standard are trying to create."[†] They were a very progressive law firm that had been providing legal assistance for civil rights workers. The lawyers wanted to have conscientious objection to the war accepted on moral grounds, not just religious grounds if you were a Quaker, or a Jehovah's Witness. My objection to the draft was on the basis of a personal moral code, which was the kind of case that Victor Rabinowitz, Leonard Boudin, and Michael Standard were trying to build. So I was interested and I wrote a statement, which they worked on with me, that I sent to the Selective Service Board. The firm was trying to collect all of these draft resisters under one umbrella and then present this case, saying that young men should be exempt from military service because of a personal moral code, because, ethically, they found the war abhorrent.

---

[*]   Heavyweight boxing champion Muhammad Ali refused military induction in April 1967 and was stripped of his heavyweight title, passport, and boxing licenses. "I ain't got no quarrel with those Viet Cong," said Ali, who had applied for conscientious objector status because of his Muslim faith. Ali said: "My conscience won't let me go shoot my brother, or some darker people, or some poor hungry people in the mud for big powerful America. And shoot them for what? They never called me nigger, they never lynched me, they didn't put no dogs on me, they didn't rob me of my nationality, rape and kill my mother and father." Ali was banned from boxing for three years, but his conviction for evading the draft was overturned by the U.S. Supreme Court in June 1971.

[†]   In January 1966 SNCC created a sensation when it became the first civil rights organization to officially oppose the war in Vietnam. The catalyst was the murder of Samuel Younge, Jr., a SNCC worker and Vietnam vet who had lost a kidney in the war. Younge, a student at the Tuskegee Institute, was murdered by a white gas station attendant for trying to use a whites-only restroom. "The murder of Samuel Young [*sic*] in Tuskegee, Alabama, is no different than the murder of peasants in Vietnam, for both Young and the Vietnamese sought, and are seeking, to secure the rights guaranteed them by law," the SNCC statement read. "In each case, the United States government bears a great part of the responsibility for these deaths." As a result of the controversial statement, the Georgia legislature refused to allow Julian Bond (SNCC's communications director) to take the oath of office and declared the seat to which he had just been elected vacant. Bond sued and won his case, *Bond v. Floyd,* in the Supreme Court. SNCC and SDS created an official partnership in defiance of the draft in July 1966.

DAVID HARRIS

In the fall of '66, my local draft board had sent me a notice saying, "You're 1-A," because I hadn't taken the student deferment. And that was followed by an order to report for a pre-induction physical. So I go to the pre-induction physical in Fresno. At that time, for the only time in its history, they were drafting for the Marine Corps, because the Marines had suffered so many casualties that they didn't have enough volunteers to cover them, so the sergeant running my physical took great pride in saying, "We're going to take you into the Marines, boy." By the spring of '67, I was essentially on notice. I was going to be drafted. At that point, myself and three other people founded the Resistance. We were essentially going to organize a national draft card return, where, on October 16, 1967, young men from around the country were going to gather at various places and collect draft cards and give them to the government. In our case, we did it in front of a San Francisco federal building. The location that got the most ink was in Boston, where Dr. Spock was. They had all these older people that the press wanted to talk about. We were just a bunch of draft-aged people. We got three hundred in San Francisco. I think there were twelve hundred that day.

The pitch was "Take your life into your own hands. Are you going to be part of the machine or are you going to be against the machine? Are you going to kill people randomly in Southeast Asia or are you going to stop that?" We went after the antiwar movement saying, "Look, saying you're against the war is nice, but it isn't going anywhere. If you're against the war, then act like it. How can you be against the war when you carry a draft card in your pocket? You've got to put yourself on the line before you start telling other people how to behave." It meant the potential of five years in prison. We were asking people to act proactively and to commit civil disobedience. In the classic sense of civil disobedience: no hiding. Which is why we didn't burn draft cards. We wanted them to have the evidence.

I can remember, in San Francisco, there was a crowd of us out in front of the federal building and we sent a basket out and it came back with draft cards in it. Then all of a sudden somebody out there would say, "Come on, back here," and we'd send it out again, and more draft cards, and send it out and more draft cards. And finally we were there on the steps of the federal building, and out came the federal attorney—who was a black man by the name of Cecil Poole. At that point, a resister from Berkeley, a guy named Dickie Harris, takes the basket of cards, walks over to Poole, and says, "Brother Poole, are you head nigger here?" and dumps the draft cards at Poole's feet. He, of course, walks off and leaves them there, so we scoop them all back up in the basket and take them up to the federal attorney's office, where the door is locked, so we leave this basket full of draft cards out in front of the door. It was an act of defiance, but it was also throwing down the gauntlet. You know who we are. We ain't hiding. You want to make your law work? Then bust us. Ultimately, the idea was to disable the Selective Service System, but short of that, to make the point.

Why am I supposed to degrade myself? Rub bear grease all over my body and stay up for five nights taking meth? Make up some crazy story? Tell them I was fucking my sister? I was standing up for me, the person I was. I wouldn't want to pretend to be somebody else in order to deal with these assholes. And whose country was it? My grandmother was in the Daughters of the American Revolution. My people have been around here a long time. Let Lyndon Johnson move to Canada. I'm not Canadian. My attitude was, We're standing up here. We're going to force the issue and make them lock people up in order to prosecute their war—because, if nothing else, people were going to notice.

Once we founded the Resistance, I left Stanford—with fifteen incomplete units short of a degree. I never have gotten a college degree. *

---

* David Harris announced the formation of the Resistance at a march in San Francisco on April 15, 1967, held by the Spring Mobilization Committee to End the War in Vietnam. Harris told the crowd: "This war will not be made in our names; this war will not be made with our hands; we will not carry rifles to butcher the Vietnamese people and the prisons of the United States will be full of young people who will not honor the orders of murder."

CHAPTER 2

PSYCHEDELIC REVOLUTION

(1960–1967)

The danger of LSD is not physical or psychological, but social-political. Make no mistake: the effect of consciousness-expanding drugs will be to transform our concepts of human nature, human potentialities, existence. The game is about to be changed, ladies and gentlemen. . . . Head for the hills or prepare your intellectual craft to flow with the current.

—TIMOTHY LEARY, *The Politics of Ecstasy*

LSD, USED WIDELY IN THE LATE 1960S, WAS THE SECRET INGREDIENT that helped to propel a transformation in attitude and lifestyle that challenged nearly every principle that had supported American society and culture in the 1950s. It was called a "revolution by consciousness," or a "psychedelic revolution." By 1970, at least two million Americans had dropped acid, and one-third of all college students had smoked marijuana. The escalation of the Vietnam War and resistance to the draft in the second half of the decade, combined with the psychedelic-fueled counterculture, created a nationwide spontaneous combustion.

RALPH METZNER (Harvard psychologist)

I was a graduate student in clinical psychology at Harvard, where Timothy Leary and Richard Alpert were both professors. They were ten years older than me. The Harvard psychology department was dominated by behaviorists. There was one part of the psychology that was behaviorism, working with rats and pigeons. That was B. F. Skinner, the arch-behaviorist. But then there was the Department of Social Relations, which was a brilliant innovation because these were PhD students in clinical psychology, personality psychology, cultural anthropology, and sociology, all working together.

Richard Alpert was teaching there. He was a junior professor. Timothy Leary was a research psychologist. He had written a book on interpersonal diagnosis of personality—he was a hardcore behaviorist.* In the summer of 1960, while vacationing in Mexico, Leary ate some magic mushrooms and tumbled through the entire evolutionary process right down to a single-celled organism and back up, which is a classical mystical experience, but formulated in the terms of somebody who has a modern education and a PhD.

I think Leary was the first person that described his mystical experience in the language of modern science; the early people described it in the language of religion or oneness with God. He said, "This is reliving the entire evolutionary process." Nobody knew that you could actually do that because people had never described it before. So Leary decided he was going to devote the rest of his life to that, which is pretty much what happened to me, too, and many other people who worked on the project.

We then started doing a number of research projects, as graduate students are supposed to do at universities like Harvard, and on one of the first ones I worked on, we recognized that LSD changes your consciousness; it doesn't change your behavior. And so right there was the first fateful step, where Leary parted company with his department chair and other professors, because they were all stuck with "You don't *take* the drugs that you're researching. You give it to a rat or a human being or a pigeon and observe their behavior." And Leary said, "Well, there isn't any behavior to observe."

It's all interior. Leary used to say, "There's no behavior to observe, the person who's taking the drug is just sitting there or lying there and not

---

* Behaviorism is an approach to psychology that studies the impact of environmental variables on controlling behavior.

saying anything, and every now and again he might say, 'Whew, amazing!'" If you want to know what's going on, you have to actually ask the person, or better still, take it yourself. It's not true of other drugs, but LSD is not like other drugs. For example, the question people were asking, "Well, what does this drug do?" You can't answer it, because it depends on the set and the setting, and the internal expectations and the knowledge that you bring to it.

DAVID HARRIS (Stanford student, draft resistance organizer)

I first dropped acid when I was a sophomore. At that time, right next door to Stanford in the town of Menlo Park, Richard Alpert was running clinical experiments on LSD. So there was a lot of pharmaceutical-grade, Sandoz-manufactured LSD floating around the underground at Stanford. In those days it was a spiritual experience to trip on acid. You read *The Tibetan Book of the Dead* before taking acid and prepared for this kind of spiritual journey. It was the spring of '65. Timothy Leary was not yet a factor on the West Coast.

I was in the second-floor dormitory room in Stern Hall with my buddy Peter Kaukonen, who was the younger brother of the lead guitarist of Jefferson Airplane, Jorma Kaukonen, and the first guy I'd ever seen with long hair. He and I took acid together. The first two hours, you're untethered. Part of what happened culturally was having the experience of being outside of control. You were suddenly in a psychic state that you couldn't control. You had no option but to flow with it. It was one of those moments where you let go. And once you let go, then all of a sudden things were a whole lot different in the world. This was still at a time on the Stanford campus when drugs were a pretty minority proposition. I can remember, with Peter, sitting in the student union passing a joint back and forth, and nobody had a clue what the fuck we were doing.

JOHN PERRY BARLOW (Grateful Dead lyricist)

I was raised a fairly devout Mormon in Wyoming, and actually became more devout than my parents were, as an early teenager, but was hit hard by adolescence. I got a motorcycle, turned my whole Boy Scout troop into a motorcycle gang, quit going to church, and stopped believing in any kind of coherent divine force, but I missed it a lot.

So when I heard that there was this substance that would make you experience the holy, I was really interested, and started trying to seek it out among the various circles that I had available to me at Wesleyan. Dick Alpert was a graduate student at Wesleyan not long before I got there—it was just that kind of a place. Wesleyan had a wonderful Indian music program where Ravi Shankar, Ali Akbar Khan, and all the big stars played. They would have these curry concerts out in a beautiful farmhouse in the woods of Connecticut on Friday nights. It's sort of surprising that I took it for the first time so insouciantly, especially now that I realize that, in some fundamental way, you only take LSD once. I was a different person after that than the person that I'd been before, and it certainly had the desired effect as far as I was concerned.

I started out getting the experience listening to Ravi at a farmhouse in Connecticut in 1966 and then wandering out into the snowy woods and looking at every snowflake individually for the miracle that it was, and became a true believer. I think the world would generally be a better place if everybody dropped acid, under the right circumstances. But I was very much of the view that it was something that needed to be done with presence of mind and a lot of care taken to be in the right setting.

DAVID HARRIS

About the same time I took acid for the first time, Ken Kesey* was doing his Trips Festival in the city. Kesey was also a figure around Stanford, because he lived up in the hills in the back of Stanford in a town called La

---

* Ken Kesey, author of the novels *One Flew Over the Cuckoo's Nest* (1962) and *Sometimes a Great Notion* (1964), first took LSD in a CIA-funded study and became a proselytizer of the creative and spiritual benefits of hallucinogens. He was famous for hosting psychedelic parties called "acid tests" at his ranch in La Honda, south of San Francisco. In 1964 Kesey captained a brightly painted bus called "Further" (sometimes misspelled as "Furthur") across the country with a group called the Merry Pranksters, who gave out LSD (which was legal until October 1966) to anyone willing to try it.

Honda. Eventually, we all knew Kesey and we actually took acid with Kesey several times.

A lot of hippies at the time were looking to get stoned and dance and play. We were all for getting stoned and dancing and playing, but the serious business was how to deal with the machine that's chewing up Southeast Asia. All those things were mingled together and they were all part of the same uprising of young people who insisted on writing their own ticket. Because the tickets that were being written for them were bad at best and criminal at worst.

And it wasn't just acid, it was the whole thing. Growing your hair out, wearing clothes that didn't come from J. C. Penney's or Saks Fifth Avenue. You've got to remember we grew up in the fifties. The fifties was a time of no options. There was one way to be. When I grew up in Fresno, we had three choices: You could be John Wayne in the *Sands of Iwo Jima,* or John Wayne in the *Sands of Iwo Jima,* or John Wayne in the *Sands of Iwo Jima.* That was it. So what happened in the sixties, in what is summarized as "hippie," was making options. There were other ways to be than the one that everyone was insisting we were supposed to be, and we were going to find them.

RALPH METZNER

I knew Albert Hofmann well until he passed on at age 102 in 2008. He liked that term, "passed on." He was a very conservative Swiss scientist— a materialist, actually. He was a chemist working for the pharmaceutical company Sandoz in Switzerland, and he accidentally ingested some lysergic acid; that's the mythology, and it's wildly improbable. Swiss chemists are probably the most compulsively exact people on the planet. Think about it. They're handling chemicals in micro amounts. But the amount of lysergic acid diethylamide, LSD, that's an effective dose is so minute you can't actually see it. It happened and he didn't know how. He didn't know that there was the possibility of a drug that would affect consciousness in that way. It wasn't a tranquilizer, it wasn't a stimulant, it didn't have any other medical properties. At first they ignored it. Then they were synthesizing all these chemicals and ergot alkaloids, and four years later he decided on an intuitive impulse, "Let's look at this one again."

It was 1943, which is an interesting synchronicity, because that was the same year as the first atomic reaction leading to the building of the atomic bomb. It's very strange when you look at all the synchronicities. It has all of the hallmarks of divine intervention. Hey, we need something here to open people's minds. Let's have this guy invent this. He was the perfect person for it, a very conservative, cautious scientist.

MICHAEL RANDALL (LSD manufacturer/dealer)

My friend Johnny Griggs had read an article in *Life* magazine in 1966[*] about these Harvard doctors and this new drug, and he told me he wanted to try it. It wasn't illegal and it wasn't on the street yet. It was still experimental. About thirty of us went to White Point on the ocean in San Pedro, took acid, and wandered off looking into these tide pools filled with little hermit crabs, and the water was clear and beautiful. It was there that I woke up and realized that there is an intelligence that has created this world and the living, breathing universe that is infinite beyond imagination. I had a deep, spiritual, religious experience. We all did, and we decided that we should form a church.

Soon afterwards, we found an old beautiful stone building that used to be a church in Modjeska Canyon just in the foothills of Laguna Beach, California. It was empty, and it was for rent, and we just said, Oh my God, this is a beautiful little canyon. Everybody started getting places in that canyon, and I wound up with a little cabin in the canyon. We then put the legal stuff in motion, a little bit inspired by Timothy Leary, and the League for Spiritual Discovery (LSD)—that was their church in Millbrook.[†] That was kind of the pattern that we followed.

[*]   Gerald Moore and Larry Schiller, "The Exploding Threat of the Mind Drug That Got Out of Control: LSD," *Life,* March 25, 1966.

[†]   In 1964 Timothy Leary and his followers established a commune in Millbrook, New York, at the Hitchcock family estate, where they operated the Castalia Foundation, an organization whose purpose was "to disseminate scientific information resulting from research into states of consciousness . . . and the results obtaining from an alteration of the state of consciousness."

We didn't have a name yet. We were going to be this, we were going to be that, and then Chuck Mundell said, "How about the Brotherhood of Eternal Love?" He was one of the great California surfers, along with Mike Hynson, who was the costar in the movie *Endless Summer*. So we called ourselves the Brotherhood of Eternal Love.

We thought, We are going to have heaven on earth. We're going to turn the whole world on, and we are all going to be living in paradise. We really thought so. It was so powerful to us, and we were young and naïve, and drunk on idealism. We thought we were going to live in teepees. We thought war was going to end. We thought, It's going to be so great, you provide the LSD, and the people do the work. It just opens your consciousness, if you're in a good setting.

JOHN PERRY BARLOW

People have a hard time thinking of 1965 as not being the core of the sixties, but the sixties did not begin, in my view, until sometime in '66. Prior to that it was Eisenhower's America. If you look at newsreels from that period, it's definitely continuous with the previous decade. So it still felt very much like the fifties to me. I felt like the real sea change was when the Human Be-In took place in Golden Gate Park in January of '67. That was where I felt like things suddenly, dramatically shifted. It was the first time Timothy Leary announced his famous counterculture slogan, "Turn on, tune in, drop out." I wasn't there. But I had a lot of friends who were, and I saw the posters in their psychedelic graphical style, which was so obviously new. Psychedelic is all I can call it. It had this profound goofiness to it. It was like postsymbolic, where you're not dealing with symbols so much as you're dealing with representations of another reality. It just had a completely different feel; it didn't feel like anything I'd seen before.

It's difficult now to really explain to somebody who wasn't there just how profound the shift was from extended fifties reality into the onset of sixties psychedelia. Because now you watch television and every ad is kind of psychedelic. The whole culture has absorbed that vision and trivialized it. I don't know if it's possible to take acid and feel anything like the thing one felt when it was a complete surprise. But it turned the entire culture on its ear, at least from where I was sitting. I had a sense that some-time toward the end of 1967, God Almighty was going to leap through the trance, and the world would be a completely different place.

MICHAEL RANDALL

Once you start taking acid, you're part of something bigger than your-self. The idea that we had is that once you understood an acid trip, you could be a guide. So we would take one person from the initial group, and that person could gather five or ten souls, and go out and lead your own trips. And then all of those people could do the same. It mush-roomed, and we got a lot of people high, and they all became LSD evangelists.

We always felt that our mission was to turn the world on to LSD. We were just certain that's what God wanted us to do. So, with that job de-scription, it was hard for us to settle into a quieter lifestyle. To tell you the truth, once you start doing the things we were doing, you don't want to go into a quieter lifestyle anyway. It becomes really fun. Dangerous fun.

PETER COYOTE (Digger, communard)

LSD was kind of the line of initiation. Once you were on the other side, once you had had this experience of wholeness and the absolute interde-pendence of everything in the universe, it was like a spiritual awakening and it was perceived as a spiritual pilgrimage. People didn't go into it lightly. Suddenly, everything made sense by showing you, first of all, that reality was not just a duality, that you couldn't express it as right against left or right against wrong. People could begin to entertain arguments about the way in which we might not be exactly right with our greed or our warfare or our racism, in terms other than political. It opened up the possibility that true creative leaps might solve this dilemma, and it seemed like a very valuable fuel for people who were trying to imagine a better future. If you have unlimited options, there's no such thing as a problem. So that was the teaser of LSD.

GRAY HENRY (filmmaker)

I dropped acid for the first time the day after I graduated from Sarah Lawrence in June '65. We were in the second Be-In in Central Park. "We" is all the artists and film studios in the East Village of New York. It was Easter of 1966. Suddenly you have on television, "Here are the hippies." The word got coined that day by the media; it was just *beatniks* before. We weren't hippies. We were seekers, after an experience of the divine. Yeah, sure, it's a shortcut to enlightenment, but what you experience is not enlightenment. I think the thing that is so incredible about it is that you have the experience that we are all one: you, me, the tree. It's the divine unity. It sounds so trite to say, "God is love," but if you're in a state of oneness with all beings, the whole energy is sheer love. It's really beautiful to experience that.

RALPH METZNER

What Tim Leary meant by dropping out was to disengage mentally, psychologically, from what he would say are the games of the culture. To retreat from it doesn't necessarily mean to go out and live in the woods, although it could for some people. But to mentally disengage, to question reality. Later on he had another slogan: "Go out of your mind and come to your senses." I think that was actually a much better slogan than the "Turn on, tune in, drop out," which was subject to misinterpretation. Of course the mainstream culture misinterpreted it as "Quit your job, quit school." He didn't care. He liked being provocative. He hated being thought of as a guru. He'd get quite pissed-off when anybody called him a guru. "I don't want you to follow me. Think for yourself," he would say. So, dropping out means drop out of your psychological commitment to the preconceived stuff that's been handed down to you. Then tune in to the natural process, to nature and the divine process. Then drop out—

find your own way. Find others who are like-minded, and maybe you'll join the Farm in Tennessee* and maybe you'll go back to school and study science, but you'll be doing it because your intuition tells you that this is what you want to commit yourself to, rather than just going in the lockstep pattern that the older generation wants you to do, like pay your taxes and get killed. That makes total sense to me.

GRAY HENRY

Millbrook was a 2,500-acre estate ninety miles north of New York City that belonged to the Hitchcock family. It had a sixty-four-room Georgian-looking mansion on it, which was the big house, and then there was a house with turrets and a bowling alley down the hill, closer to the gate. In the gatehouse lived Maynard Ferguson, the jazz musician. What happened was, after Tim and Ralph were thrown out of Harvard in 1963, Peggy Hitchcock, who had a great crush on Tim in those days, said, "Come and live at Millbrook."

RALPH METZNER

The community at the Hitchcock Estate in Millbrook came about because Leary and Alpert and Leary's children, and the graduate students that were working on the project, were meeting a lot and talking about our experiences. Even after we were forced to leave Harvard in '63, like any other graduate students we planned to research and publish papers and journals like we were supposed to do. But then as the popularity and notoriety of the drug escalated and more and more undergraduates were taking it at their universities, the research project basically stopped. But the people didn't stop. Our experience at Harvard and in Millbrook afterward had all been in small groups, and then I came to California, and in came Ken Kesey and the Grateful Dead. They were handing out acid and you had two thousand people dancing.

---

* The Farm is a commune started in 1971 by Stephen Gaskin and 420 hippies who traveled across the country in a caravan from California to settle on land in Summertown, Tennessee, fifty miles south of Nashville.

Timothy Leary (right) with his colleague Ralph Metzner at the Hitchcock estate in Millbrook, New York, August 1965. Leary, Metzner, and
a third Harvard professor, Richard Alpert, started an organization
called the League for Spiritual Discovery (LSD) and continued their
psychedelic research in Millbrook after being kicked out of Harvard in
1963.

JOHN PERRY BARLOW

My official best friend since I was fourteen in prep school, Bob Weir, had
gone off and become the rhythm guitar player of the Grateful Dead. We
fell out of contact with each other and I heard about the Kesey acid tests
and I was just appalled. It sounded like drug abuse of the first order—
people just swilling communion. I was on a very high horse about it. And
then I find out that the house band for this atrocity stars my official best
friend. So I came in late to that party because I was off in the Eastern Or-
thodox Church of LSD with Leary and Alpert and those guys in Millbrook. I spent a lot of time there.

When the Grateful Dead first came to New York and I reconnected with Weir, I arranged to drive them up to Millbrook so that they could meet Tim and the folks up there and see what was going on in that end of the culture. It was a mighty day. It was June of 1967 and the Six-Day War had just broken out, and the Beatles' *Sgt. Pepper's Lonely Hearts Club Band* had just been released. We picked up a copy of the album on our way up there. It was the first explicitly psychedelic piece of media that I think anybody ever heard. If you were an acid head, you knew exactly what that record was. And if you weren't, it would be kind of mysterious to you. But it was a fully realized way of conveying some of the obscure aspects of what was otherwise indescribable.

> *Picture yourself in a boat on a river*
> *With tangerine trees and marmalade skies*
> *Somebody calls you, you answer quite slowly*
> *A girl with kaleidoscope eyes*
>
> *Cellophane flowers of yellow and green*
> *Towering over your head*
> *Look for the girl with the sun in her eyes*
> *And she's gone*
>
> "LUCY IN THE SKY WITH DIAMONDS"*

From a cultural standpoint, we really failed to consider what a profound immediate response this could not fail to have. We had large numbers of our youth suddenly seeing the world through radically different eyes, and when you do that, there's going to be something in the way of blowback, and there really was.

JOHN HARTMANN (music agent, manager)

I'm a music agent and manager living in L.A. and I'm pretty full of myself and I keep telling everyone that Buffalo Springfield is America's answer to

---

* "Lucy in the Sky with Diamonds" is considered a classic song about the psychedelic experience; the initials of the main words in the title are *LSD*, although John Lennon denied that that was intentional.

the Beatles. There's a promoter and manager named Howard Wolf who told me, "You're crazy, you don't even know what's happened." "What are you talking about? I don't know what's happening? I *am* what's happening." He said, "No, you haven't got a clue. It's all happening in San Francisco. It's Jefferson Airplane, it's the Grateful Dead, it's Big Brother and the Holding Company, it's Quicksilver Messenger Service, it's Moby Grape, it's the Charlatans." He lists all of these bands that I had never heard of. So I get on a plane, and I go up to San Francisco.

It must have been April of '67, and I thought I knew everything there was to know about show business. I trained with the best agents. I'd been successful. I go up there, and I'm standing in a black mohair suit, chain-link watch, sapphire pinky ring, initials engraved on my shirt, hair so short it looks like it's painted on, and I am in total shock. The show was Jefferson Airplane, Grateful Dead, and Paul Butterfield. I turned to Albert Grossman, the manager of the Paul Butterfield Blues Band, who I had just met that day. He also managed Bob Dylan and Peter, Paul & Mary. I turned to him and I went, "Albert, where's it all going?" He said, "Under the sea, man, under the sea."

The Grateful Dead, with lead singer Jerry Garcia (right), play a concert on San Francisco's Haight Street, March 1968. The Bay Area's original and legendary psychedelic jam band, the Dead played their own unique blend of bluegrass, folk, rock, and improvisational jazz. PHOTOGRAPH BY JIM MARSHALL.

What blew my mind were three things that defied the rule: One was unknown acts. Number two, every guy in the room had hair longer than Sonny [Bono], and Sonny was a freak in L.A. Long hair was anything that was longer than an inch. The third thing I saw that was absolutely extraordinary, it was what is known as a liquid light show. Somebody holds a tray of oils and waters that are different colors and they pulsate it on one of those overhead projectors, in rhythm to the music. So, the whole room was going "whoo, whoo, whoo." You've seen it in videos of the era. They've got spinning lights. That's all liquid light show.

GREIL MARCUS (music critic)

I met Jann Wenner when we were both students at Berkeley, and in the fall of 1967, he started publishing *Rolling Stone*. It was the first publication that wrote about music in a way that was intelligent and interesting, and it was clearly written by people who cared about what they were writing about. I couldn't wait for every issue, and in the beginning they didn't arrive on time because their publishing schedule was erratic. The San Francisco music scene, starting in '65, going through '66, '67, was so full of life, so surprising, with every conceivable band passing through town playing the Fillmore or the Avalon. It was a thrilling time.

Jann had been involved with Ken Kesey, and the acid tests. He was much more a part of that world certainly than I was, but I was going over to the Fillmore or the Avalon every weekend in '66 and '67 and I was seeing Jefferson Airplane, Grateful Dead, Quicksilver Messenger Service, Van Morrison, the Doors—we saw the Doors lots of times, because we loved them. In '67 they played it seemed like every weekend. We'd see Country Joe play a little club on Telegraph Avenue, here in Berkeley. There was a tremendous sense of energy, of delight, of excitement, of surprise, of "Oh my God, this is thrilling, this is exciting, this is interesting." The response of some people to that would be "I want to be in a band. I want to learn how to play guitar. I want to make records." The response of some other people might be "I want to write about this," because that's your inclination. Or "I want to put out a newspaper about this," and that was Jann's inclination. He wrote a lot at the beginning. There were very few writers, and he probably wrote as much or more than anybody else. I started writing for it just because it seemed open and they had a little notice in the paper saying if you've got something to contribute, send it in. So I sent in a record review, and it was printed in the next issue. I never took acid. I was not a drug person.

JOHN HARTMANN

So, I went back to the William Morris Agency office and said, "Look, bands happen out of venues. Johnny Rivers happened at the Whisky, Buffalo Springfield happened at the Whisky, the Airplane had the Fillmore, the Grateful Dead happens out of the Avalon Ballroom. If we put Buffalo Springfield in a venue and package it, we will have the biggest act in the world. We will beat the Beatles." These guys at William Morris said, "You guys, sit down and stay out of San Francisco, and get back to work."

But I knew that we had just discovered the mother lode. What was different about this music was that it was psychedelic. They were on acid, and what was coming out of their instruments was acidesque, right? It was totally different: the sound, the feel, the energy. They had long riffs where a guy goes completely insane on the guitar. Jimi Hendrix being the best of them. We were seeing bigger bands, like five. The Beatles were four; that was the standard. Stones were five; that was acceptable. Six was starting to get big, right? A whole lot of these other bands had a large number of members. So, it was all different and we knew it was great.

Everybody smoked pot, and if you didn't, you were an idiot. Pot was the fuel. If you didn't smoke dope, who the fuck are you? What are you all about? So there was not even a contest or a challenge about pot, but it took a certain, more liberated person to get into the psychedelics. LSD is mushrooms on steroids. Once it kicks in, there's a peacefulness and then your mind opens up to the collective unconscious. So you're now in tune with the wisdom of the universe.

So that's what was happening through the music; the music was telling us who to be, how to be, and what to do, which we interpreted as revolt: resist the war, resist racism, advance the peace movement, bring

Grace Slick, a rock icon, sings with her band Jefferson Airplane in June 1969 at the Family Dog Ballroom by the Bay in San Francisco. A psychedelic light show is in the background. PHOTOGRAPH BY ROBERT ALTMAN.

some justice into the legal system, defy the corporate takeover of America. And we won.

The other thing that happened culturally was that when you were a hippie, you didn't want a job. So we were doing dope, going to concerts, and having girls take you to bed, which they were flagrantly willing to do. I was taken to bed by three girls in one day. If you met someone, and it clicked, you were doing it—there was no AIDS; no one worried about any of that stuff. I mean, you could get gonorrhea but that rarely happened. So, free love worked, and women were liberating themselves. I was all for it. It was cool, it was fun, because it gave me the ability to make powerful connections in a very short time. Like, you might never see that girl again, and in most cases, that's what happened. It just was a happening; it was wonderful. It worked for us at the time.

COUNTRY JOE MCDONALD

(rock musician, member of Country Joe and the Fish)

You had a thing called the "Super Trouper." You had spotlights and you had gels on the stage. We wore clothes that we got in a secondhand store that didn't match at all, and people used every fucking light they had and they projected liquids and slide shows and movies and everything. They had these posters that were all kinds of colors and lettering that you couldn't read. Then on top of that, you combine psychedelic drugs. It was like going from a black-and-white movie to color. It was heaven. For a creative person like myself, it was just heaven.

There wasn't any stopping it. I like metaphors. A long time ago, people ate their dinner with a knife and a spoon. Then, one day, some traveling salesman came through town with a fork and said, "Anybody want to buy a fork?" They said, "Why the hell do I want a fork?" "Just try it. Try eating your potatoes with a fork." They're all saying, "Oh my God. This thing really works good! It's a lot easier to eat my dinner with a fork and a knife and a spoon." That's what happened in the sixties. The explosion happened.

CHAPTER 3

MADISON

(1967–May 1969)

"The youth revolt means that our generation is creating its own mythology."

—JERRY RUBIN, *We Are Everywhere*

CAMPUS UNREST STARTED IN THE MID-SIXTIES WITH RESISTANCE TO parietals and demands for free speech and black studies. Then came antiwar teach-ins, sit-ins, and protests. Student activists targeted recruiters for Dow Chemical, the manufacturer of napalm, recruiters for the CIA and the military, and on-campus ROTC. Sixty percent of large universities during the 1967–68 school year had recruiting protests, half of which resulted in violence. These early antiwar protests set the stage for the more cataclysmic campus protests that would take place during the school year of 1969–70. By the late 1960s, *Rolling Stone* described college campuses as the "great youth ghetto." College enrollment increased by 37 percent in the fall of 1964 when the first year of post–World War II baby boom babies, born in 1946, reached the age of eighteen, and demographics played a role in the increasing power of college students to reshape the national agenda.

More so than Berkeley, the University of Michigan, Columbia, or Harvard, the most violent campus in the nation was the University of Wisconsin–Madison. What Wisconsin progressive movement leaders originally conceived of as a "laboratory for democracy" in the 1920s became a hotbed of radicalism in the 1960s.

———————

KARL ARMSTRONG (University of Wisconsin student)

I grew up in Madison and enrolled in the University of Wisconsin in September of 1964. My father was a machinist and a member of the machinist union pretty much his whole life. I joined the Air Force ROTC because my father was in the Army Air Force in World War II. I didn't really have any particular interest in it myself, but I checked it out because my father had been in it. At that time you wore your uniform on campus, which made me feel really uncomfortable, even though I didn't have any reason to. There wasn't a movement against the war on campus then, in 1964. But I just felt uncomfortable being around my fellow students in uniform. First of all, I didn't think I'd earned the uniform. At that stage I was just political putty. I didn't have any formed opinions. I was just basically living through the 1950s. I believed that we were the good guys, and they were the bad guys.

In October of 1967, I happened to be walking out of my econ class and demonstrators had occupied the Commerce building. They were protesting Dow Chemical recruiting on campus. Dow was one of the corporations supporting the war effort and it was particularly insidious because it manufactured napalm.* By the time I came out of class, students were milling around all over the hilltop outside the Commerce building. I thought, Well, I'll just stick around and see what's happening. When I saw Dane County sheriffs there, I said, "Well, there's gonna be problems," because I was from Madison and knew that these guys were real rednecks and basically supported the war. I knew there were going to be problems when I saw them start to amass outside.

———————

*   Napalm is a highly flammable chemical weapon that was first applied with flamethrowers and later dropped from U.S. B-52 bombers onto the thick jungle canopy in Vietnam, where it could burn up to 2,500 square yards of vegetation and kill anyone who came in contact with it. The thick, gelatinous substance would stick to humans and melt their flesh, causing them to burn alive. Photographs of Vietnamese civilians being burned by napalm helped make the weapon a symbol of American brutality in Vietnam. Between 1965 and 1973, the United States doused Vietnam with 388,000 tons of napalm.

PAUL SOGLIN (University of Wisconsin student activist)

In the 1960s, about one-third of the University of Wisconsin's under-graduate class came from out of state, and half of its graduate students were from out of state. When you look at the other Big 10 colleges, schools like Iowa, Illinois, and Indiana have 3 or 4 percent out-of-state students. That raises the question: Why was Wisconsin different? You can blame it on Fighting Bob La Follette, Wisconsin's progressive governor, who wanted to create a heterogeneous environment at the university back in the 1910s and 1920s. La Follette's theory was if you bring in all these people from all over the country, you're going to get the brightest minds. You're going to build a creative environment, which is going to be popu-list and is going to do great things for the state of Wisconsin.

It was no secret in the late 1950s and 1960s that political movements were growing in Madison, whether it was SNCC or the Committee to End the War in Vietnam, and eventually SDS. And it was no secret that Wis-consin had a disproportionate presence of out-of-state students, and Jews. Those New York Jews, and those out-of-state students, they do link up with descendants of the progressive movement here in Wisconsin. It takes a little while for this dynamic to work itself out, but by 1967–68, it's in play.

Dow Chemical manufactured napalm. In 1967 we had a sit-in and we blocked the Dow recruiter's office. The demonstration only involved about 250 to 300 students, at most. It started when the police moved in with their clubs. They did it a little after two o'clock, when classes were changing, so there were thousands of students moving across Bascom Hill. The students saw what was happening and they became angry. The police only made it worse by releasing tear gas. Before it was over, thou-sands of students were engaged, and the antiwar movement on campus just grew immense.

KARL ARMSTRONG

I saw the cops going into the Commerce building, and I could see from the outside that they were starting to hit people. I stuck around a little longer,

Our foreign policy must always be an extension of this nation's domestic policy. Our safest guide to what we do abroad is a good look at what we are doing at home.

LYNDON BAINES JOHNSON

On October 18, 1967, students at the University of Wisconsin–Madison protested on-campus recruiting and the university's research for Dow Chemical, the manufacturer of napalm. Madison police responded with unexpected brutality, instantly radicalizing many students, including Karl Armstrong. This poster was printed by an underground paper in Madison.

and then they started pulling people out of the building. That's when I saw my friend John Deverall, who lived in the same house that I did. He was a very intelligent guy from Ithaca, New York. I had a great deal of respect for this guy. I felt that he was a really centered sort of individual. When I saw him being hauled out of there, kind of like half-dragged and bloodied, I was shocked. He was being beaten and I could see his glasses getting smashed on the ground. That had a huge effect on me: a fellow student, who I had a great deal of respect for, being beaten. We hadn't even talked about the Vietnam War. It was a surprise to me that he was involved.

I was really pissed. My friend was being beaten. Then the whole top of the hill was teargassed. That was basically the first time I had seen something that really enraged me. The battle lines were drawn.

RENA STEINZOR (University of Wisconsin student journalist)

For all the bravado of the students that made this movement, most of us started as high school kids from liberal households—I was from Westchester, New York—who showed up on this huge campus that was in total turmoil, and became radicalized by events, but were still very young, and quite vulnerable.

I often compare it to Yale, where the president, Kingman Brewster, was sympathetic and tried to manage the violence. He tried to reassure the kids, and was very parental. He was out there at the demonstrations talking to the students all the time. Our faculty was hiding in its offices. There were some very notable exceptions: Harvey Goldberg, William Appleman Williams, and George Mosse were particularly radical, but they were not active with the administration. The administration of the university was very hostile about the whole thing, and therefore it was left to the police and the students, with the help of a few critical faculty, to find their way. So it just became worse and worse.

PETER GREENBERG
(University of Wisconsin student journalist)

I walked into the paper *The Daily Cardinal* and said, "Hi, I would like to join the paper," and they said, "Well, go and cover that ROTC riot," because they had nobody else to do it. So I did, and I wrote the world's worst story. But they ran it on the front page. This is a paper that every day has a circulation

Police teargas students at the University of Wisconsin–Madison Dow Day protest, October 18, 1967.

of twenty-eight thousand. And that was it. I was hooked. Within ten days we had the Dow Chemical protest. That was my first introduction to tear gas, and it was not pleasant. One hundred and sixty-five people went to the hospital that day. Once again, I ended up covering the story because everybody else was being beaten up. I saw Paul Soglin get arrested. They hauled everybody out of the Commerce building and beat the shit out of them with billy clubs. They weren't just prodding; they really whacked them.

That's when I said, "Okay, I'm not just covering a college campus for a student paper, I'm covering a war." I realized that Madison had become a combat zone and I figured the best side for me to be on was to write about it.

TOM McCARTHY

(Madison, Wisconsin, policeman)

I was a detective supervisor for the city of Madison police force, which had 293 cops. I was thirty-seven in 1967, when the Dow protests happened. At the big Dow demonstration, somebody threw a brick and it hit me in the face, broke my nose, and I lost four teeth. When I got hit they came and got me and put me on a stretcher and took me to the emergency room at the university hospital. Well, shit, there were sixty kids there with their heads shaved, getting ready to get stitched. I was on the stretcher and they found out I was a cop, so the kids came over and started spitting on me. The doctor came down and said, "Listen, we can't treat you here. You've got to go to another hospital." They had to come get me and take me to a different hospital. They got me out.

KARL ARMSTRONG

I was doing warehouse work in Madison the summer of 1968, but quit to go to the Democratic National Convention. I had campaigned for Eugene McCarthy going house to house. So I went to the convention basically to show my support for him, and my opposition to the war.[*]

LEAFLET INVITING PEOPLE TO CHICAGO FOR AN "INTERNATIONAL FESTIVAL OF YOUTH, MUSIC, AND THEATER"

A STATEMENT FROM YIP!

... Come all you rebels, youth spirits, rock minstrels, truth-seekers, peacock-freaks, poets, barricade-jumpers, dancers, lovers and artists!

It is summer. It is the last week in August, and the NATIONAL DEATH PARTY meets to bless Lyndon Johnson. We are there! There are 50,000 of us dancing in the streets, throbbing with am-

---

[*] LBJ's vice president, Hubert Humphrey, and Maine senator Edmund Muskie won the party nomination over antiwar candidate Eugene McCarthy at the August 1968 Democratic convention in Chicago. Senator Robert F. Kennedy, who was also running for the nomination on a peace platform, was assassinated the night he won the California primary, June 5. Humphrey, who supported LBJ's hawkish view of the war, did not participate in the primaries, and was nominated by party delegates at the convention in what the antiwar movement considered a behind-the-scenes power move by LBJ.

Thousands of young antiwar protesters congregate in Chicago's Lincoln Park during the Democratic National Convention in August 1968 to protest the Democratic Party's endorsement of the Vietnam War.

plifiers and harmony. We are making love in the parks. . . . Everything will be free. Bring blankets, tents, draft-cards, body-paint, Mr. Leary's Cow, food to share, music, eager skin, and happiness. The threats of LBJ, Mayor Daley, and J. Edgar Freako will not stop us. We are coming from all over the world!

KARL ARMSTRONG

I was in Grant Park on Sunday [August 25] listening to a concert, and I saw these undercover cops start fights, arrest people, and drag them off. They came in and basically broke up the concert—it was totally unprovoked. We weren't doing anything except listening to the music. And that's when I got my first taste of Chicago.

And from there, the demonstration started forming. I was really starting to get a sense that history was in the making, because you had the military helicopters flying overhead and snipers on the roofs of all the buildings. We started marching, I believe it was down Lake Shore Drive and then it came time to cross the bridge back to Michigan Avenue. On the bridge they had machine gun emplacements and all kinds of military.

We had absolutely no idea what was going to happen. I just knew there was going to be big trouble.

We decided to walk past these machine gun emplacements and across the bridge. Then we marched down Michigan Avenue, and as we got to the Conrad Hilton Hotel, I could hear panes of glass from the front of the hotel being broken, and people were being pushed through the windows. It was just the most bizarre scene. I looked up and saw Hubert Humphrey waving outside from his window above.

Right there at that intersection, I thought, This is a really safe place to be, in the middle. But that's where the cops ended up coming. The police started marching with their searchlights, up a side street. There was a wall of cops going back what seemed like a block. They came right through the middle of us, right to where I was. There were maybe a couple of people in front of me, so I said, "Sit down. Let yourself be arrested. Don't resist, just sit down!" And so people in front of me started sitting down and we all sat right in front of the cops.

The first thing I saw was the cops grabbing this guy in front of me by the hair and they started clubbing him on the head, beating him. Then all hell broke loose. People got back up to their feet, and I felt really guilty for telling them to sit down. The cops were swinging their truncheons above my head and I was trying to get out of their way. I ended up climbing a wall on the other side of the street—I guess it was the railroad tracks—and I got out of the area. At one point I was down on my knees with my head near the pavement, trying to get low enough to avoid being hit. And it was with my face down on the asphalt that I realized, I'm never going to put myself in a position like this again. In my mind, I said, If they're going to make war on us, I'm gonna make war on them.[*]

Right after the convention, I got called up for the draft. I took a bus to

---

[*] The "Battle of Michigan Avenue" was the climax of three days of skirmishes in Chicago between protesters and the police. Mayor Richard Daley deployed 22,500 police and state troopers who overwhelmed the approximately 10,000 antiwar protesters. In what was later called a "police riot," the bloody confrontation was graphically televised. Ultimately, 680 protesters were arrested, 1,100 people were injured, and 37 reporters were beaten and roughed up while they tried to chronicle the extreme police brutality. Watching the demonstrators be violently beaten by police on television shocked the nation and radicalized many viewers.

Police and state troopers roll a military tank onto Michigan Avenue in a prelude to the "Battle of Michigan Avenue," when 22,500 law enforcement officers brutally beat protesters and journalists in what would later be described as a "police riot."

the Selective Service office in Milwaukee, which was surrounded by antiwar demonstrators. I knew in my mind that if they selected me to go to Vietnam, I was going to go to Canada. I passed with flying colors, but they had this one question: "Do you ever sleepwalk?" And I said, "Yes." I answered everything truthfully, because I wanted them to recruit me into the military, so that I could go to Canada—so that I could make my statement against the war.

They sent me to see a shrink, who asked me to describe what it was like when I sleepwalked. I described my basic disorientation, and the shrink said, "Well, we don't want you." That just blew me away. I said, "I can't go to Canada, they don't want me?" And I thought, Man, this really makes it difficult, because I knew that now I had to fight in the trenches here at home. The guys they were sending over to Vietnam were the guys I went to high school with. I knew they were just going to end up being cannon fodder, so I told myself, I really have to do something about this.

PAUL SOGLIN

It was the last weekend before finals, and a couple of students made some posters that said, "Why don't we do it in the road? There'll be a block party on Saturday." When Saturday rolled around, people started gravitating to the 500 block of West Mifflin Street.

TOM McCARTHY

On May 3, 1969, the kids on Mifflin Street had a block party. What a mess. We had to break into their houses and blow the shit out of there with tear gas. We'd set little softballs—they looked about the size of softballs and they had cotter pins. If you pulled that cotter pin and you kept your thumb on the plunger, you could hold it there until you threw it and four seconds later it would explode. What we did is we left the cotter pin in and took another safety pin out, so that if you pulled the cotter pin it went off, right away. And we dropped a few of them in these houses. And the next morning, when we were examining the damage, we would hear explosions.

KARL ARMSTRONG

Mifflin Street was the hotbed of radicalism in Madison. It was the total scene. People lived communally, the underground newspapers were based out of that area, and it was basically the center for political activism. It was a place where people tried to live out the future life that they wanted to have. People were experimenting. People were learning to live with each other, no matter what their background or their preferences. I wasn't into it, though. I lived in a fraternity.

Anyway, they decided to have a block party, which to them was really not that big a deal. The police decided that they didn't want that happening. So the block party went ahead and the police tried to break it up. I was kind of an outsider. I didn't live in the area, but I came over and basically sat in front of a Mifflin Street house watching the people in the neighborhood battling the police. The police would throw tear gas, and people would pick it up and throw it back at them. Stones and bricks were being thrown. It was like a very surreal battle scene.

The cops were going around in squad cars or unmarked cars with taped-up windows. When they pulled up, four or five cops would pile out and go running after people on the street and into their houses. Everyone was getting beat on, except me. I was just sitting there on the porch, watching all this go down. I was thinking, Wow, people are fighting back! This is great stuff! They were beating on everybody in the neighborhood, even people who had absolutely nothing to do with it. They followed people into their houses. It was just crazy.

TOM McCARTHY

I thought breaking windows, destroying property, and burning buildings was despicable—they even burned down a goddamn grocery store because they'd arrested shoplifters—what the hell? I told my son, "You either go into a ROTC program, or you're getting nothing from me." And he went. He became a jet pilot in the Marine Corps.

The demonstrators were always on campus. They would go and line up in the street, they would go to the mall, but they all lived on Mifflin Street. So we thought, We're going to bring the war to Mifflin Street. They're going to have to come back. So we went down there and bombed the shit out of them. We took their bicycles and threw them in a pile, and burned them. You name it. The protesters hated me and I hated them.

PAUL SOGLIN

The music was on, and unbeknownst to the students, the second in command of the Madison Police Department, Inspector Herman Thomas, assembled a group of officers in riot gear. He said to them, "Just stay behind me. We're going to go down there and crack some skulls." The police showed up at noon, and they started arresting people who were in the streets for not having a permit and obstructing traffic. I got arrested, and by the time I got bailed out, about four thirty, one square mile of Madison was totally engulfed in a pitched battle between the students and the police: There were Molotov cocktails; the whole area was covered in tear gas; very brutal beatings. Things calmed down about midnight.

I got arrested the day of the Mifflin Street block party. The cops decided to cut the hair of the students who had been arrested, even though they hadn't been convicted of anything.

PETER GREENBERG

We were the most violent campus in America, more than Berkeley and Columbia. Absolutely. We were ground zero because we took to the streets first, and we stayed on the streets longer. The sit-in at Columbia wasn't until 1968. We were committed. It wasn't a one-off. It was going to continue. As a result, the National Guard was on campus for months with armored personnel carriers and fixed bayonets. They surrounded the capitol building, because most of our marches went straight up State Street to the Wisconsin state capitol, which drove the legislators nuts. The governor wasted no time calling on the National Guard. He perceived that the government was under attack.

Meanwhile, the focal point for the media in this country rapidly became the campuses. I was hired by *Newsweek* to be a campus stringer for twenty dollars a month. Prior to me, the campus stringer job was a fraternity handout, where once a year you got a query about whether culottes were back in style. I, however, was in the right place at the right time. There wasn't a week I wasn't filing a story. So, I was seventeen or eighteen, and by 1969 I had done six or seven cover stories on the "campuses in revolt." It was unprecedented.

CHAPTER 4

RADICALS

(1968–June 1969)

What had been a movement of nonviolent resistance, civil disobedience, and community organizing freaked out in 1969.

—DAVID HARRIS

STUDENTS FOR A DEMOCRATIC SOCIETY (SDS) BECAME THE largest leftist student organization by the end of the decade, with 400 campus chapters, more than 100,000 members, and an influential weekly publication, *New Left Notes*. Initially conceived as a civil rights organization, in the second half of the sixties SDS turned its sights to resisting the Vietnam War and the draft. As opposition to the war increased, so did black urban unrest in the wake of Martin Luther King, Jr.'s assassination, and the civil rights movement transitioned from a southern struggle to end Jim Crow to an urban war against poverty and police oppression. The Black Panther Party, founded in Oakland, California, in 1966, espoused armed self-defense and soon became the boldest and most visible black power organization of the late sixties. The Panthers' militancy and pro-third-world Marxist rhetoric strongly influenced some white members of SDS. The emerging alliance between SDS and the Panthers posed a potent threat to the social and political status quo, and J. Edgar Hoover's FBI stepped up its efforts to destroy both organizations and many others in the movement. By June 1969, crippled by factionalism between Marxist and Maoist ideologues, SDS imploded and a small group of militant radicals calling themselves the Weathermen took over.

———

MARK RUDD (Columbia student, SDS leader)

I was this middle-class Jewish kid from Maplewood, New Jersey. My parents were assiduously apolitical. But I got caught up, as millions of other kids did, in the ripples of the counterculture of the time, which was the Beat culture. So in high school I read *The Village Voice* and *The New Republic* and listened to folk music.

When I got to Columbia in September of '65, the most interesting people I met were kids who were organizing for Students for a Democratic Society, SDS.* I just fell in love with these people. They were cool, and they became my crowd. I was always a bit of a loner, I never fit into high school culture—I was a bookworm—but I suddenly found a gang. A lot of them were red diaper babies who had leftie, communist parents and had grown up organizing. They taught the rest of us how to organize.

What I fell into for three years, from '65 to '68, was an organizing culture. "How do we involve more people?" "What do we do to educate the campus, to get people to consider the problem of Vietnam, and the problem of racism?" And consider especially how they fit into it. That's what organizing is. It took time, and it took a lot of knocking on doors.

JULIUS LESTER (writer, SNCC member)

I was a folksinger in those days. My early involvement in the movement was singing at fundraising rallies for SNCC† and at hootenannies. And

---

*   Students for a Democratic Society was founded in 1960 and held its first convention in 1962 in Ann Arbor, Michigan, where University of Michigan student and civil rights activist Tom Hayden was elected president. Hayden wrote the first draft of the organization's manifesto, the Port Huron Statement, which became the blueprint for New Left student activism for the rest of the decade. Criticizing U.S. Cold War foreign policy and calling for an end to racial discrimination and economic inequity, the Port Huron Statement advocated nonviolent civil disobedience and participatory democracy.

†   The Student Nonviolent Coordinating Committee (SNCC) was a civil rights organization formed in 1960 as a more youthful alternative to Dr. Martin Luther King's Southern Christian

then in 1964, I went down to Mississippi for the Freedom Summer, as a folksinger. It really wasn't until '66 that I got involved full-time in SNCC, and that was primarily working as a photographer. I worked for SNCC for two years, out of the SNCC office in Atlanta.

One thing that has not been fully recognized is that the civil rights movement was a success. We've never observed that or celebrated that. The civil rights movement set out to end segregation in public accommodations, and to ensure voting rights. The '64 Civil Rights Act, '65 Voting Rights Act, accomplished what the civil rights movement set out to do. But the experience of people inside SNCC was that getting rid of segregation in public accommodations and ensuring the right to vote were only manifestations of a problem. There was a deeper problem, and the deeper problem was racism. And how do you picket an attitude? How do you demonstrate against an attitude? And so it was recognized within SNCC that black people lacked power to control their lives, and that having the vote was not going to give them the power they needed to control their lives. And so people started talking about power for black people. Then in 1966, Stokely Carmichael, the new chairman of SNCC, turned that around and simply started saying "black power." The combination of the words *black* and *power* shocked the nation. I mean, white people went nuts. They just went nuts.

WESLEY BROWN (Black Panther, draft resister)

I left the South at the end of the fall of '65, went back to college, kept ties with people in SNCC that I knew, and got involved whenever I could in the antiwar movement. When I graduated in '68, I came back to New York, and I went to the SNCC office. I knew about the Black Panthers, but emotionally, my ties were more to SNCC. There was a lot of paranoia in the air and it seemed that SNCC was going through a transition and there was talk about joining with the Panthers, and making one organization, which obviously was doomed from the onset. SNCC was being pulled apart in so many different directions.

Leadership Conference (SCLC). One of the largest and more radical civil rights organizations, SNCC conducted Freedom Rides and voter registration drives all over the South.

The Panthers were from Oakland, California, and Bobby Seale and Huey Newton founded the party in '66. They took the symbol of the black panther from the Black Panther Party in Alabama, which Stokely Carmichael (then head of SNCC) was involved in. And they took the notion of armed self-defense from the Deacons for Self-Defense in Louisiana.* I had kept up with what was going on when the Panthers went in May of '67 to the state capital in Sacramento, after observing the police brutality in the black communities, and learning that it was legal in California to carry a shotgun, as long as it was visible. And so, of course, when the state legislature was meeting to pass a law against carrying a shotgun openly, Bobby Seale went with a group of Panthers into the courtroom with their shotguns, wearing their black leather jackets, to protest this law.

Martin Luther King, in his famous speech at the Riverside Church in '67, came out in opposition to the war in Vietnam, and all these more traditional civil rights organizations attacked him. SNCC had come out against the war prior to that, and in 1967 the Panthers published their ten-point platform, and point six stated, "We Want All Black Men to Be Exempt from Military Service." In 1968 Eldridge Cleaver [a Black Panther] ran for president from the Peace and Freedom Party, whose platform demanded an end to the war in Vietnam.

The Panthers appealed to me partly because of their opposition to the war. They saw that blacks in this country were in a sense colonized, and I connected with that, because of what I had seen in rural areas in Mississippi. I also felt that the Panthers, while they were very race-conscious, had a perspective that seemed more international. They identified not only with liberation movements in Africa, but also with those in Latin America and in Asia. They did not have an exclusionary or nationalist perspective that did not embrace other struggles, and that was attractive to me.

---

* The Deacons for Self-Defense and Justice was an armed self-defense organization formed in 1964 in Jonesboro, Louisiana, in defiance of the nonviolent strategies of the mainstream civil rights movement.

BOBBY SEALE (Black Panther Party chairman)

May 10, 1967, Speech at the University of California, Berkeley

Why don't cops who patrol our community live in our community? I don't think there would be so much police brutality if they had to go and sleep there. . . . You've been told that the Black Panthers . . . make no bones about hating whites. That's a bare-faced lie. We don't hate nobody because of color. We hate oppression. . . . We're going to arm ourselves and protect ourselves from white racist cops. White cops are occupying our community like foreign troops. They're there to hurt us and brutalize us, and we got to arm ourselves because they're shooting us up.[*]

ERICKA HUGGINS (Black Panther Party member)

I grew up in Washington, D.C., and attended a historically black university, Lincoln University in Pennsylvania, about an hour from Philadelphia. I was in my junior year at Lincoln when I had the great fortune of sitting with Charles Hamilton and Stokely Carmichael when they were writing the book *Black Power*.[†] They would bring students together on weekday evenings and read from their work in progress.

One day I was sitting in the Lincoln Student Union and somebody brought me a *Ramparts* magazine. It's November 1967, and the featured article, written by Eldridge Cleaver, was about Huey Newton and the Black Panther Party for Self-Defense, as it was first named. I was struck not only by the words, but also by the photographs of Huey strapped to a hospital gurney with a bullet wound in his stomach and police standing guard. The picture in the article spurred something in me about what I had witnessed when I was a child in Washington, D.C. I had grown up in

[*]   From an article by Jim Hyde in the *Daily Californian,* May 11, 1967, quoted in Joshua Bloom and Waldo Martin, *Black Against Empire* (Berkeley: University of California Press, 2013), p. 80.

[†]   *Black Power: The Politics of Liberation,* by Kwame Turé (Stokely Carmichael) and Charles V. Hamilton, was published in 1967. The book defined black power as a radical way to confront and reform a racist society.

Southeast Washington, where my sister and I would regularly see the police stopping some black man or woman on the street for seemingly nothing. We would always wonder what the heck could this person have done? It was routine; it was part of the culture of living in the black community at the time, and it still is.

So by the time I read that article and saw the picture, I was so saddened to see this man who had obviously been shot, and who was accused of killing a police officer, suffering.* When I read about the purpose of the Black Panther Party, I just knew that this is the organization I wanted to join. Because of their motto, "All power to all the people," it struck me that the Black Panther Party wasn't just for African American people, though African Americans started it. It was for—as the article and later everything I read said—all oppressed people.

And so I left Lincoln University with my best friend at the time, John

A group of Black Panthers, with cofounder Eldridge Cleaver facing the camera wearing sunglasses, at a Free Huey [Newton] rally at the Alameda County Courthouse in Oakland, California, in 1968.
PHOTOGRAPH BY JEFFREY HENSON SCALES.

---

* Huey Newton was in a shoot-out with Oakland police in October 1967. Newton was shot in the stomach and police officer John Frey was killed. Newton was convicted of voluntary manslaughter in September 1968 for killing Frey, which he denied, and the charges were dismissed in May 1970. While Newton was in jail, he became an instant celebrity and darling of the New Left.

Huggins, and we drove across the country to California to join the Black Panther Party in Los Angeles.

JEFFREY HENSON SCALES (Black Panther photographer)

Huey Newton had gotten into an altercation with some cops and he was on trial for murder in 1968. It was courtroom drama. I would visit Huey at the Alameda County courthouse in jail once or twice a week. He sort of mentored me in how to organize high school students. I was fourteen years old. His gift was the idea that he and Bobby Seale developed in 1966. It was the ten-point party platform and the idea of having armed groups patrolling the police's activities. It was really sensational and it was legal, so it got a lot of attention and it got a lot of people excited to be a part of it.

As a kid growing up in Berkeley, I had been taking photographs as a hobby, and the Panthers were, of course, cool to take pictures of: the gear—the leather jackets, sunglasses—the style, the energy, the excitement

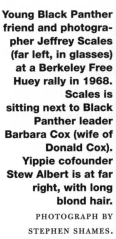

Young Black Panther friend and photographer Jeffrey Scales (far left, in glasses) at a Berkeley Free Huey rally in 1968. Scales is sitting next to Black Panther leader Barbara Cox (wife of Donald Cox). Yippie cofounder Stew Albert is at far right, with long blond hair.
PHOTOGRAPH BY
STEPHEN SHAMES.

of the movement. They had pulled together a media presence through the iconography of their uniforms and their militaristic presence. You know the famous image of Huey in the African wicker chair with the shotgun and the spear, all of that sort of business, which is image. I think their imagery was brilliant. Emory Douglas, Huey, and Bobby's style—the whole thing hit the mark and they were able to have a broader audience because they weren't black nationalists. They were more inclusive.

"Free Huey" was a rallying cry for tens of thousands of people across the country. The amount of new Panther offices that were starting up all over the country then was just phenomenal. When I first started hanging out with the Panthers in Oakland, there were three offices, and about two years later, I think seventy offices opened up across the country. It seemed like a hundred because they were just everywhere. It was exciting.*

BERNARDINE DOHRN (SDS officer)

I'm an absolute original classic Midwest radical, but I didn't come from a radical background. My parents voted Republican their entire lives, but not as ideologues. I'm a first-generation college graduate. I'm kind of a stereotype in that sense, being an innocent Midwest girl at the height of the American empire, knowing nothing about the world. So I had a very steep learning curve.

I graduated from the University of Chicago Law School in '67. There were six women in my law school class, not a single person of color in my class, and less than twenty in the whole law school. Every single guy in my class became draft eligible that day. So it was a unique moment.

I moved to New York and went to work for the National Lawyers Guild, where I started organizing student chapters. We organized lawyers and law students to support the mass arrests that were happening at antiwar demonstrations. We were mobilizing law students and lawyers to be there, to document police abuses, to get the names of people who are being arrested, to have a team of people show up in court. At the Pentagon

---

* During this period, the Black Panther Party's size and popularity spread quickly. There are varying estimates of the number of offices (probably sixty-eight to seventy) and the number of members (up to ten thousand).

demonstration in 1967,* the police drove people to armories in Virginia as they arrested them in hordes. They had a strategy for what to do with them, but we had a different strategy. We also did draft assistance and military assistance. I spoke at a lot of military bases. I traveled full-time that year, organizing student chapters of the Lawyers Guild and trying to get lawyers to join the movement.

BILL AYERS (University of Michigan, SDS member)

I grew up in an affluent Chicago family and I'm the middle of five children. One of my brothers, Rick, went to Canada to escape the draft, where he organized a home for deserters in Vancouver. John, who's younger than me, joined the Democratic Party and tried to build a peace wing within it. I joined the movement in the mid-sixties as a student at the University of Michigan, became an activist and then an organizer. We worked for three years, tirelessly, with lots of arrests, lots of beatings, lots of organizing. The hardest work in those early years was going door-to-door for three straight summers urging people to sign a petition or take my literature against the war. Our plan was, during Vietnam Summer in '67, to touch every working-class home in the Midwest—in Pittsburgh, and Cleveland, and Columbus, and Chicago, and Detroit. So, I would knock on a stranger's door, present them with an argument or evidence about the war, and have one person slam the door in my face and tell me to go back to Russia, and have the next person say, "My cousin was killed last month. Come in. Have a cup of coffee." It was heartbreaking. And it was revelatory. It was life changing.

MARK RUDD

At Columbia we developed a strategy of attacking the university's involvement with the Vietnam War. The administration was sending students'

---

* The March on the Pentagon, October 21, 1967, was organized by the National Mobilization Committee to End the War in Vietnam (MOBE) and included more than 100,000 protesters, a concert on the National Mall, and an attempt to "levitate" the Pentagon. Six hundred and fifty people were arrested during violent clashes with the military on the Pentagon steps.

class ranking to the draft board; the bottom of the class would be drafted. That was a very easy one to organize against, because students didn't want their ranking sent to the draft board. But also there was naval ROTC, recruitment to the CIA, and to various branches of the military on campus. So we'd have these little campaigns around confronting recruiters, for example, or a referendum on class rank. And in the course of these campaigns, we'd knock on doors, and hold dorm meetings, and show films, and hold teach-ins. It was a combination of educational work and confrontation.

To a large extent, the model came out of the Free Speech Movement at Berkeley in 1964. That started with an innocuous request by the Berkeley students to set up tables to recruit students to work for the civil rights movement in the South. The university opposed it and it led to a major confrontation, and the beginning of the building of a widespread student movement. So that was a model for us at Columbia.* The University of Wisconsin was another model. We learned what was happening at different campuses from *New Left Notes,* which was a weekly national publication out of the Chicago SDS headquarters.

What happened in the spring of '68, leading up to the Columbia occupation, was kind of like a perfect storm. From the end of January to April of '68 was the Tet Offensive in Vietnam,† the abdication of LBJ, and the assassination of Martin Luther King on April 4.

These three events and the response to those events politicized everyone. But at Columbia, the organizing dovetailed with all these political events, so that on April 23, we called a demonstration to protest the fact

---

* The Berkeley Free Speech Movement in 1964 was the first major student protest of the decade. Over a two-month period, almost eight hundred students were arrested in violent clashes with the police. The students demanded that the university lift its ban on on-campus political activities and occupied the main administration building.

† The Tet Offensive was a massive surprise attack launched on January 30, 1968, by the Viet Cong and North Vietnamese that humiliated the United States. In one of the largest campaigns of the Vietnam War, 80,000 pro–North Vietnamese soldiers invaded one hundred unsuspecting cities in the South. It took the Americans a month to fight back and regain the cities of Hue and Khe Sanh, for example. Even though the North ultimately suffered more casualties, Tet revealed to the American public that the communist forces were stronger and more capable than the American military had led them to believe. U.S. casualties in the week of February 11–17, 1968, reached an all-time high: 543 soldiers killed and 2,547 wounded.

that a number of people, including myself, had been reprimanded for a previous demonstration. The right wing, the pro-war jocks, as we called them, were out demonstrating in force, because they knew it was going to be a confrontation. So we met at noon at the Sundial, in the center of campus. There were speeches, and somebody yelled, "Let's go to the gym site!" There were two issues: the building of the gym in Morningside Park* and the university's complicity with war research at the Institute for Defense Analyses, or IDA.† So suddenly the crowd streamed over to the gym site, and there were fights at the gym site with the jocks, fights with the cops, and I tried to quiet the group. It was really a mob scene.

I said, "Let's go to Hamilton Hall." That was the main building of Columbia College, and the classrooms were there, and the professors' offices. And so we all streamed into it, several hundred people. By then, we had entered into a de facto coalition with the Student Afro-American Society (SAS), and we immediately formed a steering committee and started meeting continually.

There were rallies in the first-floor lobby, and the steering committee was meeting upstairs. The first thing we did was write the six demands; the first two were to stop the university's complicit involvement with IDA, and to stop building the gym, and the last one was amnesty for all concerned. So these six demands became the rallying point of the whole strike. The occupation of Hamilton Hall was totally unplanned and spontaneous, but hundreds and hundreds of people streamed in, including community support from Harlem. Harlem had blown up just nineteen days before. And so people started bringing food, and militants came in. There were rumors of guns. But at one point the blacks started meeting alone, and caucusing, and the result of that was they asked us to leave and said, "This is going to become a black occupation of students and community."

It wasn't a complete shock, because that was the era of black power,

---

*   The new Columbia University gym encroached on a park in the mostly black residential neighborhood of Morningside Heights and was opposed by local residents.

†   Among the files Columbia SDS published was proof of a $125,000-a-year contract between the CIA and Columbia's School of International Affairs, a contract Columbia's dean previously denied. Sale, *SDS,* p. 380.

and the idea of separation was very current. But there was still a kind of a tremendous feeling of unity.

JULIUS LESTER

Black power was a redefinition of who we were. We weren't Negro or colored anymore. We were black. And then also, we wanted power. I think that those were the two things that scared white people the most. To throw in the words *black power* was very incendiary. Also it was moving away from what whites had defined as the goal of the movement, which was integration. Integration had never been *our* goal. As Malcolm X put it, why would we want to integrate into a burning house? So it was a restatement of values, and in '66, when black power came out, whites certainly felt disenfranchised.

MARK RUDD

Don't forget that the most significant movement within the United States, the black civil rights movement, had morphed into a revolutionary and a national liberation movement. I can't emphasize enough the importance of black power as a challenge to white liberals and radicals, especially if you were a radical. You wanted to get to the root of the problem, and you didn't want reform, compromise, hypocrisy; that was what the liberals gave us, starting with their refusal to seat the Mississippi Freedom Democratic Party at the '64 Democratic convention.

JULIUS LESTER

In 1967 I wrote a column for *The Guardian* called "The White Radical Is Revolutionary," where I said, "It is true that the black movement at this time is a vital and dynamic one, and its energy was the largest single factor in the creation of a young, non-black radical movement. . . . The white radical, however, always saw himself in a direct relationship with the black radical, and was therefore stunned at the enunciation of black power and black nationalism. The result was a loss of direction for the white radical."

MARK RUDD

Four other buildings were taken immediately after. I remember leaving Hamilton Hall at about 5 A.M., right before dawn, and all of us straggling out with our guitars and book bags and our sleeping bags, and we wandered over to Low Library with a vague notion of going into the president's office. Well, we had to break a window, and the shattering of the glass was crossing a line. You could hear the glass shattering in the quiet silence. We forced our way up into the president's office, and it was rather amazing. We were shocked by what we were doing. That was the first of four more buildings over the next couple of days. Well over a thousand people streamed in to occupy the buildings. It was amazing.

There were abortive attempts at negotiation, arbitration, and mediation by the faculty. There were clandestine meetings with the vice president. I was involved with one of those. But eventually, a week later, the

Columbia SDS chairman Mark Rudd in front of microphones (left) as students occupy several university buildings for a week, including the office of university president Grayson Kirk. On April 30, 1968, New York City police cleared the occupied buildings, clashing violently with students—injuring more than 130 and arresting 700.

administration finally called the police. They had over a thousand police—they were later described as having spent days gnawing on their night-sticks getting ready to attack us, and they did attack, and they beat up hundreds and hundreds of people, including bystanders, professors, medical personnel. You could only describe it as a police riot. The police were out of control.

The cops at Columbia saw themselves as fighters in a class war for the government, for patriotism, for the war, against the spoiled brat middle-class white kids of Columbia, who didn't know how good they had it in this country, and were mostly Jews anyway, and they beat the shit out of us just to prove it. Just to teach us a lesson. So they rioted and arrested over seven hundred people that day, and many more later, and the lesson they taught us was that they were brutal, and that we were in a war against the pigs. We'd gotten the term "pigs" from the Black Panthers, who had just emerged into our consciousness around that time, the spring and summer of '68.

The significant thing is that after the bust, thousands of people who had been on the sidelines joined the strike because of the police brutality. And so Columbia exploded after the bust, and all classes were canceled for the rest of the year, and there was a second bust, a second occupation, and more rioting. As a result, we had created a model of student militancy and audacity, and that was the lesson the movement took from it, and I believe that led to the formation of the Weathermen.

In May of '68 I was thrown out of Columbia and I became a regional and a national traveler for SDS, and I met a lot of other people who had been thinking along the same lines, and acting along the same lines as we were at Columbia, and this kind of hypermilitancy and aggressiveness became our strategy. We formed a faction within the national SDS leadership, known as the Action Faction. And so by the spring of '69 there was a full-blown debate in SDS over strategy, and being basically intellectuals, people who work on ideas, our faction developed a set of ideas concerning how the revolution was going to happen. And people also developed opposing ideas that were hyperideological.

FBI MEMORANDUM, MAY 9, 1968

TO: MR. W. C. SULLIVAN

FROM: C. D. BRENNAN

SUBJECT: COUNTERINTELLIGENCE PROGRAM

INTERNAL SECURITY

DISRUPTION OF THE NEW LEFT

Our Nation is undergoing an era of disruption and violence caused to a large extent by various individuals generally connected with the New Left. Some of these activities urge revolution in America and call for the defeat of the United States in Vietnam. They continually and falsely allege police brutality and do not hesitate to utilize unlawful acts to further their so-called causes. . . . [I]t is our recommendation that a new Counterintelligence Program be designed to neutralize the New Left and the Key Activists. . . . The purpose of this program is to expose, disrupt and otherwise neutralize the activities of this group and persons connected with it.*

GERALD LEFCOURT (movement lawyer)

More than twelve hundred people were arrested at Columbia during the student strike led by the Students for a Democratic Society. The National Lawyers Guild formed a mass defense office to help by seeking volunteers. I volunteered and was one of the few that had criminal law experi-

---

* COINTELPRO was a secret and illegal FBI project that from 1956 until its public exposure in 1971 targeted left-leaning activists and organizations. The program first pursued groups that Director J. Edgar Hoover considered political enemies, like the Communist Party and civil rights organizations. It was under this program that Martin Luther King, Jr., was harassed and his phone illegally tapped. In response to the student protests at Columbia University, COINTELPRO initiated a new project to target the New Left and worked to discredit, infiltrate, and disrupt black liberation and antiwar groups, as well as veteran, student, GI, feminist, gay, and environmental groups. COINTELPRO also targeted food co-ops, health clinics, underground newspapers, bookstores, street theaters, communes, community centers, and rock groups. Counterintelligence tactics included spreading lies and disinformation, and encouraging violent, self-destructive behavior through the use of infiltrators and provocateurs. See Ward Churchill and Jim Vander Wall, *The COINTELPRO Papers* (Boston: South End Press, 2002), p. 177, and Brian Glick, *War at Home* (Boston: South End Press, 1989), p. 12.

ence, so they asked me to represent Mark Rudd and Martin Kenner. They were the only two who had serious felony charges arising out of the protests at Columbia.

In 1968, when I was twenty-five, I was a lawyer working for the Legal Aid Society. Because of the outrageous caseloads and no training, we were unable to provide quality representation for the poor. I began organizing a lawyers union and was fired after several organizing meetings, but the union was formed in protest of my firing.

As a result of the political upheaval caused by the antiwar and civil rights movements a group of us formed the New York Law Commune, which was committed to fight for those struggles. The Law Commune represented every part of the movement. With several women lawyers, we were deeply involved in the emerging women's movement led by my sister-in-law Carol. I used the term "movement lawyer," because we were fighting for "the movement for social change."

In the spring of '68, the Panthers were forming a chapter in New York. My first call was that three Panthers were arrested in Brooklyn charged with assaulting the police. That call was from Charles R. Garry, who represented Huey Newton in Oakland, to William Kunstler, who asked me to handle the case because of my criminal law experience as a public defender.

ERICKA HUGGINS

The Black Panther Party was created on the heels of the civil rights movement. We were the peers of SNCC and other more nationalist organizations within the community, but we were not a nationalist organization. We were talking about redistribution of the wealth. Huey and Bobby were talking about conditions of poverty that need to change. Racist and classist notions keep us from recognizing what great people we are.

Mass media would never, ever speak truthfully about the Black Panther Party. People in the communities around the U.S. who experienced the benefit of our community programs—of which there were many— loved us and protected us. Programs like the Oakland Community School, that I was a director of, were created by the Black Panther Party, the People's Free Medical Clinics, the housing cooperatives, the busing to prisons programs. The Free Breakfast for Children Program was the first community program we developed. J. Edgar Hoover tried to stop them. He worked with local law enforcement to shut things down. For instance, I can remember being in Oakland when the police came into a breakfast program in a church basement with their guns pointed at us—with the children right there. There was nothing going on but eggs and milk and bacon. But our stance was, you can't ask people to step forward to make change in the world if they're hungry, their children are starving, and no one in their house has shoes, or heat in the winter.

So the Black Panther Party was created with a feeling of love for the people it was serving and that's my memory of it. Our community survival programs were full of love for people. All of these people, some of whom are now grandparents, would tell you that having a free breakfast or a free lunch, or the school, or the free clinic, which tested men, women, and

The Black Panther breakfast program served hot meals to children and was one of many inner-city community programs the Panthers provided, including free medical clinics, housing cooperatives, busing, and prison programs. At its height, during the school year of 1969–70, the breakfast program served one hundred thousand children in thirty-six cities. PHOTOGRAPH BY STEPHEN SHAMES.

children for sickle-cell anemia and saved their lives, literally—that their lives would not have been the same without the Black Panther Party. We were called the vanguard of the revolution. Why? Because of our way of organizing people, which was grassroots community based. The Black Panther Party drew lots of visionary young people. And the median age of party members was only nineteen!

J. EDGAR HOOVER TO FBI SPECIAL AGENT IN CHARGE, SAN FRANCISCO, MAY 27, 1969

One of our primary aims in counterintelligence as it concerns the [Black Panther Party] is to keep this group isolated from the moderate black and white community which may support it. This is most emphatically pointed out in their Breakfast for Children Program, where they are actively soliciting and receiving support from uninformed whites and moderate blacks. . . . You state that the Bureau under the [Counterintelligence Program] should not attack programs of community interest such as the [Black Panther Party] "Breakfast for Children." You state that this is because many prominent "humanitarians," both white and black, are interested in the program as well as churches, which are actively supporting it. You have obviously missed the point. The BPP is not engaged in the "Breakfast for Children" program for humanitarian reasons. This program was formed by the BPP . . . to create an image of civility, assume community control of Negros, and to fill adolescent children with their insidious poison. . . .*

BERNARDINE DOHRN

I went to the SDS convention in June of '68 and lo and behold, by the end of it I had put my name up and was one of three people elected as

---

* FBI COINTELPRO operatives were directed to "eradicate" the Panthers' "serve the people programs." One of many ways the FBI tried to discredit the breakfast program was by spreading rumors that members of the Black Panther leadership were infected with venereal disease. Churchill and Vander Wall, *The COINTELPRO Papers*, pp. 145–46.

national secretary. I was twenty-six. I was old compared to most of the SDS people.

In August of '68, I took a delegation of thirty people to Budapest, where we spent ten days meeting with a delegation of twenty-five Vietnamese from North Vietnam. It was a life-altering experience. They convinced us of two things. One is that the struggle to expel the United States from occupying Vietnam was a decisive struggle in the world at that moment for a variety of reasons—mainly because the United States had committed to interrupting the unification of Vietnam. The Vietnamese reminded us of that history, and of their determination to do anything and everything to reunite Vietnam and get the Americans out.

The trip gave me a very strong sense that we had a unique role to play, and that our job was to mobilize the broadest possible opposition to this immoral, illegal, and genocidal war. I can remember coming back to New York and having a hard time talking to people because I felt like I had really changed inside. I felt that history had thrust us into this moment, and the moment was calling on us to act as our most aggressive moral selves to stop the slaughter. We knew that almost two thousand people a day were being killed in Vietnam by the Americans.

BILL AYERS

In 1968, there was a convergence of unprecedented events—it's important to remember that we were twenty-one, twenty-two, twenty-three years old then. We were kids. Most of us did not come out of a political background or framework. We were just learning. And we were learning as New Leftists, meaning we were *not* part of the old communist left. We were people who'd learned and developed our politics in the streets; we'd come up in activism. We were born in the civil rights movement. We were, then, born in the antiwar movement. We were born in the women's movement, and the beginning of the queer movement. And there was an environmental movement, and movements of Mexican Americans for land in the Southwest, and of Puerto Ricans for independence. So, all of this ferment was bubbling up and setting the context.

I was an SDS regional organizer in '68, '69 in Michigan and Ohio. My district went all the way from Lake Michigan to Lake Superior, and I was on a lot of those campuses all the time. Come the spring of '68, Lyndon Johnson announces that he won't run for reelection and that he will work to end the war. It was March 31, 1968. I was in Ann Arbor that night, and we just went nuts. There were, suddenly, thousands and thousands of people in the streets. We exploded in Ann Arbor, but they exploded all over the place—Cambridge, Berkeley—everywhere there had been an organized antiwar presence.

We ended up on the steps of the president of the university's house. We were raucous, and having a good time. He came out and he said to us, "Congratulations. You've won a great victory. Now the war will end. And you should go home and be happy." And we agreed. I thought we had ended the war. There were a million unnecessary deaths. It was a cataclysmic catastrophe for the Vietnamese people, but it was over. So, we should be happy. Four days later, King was killed. And two months later, Bobby Kennedy was killed. And a couple of months after that, Henry Kissinger emerged from the swamp he was living in, which happened to be Harvard. He had a secret plan to end the war. And that secret plan was a plan, it turned out, to expand the war.

So not only did the revolution not happen in '68—of course, none of us would have known how to pull that off anyway—but Nixon was elected, and Kissinger came along. And they expanded the war under the guise of shutting it down. They made it an air war and a sea war. They expanded into Cambodia and Laos. And all of our efforts were for nothing. And so, what should we do?

GERALD LEFCOURT

After I was fired from Legal Aid for organizing the union and a *New York Times* story about it made me a cause célèbre, Abbie Hoffman called me. It was late August or early September of '68. He said, "I have a dentist and a doctor but because I have three criminal cases I really need a lawyer." I didn't know who he was, but I went to his apartment and we talked all night. By the morning, we had a pact. He said he would make a revolution if I kept him out of jail. I believed him. I was twenty-six years old.

I started representing Mark Rudd after his arrest during the April Columbia uprising, and Abbie* in August–September. So, within three months in 1968, I was counsel for Abbie, Mark, and the Panthers. Because I knew all their cases and talked about them to each other, I remember introducing Mark to Abbie, Mark to the Panthers, and Abbie to the Panthers. It seemed like I was in the middle of everything.

Ericka Huggins dropped out of Lincoln University in Pennsylvania at age eighteen to join the Black Panther Party. She drove across country with classmate and soon-to-be husband John Huggins, and they both became leaders in the Black Panther Party's Los Angeles chapter.
PHOTOGRAPH BY STEPHEN SHAMES.

ERICKA HUGGINS

John [Huggins] and I got married and joined the Black Panther Party in Los Angeles. They had an office in South Central and we met the leader of the L.A. office, Alprentice (Bunchy) Carter. John and Bunchy became immediate friends. Bunchy was a natural leader, and John worked directly

---

* Abbie Hoffman was facing several months in jail for a series of charges including resisting arrest, trespassing at Columbia University, and public obscenity for writing "Fuck" in large black letters on his forehead during a protest.

with him. They became students through the High Potential Program at UCLA and were supporting students who wanted to make changes on the UCLA campus.

FBI MEMORANDUM, SEPTEMBER 25, 1968

```
To: Director, FBI
From: SAC, Los Angeles
```

Information has been received that there is considerable friction between the Black Panther Party (BPP) and the "US" organization headed by RON KARENGA. Several sources have reported that the BPP has "let a contract" on KARENGA because they feel he has sold out to the establishment. . . . It would appear that most black nationalist organizations are now afraid of the BPP and in some cases are looking to the BPP for approval of their own actions. It is believed that in the future, there will be additional trouble between the BPP and other Negro groups. Los Angeles will utilize every technique in an attempt to capitalize on this development.

ERICKA HUGGINS

On January 17, 1969, after a meeting on [the UCLA] campus to discuss the election of the High Potential Program presidency, two men created an argument and then when John and Bunchy walked into the room to talk to those men, one was shot in the chest, the other in the back. Bunchy and John died immediately. Two other men were arrested, but they were not the men who shot or killed anyone. Long story short, those murders were orchestrated by the FBI, although mass media stated that two black rival organizations had a shoot-out.*

---

*   Huggins and Carter were shot by members of a black nationalist organization called US (United Slaves), at the time when the FBI had intensified its program to undermine the Black Panthers by creating conflict with US and other black liberation groups. The assassin escaped, and later two other US members, George and Larry Stiner, were convicted for conspiring to commit murder. The Panthers considered the Huggins and Carter murder a political assassination ginned up by the FBI. Bloom and Martin, *Black Against Empire*, p. 220.

When John was killed, I was a widow and a single mom immediately. Our daughter was three weeks old.

BERNARDINE DOHRN

By the spring of 1969, SDS had become a mass organization. There were SDS chapters where they'd never been—in community colleges, in high schools, in working-class technical schools. SDS had existed by and large in the big Midwest universities and in the elite schools until that time. Suddenly the national office was scrambling to keep mailing lists and enough pamphlets in people's hands, and buttons and things like that. But in the face of getting that big, we were set upon by these organized, ideological groups with ties to particular Maoist organizations.

CATHY WILKERSON (SDS officer)

SDS was so huge! Nobody had any clue how to run an organization like that. Unlike the civil rights movement, which sometimes had a lot of money—we had none. The rent was never paid on time. We didn't have money for travel. We couldn't pay the phone bill. And yet we had one hundred thousand members participating.

MARK RUDD

In June of '69, two things happened. SDS split into two entities. One was the Progressive Labor (PL) Party, and it's almost impossible to describe what it was about. It was about these people who were absolutely certain that Mao Zedong had defined the way the revolution was going to happen in the United States. They were one group. And then there was the other group that was absolutely certain that Che Guevara had defined the way the revolution was going to happen in the United States. Our belief was that the nonwhite people of the world are going to bring down American imperialism. This was happening around the world in Cuba, China, Vietnam—especially Vietnam—the revolts in Latin America. Internally, the African American struggle and the various Latino struggles and the

Native American struggle were all part of the movement of national liberation against U.S. imperialism.

We became followers of Che Guevara, and not only did we see this happening around the world, but we fantasized that it was going to happen in the U.S. We had a pro-third-world view, whereas the other views tended to put workers, and especially white workers, at the center of things. And we knew we were right, and we knew they were fuckheads, and they knew we were wrong, and that's what we split over. Of course, all of these positions were wrong, they were all fantasies, but I think the context is important.

BILL AYERS

Let's talk about the movement. At that point, the black movement splintered, the antiwar movement splintered, the student movement splintered. Radical feminism was born, and that eventually splintered. In other words, it wasn't like there were some crazy people in SDS driving this thing. There were forces much bigger than the pretty small individuals, who were either in positions of leadership or emerging as leaders. So, it's too narrow a lens to think that SDS did something that was so unique and bizarre that nobody else was doing. It was in the water we were drinking and the air we were breathing: Nobody knew what to do. No one knew the way forward. We had tried everything that we could think of: organizing, knocking on doors, mass demonstrations, getting arrested, militant nonviolent resistance, disrupting draft boards, stopping troop trains, a little bit of sabotage here and there, burning draft cards. People had tried everything. And we had won the hearts and minds of the American people. So, all of this is going on, and here comes the summer of 1969.

So in '69, a dozen of us got together as a study group, and those discussions resulted in drawing up this paper, which was basically a resolution to SDS. The thesis was simple: The world was on fire. At the last minute Terry Robbins put this whimsical title on it: "You Don't Need a Weatherman to Know Which Way the Wind Blows," which is a line from Bob Dylan's song "Subterranean Homesick Blues." Terry offered a bit of self-mocking irony with the title to this insufferably dense and difficult text about the world situation that can be summed to a rock-and-roll beat.

Maggie comes fleet foot
Face full of black soot
Talkin' that the heat put
Plants in the bed but
The phone's tapped anyway
Maggie says that many say
They must bust in early May
Orders from the DA
Look out kid
Don't matter what you did
Walk on your tiptoes
Don't try "No-Doz"
Better stay away from those
That carry around a fire hose
Keep a clean nose
Watch the plain clothes
You don't need a weatherman
To know which way the wind blows.

GREIL MARCUS (music critic)

In "Subterranean Homesick Blues," when Bob Dylan says, "You don't need a weatherman to know which way the wind blows," he's saying you don't need a protest singer to tell you what's going on in the world. That's one way of reading that line. And then you have the Weathermen naming themselves after that. In essence they are saying, "You *do* need a weather-man to tell you which way the wind is blowing, and we're the Weather-men." On the other hand, the last line of that song is, "The pump don't work, 'cause the vandals took the handles." And they at one time considered calling themselves the Vandals, not Weathermen, which probably would have been a better name.

> *Better jump down a manhole*
> *Light yourself a candle*
> *Don't wear sandals*
> *Try to avoid the scandals*
> *Don't wanna be a bum*
> *You better chew gum*
> *The pump don't work*
> *'Cause the vandals took the handles.*

MARK RUDD

There were about two thousand people in the Chicago Coliseum for the ninth annual [June 1969] SDS convention, representing this enormous organization of over one hundred thousand members, screaming at each other and waving the Little Red Books of Mao Zedong quotations. All of us were in a frenzy of sectarian infighting. On one side of the hall there were chants, "Ho, Ho, Ho Chi Minh, the Viet Cong are gonna win." And on this side, "Mao, Mao, Zedong . . ."

MICHAEL KAZIN (Harvard SDS)

The convention in Chicago was crazy. The Panthers were there, talking about pussy power. PL [Progressive Labor] was incensed because they thought the other people were trying to drive them out of SDS, which they kind of were. Bernardine Dohrn was an avatar of a certain kind of rebellion. She was very smart and charismatic and other people from her faction of SDS were arranged behind her, like John Jacobs, and Mark Rudd—people who formed the Weathermen, mostly from Columbia and Michigan. All of them I knew by then. About halfway through the meeting the non-PL people started to have separate meetings, and they eventually walked out and went to a nearby church. The main convention took place in the Chicago Coliseum, which was known for having wrestling matches, which I believe was appropriate.

MARK RUDD

We were being disrupted by what we later learned was COINTELPRO. We knew we were being fucked with because suddenly leaflets appeared putatively from us, saying things that we didn't say. And then there'd be other leaflets appearing, putatively from the Progressive Labor people, with sexist drawings of Bernardine in bed with Black Panthers and shit, and then we would get pissed-off. "PL's really unprincipled bastards." But it wasn't PL. It was somebody else.

FBI MEMORANDUM, JUNE 30, 1969

```
To: Director, FBI
From: [blackout] Chicago
Subject: COINTELPRO-NEW LEFT
```

1. POTENTIAL COUNTERINTELLIGENCE ACTION

The recent split between pro–national office and pro–Progressive Labor factions of Students for a Democratic Society (SDS) presents possible opportunities for counterintelligence action with the objective of widening the split and preventing possible reunification of SDS. . . .

2. PENDING COUNTERINTELLIGENCE ACTIVITY

A recommendation was made to attempt to weaken or destroy an alliance between SDS and the Black Panther Party (BPP). The Bureau approved use of informants to attempt to point out that SDS was exploiting the BPP, intending to use them as a black army for a white revolution. This has been done, but no tangible results have been noted from this action at this time. . . .

BERNARDINE DOHRN

The issues seemed so important at the time. At that point, the Progressive Labor group had built up strength inside SDS, arguing that we should support workers, and that the National Liberation Front and North Vietnam had betrayed the workers' struggle. They took the Chinese position. They also denounced the Black Panther Party. But our view was that Americans had invaded Vietnam, and our job was to get the United States out of Vietnam. And the Vietnamese should decide their own destiny; for us to denounce the Vietnamese was the height of white chauvinism and arrogance—and the same for the Panthers. The Panthers were being shot and murdered by now. I'd been to Panther funerals on the West Coast— the first funerals in my life. We thought it was dangerous and wrong and we couldn't go along with it.

So that all came to bear at the national convention in June of '69 and resulted in me giving a speech about the history of SDS, and about our core values in terms of participatory democracy, which is a different idea than democracy. It wasn't parliamentary rules and voting, but it was democracy at the grass roots. So that led to us walking out and pretty much the end of SDS, the meaning of which has been fought over ever since.

MARK RUDD

I was on the stage next to Bernardine, who was accusing the other side of being racist. So in effect, she read them out and we physically left the building. People screamed all kinds of stuff like "Shame! Shame!" at us, and other people were screaming "Racist!" at the Progressive Labor faction. It was pandemonium. Bernardine was the central organization secretary, the most recognized leader in SDS. She took the stage and expelled PL. Now, there was no basis to do it. But the handwriting was on the wall. In our arrogance and our fantasy, we saw this as the moment that we became true white revolutionaries.

SDS leader Bernardine Dohrn gives a defiant speech at the June 1969 SDS convention in Chicago. Standing at Dohrn's left are fellow activists Susan Stern and Mark Rudd. Dohrn's radical group, the Action Faction, split off from SDS to create the Weathermen. "Bernardine was very charismatic," Mark Rudd told me. "She's the most seductive person I have ever met in my whole life, without exception, and without even trying to be. She just is."

PHOTOGRAPH BY
DAVID FENTON.

MICHAEL KAZIN

Bernardine's speech was impressive, but also a little scary because I was beginning to learn what the Weathermen were all about. They were about urban guerrilla warfare. They were emulating the Panthers, they were emulating the Viet Cong,[*] emulating the Cubans—all of us in my faction were, too, but that didn't mean we were ready to go out and pick up guns and start shooting people. But the way she was talking, it was clear that we might be ready to commit violence. She basically said people who don't support all these revolutions in all these communist countries are counterrevolutionary. I remember she mentioned Albania. I thought, Do I

---

[*]   From Vietnamese, *Viet Cong* (or VC) was short for "Vietnam communist" and was applied to anyone fighting alongside the National Liberation Front (NLF), who were South Vietnamese who opposed the U.S.-Saigon government and wanted unification with Ho Chi Minh's North Vietnam.

want to go to war for Albania? I don't think so. I didn't have the same feeling about Albania as I did for the Vietnamese and the Cubans.

DAVID FENTON (movement photographer)

I have some of the very few photos from that SDS convention in Chicago of '69. I was seventeen and had just dropped out of high school to be a photographer for Liberation News Service, which was a chapter of Students for a Democratic Society. Liberation News Service* was the AP, UPI, Reuters of the underground, countercultural, antiwar press. One of the people that had started it, Allen Young, was a former *Washington Post* reporter who was so fed up with the *Post*'s bullshit coverage of the Vietnam War that he quit and helped start the Liberation News Service.

It was small, but influential, because there were several hundred underground antiwar newspapers. There was one in every major city and on every major campus at that time, and LNS was the news service for all of them. We actually printed a packet of photographs and news and mailed it to people. Imagine! We had correspondents traveling with the North Vietnamese and the Viet Cong, and with the early precursors of the Palestine Liberation Organization, and the guerrilla movements in Latin America and in Cuba. We had correspondents all over the place.

When I joined Liberation News Service, it was obligatory to go to SDS conventions, so they sent me to Chicago, and I went into this huge hall and saw these people waving the Red Book and chanting. That was the Progressive Labor Party. They were extremely ideological and rigid and incredibly sectarian. Culturally, they were very straight—no sex, drugs, and rock and roll for them. And I think that was part of the nature of the split. It was a cultural split, not just an ideological split. Bernardine Dohrn and Mark Rudd, Terry Robbins, and Bill Ayers stormed the stage, guarded by a bunch of Black Panthers, and took over the convention and expelled the PL people.

---

*   An underground wire service, Liberation News Service (LNS) reached one million readers who read six hundred New Left and GI underground newspapers with names like *The Guardian, Ramparts, Berkeley Barb, East Village Other, Rag, Paper, Space City, Great Speckled Bird, Ann Arbor Sun, Avatar,* and *Rat.*

David Fenton dropped out of high school at age seventeen to join the movement as a photographer for the Liberation News Service (LNS), which provided news and photographs to six hundred underground newspapers reaching one million readers.
PHOTOGRAPH BY STEPHEN SHAMES.

The Weathermen faction of SDS romanticized that they were going to get high school students from the working class to rebel and storm out of their schools and fight the police and have a revolution. They really thought that. You have to be completely delusional to think something like that. They were fucking out of their minds.

MARK RUDD

Part of our Weatherman ideology was the concept of a revolutionary youth movement, and that young people would rise up to support third-world revolution. So we set about trying to prove that by organizing the white youth, and the point of all the organizing was to bring them to Chicago in October '68 to demonstrate our militancy.

The theory was if we started armed struggle it would grow into a mass

phenomenon, and we would be the vanguard of this large mass movement. It would take on the issue of power. Political power grows out of the
barrel of a gun—Mao Zedong had written that, and we believed that. The
Vietnamese were engaged in a war for liberation. The Cubans had to engage in a war for liberation. The black struggle had turned from nonviolence to by any means necessary. Malcolm X was our hero, not Martin
Luther King. These are all to a large extent intellectual phenomena that
were present in our milieu at the time. We had all read *The Autobiography
of Malcolm X,* an absolutely critical book.

We split into two entities, and I found myself as the national secretary
of our faction of SDS, which was now in control of the national office and
the regional offices, and in touch with the chapters; we had four hundred
chapters, and a national membership of about 120,000 and a national
weekly publication called *New Left Notes.* We decided that a small group
of people would take over this major national organization, which had
democracy in its name, and would reorient the work of the organization
towards struggle in the streets, and eventually armed struggle. We were
totally out of touch with our membership. But we knew we were right.
Terrible arrogance, you know?

JULIUS LESTER

By the time SDS broke up in '69, I was aware that the movement was falling apart. I was aware that the movement was becoming ideological. And
when movements become ideological, they lose sight of people. Ideology
becomes more important than people. I'm talking about all movements.
I'm talking black movements, white movements. The Panthers were also
very ideological.

MICHAEL KAZIN

People who study it tell you different things. Some think that the SDS
membership was about 120,000 strong. The problem is, I went to the
national office and I saw people open up an envelope with membership
cards in them, sometimes from a whole chapter, put them on a table, and

then somebody would spill cheap wine on it and throw them away. I mean there was no way of knowing how many members there were. People called themselves SDS members who never saw a membership card, because they felt like SDS members. SDS was a name.

SDS petered away. Some chapters tried to keep going. The irony was that the national office didn't matter that much, but if there was no national office, there was no newspaper, there was no sense of being part of a national organization, and then you might as well just be an antiwar group rather than SDS. A lot of SDS chapters were not full of revolutionaries. They were full of kids who called themselves pacifists, didn't like the war, were for civil rights, but they were not revolutionaries, and were not looking to pick up a gun and smash the state.

TOM HAYDEN (founder, SDS)

That was the end of SDS. It was really bizarre, because this was before Kent State, Jackson State, before the Moratorium, before Earth Day. There were many student uprisings to come, and the group that had triggered it, and had gotten all the blame and all the credit, was actually dead. Unbelievable. And this was not seven years from the time when SDS was formed.

CHAPTER 5

RESISTERS

(1967-August 1969)

"Vietnam, Vietnam, Vietnam, we've all been there."

—MICHAEL HERR, *Dispatches*

BY JUNE 1965, 117,000 U.S. TROOPS WERE STATIONED IN VIETNAM AND the ground war escalated swiftly. By the end of 1967, the number of U.S. military personnel in Vietnam had grown to 500,000. Annual American casualty rates peaked in 1968, with 16,899 soldiers killed that year. The average age of the Vietnam soldier was nineteen, compared to twenty-six in World War II, and nearly 76 percent of the American GIs came from working-class backgrounds. With the rising deployment and death toll came a corresponding increase in draft resistance. By 1967, three thousand young men had signed "We Won't Go" petitions. Five thousand had turned in their draft cards, and anti-draft protests took place on campuses at half of the nation's public universities. The resistance movement swelled into a grassroots uprising with thousands of participants in most major cities sabotaging draft boards by destroying records, returning and burning draft cards, and counseling others in draft resistance.

RANDY KEHLER (draft resistance organizer)

I grew up in Scarsdale, New York, went to Exeter Academy, a private boarding school in New Hampshire, and graduated from Harvard in '67. In September of '67, I started at Stanford in the teaching program, and when I first got to campus I met David Harris. I had heard the story about how they had shaved his head one night as a fraternity boy prank. He was organizing this group called the Resistance, which I quickly joined. The Resistance was based on getting young men to turn in their draft cards. He was going up and down the West Coast with this bunch of people; they all lived in a commune in East Palo Alto called the Peace and Liberation Commune.

So, I immediately thought, I've got this draft card that's burning a hole in my pocket. So, before classes even started, I wrote this letter to the Selective Service System, the national draft board in Washington. General Lewis B. Hershey was the head of it. I essentially said, "I can't cooperate anymore with any part of this. Here's my draft card. Don't call me. I'm not your boy."

The law said that you had to carry your draft card. If you were apprehended by an ordinary police patrolman, and they happened to ask to see your draft card, if you didn't have it somewhere on your body, in theory you could get up to five years in federal prison. No fooling around. I sent it back in September of '67, full of fear and trepidation. I remember sticking my hand inside the mailbox before I let it go, thinking, All right, think again on this. Is this really what you want to do? The minute I let it go, I thought there was going to be this hand clapping me around the back and hauling me off. Of course I was being ridiculous.

RICK AYERS (draft deserter and GI organizer)

The big thing in the fall of '67, which was my junior year, was resistance against the draft. I turned in my draft card in October. I knew about David Harris and I was in the Resistance. I was also in SDS. But you could be in everything. The Resistance had a lot of Quakers, who were also highly regarded in the movement. They were big in Ann Arbor. So I decided, "Okay, I'm going to do this."

I grew up in an affluent suburb of Chicago and went to college in Ann Arbor at the University of Michigan, and was very involved in the agitation around Vietnam. My father was the president of Commonwealth Edison in Chicago. He was a big muckety-muck, and a liberal businessman, a friend of labor.

My choices were: I could still stay in school and be a good boy; protest, but try to not get in trouble. Or, like the Mario Savio* line, you could "put your body upon the gears" and say, I'm going to stop this. In other words, instead of avoiding the draft—I got my 2-S [student deferment]—I decided that I would walk into the draft board and say no.

Demonstrator holding an anti-draft banner at a protest outside the Whitehall Street military induction center, New York City, July 2, 1968.

RANDY KEHLER

I wasn't happy in the Stanford graduate teaching program and I really wanted to be working full-time against the war. I signed up for a course in what was then a free university. In those days, there were these free univer-

---

*   Mario Savio was a Berkeley student, a gifted orator, and a leader of the Free Speech Movement. In Savio's often-quoted December 2, 1964, speech about civil disobedience, he references Henry David Thoreau's "On the Duty of Civil Disobedience": "There's a time when the operation of the machine becomes so odious, makes you so sick at heart, that you can't take part. You can't even passively take part. And you've got to put your bodies upon the gears and upon the wheels, upon the levers, upon all the apparatus—and you've got to make it stop!"

sities popping up all over. There was one called the Mid-Peninsula Free University, where anybody could offer a course on anything, and anybody could take a course for a ten-dollar registration fee. There were no grades and people met outside under trees, or in living rooms, or basements. And there was everything from astrophysics to making candles, singing gospel songs, to the history of Vietnam.

So, I signed up for a course on Gandhi and nonviolence, which was being led principally by Ira Sandperl, Joan Baez, and Roy Kepler. Sandperl* was Joan Baez's mentor, who got her into nonviolent civil disobedience and activism when she was just a Palo Alto High School kid. All three had a big influence on me. Roy Kepler had been a World War II CO, and started and owned the largest bookstore in Northern California at that time, Kepler's Books in Menlo Park. So I signed up for this course. I knew nothing about nonviolence; the word *pacifism* wasn't even really part of my vocabulary.

But it turned out that these three rascals were also planning a demonstration for the fall of '67, which they invited everybody in this little seminar to be part of. So, I went by just to witness. I had never thought of being arrested. It was so amazing to see it. It was such a beautiful demonstration. I thought of demonstrations as just this kind of thing on the street, yelling and confronting the police, which is a lot of what was going on then. But this was a really dignified, peaceful sit-in, blocking bus after bus of inductees who were being led into the Oakland induction center. I couldn't help but join. I sat down, and I went to the Santa Rita jail outside of Oakland for ten days with three hundred others, including Joan, Ira, Roy, and the whole gang.

RICK AYERS

There was a march from [the University of Michigan] campus to the Ann Arbor draft board, and there were like two thousand people in this march.

---

* Ira Sandperl was a pacifist and a student of Gandhian teaching who worked at the renowned Kepler's Books in Palo Alto for thirty years and is credited with teaching a generation of men how to resist the draft nonviolently. He became folksinger Joan Baez's mentor after meeting her in 1959, when she was a high school senior, and traveled with her to Mississippi in 1966 to help with Martin Luther King's school desegregation campaign. Together, Sandperl and Baez founded the Institute for the Study of Nonviolence.

Police officers arrest a protester outside the armed services induction center in Oakland, California, October 1967.

It had been planned ahead who was going to get arrested. It was very moving. They went in; they sat down; they wouldn't leave. There were police lines and chanting outside. We stayed there while they carried people out and threw them into police vans. It was quite dramatic. Ann Arbor was a big activist center around anti–Vietnam War work. I mailed my draft card in, in a big protest. We all got our envelopes and threw them in the mailbox. Six days later it came back. "You're reclassified 1-A."

So I got drafted, which was a shock, because I still thought, This ain't going to happen. And it did happen. I was very concerned, because the choices didn't look good. I didn't want to go to jail. I was too young and scared of what happened in jail. I was scared of the army because I thought, being antiwar, I would get beat up.

My brother Bill was also at the University of Michigan. He was very active in SDS, but he hadn't taken this path, and I asked him, "What am I going to do?" We went around and around, and we finally decided I'd go to Canada. We had friends in Toronto. It's not that far from Ann Arbor. I went up to Canada and got a job offer letter, and I got a recommendation letter from the vice president of the University of Michigan, because I was on his advisory board. He was heartbroken that I was leaving. I had to tell my Greek professor. I didn't tell my parents because I didn't know if they would rat me out. So I drove with a friend to a border crossing and presented myself at the immigration board as requesting immigration—we had consulted lawyers, and that was a pretty fast way to get it if you have all your paperwork lined up. If you asked for immigration, they were not allowed to ask you about your draft status, but everyone knows what it is, and you become a landed immigrant. A landed immigrant status was temporary until they verified a lot of stuff. So they gave me papers, I walked right in, and I was a landed immigrant in Canada, and I went to Toronto and got a job at a movie theater. It was 1968 and I was twenty-one.

DAVID HARRIS (draft resistance organizer)

I was traveling up and down the West Coast giving speeches, and then I also start traveling nationally. I'd fly into Portland, I'd be met by the guy from the Portland Resistance, who had set up a bunch of gigs. I'd give anywhere from four to nine speeches a day, trying to get people to send their draft cards back, and then I'd move to the next city. I did that from 1967 essentially through the time I got incarcerated, July '69. I was an organizer. That's what I did.

We took donations wherever we could. That's how I met Joan Baez. There was a guy named Roy Kepler, who ran Kepler's Bookstore in Menlo Park, which was kind of a hip left outpost. He had been one of the founders of KPFA, a local listener-owned radio station. He had been a draft resister in World War II. He also was Joan's business manager. And he said to me, "You ought to talk to Joan about this. She'll give you some money." So he set up an appointment. I went down to her house in Carmel and got a check.

She's five years older than me, and at the time she was paramount. She was Ms. Folk Song of the Universe. She'd been on the cover of *Time* magazine in 1962. She was just coming off a romance with Bob Dylan. She was as big a star as there was in the music world at that point. Folk music was our own invention. The space between the Beats and the hippies was folk music, which had icons like Woody Guthrie and Pete Seeger, who were all lefties. People sometimes sang with bare feet, which Joan did. She had long, straight hair down to her shoulders, which was not the way women were supposed to look at that time, so there was a counterculture aspect to it which soon became popular.

Her father, Al Baez, was a physicist who refused to do war work during World War II, and he was a Quaker. So she came by her politics that way. She had been an outsider girl in high school and started singing and became this major celebrity. I liked her music before I ever knew her. Five months after I got that first check, we were married. What can I say? In that era, people got married a lot earlier. Also, we were on a speaking tour together. She was doing concerts and I was giving speeches, and we just kind of decided on the road, "Okay, let's go get married." We got married in New York City, and for a couple of years, I was part of Mr. and Mrs. Peace in America.

Resistance founder David Harris with his wife, folksinger and activist Joan Baez, at a war resistance demonstration in New York's Central Park, April 1968.
PHOTOGRAPH BY
ROBERT ALTMAN.

WESLEY BROWN

I graduated from college June of '68, and I was called to report to my draft board in September, but I never showed up. By that time, I was living in Rochester [New York], and there was a chapter of the Black Panther Party there that I became involved with. In Rochester, I was doing community stuff, selling the Panther newspaper, connecting with local groups who were involved with school issues. We were trying to do things with regards to free lunch, free breakfast programs in schools, having more accountability with parents' involvement in the local schools.

In March of 1969, I wrote a letter to my draft board, quoting the Black Panther platform as an explanation for why I refused to sign up:

> Point six of the Black Panther Party platform and program states: "We want all Black men exempt from military service. We believe the Black people should not be forced to fight in the military service to defend a racist government that does not protect us. We will not fight and kill other people of color in the world who, like black people are being victimized by the white racist government of America. We will protect ourselves from the force and violence of the racist police and the racist military, by whatever means necessary."
>
> This position I adhere to. Therefore, since the government grants no rights, I owe it no duties. And if you can't relate to that, you can walk chicken with your ass picked clean.

DAVID HARRIS

I was ordered for induction in January of '68. I rode the bus up to the induction center and then turned around and told them, "I'm not going any further. I'm done." They indicted me thirteen days later—only Muhammad Ali got indicted faster than me. I know people who refused induction who have never heard from the government. By 1968, if you wanted to prosecute every violation the Selective Service had in the northern district of California, you would have to close the courts down for two years and just do draft cases.

Two months later, Joan and I got married. Two months after that, I went on trial. We were always trying to find ways to talk about the war in the courtroom, because the courtroom is theater. That was part of our approach. If you're going to be on trial, you make your trial a propaganda mechanism as much as you can. My lawyer was a guy named Francis Heisler, who was a longtime civil liberties lawyer. What we used for a defense was, in order to be convicted of a felony, you have to not only prove the facts of the case, they have to prove that you acted with intent and bad purpose. So we used intent and bad purpose to try and give testimony. "What was your intention, Mr. Harris?" I said I thought the war was immoral and I wasn't going to be part of it. I had the jury out for eight hours. There were two holdouts. There was a Quaker lady on the jury and a black housekeeper. The Quaker lady caved first. The last holdout was the black housekeeper, who finally, after they worked on her for eight hours, gave in. My trial judge was a guy named Oliver Carter, whose nickname was Death by Elocution. He said, "You may not need to be real ill-fated, but you're going to be punished," and gave me twice the length of any sentence that had been handed out in San Francisco ever for a draft case, which was three years. Normally you'd find, around the country in judicial districts, there was a standard length of sentence. In San Francisco, it was eighteen months. I spent the next year on appeal.

RANDY KEHLER

I registered for the draft, because at age eighteen I happened to be working on a cattle ranch near Cheyenne and the law then said when you turn eighteen, you register at the closest draft board, and that's your permanent board.

Around that time, I got a letter telling me to report for induction. So I went to the Oakland, California, induction center and there was a long line of young men who were about to be inducted that day. There was a line on the floor, and once you stepped over it, you were in—you were a member of the military. I remember getting closer and closer to the line. I had rehearsed this in my mind with trepidation. Just before I got to the line I turned around—thinking that I might be beat up or shot, or hauled off and arrested for what I was about to do—and I turned around to the guys behind me and I said, "I'm not going. This war is wrong. We should all be refusing to fight in this war. Let's all go home." And I walked out. Nobody blinked. Nobody did anything.

In the end I was indicted out of Wyoming on five counts, carrying a potential of five years on each one. I only remember four of them. One was nonpossession of a draft card. One was failure or refusal to give current address. I would get mailings asking for my current address and I'd just throw them away. Another one was refusing a physical examination. Another was refusing induction.

DAVID HARRIS

When my appeal was finally turned down, I chose not to take the appeal any further. I wanted to get my time done. At that point Joan was five months pregnant, and the issue was, do you go in and get out earlier, or do you wait? It was a hard call. So she ended up having to go through childbirth by herself—she had people there, but not me. I'd been looking down the barrel of prison for three years at this point. I wanted to get going.

On July 17, 1969, there I was, in San Francisco County Jail, where I was for a month. We staged a hunger strike, "we" being all the prisoners in the federal cell block. I was the only draft prisoner; the rest were you name it: car thieves, dope dealers, whatever. A month later they moved me to a prison in Safford, Arizona, where they were concentrating the West Coast draft prisoners. I walked in and it was full of people I had organized. At one point I shared a cell with another resister who I had organized, who had started as a defensive halfback in the Rose Bowl for UCLA, and then walked into the induction center in Los Angeles, grabbed a stack of files, and walked out into the street and burned them.

RANDY KEHLER

Instead of facing trial in Wyoming, and then prison, I could have gone to Canada, but I thought that was the most difficult and horrible option, because I thought I wouldn't ever be able to come back home. I didn't know that later there would be amnesty. I didn't want to be separated from my family, my community, and all the people I knew and loved. I said, "I'm not going to let them chase me out of my country. I refuse to flee."

The other option was to start cooperating. I definitely wasn't going to do that. I could have gone underground—Dan Berrigan* was underground at the time. I heard him speak, but I didn't then know him. I thought, Hiding? I would need to go from place to place, cloak-and-dagger stuff, surfacing and then going back under. I thought, I'm not into that. You couldn't be in touch with your family and friends, and you had to keep moving because you would be somewhat of a burden for whoever was hiding you; you would risk their well-being and safety. I just thought, I can't imagine doing that, any more than I can imagine being forced out of my country.

RICK AYERS

We created a hostel for deserters only. It was a house we rented that only had three bedrooms, but it had a basement, and at any time we'd have between twelve to fifteen people. We learned to do fake IDs, because we were very defiant, so it wasn't just getting them legal, although we had a bunch of lawyers helping us; but it was also getting ID for those who couldn't get legal. We openly did marriages with Canadian women, and interestingly enough, a few of them turned into love. A lot of Canadian activist women did that. We had these GIs who would come to us and say, "I ran away from my base, and was hitchhiking. I had short hair, and

---

* Daniel Berrigan was a radical antiwar activist, poet, and Jesuit priest, who along with his brother Philip (also a Catholic priest) and seven other Catholic activists used homemade napalm to burn hundreds of draft files from the Catonsville, Maryland, draft board in May 1968. The group was called the Catonsville Nine. Berrigan was sentenced to three years in prison, but he and others skipped bail and went underground. He was eventually apprehended in 1972.

someone picked me up, and I said, 'I'm a deserter, help me.' And they said, 'Okay, I'll help you. Get down.'" There was so much support in the land that these guys got across the border because they threw themselves at the mercy of the public, and the public would say, "What can I do for you?" It was very moving, and very beautiful. We had people who were in the Presidio 27 who were charged with mutiny, which you can get executed for.*

GIs in uniform brazenly lead an antiwar march in San Francisco on October 12, 1968. In 1968, 155,536 soldiers deserted or went AWOL (absent without leave). Two days after this march, 27 soldiers in the Presidio military jail staged a sit-down protest. PHOTOGRAPH BY STEPHEN SHAMES.

DANIEL ELLSBERG (RAND defense analyst)

When President Nixon was elected he promised to end the war, and in August of 1969 everybody thought that the war was ending, so the em-

---

*   The Presidio 27 was one of the largest cases of resistance to the war from within the military. On October 14, 1968, twenty-seven prisoners who were being kept in the stockade at the military base in San Francisco's Presidio staged a sit-in during morning formation and sang "We Shall Overcome." They were tried for mutiny, and the first three sentenced were given fourteen, fifteen, and sixteen years of hard labor, which caused a national uproar. Their sentences were eventually reduced on appeal. Three of the GIs escaped to Canada.

phasis of the War Resisters International* conference that I attended that month was on other liberation movements around the world. But I'd been talking to my friend who worked with Kissinger on the National Security Council [NSC], Mort Halperin, and he told me that not only was the war not going to end, but it was going to get larger.

RANDY KEHLER

Every three years War Resisters International would have a conference, and that August of '69 it was held in the U.S. for the first time, at Haverford College, which has a Quaker background, and I was asked to give a talk there. Probably I'd been indicted and was about to get sent to prison. So a bunch of us from the War Resisters League in San Francisco jumped in a VW van and drove across the country to Haverford. That's where I met Dan Ellsberg. He was with a brilliant young Indian woman named Janaki Tschannerl and, frankly, I think Dan was in love with her. She was a Gandhian and she'd introduced him to Gandhian thought, which blew his mind. "What do you mean, you don't believe in an enemy? In Gandhian thinking, no one's your enemy?"†

DANIEL ELLSBERG

I chose not to potentially embarrass RAND by going to the conference on RAND money, and I paid my own airfare and took vacation time. But nev-

---

* Founded in the Netherlands in 1921, the War Resisters League is an international antiwar organization that has helped war resisters since World War I. The league had a close working relationship with the Gandhian movement.

† Daniel Ellsberg had spent most of his career as a Cold War hawk. A former marine with a PhD from Harvard in economics, he worked as a strategic analyst specializing in nuclear weapons at the RAND Corporation starting in 1959. In 1964 Ellsberg moved to Washington, D.C., and worked as a special assistant to Assistant Secretary of Defense John McNaughton, in which post he became a proponent of escalating the war in Vietnam. But in 1965 Ellsberg went to Vietnam for two years, with the State Department, to see for himself what was happening on the ground. He spent months in the jungle witnessing the horrors of the war firsthand and came back home a changed man. He spent the next two years at RAND writing part of Secretary of Defense Robert McNamara's top-secret study of U.S. decision-making in Vietnam from 1945 to 1968 [later known as the Pentagon Papers] and trying to convince the powers that be that America needed to withdraw from what he believed was a criminal and unwinnable war.

ertheless, I was a consultant to Kissinger at that point so I was not anxious to be photographed in a vigil line for one of the resisters who was about to go to jail, Bob Eaton, in front of the Philadelphia post office. I seriously tried to think how to get out of this. I thought of being sick, but there were several more days of the conference, so was I going to stay sick? Or did I have to turn up miraculously recovered the day after the vigil? And that was embarrassing. I couldn't tell them I can't bear to be photographed at these things. And finally I figured I just had to go. I didn't have the guts to refuse. So we go out to the first vigil and stand around outside the post office. Bob Eaton is going to be sentenced and sent away inside the courthouse. We were standing arm to arm outside the courthouse in a vigil and I was think-ing, Boy, if there is a photograph of this, my colleagues in the Pentagon and at RAND would think that I'd gone insane, because they would consider this the lowest-prestige-imaginable way of influencing policy, to be stand-ing on a street corner, literally like somebody on a soapbox, or a homeless person dragging a cart with a sign on it. I was obviously giving up the chance to write memos to the president, and to Henry Kissinger. I was with long-haired hippie types from all over the world, and they were all pacifists, the lowest of the low. But you get used to anything. As the hours went by, I began handing out leaflets myself. I finally got enthusiastic about it. I would even go into the street and give leaflets to cars at the stoplight.

RANDY KEHLER

I'd been introduced to Dan before I gave my speech. I wasn't even sure what his background was, but I was told that he was not one of us. Not hostile in any way, but just from a different background. I wondered, What's he doing here? It turns out he had just finished working on a top-secret Pentagon study. He'd risen through the ranks of the Defense De-partment under McNamara and then RAND.

DANIEL ELLSBERG

Randy Kehler was speaking to a full auditorium about how he had gotten into the War Resisters League through the people he met at the Santa Rita jail, from draft resistance in Oakland. I was watching in this auditorium with people from all over the world, from India and Vietnam and Japan and East Europe, and I was thinking, I'm so glad that they can see this man, Randy Kehler, because he's the best we've got. He's the best young American. I was proud of being an American, and that they were seeing him. And so here I'm hearing that the best thing he can do with his life is go to prison.

Randy said he was the only man left in the San Francisco War Resisters League office, because all the other men had been imprisoned—David Harris and several others. He said, "Pretty soon it'll be all women when I go to prison." I think that was the first moment that everybody in the audience had heard that he was going to prison. His trial was just after this, but he knew he would end up going to prison. "But," he said, "I know that it'll be all right, because all of you people will still be working against the war." So it was hitting everybody at once. He was crying slightly at this point. His voice was choking. And one by one, people were standing up, and eventually everybody was standing up and nearly everybody was crying in the audience. Everybody was crying. I was crying.

I got out of my chair and found the men's room, and as soon as I got there I began sobbing hysterically. My chest was heaving, and it was hard to breathe. I'd only cried like that one other time in my life, when I learned that Bobby Kennedy was shot. I had seen Bobby just days earlier and I had drafted the policy framework for his last speech, which was in San Francisco. So here for the second time, and only other time in my life, I was crying—but not just crying, really hysterically racked. I thought, Randy Kehler is right. Resisting the draft and going to jail is the best thing he can do at this point. That's what we've come to. The lines of a Leonard Cohen song called "Dress Rehearsal Rag" kept going through my mind. It's about a guy contemplating suicide. The refrain of the song is

> *That's right, it's come to this,*
> *yes it's come to this,*
> *and wasn't it a long way down,*
> *ah wasn't it a strange way down?*

I was sitting on the floor of the bathroom, sobbing and thinking, This is what my country has come to, that the best thing a young man can do is go to prison. And that's when I thought, My son is born for prison. He was fourteen then, and indeed the war was still on when he turned eighteen. Finally I got up, and I washed my face in the basin, and went back still crying.

I was in there a good hour, and toward the end I was thinking, Okay, now what should I do to help end the war, now that I'm ready to go to prison? I just realized that going to prison could be an effective thing to do. Was I ready to go to prison? Well, sure. Here were these people who were perceiving that it made sense for them to go to prison. So the point was not that I wanted to go to prison—I didn't, I never did—but that I should be willing to do everything up to and including prison, or being killed, like these other Americans. And that meant, more significantly, risking my clearance, my job, my career, all the other things that you risk short of prison. These risks prevented all my colleagues at RAND, who felt exactly the same way I did about the war, from meeting a Bob Eaton or a Randy Kehler or Janaki Tschannerl.

RANDY KEHLER

Some weeks or months after my talk, Dan said, "The question that I never, ever asked myself, that never occurred to me, was what might I do if I, too, were willing to go to prison?" And as soon as he asked himself the question, the answer popped up. "I would release this study, revealing decades of lies by four different administrations, Republican and Democrat, to Congress, to the press, to the American people, about what Vietnam was all about. And what was happening on the ground there, and what our real objectives were." And that's what he did.

DANIEL ELLSBERG

What Randy had done was put in my mind the willingness to go to prison for life, for the small chance of ending the war.

CHAPTER 6

WOODSTOCK

(August 1969)

It was a phenomenal burst of human energy and spirit that came and went like a tidal wave up there in White Lake, Bethel, Woodstock, Aquarian Exposition, Music Festival, Happening, Monster, or whatever you called the fucking thing. I took a trip to our future.

—ABBIE HOFFMAN, *Woodstock Nation*

POSTERS ADVERTISED "AN AQUARIAN EXPOSITION: THREE DAYS OF Peace and Music," and on August 15–17, 1969, half a million people descended on a six-hundred-acre dairy farm in the Catskill Mountains, ninety miles north of New York City. Another million tried but were kept away by massive traffic jams. Thirty-two musical acts played, including Jimi Hendrix, the Who, Janis Joplin, the Grateful Dead, Jefferson Airplane, Crosby, Stills, Nash & Young, Joe Cocker, Richie Havens, Santana, and Ravi Shankar. Joan Baez sang "We Shall Overcome" in a thunderstorm. A New Mexico commune called the Hog Farm, led by the charismatic Wavy Gravy, provided security and catering. Young people camped out and were sleeping, eating, making love, singing, and swimming in the nude together. It was not just a musical festival. "We used to think of ourselves as little clumps of weirdoes," said Janis Joplin. "But now we're a whole new minority group." The size and success of the event convinced millions of young Americans who didn't attend but had already embraced the counterculture that they were part of a larger community. "It was as much of a fair as the French Revolution or the San Francisco earthquake," wrote journalist Andrew Kopkind.

RICHARD REEVES (*New York Times* reporter)

I was chief political reporter for *The New York Times* and was driving up to the Catskills to cover Mayor John Lindsay, who had just decided that he was going to become a Democrat, and suddenly the roads were totally blocked. There were cars parked in the fields everywhere. I go up to a state trooper and I say, "What the hell is going on?" He says, "Ten miles up that way, there's a music festival called Woodstock, and people are coming from all over. They're leaving their cars and walking." And I said, "How can you get up there?" And he says, "The only way you can get there is by helicopter." And I said, "Whose helicopter is that?" I was pointing across the field, and he said, "That's Canned Heat," which was a group at the time. And so I run over to Canned Heat. I'm just a thirty-three-year-old *New York Times* reporter wearing a jacket and a tie. So I get on the helicopter and I go up to Woodstock. Woodstock was an extraordinary story.

GERALD LEFCOURT (Abbie Hoffman's lawyer)

The Chicago Eight were indicted in April,* and then these rock promoters announce a concert at Woodstock in August. The trial was scheduled for September. Abbie is enraged that they were going to rip off all these young people while "our movement is going on trial for our lives," as he would say.†

So he stormed into the offices of the people putting on the concert and said, "We're going to protest the concert, unless you put performers on

---

* Abbie Hoffman, Jerry Rubin, David Dellinger, Tom Hayden, Rennie Davis, John Froines, Lee Weiner, and Bobby Seale were all charged with conspiracy to incite a riot during the protests outside the Democratic National Convention in August 1968.

† The four organizers, Michael Lang, John Roberts, Joel Rosenman, and Artie Kornfeld, planned to make a profit from the concert. Ultimately, so many people flooded the venue that fences were torn down and the concert automatically became free.

the program who are antiwar." The promoters folded and gave ten thousand dollars to Abbie to bring whomever he wanted. Abbie picked Phil Ochs, Country Joe, and some others.

COUNTRY JOE MCDONALD (rock musician)

They were putting on a festival to make money. That was their idea. But everything that the counterculture did was political because none of it was traditional. So it was political, and you couldn't really separate the two. It was shocking to the status quo and to the old-line, World War II generation. I've talked to some people who went to Woodstock, and they were just hippies in a small community, and didn't realize that there was this bigger national community of hippies until they got to Woodstock and realized, Wow, I'm not alone!

STEPHEN STILLS (Crosby, Stills, Nash & Young)

Everyone was fist-pounding, and angry about the war, and our music gave them something to do besides just be mad at everything. Woodstock, of course, everyone thinks it was a conspiracy—it's so simple. There's Bethel, New York. There are three hundred colleges within one hundred miles. Everybody came, and nobody realized how many hippies there were. They all decided to just gut it out, because all their favorite bands were going to be there. And then the promoters, and Michael Lang, happened to handle several things rather adroitly on the spot. It was a complete accident that it did not turn into hell.

RICHARD REEVES

I called up the paper [*The New York Times*] and I said, "Look, there's something going on up here, there are hundreds of thousands of people in a field, and I'm going up there." I didn't ask. I said, "I'm going." The news desk didn't even know the concert existed. Then I got another break. The *Daily News* called for bringing in the National Guard and cleaning out Woodstock because it was a health hazard; arrest all of the people and move them out. And that might have happened. They were calling for bringing in the army. "This is a danger to national security" because of drugs, and sex, and mud.

So I set myself up on the stage for three days, and I wrote a story saying, "Except for the fact that they're dirty," because there was mud, it was raining, "these people are no danger to anybody." And I think that the guys who organized it, and some of the stars, realized that the *Times* was keeping them alive.

Organizers of the Woodstock festival were caught by surprise when hundreds of thousands more people attended than they expected. The traffic on the way to Bethel, New York, stretched for miles, and eventually people abandoned their cars and started walking.

THELMA SCHOONMAKER (documentary filmmaker)

I was an assistant director with Martin Scorsese on Michael Wadleigh's production of the Woodstock documentary, but little did we know what the concert was going to be. We had no idea it was going to be that many people, or that it would get to be a little bit of a nightmare in terms of the blocked highways and people not being able to use their cars and not being able to get things in, and us not being able to get to our motel to sleep or eat anything for three days.

Half a million people, and that was absolutely terrifying. Some of them were flying over the fence, because they were just so excited. The great gift of Woodstock was that the security was handled really beautifully. People talked to the kids, calmed them down, took them to the medical tent. There were no police hitting kids over the head. Everybody had the same feeling of love and the same political commitments and values, and it was just a wonderful feeling, even though for me it was quite a personal strain. I was terrified. I had no idea if we were getting the footage, if it was being damaged. So many of our magazines would jam, because it was very humid and raining a lot, and the cameramen would throw off the magazine, and I would try and get them another one from under the stage where we had eighty people loading magazines. It was insane! I remember the first time I looked up and saw half a million people out there. I'll never forget it. It was absolutely stunning. I mean none of us expected it.

GREIL MARCUS (music critic)

I went to cover Woodstock for *Rolling Stone* magazine and I went for a simple reason, which was that there were lots of bands there I'd never seen and it seemed like a good way to see them. I went with a *Rolling Stone* photographer and another *Rolling Stone* writer. We even had tickets and a motel room. The first day I was there I completely hated it. I thought it was just awful. It was hot. There were a lot of people in distress. There were a lot of people without anything to eat, without water. It was a mess. It was this just enormous rural slum, and a lot of people were miserable. It was distressing. And it was raining all the time.

What was most surprising to me were the number of performances that were just magnificent. Playing for this enormous crowd, people really seemed to come out of themselves and they made music that was bigger, that had more of a reach and an ambition, and I thought, God, crowds like this make for better music. Which probably isn't remotely true—but that was the feeling I had then.

A pregnant Joan Baez plays at Woodstock and tells the audience about her husband, David Harris, who is in jail for resisting the draft.

JOAN BAEZ (political activist, folksinger)

August 15, 1969, Bethel, New York

I'd like to sing you a song that is one of my husband David's favorite songs. And let me tell you that he's fine. . . . [Pause and applause.] And we're fine, too. [Pats her pregnant belly.] David was just shipped from the county jail, which is very much of a drag, to federal prison, which is kind of like a summer camp after you've been in county jail long enough.

Anyway, this is an organizing song, and I was happy to find out that after David had been in jail for two and a half weeks he already had a very, very good hunger strike going with forty-two prisoners, none of whom were draft people.

From August 15 to August 17, 1969, half a million hippies camped out on a six-hundred-acre dairy farm in the Catskills for the Woodstock Music and Arts Fair.

I dreamed I saw Joe Hill last night
Alive as you and me.
Says I, "But Joe you're ten years dead."
"I never died," said he.
"I never died," said he.

COUNTRY JOE MCDONALD

The size was surprising. It was the biggest stage I had ever seen before—the biggest sound towers, and the biggest audience—I mean, half a million people, you know?

Then I was on the stage at Woodstock, the band was breaking up, but we got booked two weeks before. We're not on the poster. I went early because I didn't like to travel with the band. I liked festivals because you could see all kinds of acts. Saturday, I was just hanging around the stage, and Santana couldn't get through the traffic on the road and the organizers said, "How about starting your solo career?" I said, "What the fuck?" And they said, "Just go do something, because Santana can't get in here. We want to keep something happening onstage."

It was Saturday afternoon. I said, "I don't have a guitar." They went and they got me a guitar. I said, "I don't have a guitar strap." They got a piece of rope and tied it onto the guitar. Then they said, "Okay, go out there and do something." I hadn't performed solo for three or four years, and I sang some country-western songs and nobody was paying any attention to me, because nobody knew who I was. Most people knew Country Joe and the Fish.

I walked offstage to ask the tour manager for Country Joe and the Fish, Bill Belmont, "Should I sing 'Fixin'-to-Die Rag' and the cheer? Because I'm saving it for when the band plays later tonight." He said, "Nobody's paying any attention to you. What the hell difference does it make what you do?" I thought, Okay. All right. So I went out there and yelled, "Give me an *F*!" I mean, they all responded and stood up and started singing along. They stopped talking, and they started yelling, and they paid more and more attention to me, and I realized, Whoa, what the hell is going on here? Then I got pretty brave in the middle and started yelling, "How can you expect to stop the war if you can't sing louder than that?"

THELMA SCHOONMAKER

When we cut Country Joe singing his anti-Vietnam song, I chose the shots of these beautiful young men who were going to be cannon fodder if they ended up in Vietnam. We particularly wanted to illustrate that. We had so much rich material. We couldn't even use it all, of course, but we knew something special had happened. We didn't know it would never happen again, but we knew it was special. It was very much connected with Vietnam, very, very much.

COUNTRY JOE MCDONALD

I didn't know Michael Wadleigh was there filming me. I didn't see him. I was concentrating on the crowd. I was surprised they paid attention to me, because they weren't paying any attention to me before that. Then they started standing up. It was exciting. I thought, This is amazing. Then they all stood up and they sang along. I didn't know what the hell to do next. So I went back out and sang a little bit more of it.

And it's one, two, three,
What are we fighting for?

The unique thing about "Fixin'-to-Die Rag" is that it is not anti-soldier. It's just about a person who's doing a job that he thinks is stupid and doesn't want to do it, but is going to go ahead and do it anyway.

GREIL MARCUS

You're talking about a time when life was politicized, when people are talking about and arguing about political issues all the time, whether it's the war, whether it's Nixon, whether it's Humphrey, whether it's Eldridge Cleaver, whether it's the Black Panthers, whether it's SDS, or Weathermen. All these things are being discussed all the time. Everybody is aware of these things. And people are living more politically than they had before and most likely than they have since. So politics just becomes a dimension of life. It isn't something foreign. It isn't something over there.

So you've got David Crosby writing "Almost Cut my Hair," which in a way is a ludicrous kind of song, except it was about something real, which is all kinds of people had grown their hair long, and most people had done it because it looked good. Then they said, "Actually having long hair is kind of distracting, and it gets in the way of things, and do I really want this? But now if I cut my hair, I'm saying I'm disaffiliating with people who have long hair. Maybe I don't want to do that." In other words, it was a real dilemma. So he wrote a song, and it was this very heartfelt song, and maybe overdone, but it was about something that people were actually living through, so in that sense it was a good song.

Almost cut my hair, it happened just the other day.
It's gettin' kinda long, I coulda said it wasn't in my way.
But I didn't and I wonder why, I feel like letting my
    freak flag fly,
'Cause I feel like I owe it to someone.

Must be because I had the flu for Christmas and I'm not
  feeling up to par.
It increases my paranoia, like looking at my mirror and
  seeing a police car.
But I'm not giving in an inch to fear 'cause I missed myself
  this year.
I feel like I owe it to someone.

STEPHEN STILLS

We got there on the second day; we flew in and saw six hundred acres covered with wall-to-wall people. You have no idea what that looks like. It's unbelievable. And as I said to a German reporter who was getting under my skin, I said, "Do you know the last time in history that this many people got together for anything? Normandy." Actually, Normandy was less. But it was just a sea of humanity.

JOHN HARTMANN (music agent, manager)

Everyone knew CSN&Y even though they had never put out a record or played in a gig other than in Chicago the night before, because they all came from supergroups. Crosby came from the Byrds, probably the first big folk rock band; Stills and [Neil] Young came from Buffalo Springfield, hit act, well-known. [Graham] Nash came from the Hollies; he wrote most of the Hollies' hits. They get up on this stage and Stephen Stills says, "This is only the second time we've performed in front of people. We're scared shitless." Then those three-part harmonies hit and it was all over. They owned that place and they became the star of the event—until Jimi.

COUNTRY JOE MCDONALD

One of the more political moments of Woodstock was when Jimi Hendrix shredded the national anthem, which the establishment still doesn't know what to do about. Is it a dis? Is it not? He was a musical genius.

David Crosby, Stephen Stills, Graham Nash, and Neil Young (who is not in this photograph) take the stage at Woodstock at about 3 A.M. on the festival's final day. It was their second live performance as a newly formed band.

When he played the national anthem, I knew that he changed playing the guitar forever. He just did stuff with the guitar that nobody had ever done before—made sounds and improvisations. There's really no language to describe it. But you know when you hear it. No one had ever done that before—taking a traditional song and trashing it like that. Not trashed—it was just gorgeous. It was unbelievable—really unbelievable—creative, artistic, not intellectual, impulsive—all those things, without a word of language. Then a whole generation of kids grew up playing like that.

THELMA SCHOONMAKER

I remember that at the very end we were so tired. I just cannot tell you how tired we were. We had rented motel rooms but there was no way we could get to them, so we had no place to sleep. We just laid down in the mud whenever there would be an hour we could sleep, which was about all we got, because we were shooting all night and all day, and there was nothing

Guitar legend Jimi Hendrix (1942–1970) plays "The Star-Spangled Banner" early in the morning on August 18, 1969, as the final act at Woodstock.

to eat. It was insane. I'll never forget the smell of the mud. It must've been like it was in the trenches in World War I, you know, the mud mixed with garbage, and we were covered in mud ourselves. We had decided to go out in the field and film the remnant of the field as if it was Vietnam. We got beautiful footage, and we used that against Jimi Hendrix playing, massacring "The Star-Spangled Banner" with Vietnam sounds.*

GREIL MARCUS

The most powerful political statement that was made musically—or for that matter verbally—was Jimi Hendrix on the last morning, Monday at

---

*   The three-hour documentary *Woodstock* was edited in seven months and won the Academy Award for best documentary feature in 1971. Thelma Schoonmaker earned a nomination for best documentary film editor. Woodstock was the sixth-largest-grossing film of 1970—it made $51 million and the production cost $600,000. After the film was released, Abbie Hoffman called Warner Bros. and complained that the film had left out the antiwar music.

eight in the morning. The show went way long and there was almost no-body there by the time he played. He was the last performer, playing his version of "The Star-Spangled Banner," which is a very complex, deep piece of music. I always think of it as the greatest protest song ever, but it's not just a protest song, it's an incredibly layered, ambiguous piece of music. To take the national anthem and distort it, when people saw it in the *Woodstock* movie, when they heard it on the soundtrack album, be-cause, again, very few people were actually there to hear the performance—it was taken as an attack on the United States for its crimes in Vietnam, which is not an unreasonable way to hear it, but it's also a great piece of music. No art that has its own integrity is ever going to be about one thing or be one thing.

NEW YORK TIMES EDITORIAL,

AUGUST 18, 1969

NIGHTMARE IN THE CATSKILLS

. . . What kind of culture is it that can produce so colossal a mess? One youth dead and at least three others in hospitals from overdoses of drugs. . . . The adults who helped create the soci-ety against which these young people are so feverishly rebelling must bear a share of the responsibility for this outrageous epi-sode. . . .

RICHARD REEVES

When things started to break up, I went back with the bands, and their managers, and maintained contact with them, and wrote a *New York Times Magazine* piece about Woodstock. At that time, it was the most resold *Times* piece that had ever been written, because everybody in the world was interested in Woodstock.

GERALD LEFCOURT

Within one week of the concert, Abbie wrote a book called *Woodstock Nation*. He wrote it on the floor of Chris Cerf's apartment in New York.* He slept in his living room for a week. The book comes out, and then they [the Chicago Eight] go to trial in September.

---

* Chris Cerf's father, Bennett Cerf, was the cofounder and publisher of Random House, which published *Woodstock Nation: A Talk-Rock Album* in 1969. The book became a must-read within the movement.

CHAPTER 7

WEATHERMEN

(August–October 1969)

Revolution: how had it come to that? It was a blend of many things: bitterness, hatred, and alienation, hope, confidence, and conviction, energy, passion, and need. It was the pattern woven by all the threads of the sixties, the inevitable product of the awakened generation as it probed deeper and deeper into the character of its nation.

—KIRKPATRICK SALE, *SDS*

A MAJORITY OF AMERICANS HAD ALWAYS SUPPORTED THE U.S. efforts in Vietnam, until 1969, when a September Gallup poll showed that the tide had changed and 55 percent believed the United States had made a mistake sending troops to fight there. Troop strength in Vietnam peaked at 543,480 in April 1969, and an average of two hundred American soldiers were being killed every week. In April, Nixon announced his first troop withdrawal, promising that twenty-five thousand soldiers would be home by the end of August and initiating his Vietnamization strategy of training and arming South Vietnamese troops while beginning to withdraw American combat troops.

But frustration with American casualty rates and media images of napalm-burned Vietnamese civilians turned some antiwar activists to violence. The Weathermen adopted the slogan "Bring the war home," and they worked to transform the student movement into a revolutionary force. Former SDS president Todd Gitlin expressed a commonly held view among older members of the New Left when he said, "I sat in horror watching the Weathermen run away with the student left."

MICHAEL KAZIN (Harvard SDS)

I was in Berkeley in the summer of '69, where I had a job ghostwriting papers for undergraduates, which paid pretty well. I wasn't sure if I'd go back to Harvard or not. I was pretty disillusioned with being a good Harvard boy at the time. On my way back east in August, I met with Mark Rudd in Chicago, where the Weather people were still in charge of the SDS national office. I asked him, isn't this Weatherman stuff kind of adventurist? That's an old Leninist term for going far beyond what the people will stand for. He said, "When have we ever done too much to stop the war? When have we ever done too much to help black liberation?" He kind of gut-checked me. I said, "Well, I guess you're right." So I took the fall of '69 off from Harvard to join the Weathermen, and I moved into the Cambridge collective when I got back in late August of '69. We lived near Central Square, in a small apartment with too many of us.*

DAVID FENTON (movement photographer)

I had dropped out of the Bronx High School of Science to join the revolution when I was sixteen. Tenth grade was the end of my formal education. Tim Leary said, "Turn on, tune in, and drop out," so I decided to follow him faithfully and I did all three. But I was also very responsible—I was a photographer and I made a living. After the SDS convention in June, the Weathermen took an interest in me and some of my friends because we were high school students, so they kept trying to get me to join them. Not

----

* In April 1969, more than three hundred students occupied Harvard's main administration building, University Hall, for fourteen hours until they were forcibly removed and severely beaten by a hundred Cambridge police officers. Students then rioted in Harvard Square, fighting police, burning three police cars, and trashing stores. More than three hundred arrests were made.

too long after that convention in Chicago, the Weathermen faction took over SDS's staid, boring newspaper, which had been called *New Left Notes,* and they changed the name of it to *Fire!* and printed it in full color. It became a hippie, psychedelic underground paper, only it was filled with violent, crazy rhetoric—"Off the pigs," "Overthrow the government." They wanted me to move to Chicago and work with them on this newspaper.

Mark Rudd was pushing me to do it. I remember he'd call me up and say, "This is where you belong. We're going to make a revolution. You should be part of it. We're going to overthrow the state, and we're going to have a good time." I was on a cross-country national park camping trip, and Mark had given me these deadlines. "You need to let us know by this date." This would have been that summer of '69, and I remember I called him from a phone booth in South Dakota to say, "You know, I'm really not going to do this." Because I just thought they were nuts. I admit I was a little attracted to it. It was exciting and vibrant and different and interesting, but politically crazy. Plus it was so clear to me, and a lot of other people, that they were playing right into Nixon's hands. They were turning the public against the antiwar movement and they had no awareness of this. If you tried to talk to them about it, they'd say, "You're a counterrevolutionary."

MICHAEL KAZIN

It was exhilarating and a little scary, because we were taking karate classes, we were planning on taking weapons classes, but we never ended up doing that. We would do these actions, as we called them. In one of them we went to Boston Latin School and we'd go on the steps of the school and start giving speeches about how schools were jails and how you should break out. On this particular occasion the football team tried to beat us up, because they were really pissed. We went to a mixer at BU [Boston University] to denounce them for being sexist, because women's liberation was beginning then, too.

Our big action, which I planned, was at the Center for International Affairs, a think tank to train grad students in international relations and government, that Kissinger helped start. Because Kissinger was involved, and Kissinger was of course Nixon's national security advisor at the time, this was clearly a cornerstone of U.S. imperialism right on [the Harvard] campus. I thought it would be a good target for an action. So about twenty of us went into the Center for International Affairs. We pushed the people who worked there out of the building; some of them resisted, some did not, and we spray-painted all kinds of slogans on the walls like "Long live the victory of the people's war," and "Down with U.S. imperialism." And then we fled through the Peabody Museum, through the glass flowers exhibit. I worked out the escape route very well. It was like being a little guerrilla fighter. Two of the people got arrested and served two to three years of jail time for assault. Luckily I did not. I didn't beat anybody up.

I remember when Ho Chi Minh died in early September in '69, and we went to Dorchester to get in a fight with white working-class kids to show them how tough we were. Completely absurd in retrospect, but this was a middle-class kid's idea of revolution. A lot of my friends who didn't join Weatherman thought we were nuts, and in retrospect, they were right. But at the time I thought we were at the cutting edge of the revolution. It taught me something about what it might be like to be a terrorist suicide bomber, even though I didn't make any bombs. Well, actually, I did make a Molotov cocktail at one point, put it next to the ROTC building at Harvard, and it didn't go off, luckily. I've never been very mechanical.

BERNARDINE DOHRN (Weathermen leader)

The Cleveland Conference in late September '69 was our own internal conference. The culture had actually been developed in the collectives, but it got spread to everyone, and unified or homogenized. At Cleveland the idea of criticism, self-criticism, and "total commitment," and "gut check," and "are you strong enough to be a revolutionary," and "smash monogamy," came in. A collective was a group of as many as eight to twenty people who united in trying to organize together. And everyone threw everything they had into it: time, money, goods. Everything was subordinated to this one idea of organizing together.

At the Cleveland Conference the collectives reported on their work, and there were all kinds of fantastical reports like "We're chartering a train from Detroit to take hundreds of people to Chicago," things like that. Or we did this action at a high school and this action at a suburban mall, and we broke windows, and we attracted support. It was all fantasy. It was all self-serving lies.

CATHY WILKERSON (Weathermen member)

I was coming from the civil rights movement, and from SDS at my college, Swarthmore, and being in the national office in Chicago, working on the newspaper and then starting a region in Washington, D.C.

For me, the Cleveland Conference was the beginning of the cult period during which people were humiliated and undermined—it's embarrassing to think about it now. Many of us were required to stay up all night, leaving us sleep deprived. Then a further shift away from bringing people into the movement became apparent, replaced by even more emphasis on militancy and changing consciousness through demonstrations of our own rage. I think most women were not entirely sure how to interpret all that.

But there was also this feeling that the women's movement was very strong and that the men in Weathermen would lose legitimacy unless they dealt with that. So their response was to create this very militant women's action. And certainly the women didn't want to be left out, which we generally were. So we were easy targets for the argument that the way to liberate women was to show women being militant.

BILL DYSON (FBI agent)

Sometime in May of 1969 I get a call, and it's the special agent in charge's secretary. And she says, "The special agent in charge would like to see you immediately." I had never met the man. When you came into a major office, you didn't even get a chance to meet the special agent in charge. He was sort of like God. I mean, Hoover was God, this is God's right-hand man. So I met the assistant special agent in charge in Chicago.

There were a half a dozen of us, all similar seniority, all of us worried what the heck have we done wrong? His name was Marlin Johnson, and he says, "You gentlemen know what's going on on college campuses?" I didn't know what to say. Learning? And he says, "Well, you've got all of this picketing, and demonstrating, and protesting, all this disruptive thing going on on college campuses against the war in Vietnam." Well, everybody knew that. He said, "We're not interested in that. We're interested in the bombings. The arsons. The physical attacks on corporate people, governmental agents, and so forth." I didn't know anything about it. Well, I soon found out that between the middle of 1968 and the middle of 1969, there was something like one hundred and twenty bombings on or around college campuses in connection with the war in Vietnam. I had no idea. And that's what he was asking me to work on.

MARK RUDD

In the late fall of '69, our little clique of eight or ten people made a decision to close the national offices of SDS, and the regional offices, under the belief that we needed to start armed struggle, so that the revolution could happen. And that would be our contribution. We assumed somehow that the mass movement would just carry on, and that SDS would continue, but we would be out front. There was no more SDS regional office; there was no more organizing on college campuses that was coordinated or advanced in any way by SDS. SDS ceased to exist, and it was during the height of the war. We didn't put our ideas up to a vote. We just did it. It was like a coup.

BILL DYSON

Our squad supervisor, Hugh Mallet, who was a wonderful mentor, said, "We're going to be putting in a wiretap." I said, "A wiretap? I don't even know what a wiretap is. I've never really experienced that." And I'm led through the bowels of the Chicago office, to a place I never knew existed. It's a windowless room with machines all over the place. I never saw anything like this before. And they said, "Here's your machine." And they sit me down and there's three recording machines. That's what my first assignment was, and it was on the SDS national office. As far as I knew, everything was perfectly legal. I mean, it's not as though this was clandestine. There were no microphones at the old SDS National Headquarters at 1608 West Madison Street.

I knew nothing about these people at first. I'm being assigned to this squad and I worked the night shift. I would come in at four o'clock, and it was like I never went home. I would just be so fascinated with these people. I would stay there until the relief came in the next morning. And sometimes I wouldn't even leave then. It was fascinating.

Now, I'm only hitting the recorder when they're saying something that's pertinent to violence. So I'm hearing about their whole personal life. And I'm hearing all sorts of things—I'm getting to know these people very, very well, better than anybody else would know them. You can go out and interview and learn about a person to a certain degree, but that's not the same as when you're monitoring them constantly. They may be militants, they may be terrorists, whatever word you want to use, but they're still human beings. They've still got gossip, they've still got their personal life, and their personal problems, and everything else. And I'm just listening, and listening, and I'm really getting to know these people very, very well. I lived with these people sometimes twenty-four hours a day, seven days a week.

I mean this was exciting! We were monitoring the Students for a Democratic Society and I watched them become the Weathermen. I was with them when they became clandestine. If you work a wiretap, a good wiretap, you will become that way. And to me, it was exciting. I was watching history.[*]

MICHAEL KAZIN

I was scared to death. I was a nice upper-middle-class Jewish kid from the New Jersey suburbs. I did judo as a kid but I didn't like fighting. That's why I left the Weathermen in the end, because I wasn't ready to die, which we were talking about doing. We were talking about confronting PL [Progressive Labor] people, maybe with guns. Mark Rudd came to town as a

---

[*]   I interviewed Bill Dyson at his home in Florida on January 20, 2014, but this last paragraph is taken from Dyson's FBI oral history interview, January 15, 2008.

member of the Weather Bureau, and this shows what a sect we were. The gospel was that you couldn't leave Weathermen; you had to be expelled. So at an all-night meeting I convinced Mark to expel me. But even so, I was still sympathetic with the politics. I felt guilty for leaving, but I was already beginning to question it.

BILL DYSON

What fascinated me? You got to understand, my background is different. Most of these people came from affluent backgrounds. And it's almost like they're just throwing away their education. They're throwing away their lives. And here I am, I've spent so much time trying to get this education at the University of Miami, I've fought and battled to get this education, but with these people, it was just given to them on a silver platter. I came from a very working-class family. My parents always wanted to go to college, and they couldn't; it was the Depression era.

It caused me confusion in that sense, but it also showed their [the Weathermen's] dedication. I mean somebody just throws away their life for this movement. I couldn't understand—a lot of the philosophy didn't make any sense to me. The war in Vietnam wasn't the only issue. It took me a while to learn that. And when I figured that out, then I could understand these people.

Their bag was they wanted to overthrow the U.S. government and set up a communist state here. To them the war in Vietnam was the outward manifestation of all the evils of capitalism. We were over there because we needed new markets for our products. We were over there because we needed resources to build our products. That's what their belief was. Whereas for the people who were picketing and demonstrating, and doing all the things that are legal or maybe cross the line to a misdemeanor, the average person who's opposed to the war, that's what he was opposed to: the war, and the principle of it—like me. As far as the war in Vietnam was concerned, I really didn't know why we were there. I'm not picketing and demonstrating, but I don't understand why we were fighting a war in Vietnam. I don't think my brother understood, either, and he was in the air force stationed in Thailand. He was two years younger than me.

MARK RUDD

We formed these goofy collectives, where everything was owned together, because the future was going to be a collective, not private property. And everything was owned—all clothes were owned together, you know? Therefore, nobody had any clean clothes.

I don't know if you've ever noticed this, but if you take a bunch of nineteen- and twenty-year-olds and put them in an apartment together, there is a tendency for them to engage in sexual intercourse. It's not unique to the Weatherman phenomenon, but we did have a kind of an ethic that we were all revolutionaries, and that the way to build intimacy in the collective is through sex. But that was heterosexual sex. Except for sex among women, which was okay, but not sex among men. Not okay. The poor gay guys who were not open, I heard from them later, they were pretty miserable.

It was totally sexist from the start. Monogamies were smashed. There was a line that monogamies were like a deal where women especially were protected from criticism by being in a couple. And so that's a form of liberalism, because a radical communist thing to do is to open yourself up to total criticism. So all monogamies were smashed. Except those that Bernardine was involved in.

For one thing, sexually transmitted diseases were very common—crabs, pelvic inflammatory disease, gonorrhea. There were always some doctors in the periphery who we could get some help from. It was terribly unhygienic. In fact, there was also a low-level infection, a cold-type thing which we called the Weather crud.

There was an apartment in Park Slope, Brooklyn; it was before Park Slope had become gentrified. There were maybe twenty kids living there, and maybe half of them were women, and I opened up a closet once, and there were all these hair dryers piled up inside. It was hilarious. I mean clearly they weren't going to use them anymore. There was no housekeeping—there might have been some spaghetti, but there was no housekeeping. There was no cleaning; there was none. There was no laundry; there was nothing. People would stage phony weddings, and get money from their parents, and give it to the collective.

BILL AYERS

We had no sleep and did lots of speed. It was all about the next meeting, and the next meeting, and living on drugs and hot dogs. It was really not a good way to live—sleeping in the national office under the printing press. To the extent that anyone had a sex life, it was kind of an animalistic sex life of necessity. It wasn't joyful. That's not 100 percent true, but it's true enough. It lacked a certain amount of intimacy; when there was intimacy you were often ratted out for it. So you would have an intimate moment with somebody—a friend, a lover—and then you'd be in some group-criticism session and you'd be told what a backward-sliding person you were. And you'd always agree.

CATHY WILKERSON

Marriage was inherently unequal in the social structure of the time. And also many women—myself included—felt like to really participate in the movement, the movement had to come first. And so it would make it hard to have a traditional marriage. People had relationships, but they came and went.

I don't know who cooked up smash monogamy, but the effect of it was that there was open season on women by the men all under the guise of women's liberation. What it really did was disempower women—another decision we're taking away from you. It didn't impact me because I wasn't in a relationship that I particularly wanted to stay in so it was an easy out, and I think that was true for a number of women. The smash-monogamy policy only existed for a few months, but while it lasted it caused a big commotion.

All the talk of guns and violence and being strong, and nothing about families and children and social life, was very disorienting; no day-to-day substance to ground us. It contributed to an eroding of intellectual self-confidence. Increasingly, I think women were devastated and wiped out and disempowered by being humiliated in these criticism sessions. That was how I experienced it. The criticism sessions were like rehab therapy: Someone humiliates you and strips you down and tells you you're a worthless piece of shit, and then builds you back up again in their own image.

BERNARDINE DOHRN

Self-criticism sessions were terrible. It was kind of on the Chinese Maoist model, or what we thought it was. The great side of it was we were trying to break out of the traditional nuclear, patriarchal family and insist that in order to be a revolutionary you had to not have children; you had to not be in a monogamous relationship; and that you had to sleep with lots of people, which was obviously terrible, self-righteous, and hurtful. But again, how do you change these big systems without confrontation?

BILL DYSON

Of course, there were other problems with the Weather Underground, some of which I knew, some of which I learned later. There was male chauvinism. The females felt that they were not being treated as equal to the men. But I'm not so sure about that. I think it may have been the opposite extreme that the women seemed, in some cases, to be more dominating than the men were. They had Bernardine Dohrn, Cathy Wilkerson; they had Kathy Boudin, and many others—they had women in prominent positions. And yet there seemed to be this thought within people in the Weather Underground that the women were being regarded as secondary. I don't think it was true. I'm looking from the outside and saying, "Wait a minute, it's the exact opposite!"

BERNARDINE DOHRN

We were planning the Days of Rage, which we called the National Action, in Chicago for October. The Vietnamese, the Cubans, and the Black Panthers all told us not to do it, and we said, "No, you don't understand. We know better, and we have to do this. And the 'this' that we have to do is we have to bring young, white kids to Chicago to fight cops." Totally suicidal. We thought we would bring thousands to the streets. In fact, we brought fewer people than we started out with in June of '69. We probably had five hundred Weather supporters in June, and by October we probably had maybe two hundred and fifty people, despite four months of effort.

MARK RUDD (Weathermen leader)

I remember sitting in Central Park with a guy I knew from Columbia named Marty Kenner. Marty had been in touch with the Cubans, and he said, "So-and-so, of the Cuban consulate, says that you shouldn't be doing the Days of Rage." And I thought, Really? Wow, why did they say that? He says, "You're way too far ahead of where the base is, and not only that, but the Vietnamese want a united antiwar movement. And you're already calling for revolution." I'd say, "Oh, that's interesting," and then I'd go back to my comrades at the Weather Bureau and I'd report this, and they'd say, "Well, that's ridiculous, we understand that the time is right now for a revolution, and we've got to go all the way. The Cubans and the Vietnamese don't understand our situation." So I'd say, "Really? I guess so." But I was conflicted, because I'm not totally crazy. Even at that time I wasn't. I mean I was crazy enough to be in it, and not to get myself out of it. But I wasn't crazy enough to really believe my own shit.

I felt it was my own failing. A lot of what we were presenting to the rest of the New Left was what we called a gut check. "Are you strong enough?" "Do you believe in revolution enough?" "Are you really willing to lay your life on the line?" And "Do you carry a gun?" I've got a gun, you know?

BILL AYERS (Weathermen leader)

We were convinced that militancy was essential. That is, putting our bodies on the line, showing what we're willing to do, taking the consequences. That's why we organized the Days of Rage. We organized the Days of Rage under the theory that the problem with the mass mobilizations at that time was that the militants—us—were always contained. We were pushed aside by peace marshals and demonstration marshals. But actually we were the real energy of the thing, so why don't we organize our own action with the militants in the open and in the lead? Well, that was a miscalculation, to say the least, because it's one thing to be the militant in a one-hundred-thousand-person demonstration. It's another thing to be the militant with two hundred other militants. It was isolating, and we did it to ourselves.

BRIAN FLANAGAN (Weathermen member)

I was a soldier rather than a leader. I wasn't part of the Weather Bureau, which were the people who had written the Weathermen's statement, you know, J.J. [John Jacobs], Bernardine, Billy, Mark, all the people with the big names, and a few that just faded away.

They're carpet bombing Vietnam, and Cambodia and Laos. So there has to be something done to try to make this country unlivable as long as they're slaughtering Vietnamese; we're going to make big trouble here, and so a big march on Washington is not enough. Getting more and more people to a big demonstration isn't going to do any good. So the Days of Rage was sort of our coming-out party.

MARK RUDD

We went into it thinking we were going to have ten thousand people, and about two hundred and fifty to three hundred showed up the first night. I was in hiding. They were keeping me for the next day. What we did was, we rotated responsibility. I was going to handle the bail money and then on the third day I was going to lead the demonstration.

So I was handling bail, and getting people safe away from the police, and all kinds of crazy things. A cop got beat up in one of our movement centers, and all kinds of things were happening. I was in charge of leading the last march, which was Saturday morning, October 11. I had this crazy little mustache disguise, the kind you buy in a magic shop, and I got to the location of the rally about forty-five minutes early and immediately the Red Squad came and beat me up and busted me. Just immediately, before the rally ever formed. There was this group that was part of the Chicago Police Department called the Red Squad. They always followed us around.

I stopped fighting at one point, and the cop who arrested me said that he was surprised I had stopped fighting. It stuck in my mind. I must have had some sense of self-preservation, a concept that if you don't fight, they won't—they'll lay off. I'm not much of a fighter; I never was. So the whole thing was macho posing. They charged me with assaulting an officer and I went to jail.

DAVID FENTON

The Days of Rage was one of the scariest things I've ever seen in my life. The Weathermen all took nightsticks and police truncheons out from under their jackets and went running in a mad frenzy down the streets of Chicago's Gold Coast breaking every window in sight. This was their big revolutionary action. And the police freaked out, and opened fire on them, which is well documented, but forgotten. Nobody was killed. So I watched the police shooting at these people—I think six people were shot. And I'm like, Oh, my goodness! Maybe I should get out of here. But my job as a

Leaders of the Weathermen—(left to right) Jim Mellen, Peter Clapp, John Jacobs, Bill Ayers (wearing glasses), and Terry Robbins (1946–1970)—march at the front of a group of demonstrators on October 11, 1969, during the Days of Rage action in Chicago, where they attacked the police and were beaten and shot at with live bullets. PHOTOGRAPH BY DAVID FENTON.

photographer was to go where the action was. And that's when this guy Richard Elrod got knocked over.

The Days of Rage were really an anarchist act, not a political act. The whole thing was emotional. That's the main thing I would say about the Weather Underground. It was a huge emotional explosion.

BRIAN FLANAGAN

On the morning of October 11, we had no sleep the night before and J.J. [John Jacobs] is standing on the Haymarket statue that we'd just blown up.* He's wearing a red football helmet and a black leather jacket and he gives a speech to a group of us and says, "We'll probably lose people today. We don't really have to win here . . . just the fact that we are willing to fight the police is a political victory." When I heard that, I thought, Oh my God, I really don't want to die. I have a lot of things I want to do with my life. It was about ten days before my birthday. I had my twenty-third birthday in jail.

So we are marching along, and I'm not wearing a helmet. The only real piece of equipment I'm wearing is my boxing cup underneath my pants, because I don't feel like getting hit in the balls. I boxed while I was at Columbia from '64 to '69 in the New York Golden Gloves and AAUs. I was a light heavyweight. So I was not afraid to fight, let's put it that way. I knew how to fight better than other people.

As we're marching down the street, people are chanting and screaming and we're headed towards point zero, which is State and Madison streets, which is basically the Times Square of Chicago. And then somebody smashes a cop through a plate glass window, and then the thing was really on. People pull out their pipes and chains. We were battling the cops. It's just total mayhem in the streets. I didn't have a weapon. I didn't know what to do with a pipe. I was good with my fists. I was a street fighter, so I wound up getting into a fight. A cop jumped this girl who was next to me. And I got him, and I slugged him, and I kicked this other guy.

---

*   Four days before the Days of Rage, on October 6, 1969, the Weathermen bombed a monument in Chicago's Haymarket Square that was a memorial to the seven police officers killed in 1886 by anarchists (who were later hanged) and workers who were on strike demanding an eight-hour workday.

Then I got one guy—the guy who was on the right side, I hit this guy harder than I ever hit any human being. It was an absolute perfect clock. And he went down. I can't believe this guy ever got up after that, but within the next ten minutes, he wound up with the other guy I'd been fighting, chasing me down the street. So there's a posse of uniform and plainclothes cops chasing me, screaming, "Get him, get him!"

So I take off and I'm faster than any of them, and I'm going east on Madison, towards State. I'm thinking, what in the hell was I going to do to get away from these guys and save my ass?

Now at that point, Richard Elrod was across the street talking to a reporter, and people are screaming "Get him," and I see this suit come running across the street at me. I'm thinking, I've got to get up on the sidewalk to get away from this guy. He takes a flying tackle block at me, hits me, and knocks me sideways through an opening that leads to two short flights of stairs. I don't know what happened to him after he hit me. I never touched him again. I'm knocked through the doorway and almost tumble down the stairs. So I right myself and as I try to come back up the stairs, in come about four cops and they throw me down the stairs.

They were all beating on me, and they're swinging at me, one guy's going boom, boom, into my cup. He's trying to ram me in the balls, but I've got the cup, so it's not hurting me, but he really wants to rip my balls off. So they're swinging and hitting me. I'm trying to protect my head. So now, the beating's over, they're tending to their friend, they throw me out on the sidewalk, and here is Elrod, lying on the sidewalk saying, "I can't feel my legs, I can't feel my hands."

Now I'm thinking, Maybe I should run, and split, but I made one of the best decisions I've ever made in my life. I said, This is it. I did what I could, we made our statement, I'm going to jail like everybody else. I quit. So they threw me into the paddy wagon and took me into a holding cell with all my Weather people. About a hundred of us were arrested. I later found out that Elrod's neck was broken and he was partially paralyzed, and that he was a lawyer for the corporation counsel for the city of Chicago and a protégé of Mayor Daley.

Waking up in jail the next day, my head was so sore, oh my God. Soft spots and everything. I think I still have some of them. At a hearing I had five charges against me for attempted murder, aggravated battery, felonious mob action, and resisting arrest, and my bail was set for one hundred thousand dollars. SDS had a quarter-of-a-million-dollar bail fund, and I used up a whole lot of it.

BERNARDINE DOHRN

Almost everybody was arrested by the second or third day. I was arrested at the women's demonstration. Right away, before we took a step, right after speaking. So I spent the next three or four days in Cook County Jail. By that time we had three or four hundred in Cook County Jail. I remember we were doing karate on the floors of the jail. I was brought down to meet the warden of the jail. He was a very large, African American, bald man, a very intimidating physical presence. He basically said, "You're in my jail. I run this building. And you will do what I say while you're in this building." I said that we didn't ask to be here, and we weren't breaking the law in his building. Having political discussions, and exercising, and having our meetings was not a violation of his law.

SDS *NEW LEFT NOTES*, OCTOBER 1969
(after the Days of Rage)

We did what we set out to do, and in the process turned a corner. FROM HERE ON IN IT'S ONE BATTLE AFTER ANOTHER—WITH WHITE YOUTH JOINING IN THE FIGHT AND TAKING THE NECESSARY RISKS. PIG AMERIKA—BEWARE: THERE'S AN ARMY GROWING RIGHT IN YOUR GUTS, AND IT'S GOING TO HELP BRING YOU DOWN.*

MARK RUDD

We made a decision to go underground toward the latter part of 1969, after the Days of Rage, which was a failure. But like a lot of failures, there's

---

* Kirkpatrick Sale, *SDS,* p. 613.

always the tendency to double down. Days of Rage didn't work out. People didn't come. So we said, well, we've got to get even more serious about it. So, intellectually, I was still committed to that course, but somehow in my deepest gut I couldn't do it. I wasn't strong enough; I wasn't the revolutionary fighter that I was posing as.

It took a long time for me to first understand that our strategy was wrong. It was doomed to failure. I was loyal to my friends. However, very early on, even before we went underground, I realized that I could not be the revolutionary hero that I needed to be. I couldn't pose as being a revolutionary hero anymore, because I was just this kid from New Jersey. I didn't know anything. I wasn't particularly brave, and I didn't particularly want to die. I saw it as my own failure.

I believe that results are what counts, and had we not been so enamored of our own heroic morality, we might have been able to judge the fact that our theories were not working. For example, nobody came to the Days of Rage. But we were deeply involved in our rightness.

FBI REPORT

As reported by the Statistical Section of the Records and Identification Division of the Chicago Police Department, 287 arrests occurred for various charges of mob action, resisting arrest, disorderly conduct, aggravated battery and other offenses during the Weatherman "Days of Rage" mob activity October 8 through 11, 1969. During this period 59 police officers sustained personal injury including abrasions, contusions, cuts and bruises on the arms, legs, groins, body and head; human bites on the arms and hands, loose teeth and injury to eyes and ears. . . .*

DAVID HARRIS (draft resistance organizer)

By 1969, suddenly the most visible part of the movement was the Weathermen. Who are these people? They haven't done shit. They're spouting this

---

*   FBI Weather Underground summary dated August 20, 1976.

stuff, "Oh, we tried nonviolence." Oh, did you? Where was that, in your three months at Bryn Mawr? Is that what you did? First they were a bunch of white kids trying to pretend they were like black people. They had this bullshit revolution they were talking about. What did they do? They blew up a urinal in the Capitol Building [in 1971]. There's the Weathermen for you. They talked a lot of talk and got a lot of ink, and they didn't deserve any of it. They didn't do any work and they hadn't been in the movement long enough to be given any kind of stature like that. They were rich kids playing out fantasies. Today we call it a virtual revolution. It's like this big pretend game.

So needless to say, I didn't like these guys. Didn't like what they stood for. Our ethos was we never called anybody pigs. We're trying to get the cops to come over to our side. I went to high school with the cops. As soon as the movement got into a place where it started saying, "You're either with us or against us," the movement died. What worked for us was that we always were open and inclusive. We always took new people in, and we recognized that everybody started out on the wrong side. All of us had gone through a transformation to get to where we were. Our movement would thrive because everybody was going to go through that transformation, and we had to empower that transformation, which means we had to embrace whoever was out there. And that included the police.

MARK RUDD

The Weather made a fundamental mistake in forgetting about base-level organizing, which is relationship building, coalition building, all the things that built the antiwar movement up to that time, had built the civil rights movement, had built the labor movement. That's all we did, up until '68. But then we made such a big leap, and got so much press, and publicity. It went to our heads. Our actions, our guts, our courage, holding buildings at Columbia, we identified that as being what built the movement. Also, that dovetailed with Che Guevara's theories of taking action. Which if we had looked at it objectively and dispassionately, all of Che Guevara's theories were proven wrong by '67. Everything he tried had turned to shit. He died behind these theories, but we weren't willing to reject them, because we knew they were right. We were so arrogant.

DAVID HARRIS

What had been a movement of nonviolent resistance and civil disobedience and community organizing freaked out in 1969. We had been the New Left, which meant we had values and were looking for new ways to express them. Everything started in '68 and reached fruition in '69, all this neo-Marxist bullshit. I am not a Marxist. I've never been a Marxist, and I have no interest in being a Marxist. So there was this dynamic in the movement over the years of everybody trying to be more radical than six months ago. That eventually played itself out into all these white kids pretending they were Black Panthers, and Black Panthers pretending they were third-world revolutionaries. And all of it was bullshit. When I was on the streets organizing, I would often get heckled by SDS members. There were a bunch of Marxist assholes in SDS in Los Angeles, and they'd come out and literally heckle us.

They were threatened, because we were saying to them, "Where's your draft card, sucker? Oh, you're the big revolutionary, but you can't put your ass where you want everybody else to put theirs, can you?" That was the issue. They derided us as martyrs. We weren't revolutionaries. "Oh, you guys are all middle class," they would say, and I'd say, "Well, what the fuck are you, man? You're a goddamn college student. Of course you're middle class. We're here to organize the middle class, don't you get it? We're not here to pretend that we're something we're not."

MARK RUDD

It was a macho dead end; it played into the hands of the government very well. We destroyed SDS at the height of the war. Don't you think that's what the FBI wanted us to do? Maybe I was a paid informer. I mean, I could have been, except I know I wasn't. And I know that none of us were. We just did it because of our own arrogance. That's why I have a bumper sticker on my car that says, "Don't Believe Everything You Think."

We gave Nixon the ammunition to use against the entire movement. Our arrogance undermined the entire antiwar movement.

CHAPTER 8

THE CHICAGO EIGHT

(September–November 1969)

For us as a generation the courtroom and jails may be becoming more important than the universities.

—JERRY RUBIN, *We Are Everywhere*

FOR THREE DAYS DURING THE DEMOCRATIC NATIONAL CONVENTION in August 1968, the nation watched as the Chicago police and antiwar protesters clashed in a series of violent riots. "The whole world is watching" became the protesters' refrain as they were bludgeoned by Mayor Richard Daley's policemen's nightsticks. The whole world continued to watch a year and a half later as eight movement leaders were charged with conspiring to use interstate commerce to "incite, organize, promote and encourage" riots at the Democratic convention.

The Chicago Eight (later Seven) conspiracy trial (*United States v. Dellinger et al.*) opened on September 28, 1969. Seventy-three-year-old judge Julius Hoffman presided for five months over what was called "the political trial of the century." Developments in the Chicago courtroom captivated the nation and became a mainstay on the evening television news. William Kunstler, the lead defense attorney, pursued a strategy of putting the Vietnam War on trial and wore a black armband to court to commemorate the war dead. The defendants mocked the premise of the trial by turning the courtroom into a stage for their ribald, countercultural antics, and Judge Hoffman played the conservative, angry lead like someone right out of central casting. The division between the government and the defendants soon came to symbolize the nationwide cultural and political split.

GERALD LEFCOURT (Abbie Hoffman's lawyer)

The case was called *The United States v. Dellinger* because Dave Dellinger* was supposedly the architect of the conspiracy. The government picked out leaders from various parts of the antiwar and civil rights movement. I guess they were a conspiracy in what they believed. They were trying to stop the war and end racism and poverty.

I remember the arraignment day [April 9, 1969]. The first day we all had to go to Chicago. The defendants barely knew each other. We're all in a room, lawyers and defendants. Bobby Seale was asking lawyers for cards and he asked Dave Dellinger for his card thinking he was one of the lawyers instead of being his codefendant. Some conspiracy.

Bobby Seale's lawyer was Charles R. Garry. Garry needed a gallbladder operation. He was seeking adjournment for a month or two and Judge Hoffman refused. So Bobby showed up for trial in September without a lawyer.

STEVE WASSERMAN (Berkeley student activist)

The Chicago Eight trial was significant because the eight people charged embodied and represented the rest of us. Bobby Seale, the cofounder of the Black Panther Party, was a proud, defiant, unbowed, and enormously articulate black American; Tom Hayden with his Catholic midwestern roots was an organizer extraordinaire and something of a theorist of radical change; Rennie Davis was an activist of striking intensity of purpose and plainspoken common sense; David Dellinger, the oldest of the defendants, a graduate of Yale who had gone to prison as a pacifist during the

---

*   David Dellinger was a longtime veteran of the peace movement. Born in 1915, about thirty years before most of the sixties activists, Dellinger was a conscientious objector during World War II and founded the Committee for Nonviolent Revolution in 1946. He was also active in the civil rights movement in the 1950s and 1960s.

The Chicago Eight defendants—(top, left to right) Jerry Rubin, Abbie Hoffman, Tom Hayden, Rennie Davis, (bottom, left to right) Bobby Seale, Lee Weiner, John Froines, and Dave Dellinger—were charged with conspiracy and inciting a riot during the 1968 Democratic National Convention in Chicago.

Second World War, was a stalwart elder statesman of dissent; Lee Weiner and John Froines, among the least known of the eight defendants, seemed to be ordinary citizens, like so many other Americans, whose activism had been spurred by deepening outrage over the continuing horror that was the Vietnam War; and rounding out the group were Abbie Hoffman and Jerry Rubin, gifted rapscallions who had their fingers on the pulse of the counterculture—a counterculture dubbed Woodstock Nation.

Whoever you were you could see a reflection of yourself in one or another of the defendants—unless, of course, you were a woman, since there weren't any in this case. Still, the defendants appeared to be a more pronounced, edgier, more daring version of oneself. It wasn't only they who were on trial. It felt as if our whole generation had been indicted. Even if you had only gone to a single protest, you could easily imagine yourself as, say, John Froines, a graduate student essentially minding his own business but roused to action by what the government was doing in his name. You didn't have to be in the upper echelons of the movement's leadership to feel that you too were under attack, that your fate was bound up with theirs.

GERALD LEFCOURT

After the demonstrations at the '68 Democratic convention, the FBI put together a case against the leaders of the protest movement and tried to get the Justice Department to indict the Chicago Eight for crossing state lines with the intention of inciting a riot. Ramsey Clark, who was LBJ's attorney general at the time, refused. This was a demonstration that was determined to be a police riot.* But after Nixon was elected promising law and order, his attorney general John Mitchell decided to bring the case. It was political repression, pure and simple.

TOM HAYDEN (FOUNDER, SDS)

It was a spectacle from day one: the judge, the Yippies,† the mood of the times. It felt like we were on television every day from the day the trial

---

* The Chicago Study Team of the National Commission on the Causes and Prevention of Violence investigated the 1968 Democratic convention protests, interviewing 1,400 witnesses as well as reviewing 180 hours of film and 20,000 pages of eyewitness statements. The so-called Walker Report, named for lead investigator Daniel Walker, was issued on December 1, 1968, and characterized the violence at the convention as a "police riot." Here is an excerpt: "During the week of the Democratic National Convention, the Chicago police were the targets of mounting provocation by both word and act. It took the form of obscene epithets, and of rocks, sticks, bathroom tiles, and even human feces hurled at police by demonstrators. Some of these acts had been planned; others were spontaneous or were themselves provoked by police action. Furthermore, the police had been put on edge by widely published threats of attempts to disrupt both the city and the Convention. That was the nature of the provocation. The nature of the response was unrestrained and indiscriminate police violence on many occasions, particularly at night. That violence was made all the more shocking by the fact that it was often inflicted upon persons who had broken no law, disobeyed no order, made no threat. . . . Newsmen and photographers were singled out for assault, and their equipment deliberately damaged. Fundamental police training was ignored; and officers, when on the scene, were often unable to control their men. As one police officer put it: 'What happened didn't have anything to do with police work.'"

† The Youth International Party, or Yippies, was cofounded by Abbie Hoffman, Jerry Rubin, and Stew Albert with the goal of politicizing the hippies, bringing social change, and becoming a media sensation. The Yippies were an anarchist guerrilla theater group who communicated their revolutionary message with humor and outrageous antics, like throwing money from the balcony of the New York Stock Exchange and trying to levitate the Pentagon.

began. So it was not unreasonable for Jerry and Abbie to plan a media strategy. Because the media sort of expected it, otherwise there would be no news.

They were McLuhanites.* They believed that little mattered beyond being on television. If you dressed appropriately, if you had long hair, specifically, that image would reach your base. Words would be useful also, but it was mainly the image, because your image would offend the right people, and attract the right people, as they saw it. Jerry Rubin called it the Academy Award of Protest before the trial began. Jerry and Abbie were partners, but they were also in a rivalry with each other over who was the king.

I think that Abbie was probably the greater performance artist. He was a natural. From the first day of the trial, they just set forth to create what they called the Yippie myth. It was not an organization, not a political party; it was a media-projected myth that did attract a number of people. It was a platform to act out a myth, which I think was meant to be a generational revolt and also antiracist, and antiwar.

GERALD LEFCOURT

Abbie takes the stand and the clerk says, "Name and address." He says, "Abbie Hoffman, Woodstock Nation." And the judge says, "What are you talking about?" And Abbie says, "I live in Woodstock Nation. It is a nation of alienated young people. We carry it around with us as a state of mind in the same way as the Sioux Indians carried the Sioux Nation around with them."

It was a state of mind—it was a new generation, a new way of being. We talked in terms of "We" instead of "I." It was people helping people.

STEVE WASSERMAN

I remember the courtroom well. It was exactly as Abbie had described it: a "neon cave" of extremely high ceilings with a bullying sterility of archi-

---

* Marshall McLuhan was a Canadian philosopher and public intellectual who became famous when he published a pioneering book on media theory, *Understanding Media: The Extensions of Man,* in 1964, in which he argued that "the medium is the message."

tecture that could have been appreciated only by Mussolini. Everything about the courtroom seemed to embody values utterly opposed to everything we thought we stood for. The very architecture announced its mission: to regiment, to confine, to erase individuality, to crush the anarchic and mischievous spirit of joyous rebellion. Our minders and oppressors wore suits and ties; we affected bell-bottoms and tie-dye shirts. They wrapped themselves in the American flag as if to shield themselves from what they were convinced was our assault on all that was holy; Abbie wore the flag as a shirt to advertise our patriotism.

The prosecution's intent, it seemed clear, was to intimidate the rest of us, to suppress our opposition, by trying to decapitate our leadership, to make examples of them, to prosecute and persecute them and, by extension, their allies. Not least of the government's considerations was to distract us by draining the always-meager treasury of opposition of its few dollars by having to pay ever-mounting legal bills.

GERALD LEFCOURT

Within days of the opening arguments, Judge Hoffman cited all the lawyers for contempt. Bobby Seale showed up without a lawyer and the government said, "What about these other lawyers who were in the case?" The government tried to force us to represent somebody who we'd met but didn't know. I was representing the Panthers in New York and Bobby and I were on the same page, but Charles Garry represented the national Black Panther leadership in Oakland. He was their lawyer from the founding of the Panthers on, and Bobby wanted Charles Garry. So we refused the order to represent him, and the judge held us in contempt and he ordered our arrests. Michael Tigar was in Southern California, Dennis Roberts and Michael Kennedy were in San Francisco, and I was in New York. We had a conference call when the arrest orders were announced, and we decided to sue in our own districts to quash the arrest warrants.

I went to Chicago, where Michael Tigar was already in custody. As soon as I entered the courthouse, I was arrested and brought into the lockup with Tigar, Bobby Seale, and Jerry Rubin. Bobby Seale was in jail because he was awaiting trial on a murder case in New Haven. Jerry was serving a sixty-day demonstration sentence. So the four of us were in a jail holding pen together.

I remember it was a Friday because what occurred was truly amazing. Bill Kunstler came to the jail to tell us that because it was a Friday at 5 P.M. the appellate court was closed and we had to stay in jail until Monday, when Judge Hoffman would sentence us for contempt. But the U.S. Court of Appeals, hearing the news that lawyers were jailed on this basis, decided on their own to order our release that Friday night. This was a turning point in that trial that got the media all up in arms at how outrageous the government and the trial judge were acting. I mean, to jail lawyers for refusing to represent a defendant they had no relationship with and who had his own lawyer was pretty shocking. Lawyers from around the country demonstrated against our contempt citations, the judge backed down. The contempts were dropped on Monday, September 29, and the four of us held a press conference slamming the government and *The New York Times* ran a huge front-page story about us. A month later, Bobby Seale was in the chains and gagged while demanding to represent himself. He was finally severed from the trial. By that time the whole country was watching and this became the trial of the century because the movements for change were at war with the government.*

The war in Vietnam was raging and the antiwar movement was on trial. In October in Washington, hundreds of thousands of demonstrators [the Moratorium] marched to the Department of Justice screaming, "Stop the trial!" And every night, one or more of the defendants would fly to a rally. Abbie's effect on this was incredible because he planned what he called TDA, The Day After. He would go to a campus and there'd be five thousand people at a rally, and he would say, "What are you going to do on the day after?" Meaning, the day after they convict us, we need you to go into the streets. You have to respond.

---

* In one courtroom moment when Seale demanded his constitutional right to defend himself, he said to Judge Hoffman, "You have George Washington and Benjamin Franklin sitting in a picture behind you, and they were slave owners. That's what they were. They owned slaves. You are acting in the same manner, denying me my constitutional rights." Bloom and Martin, *Black Against Empire*, p. 252.

The Chicago Eight's defense lawyers, (from left to right) Dennis Roberts,
Michael Tigar, Gerald Lefcourt, and Michael Kennedy, hold a press conference
at the Federal Building in Chicago on September 29, 1969, after Judge Julius
Hoffman dismisses contempt charges against them for refusing to represent
Bobby Seale against his will.

BERNARDINE DOHRN

The first time I was arrested was September 26, 1969, the day before the
opening of the Chicago Eight conspiracy trial. There are pictures of me
being thrown into the police car. I was charged twice in that period with
resisting arrest, disorderly conduct, and mob action. Those were the
demonstration arrests; if you were at a demonstration and you got arrested, that's what you were charged with. The conspiracy trial was the
epicenter of activity here in Chicago.

We didn't know that there was such a thing as COINTELPRO, and
yet we knew because we were experiencing it. We knew that we were
being followed and harassed, and we knew that people were being hung
out of windows by their feet. The Red Squad knew us by sight. There was
this organized group of Chicago cops who were all Korean War veterans
who were called the Red Squad—they were out to disrupt us, and to jail
us. What was to emerge over the next year was many conspiracy trials

across the country, against lots of antiwar groups including the Vietnam Vets Against the War, and so on.

Part of the Justice Department's strategy was to tie people up in long, costly trials or their own small, petty trial. Once you're on trial, once you're charged, and you have to keep making court appearances and you're in the hands of lawyers, even radical lawyers, you're in a different posture. You're off the streets and you're worrying about your own defense, and you're not organizing, and you're not planning ahead for the next thing, and you're not thinking about what the opportunities are to grow.

So we began to plan to have some small groups of us disappear, to protect ourselves from that kind of arrest and constant scrutiny. Our phones were tapped at this time and we were being followed all the time. We did some very funny things: We all learned sign language, and we had whole meetings in sign language. We developed code words—a lot of them were from songs or from drug culture, or from underground culture. We were hardly part of drug culture at that time; if anything, speed was our drug—coffee, speed, and bad food. But we were trying to figure out how to continue to grow and be a force and not be tied up in trials and nonstop arrests.

DAVID FENTON (movement photographer)

When the charges came and the trial started, I went to Chicago to photograph activities around the trial for Liberation News Service. Given that I knew Abbie and Jerry, I was hanging out with them every day after the trial. So I became part of the team that would go back to the offices and plot strategy for the next day in the courtroom. We'd watch Walter Cronkite and the other news reports of that day's trial—it was on every night—and then we'd figure out what antics we were going to do the next day to drive news coverage.

Abbie and Jerry showed up wearing judge's robes one day, and Judge Hoffman just flipped out and cited them for contempt. Another day they'd show up wearing Revolutionary War uniforms. All the world's a stage. I really didn't see them concerned about the trial at all, until they were cited for contempt of court because of the accumulated actions that the judge just couldn't bear.* They were facing serious jail time at that time on the contempt charges.

The Yippies were one of the first great myths of the television era. They were basically the Youth International Party. It was Abbie and three guys. That's it. And the reason I say it was the first great myth of the television era is that the television network news and *The New York Times* would faithfully report on the pronouncements and actions of the Youth International Party—which were three people. So it was complete and total manipulation. It was hysterical. Nixon thought there were really Yippies, as a result. There weren't any Yippies. It was Abbie, Jerry, and Paul Krassner. They were master showmen.

Abbie's insight into what television was going to do to the political situation in America was amazingly prescient. The only other person in that period who understood it was Roger Ailes, who went to work for Nixon and used his insight to get Nixon elected in '72. They both saw that TV was going to become everything.

GERALD LEFCOURT

The Panther 21 case in New York† and the Chicago Eight case were scheduled to go to trial at the same time. Bill Kunstler and I were counsel in both cases, so a decision had to be made. Kunstler basically made the decision that the Panthers needed me. It was a rough thing for me. I was so young to be the lead counsel. The Panthers were facing life in jail. They had no bail—one hundred thousand dollars might as well be no bail. By comparison, Abbie and the other Chicago Seven defendants were re-

---

*   At the end of the trial, Judge Hoffman cited the defendants and their two lawyers, William Kunstler and Leonard Weinglass, with 159 counts of contempt of court for courtroom outbursts and profanities, disrespecting the judge, challenging the judge's rulings, and personal insults. All of the contempt charges were overturned on appeal in 1972.

†   On April 2, 1969, twenty-one members of the New York Black Panther Party were indicted and charged with conspiracy to kill police officers and bomb several buildings, including five department buildings and the New York Botanical Garden. Bail was set for each defendant at $100,000. The trial, which lasted eight months, ended on May 12, 1971, when the defendants were acquitted of all 156 charges.

leased on their own recognizance and were facing five years for a protest demonstration.

So I worked all summer on the Chicago case until September, when Lenny Weinglass took over Abbie's representation at trial. Then the Panther 21 case in New York adjourned until February. So I kept coming out to Chicago on weekends to help prepare Abbie's testimony.

STEVE WASSERMAN

I was a senior at Berkeley High School and had been elected student body president on a radical platform. Several years earlier, in 1965, I began to participate in the Vietnam Day Committee, organized by Jerry Rubin and others to hold teach-ins to educate people about the escalating war. Four years later I attended the Chicago trial as one of Rubin's many "cousins," since only members of a defendant's family were permitted to view the proceedings. I arrived at the apartment of Leonard Weinglass, one of the defense attorneys, which was serving as both de facto legal headquarters and crash pad for the far-flung tribe of radical nomads, unafraid to let their freak flags fly, who sought to muster support for the beleaguered defendants. I walked in and was greeted by a haze of pot smoke. On the turntable, the volume cranked high, was the new Beatles album, *Abbey Road,** playing George Harrison's "Here Comes the Sun." Later, about midnight, Fred Hampton, the legendary and charismatic head of the Chicago chapter of the Black Panther Party, dropped by looking in his black leather coat like a glamorous paladin of the Resistance.

COUNTRY JOE MCDONALD (musician)

Judge Hoffman was really an oddball character. He kept asking me questions. I just stalled. They wanted me to testify that Jerry and Abbie and everybody else had conspired to cross state lines to start a riot, and I

---

*   *Abbey Road,* the Beatles' last recorded album, was released October 1, 1969, in the United States.

wasn't going to do that.* Kunstler was cross-examining me. That was their defense strategy, to have people come and talk about the problems of bringing the Yippie thing to Chicago and make a counterculture statement of some kind. I did that, and then I started singing. Well, the judge says, "No, no, you can't sing. Stop him." The sergeant-at-arms came over and put his hand over my mouth, and I stopped.†

TOM HAYDEN

On October 29, 1969, Judge Hoffman suspended the Chicago Eight trial proceedings and ordered a defendant to be taken out and dealt with. A few minutes passed, and Bobby Seale was carried back in the courtroom in a chair. They took him through the door, shut the door, chained and gagged him, put him in a chair, and carried him back. It was swift, as I recall. It might have been ten minutes.‡

When I get stunned, I sort of sink while I'm trying to comprehend what's going on. Other people were acting out of shock, including some reporters who were gasping. There must have been Panthers in the courtroom. I remember some yelling. But the judge or the FBI had brought in a lot of extra muscle, and there were a lot of armed marshals in the courtroom, maybe twenty-five to thirty. It was not a big courtroom, so we knew who they were.

---

*   A provision tacked on to the 1968 civil rights bill by conservative southern senators in response to the civil unrest made it illegal to cross state lines in order to start a riot. It was called the "H. Rap Brown law."

†   Judy Collins sang "Where Have All the Flowers Gone?" Other character witnesses for the defense included Arlo Guthrie, Norman Mailer, William Styron, Phil Ochs, Timothy Leary, and Allen Ginsberg.

‡   Because Bobby Seale had very little involvement in the Democratic convention protests, his indictment seemed to most observers to be only to repress and intimidate the Black Panther Party. When Judge Hoffman demanded that William Kunstler represent Seale, Seale insisted that he had a constitutional right to defend himself. Seale refused to be silenced and called Hoffman a "racist," a "fascist," and a "pig." The image of Seale bound and gagged in the courtroom became a powerful symbol of government racism and oppression and galvanized thousands of white activists to support the Panthers.

WESLEY BROWN

I think one of the most striking things about the Chicago Eight trial was the perception that Bobby Seale was a far greater threat than Tom Hayden, Rennie Davis, Abbie Hoffman, or Jerry Rubin. Seale was just saying you do not have the right to try me or to bring me up on charges. I don't have to defend myself, because I don't acknowledge you as a legitimate arbiter of my fate. And he kept saying that until they gagged and tied him up.

Courtroom drawing of Black Panther Party cofounder Bobby Seale, who, on the order of Judge Julius Hoffman, was carried into the courtroom bound to a chair and gagged.

TOM HAYDEN

We went through a couple more rounds where the judge was criticized by our attorneys for the condition that Seale was in, the manacles were too tight, he couldn't be heard because his mouth was covered, it was barbaric, it was torture, you don't chain a black man in America. And this all seemed over Judge Hoffman's head. I'm not sure he was in control of his senses to begin with. He was very old, and his condition was known to the Chicago defense community as either senile or totalitarian. Nobody had a good word to say about him. But in the culture of the federal courts, it meant you never crossed him. You just said, "Yes, sir."

WESLEY BROWN

The image of Bobby being tied and bound had historical continuity with the efforts of blacks who have had the audacity to raise their voices and say, "I'm not recognizing your right to judge me, and so I'm not going to participate." Eventually they separated his case from the others.

TOM HAYDEN

So they take Bobby out and bring him back about two or three times. Defendants would rise and rebuke the judge, and the marshals would push people down, or stare them down. People in the courtroom were so upset, so outraged, that I think the courtroom was cleared, and they took Bobby away and he never came back. Somebody prepared the document, the judge read it, declaring many counts of misconduct, and then he was severed from the case. Mistrial.

It served the purpose because Bobby was facing a murder conspiracy charge in Connecticut.[*] Chicago was a way station in his journey. And Chicago was trivial compared to anything else. He had made one militant speech for about thirty minutes in the Chicago park during the '68 Democratic convention, and otherwise, he wasn't even around. He had nothing to do with Chicago.[†]

I met one night with Bernardine Dohrn, and she was criticizing me for not tearing up and destroying the courtroom when Bobby Seale was

---

[*]   Seale was one of the "New Haven Nine" and was very loosely implicated in the murder of nineteen-year-old Black Panther member Alex Rackley. The high-profile trial started in May 1970 and a year later charges against Seale were dropped.

[†]   After shackling Seale, Judge Hoffman on November 5 cited Seale with sixteen counts of criminal contempt of court, declared a mistrial, and severed him from the case.

chained and gagged. She had the power of provoking guilt when she said things like "Why didn't you? What would John Brown have done?" And I wondered, Was I just trying to save my white skin? Why didn't I tear up the courtroom? I didn't think I had a very good answer, but I didn't think that her logic went very far, either, because when you tore up the courtroom and were put back in jail, then what would you do next? What's the day after about? So we would go around and around on this. Turned out, of course, I wasn't John Brown.*

---

* On February 19, 1970, after the twenty-one-week trial, the jury acquitted all seven defendants of the conspiracy charges but found five defendants (excluding Weiner and Froines) guilty of traveling across state lines with the intent to incite a riot. Judge Hoffman imposed the maximum five-year jail sentence. On November 21, 1972, the U.S. Court of Appeals for the Seventh Circuit unanimously overturned the defendants' criminal convictions and criticized Judge Hoffman and the prosecutor for their failure to fulfill "the standards of our system of justice." The contempt charges against the lawyers and defendants were also overturned, in a separate proceeding, in May 1972.

CHAPTER 9

ELLSBERG

(1967–October 1969)

The irony was that just as the Weathermen were giving up on the establishment, members of that very establishment were beginning to risk treason charges.

—TOM HAYDEN,
*The Long Sixties: From 1960
to Barack Obama*

IN JUNE 1969, *LIFE* MAGAZINE PUBLISHED A CONTROVERSIAL cover story called "The Faces of the American Dead in Vietnam: One Week's Toll." Photos of the 242 soldiers who were killed during a single week in June covered a ten-page spread. The previous year, in February 1968, *CBS Evening News* anchorman Walter Cronkite returned from a reporting mission in Vietnam after the Tet Offensive and declared the war "mired in a stalemate." Cronkite's short editorial suggested that the United States should withdraw. "It is increasingly clear to this reporter that the only rational way out will be to negotiate, not as victors, but as an honorable people who lived up to their pledge to defend democracy, and did the best they could." President Johnson, who was watching the broadcast live, famously said to his aides, "If I've lost Cronkite, I've lost middle America."

Daniel Ellsberg was intimately familiar with the news from the front, and his knowledge about the hard truths of the war motivated him to act. A product of the Cold War U.S. defense intelligentsia and a former hawk,

Ellsberg became convinced after spending two years on the ground in Vietnam with the State Department that the war was both immoral and unwinnable. Ellsberg's inside knowledge that Nixon and Kissinger intended to escalate the war at a time when the general public believed it was winding down led him to risk everything to try to stop it.

––––––––

MORTON HALPERIN (Defense Department expert)

I was sitting in my office one day in June of 1967 and there was a phone on my desk, which rang from Assistant Secretary of Defense John McNaughton's office, who was my boss. I was then his special assistant. My office was two feet away from his. My instructions were straighten your tie, put on your jacket, make sure you look presentable, and then come immediately into his office. So I did. And there was an old friend of mine—a guy named Colonel Robert Gard. Bob was then the second military assistant to Secretary of Defense Robert McNamara, and he was there to say Mr. McNamara wanted an encyclopedic history of the Vietnam War. And he wanted a memo about how to do it, which he would then approve, and then he wanted the study done. So I said, "Okay."

So I wrote a memo that laid out that we had to do it in his office in order to get the cooperation that we needed; we needed twelve people, and it would take six months. It turned out, of course, to take three years. The memo said, "Since you attach this high importance to this, I propose that I spend full time on this for six months." McNamara responded, "All approved except I want Halperin available for other things. Get somebody else to run it." So I recruited the deputy director of my policy planning staff—a guy named Leslie Gelb—and put him in charge full-time to run the study. I was involved mostly in recruiting people, so I recruited Dan Ellsberg to write a chapter.

Dan and I had been good friends since 1960, and he was at RAND,* which was one of the places we looked for people. These were people on

* The RAND Corporation is a large think tank based in Santa Monica, California, that originally provided quantitative research and analysis to help the U.S. armed services during the Cold War. It has since expanded its mission but is still a major Pentagon contractor.

contract with the Defense Department who were accustomed to being told by the government, "This is urgent. Stop what you're doing. Do this for six months." So we got a lot of our good people from there. Dan was a trained academic and he had spent time in Vietnam. He had six qualities of which any three would have been enough for us to want him to do this. So he was a natural for this.

When it was finally finished during the very beginning of the Nixon administration in January '69, Mel Laird, Nixon's secretary of defense, took the position that it wasn't his study, it was McNamara's study. Clark Clifford, who succeeded McNamara as LBJ's secretary of defense, took the position it wasn't his study, it was McNamara's study. McNamara took the position that he had made it clear he wanted nothing to do with the study. So Laird asked Paul Warnke, who had replaced McNaughton as the assistant secretary; Gelb, who ran the study; and me to decide on a distribution list. We decided there should be fifteen copies. One went to the NSC [National Security Council], one went to the State Department, one went to the Kennedy Library, and one went to the LBJ Library. And the fateful copy went to me, Warnke, and Gelb, which we put at the RAND Corporation. It was forty-nine volumes, and each volume was one hundred, two hundred, three hundred pages. So, it was very long, about seven thousand pages.

Basically, what the study revealed is that the U.S. government systematically lied to the American people about the nature of the war, from the very beginning. Harry Truman was told that Ho Chi Minh was the nationalist hero of Vietnam, that he had the legitimacy and the support of the people, and that the people on our side had been the stooges of the French, and then of the Japanese, and had no credibility. He was also told that France would elect a communist government if we forced them out of Vietnam. And so he decided he had to support the French going back into Vietnam, because he believed this nonsense that the French in France would vote to be communist if we didn't support them going back into Vietnam. And then the American people were told that Ho Chi Minh was a tool of the Chinese, Sino-Soviet bloc, and that we were going in to fight for the independence of the Vietnamese people. That was one big lie.

The second biggest—in a way, the most important lie—was that we sent combat troops into Vietnam at the urging of the South Vietnamese government. In fact, the Pentagon Papers make clear that we sent them against the bitter opposition of the South Vietnamese government. They thought they'd lose their sovereignty, and of course, soon after, we helped overthrow them. So, Diem* was right in not wanting us to come in. But we did flat-out lie. We said we're doing this at their invitation, that they were urging us. Meanwhile, we told them we would withdraw more military aid unless they publicly said they wanted us. So they did. But the study showed, absolutely clearly, that they did not. There were many other places in which the government clearly, explicitly lied about what was going on. Those were the two that come to mind, and the most important.

I knew Henry Kissinger because we both taught together at Harvard and in November of '68, after Nixon had won the presidential election, Kissinger asked me to work for him. At the time I was a deputy assistant secretary of defense in the LBJ administration. I liked being in the government, and I thought if you care about public policy issues, you want to be in the government. I've always believed that you can have more influence on an issue in an hour in the government than you can in five years outside the government. I thought as long as I had a chance to influence our getting out of Vietnam, I had to stay in the government to do that.

So I spent some of November and December and the beginning of January in New York, at the Pierre hotel, working with Kissinger on the Nixon transition. We wrote a memo on Vietnam for Nixon with the help of Dan Ellsberg and others at the RAND Corporation, which had a series of options, ranging from staying in at the current level to getting out of the war right away. We sent it to Nixon, and it came back saying there's a missing option. Kissinger said, "What's that?" Nixon said, "Escalation." So we wrote in an escalation option, which is what was eventually carried out. So it was clear early on that Nixon thought escalation was a real option. Kissinger did not think it was until he realized Nixon thought it was, and then Nixon and Kissinger became very attached to escalation as an option.

---

*   Ngo Dinh Diem was the first president (and an anticommunist Catholic) of South Vietnam from the nation's formation in 1955 until his assassination in 1963.

ROGER MORRIS (national security expert)

I came over to the National Security Council in June 1967 as special assistant to McGeorge Bundy, LBJ's national security advisor. After that assignment expired at the end of 1967, I was asked to stay on the staff under then–national security advisor Walt Rostow. This was all under President Johnson, of course. After Nixon's election, they didn't really have a very clear idea of what the new NSC staff was supposed to look like, except that the Nixon people wanted it to be Republican loyalists who reflected the administration's view of things, and only two of us were kept on from Johnson's NSC staff.

There was a great disparity between the public story, which was "We've got this in hand, the North Vietnamese are exhausted, and Tet is not an American defeat, it's just a last spasm and we're going to turn things around." That was the rah-rah military view of the Pentagon and its people in Saigon, as opposed to the CIA view, which was a much more realistic and grim appraisal of what the political impact of the Tet Offensive was.

The common antiwar interpretation of all of this at the time was that Tet was a devastating blow to Lyndon Johnson, and eventually it drove him from office to the extent that it accounted for Eugene McCarthy's 42 percent showing in the New Hampshire primary and Bobby Kennedy's emergence. But there was the other dimension, which didn't get much attention, which was Tet was devastating politically in South Vietnam. The war had already been lost politically in so many ways, but this was a numbering of the days for the South Vietnamese government that no one had been very realistic or honest about. And so the attacks showed the endurance, the resiliency, the creativity—the sheer effectiveness—of the other side. It showed that the more indigenous South Vietnamese Viet Cong were still a very formidable force. And though the VC took enormous casualties, the CIA was saying, "This is not a knockout blow. This is not the kind of last spasm that the Pentagon was seeing."

The public story may have had elements of what the government thought it knew, but for the most part it was a deliberate misinterpretation of events. So it's an intelligence mess. It's an intellectual disgrace, really, when you think about it. We never really got a grip on the political character of the war in South Vietnam. Tet was an American political atrocity, as well as a disaster in the field, and my feeling at the time was that the war needed to end as soon as possible.

If you were not too cynical about things, one could take some hope from the Nixon campaign message, "I have a secret plan to end the war, and I'm going to start bringing the boys home; we're going to recalibrate the negotiations." Melvin Laird, this Wisconsin congressman who was secretary of defense, coined the term "Vietnamization," a rather ugly little term, which just meant that we were going to have a withdrawal of U.S. forces and shift responsibility to the South Vietnamese. This plan had been on the table during the Johnson administration for years. But I think, looking back, there was serious reason to believe that the administration would move with some dispatch to do something about the war.

MORTON HALPERIN

I was inside enough to know that we were not getting out, and that Nixon was fighting with his secretary of defense, Melvin Laird, who definitely wanted to announce the next troop withdrawal and was clearly stringing it out as long as he could. It was clear to me that Nixon was going to get out slowly, and that he thought the key to U.S. popular support for the war was to end the draft, and that he was going to do that, and he was determined to stay in Vietnam until he got a deal that he thought was satisfactory. So I told him that this was not going to happen.

I found out about the secret bombing of Cambodia the day it started, March 18, 1969.* It was by accident. I was in Kissinger's office talking to him about something else, and [Kissinger's military advisor] Al Haig burst in and said, "We've gotten a whole slew of secondary explosions," meaning that they had hit ammunition depots in Cambodia. Then he realized that I was in the room, and that I wasn't one of the people cleared to

---

* The Nixon administration's secret bombing campaign against North Vietnamese military bases in (neutral) Cambodia and Laos, code-named "Operation Menu," began on March 18, 1969, and ended May 26, 1970. Nixon authorized the use of B-52s to carpet bomb the region along the border of Vietnam, and the campaign was kept secret and records falsified or destroyed so that even members of the military command didn't know about the bombing.

know about the Cambodian bombing. I was not involved in drafting any of the papers, and I was not involved in anything afterwards.

I was unhappy about Nixon asking for an escalation strategy, but I still didn't know that it meant he was going to implement it. But I gradually came to understand that he really was going to implement it, and that, along with a lot of other things, led me to decide that I could not fight the Vietnam War from inside anymore, and it was time to leave.

DANIEL ELLSBERG (RAND defense expert)

Mort Halperin called me midsummer of '69, when everyone thought that Nixon was planning to get us out of the war, and told me elliptically, "Nixon's staying in; he's not getting out."

In March of 1969, Nixon told the North Vietnamese, "The gravest consequences will follow if you don't accept our terms." The terms were basically for mutual withdrawal of North Vietnamese forces and U.S. forces from South Vietnam—a proposal which seemed to Mort and me to have some promise. It would have been good for them to accept it. But the North Vietnamese rejected it very quickly. They never came close to accepting it, and the North Vietnamese forces never did get out of South Vietnam.

And so it was clear to Mort and me by the spring that this thing is a dead letter that's not going to happen. So what do you do? What's next? As we saw it, a unilateral U.S. withdrawal was what you ought to do. If they weren't going to agree to a mutual withdrawal, we had to get out. But that was not the conclusion that Nixon and Kissinger drew. Rather, they thought they would get mutual withdrawal by threatening that if the North did not accept those terms, they would be wiped off the map, both by conventional and nuclear weapons. So the threat was communicated by Kissinger to the North Vietnamese when he started talking to them in Paris August 4, 1969.

MORTON HALPERIN

When a story about the secret bombings in Cambodia appeared in *The New York Times* story by William Beecher on May 9, 1969, there was much detail in the story that I did not know. I could not have been the source for most of that story, because the only thing I knew was the fact that we were bombing. I didn't know anything about the double targeting and all this other stuff.[*]

The day the story was published, Kissinger called FBI director J. Edgar Hoover and said, "The president's very disturbed about this. He wants to know what you think should be done." And of course, Hoover's answer to all problems was wiretap people. So Hoover then called his sources, who were journalists friendly to the administration, and said, "Who do you think leaked this?" And one of them said, "It must be Halperin. He's against the war. He was trying to get us out of Vietnam when he was in the LBJ Pentagon. He would do anything to get us out of the war." So Hoover told Kissinger, "My sources tell me Halperin leaked the thing." And then Hoover, without waiting for White House approval, put a wiretap on my phone.

DANIEL ELLSBERG

I knew from Mort that Nixon was threatening escalation, and I was sure that it would not lead to mutual withdrawal, which was what he was asking, because his earlier offers of mutual withdrawal had been rebuffed. After studying the Pentagon Papers, I felt that Nixon, having made such threats, was likely to carry them out, and that would do nothing but escalate the war and prolong it. My incentive for deciding to start the process of trying to publicly expose the Pentagon Papers was that Nixon's plan would ultimately lead to the use of nuclear weapons.

ROGER MORRIS

By the end of summer '69 my stock was reasonably high with Kissinger. I think it must've been August that he began to ask me to sit in on meetings dealing with Vietnam, and he was obviously putting together a little work-

---

[*]   William Beecher, "Raids in Cambodia by U.S. Unprotested," *New York Times,* May 9, 1969, p. A1. The government kept the bombing raids secret by officially reporting false bombing targets in Vietnam.

ing group. By the summer, time was running out with the antiwar movement, it was running out on the Hill, and it was plain that the covert
bombing in Cambodia and a lot of other covert stuff, a lot of raiding across
the parallel and mucking around with North Vietnam, was not going to
affect policy. So something more forceful in terms of coercion of [North
Vietnam] would have to be done to open things up.

Kissinger convened a special NSC staff planning committee called the
September Group, and we were asked to look at the political, military, and
economic contingency plan of a massive strike at North Vietnam, including what would later materialize as the carpet bombing of Hanoi* and the
very risky bombing of the Haiphong Harbor, which involved a lot of Soviet and Chinese shipping, the bombing of the rail line to the North,
through China, and through the Mu Gia Pass [to Laos]. There was talk of
using a nuclear weapon on the Mu Gia Pass. The code name for this escalation plan was Operation Duck Hook.

TONY LAKE (White House national security expert)

I was Kissinger's special assistant. Kissinger knew that I did not believe
that after all of that effort and sacrifice, we could win, and therefore we
should find the best negotiated settlement we could, as quickly as possible. He had me be his Vietnam person as well. So I accompanied him to
the secret negotiations with the North Vietnamese in Paris, and it gave me
an entry point for writing him occasional memos on why I thought the
administration was taking the wrong approach.

ROGER MORRIS

So in August of 1969 there began a succession of secret meetings with the
Vietnamese that goes through the winter and spring of 1970. We'd get
flown to Paris, land in an outlying military airfield, and be whisked off to
a safe house. The French government knew something was going on but

---

* In December 1972, B-52s carpet bombed Hanoi, the capital of North Vietnam, in the so-
called Christmas bombings.

they were not informed. They would have had the house bugged, so they probably knew. But we were not telling anybody.

TONY LAKE

Kissinger argued that we had to be more threatening with the North Vietnamese in an effort to bring them to the table to reach a better diplomatic solution, which was a part of the strategy leading up to November 1, 1969, the anniversary of Johnson's bombing halt. Nixon threatened the North Vietnamese with measures of great force if they didn't come across with the kind of deal that we were looking for by November 1, and the North Vietnamese called what turned out to be Nixon's bluff.

MORTON HALPERIN

My decision to resign was a long, gradual process. After the wiretap, Kissinger cut down my access and I kept saying, "Henry, I'm going to leave. I don't have enough to do. I don't like just knowing about parts of things." And he would say, "You can't leave." I resigned in September of '69.

DANIEL ELLSBERG

In September, a month before I started copying the papers, I contacted Ted Kennedy and Averell Harriman and various other prominent Democrats like Harry McPherson, who was assistant to Johnson, and Paul Warnke, and tried to get them to make a statement saying, "This is not your war, this is our war." That was the message. What I knew from the Pentagon Papers is no president will get out of Vietnam if he has to take the full responsibility for it. It would only work politically if the opposition party will take responsibility, which was fair enough for the Democrats. It was the Democrats' responsibility, and if they assured Nixon that they will not call him weak on communism, and a sellout, but on the contrary will say, "We stand with you, this is the right thing to do"—only if he could share that responsibility with them, I thought, would the president ever get out.

What I found in each case, one by one, was that none of them was will-

President Richard Nixon convenes his war council on September 1, 1969, to discuss Vietnam War strategy. From left: National Security Advisor Henry Kissinger, Attorney General John Mitchell, Vice President Spiro Agnew, Admiral John S. McCain, Jr., General Creighton Abrams, CIA director Richard Helms, peace delegate Philip C. Habib, Ambassador Ellsworth Bunker, Secretary of State William Rogers, President Nixon, Secretary of Defense Melvin Laird, and General Earle Wheeler.

ing to do that. Not the right time, you know, later, and so forth. And what I came to realize was they wanted it to be *Nixon's* war. Not just the Democrats' war—and then they could conceive of giving him a break and standing with him. But my conviction was that by then it will be too late. Once he has made it his war, and has committed a lot of troops, and suffered a lot of casualties, he ain't going to get out, even if you are willing to stand with him. It's his war by then. So either you do it *now* or it's not going to happen. That was my feeling.

I started copying the Pentagon Papers on October 1, or the day before. Tony [Russo] and I were never able, best we tried, to decide whether it was September 29 or the 30, or October 1. So in my book I say it's October 1. I tell the whole story in the book:

> In the early evening of October 1, 1969, I opened the top secret safe in the corner of my office and started to pick out volumes of

the McNamara study to copy that night. The forty-seven volumes filled two drawers, about eight feet. I thought I'd better start with the highest-priority studies. . . . I chose the volumes on 1964–65 to start with. They had the most relevance to the current movement. That was history I was trying to keep from recurring: a president making secret threats of escalation, and secret plans to carry them out if they didn't work, as was almost certain; a war on the way to getting much larger and longer, with the public wholly unaware. . . .

I opened the doors to the lobby [of RAND in Santa Monica]. There were two guards behind the desk as usual. I was wearing my badge, but they knew everyone by sight. They said, "Good night, Dan," friendly as usual, and I waved my free hand good night as I passed the desk, where one of them was checking my name off on a list and noting the time. I walked past the posters on tripods that had World War II security reminders on them: "Loose Lips Sink Ships"; "What You See Here, What You Say Here, Let It Stay Here." . . .

I went over directly to my former colleague Tony Russo's apartment. Lynda Sinay [his girlfriend] was with him. . . . We drove to her office at the corner of Melrose and Crescent. It was on the second floor, above a flower shop. . . . The Xerox machine was just inside the glass door at the top of the stairway, on the left in the reception room. . . .

The top secret markings on the top and bottom of every page reminded me constantly of the stakes. I didn't know yet how I was going to get this information to the public, but however that happened, it was going to change my life very drastically and suddenly.[*]

Meanwhile, during the daytime, the next thing I thought of was, Let's get a bunch of people from RAND who are against the war, who know

---

[*]   Daniel Ellsberg, *Secrets: A Memoir of Vietnam and the Pentagon Papers* (New York: Viking, 2002), pp. 299–303. I interviewed Daniel Ellsberg at his house in Berkeley, California, on March 10, 2014. During our five-hour meeting, Ellsberg resisted describing his experience of copying the Pentagon Papers and asked me instead to quote directly from his memoir.

how hopeless it is from their research, to write a personal letter. We spent days drafting this letter. I was not a key drafter because I was spending the nights copying the Pentagon Papers, which none of them knew about of course. They were all naturally concerned about their jobs. I wasn't too concerned about my job, because I expected to be in prison within weeks. I was also pretty tired during the day. I was copying all night, so I think I was rather passive in the group get-togethers where we were drafting this letter, but we all took part in it. There was a lot of back-and-forth, and then we all agreed that we would not send it out without showing it to Harry Rowen, who was the president of RAND.

I think they all assumed that this was a good exercise but that Harry would never agree to let the letter out. And to their surprise, Harry's reaction was, "Why isn't this on RAND letterhead?" We said, "Well, we weren't trying to embarrass RAND here. We put it on a plain letter." And he said, "No, no, it'll come out that you were all from RAND, and it'll look as though we had censored you." He said, "Put it on RAND letterhead." The whole point was we were people who have had access to the classified information, and we say America should get out of the war. We were opposed to the attitude that the only people who supported withdrawal had to be either irresponsible, reckless America haters or totally ignorant of the situation. On the contrary, we had all worked on the Vietnam War for the government, and we had seen the information, and we say it's not going to get any better. There may be some bad consequences to withdrawing now, but they will not be better a year from now, or two years from now if you postpone it.

Dear Sirs,

Now that the American people are once again debating the issue of Vietnam, we desire to contribute to that discussion by presenting our own views, which reflect both personal judgements and years of professional research on the Vietnam war and related matters. We are expressing here our views as individuals, not speaking for Rand, of which we are staff members; there is a considerable diversity of views on this subject, as on other issues, among our Rand colleagues.

We believe that the United States should decide now to end its participation in the Vietnam war, completing the total withdrawal of our forces within one year at the most. Such U.S. disengagement should not be conditioned upon agreement or performance by Hanoi or Saigon—i.e., it should not be subject to veto by either side. . . .

We do not predict that only good consequences will follow for Southeast Asia or South Vietnam (or even the United States) from our withdrawal. What we do say is that the risks will not be less after another year or more of American involvement, and the human costs will surely be greater.

> Daniel Ellsberg, Melvin Gurtov, Oleg
> Hoeffding, Arnold Horelick, Konrad
> Kellen, Paul F. Langer
>
> THE RAND CORPORATION

I called up *New York Times* correspondent Steve Roberts and said, "Be in the parking lot at RAND, and I'll come out. I have a letter for you." I walked out to the parking lot, and there was Steve, and I said, "Okay, Steve. Here's your letter. Now, stay away from the phone until this thing appears, don't take any message from me or anybody else on this. Get it out." I thought there would be second and third thoughts, and they'd want to take it back.

In the end, it was printed as a news story on October 9, 1969, which we had mixed feelings about, because it meant they didn't print the whole letter. We had been very careful to express ourselves and show how nuanced and broad-thinking we were but only a few paragraphs of the letter got in the news story. But because it was a news story, it got a little more attention. It was news that six people at RAND said this. The headline was "Six Rand Experts Support Pullout: Back Unilateral Step Within One Year in Vietnam."

Because the *Times* hadn't carried our letter in full, we offered it to *The Washington Post* as well, and it printed the whole letter prominently in the center of its editorial page on Sunday, October 12, with the headline "A

Case Against Staying in Vietnam." I was told later that it was the most quoted item in the Moratorium rallies, which took place all across the country on October 15. That was what I was hoping for. It was the very point I was making. You didn't have to be ignorant of the specifics of the war to be for getting out. Our letter had the kind of authority I wanted these Democratic policy makers to use, and since they wouldn't do it, we did it.

The only other people who'd called for unilateral withdrawal before now were great men like Abbie Hoffman and Howard Zinn—who'd written a little book on it, *The Case for Withdrawal.* Abbie Hoffman, Jerry Rubin, and the hippies and Yippies, people like that, were dismissed as radicals who didn't know anything. No establishment figure had come out publicly for getting out altogether. Bobby Kennedy had told Johnson that we should get out in early '68. He'd come back from Vietnam, and Johnson shat all over him and said, "It's unthinkable." Bobby didn't say it publicly after that, and he did not run on saying we should get out unilaterally. Eugene McCarthy did not run on it, either. No establishment person had done it. After the RAND letter came and got nationwide press coverage, we got over two hundred and fifty letters from professionals at RAND denouncing us.

About a week after the letter was published, Senator [Walter] Fritz Mondale wanted to see me. So I met him in the cloakroom, off the floor of Congress. I remember him saying he wanted to congratulate me on the RAND letter. He said that took real guts, real courage. He said, "I don't have that kind of courage." And I said, "Well, you don't know what kind of courage you have until you come up against the actual situation." And he said, "No, I know myself. I don't have it."

CHAPTER 10

MORATORIUM

(June–October 1969)

ATTENTION ALL PEACE MARCHERS: Hippies, Yippies, Beatniks, Peaceniks, Yellow Bellies, Traitors, Commies and their agents and dupes—HELP KEEP OUR CITY CLEAN . . . just by staying out of it.

—HEADLINE OF THE *Manchester* (N.H.)
Union Leader, October 15, 1969

WHAT MIGHT BE REFERRED TO AS A SINGULAR PEACE MOVEMENT OF the 1960s was in fact a loose coalition of many organizations, each with its own distinct agenda: SNCC, SDS, the Weathermen, the Black Panthers, MOBE, the Resistance, the Yippies, Women Strike for Peace, McCarthy supporters who were "Clean for Gene," Vietnam Veterans Against the War, and many more. By October 1969, none was more threatening to the Nixon administration than an organization with only thirty-one paid staffers called the Vietnam Moratorium Committee. Made up of young Democratic Party operatives who were alumni of Senators Eugene McCarthy's and Robert F. Kennedy's 1968 presidential campaigns, the M-day committee appealed to moderate middle Americans— housewives, priests, white-collar professionals, and midwesterners—which is why it was so menacing.

DANIEL ELLSBERG (defense expert, RAND consultant)

Sam Brown called me and asked me if I would join the moratorium group as an advisor. It was just four students: Sam Brown, Dave Mixner, Marge Sklencar, and Dave Hawk. So, fine, good luck, I didn't imagine that it would amount to very much.

DAVID HAWK (Moratorium Committee organizer, peace activist)

I had worked for SNCC in the South. I had come out of the same places as many of the Weathermen. I had been through some of the same experiences. But the "Days of Rage" stuff was kooky. It was crazy. At the time we thought, Oh, well, they're going to do their thing, and we're doing ours.

DAVID MIXNER
(Moratorium Committee organizer, peace activist)

We felt that at this stage that some Americans who were against the war were being turned off by the tactics and rhetoric of the more strident people in the movement like the Weathermen. A classic yet small example was showing up at peace rallies with Viet Cong flags, which would alienate anybody who might have had a family member serve in Vietnam. I had relatives serve and die in Vietnam, and my family would have been turned off by that Vietnam flag even though they were antiwar. I had lost four first cousins, including one that was my best friend, in the war. Actually, I was one of the only ones on the Moratorium Committee that had actually lost somebody.

SAM BROWN

I had been the chair of the National Student Association. I probably knew people on a hundred campuses around the country. College Young Dems then had some of the same elements it probably has now; it was a little bit goody two-shoes, "Let's be the next generation of political leaders." We wanted to show the administration that there was a group of people opposed to Lyndon Johnson who weren't Abbie Hoffman, and Jerry Rubin, and a bunch of crazies.

Back then, the antiwar left had been portrayed as loners, outsiders, radicals, and not someone you'd want to have as a child. So we thought it was important, when kids show up on the doorstep campaigning for Eugene McCarthy, that people couldn't dismiss them for their appearance, that they had to listen to their argument. Being Clean for Gene* was a door opener to a conversation. It was very important to get that door open and have people not dismiss you. So it was all part of the broad strategy to show that young Dems who were wearing neckties, coats, and were clean-shaven with short hair could be against the president.

DAVID HAWK

I had been involved with Sam Brown and the "Dump Johnson" movement. After the campaign, he went back to the Kennedy School at Harvard. I went to the National Student Association, where I organized a "We Won't Go" petition. We got about two hundred student body presidents and college newspaper editors, and sought a meeting with Nixon so we could tell him how strong the antiwar opinion was on college campuses. We didn't get a meeting with Nixon, but we got a meeting with Henry Kissinger and John Ehrlichman [the White House counsel] in the Situation Room of the White House. Kissinger was at his Harvard professor, meeting-with-graduate-students best. He was making the claim that they [the Nixon administration] inherited the war, and they were going to end it with honor, but we had to give them time. He was acting like a professor of international relations meeting with a group of graduate students.

We had a dozen people who had signed this letter at the meeting. Kis-

---

* Democratic U.S. senator from Minnesota and ardent Vietnam War opponent Eugene McCarthy challenged Lyndon Johnson in the 1968 Democratic primary. College students flocked to work on McCarthy's campaign. The "Get Clean for Gene" slogan was born in New Hampshire, where long-haired New Left student volunteers cut their hair and beards before canvassing for McCarthy, who with 42 percent of the vote came within 6 points of beating Johnson, thus signaling LBJ's political vulnerability. Days later, New York senator Robert F. Kennedy jumped into the Democratic primary race.

singer made his plea and left, and Ehrlichman took over the meeting and read us the riot act. He told us, "If you people think you can break laws now just because you don't like them, you're going to force us to up the ante to the point where we're giving out death sentences for traffic violations." So, as thoughtful and rational as Kissinger had been in making a plea for a war they inherited and that they were going to try to end, Ehrlichman undid whatever public relations boost might have come out of the meeting by being the hard-liner that he was. So, of course, the student leaders were shocked, and the exit from the Situation Room, perversely, led through the Press Office. The letter to the president had been public. It had gotten small stories in the press; the press knew the meeting was taking place. So they asked the students what they thought, and their response was that these guys were going to be worse than the former administration. Ironically, Ehrlichman was the one who ended up going to jail, not the students.*

SAM BROWN

I taught a study group in the spring of '69 at the Harvard Kennedy School on contemporary American politics, and we spent the entire semester discussing what we could do to end the war in Vietnam. We talked about having a national strike, but the language wasn't right, it was too Old Left industrial sounding. So during the course of the spring this became a discussion about what the real levers of power were. What are the ways you can influence those people in power? We had failed in the political realm by losing the '68 election to Nixon, but we had failed in a broader realm to convince people that they could be against the war, and also be good Americans, and that was a decent, honorable, pro-American position to have. The unions hated the antiwar movement and hated Gene McCarthy. We had not figured out how to build a political movement that was going to make this change.

---

*   John Ehrlichman was Nixon's assistant for domestic affairs and the architect of the White House "Plumbers." He was convicted of conspiracy, obstruction of justice, and perjury in the Watergate scandal and served one and a half years in prison.

DAVID MIXNER

Sam approached me about this idea of working with him on this thing that they originally called Strike for Peace, and we thought that was too strident of a word, so we changed it to Vietnam Moratorium. People would take a day off and campuses would shut down, and people would read names of the war dead, and ring bells, and have interfaith services, and do it in their own communities, instead of all coming to one place, and they would talk about the war. I loved it. I had often talked about the need to have a broad-based antiwar movement that didn't have Viet Cong flags, and that would reach into America's middle class, and be able to have labor join us, and corporate leaders join us, which just wasn't happening. I mean, even the UAW [United Auto Workers] at that time wasn't against the war.

SAM BROWN

I called David Hawk and David Mixner, who I knew from the McCarthy campaign, and I talked to a bunch of other people around the country, and over the course of the spring we developed this idea, and kept refining it, and "moratorium" became the operative word. It meant to take a pause. It grew from the discussion about strike. It wasn't the image of "Let's take a picket sign and go someplace." Rather you could simply stop what you were doing and have a discussion for an hour, or a day, a teach-in on a college campus. You could honor the dead by a set of crosses on the campus. You could do a silent vigil. You could pick from the menu, or make up your own. The name "Moratorium" had a ring of respectability—people could choose their own path to it. In June of '69 three of us went to Washington, opened an office, held a press conference, and said, "We're going to end the war in Vietnam, and we're going to do it starting in October."

SAM BROWN

I had been involved in a lot of past demonstrations, and I knew that if you're going to do a big demonstration that involves college students, you want to do it in the fall. You don't want to do it when people are just arriving back on campus, or when they're already in exams. You need to do it when the weather is decent, so people can actually be outside. You need to understand that lots of people may have an equal interest in the social aspect of it. There were a lot of guys who came to this march who were thinking that they were going to get lucky. Maybe a lot of women came thinking they were going to get lucky, too. The women didn't tell me. The men all told me. So the October–November window was when you could do something substantial and make it work. But you needed a month or so after people got back to campus to get it organized, and we always knew that students would be the core. We settled on the date of October 15.

I thought the organization was just right. It was complete chaos at all times. Our notion from the beginning was that it should be as decentralized as possible, as locally controlled as possible, that the only rules were that it needed to be nonviolent, that it needed to focus on bringing more people in. It was not to be a vanguard action. It was to be a mass action. For that reason we set up four or five regional offices around the country.

DAVID MIXNER

I'm from southern New Jersey. My father worked on farms, and my mother worked shift work in a factory. We were poor. We even had an outdoor john for a while. My family fit the profile of those who were drafted, or went into the military to escape from where we were raised. They were deeply segregationist, but vehemently antiwar. I had a cousin named Russell Garrison who was my best friend. We grew up together, across the fields. His daddy was a dairy farmer, and Russell worked on a dairy farm. He had to drop out of college because he couldn't afford it. I was smart enough to get a scholarship, but he joined the military in order to get them to pay for his education—the biggest scholarship fund for my people. He was shipped off to Vietnam and killed in March of 1967.

Ever since World War II, my family never was a big fan of war. I guess you can come back from World War II in many ways. My uncles were in the Battle of the Bulge and saw a lot of mass death. You can come back as a superpatriot, my country right or wrong, or you can come back and say, "I hope my kids never have to go through that hell."

It was the first televised war. We could see instantly these horrible images of napalm, and as we used to say back home, "It ain't right." I was concerned about appearing unpatriotic. I'm still the guy that tears up at the national anthem. I come from that kind of folk. I was the conservative one on the Moratorium Committee. I insisted on carrying a tiny American flag on the big march, which drove David Hawk nuts. I said, "David, y'all just be grateful it's not a big one."

SAM BROWN

David Mixner, David Hawk, and Marge Sklencar came to work. Mixner was a political strategist. He was a young man, very wily, very clever, a very smart guy about how politics work. He was a deeply closeted gay person at the time. Hawk was probably the most left of us. He was a draft resister. We all went to his arrest ceremony at Riverside Church, where Bill Coffin* spoke. He had the deepest, real roots in the civil rights movement. He was with Charlie Sherrod, in the Southwest Georgia Voter Project, which is one of the toughest places to be in '64. Marge Sklencar was from Mundelein College in Chicago, and she helped us largely with women's Catholic and liberal arts colleges. We didn't want it to be just some Ivy League, West Coast, or Madison, Wisconsin, operation. We wanted to make sure that we had roots more broadly than that.

DAVID HAWK

Over the summer, our small office at the Vietnam Moratorium Committee started to call the dean of students' offices at hundreds of universities and getting the phone numbers of next year's student body president, finding them at home and convincing them to start organizing the week school started. Toward the end of the summer we were being covered by the press corps in Washington that covered the student beat. *The New York Times, The Washington Post, Newsweek, Time* magazine, all had journal-

---

* William Sloane Coffin (1924–2006) was the chaplain at Yale University and later a minister at Riverside Church in New York. He was a civil rights and peace activist and a leading voice of the Vietnam peace movement who espoused the use of civil disobedience.

ists whose beat it was to cover students. The journalists who were doing this would contact us over the summer, wanting to know what was going to happen when the campuses opened in the fall. I started telling them, with increasing confidence, that we were going to have this thing called the Vietnam Moratorium.

DAVID MIXNER

Before the Moratorium, the Nixon people had seen what the students were able to do to Johnson, and so they were making outreach like mad. They contacted me through their liaison, Jay Wilkinson, and a guy named John Campbell at the White House. And they actually took a group of us to the Airlie House retreat. I think it was a CIA retreat place, quite honestly. They flew us in a helicopter, from the White House lawn. Ehrlichman was there. [Chief of Staff H. R.] Haldeman was there, and [White House counsel] John Dean. We talked about war, and what students wanted. It was a bullshit meeting. But we were all gaga. I mean, come on, we just flew out on Marine One! I was twenty-three, and all these people were asking my advice on the war. Hello?

STEPHEN BULL (Nixon aide)

I enlisted in the Marine Corps after graduation in 1963. By 1965 I would go to Okinawa, and then to Vietnam. We were part of the initial buildup. I was with a motor transport outfit. We got shot at from time to time, but they missed. 'Sixty-five was the beginning of a transitional year. There was a huge revolution, in about an eighteen-month period. I left the country around the time—do you remember Berkeley, and the Free Speech Movement in 1964, otherwise referred to as the dirty word movement? Mario Savio was leading it. When I was in Vietnam, Watts blew up.* I remember there was a notification that went around to various units in the Marine

---

*   A race riot broke out in the Watts neighborhood in South Central Los Angeles in August 1965 that lasted six days and caused thirty-four deaths, more than 1,000 injuries, and $40 million in property damage. The extensive violence shook the country and sounded the bell for black discontent over chronic unemployment, police oppression, and racial discrimination.

Corps, saying in effect, be on the lookout for troops smoking marijuana. I thought, Marines didn't smoke marijuana. Marines don't do drugs; they're marines. Drugs were not part of my generation. But when I came back home, drugs were ubiquitous. The antiwar movement had just started. I got back in the summer of '66.

I grew up on Long Island, and when I started job seeking in Manhattan after only being home for two weeks, the first thing I see is a bunch of raggedy kids marching down the street, carrying Viet Cong flags, chanting, "Ho, Ho, Ho Chi Minh, the NLF is going to win." And I'm thinking, What in the heck is going on? And they're smoking dope, and all of this stuff is going on, and I'm thinking, What happened in this one-year period? Fortunately, I was there at the beginning of the Vietnam War. And perhaps because I had it all behind me, I could be more cavalier in my attitude because it didn't really affect me directly. I wasn't going to be drafted and be sent back over there. I was done.

SAM BROWN

What happened was almost incomprehensible. In August our office was quiet, and we were developing relationships, reaching out to people, but September and October blew our minds. People were constantly contacting us—people we didn't know at all. They'd call us and say, "I'm in Wichita. What can I do?" "Well, what do you want to do? Let's think together about what you might do in Wichita, and if it makes sense in Wichita. What do you think works? Who do you know? Who can you talk to? Who are the people you would reach out to in the community?" We were helping people think through what they could do.

Interest built steadily in the last six weeks. And so, when you asked me to describe it, I said "incomprehensible" because of the waves of stuff that was happening every day. We were living together in a house out on Eighteenth Street, seven of us, sharing a house, and cooking spaghetti at one o'clock in the morning when we got home. I mean, we thought it was us against the world, and then suddenly it seemed like the whole world was standing outside our door.

Anyway, the momentum grew, and grew, and grew, and it became more and more respectable, even in little towns like the one where I grew up, Council Bluffs, Iowa. But it was very tough on my parents. I would say the worst night was when they got a phone call at three o'clock in the morning saying, "Your son is dead, and we're glad," and then they hung up. They had been pillars of the local Methodist church all of their adult life, and there were many people who stopped speaking to them and wouldn't shake their hand in church. It was nasty. The world was really split, and in those little towns I was considered a communist crazy, and it didn't matter that I was the right wing of the antiwar movement. I was still a communist crazy by their reckoning.

DAVID MIXNER

Suddenly we were on the cover of *Time* and *Life* and *The New York Times*. The press practically organized it for us. At that time, that was the organizing tool. There were no chat rooms, no email—we had to do mailings. We had hundreds of volunteers on the floor of our offices stuffing envelopes and putting packets together to send to the organizers at these colleges. Then we'd take them to the post office, and mail them to the organizers. There was no FedEx; the post office didn't do next-day delivery.

STEPHEN BULL

There weren't that many of us working in the White House who had served in Vietnam. In fact, of the people that I was working with, I may have been the only one who had any real experience there. I mean there might have been a couple of guys on the National Security Council who may have been there. But I was about the only one who had any real experience. Some of the other guys who were my contemporaries, they somehow had avoided military service. So anyway, my only point is, I've got a prejudice against those who are, in my mind, trying to tear down the country.

I'm carrying that prejudice into my position at the White House. And I'm going to try to be careful not to project too much of my own attitude, which was, these are a bunch of raggedy-ass kids and I have absolutely no sympathy for you guys. I think you're a bunch of commie pinkos and you all ought to be in jail. Now that's perhaps an exaggeration of my attitude.

I was a Nixon advance man in the '68 campaign. The reason I came to Washington was because the Nixon administration had an old man's image as a bunch of old pols. They needed some young faces down here, so the chief of staff, Bob Haldeman, invited me and a couple of other young guys to the White House. Initially we all worked for Haldeman, and in the spring of '69 I moved into the position of Nixon's personal slave. I was essentially the civilian aide that ran the Oval Office.

DAVID HAWK

On September 26 Nixon held a press conference, and we got some of our friends in the press corps to go and to ask the president what he thought about the announced student demonstrations for the fall. Nixon made a terrible comment that he didn't care what the students did. He said, "I understand that there has been and continues to be opposition to the war in Vietnam on the campuses and also in the nation. As far as this kind of activity is concerned, we expect it. However, under no circumstances will I be affected whatever by it."

RICHARD NIXON (*RN: The Memoirs of Richard Nixon*)*

I was fully aware of the furor that this statement would cause. But having initiated a policy of pressure on North Vietnam that now involved not only our government but foreign governments as well, I felt that I had no choice but to carry it through. Faced with the prospect of demonstrations at home that I could not prevent, my only alternative was to make it clear to the enemy that the protests would have no effect on my decisions. Otherwise my ultimatum would appear empty.

---

* *RN: The Memoirs of Richard Nixon* (New York: Simon & Schuster, 1978; second edition, 1990), p. 399.

DAVID HAWK

So, needless to say, after that press conference, the press came to us for our comments. We had learned how to do this kind of stuff from working in presidential campaigns, and instead of responding immediately, we called a press conference for Saturday morning, which was an unusual time. We had, in the meantime, been lining up endorsements from McCarthy and McGovern and Coretta Scott King and a whole bunch of grown-ups. Congressmen, senators—if we had a Democratic senator, we were careful to have a Republican. If we had a Republican member of the House, we'd have a Democrat member. We were always balanced and bipartisan, and we also had leading academics like John Kenneth Galbraith.*

So, Sam and I called this press conference, and our response was that the president misspoke, that no elected leader in a democracy would disregard the opinion of the public. Furthermore, we said it's not just kids. It's not just students. Here are our endorsers. And this effort is not going to be limited to students. It's just starting with students. Sam and I ended up having our pictures on the front page of *The Washington Post.* The headline was "The President Misspoke." So, here are these kids in their early twenties claiming that the president misspoke, not denouncing him as a baby killer. We were speaking Washington-speak. Our endorsements were included in the story, and it knocked us from the press who were assigned to cover students to the mainstream political reporters in Washington.

RAY PRICE (Nixon aide)

I worked at the *New York Herald Tribune* for nine years and was the last editor of the editorial page before the paper died in 1966. Nixon called me in 1967. He was a full-time lawyer in New York at Nixon, Mudge, Rose, Guthrie, and Alexander, but he was also preparing for a presidential campaign in '68. I started working and traveling with him a lot, and

---

* Seventeen senators and forty-seven members of the House of Representatives announced their support for the Moratorium, or M-day, as many called it, and presidents of seventy-nine colleges and universities signed a statement calling for a U.S. withdrawal from Vietnam.

he became a good friend. I became the head of the White House writing staff.

As the first of the moratoria neared, there was extensive debate within the White House about what kind of stance to take toward it. Nixon's decision was to pick up the gantlet and hurl it squarely back, which is why Nixon said, at the press conference September 26, that "under no circumstances will I be affected whatever by it."

The protest was an organized attempt to disrupt the process of government, which was not helpful, especially when you're in a time of war. And also, of course, it delighted the enemy. It encouraged them to fight on. The protesters were operating on an entirely upside-down notion of the way policies should be conducted. Policy is not just for emotions; it's for reason. And they didn't know what they were talking about, most of them. And they didn't want to take the time to learn about it.

DAVID MIXNER

Rutgers University was the first to announce that they were closing on October 15, and urging its students and faculty to talk about the war. It was the big break. It was a traditional state university, it wasn't an Ivy League school, it wasn't a Catholic school; it was a state university that had no history of activism. It was the ideal fucking poster child. It couldn't have been a bigger gift from God. After that we were in business. University after university, all we had to do was say, "Well, Rutgers is," and then you had ten, and then you had twenty. It was the classic organizing model. It was decided by the university presidents, and students demanded it. Then suddenly communities were adopting it, because it started getting press.

By the time we got to the Moratorium we were all pretty well known from the Eugene McCarthy campaign, or the National Student Association, or the march on Washington in '67. The press loved us. It was a perfect combination, they loved Sam, they loved me, they loved Marge. Everyone loved the fact that the young people were making the president quiver. Who doesn't like a David-and-Goliath story? We had created the Eugene McCarthy campaign to force the sitting president to resign. We had been beaten up in '68 at the Democratic convention in Chicago. I mean it's not a bad opening for your story when you're trying to get on the front page. We were clean, and not hippies, and the press liked us personally. They loved the fact that I was this poor kid who actually knew someone who died in Vietnam, and Marge was this big, boisterous, great female organizer who was sort of a Mother Earth figure, and Sam was the son of a wealthy shoe company president who went to Harvard, and maybe someday would be president. David [Hawk] was this clean-cut, all American, good-looking swimmer who said, "Hell no, I ain't going." Come on, what's not to love? They also fell in love with the poster: fathers and sons against the war.

A full-page newspaper advertisement urging citizens to participate in the October 15, 1969, Moratorium to End the War in Vietnam reads: "To be against the war in Vietnam and to do nothing about it is indefensible. To see your son or your neighbor's son dragged off to the slaughter or to prison, and to do nothing about it is inexcusable."

SAM BROWN

We ran a series of ads in *The New York Times.* One of them was a picture of an old-fashioned doorbell and it said, "Push button to end war." It described people going door-to-door to talk to their neighbors about ending the war in Vietnam. Another one was a picture of a long-haired son and a very burly, hard-hat-y kind of father, and it said, "Fathers and Sons To-gether Against the War. October 15: An opportunity for generations to—" I don't remember what the copy was, but it was focused on, "Look, this is a time for people who are having trouble with each other to figure out how to talk to each other again."[*]

DAVID MIXNER

My job was the unions and the Hill because I came from a constituency that was different. I worked with a guy named Bill Dodds, who was head of the political action stuff for the United Auto Workers, and we laid the groundwork that got me into a meeting with Walter Reuther, the head of the UAW.

The argument I made to Mr. Reuther was, sitting across this desk from you is a man who's buried four of his cousins, and they were workers. All the men who were being killed and brought home at the time were his membership's sons. It certainly wasn't the sons of Harvard, is how I put it. I could speak with some authenticity.

Reuther became the first labor leader of the major unions to come out against the war. He was real nervous because his members were not necessarily antiwar. I remember when I was leaving his office, Sam was with me, and it was a done deal, and I remember Mr. Reuther putting his hands around our shoulders and telling us the famous story about the dentist: The man hated going to the dentist more than anything in the world, but he got in the dentist chair because he knew he had to do it. Just as the dentist had the drill coming towards his mouth, the guy grabbed ahold of the dentist's balls and said, "We're not going to hurt each other, are we, Doctor?" I looked at Mr. Reuther and said, "No, sir, we're not. I give you my word." And I kept it. When he agreed to come out against the war it was a huge victory, and I was very proud of it.

---

[*]   Jasper Johns also created a print for the Moratorium that became one of the iconic images of the antiwar movement. It was a "toxic" American flag painted in camouflage green and black stripes, with black stars and a white bullet hole in the middle. Stenciled under the flag was one word: "Moratorium."

DAVID HAWK

We had enough bipartisan, mainstream political support that the mainstream politicians wanted to jump on this bandwagon. Nixon was in the process of making it a Republican war. So you had a lot of elements of the Democratic Party that weren't outspoken when it was the Democratic president, but who became very outspoken. It was hard to maintain the bipartisanship, but we had Senator Mark Hatfield [Republican from Oregon] and Senator Charles Goodell [Republican from New York], and there were a dozen House Republicans. We had Hugh Scott, a Republican senator from Pennsylvania, the Senate minority leader. It was a very, very, very different Republican Party. You still had Chuck Percy in Illinois. You had moderate and liberal Republicans.

Vietnam Moratorium Committee members Marge Sklencar, Sam Brown, and David Hawk give a press conference on October 19, 1969. David Mixner, the fourth committee member, who at the time was being blackmailed for being gay, is notably absent.

DAVID MIXNER

I was terrified to tell my dad that if I was drafted, I wouldn't serve. Which is sort of a joke now, because all I had to do was tell them I was gay and I'd have been out instantly. But being in jail for five years appealed more to me than letting anyone know that I was gay. It's pretty powerful, isn't it? That's all I had to say. I would rather have gone to jail than have anyone know the truth about me. I wouldn't have been allowed to do anything I was doing. I wouldn't have been a cochair of the Vietnam Moratorium if I were gay. Hell, I had to fight to get Marge aboard. Women were not given good roles. I was one of Marge's supporters. The movement was still misogynist at that time. Gay? Not a chance in the world would I be allowed to do any of it. I would have immediately been discarded.

The Stonewall Riots in late June 1969* were hardly discussed at the Moratorium. It was like it didn't happen. I don't ever remember anyone saying, "Oh my God, did you hear about the gays in New York?" I had a mixed reaction to it. I was intrigued and in awe of it. I remember cutting the *New York Times* story out and putting it in my wallet. I have no idea why. I carried it around with me for two years. But then on the other hand, since many of those who were brave enough to be out [of the closet] and fight back tended to be the more marginalized and the more persecuted of those in our society, I didn't identify with them. I was a twenty-three-year-old boy and I knew that if I got caught, I would do enormous damage to the movement, great shame to my family, and great shame to my compatriots.

SUSAN WERBE (Moratorium press secretary)

We didn't know David was gay. There wasn't even a suspicion. He always talked about having a girlfriend. I don't think any of us understood gay rights; the movement hadn't really started by then, at least no one ever

---

* On June 28, 1969, police raided a gay bar called the Stonewall Inn in Greenwich Village, sparking a riot that continued for several days. This marked the beginning of the gay liberation movement. In 1969, sodomy between consenting adults in the privacy of their own homes was illegal in forty-nine states, and homosexuals faced job and many other forms of discrimination. The first gay pride marches were held in New York, Los Angeles, and Chicago a year later, on June 28, 1970.

talked about it. So when he came out years later it was a surprise at first, and then an "aha." It all fell into place. Because he'd disappear and nobody knew where he was. He always projected himself as melancholy.

DAVID MIXNER

One night I got drunk, went to this really remote, dingy bar, and this vision from God came in, who was exactly my type: intelligent, handsome, masculine. And we ended up going home together. He said, "I know who you are, I work for the federal government, I don't want you to panic. I want to create a safe place for you. I really have feelings for you." He had everything I loved at his house: Tennyson, Neruda, Yeats, all the great poets that I loved, and Elvis Presley and Janis Joplin records. Anyhow, to make a long story short, we started an affair, and he did become a very safe place for me.

About thirty days into it, he said he had to go away for the weekend. When he got back he said, "Let's meet for lunch on Monday. I'll come straight from the airport." I said, "Great." So I went to the Hot Shop on K and Sixteenth and sat in a booth waiting for him. Two guys in suits pulled into the booth and sat across from me and showed me their badges. When someone shows you a badge, how many times have you taken a look at it—especially in those days? I don't know if they were real. They poured out on the table some naked pictures of the two of us having sex. It just was as if someone had stuck a knife into my gut. My first thought was, I have to warn Frank. So immediately afterwards I ran to his apartment to warn him. I used my key, got in, and the place was totally empty. There wasn't a dust ball or anything else in the apartment. I never saw him again. The suits gave me three days to get out of the Moratorium or they were going to send these pictures to my family and the press. So I got very, very drunk and told my friends I had a heart condition and was very sick.

I decided to kill myself. I bought a gun and put it underneath my mattress, and was going to kill myself, but I wanted to get drunk enough to do it. But then I had this moment of clarity and I realized that there was no way they could send the photos to the press, because how were they going to explain it? Did the government really want the press to know that they were filming homosexuals, and blackmailing them? Maybe they had as much to lose as I did? So I sobered up, and when they met up with me three days later and asked me, "Are you getting out?" I said, "Send it to them, I don't care," and walked away.

Every time the phone rang and someone said, "Your mom and dad's on the phone," I thought they had gotten the pictures. I dreaded hearing from them. Or if the press called and said, "We want to speak to David," every single time I worried that they had the photos. So I immediately pulled back and stopped speaking to the press.

RICHARD NIXON (*RN: The Memoirs of Richard Nixon*)[*]

On October 14, I knew for sure that my ultimatum [to the North Vietnamese] had failed when Kissinger informed me that Radio Hanoi had just broadcast a letter from [North Vietnamese] Premier Pham Van Dong to the American people. In it Dong declared:

> This fall large sectors of the U.S. people, encouraged and supported by many peace- and justice-loving American personages, are launching a broad and powerful offensive throughout the United States to demand that the Nixon administration put an end to the Vietnam aggressive war and immediately bring all American troops home. . . .
>
> We are firmly confident that with the solidarity and bravery of the peoples of our two countries and with the approval and support of peace-loving people in the world, the struggle of the Vietnamese people and U.S. progressive people against U.S. aggression will certainly be crowned with total victory.
>
> May your fall offensive succeed splendidly.

To indicate the seriousness with which I viewed this blatant intervention in our domestic affairs, I asked [Vice President Spiro]

---

[*] Nixon, *RN,* p. 402.

Agnew to hold a press conference at the White House. . . . He said, "The leaders and sponsors of tomorrow's Moratorium, public officials, and others leading these demonstrations should openly repudiate the support of the totalitarian government which has on its hands the blood of 40,000 Americans."

. . . I had to decide what to do about the ultimatum. I knew that unless I had some indisputably good reason for not carrying out my threat of using increased force when the ultimatum expired on November 1, the Communists would become contemptuous of us and even more difficult to deal with. I knew, however, that after all the protests and the Moratorium, American public opinion would be seriously divided by any military escalation of the war.

STEPHEN BULL

I think Nixon was very, very frustrated trying to wind down this war, and on the exterior you had what almost appeared to be resistance to the ability to wind it down. It's not a big help when you have five hundred thousand screaming banshees carrying torches calling him a killer when he's trying to end the war so the killing can stop. I'm just saying that there's a belief among some people that if there hadn't been so much active, violent resistance to the Vietnam War, that the U.S. would have had a stronger hand in negotiating with the North Vietnamese and the Viet Cong to end the war. But rather, the antiwar activity weakened the hand of the negotiators.

RAY PRICE

It was very important that the war end the right way. Not the wrong way. All the critics wanted to end it the wrong way by just cutting and running. That would have been the worst thing we could do. We would have lost all credibility if we did that. I used to call the protesters "the Arlo Guthrie Woodstock pot rock love contingent." I disdained them. They were passionate, but they didn't know shit about what they were passionate about. Most of them were too busy getting high to understand anything about the way the world works. Their arrogance was exceeded only by their ignorance.

STEPHEN BULL

On October 15 I walked out onto the Ellipse, and there I was, dressed in a coat and tie, with a short haircut, and here were all these scraggly kids. There's free love, and they're all doing drugs, and they're having fun and drinking, and all that. And I'm thinking, Now wait a second, we're the same age. Why am I here? They were having more fun than I was. I was a straitlaced guy. There was a major disconnect.

DANIEL ELLSBERG

The vice president's thirteen-year-old daughter wore a black armband, for which she was grounded for a month or something. I thought one of the better buttons of the whole war movement was "Free Kim Agnew."

I went to the L.A. march on October 15 with Jan Butler, who was the top-secret control officer of RAND, and a former girlfriend of mine, and my two kids. I remember we were at UCLA during that day and I wasn't worried about being seen because I was in the middle of copying the Pentagon Papers, and I was expecting to be in prison shortly.

CARL BERNSTEIN

My beat at *The Washington Post* was covering the demonstrations in Washington. What was so extraordinary was that the last time numbers of people like this had taken to the streets was in the early part of the twentieth century. This is not a revolutionary country, despite our origins. The biggest demonstration that Washington had ever seen since the twenties or thirties had been the March on Washington, August 28, 1963. But the amazing thing about the antiwar movement was that it reached the proportions that it had reached, and that it was affecting policy, that Lyndon Johnson had been driven from office, not by the war, not by the coverage of the war, but by people in the streets.

DAVID MIXNER

On October 15 we all holed up in our office. No press was allowed in to see us while we were waiting to get reports on what was happening. There were thousands of events in smaller towns like Muskogee, Oklahoma, where they read the list of the war dead. Church bells ringing for each of the war dead—it was extraordinary. Thousands and thousands of events in towns in Montana with fifty people, you know, one or two people reading the names of the war dead in the town square. The biggest events were where we least expected them. I mean we had 100,000 on the Boston Common, and 100,000 in Bryant Park. But it was like, 6,000 in St. Louis, which had never happened before. There were 10,000 in Denver, which had never happened, or Las Vegas, places where there had never been demonstrations. I'd say two million people participated, all over the country, in the Moratorium. It was truly remarkable.

More than one hundred thousand protesters came to the Moratorium to End the War in Vietnam rally on the Boston Common on October 15, 1969. Two million people participated nationwide in peaceful teach-ins and demonstrations. It was the country's largest ever protest against the war in Vietnam.

DAVID HAWK

On October 15 about two million people participated. It was enormous. There was now a recognition that the demonstrations were so mainstream and so big and nationwide—it was the largest nationwide demonstration ever, at least until Earth Day the next year.

DAVID MIXNER

That night Sam was on *The Tonight Show* and David was on another show, and poor Marge was never asked to be on anything, because she's a woman. I was alone that night. I turned down all interview offers because I didn't want to be visible. I lay down on this old couch in the lobby of the Moratorium office, and I played "We Shall Overcome" on my harmonica.

RICHARD NIXON (*RN: The Memoirs of Richard Nixon*)[*]

A quarter of a million people came to Washington for the October 15 Moratorium. Despite widespread rumors that some of the more radical left-wing organizations would provoke violent confrontations with police, the demonstrations were generally peaceful. . . . On the night of October 15 I thought about the irony of this protest for peace. It had, I believed, destroyed whatever small possibility may have existed of ending the war in 1969. But there was nothing I could do about that now. I would have to adjust my plans accordingly and carry on as best I could. At the top of the page of preliminary notes I was making for my November 3 speech, I wrote: "Don't get rattled—don't waver—don't react."

DANIEL ELLSBERG

Nixon himself says in his memoir something like, "I realized that my threat had failed because of the Moratorium," and his logic was simple:

[*]   Nixon, *RN*, p. 403.

first, that the North Vietnamese hadn't accepted his threat to escalate the war by that time, and second, with this amount of mobilization, without having used nuclear weapons yet, there was every reason to believe that if he were to carry out that threat in the next two weeks you would see not two million people on the streets, which is what you had on October 15, but ten million.

DAVID HAWK

The first Moratorium had exceeded our expectations, blown our strategy out of the water. We thought it might take three, four months to build up, so that we'd be coming into our strength in early spring. Essentially there was nothing that could be done to redo or build on what we did in October, and then the politics changed with Vietnamization and the "silent majority" attack on the students.

CHAPTER 11

SILENT MAJORITY

(November 1969)

He declared the United States of Nixonland, and planted Old Glory on her surface.

—**RICK PERLSTEIN,** *Nixonland*

AFTER THE OCTOBER 15 VIETNAM MORATORIUM THE COUNTRY SEEMED to be at the cliff's edge of a revolution. *The Washington Post* heralded a new era of "plebiscitary democracy." When Attorney General John Mitchell watched protesters exchange the American flag on the Justice Department flagpole with a Viet Cong flag, he said he felt like he was witnessing the storming of the Winter Palace in St. Petersburg, Russia, in 1917.

With the peace movement's success came the Nixon administration's most effective retaliation—an appeal to middle Americans who were not demonstrating in the streets against the war. Nixon called them the "silent majority" and asked for their support in ending the war. "The speech made the case brilliantly," wrote historian Rick Perlstein. "That if you were a *normal* American and angry at the war, President Nixon was the peacenik for you."* The November 3 Silent Majority speech succeeded beyond Nixon's highest expectations.

---

* Rick Perlstein, *Nixonland: The Rise of a President and the Fracturing of America* (New York: Scribner, 2008), p. 435.

DAVID MIXNER (Moratorium organizer)

The success of the Moratorium created Nixon's November 3 Silent Majority speech. They knew that they were going to be brought down unless they went on the offense. I remember all of us watching the speech together crammed into the Vietnam Moratorium offices. We had this television with antennas wrapped in aluminum foil, and this big old box.

DANIEL ELLSBERG (RAND analyst, peace activist)

On November 2, Sam Brown invited me to come and help him do a response to Nixon's November 3 speech. I said yes, and I flew from Los Angeles with my then girlfriend, now wife, Patricia, to D.C. on November 3. We went directly from Dulles Airport to Moratorium headquarters and got there minutes before the speech started. I come into the headquarters, and here were all these young kids with their long hair. Sam Brown, Dave Mixner, Marge Sklencar, and Dave Hawk were all there.

DAVID HAWK (Moratorium organizer)

In response to the Moratorium, Nixon made the November 3 speech outlining his Vietnamization plan. They were going to withdraw American troops but increase the use of U.S. airpower.

RICHARD NIXON SPEECH, NOVEMBER 3, 1969

Under new orders, the primary mission of our troops is to enable the South Vietnamese forces to assume the full responsibility for the security of South Vietnam. . . . After five years of Americans going into Vietnam, we are finally bringing American men home. By December 15, over sixty thousand men will have been withdrawn from South Vietnam—including twenty percent of all combat forces. The South Vietnamese have continued to gain in strength. As a result they have been able to take over combat responsibilities from our American troops.

DAVID HAWK

To us, all Vietnamization did was change the color of the corpses. This was the policy Nixon embraced. There was no more secret plan to end the war.

RICHARD NIXON SPEECH, NOVEMBER 3, 1969

... I recognize that some of my fellow citizens disagree with the plan for peace I have chosen. Honest and patriotic Americans have reached different conclusions as to how peace should be achieved.

... And so tonight—to you, the great silent majority of my fellow Americans—I ask for your support.

I pledged in my campaign for the presidency to end the war in a way that we could win the peace. I have initiated a plan of action which will enable me to keep that pledge.

The more support I can have from the American people, the sooner that pledge can be redeemed; for the more divided we are at home, the less likely the enemy is to negotiate at Paris.

Let us be united for peace. Let us also be united against defeat. Because let us understand: North Vietnam cannot defeat or humiliate the United States. Only Americans can do that.

DAVID MIXNER

Nixon went for a scare. I knew we were in trouble. That was when it shifted, and it really polarized the country, and they were successful.

ROGER MORRIS (Nixon national security aide)

I know the November 3 speech because I wrote some of those lines. The purpose of the speech was to say in blunt terms, "I'm going to do this on my own terms. I think that the majority of the country is behind me. I want peace in Vietnam, but not at the cost of our honor." These are all deliberately nebulous terms, but it was a way of saying, "I'm going to conduct this policy. You can put another million people in the streets tomorrow, and I will still have the great silent majority with me, and I will still have my conviction that we will not be a party to a dishonorable settlement."

This is Nixon saying Frank Sinatra's "I'm going to do this my way and fuck you." And moreover, "I'm not in the minority. I'm not a president without major support. I'm morally sound and I'm politically okay." It was Nixon's declaration of independence from what the rest of the country had hoped would be a hostage taking by public opinion and public protest that they thought they had achieved with Johnson.

TONY LAKE (Nixon national security staff)

Roger Morris and I had written an early draft of the November 3 speech and we argued that it was a mistake for the president to take such a hawkish position on the war. We said Nixon would "sink into the Johnsonian bog" on Vietnam and make it his war. It wasn't quite Nixon's war yet. That was the heart of the argument I was trying to make, as Kissinger's special assistant, and while working on the secret negotiations with the North Vietnamese, in which Kissinger and Nixon failed to scare them into a settlement.

RAY PRICE (Nixon speechwriter)

The president wrote the November 3 speech himself, working long and laboriously, late into the night, day after day at the White House and Camp David. "Silent majority" was a very apt description, because the people making the noise just wanted the country to think that they were everybody. They were a small part of it, but they were the noisy part. The serious people were not making the noises; it's just not their nature. The media were mostly listening to the screechers and the screamers, and the yellers and the shouters, and the kickers, because that was more their style.

TONY LAKE

I remember writing a memo to Kissinger, which said once you start Vietnamization it's going to be like salted peanuts. When the American public has developed a taste for one withdrawal, it's going to keep demanding more and more. Therefore, our negotiating position is stronger now than it will be in six months or a year or two years, and we should get the best deal we can and get out now. Kissinger used the memo as a memo to the president opposing Vietnamization.

STEPHEN BULL (Nixon aide)

I remember the outpouring of support after the Silent Majority speech. It was not, to my knowledge, fabricated. People sent telegrams back then, huge piles of telegrams, and telephone calls were coming in—apparently there were fifty thousand telegrams and thirty thousand letters, mostly approving of the speech. There was a picture that we had of telegrams and letters piled on the president's desk. It had quite an impact on the public, and the president's approval ratings increased as a result of it. He was pleased at the reaction, and pleased at the success of it.

RICHARD NIXON (*RN: Memoirs of Richard Nixon*) *

Very few speeches actually influence the course of history. The November 3 speech was one of them. Its impact came as a surprise to me; it was one thing to make a rhetorical appeal to the Silent Majority—it was another to actually hear from them. . . . The November 3 speech was both a milestone and a turning point for my administration. Now, for a time at least, the enemy could no longer count on dissent in America to give them the victory they could not win on the battlefield. I had the public support I needed to continue a policy of waging war in Vietnam and negotiating for peace

---

* Nixon, *RN,* pp. 410–11.

After Nixon's November 3, 1969, Silent Majority speech, the White House was flooded with fifty thousand congratulatory telegrams and thirty thousand letters. Some were suspected to have been ginned up by the White House staff.

in Paris until we could bring the war to an honorable and successful conclusion.

During the weeks after November 3 my Gallup overall-approval rating soared to 68 percent, the highest it had been since I took office.

ROGER MORRIS

It was a climactic moment after the November 3 speech. [White House special counsel] Chuck Colson and the boys ginned up a lot of artificial stuff, but there was also a genuine avalanche of cables and telephone calls and support for the president. It's easy for the antiwar movement now to look back and to say the country was on our side, but that's a function of history that's not yet taken place in 1970. The country was brutally divided.

DANIEL ELLSBERG (RAND analyst and peace activist)

After the [Silent Majority] speech we all went to the Dupont Plaza [Hotel], where I spoke at a press conference, along with others. Meanwhile, I had one thousand pages of the xeroxed Pentagon Papers in my suitcase. There were seven thousand pages in the whole study. I hadn't copied them all, by any means, by that time. I had in my suitcase top-secret documents to give to Senator [William] Fulbright, which I did later that week.

I joined the movement that week, and I may have been its highest-ranking government insider. Plenty of people were resigning, or turning to other subjects, but none of them joined the movement. That would've ended their careers. They also probably despised the movement, and thought, These people have the right idea, but they're not respectable. So none of them really took part, even in a peripheral way, in the movement, which was pretty broad at that time.

I finally felt I was surrounded by people who, like myself, thought about Vietnam all the time. I don't think an hour went by during the day, even during a movie, when I didn't think thoughts about how to get out of Vietnam. There wasn't an hour. So, in other words, we were obsessed, and that was the right way to be. That's what people should've been thinking about. These were people who were determined to do whatever they could possibly do to end the war.

RICHARD MOOSE (Senate staffer)

I was on the staff of the Senate Foreign Relations Committee [chaired by Senator Fulbright] and I knew Dan Ellsberg slightly. When he came to Washington, his objective was to get the Foreign Relations Committee to release the papers, or if not the committee, then some member of the Congress. There was no way that the committee was about to do this. I saw a fair amount of Dan during that period, and I was not familiar with the papers myself. I had skimmed parts of them.

DANIEL ELLSBERG

It took Fulbright until December 1970 to decide *not* to put out the Pentagon Papers. He said, "After all, isn't it just history?" I said, "Well, yeah, but I think it's pretty important history, and it's being repeated," but I didn't have the proof that it was being repeated. Mort Halperin and John

Vann had led me to understand that it was being repeated, but I didn't have documents to prove that. If I'd had the documents, I would've put those out and not even bothered with the Pentagon Papers.

So when people say to me now, "Well, unlike Edward Snowden, who's putting out all this current sensitive stuff, and Bradley Manning, Ellsberg just put out history. That's why he was all right. He was a good guy. He was discriminating." That's what I've been hearing the last few years. But if I'd had current documents, I would not have put out the history. I would've put out the current documents. I give Snowden and Manning credit for putting out stuff that's current, because that makes all the difference.

RICHARD MOOSE

I never felt that the Pentagon Papers really substantiated the most extreme claims made about them. They were far more careful than the press and the antiwar movement chose to believe. It was the struggle over their release that really drew more attention to them, but also led to the overcharacterization of them as bearing out the proposition that the administration had lied to the public. I mean, untruths were told, and some bald-faced lies, but it was a far more complicated situation than that.

It was the executive branch misrepresenting things up and down the line to each other, for example. The CIA and MACV [Military Assistance Command, Vietnam] were more or less in continuous disagreement about key aspects of the war, like how many Viet Cong or North Vietnamese had been killed. So MACV had one view, the CIA had another view, the army had one view, the Defense Department, the State Department; everybody had their own slant on the thing.

DANIEL ELLSBERG

After the November 3 speech, Senator William Fulbright canceled the [Foreign Relations Committee] hearings, which were calling on Nixon to get out of Vietnam within one year. Fulbright told me that his committee was not with him anymore. They were convinced Nixon was getting out, and we didn't have to take this stand and split from him.

DAVID HAWK

In mid-November, you had the preplanned Vietnam mobilizations, which weren't dispersed nationwide—it was a march on Washington.* It was centralized, and very much focused on Nixon and Kissinger and John Mitchell, the attorney general. Mitchell because the Chicago Seven trial was going on, which was for the radical pacifists, the student left, and the Yippies, and the Black Panthers. John Mitchell's Justice Department had put together a conspiracy trial in Chicago.

SAM BROWN

In early November, Bill Ayers came to see me. He gave me this long pitch about how he thought that we didn't share the Weathermen's vision of the future, and we didn't have the same sort of dialectical understanding of the nature of American society. I don't think he ever used the word *sellout,* because he had a purpose for this meeting. His point was we didn't actually get it about how America worked, and he did, but if we were prepared to stand in fraternal solidarity with them, instead of going to the Justice Department the day of the march [November 15], they would withhold their action and not screw up the march by diverting the inevitable: when a hundred radicals get the same attention as five hundred thousand sensible people. For twenty thousand dollars we could show fraternal solidarity, and I explained to him that I might not know much about American politics, but I understood the words *blackmail* and *extortion* when I heard them, and I thought he should just leave the office.

And as it happens, there were two or three other people in the office at the time, which is how it ended up in *The New York Times*. Anyway, that was the texture of the relationship. It was a very strange, fraught relation-

---

* A month after the first Moratorium came the second one, on November 15. Undaunted by Nixon's successful appeal to pro-war, patriotic middle America, the antiwar movement upped the ante and produced a three-day march on Washington, bringing more people to the capital city than there had ever been for one peace protest.

ship, not just with the Weathermen, which was understandable, but also with a large part of the leadership of the MOBE,* and it came down to fights about who was going to speak on November 15.

DAVID HAWK

SDS had gone off the deep end. They were living in some other political universe; the New Left had lost its moorings. These people just got deeper and deeper into anticapitalist, anti-imperialist rhetoric and analysis that was ever more detached from intellectual, political, and even moral bearing—some of these people ended up committing armed robbery to get money for political action, or bombings that were going to kill civilians. This was not only intellectually but morally despicable.

DAVID MIXNER

The night of November 14 there was teargassing and the breaking of windows at Dupont Circle when the Weathermen tried to storm the South Vietnamese embassy.

STEPHEN BULL (White House aide)

I remember noticing that the Washington Monument, which is ringed with flagpoles, the American flags had been torn down, and Viet Cong flags were flying. Which annoyed the heck out of me. I had no sympathy for the Viet Cong, and I didn't like the idea of the American flag being desecrated. I figured these were all a bunch of commies. You have to understand where I was at the time.

---

* The MOBE, the National Mobilization Committee to End the War in Vietnam, was a coalition of antiwar organizations founded in 1967 to organize large antiwar demonstrations.

On Saturday, November 15, 1969, the Moratorium March on Washington drew five hundred thousand peaceful antiwar protesters—the biggest ever single antiwar protest. Five speakers, Senators Charles Goodell and George McGovern, David Dellinger, Coretta Scott King, and Dick Gregory, were accompanied by musicians: Peter, Paul & Mary, Richie Havens, Joan Baez, and Pete Seeger.

DAVID MIXNER

At the big demonstration November 15, a group of people with Viet Cong flags tried to get up to the stage, but we barricaded them into just one little section. There was just one little pocket up near the front with Viet Cong flags, but it was so clear that they were isolated, and we were policing them.

There were huge battles with the MOBE, over whether Sam [Brown] would speak, or someone from the MOBE would speak. So we agreed on five speakers: Senator Charles Goodell, Senator George McGovern, Dave Dellinger, Coretta Scott King, and Dick Gregory. I said we ought to have a lot of music, and we did. There was Peter, Paul & Mary; Richie Havens; Joan Baez; and Pete Seeger.* The cast of *Hair*, which was playing on Broadway at the time, sang "Aquarius" and "Let the Sunshine In."

As far as the eye could see there were people. I've never seen anything like it.

The police said that there were six hundred thousand people there. It was the biggest-ever march on Washington at the time. It was incredible.

ROGER MORRIS

Tony [Lake] and I and Bill Watts all had wives and kids who were marching in these demonstrations. I remember standing with Bill and Tony on the South Lawn of the White House watching the November Moratorium coming down Pennsylvania Avenue. There was this sea of people coming from Capitol Hill to the White House, and there were machine gun nests on the South Lawn, and buses turned over. I remember standing there thinking, It's going to climax at the Washington Monument, and my wife is out there with one toddler and another in a stroller, and Tony's got two kids and his wife, and Bill's wife and kids.

We were on the wrong side of the fence. But we were on that side of the fence because up until the spring of 1970 we thought we really could make a difference, and really could bring this thing to an end. You knew, given the mentality, as Henry would say, "Policy will not be made in the streets," that the demonstrations were never going to do anything.

RAY PRICE (Nixon aide)

When the protesters marched outside the White House on November 15, Nixon drove home his point by letting it be known that he had spent the afternoon watching football on television.

---

*   Pete Seeger led the crowd in singing John Lennon's new song, "Give Peace a Chance."

DANIEL ELLSBERG

The strategy inside the White House was to put out the word that the president was watching a football game, and he didn't take the protest seriously, which was, of course, untrue. Every ten minutes he was calling the Situation Room and finding out what was going on, getting the reports from the U-2s on crowd size, and that sort of thing. He was totally absorbed with the Moratorium. Many people remembered that. I used to ask auditoriums, when I used to discuss the subject, "How many of you here remember the football game?" It turns out that everybody remembers the football game. It was very effective.

DAVID MIXNER

My proudest moment was organizing the March Against Death. Someone had the idea that people would start at Arlington National Cemetery, and there would be placards that you'd hang around your neck with forty-five

The March Against Death began Thursday, November 13, 1969, and continued until the morning of November 15 as more than forty-five thousand people walked single file from Arlington National Cemetery down Pennsylvania Avenue, past the White House to the Capitol Building carrying placards with names of dead American soldiers and destroyed Vietnamese villages.

thousand names of the [American] war dead on them, and the names of villages in Vietnam that had been destroyed. One by one with a candle, we left Arlington Cemetery, we went across Arlington Bridge single file to the Lincoln Memorial, we went around the Lincoln Memorial, and we walked in front of the White House, and as we got in front of the White House, we shouted out the names of the war dead. I shouted out Russell's name. Then we walked up Pennsylvania Avenue, single file, and put the placards in wooden caskets that were built by the carpenters outside the Capitol.

It started Thursday night [November 13] and it went for thirty-eight hours all Thursday night, all Friday, all Friday night, and into Saturday, November 15, which was the Moratorium—single file, unbroken, uninterrupted, hour after hour. It was one of the most powerful experiences I've ever had. On the day of the Moratorium, we closed the caskets, and they were carried ahead of us, with the names inside, down to the White House.

When the March Against Death finished in front of the Capitol Building, the forty-five thousand placards with names of dead American soldiers and destroyed Vietnamese villages were placed in wooden coffins. The march lasted for thirty-eight hours, from Thursday night until Saturday morning, November 15.

CHAPTER 12

MY LAI

(October–November 1969)

The war wasn't all terror and violence. Sometimes things could almost get sweet. For instance, I remember a little boy with a plastic leg. I remember how he hopped over to Azar and asked for a chocolate bar—"GI number one," the kid said—and Azar laughed and handed over the chocolate. When the boy hopped away, Azar clucked his tongue and said, "War's a bitch." He shook his head sadly. "One leg, for Chrissake. Some poor fucker ran out of ammo."

—TIM O'BRIEN, *The Things They Carried*

A NEW ANTIWAR SLOGAN APPEARED ON SIGNS AT THE NOVEMBER 15, 1969, Moratorium in Washington, D.C.: "Free the Pinkville People." Just two days earlier thirty-two-year-old freelance investigative journalist Seymour Hersh had published a story that exposed one of the war's most horrific atrocities. Hersh discovered that U.S. soldiers had killed hundreds of unarmed Vietnamese civilians, most of them women and children, in the South Vietnamese village of My Lai, an area called Pinkville by the American military, on March 16, 1968, and that the Pentagon was in the process of covering up the crime. The story exemplified the Pentagon's unwritten "kill anything that moves" policy and its quest for high body count over all else. It also exposed a deeper truth—that American soldiers could not distinguish their allies from their enemies. They were on a mission to nowhere. On December 5, *Time* magazine summed up the significance of Hersh's story: "[M]en in American uniforms slaughtered the civilians of My Lai, and in so doing humiliated the U.S. and called in question the U.S. mission in Viet Nam in a way that all the antiwar protesters could never have done."

———

SEYMOUR HERSH (investigative reporter)

I quit the AP [Associated Press], where I covered the Pentagon, and did a stint as Eugene McCarthy's speechwriter. By 1969, I'm freelancing and doing my nickel-and-dime stuff, trying to make a living. I get this tip in October '69. I couldn't say for twenty-five years who it was, but it was Geoffrey Cowan, an antiwar lawyer, whose brother was a reporter for *The Village Voice*. I didn't even know who he was. He just knew who I was because of what I'd been writing for the AP and as a freelancer for a little news service called Dispatch News Service, which would publish my antiwar rants.

So Cowan calls me and he says, "Sy, there's been a terrible massacre. Some GIs have gone crazy and killed a lot of people. I think fifty or seventy," and he said the GI [William Calley] was at a base in South Carolina. So I go to the Pentagon and talk to my source. We're walking down a hallway and I say, "So, what about this guy that shot up things?" He hit his bad knee with the side of his hand, hard, and he said, "Sy, that guy, Calley, he didn't kill anybody higher than two feet, little kids. I don't think they were Viet Cong, do you?" So I had a name.

Sure enough there it was in the clip file, a one-graph announcement two months earlier of a lieutenant named William L. Calley, Jr., who was being investigated for a possible crime against unspecified noncombatants. *The New York Times* ran it on Saturday on something like page fourteen or sixteen. It said he was from Florida. I called the PR guy at Fort Jackson, South Carolina. He looked him up and said Calley "shot up a gin mill." Which is what they were told to say. He wasn't lying. Calley had been reassigned there and was waiting for the investigation. There was nothing to it. He said there's nothing here. I didn't say I thought there was more to it.

WAYNE SMITH (Vietnam vet)

I knew I would have gotten drafted, and would have gone into the infantry; so volunteering was a way to have some control over what I did. I wanted to be a medic. I really wanted to save lives, and I thought that I had a knack, or some kind of gift.

When I first got off the plane in Saigon, it was shocking—my first inhalation was of this putrid air and rotting vegetation. You couldn't smell death at first, but diesel fuel, and humidity. It was an assault on your senses. The heat was another thing that you felt immediately, and you had to defend yourself with a towel and water, just to keep hydrated. As we got off the plane, we got on these buses that had corrugated steel covering the windows. Someone asked, "Why are these things on the window?" and they said, "So grenades won't come inside the bus. Welcome to Vietnam, guys."

It was September of '69 when a medic with the Second Battalion, Sixtieth Infantry, of the Ninth Infantry Division was killed. I believe his last name was Best—Doc Best. So I replaced Doc Best, and was assigned to a base called Tan Tru, the Ninth Infantry Division, Company D. This is a hot area. The Second of the Sixtieth boys loved combat. I introduced myself, "Yeah, I'm Wayne. I'm from Providence," and the first thing they all wanted to know was, "You know, Doc, if I get hit, are you going to come get me?" They waited until I answered. I was like, "What do you mean? Of course I'm going to come get you. Aren't we in this together?" Some of the training was "Don't get too close to people. You are the medic. You are the one they're going to confess themselves to. They're going to tell you their secrets. They want to be your friend because if there's a bunch of casualties, they want you to go to them first."

SEYMOUR HERSH

I said I need the name of Calley's lawyer and he said there's a guy named George Latimer, who had been an army lawyer for years and then became an army judge and then got on the Court of Military Appeals, and he apparently was representing Calley. He was a Mormon out of Salt Lake City.

So I called him up in Salt Lake City and I said, "I'm going to be going to the West Coast and there's a plane that stops in Salt Lake. I want to talk to you about the Calley thing." And he said, "Oh yes, it's a terrible case. What a miscarriage of justice." So I got the right guy.

When I met Calley's lawyer in his office in Salt Lake City, he told me that it was just a mistake. There was a firefight and Calley got in the cross-fire. There weren't a lot of casualties, but it was a terrible battle, and he fought his way out. They were fighting the North Vietnamese division. That's what he was told. That's what he believed, and that was his defense. Calley wouldn't plead. They wanted him to plead but he wouldn't plead. He's now back being processed. They investigated and they're going to make a determination whether he's going to be held for a court-martial. I'll never forget this part. He opened up his desk and he pulled out a piece of paper and he put it in front of him. It was the charge sheet against Calley. I saw the first sentence of the charge sheet, which said, "Lieutenant William L. Calley, Jr., is accused of the premeditated murder of one hundred and nine," get this, "Oriental human beings." I'll never forget that. So I went to Fort Jackson.

OLIVER STONE (Vietnam veteran, filmmaker)

I was raised conservative Republican in New York City. I'd dropped out of Yale twice. I didn't have a future, and I didn't like those elitist, privileged kids at Yale, like George Bush and that whole gang. The cliques of kids were snotty and preppy and all that shit. I wanted to see the wider world, so I decided I would volunteer for the draft and I insisted on them sending me to Vietnam infantry, frontline duty. I wanted to see the whole hog. I didn't want to be sent to some camp in Germany or Korea. They obliged me. They offered me to apply to Officer Candidate School and I refused.

I ended up in Vietnam in September '67, which was the beginning of the really heightened phase of the war. I was in three different combat units. I was there from basically September '67 to November '68—fifteen months. Vietnam was scary. I mean, within one week in the jungle I just knew that I was in for far more reality than I thought. I got wounded within a couple weeks.

I was doing my duty. I was trying to become a better soldier. At first I didn't have any friends. I was on my own, just trying to stay alive. Becoming a better soldier means to really fucking get your shit down, get tight, listen to the jungle. I became a jungle animal. You live on your feet. You don't sleep. You read your nerves. You're always watching.

SEYMOUR HERSH

So I go to Fort Jackson and I start driving around and it's a big base. They do basic training. They do ranger training. They do parachute training. They do all sorts of stuff. I start driving to the brigs, the jails. There were five different camps and I drive to three of them. I was wearing a ratty suit and I had a briefcase. I walk into the brig and there's always some sergeant dozing off. "Sergeant! I want Bill Calley out here right now." "Who?" "Bill Calley." If they wanted to think I was a lawyer let them think that. But I didn't say. If they'd asked me who I was I'd say I'm a reporter named Hersh from Washington. I would always do that, but you don't have to give everything away.

I struck out at three of those jails and by now it's twelve noon and I had a hunch that he's not there. So I go into the phone booth in the PX and ask the operator, "I would like to get the new listings for the June phone book." And she said to me in this deep southern voice, "Yes, I got him. He's in . . ." He was in an engineering battalion.

WAYNE SMITH

As a medic, I would write medical notes for guys. If they had medical maladies, I would try to keep them out of combat. It wasn't uncommon. There were other soldiers who asked me to break their legs, to injure them, so they didn't have to go out into the jungle. They would take medications and things to underperform, and not be ready for duty. Let's face it, when you're going out into combat, you want to have everybody clear-headed, clear-eyed. There was no smoking dope out in the boonies, at least in my unit. Coming back into the rear area, absolutely. But one of the ways that we were able to keep some men out of combat was giving them a sick call and they would get a three-day out-of-combat order from the doctor, based on a medic's recommendation. So it was the system itself that was breaking down from within.

OLIVER STONE

What I saw, in three different combat units, was definitely that there were those people who could think for themselves a little more freely, and those who didn't. Those who were locked into a rigid, racist, anti-Vietnamese point of view, in which there was no margin between the enemy and the villagers. The general treatment of even the civilians around the military bases was pretty shoddy. You know, fuck 'em but don't trust 'em, that kind of attitude. There were a lot of people who, I would say, were not educated. But there were also some educated people. I hung out with a few.

We were fucking with the villagers. They were fucking with us, too—there was all kind of hidden shit. We were scared, and there was anger, too. We'd lose guys to snipers, booby traps. . . . Sometimes the guys were stupid enough to blame the villagers. They would say, "The villagers knew where the booby trap was." But they didn't.

The villagers were on both sides: Their sympathies may have been with the North, because what'd they get from the southern government except get kicked around? The South Vietnamese troops were more brutal than we were. And, of course, their sympathies may have been with the North, too, but they were trying to stay alive in a very impossible situation. I didn't like it. I got very upset with some of the villagers but I didn't kill them.

SEYMOUR HERSH

So I get to this building where he's supposed to be, an engineering battalion. And I park about a couple blocks away and go in the side entrance and it's midafternoon and it's three floors of double bunks. Sure enough on the second floor some kid's asleep in a bunk. Figured I got Calley. So I go in and I'm aggressive and I kick the bunk. Bam. And I said, "Get up, Bill!" And some blond kid about twenty has a name tag with a Polish name. I'm disappointed because I thought it would be Calley and it wasn't. I just said, "What's your job?" He said, "I'm the mail clerk." I said, "Oh yeah? Ever hear of a guy named Calley?" And I'm telling you, the next sentences are literally what happened: He said, "You mean the guy that shot up everything? I get his mail. He's not here." I said, "Where does it go?" He said, "He's in an engineering company at battalion headquarters. Smitty, the mail clerk at battalion headquarters, comes every week to pick up Mr. Calley's mail."

And I said, "Okay, in eight minutes I'm going to pull up to the back door here with a blue Chevy, and you come out in eight minutes and take me over there." He said, "Okay." So I drive him there and I remember it was a one-story wooden headquarters building, and there was a big fat sergeant leaning against the door picking his teeth. Now Smitty's just been cashiered, so I said, "Sergeant, get Smitty out here right now." And he starts laughing. What's Smitty done now? So out Smitty comes, slumping. I said, "In the car!" It's amazing how you can pretend some authority. And he gets in the car and I say, "Hey, I've got no problem with you. I'm just a crummy reporter. I'm looking for a guy named William Calley. You know who I'm talking about?" He said, "Yeah. He's in big trouble." I said, "Where is he? What's the story?" He said, "He lives off-base." I said, "What do you know about him?" Then he said, "We have his personnel file." If you have his personnel file in the military that's big. It's called a 201 file. "You have his personnel?" "Yeah, we're still storing it here in a special safe." I said, "Get it." He looked at me and he said, "Okay." I said, "Put it in your shirt." So he goes back inside and a minute later he comes out and gets in the car and he opens up his shirt and he pulls out the 201 file and the first page is the same page I'd seen the day before in the lawyer's office in Salt Lake. I copied it down—got the serial numbers and what the date was. And also there was an address where he was living.

WAYNE SMITH

In my view, most of these officers were looking to get their ticket punched. They wanted to get their medals. They wanted to fatten their résumés for their career path. But the infantry soldiers were all pretty cool. There were some guys who didn't know Rhode Island was a fucking state; they called me "Long Island." Like "Where are you from? Are there black people in that place?"

You've got to also remember that one of McNamara's great sins was Project 100,000.* Project 100,000 began in the mid-sixties when the government could not get the number of people they needed. So one way to simply get one hundred thousand soldiers in the war ASAP was to lower the intelligence standards and physical qualifications that ordinarily would have kept people out of the military. They lowered the floor level so that they could add these people who had real limited abilities. I mean, fucking crazy and dangerous.

BARRY ROMO (Vietnam vet)

When I went to join up, my father sat me on his lap and cried. He was sixty-six years old and he said, "I don't want you to go." And I said, "You and my brother Harold went off in the Second World War. I'm just doing what our family does."

I wanted to go. I was volunteering for Vietnam. I didn't listen to my dad, who was forty-eight years old when I was born. My dad said to me, he had a fourth-grade education, "Your brother and I went off to fight people that were putting human beings in ovens. You're just going to go fight some poor farmer who doesn't want to be bothered with you."

I was a nineteen-year-old second lieutenant, infantry. I was assigned to the 196th Light Infantry Brigade at Chu Lai, and a short time later we were sent to Tam Ky. I was supposed to have forty-five men in my brigade, but depending on how many casualties we would take, it was anywhere between eighteen to forty-five men.

---

* Secretary of Defense Robert McNamara described Project 100,000, which drafted thousands of men who had failed the Armed Forces Qualifications Test, as a liberal extension of Johnson's Great Society. "The poor of America have not had the opportunity to earn their fair share of the wealth of this nation's abundance, but they can be given an opportunity to serve in their country's defense and they can be given an opportunity to return to civilian life with skills and aptitudes which, for them, and their families, will reverse the downward spiral of human decay." George Mariscal, ed., *Aztlán and Viet Nam: Chicano and Chicana Experiences of the War* (Berkeley: University of California Press, 1999), p. 20.

BOBBY MULLER (Vietnam vet)

I grew up in Great Neck, New York, in Nassau County, just outside the city line. Unless there was something special, you didn't have a choice but to go into the service. So if you're going to go, I said, "You think I'm going to have some fucking hillbilly from the South get me fucking killed? I'd rather take charge of it myself." So I enlisted as opposed to simply getting drafted. So it's good morning, Vietnam!

All the guys in my Marine infantry company, except for the NCOs, were eighteen. They asked for five guys out of the company to go work with the CAP program, the Combined Action Platoon, which is a thing the Marines had where you work with local people in a small unit. They said, "We need guys who have at least a high school diploma." The company clerk went through the record, and out of a hundred and fifty-five guys in my Marine infantry company, we didn't even have two with a high school diploma.

BARRY ROMO

I had Mexicans, Puerto Ricans, and Cubans who could barely speak English in my platoon. I had whites from Appalachia who couldn't read and write. I had African Americans from Mississippi, and we would have to write their letters home for them. It was the lowest of the low, the people who had the least to gain from society. I mean, black servicemen were still being killed and beat up in the South for just trying to vote.

SEYMOUR HERSH

By midnight, after knocking on about a hundred and twenty doors, I finally find Calley in the senior officers' quarters. He is five foot six, a hundred and thirty-five pounds, and his skin is translucent. We had a beer or two and he was telling me that it was just a setup, just a firefight. I'm taking notes. It's now about 2 A.M. Calley's girlfriend gets off from the hospital, so we're going to go get her and get a steak and some more bourbon. Then at five or six in the morning we're going to call Ernie Medina, his captain, who will tell me how he did everything under orders. So Calley's telling me all this stuff and I'm taking notes. At one point he goes to take a leak but the door to the bathroom is open a little bit and I see that he vomits arterial blood. He's got an ulcer. So I know it was eating him up, and there was a lot more to the story.

At about 5 A.M. we drove to the hospital to pick up his girlfriend, who was doing the night shift, and we had a steak. She was plenty pissed when she found out that I was a reporter. So now it's six, when the day starts, and Calley's got no assignment, he's just waiting for doom. He's going to have a court-martial. He said, "Oh, we're going to beat that. Don't worry. The army's just out to get me." And we call Ernie Medina. Calley says, "Hey, Captain, hi. I've got a reporter here. You've got to tell him how I had nothing to do with it." And he puts me on the phone and Medina said, "I have no idea what he's talking about." He hangs up, and Calley was stunned. Captain Medina ran away from him so fast it wasn't funny because it was either Medina or him. Medina got off even though he shot somebody point-blank in front of witnesses. But anyway, everybody shot somebody point-blank.

WAYNE SMITH

We were the first integrated army since the Revolutionary War. Before Vietnam there were a couple of isolated integrated units in the Korean War. But that son of a bitch Truman didn't desegregate the military until '48. So here was Vietnam, the first fully integrated military. I didn't have rank superiority, but as a medic I was viewed as a leader of sorts, and a high target for the enemy.

There was a lot of black pride. We African American brothers called ourselves "soul brothers." And the Vietnamese called us soul brothers, too. I mean, it was straight up. They left propaganda sheets for us all around the Mekong Delta when we were on patrol that said, "Soul Brother, no Vietnamese ever called you nigger. We treat you with respect if you treat us with respect." Like, "Look at what's happening in your cities."

The riots had been jumping off the summer before—the '68 riots. Everybody knew about that.*

It was powerful, just for brothers to see each other on the street. We would do this thing called "dap." *Diệp* is the Vietnamese word for beauty, but we called it "dap," an American bastardization. We would slap fives and do all this other stuff. To call it a special handshake would be an understatement. Some brothers would do the special handshake to Santana's "Black Magic Woman." This is love. It was really beautiful that men could show emotion, regard, real care and love for another man. This was a unique kind of relationship that I believe happens mostly in war.

> *Got a black magic woman*
> *Got a black magic woman*
> *I've got a black magic woman*
> *Got me so blind I can't see*
> *That she's a black magic woman*
> *She's trying to make a devil out of me.*
>
> —"BLACK MAGIC WOMAN," WRITTEN BY
> PETER GREEN (FLEETWOOD MAC)

OLIVER STONE

Most of my friends, frankly, were black guys. I don't know why. I never had experienced many black men in my life. I liked them. They introduced me to dope; they introduced me to music that I had never heard before. I was a classical conservative—Beethoven and all the great classical scores. But the first time that I heard soul music out of Detroit, I was

---

* Black GIs would become the most militant members of the GI resistance movement, and by 1970 many black soldiers were considered unreliable in combat. The top brass considered black radicalism a hindrance to U.S. fighting capabilities. In August 1968, black GIs led two U.S. military prison rebellions in Long Binh and Da Nang. Black separatist antiwar groups cropped up among GIs called the Black Brothers Union and the Black Liberation Front of the Armed Forces, led by Black Panther Party supporters. See David Cortright, *Soldiers in Revolt* (Chicago: Haymarket Books, 2005 edition), pp. 39–40.

blown away. They made me understand the Detroit sound, and then the blues sound, and then the southern sound, the Memphis sound.

We had hangouts, and we would smoke dope. We kept our humanity, and humanity's very important. When you live in a military existence with other men, it's like jail: You can become very brutal and inhuman. A lot of the guys were. I saw it everywhere in the three units I was in.

Oliver Stone (left) with a friend. They were both in the First Cavalry Division stationed at Camp Evans, west of Qui Nhon and Da Nang in Vietnam, 1968.

WAYNE SMITH

There was a division between the boozers versus the heads. It didn't always break along those lines, because there were some African Americans that wanted nothing to do with socializing with white soldiers. There were some white soldiers that wanted nothing to do with African Americans or Hispanics—God forbid, Native Americans.

But then there was an integrated group that I traveled in that we called "blue-eyed soul brothers." Some of us, in combat especially, formed a brotherhood. This guy with red hair and freckles is closer to me than my own brothers and sisters. When one goes through experiences that are so horrendous, so indescribable that you cannot find the words for it, but you can look at this guy and he knows. And he knows that you know. "You're my brother. This is no bullshit. I'm willing to put my life on the line for you. Are you willing to do that?" And that's not even a question. That was very powerful in Vietnam.

SEYMOUR HERSH

It's 6 A.M. and I was done but Calley wanted to go bowling with me. I said no. I think he knew that I was the last reporter he was going to talk to in that way. So we said goodbye and I flew back home and wrote the story. I couldn't get anybody to buy the story. I showed it to editors at *Look*, *The New York Review of Books*, and an editor at *Life* magazine, who I later learned had been told about My Lai months earlier by an American GI, Ron Ridenhour. Nobody would touch it. No one wanted to be the first to publish.

BOBBY MULLER

I took a bullet through the chest forty-four years ago, on April 29, 1969. It went through both lungs and severed the spinal cord on the way out. It was absolutely a series of miracles that I lived. Unbelievable. I got mede-vaced virtually right away. With my luck, the hospital ship, *Repose*, was right off the coast of where we had been operating, and the medical ship is the best provider of trauma care that you'd ever want, right? Just getting steady fucking casualties. They put in my medical record that had I ar-rived one minute later, I'd have been dead. Both lungs had collapsed. I had blown-up chest tubes, both sides. So I'm in intensive care. I don't know how long. At some point a psychiatrist comes to me and says, "You want to talk about anything?" Presumably he thought that I want to talk about being paralyzed. But what I wanted to talk to him about was some-thing else.

A few days earlier I had sat down amongst a bunch of dead bodies and ate lunch. I said, "How come it doesn't bother me anymore? Is there something wrong with me?" The psychiatrist said, "No. Your mind has defense mechanisms. When you are in extreme circumstances, those mechanisms come in to protect your mind. They will soften things and let you endure it." He said, "When you go back to New York, next year, if you see somebody get hit by a cab, you will be as affected as anybody else." What I came to understand, and in a way I'm actually grateful for it, is that when you go to war, going down what I call a dark path, you change. Whether you realize it or not, you change. Depending on how far down that path you go is the amount of change that takes place.

SEYMOUR HERSH

I knew this was a loaded story and if we were going to send it out over the wire I needed a lawyer. I had a lawyer named Michael Nussbaum, who was a lot of people in the antiwar movement's lawyer. He's a First Amendment lawyer. I went to see him at his little house in Georgetown and I said, "Mike, I need you to be my lawyer on this." He read my story and said, "Why don't you call Calley's lawyer? You know you're screwing Calley by quoting him. I mean it's your job, but you've basically put him in jail, and you should tell them everything Calley told you."

So I called George Latimer and I said, "Here's what I'm writing." He said Calley's comments conflicted with his sworn testimony and if I published the interview this way, I would possibly be denying Calley his constitutional right to a fair trial. He offered me a deal: If I would avoid saying outright that Calley's comments were made directly to me in an interview and be ambiguous enough to leave open the possibility that I had heard them secondhand, he would go over my story, line for line, and correct any factual mistakes he could. I said, "Fine. That's a deal." And I said, "If I do these changes and editors want to know if the story's correct, will you talk to them?" He said, "Yes. I'll tell them I read the story and it's correct." And that's what did it.

WAYNE SMITH

We had one guy, his name was Jordan, and he was nicknamed "Jungle Jordan." This son of a bitch was one of these kill-happy people. He just wanted to kill anything. It's hard to even understand that, but there were people like him who were willing to do anything just to kill. It was the objective, not that we were advancing a cause. We didn't necessarily know if they were enemy or not.

In the summer of '69 our division received the Presidential Unit Citation because we killed so many Vietnamese. Operation Speedy Express* had ended just shortly after I came to Vietnam. But this was another one of these big campaigns that was totally dedicated to killing anything that moved. We had free-fire zones; these areas were assumed to be enemy, day or night, and subject to being fired on and asked questions later. When you go into combat, you think, Well, it's going to be pretty clear that there's us, and then there's them. But they had no uniforms. They had no real, formal lines. So it was an atmosphere of wanton killing.

We killed an awful lot of people, in all kinds of ways. I didn't see it, but it was accepted that some of the Vietnamese were taken up in planes and thrown out. Some would drown. Some didn't take prisoners. There were all kinds of snipers; we just killed huge numbers of people in ways that were largely by design. The Vietnam War was all about body count. That's how we measured success. When one of my men had a confirmed kill he would get a three-day pass to an in-country R-and-R center like Vung Tau, where this gorgeous beach was. It was a so-called war of containment—we would contain the enemy in certain areas, free-fire zones. So it was very depersonalized. It wasn't people that we were killing—they were gooks and dinks. The way to progress and win the war was by killing more of them than they killed us. Hence the daily body counts. "Last night, American forces killed a hundred and ninety-nine NVA regulars, and only thirteen Americans were killed." I'm not going to hold us [soldiers] harmless. We have personal responsibility.

---

*   Operation Speedy Express was a military offensive in the Mekong Delta that lasted from December 1968 to May 1969, in which 10,899 enemy soldiers were killed and only 267 Americans. Though thousands of civilians were killed, the U.S. Army later covered up the full civilian death toll. Details about Operation Speedy Express were revealed by Nick Turse in "A My Lai a Month: In Operation Speedy Express, New Evidence of Civilian Slaughter and Cover-Up in Vietnam," *The Nation*, November 13, 2008.

SEYMOUR HERSH

David Obst, my twenty-three-year-old neighbor who ran Dispatch News Service, gets on the phone and starts talking to managing editors of major daily newspapers saying, "I have a great story by Seymour Hersh." He called editor after editor. Obst had the gift of gab; he had incredible charm. On the night of November 12 we sent the story by telex to fifty papers. This is right before the November 15 Moratorium. The next day we didn't hear anything. Communications were different then. The AP and UPI wires didn't touch it. They didn't know what to do with it. I had an office in the National Press Building on the eighth floor next to Ralph Nader, and Obst and I waited in the library for the regional papers to come in at 3 A.M. Everybody paid a hundred bucks for the first story. The first paper we saw was the *Chicago Sun-Times* and it was a banner. The *Boston Globe, Miami Herald, Seattle Times* all carried it. We even sold it to the Billings, Montana, paper. The *St. Louis Post-Dispatch*'s front-page headline was, "Lieutenant Accused of Murdering 109 Civilians."

ST. LOUIS POST-DISPATCH, NOVEMBER 13, 1969

LIEUTENANT ACCUSED OF
MURDERING 109 CIVILIANS

By Seymour Hersh

FORT BENNING, GA., Nov. 13—LL William L. Calley Jr., 26 years old, is a mild-mannered, boyish-looking Vietnam combat veteran with the nickname "Rusty." The Army is completing an investigation of charges that he deliberately murdered at least 109 Vietnamese civilians in a search-and-destroy mission in March 1968 in a Viet Cong stronghold known as "Pinkville."

The *New York Post* and *Newsday* ran it big. But *The New York Times* wouldn't buy it. They assigned a reporter to go to My Lai and he wrote a story a couple days later. It also ran in some British papers and it led to a debate in Parliament. The story ran Thursday in thirty-seven papers, and in the antiwar demonstration that weekend there already were signs, "Free the Pinkville People." The area was called "Pinkville" because on the military maps My Lai was colored in pink because it was communist territory.

BARRY ROMO

I was now a first lieutenant at twenty years old; I'm at First Battalion headquarters. I had volunteered to go back [into combat], so they sent a bunch of us down to the Eleventh Brigade to be briefed. We got incredibly drunk, and the next morning in a briefing we were told, "This is really a great unit you're going into, they've just come into country a short while ago, they've got this really incredible body count going on."

It was something close to a five hundred confirmed body count. And all of a sudden we all fucking sobered up. One guy asked, "How many American casualties?" And he goes, "One, self-inflicted. Not a single American wounded by enemy forces." So, five hundred, and one American—fuck, you know? Normally we would have the same number of casualties. Not the same killings, because we had much better medical care, so if we took five hundred, there might be a hundred people killed and four hundred people wounded. We had never seen combat like that.

So we're really sober now, and one full colonel, G-2, goes, "How many weapons did they capture off these dead Viet Cong?" And he says, "Three." Three could have been two hand grenades and a pistol. Three could have been on one person. Three could have been found in a pigsty. Three could have been what they carried into the area. One of us said back to the colonel, because we really didn't care, "They're killing civilians, aren't they?"

He called an end to the meeting and sent us to the Eleventh Brigade. When we get there after that, people didn't talk about it.

SEYMOUR HERSH

That Sunday, November 16, a paper in Phoenix wrote a story about the My Lai story, as everybody else did. At the bottom they had a little squib that said Ronald Ridenhour, a native of Phoenix, said that he was the first to investigate it. This is true. The army started its investigation because this kid Ridenhour was what they call a LRRP [long-range reconnaissance patrol], an advanced patrol guy, very elite unit in the army. He had been told about it by some of the kids in the unit the next day after it happened, and he got a helicopter and flew over it. He saw the scene. He saw ditches and bodies smoldering. He couldn't believe it. He waited until he got out of the army, and about six months later he reported it to the army and they began an investigation. I didn't know any of this.

I found out Ridenhour was at Claremont College in California and I flew out the next morning to see him. He couldn't have been more gracious, and he said, "I always wanted to write it but you can do it, I can't. I couldn't get anybody interested in the story. You've got it in print." It turned out that Ridenhour had given the whole story to *Life* magazine and they'd passed on it.

BOBBY MULLER

You come back, you're in a normal place, you're not in a war zone, you think about the shit that you did, and you don't believe that you fucking did this. What the fuck? And you then live with the memory. Because not only did those defense mechanisms protect you from shit by lessening their effect; it also enables you to do that which you would never have done because it doesn't have the effect. You look at all the reports of what the good guys, the American soldiers, do, whether it's in Iraq, Afghanistan, Vietnam, massacring people, innocent people, and you remember, hey, these are Little Leaguers. These are the good guys. We look at what goes on in the world and we think it's a subspecies of human beings. It's not. It's us.

SEYMOUR HERSH

Ridenhour said to me, "Here's a company roster and I know one of the guys." There's a guy named Mike Terry and Mike lives in Orem, Utah. I flew to Salt Lake, rented a car, and I drove over a snowy pass. He was one of about six or seven kids, Mormon. So I knocked on the door and one of the kids answered it and I said, "I'm looking for Michael Terry." He comes out and I said, "Hi, my name is Hersh. I'm a reporter. Ron Ridenhour gave me your name. . . ." "Oh yeah," he says. He couldn't have been nicer. And I said, "I want to talk to you about what happened." He said, "Well, do you want me to tell you the same thing I told the colonel?" I said, "Sure." "Well, it was a Nazi-type thing, how they mowed down people." That was the line I used and I called Obst up from the airport and I said I'm going to dictate. David sold the second story, which ran in lots of papers on Thursday, November 20.

ST. LOUIS POST-DISPATCH, **NOVEMBER 20, 1969**

Hamlet Attack Called
"Point-Blank Murder"

By Seymour Hersh

. . . Why did it happen?

"I think that probably the officers didn't really know if they were ordered to kill the villagers or not. . . . A lot of guys feel that they (the South Vietnamese civilians) aren't human beings; we just treated them like animals."

SEYMOUR HERSH

Then somebody finally told me about Paul Meadlo. Meadlo was a Project 100,000 kid. He fired clip after clip into the people. Calley told him to fire. There was this moment when they had shot everybody in the ditch and they were eating their K-rations lunch right next to the ditch. War is war. And if you don't dehumanize the enemy you can't do anything, so you have to. They were dehumanized. They heard a keening, a noise. And from the bottom of the pit, even though they thought they'd killed everybody by shooting repeatedly into the pit, there were three pits, each with hundreds of people—the number was staggering. So a kid crawls up to the surface full of other people's blood and he's a two- or three-year-old and he starts running across the ground and Calley with his big show of he-man braggadocio, went up behind him and blew his head off.

That next morning they were interrogated by the colonel and they said, "Sir, nothing unusual happened." The colonel said, "I take your word for it, men. Thank you very much." That evening the officers said, "No, sir, nothing untoward. We were in a firefight, sir. We did a good fight." They got on the front page of *The New York Times* for that fight. GIs kill one hundred and eighteen in combat. Three weapons captured. I mean I can't believe it made the front page. Westy [General William Westmoreland] flew out to congratulate them right in the middle of all this shit. It's just amazing.

Anyway, the next morning on patrol a couple miles away, Meadlo gets his leg blown off by a land mine. And while he's lying there waiting for the medevac, he's issuing an oath, "God will punish me. And Lieutenant Calley, God will punish you." And the kids were all saying, "Get him out of there! Get him out!" Finally, they take him away and he spends months recovering from his wound in Japan. He never spoke; he was totally comatose.

WAYNE SMITH

I was in this aid station in Dong Tam. There was a supply building behind a little hospital. I had to go out and get some supplies, and there was a key that you needed to get in there. It was the morning shift; I went out there, opened it up—and some casualties, some dead Americans had come in the night before. Typically, they're either in a body bag or had a body bag over them that they're going to be put in. So, there was this dead soldier, a white guy, he had a peace ring on his finger. I'll never forget this. I believe it was a Sunday morning. And it was, like, Holy shit. Here's this dead guy. His family is probably on their way to church, maybe having Sunday dinner without a fucking clue that their life has changed forever. Here I had this almost privilege, of being with this dead fellow. I said a little prayer, "Our Father." I was just so totally demoralized; so struck by the contradictions of life and death. Who knows, his family could be telling stories like "Johnny's over there fighting the war." Unbeknownst to them, Johnny's dead. I also realized that it could be any one of us. It could be me. One tried to suppress those kinds of thoughts. But reality would find strange ways of breaking through into your psyche.

SEYMOUR HERSH

Finding him wasn't that easy. The only thing I knew from the company roster was M-E-A-D-L-O was from Indiana, and so I just phoned every Meadlo I could find in the whole state. I finally found somebody near Terre Haute, in a place called New Goshen. I called and I said, "Hi, I'm looking for Paul. Is he okay?" "Well, what do you mean?" I said, "You know, how's his leg?" "Oh, well, he's doing all right. Who are you?" And I said, "I'm just a reporter. I want to talk to him about what happened in the war." And she said, "Well, I don't know if he'll talk to you." I said, "Is it okay if I come?" She said, "I can't promise." She had a very deep, Indiana rural voice.

So the next day I flew to Indianapolis, rented a car, and drove. It might have been ten in the morning when I got to New Goshen. I couldn't find his place for a long time. It was a chicken farm. But when I pulled into the farm I could see that it was all messed up and there were chickens all over the place. His mom comes out and she's this little old lady. She's fifty but looks closer to seventy—just beat down, and living in this old wooden shack. So I say, "Is he in there? Is it okay if I go in?" She said, "Yes, of course." And then she said this great line: She looked at me and she said, "I sent them a good boy and they made him a murderer." It's one of those lines that'll stick with you forever.

I sat down and first I asked him about his leg, which is always what you do. You've got to do that. I said, "I want to see the stump." And he showed me his stump and after a few minutes I said, "Okay, tell me your story. What's your story?" And he smiled. Happy to have somebody not pretend that nothing ever happened to him.

He said, "I just began to shoot people. Calley told me to shoot and he shot and shot." And I'm taking notes. "I just shot and shot." I spoke to seventy of the kids in the next six months, to write the book, after doing the first five articles.

Investigative reporter Seymour Hersh tracked down Private Paul Meadlo at his family's remote Indiana farm, where Meadlo told Hersh the disturbing details of the My Lai massacre. Meadlo's mother told Hersh, "I sent them a good boy and they made him a murderer."

ST. LOUIS POST-DISPATCH, **NOVEMBER 25, 1969**

Ex-GI Tells of Killing Civilians at Pinkville

By Seymour Hersh

TERRE HAUTE, IND., NOV. 25—A former GI told in interviews yesterday how he executed, under orders, dozens of South Vietnamese civilians during the United States Army attack on the village of Song My in March 1968. He estimated that he and his fellow soldiers shot 370 villagers during the operation in what has become known as Pinkville.

WAYNE SMITH

I saw a lot of heroin. When I first got there, there wasn't much. But by '70 it was a snowfield. There were these little plastic vials that could be bought for dollars. It was very inexpensive, very powerful, and very pure. In fact, even some of the marijuana was laced with opium and laced with heroin. Hundreds of thousands of soldiers got addicted. The counterculture went to Vietnam. Some of them got caught up in it. There were people that, clearly, knew about marijuana cultivation, and so much of the music was antiwar and, you know, anti-imperialism.

I started using drugs and was self-medicating—marijuana with opium, some heroin. At first I was smoking it. It was awful. I eventually did shoot some heroin. If one is in pain, almost of any kind, one of the worst things you can do is heroin. Because it is, dare I say, the almost perfect solution to ending your pain. For me, it was ghosts. Seriously, it was voices. It was noise in my head that I couldn't quiet. Honestly, it's not about getting high. It's about just avoiding pain and avoiding the noise. It wasn't uncommon—I mean, it was an epidemic.[*]

I always found it bizarre how anyone had PTSD (post-traumatic stress disorder). I had immediate stress disorder. Delayed? Hell no. It was immediate. I was depressed, I was angry. There was a part of me that thought, Hey, the world would be better off if I wasn't here.

SEYMOUR HERSH

Walter Cronkite knew me from being Eugene McCarthy's press secretary, and he wanted this story on the air, so he pushed me to get Meadlo. When I asked Meadlo, he said, "I'll go." I said, "Well, you can bring your wife and the baby. And they'll pay to fly us." He agreed. So the next morning we flew to New York. It was November 25. I'll never forget. We were doing a pre-interview with Mike Wallace, who asked, "So what happened?" Meadlo said, "Well, I began to shoot." I remember Mike stopped and he said, "Roll the camera." That was the great interview. Mike won prizes for it, and it became a famous antiwar poster.

---

[*]   An army survey of returning GIs found that 44 percent of the men contacted had tried either heroin or opium while they were in Vietnam, and 10 percent were using narcotics every day. Ninety-three percent of those who used heroin had their first contact with the drug while in Vietnam. Another army survey showed that 51 percent of the soldiers stationed in Vietnam smoked marijuana. Cortright, *Soldiers in Revolt*, pp. 29–31.

WALLACE: How many people did you round up?

MEADLO: Well, there was about forty to forty-five people that
we gathered in the center of the village. And we placed them in
there, and it was like a little island, right there in the center of
the village, I'd say.

Q. What kind of people—men, women, children?

A. Men, women, children.

Q. Babies?

A. Babies. And we all huddled them up. We made them squat
down, and Lieutenant Calley came over and said, "You know
what to do with them, don't you?" And I said yes. So I took it
for granted that he just wanted us to watch them. And he left,
and came back about ten or fifteen minutes later and said,
"How come you ain't killed them yet?" And I told him that "I
didn't think you wanted us to kill them, that you just wanted
us to guard them." He said, "No, I want them dead."

Q. He told this to all of you, or to you particularly?

A. Well, I was facing him. So, but the other three, four guys heard
it and so he stepped back about ten, fifteen feet, and he started
shooting them. And he told me to start shooting. So I started
shooting, I poured about four clips into the group.

. . .

Q. And you killed how many? At that time?

A. Well, I fired an automatic, so you can't—you just spray the
area on them and so you can't know how many you killed
'cause they were going fast. So I might have killed ten or fifteen of them.

Q. Men, women, and children?

A. Men, women, and children.

Q. And babies?

A. And babies. . . .

. . .

Q. Obviously, the thought that goes through my mind—I spent
some time over there, and I killed in the Second World War,
and so forth. But the thought that goes through your mind is,

We've raised such a dickens about what the Nazis did. Or what the Japanese did, but particularly what the Nazis did in the Second World War, the brutalization and so forth, you know. It's hard for a good many Americans to understand that young, capable American boys could line up old men, women, and children and babies and shoot them down in cold blood. How do you explain that?

A. I wouldn't know.

Q. Did you ever dream about all of this that went on in Pinkville?

A. Yes, I did . . . and I still dream about it.

Q. What kind of dreams?

A. I see the women and children in my sleep. Some days . . . some nights, I can't even sleep. I just lay there thinking about it.

SEYMOUR HERSH

My story ran that same morning, and that night, the buzz was big.

The first story we sold for a hundred bucks, and by the third and fourth stories, it was five thousand dollars, and ten thousand dollars per story. Money was coming in like crazy—enough so I could buy a house.

Then *The New York Times* and other people began to use the stories, so that's how I ended up getting a Pulitzer Prize, because the establishment press finally bought into the story, which was a lucky thing.

"TOP-SECRET" NOTES FROM CONVERSATION WITH PRESIDENT NIXON, NOVEMBER 27, 1969, BY ALEXANDER BUTTERFIELD, AIDE

Check out Claremont man [Ron Ridenhour] . . . Check out all talkers. Pentagon too scared to investigate adequately . . . Another vulnerable spot—Claremont fellow Jewish (lib Jew) . . . Get backgrounds of all involved—all must be exposed . . . Meadlo too

Army photographer Ron Haeberle was assigned to Charlie Company during the My Lai massacre and took photographs both with his official army camera and his own "unofficial" camera. Haeberle kept the film from his personal camera and released the photos to *Life* magazine and his hometown paper, the Cleveland *Plain Dealer,* after he was discharged. This graphic photo of a pile of dead Vietnamese women and children became an iconic image, frequently reproduced in antiwar posters.

smooth for a farmer . . . Extent to which it happened greatly exaggerated . . . Let's check this Mike Wallace too. He's far left.

ALEXANDER BUTTERFIELD, DECEMBER 17, 1969, MEMO TO PRESIDENT NIXON RE: RONALD LEE RIDENHOUR (and Other Information re My Lai)

—Seymour Hersh, the 32-year-old former McCarthy campaign press secretary, received a $1,000 grant to pursue development of the My Lai story. The grant came from the Edgar B. Stern Family Fund which is clearly left-wing and anti-administration. . . .

Lieutenant William Calley, Jr., on the cover of *Time* magazine, December 5, 1969. Calley became the poster child for atrocities committed in Vietnam against civilians by American soldiers.

—Our current aim is to compile discreet investigative reports on Ridenhour, Haeberle, Hersh, Meadlo, the Edgar B. Stern Family Fund, and Dispatch News Service (to include a run-down on its present editor, 22-year-old David Obst).[*]

PLAQUE AT THE MUSEUM OF
SON MY MASSACRE, VIETNAM

504	dead
247	families
182	women
17	were pregnant
173	children
56	were infants
60	men over 60

[*]   These "Butterfieldgram" memos were first published by Bob Woodward in *The Last of the President's Men* (New York: Simon & Schuster, 2015), pp. 206–7, p. 211. Nothing ever came of Butterfield and Ehrlichman's investigation. Calley was convicted of premeditated murder of twenty-two Vietnamese civilians and sentenced to life in prison. Captain Ernest Medina was acquitted of all charges, and no other member of Calley's platoon was convicted. The day after his sentence, Nixon ordered Calley released from military prison and put under house arrest at Fort Benning, where he stayed for three years. In 1974 Nixon granted Calley a presidential pardon. No one else was prosecuted for the crimes at My Lai.

CHAPTER 13

EXILE

(November 1969–February 1970)

The first rule of our [Woodstock] Nation prohibits any of us from serving in the army of a foreign power with which we do not have an alliance. Since we exist in a state of war with the Pig Empire, we all have a responsibility to beat the draft by any means necessary.

—ABBIE HOFFMAN, *Steal This Book*

BY THE END OF 1969 MANY YOUNG MEN WERE WILLFULLY BREAKING the law by resisting the draft, and many of those who were in the military refused to fight. The Great Refusal was in full swing. Statistics paint a clear picture of the havoc that the war and the draft visited on America in 1969 and 1970. Of the nine million men enlisted in the military during the Vietnam War era, 2.2 million were drafted, 570,000 violated draft laws and did not serve, 25,000 were indicted, 9,000 were convicted, and 170,000 were granted conscientious objector (CO) status. The Justice Department sent 3,250 draft resisters to prison and draft resistance activists disrupted 300 local draft boards between January and September of 1969.

Protesters who attacked draft boards in Delaware and Rhode Island in 1970 destroyed nearly all of the records, crippling the system in those states. In Oakland, California, between October 1969 and March 1970, 50 percent of those called did not report to the Selective Service office.

Eleven percent of the men who did refused induction. Army Conscientious Objector status applications jumped 400 percent between 1967 and 1971, and desertion and AWOL rates were the highest in modern American history. Secreted out of the country by an underground railroad, draft resisters and GI deserters congregated in Canada and Sweden.

By 1970, American soldiers regularly refused commands to fight in the field and military accounts recorded 68 cases of fragging—attacks by soldiers against their own officers—and many more cases went unreported. GIs rioted at more than 30 military bases and military jails, and GIs circulated 250 antiwar underground papers. Widespread draft resistance, desertions, and dissent inside the ranks drove the American armed forces to near collapse.

DAVID HARRIS (leader of the Resistance)

I remember Joan [Baez] telling me that she'd been at this thing, Woodstock. You have to perceive how remote it all was in the federal prison camp in Safford, Arizona. You survive prison by not being anyplace else—you go crazy if you try to live outside the walls. If, in your mind, you are out there, then you're fucked, because you're not there, and that means you're going to go batshit. So the way you do time is not to pretend you're anyplace else. The guys who identify themselves by the car they're able to drive have a hard time doing time. Some people I knew wouldn't take visits, because it's really disorienting. No question I was going to take them. There was my son.

RANDY KEHLER (draft resistance organizer)

I got arraigned in November of '69, in Cheyenne, Wyoming, and the trial was the first week of February 1970. So there were several months between the arraignment and the trial. At the trial itself, one of the probation officers said to me in front of my parents, "Look, here's the address form. Tell you what, if you just give us your current address, we'll drop all the other charges." My parents were totally elated, but I said, "No." I wanted to resist. It's like the great line from Thoreau's *On the Duty of Civil Dis-*

obedience. I wanted "to be friction against their wheel." However insignificant my action might be. I remember not even being tempted. I remember being clear. I had come this far. I ticked off the names of my friends, including David Harris, who were already in prison and I said, I will be proud to be joining them. So I had my mind made up: prison or let me go free. Those were the only options I would entertain.

DAVID HARRIS

On December 2, 1969, they cut me a special dispensation and let me stay up in the rec room and wait for the phone call to tell me that my son had been born. After that, for eight hours every month was the only time I got to see my son, Gabe. Joan would bring him and we'd take our eight hours. Eight hours a month to get to be a father, that's it. So I was always going to take those. But it put your head in a twist. Because all the sudden, for eight hours, you're part of some life that's out there somewhere. And then they leave and you're back in your cell block. Visits are definitely a mixed bag.

The guards would do shit like I'd be sitting in my cell one weekend. I knew I was getting a visit. You had to dress up. I have my bonnaroos on, which means my khaki pants and shirt—like an army uniform. They called my name and number over the loudspeaker, "Harris, 4697-159. Visit." So I'd then stand at my gate waiting for them to open my cell. They'd do the thing just like in the movies. You step out, get through the next gate, get patted down, get through the next set of gates. You make a left-hand turn. You have to go through another gate to get to where the visits are, but you get through that gate and then you have to go into this room, and they strip-search you. "Take your clothes off, bend over, show us your asshole."

So you'd go through that whole process, and then you're there at the last gate and I can see Joan and Gabe there waiting for me, and all the sudden the guard would say, "Oh, Harris, man, look at those sideburns. God, those are at least a quarter inch too long, man. You've got to go back and cut those things." So I'd have to turn around and go through the strip search again, get my clothes back on, and go back through all the gates, go up to my cell, cut my sideburns, turn around, go do the whole thing over again. They just like to fuck with you. That's the game that's going on all the time between you and the guards.

I remember once they cut my visit short, because there were these water faucets on the wall they use for the lawn. It was hot and we took Gabe's clothes off and put him under the water fountain and dripped some water on him. They busted my ass. "You can't do that! You're done." That was the end of my eight hours of visit, for having a naked baby.

"Mr. and Mrs. Peace in America," David Harris and Joan Baez, with their newborn son, Gabe, on the cover of *Look* magazine, May 5, 1970. The photo was taken while Harris was still serving time in jail for resisting the draft.

RICK AYERS (draft dodger, GI organizer)

I showed up at the induction center in Chicago on November 5, 1969, and it was basically a bunch of working-class dudes—the big south-side African American group, and a big west- and north-side white, working-class group. There were very few middle-class people.

I was scared, very scared, but very clear on my politics and what this was about and what I was going to do. We took a bus down to Fort Leonard Wood, Missouri, which is where all the Chicago boys go for basic training, and did all the classic things of getting our heads shaved and going through training.

The weird thing about training was, I liked that part. I liked getting up at 4:30 A.M., and I liked the food, and I liked the physical training, and I liked the weapons training. I just didn't like the mission. But I was definitely shit-talking, complaining about things, and especially trying to bring up Vietnam. What was really weird is they never once—this is the height of the war—gave us a political indoctrination. They never said you're fighting communism; you're fighting for the survival of our way of life. Nothing. The only indoctrination was, Don't be a pussy, don't be a faggot. Your girlfriend is fucking someone else. It was all sexual politics, and it was all about your buddies.

I would talk to the guys about how the war was wrong. How you could be the last one killed, but the U.S. wasn't going to win and what the conditions were for the Vietnamese. Whatever I could talk about. It wasn't all the time. It was little talks here and there, but they knew me as the antiwar guy, and they also knew that I knew lawyers.

PHYLLIS MENKEN (girlfriend of draft dodger)

I had a really hard adolescent relationship with my parents, so as soon as I graduated from high school in 1969, I left the country and moved to Paris, where I got a job teaching English in a French public school. That was my excuse for getting out of town. My parents signed on to this only because they thought that they were going to get me away from my boyfriend, who was an Irish kid from the wrong side of the tracks, and who was older than I was. He was poor and his dad had died when he was little and he was addicted to heroin, so they wanted to separate me from him. So they signed on to this idea that I would go to Europe and have this job and get an apartment. But I sent my boyfriend money to come and be with me as soon as I got to Paris, and then I ended up getting pregnant.

We ended up going to Sweden because he was avoiding the draft and in Sweden we could get government support. I was going to have a baby, and there was a network of people supporting the Black Panthers and supporting the draft resisters and the war deserters in Paris, and they sent us to Amsterdam and we stayed with this incredible Dutch woman who had this beautiful art-filled apartment and she welcomed us. At that point I was probably six months pregnant, an eighteen-year-old kid.

ABBIE HOFFMAN (*Steal This Book*)[*]

If you've totally fucked up your chances of getting a deferment or already are in the service and considering ditching, there are some things that you should know about asylum. . . .

. . . Sweden will provide political asylum for draft dodgers and deserters. It helps to have a passport, but even that isn't necessary since they are required by their own laws to let you in. There are now about 35,000 exiles from the Pig Empire living in Sweden. The American Deserters Committee . . . will provide you with immediate help, contacts and procedural information once you get there.

RICK AYERS

I learned it's very easy in jail or in the army to hang out with the black guys if you're the white radical, because they like you. They like a white guy who gets them. So there was a part of the barracks called the Soul Hole where all the black guys hung out. They were like, "Ayers, you're cool, man. What's up?" I'd sit with them.

My girlfriend Melody and another guy from SDS came down to visit me, and I was telling them things I learned: One, they called me the hippie. I was trying to blend in and be a working-class guy. And so Melody said, "So what do they think a hippie is?" "Well, a hippie has access to drugs, a hippie is against the war, a hippie is anti-authority." "Well, those are good things. So be that." So instead of trying to hide and blend in, I decided to be the oddball. The second point they raised with me is that I shouldn't just hang in the Soul Hole. The black guys are already revolutionaries. Talk to those white guys. I was doing it for comfort. I pushed myself to push the white guys. That was good for me.

[*]   Abbie Hoffman, *Steal This Book* (New York: Pirate Editions, distributed by Grove Press, 1971), p. 195.

Basic training was from November to late January. I figured I'd be sent to Germany or something. I'd be a clerk, because they'd figure out I was just going to create problems in Vietnam, and I'm a college boy; I can type. But of course that didn't happen. I got 11-Charlie. That means that you're a mortarman. Eleven-Charlie is infantry mortar, which means you're in the infantry platoon; you're in combat.

PHYLLIS MENKEN

Sweden was giving political asylum and humanitarian asylum to American draft resisters and draft deserters, because Sweden was opposed to the war in Vietnam. We ended up in Stockholm applying for asylum and getting all kinds of social service support. We were given an apartment and Swedish lessons, free healthcare. We became enmeshed in this political network of people who were asylum seekers, people who were draft resisters and draft deserters, and we also coexisted with a subculture of immigrants from North Africa who were in the same language classes, in the same housing, in the same welfare lines, with absolutely nothing and completely dependent on the largesse of the state. There was this big underground economy and subculture, and there was a lot of illegal dealing going on, of drugs and goods. You'd go to your place to buy or sell and then the police would make a sweep a couple of times a day. Somebody would say, "Here they come," and everybody would scatter. It was like a flock of crows and then everyone would settle back down again when they left and continue about their business.

It was a kind of a tight community and the deserters were in really rough shape. They were lower-class, middle-America guys whose minds had been completely blown in Vietnam, and who said, "Get me out of here." Where do I go, how do I go? How do I leave? And then of course they could leave Vietnam but they couldn't get Vietnam out of their heads. So there was a tremendous amount of drug abuse, a tremendous amount of speed addiction. Sweden had this huge underclass and this huge drug culture. People would go down to Spain and they would buy all of these drugs and bring them back. They'd sell pharmaceuticals pill by pill. There was also a lot of hash and opium, and a lot of opium addiction.

ABBIE HOFFMAN (*Steal This Book*)*

We feel it's our obligation to let people know that life in exile is not all a neat deal, not by a long shot. You are removed from the struggle here at home, the problems of finding work are immense and the customs of the people are strange to you. Most people are unhappy in exile. Many return, some turn themselves in and others come back to join the growing radical underground making war in the belly of the great white whale.

WESLEY BROWN (draft resister)

There were a lot of young men who didn't get CO [conscientious objector] status but were given some kind of community service that was short of going into the army. But given that I was in the Black Panther Party, and had used language that clearly was offensive to the authorities, they were not going to cut me any slack.

Finally, after about another year or so, my lawyer Michael Standard got the call that I should report to a three-judge panel for sentencing, and the maximum penalty was five years. They were not going to listen to any speeches about my ethical stance on the war in Vietnam. So I went to court in Brooklyn with two friends and my mother and was sentenced to three years.

I think my mother was in shock that I was actually going to jail. My parents felt that if I had taken a teaching job it would have shielded me, but getting involved with the Panthers pretty much sealed my fate in terms of there being any latitude that the court would have exercised in sentencing me. I knew that I wasn't going to leave the country. I didn't feel like that was an option for me. It was going to be hard enough for my parents as it was, but if I left the country, there was not a finite amount of time that I would be gone. With prison there was. I didn't know how long the war was going to last. If my parents would have tried to see me if I left the country, I would be putting them in the position of aiding and abetting a

---

* Hoffman, *Steal This Book*, p. 197.

felon. The feds probably would have put pressure on them. So I felt that if I was in prison, at least they would know where I was, and they could visit. And so as soon as I was sentenced, I was taken into custody and placed in a holding cell. I ended up spending eighteen months in the Lewisburg Federal Penitentiary.

RANDY KEHLER

We went to trial and I chose to represent myself because I wanted to speak for myself. I started out telling the jury right off the bat that I did what I was charged with doing. "I did refuse to obey a draft order," I said, "but I want to tell you why." I called my parents as character witnesses, thinking maybe I could get a little sympathy out of the jury. My father, Gordon Kehler, was a retired businessman. I was raised in a privileged Scarsdale, New York, family. My father never made much himself, but it was enough to live in Scarsdale. He was a Republican, although not really active, and he was a businessman; not a very successful one. But he was very dignified looking: His hair was silver. My mother was a mainstream American housewife from the forties and fifties. She was nominally a Democrat, but not involved in politics at all. There was no talk in our home, or in our schools, or in our church, about war, peace, pacifism, nonviolence. I never heard any of those words. I was raised, I think, with really decent values. You should be honest, always tell the truth, you should try to help other people, and be a good person.

My father got up on the witness stand and I asked him, "What were the values that you and Mom tried to instill in us as children?" I have an older brother, and a younger brother, and a younger sister. My father took the cue, and he mentioned that killing is wrong. He totally blew my mind. He turns to this old judge, who was a World War II judge advocate general in Italy, postwar, and he was the only federal judge in Wyoming, a very powerful man, crusty old guy. My father, who could be just as crusty and was just as old, turned to him and said, "Your Honor, if you want to put somebody in prison, put me in prison. Because he's just following what we taught him." That was one of the most moving things that happened in all that time.

RICK AYERS

After you finish basic you go to advanced training. I got orders for Fort Polk, Louisiana, which is all Vietnam training because it's just swamps there. So as soon as I got those orders, I started smoking cigarettes again, because I really didn't think I was going to live. So I go to Fort Polk, Louisiana, which was really interesting. It's the deep, bad South. It's in a little town called Monroe, Louisiana. Here's the kind of shit that would happen: First of all, the sergeants and lifers, who are supposed to be the big enemy because they kick your ass—the sergeants in the South were all black, southern guys, and they had already been to Vietnam, sometimes a couple of times. They were so antiwar. They would say to us, "You guys, *this* is bad. This is a *bad* deal."

So it wasn't that kind of the sergeant-gung-ho-let's-fight rhetoric I had expected to hear. Lieutenants who come out of ROTC, they're more gung ho, let's fight. The way the military is, lieutenants are supposed to be from the higher classes. Sergeants come out of the working class, they are like a foreman in a factory. So you know who got killed a lot in Vietnam? Second lieutenants, which were these college boys, because they were like, "Come on, men, let's go," and everyone else is like, "Fuck, no!" So the lieutenants got killed by their own people. There was a lot of fragging, mostly of second lieutenants. If you had a gung ho second lieutenant, he was dead.

RANDY KEHLER

Besides saying that I thought the war was a violation of international law, I cited chapter and verse, and I told the jury that international treaties ratified by the United States Senate, according to Article Five of the United States Constitution, are to be considered the "supreme law of the land." I said, "This is not some little thing. And there's been no declaration of war."

I had researched the concept of jury nullification, which I thought would be my ace in the hole. It goes back to the Peter Zenger trial, in the colonial days of New York. He was accused by the British, and taken to court for printing something the British considered libelous, or slanderous. But the jury acquitted him. My instruction to the jury in my trial, which I submitted to the judge, was "Even if you find that the defendant has violated the law as charged, you have the right to acquit the defendant based on other considerations." The judge read it and said, "I'll include that." I thought, Oh my God. I'd been told no judge had ever agreed to tell that to a jury. I thought, Holy shit. This could be an incredible precedent for lots of people. So then he starts reading all the instructions to the jury, and he reads my instruction, too. But in the very next breath he says, "However, if you find that this defendant did in fact violate the draft law, you have no choice but to find him guilty as charged."

I rose up and I said, "Your Honor, I object." He said, "Sit down. I will record your objection for the record." Well, the jury—a good Wyoming jury—took no more than about forty-five minutes to find me guilty.

The sentencing was right away and the judge said, "Well, since you would have had to serve two years if drafted, I'm going to sentence you to prison for two years." Which was a very light sentence, considering. Then he said, "Do you have a preference as to which prison I send you to?" I was living in San Francisco. I said, "I have some friends who have already been sentenced to prison down in Safford, Arizona." I was thinking of David Harris and a couple others. He said, "All right." And he said, "Do you want me to have the federal marshals take you there, or will you show up under your own steam?" I said, "I'll show up." He said, "Okay," and gave me one week to turn myself in at the prison, which I did.

RICK AYERS

You did these chants when you marched to stay in step. *I don't know but I've been told, streets of heaven are paved with gold.* But there'd be different, political ones that were often antiwar. They called them cadences. Here's one: *Vietnam, Vietnam. Late at night when you're sleeping, Charlie Cong comes a-creeping around in Vietnam.* I mean, usually we didn't even talk about Vietnam in training, except for things like "Don't be a pussy." Here's another verse: *You write your girl a letter,* and then the guys repeat, *You write your girl a letter; to you, she's mighty dear. You're wishing you were never, never here.*

The last one was *You hear the bombs a-dropping. What is it? You think that they're all gone, here comes another thousand Cong.* And then the chorus: *Vietnam . . .* I get teary-eyed just saying it. It was so scary. These kids were going to die; you could just feel it. The big decision coming up for me by the end of March was, What am I going to do now?

RANDY KEHLER

Safford was a minimum-security federal prison. What helped me all along, even before I went to trial, was knowing that I had friends there, and they were surviving. Nobody was being beaten. There were no race riots or brutality. Federal prisons in general tend to have less of that than state prisons. So I felt sure I could do it, but I was still scared shitless.

The next morning, my wife, Jane, drove me up to the door. We hugged and kissed goodbye, and cried. I dried my tears and walked in. It was just like any other big bureaucracy. I could have been walking into a hospital: There's the registration line where you fill out these forms. We need your fingerprints, and let's see your possessions, put them in this bag, and you're assigned to this, and you have to wait for that, and you have to get shots for this. Here's where you're going to be living. It's very routine. It's probably like the first day of the military. You had to wear a military-type prison uniform.

DAVID HARRIS

We fucked around a lot. Visitors would come on the weekend, and every Monday people would get to the work site and scramble out into the woods where people had left all kinds of dope, so we were smoking a lot. At one point a guy came in who had been busted on dope charges. He was part of what was called the Brotherhood of Eternal Love, which was a big Orange County acid manufacturing group. Orange Sunshine was the product of the Brotherhood of Love, who had kind of taken over the acid business after "Bear" Owsley [Stanley] went to jail. A week after that guy showed up, there was all this Orange Sunshine floating around and people taking acid. I never took acid in the joint, though. I'd smoke reefer anytime, but the thought of having to deal with these guys for twelve hours while I sparked up, no thanks.

RANDY KEHLER

We were in the desert, and there were no walls around this place—there wasn't even a barbed-wire fence, but there were lines, a perimeter which you weren't supposed to go beyond. If they knew you were gone, they would chase you down in jeeps with rifles and dogs. You would be wearing shoes with a pattern cut out of the sole, so they could track you better through the desert. You wouldn't want to go out in the desert barefoot. One of the hard things about being in this prison—which I was only in for six months before I was sent to a much bigger, medium-security place—was that there were no walls, and there was even a road going right by it.

We would say to ourselves, "Why do we stay here?" We could so easily have somebody pick us up and just be gone. I knew that none of my draft resister friends ever did that. There were three hundred prisoners there, of which maybe fifty were draft resisters. But half of them were Jehovah's Witnesses, which is a different category. They were truly against war, true conscientious objectors, but they wouldn't even apply for CO status, and they kept to themselves totally. It surprised me, I had thought the non-JW draft resisters would all be organizers, because we thought they were selectively prosecuting us.

Out of the hundreds of thousands of people who were disobeying the draft law, it appeared that they were picking out key organizers who were in the public eye. Of which I was one, and David was one. But most of the guys there were not organizers. They were sweet, conscientious young men from all over the West Coast or Southwest who had just decided that they couldn't cooperate.

My wife, Jane, and David's wife, Joan Baez, and another guy's girlfriend used to drive down together to visit us, and one time they were outside the fences near the road. Joan and others were singing for us, so we sang back our strike song. We were on a food strike. I was playing away at the guitar. The guards broke it up pretty fast.

CHAPTER 14

DECEMBER

(December 1–31, 1969)

You can jail the revolutionaries, but you can't jail the revolution.
—FRED HAMPTON, SPEECH, 1969

DECEMBER 1969 WAS PLAGUED BY VIOLENCE AND DESPAIR. AS
bloodshed in Vietnam escalated, so did violence at home. The ranks of
Americans who considered themselves "revolutionaries" swelled to as
many as a million, and militant resistance threatened nearly all government institutions related to the war effort. Nonviolent civil disobedience
of just months earlier, with the October and November Moratoriums, had
evolved into violent clashes with police, rioting, arson, and bombings. In
the fifteen-month period between January 1969 and April 1970, an average of fifty politically motivated bombings occurred each day.

At the vanguard of this domestic rebellion was the Black Panther
Party, which, in reaction to police brutality and FBI harassment, publicly
declared war against the police. Two dozen Black Panther chapters had
opened across the country, and in 1969 the police killed 27 Panthers and
arrested or jailed 749. J. Edgar Hoover announced that the Black Panther
Party was "the greatest threat to [the] internal security of the country,"
and he assigned two thousand full-time FBI agents to "expose, disrupt,
misdirect, discredit, and otherwise neutralize" the Panthers and other

New Left organizations. In a 1969 speech to Congress, Hoover declared that the New Left was a "firmly established subversive force dedicated to the complete destruction of our traditional democratic values and the principles of free government."

Meanwhile, the Vietnam War raged on. From 1961 until 1971, the U.S. military dropped more than 19 million gallons of toxic chemicals— defoliants or herbicides, including Agent Orange—on 4.8 million Vietnamese. In 1969, 11,780 American troops were killed, bringing the death toll to 48,736. It was not a festive Christmas for those in the peace movement. John Lennon and Yoko Ono displayed huge billboards in Los Angeles, London, and other cities that read: "War is over! If you want it. Happy Christmas from John & Yoko." On New York City's Fifth Avenue during the holiday shopping rush, a woman blocked the street with a sign that read, "How Many Shopping Days Until Peace?"

KARL ARMSTRONG

(student, University of Wisconsin–Madison)

I remember sitting in the student union with my brother Dwight and watching news accounts of the My Lai massacre, and I couldn't believe our country had sunk to such low depths. Even before the My Lai story came out, I had come to the realization that we were basically fighting these peasant people in Vietnam, and it was a very asymmetric sort of war, using all of this technology and bombs, killing hundreds of thousands of people who were basically fighting back with limited resources.

At some point I felt like I became Viet Cong. My allegiance had switched. I thought, I would rather be with these people and lose, than be an American and win. And that's when I realized that I was no longer an American. I was really a citizen of the world.

I was of the opinion that any kind of demonstration against the war was important, but I just didn't feel it was going to go anywhere. The war could carry on, and the demonstrations would be ignored. They could do that for the next ten years and it'd be the same thing. I had no problem

One of John Lennon and Yoko Ono's several anti–Vietnam War campaigns, this Christmas 1969 message was posted on billboards in a number of American cities and London.

with the demonstrations, they were my brothers and sisters out there, but I realized that I was in a very special place, because I didn't have a family of my own and I wasn't tied up in corporate America. I didn't have a job. I felt like I wasn't risking anything. I was a free actor, and I had a responsibility. I decided I would remove all the obstacles in front of me in order to help bring this war to an end.

DECEMBER 4, CHICAGO: FRED HAMPTON

MARK RUDD (Weathermen leader)

When Fred Hampton was murdered on December 4,[*] it confirmed our whole strategy, which was that a war was taking place already, and we'd better get ready to respond to it.

BERNARDINE DOHRN (Weathermen leader)

Fred Hampton had talked to his friends and to his mom about being a lawyer. He had Bill Kunstler's book by his bed. He was one of those absolutely charismatic, magnetic people. He was young, twenty-one, but had a great sense of people, and a theatrical ability to make gestures that were very powerful—for example, commandeering ice cream trucks in the summer for kids, and then getting arrested for it. Even in his high school days with the NAACP he did things like demand access to segregated swimming pools on the west side of Chicago.

By the time I knew him he was saying, "I'm high on the people. I'm high on freedom," and he'd become the chairman of the Black Panther Party here in Chicago. We shared a printing press with the Panthers. They were down the block from us. We agreed about some things and disagreed about other things, but they knew us pretty well and we knew them pretty well. We had an intense relationship with the Panthers; we saw them all the time.

---

[*]   In one of the most brazen examples of police violence and FBI dirty tricks, Fred Hampton, the twenty-one-year-old chairman of the Illinois chapter of the Black Panther Party, was gunned down in his sleep at 4:30 A.M. on December 4, 1969, by the Chicago police. Mark Clark, another Panther leader, was also killed in the raid. Though the police claimed they acted in self-defense, they were proven wrong by evidence showing ninety gunshots going one way through the front door of Fred Hampton's apartment, where he slept with his fiancée, who was eight months pregnant. Hampton was killed by two bullets fired to his head at point-blank range in a cold-blooded assassination. The FBI assisted the Chicago police by giving them a map of the floor plan of Hampton's apartment that they obtained from William O'Neal, an FBI informant who was Hampton's trusted bodyguard. O'Neal had slipped a sleeping pill into Hampton's drink when they had dinner together that night, sedating him so that he could not defend himself.

Charismatic and eloquent, the chairman of the Illinois chapter of the Black Panther Party, Fred Hampton, was perceived as a particular threat to the FBI's J. Edgar Hoover because he appealed to both white and black leftists.

FRED HAMPTON (1969 speech)

A lot of people don't understand the Black Panther Party's relationship with white mother country radicals. . . . What we're saying is that there are white people in the mother country that are for the same types of things that we are for stimulating revolution in the mother country. And we say that we will work with anybody and form a coalition with anybody that has revolution on their mind.*

BERNARDINE DOHRN

I knew the National Lawyers Guild people and the People's Law Office people very well, so on December 4, when Fred was murdered, they imme-

---

* J. Edgar Hoover was particularly threatened by Hampton because he preached racial solidarity against an oppressive U.S. government. He appealed to white as well as black radicals and moderates and had a charisma and way with words that enabled him to unite a fractured movement. One of the FBI's COINTELPRO objectives was to "prevent the rise of a 'messiah' who could unify, and electrify, the militant black nationalist movement." In 1967 the FBI opened a file on Fred Hampton that would eventually fill twelve volumes and more than four thousand pages.

diately took charge of the situation and seized the crib—as the apartment was called—door for evidence of bullet holes. We, the Panther Party survivors, and the People's Law Office responded in a way that kind of reenacted the murder of Emmett Till—with a massive, public, visual look at what the police had done. And of course the police and the FBI—who we now know conspired to murder him—were both on the scene, and participants.

On December 5, 1969, Fred Hampton, age twenty-one, was gunned down in his sleep in a predawn raid by the Chicago police with help from the FBI. Hampton's colleague Mark Clark was also killed in the raid. The police claimed they acted in self-defense, but an investigation revealed that they fired ninety shots to the Panthers' two.

ERICKA HUGGINS (Black Panther Party member)

When Fred Hampton was murdered, I knew immediately, even though I was incarcerated at the time,[*] that Fred did not die just at the hands of the police officers that invaded his home. It was a setup, and later it was proven

---

[*] Ericka Huggins, along with Bobby Seale (cofounder of the Black Panther Party), was in jail awaiting trial on murder charges that were part of the New Haven Nine conspiracy trial.

that it was set up—that he was drugged. He was killed in his sleep in the middle of the night by the police who arrived in borrowed Chicago Phone Company trucks. So it was orchestrated. J. Edgar Hoover, who was the head of the FBI for forty-seven years, created COINTELPRO as the counterintelligence program. You can read their mission online. I wish I was making it up; I wish it hadn't occurred. But the fear that is at the root of racism will prompt people who have that fear to do very inhumane things.

Fred was an amazing human being. He was very dedicated to working with all communities. If you just listen to him and just watch him on video, you'll see why J. Edgar Hoover wanted him dead.

FBI surveillance and harassment was something we were all used to. Our phones were tapped and we were followed all the time. They would leave notes on our car windows threatening us, "Hi John, hi Ericka. We're watching you." Every night when we would leave the party office in South Central, unmarked police cars would shine their floodlights on the windows and the doors of the office. This is how we left the office every night. We got used to it. I always remember that whole period in Los Angeles as living in a state of war. But we weren't warring; something was warring against us.

VIVIAN ROTHSTEIN (SDS organizer)

I was organizing high school kids. They were all white, living in Berwyn and Cicero—very right-wing white communities in the Chicago suburbs. I got to know Fred Hampton in Maywood, where he was head of the NAACP chapter, and I invited him to come and talk to the students. These kids' parents were so racist; they'd never talked to a black person before. Fred would sit with them for a whole evening and talk to them. He was so warm and understanding and charismatic. They fell in love with him. He was just wonderful.

When he was killed, I took the students that I was working with to where his body lay in state in a Baptist church in Chicago. It was this incredible scene. The kids I worked with knew him before he was this big public figure. He was lying in state with a rifle by his side in the coffin, and beads, and the Black Panther Party newspaper. All these Black Panthers were standing guard around the coffin with their berets and their black leather jackets. I was with a group of white girls and we stood in line for hours, and then we finally went by his casket. I almost passed out in his casket because I'm Jewish and we don't do viewings. But it was quite an experience having this gaggle of young teenage white girls going through a black church with all of these Panthers around, and they all loved Fred, so they were all crushed.[*]

A young boy holding a copy of the *Black Panther* newspaper listens to Black Panther leader Fred Hampton speaking at the bandshell in Grant Park, Chicago, 1969.

CATHY WILKERSON (Weathermen member)

When Fred Hampton was killed it felt like the police were going to end democracy in the United States. It also felt like the warmongers, the "U.S. must rule the world" people, and anti-women and anti-black leadership of the country were going to win and solidify control. We were young. We were in a complete panic. It was pretty scary.

[*] Five thousand people attended Fred Hampton's funeral.

MARK RUDD

When the Panthers came along, and they were carrying guns and spouting "by any means necessary," and the government reacted by taking them seriously, and murdering them, we said, "It's war. And we've got to be out there, and not just applauding from the sidelines." See, there's always a tendency for white people to hold back and applaud from the sidelines, but we identified that as being racist, to not take any risks. We didn't want to be liberals. To be a liberal was to be a hypocrite, and to be a betrayer. So part of our thinking was, Which side are you on? "Avenge Fred Hampton!" became our battle cry.

Black power then became an enormous challenge to white kids. Would we be good Germans? Would we be racist and ignore what's happening? Or would we support the people who are fighting and taking the risks? That became the challenge for the Weathermen. Most young whites don't understand the extent of the challenge that the black movement posed to the Weather Underground, and to the movement.

MICHAEL KAZIN (Harvard SDS leader)

The Panthers saw themselves as urban guerrillas. I mean, the whole carrying guns and taking them to the statehouse in Sacramento and taking on the police—they saw themselves as being in an almost fascist country. Huey Newton used to say, "If the pigs are going to act like Nazis, we're not going to act like Jews." Which, you know, for a Jew like me, made me feel a little strange. But I understood what he meant. If you didn't have the Panthers on your side, then you were doing something wrong, because they were the black vanguard.

BERNARDINE DOHRN

It took seven more years to prove it in the court case *Iberia Hampton v. Hanrahan,* which the People's Law Office represented. I always tell my law students Fed Supp. 600 is one of the most astonishing cases you'll ever read, because the federal appellate court found that there was a conspiracy to murder Fred Hampton, and then an elaborate cover-up and the FBI and the Chicago Police Department had lied and withheld documents ordered by the court and had an informer present inside the Panthers who had given them a map of the apartment where Fred and his wife were sleeping. So it was a deliberate assassination. But we knew that; we assumed that from the beginning.*

JULIUS LESTER
(writer, photographer, civil rights activist)

It's very interesting, the different reactions of whites and those of us who were in SNCC had to the murder of Fred Hampton. Our feeling at SNCC was that the rhetoric of the Panthers led to his death. The Panthers had this rhetoric of violence, and if it's one thing that white America knows, it's violence. You don't challenge somebody on their strength. So you don't get violent with white America, because they're itching to kill you. Our feeling was that Fred Hampton did not have to die. That was the Panthers' doing. So our response was very different than the response of SDS. The other deaths of the Panthers were senseless as far as we were concerned. You don't challenge white policemen with guns; they're eager to kill you.

WESLEY BROWN
(draft resister, Black Panther member)

After Fred Hampton and Mark Clark were assassinated, I realized that I had implicated myself in the kind of rhetoric that could bring about my own undoing. We [the Panthers] got revved up in a frenzy of rhetoric and began to believe our own bullshit about revolutionary change. Huey Newton[†] fa-

---

*   The police officers were found not guilty in a 1972 trial, but after thirteen years of litigating the civil rights case, which went all the way to the Supreme Court, the families of Fred Hampton and Mark Clark were awarded $1.8 million—the largest settlement of its kind at the time. In 1990, FBI informant William O'Neal, who was Fred Hampton's bodyguard, died in what some believe was a suicide.

†   Huey Newton, who with Bobby Seale founded the Black Panther Party in 1966, wrote an autobiography titled *Revolutionary Suicide,* which was published in 1973.

mously called it "revolutionary suicide." And so I think all of us had to acknowledge that we were in some ways collaborating in a presentation of
ourselves in a flamboyant way that would bring the very thing that we said is
going to happen, to us. And then we were surprised when they believed
what we said we were trying to do. I didn't even know if I believed it. I had
to examine if what I was doing had contributed to an ongoing struggle for
people to better the circumstances of their lives, and where that becomes
less the issue, and more about whether you are going to try to kill the police,
or bring revolution to the streets.

To what end is it going to serve if I get up in the face of authorities
where the pushback can be lethal? What does that achieve if confrontation and escalation of confrontation is the primary strategy to get attention
for things that need to be paid attention to? So that's what I had to ask
myself.

FBI REPORT

December 6, 1969: Several Chicago Police cars parked in a pre-
cinct parking lot at 3600 North Halsted Street, Chicago, were
bombed. No suspects have been developed in this matter and no
organization claimed credit until almost five years later when the
WUO [Weather Underground Organization] admitted that it was
responsible in their book "Prairie Fire." The WUO stated that
they had perpetrated the explosion to protest the shooting deaths
of Illinois Black Panther leaders Fred Hampton and Mark Clark on
December 4, 1969, by police officers.

DECEMBER 6, NORTHERN CALIFORNIA: ALTAMONT

PETER COYOTE (Digger, communard)

The story of Altamont is that Sam Cutler,[*] the manager of the Rolling Stones, came to Peter Berg[†] and myself, because we were known for throwing these huge parties, where there was no violence, no trouble, no nothing. The reason there was no violence and no trouble was because we never made the concerts hierarchical—there was never one stage, there were multiple stages. If you throw a party for the summer solstice, everyone is equal under the sun, so what's to fight about? You can be exactly who you want to be. You're not taking anything away from anybody.

Peter and I both said the Rolling Stones are not an occasion for a party. There will be one stage, the Stones will own it, and everyone else will be the audience. That's not the spirit of San Francisco. We'll have a party, we'll have six stages, and the Rolling Stones can have one of them. We'll give everybody redwood trees to plant and yards of silk and this and that, and come up with a party. And Sam said, "Oh, no, we can't do that for the Rolling Stones."

We also knew by that time that the Rolling Stones were going to make a documentary, so it's not a free concert.[‡] The audience was going to be extras. So free doesn't mean there's no admission ticket. Free means the audience are co-creators of the event. You don't need security. You only need security when there's a treasured space that has to be kept clear of everybody else. So the idea of bringing in the Hells

---

[*]   After Altamont, Sam Cutler left the Rolling Stones and began working as the Grateful Dead's tour manager.

[†]   Peter Berg, Peter Coyote, and Emmett Grogan cofounded the San Francisco improv and radical community action group called the Diggers. They were fixtures in San Francisco's Haight-Ashbury hippie scene in the mid- to late sixties.

[‡]   Albert and David Maysles made a documentary, *Gimme Shelter*, about the last weeks of the Rolling Stones' 1969 tour, which ended with the Altamont Free Concert in Northern California.

Billed as "the Woodstock of the West," the Altamont Speedway Free Festival in Alameda County, California, drew three hundred thousand fans on December 6, 1969, to see Santana, Jefferson Airplane, the Flying Burrito Brothers, Crosby, Stills, Nash & Young, and the Rolling Stones.
PHOTOGRAPH BY ROBERT ALTMAN.

Angels[*] was a terrible mistake. We said, wrong place, wrong time, there's going to be trouble, and none of us went, and there was trouble.

GREIL MARCUS (*Rolling Stone* music critic)

I went to Altamont, December 6, with a couple of friends, but I went there as a *Rolling Stone* writer, to write about it. We drove to the Altamont Speedway in Northern California and got there with no problem. Somehow we missed all of these horrible traffic jams. We knew that the Hells Angels were going to be there providing security. You could tell from the minute you got there—it was quite early, nine in the morning—that the crowd was angry, unfriendly, and pushy. Nobody made room for you— and that was before the Hells Angels started beating people up.

There was this big Hispanic guy, probably six four, very fat, and he

---

[*]   The Hells Angels were a motorcycle gang with a violent, outlaw history who rode Harley-Davidsons and were affiliated with parts of the counterculture, and were sometimes used to provide security.

took off all his clothes and started dancing. This is right in front of the stage where I was sitting. And he was acting like, "Oh, we're all free, and I'm dancing to the music, and I'm full of enthusiasm," but people began to move away because he was trampling people. So the Hells Angels leaped out and started beating him, and they beat him to the ground, and kept beating him. The crowd just immediately clears this huge area. They finally drag him backstage and the crowd comes back like some gigantic insect colony. From that day on it was just ugly. And it was angry. And it was mean, and there were a lot of crazy fucked-up people there.

The Hells Angels killed Meredith Hunter [who was black], because he was right at the front of the stage with his white girlfriend, and they didn't like that, and they jumped off the stage and started chasing him and beating him. He was stabbed before he pulled a gun out, but he did pull a gun.

MICHAEL RANDALL (Brotherhood of Eternal Love acid dealer)

I was at Altamont. I left before all that happened. You could've been there and not known it was going on. It was really huge, three hundred thou-

The Rolling Stones (lead singer Mick Jagger, left) stopped playing "Under My Thumb" when the Hells Angels, who were providing security for the concert, stabbed Meredith Hunter to death.

PHOTOGRAPH BY ROBERT ALTMAN.

sand people. I was there for the music, but I had a meeting that I had to go to and one hundred and twenty million doses of acid to sell all over America, so I was busy.

GREIL MARCUS

For all of us involved, we understood it as the end of something, as this overwhelmingly symbolic end of so much that we had believed in and invested ourselves in. And it just so happened that the Rolling Stones had put out an album at that time, *Let It Bleed,* and the album was about the end of the sixties. That was its explicit subject. "You Can't Always Get What You Want"—what an ultimate anti-sixties thing to say. That song and "Gimme Shelter" were about the moral collapse of the counterculture, just to put it in a nutshell.

When they were playing "Gimme Shelter" at Altamont, which was in the middle of their set, I was pushed off the stage, and later I was on top of the VW van behind the stage when the van collapsed. I could tell that something terrible was happening, because you heard screaming, and you heard Keith Richards berating the Angels, and Mick Jagger pleading with them. I said, "The hell with it," and I left. I started walking away in the dark to go back to my car. At one point I tripped, because it was pitch dark. I was lying on the ground and I could hear them playing "Gimme Shelter," which at that point I'd heard on the record, and had been overwhelmed by. I heard them playing it and I thought I'd never heard anything sound as good as this sounds. It was so powerful.

> *Oh, a storm is threat'ning*
> *My very life today*

I went back to my car, where I found my radio had been stolen. People believed they were moral and high-minded. People believed that they had somehow escaped the endemic moral, political, and economic corruption of American society, and they found out that day that that wasn't true.

JOHN HARTMANN
(music agent, manager)

It was sort of like the funeral where they buried King Hippie. Altamont was a big damaging blow to the hippie peace and love ethic. This wasn't peace and love, this was violence and death. The Stones' image was as bad boys, not good boys like the Beatles. The Beatles, who started out dirty, became clean in the minds of the public. With the Stones, the whole thing was about the devil, and cross-dressing, and everything that was taboo, you could see manifested in various songs like "Sympathy for the Devil." So they were the bad boys; they made a huge mistake, because they got the Hells Angels to be the security for Altamont.

GREIL MARCUS

It was probably the worst day of my life in a lot of ways. When it was over, we had a meeting at *Rolling Stone* among those of us who had been there, and we thought, this was so awful, that we shouldn't even dignify it by covering it. Jann [Wenner] said, "No, we're going to cover this from top to bottom. We're going to use every resource we have and we're going to lay the blame." The whole issue was devoted to Altamont as this day of calamity, horror, and bad faith on the part of all different kinds of people.

MID–DECEMBER, NEW YORK, CHICAGO: SDS

MARK RUDD

I was one of the people who implemented the closing of the SDS New York regional office and the closing of the national office. That decision was made in conjunction with the decision to go underground. Now I consider the closing down of those SDS national and regional offices to be the largest single political error that I've ever made.

CATHY WILKERSON

I remember being at the SDS national office in Chicago when the cops were lined up outside. We called the University of Wisconsin, who kept an archive on SDS, and said, "Do you want the remaining papers?" And they came down at the drop of a hat with a van and literally shoveled the papers off the floor into the van, because the [SDS] office had been trashed by the cops.

MARK RUDD

I had a Volkswagen van, and I remember picking up the mailing addresses for the whole New York region; they were in a couple of big boxes. We had a loft on 131 Prince Street that somebody had given us, and Ornette Coleman was practicing the saxophone above us. I remember around the end of December picking up these mailing stencils and taking them with Ted Gold to the West Street Pier, at the end of Fourteenth Street, and dumping them into the garbage barge that was parked there. That was the end of SDS. If I had been an FBI agent, I couldn't have done it better.

BERNARDINE DOHRN

We felt a lot of despair, and that's always unhealthy—it's a human feeling, obviously, but it's also politically very unhealthy. We felt the holidays taking over—Christmas lights by Thanksgiving, and people going about their lives as if bombs weren't raining on the Vietnamese—was unspeakable. And everything that captured the public mind—Nixon's stupid stuff and ultimately the Charles Manson* murders—things that obsessed people were just sideshows and circuses. We had to find a way to bring peo-

---

*   Charles Manson, a mentally disturbed musician who created a small cult called the Manson Family, was responsible for nine grisly murders committed in Los Angeles in July and early August of 1969, the most famous one being Sharon Tate, the pregnant wife of director Roman Polanski. Manson and his accomplices were indicted for the Tate and other murders in December 1969. The high-profile trial began in Los Angeles in June 1970.

ple's attention back to the crisis of our time, which in our mind was the Vietnamese struggle and the black freedom movement.

By the time of Flint, a lot had happened. The Days of Rage had happened. We had had lots of arrests, and lots of charges against us. The [Chicago Seven] conspiracy trial was ending, and SDS as such didn't exist. There was still a campus movement around the country, and a huge antiwar movement, but there was also a growing military assault against Vietnam, and against Laos and Cambodia, and Fred Hampton had been assassinated. All of that was right before Flint.

DECEMBER 27, FLINT, MICHIGAN: NATIONAL WAR COUNCIL

MARK RUDD

The War Council meeting in Flint, Michigan, December 27–31, was kind of a strange hybrid, because on the one hand it was the continuation of an SDS tradition, which was bringing people together a few times a year for conferences and conventions. SDS typically had three of them. And this was the same kind of thing. But we called it the National War Council meeting and sent out pamphlets calling it a "wargasm." And it was more like a rally. It also was crazy because it was obviously infiltrated by many, many undercover cops.

Flint was insanity. The venue was a dilapidated dance hall in the black neighborhood. There was a giant cardboard machine gun, and pictures of Che [Guevara] and Fred Hampton all over the walls, and orgiastic dancing to Sly and the Family Stone, but we made up our lyrics. "Che vive, viva Che! Che vive, viva Che." Sly and the Family Stone were very cool.*

---

*   Sly and the Family Stone, who played at Woodstock, was a racially integrated soul/funk band that created an original blend of the black Motown and San Francisco white psychedelic sound. The band released the album *Stand!* in May 1969; it sold three million copies and is considered one of the most successful albums of the sixties. The single "Stand!" reached number three on the charts in 1969. "Sly was less interested in crossing racial musical lines than in

Stand
In the end you'll still be you
One that's done all the things you set out to do
Stand
There's a cross for you to bear
Things to go through if you're going anywhere
Stand
For the things you know are right
It's the truth that the truth makes them so uptight
Stand
All the things you want are real
You have you to complete and there is no deal
Stand, stand, stand
Stand, stand, stand

TOM HAYDEN (founder, SDS)

The meeting in Flint was in late December, just a month and a half before the [Chicago Seven] trial ended. I went there and taught a karate class. But frankly, I thought it was spooky. I think people might've been on speed—it could be that simple. They were already in another world. The inner group had made a decision to go underground; they weren't sharing it.

I was feeling very bourgeois. I was with my girlfriend, and some other couple, and a kid might've been with us. It was no place for couples. They had smashed monogamy, which was a way of giving yourself to the revolution. Monogamy was a form of possessive individualism to be abandoned.

If I had been footloose and not on trial, it might've been seen slightly different. If I hadn't been in a relationship where there was a small child at stake, it might've been different. I think it's more that I was older, and I had this residual foundation of the early sixties in my soul, which the

---

tearing them up," wrote Greil Marcus in *Mystery Train: Images of America in Rock 'n' Roll Music* (New York: E. P. Dutton, 1975), p. 65.

Weathermen were dismissive of. My rock foundation was the early sixties. Theirs was the mid to late sixties. It doesn't sound chronologically like it's much distance in time, but it's an eternity. If you were a college freshman in '64 as opposed to a freshman in '57, that's an eternity. The only thing I can add, now that I look back on it, was that I was becoming out of touch. I mean, these people were having flat-out naked, wild orgies as a political act.

MARK RUDD

I've always respected and adored Tom Hayden, and I was really very, very pleased that he came to Flint. You have to understand that from 1962 to 1969, SDS leadership had gone through three generations in seven years. I'd be of the last generation, and Tom being of the first. I think he was the only person there from that first generation.

Tom Hayden has a very clear view of it. He says in one of his essays, as the violence escalated in Vietnam, the violence at home escalated in response. That's it, that's a simple way to look at it, and I agree with him.

My FBI files report has me saying at Flint, "We are going to meet and map plans to avenge the deaths of Fred Hampton and Mark Clark." My own madness slipped out of my mouth when I said, "It's a wonderful feeling to kill a pig or blow up a building."

BILL AYERS (blog, March 3, 2008)

Bernardine was reported to have said in the middle of a speech at an SDS meeting in Flint, Michigan, "Dig it! First they killed those pigs and then they put a fork in their bellies. Wild!" I didn't hear that exactly, but words that were close enough I guess. Her speech was focused on the murder just days earlier of our friend Fred Hampton, the Black Panther leader, a murder we were certain— although we didn't know it yet—was part of a larger government plot, the Gestapo-like tactics of an emerging police state. She linked Fred's murder to the murders of other Panthers around the country, to the assassinations of Malcolm X and Patrice Lumumba, the CIA attempts on Fidel's life, and then to the ongoing terror in Vietnam. "This is the state of the world," she cried. "This is what screams out for our attention and our response. And what do we find in our newspapers? A sick fascination with a story that has it all: a racist psycho, a killer cult, and a chorus line of Hollywood bodies. Dig it! . . ." So I heard it partly as political talk, agitated and inflamed and full of rhetorical overkill, and partly as a joke, stupid perhaps, tasteless, but a joke nonetheless—and Hunter Thompson for one, was making much more excessive, and funnier, jokes about Charles Manson then, and so was Richard Pryor.

ROBIN MORGAN (radical feminist)

When I was noticeably pregnant with Blake, I ran into Bernardine. This was right around the time when she made the pronouncement about Sharon Tate—that the Manson people stuck a fork in her belly after they killed her, adding, "Wasn't that cool?" I was pregnant and she said, "Is that a pig child?" And I said, "You mean is the father white?" Because if the father was black then the child was acceptable. "As a matter of fact, as it turns out the father is white," I said. And she said, "So why are you having it?" I said, "What would you have me do, abort a planned, wanted child? Or perhaps I should just stick it in a trash can when it's born." She said, "Now, that would be a good idea." So, frankly, I have never quite forgiven Bernardine, despite her claims of having revised her virulent anti-feminist politics.

BERNARDINE DOHRN

I feel self-critical about those days. I think that that's the period of time when I feel like the metaphor of bringing the war home took over my language, and the way that I thought about the movement. I can understand that, because I feel like we had this fierce sense that somebody had to stand up and object to the war, and the bullets were flying. People were dying in the thousands every week in Vietnam and Southeast Asia, and were being assassinated at home. So that part I can understand, but obviously I feel now that the language of war, even revolutionary war, made us harsh, made me harsh; and made me speak about war without doing everything to avoid it without recognizing the horror and the harm; and how it turns people, even people who are fighting for freedom, into something else. So I think that period was harsh.

I have vivid memories of that December: the horror of people going shopping, and Christmas bells. You know how in an election cycle like this you can get really cynical about the American people. We can't talk about the world? We can't be part of the world? We can't talk about the environment? That was the feeling times a thousand, because of having the images of war on TV, and having the vets coming home, and knowing from the Vietnamese what the cost was on the ground.

MARK RUDD

The decision was made at Flint that I would step out of the Weather Bureau. I was suffering enormous self-doubt. I didn't question the rightness of our strategy or of our method, but I questioned my ability to do it. I knew I was posing and it didn't feel right, and so I experienced this as depression. The other members of the Weather Bureau, which was the leadership of the Weatherman faction of SDS, could see that I was flagging, I was wavering. So, by mutual agreement, we agreed I would demote myself out of the top leadership, down into what you might call a regional leadership position.

Also one of the craziest things that happened was after Flint, I went to Ann Arbor and shacked up with a girlfriend of mine, and we both did acid for the first time. You can imagine what that was like—total paranoia, plus the feelings of exhilaration around psychedelics. I took my first acid trip on December 31, 1969, and took my last acid trip on December 31, 1970, and in between I became a fugitive.

I spent the month of January traveling around the country, trying to recruit people in the organization to go underground. By the time that I got to New York in February, I was still aboveground, and I was still using my own ID. I still had contact with my parents and old friends, and was using regular telephones. But we set up a series of houses in Manhattan that were completely clandestine. We rented apartments under clandestine names and we began living there and operating. And that included an armed robbery to finance the operation.

There were circles of support. And it involved some people being willing and able to go underground and other people wanting to help. It's not as if there was a clear line between those in the organization and those outside the organization. There were sort of circles of agreement and of support. And I suspect that lawyers felt maybe that they should have been on the front lines but their skill kept them doing legal stuff. We were getting money from wherever we could get money. It wouldn't matter. We'd get it from our parents; we'd get it from anybody who had money.

TOM HAYDEN

As my day job, I was working inside the system, which the Weathermen considered wrong, and they thought I should go underground with them. I wouldn't do that because I didn't feel that I fit in with them. However, I didn't know if they were right or wrong. This is what was so existential about it. Maybe a police state was coming. Certainly towards the Panthers it seemed to be coming. The Berrigan brothers had gone underground. There were different undergrounds. There was a Catholic underground against the draft. There were Panther undergrounds. There were draft resistance undergrounds. Drug dealer undergrounds, marijuana undergrounds. All across America, a lot of people were breaking one law or another. So it wasn't a completely strange idea.

So in that sense, I took seriously the Weathermen analysis of repression and I thought it was legitimate, but I wasn't going to do it. I knew all sides of the debate but I wasn't leaving my legal defense work in the court [at the Chicago Seven trial]. And I wasn't giving up on the idea of persuading public opinion, or persuading an appellate judge. It could be that

I was trained all my life to use words, and to abandon words for guns just didn't seem the best use of my talents.

BRIAN FLANAGAN

In December of '69 we started dumping the collectives, and starting other collectives that were doing violent stuff. The mass collectives that were living openly in apartments we dumped and started going into safe houses and doing arson and various low-level bombings. All of the big names went underground.

DECEMBER 27, MADISON, WISCONSIN: CHRISTMAS BOMBINGS

KARL ARMSTRONG

It was winter break, so there was no one on campus. I felt like I was out there in the emotional wilderness. I had reached an emotional low point, where I said, "I really have to act." The armory was half a block away from where I was living, and half of the building was devoted to ROTC. There had been lots of demonstrations at the armory. First of all, I thought it was a beautiful building. I played basketball there. But I realized what it meant symbolically. I was of very mixed mind about it. It went against my grain to destroy property, but I knew that the symbolism was really important.

On December 27, 1969, at two o'clock in the morning, I walked up to the building, threw a jar of gasoline in, and burned the building. Basically it was my declaration of war. I was now at war with the United States. To me it was laughable: It felt like puny acts against the war machine. But it was important, because this was a way of committing myself. After the first act I said, "There's no turning back." It was just a matter of marshaling resources, picking the right targets, and trying to be smart. I truly felt out there, and yet, in another sense, I felt really comfortable because I was finally active.

WISCONSIN STATE JOURNAL,

DECEMBER 29, 1969 (front page)

FIREBOMBS DAMAGE UW
ROTC BUILDING

Firebombs were thrown through three windows of the ROTC building at Linden and Babcock Dr. on the University of Wisconsin campus early Sunday, damaging several desks and scorching the ceiling of a lecture hall.

No one was injured.

KARL ARMSTRONG

After the firebombing of the armory, I talked to my brother Dwight and I said, "I'd like to do an aerial bombing of the Badger ordnance plant."* And he said, "Are you crazy? What are you talking about?" And I said, "Well, remember the firebombing of the ROTC building a couple of nights ago? That was me." I said I thought a bombing of the Badger ordnance plant on New Year's Eve would be the perfect symbolic bombing against the war. The Badger ordnance plant was producing the bulk of the rocket powder used in Vietnam. It was a huge plant. I picked New Year's Eve for the symbolic starting the New Year. I thought that symbolically it was the time to do it.

My brother had been a gas jockey at the airport, so he did the flying. We went to Morey Airport and we pulled an ROTC training plane out of the hangar. Dwight wasn't a certified pilot, and he had never flown at night before. Lynn, my girlfriend, Dwight, and I loaded up a big metal ashtray from the fraternity house and a couple of mayonnaise bottles filled with ammonium nitrate. I knew about bombs from the *Encyclopaedia Britannica*. But we didn't have a detonator. So I knew they probably wouldn't go off. The symbolic act seemed more important than the actual damage,

---

* The Badger Army Ammunition Plant, or Badger Ordnance Works, in Baraboo, Wisconsin, made ammunition during World War II and the Korean and Vietnam wars. During World War II it was the largest munitions factory in the world.

because if the bombs did go off, we'd probably have been blown out of the air. We followed the road up to the Badger ordnance plant, and we could see Lynn from the air as she was going in to make the phone call to warn them at the plant that we were going to bomb it in protest of the Vietnam War. I didn't think anyone would be working there because it was New Year's Eve.

We flew over in a snowstorm and I dropped one of the bombs out. I told my brother, "I don't think I hit anything except snow. You have to go a lot lower." And he said, "If we go any lower, and that bomb goes off, we are dead ducks." And I said, "You're going to have to go lower if we're going to hit anything." So we made another pass, and by that point I was thinking, Well, it's just symbolic anyway. And I just dumped the bombs out of the door as we flew over the fuel tanks.

We landed at the airport outside of Prairie du Sac, left the plane in the middle of the runway, and ran to the car with Lynn to go back to Madison. When we got back to Madison, I thought, Maybe we should call the newspapers and tell them what we did. So I called the *State Journal* and I said, "I just firebombed the Badger ordnance plant." And the guy says something like, "Yeah, yeah. And what's your name, please?" And I said, "No, we firebombed the Badger ordnance plant from the air." Then I remember calling *The Daily Cardinal* and I believe the *Kaleidoscope,* the two student newspapers, and told them the bombing was because of the Vietnam War. Basically I wanted to lock into people's minds that we were acting like Nazi Germany. That this aerial bomb was symbolic of the Allies' bombing of munitions plants in Germany. It was my way of bringing the war home, so people would be able to see it in a different light.

BILL DYSON (FBI agent)

These leads start coming in and the supposition then was "This guy must have been a Vietnam pilot, because he landed with the wind!" I mean, there's a snowstorm, he comes in, and he lands the wrong way. And it was like, "Oh my God, this guy stole the plane, and he was actually able to land it? He must be really a tremendous pilot!" And hell, the guy didn't have a license, and it was miraculous that he was able to land the plane that way. They dropped the fuel. I don't know where the bombs went. They had no detonator. Maybe it was the Weathermen, we didn't know.*

STEVE REINER (editor of *The Daily Cardinal*)

After the Christmas bombings by what we would later call the "New Year's Gang," there was a debate at the *Cardinal* about the difference between property damage and personal damage. I think the fact that no one was hurt and that these episodes all seemed to be calculated to destroy property, but not to harm people, helped us rationalize it. We made a distinction between political sabotage and terrorism. I think it was obvious that these guys never intended to hurt anybody. We rationalized it because the levels of frustration, anger, and exasperation that were welling up in all of us had reached a crescendo. We rationalized it because no one was hurt.

This is what I wrote in an editorial: "And if acts such as those committed in the last few days are needed to strike fear into the bodies of once fearless men and rid this campus once and for all of repressive and deadly ideas and institutions, then so be it." It was the line "then so be it" that I regret writing now. I don't really regret anything else in the editorial. I think saying that that kind of manifestation is inevitable is absolutely correct. And I think it was. It's easy to say that it's inevitable after it happens. But it was inevitable.

---

*   Armstrong and the New Year's Gang didn't know the Weathermen and were acting independently, but according to FBI informant Larry Grathwohl, Bill Ayers sent a cell of Weathermen to Madison to try to make contact with the New Year's Gang and scout out more locations in Madison to bomb in February 1970, but the plan was scrapped after events that occurred on March 6. See Larry Grathwohl, *Bringing Down America* (New Rochelle, NY: Arlington House, 1976), p. 159.

CHAPTER 15

WAR CRIMES

(January–April 1970)

The country doesn't know it yet, but it has created a monster, a monster in the form of millions of men who have been taught to deal and to trade in violence, and who are given the chance to die for the biggest nothing in history; men who have returned with a sense of anger and a sense of betrayal which no one has yet grasped.

—LIEUTENANT JOHN KERRY,
TESTIMONY BEFORE U.S. SENATE
COMMITTEE ON FOREIGN
RELATIONS, April 23, 1971

ON DECEMBER 5, 1969, *LIFE* MAGAZINE PUBLISHED A COVER story about the My Lai massacre with graphic color photographs taken by army photographer Sergeant Ron Haeberle, who had witnessed the extermination of the village. Haeberle took photos with his army-issue black-and-white camera and with his personal color camera. After he was discharged, Haeberle sold his color photographs to *Life*. Haeberle's images of piles of bodies of women and small children hit newsstands all over America soon after the publication of Seymour Hersh's vivid reporting of the massacre. The collective force of these stories galvanized an increasingly violent and radical resistance to the war.

The Pentagon called My Lai an aberration. It was the only civilian massacre recorded by an official photographer, but Vietnam veterans recently home from the war were beginning to disclose that the systematic slaughter of civilians was part of an unofficial "kill anything that moves" policy. This coincided with the objective to generate high enemy body counts on battlegrounds where American soldiers could not distinguish between villagers and enemy forces. A secret Pentagon task force, the Vietnam War Crimes Working Group, later unearthed by author Nick Turse, chronicled three hundred incidents of massacres, rapes, torture, mutilations, and other atrocities similar to My Lai. Of the estimated three million Vietnamese war casualties, two million were civilians.

TOD ENSIGN (GI antiwar activist)

When I first read the My Lai story, it had a big impression. I thought, Damn, this is big. This is big. This just breaks the whole mythology of the war open. The Pentagon responded to the furor over the atrocity by claiming it to be an isolated incident. Vice President Spiro Agnew blamed the incident on a few "bad apples" who should be rooted out and punished. Only the Tet Offensive did more to shake the public's faith in the American military than the revelations about My Lai. The disclosure lent strong support to the antiwar movement's claim that we were waging a genocidal war against the Vietnamese people.

I went to law school at Wayne State in Detroit from 1963 to 1966. Those years are relevant because they're the peak Vietnam War years, and I was avoiding the draft. But when I got out of law school, I realized I still had five months to avoid draft eligibility. So I came to New York and in a year I got an LLM from NYU Law School. And that got me out of Vietnam, thank God.

About two weeks after the My Lai story broke, my friend and fellow activist Jeremy Rifkin told me about this guy Ralph Schoenman, who was the secretary to English pacifist Lord Bertrand Russell. In reaction to My Lai, Schoenman called for a Citizens' Commission of Inquiry into U.S. war crimes in Vietnam. Schoenman had organized the Bertrand Russell International War Crimes Tribunal in 1967 in Stockholm, Sweden, and Roskilde, Denmark, which was the first time American veterans testified about Vietnam War crimes. The first three veterans to testify were Peter Martinsen, David Tuck, and Donald Duncan, and their eyewitness testimony of wanton killing and torture reportedly had a powerful impact on many illustrious tribunal members who attended, like Jean-Paul Sartre, James Baldwin, and Simone de Beauvoir.

The hearings received wide attention in Europe but were largely ignored by the American media. *The New York Times* did, however, find the space to print an editorial lambasting the tribunal as a kangaroo court, which lacked any legal or moral authority. We had read about the tribunals in the leftist newspaper *The Guardian*. They covered the Bertrand Russell Tribunal extensively. So I was impressed with Russell, who was in his late eighties at the time. I really liked the fact that despite his age and his respectability and his esteem he said, "This must be done."

JANE FONDA (actor, peace activist)

One of my close friends in Paris was Simone Signoret, who was probably the most famous French actress at the time. She was married to Yves Montand. She took me to antiwar rallies to hear Simone de Beauvoir and Jean-Paul Sartre speak. I was becoming really uncomfortable about being an American, living in Paris. I didn't want to be in France, talking against the war, because I also felt kind of defensive. Simone had been one of the people who had stood in front of trains during the French-Indochinese conflict. She was very active against the French war in Indochina, and she had been a member of the French Resistance when she was very young, during the Second World War. She helped me understand the history of the Vietnam War.

TOD ENSIGN

Ralph Schoenman said that he wanted to hold hearings in this country to show that soldiers at the low ranks are not responsible for policies and that My Lai was the logical conclusion of "search and destroy" and other policies of the Vietnam War that were conceived in Washington. We knew that colonels, generals, secretaries of defense were responsible for war crimes, not some fucking lonely jackass soldier from Kansas who had never even seen an Asian person before.

So Jeremy and I, we went to see Ralph. He had an office down on Twentieth and Fifth Ave—at that time it was called the Movement Building, 156 Fifth Avenue. The ACLU was in there, Workers World [Party], a bunch of groups were in there. We said to Ralph, "Look, we're interested in what you're proposing. How can we work with you?" And he said, "Well, I need a lot of money to do that." And we said, "We're from the New Left; we don't need money. We'll do it." And he believed us.

I said, "We believe this is everywhere, in every city; let's just pick cities and go out and find vets who will testify." We saw it as a way of organizing veterans—coming together, speaking out, taking action against their own victimization. We also thought that most combat veterans would feel threatened and angered by the Pentagon's insistence that war crimes were caused by aberrant or sadistic GIs—rather than the logical consequences of military policies designed at the highest levels of the command.

At that time, there were only two national veterans groups that were antiwar—the Vietnam Veterans Against the War, then headquartered in New York City, and the Chicago-based Vets for Peace. Both groups were quite small, with VVAW consisting of only a few active members and no regular staff.

JAN BARRY (founder, Vietnam Veterans Against the War)

After Sy Hersh's series of My Lai stories were published, I started getting phone calls from journalists who knew me from the days when I worked for the *Bergen Record* and knew I was active with the Vietnam Veterans Against the War, and they said, "Tell me your worst atrocity stories." I said, "That's not what this is about." This wasn't just an individual lieutenant going amok. This is an unwritten policy. In fact, we'd been trying to speak about this, but nobody wanted to hear it.

Starting from the time that I was in Vietnam in late 1962, and going into early 1963, we were told that there were free-fire zones in which anything that moved could be killed. I went to West Point and studied military history. You can't find a policy like that in World War II. They didn't arrive on D-Day in France and were told, "There's a huge area of France where you can kill anything that moves—the farmers, the people in their homes." Furthermore, it's a violation of various international laws to target civilians. But that was a policy that was there when I arrived in Vietnam.

When the My Lai revelation came out, it clicked for an awful lot of Vietnam veterans that this was the larger version of smaller things that just went on on an almost daily basis. The civilians had become the targets in all kinds of ways. I got involved in helping to start VVAW because in early 1967 I read something in *The New York Times* about how yet again we'd bombed a friendly village. I just blew up—you can't make this mistake over and over and over again. It reminded me of the very first statement that I heard the first night I got into a chow line when I arrived in Vietnam, at Tan Son Nhut, which is the air base next to Saigon. It was December 1962, and I get into line, and there are helicopter crews coming back from a mission, and these two guys in line next to me are bragging about how they had just attacked a village and created some more Viet Cong.

That was part of the policy when we were there in the early sixties—to start a war, to stir up somebody to fight us, so that we could say, "There's a war going on," because they're shooting back at us. And no matter how many times I mentioned this previously when I spoke to various audiences, people would say, "American boys don't do things like that."

We were asked to speak at all kinds of teach-ins, and we did our research. We insisted everybody speaking on behalf of VVAW in the early days learn about the Geneva Accords of 1956. Now we could start putting My Lai into a larger context, which was that we had utter contempt for the people who we were supposed to save and protect. Since we couldn't find the army we were fighting against, because it was guerrilla warfare, the people who were in sight were the ones who took the brunt. Their villages got attacked, and they got attacked if they were working in their fields, they got attacked if they were going to market on a road. In many cases they were deliberately driven to these hamlets—they were called strategic hamlets—and basically surrounded by barbed wire. They were prison camps.

Initially, people in the peace movement were harassing Vietnam vets.

When I started speaking to peace groups I said, "Don't rush up to some guy in uniform and start calling him a baby killer, whether or not he was participating in things that ended up with babies being killed. If you want to get him on your side to protest the war, you don't rush right up and immediately accuse him of being a war criminal."*

MICHAEL UHL (veteran antiwar activist)

My Lai opened a gate for us to mobilize within the antiwar movement. I don't think you could ever suggest that My Lai wasn't a particularly vile expression of all of those military policies that came together at that one particular moment. It's just that all those policies like search and destroy and forced relocations were being acted out—in most cases—on a less grand scale. There were a couple of other large massacres like that, but it was more the small, everyday atrocities. That's what we were trying to show, the overall pattern of the war. We could not allow My Lai to become just a singular isolated event and we couldn't allow Calley to become the person that somehow took the blame, had to fall on his sword or had to be pushed on his sword, when we should be indicting the architects and managers of the war as the true criminals.

I volunteered to serve in Vietnam and was a first lieutenant in the Counterintelligence Corps attached to the Eleventh Infantry from November '68 to April '69. I was evacuated from Vietnam because I had tuberculosis and I was in Valley Forge Army Hospital for four months, where my anger was sizzling to the point where I got in trouble and got kicked out of the army hospital. I was quietly, honorably medically discharged and sent to the VA in Manhattan.

JANE FONDA

In 1969, as my husband [the French film director Roger Vadim] was finishing editing *Barbarella,* I began to hear from American resisters who

---

* Vietnam Veterans Against the War (VVAW) made its first public appearance in April 1967 when Jan Barry and others carried a banner at a giant antiwar march led by Dr. Martin Luther King, Jr., in New York City.

had left the army in Vietnam and were living in Paris. These had been active-duty servicemen, and they were looking for American expats who could help them with money, doctors, dentists, clothing, stuff like that. And I did. I met with them frequently, and gave them money, and gave them Vadim's old clothes. Interestingly enough, I didn't find out until later, many of them were housed at the farm of the sculptor Alexander Calder.

All they wanted to talk about was what was happening in Vietnam. My father [Henry Fonda] had fought in the Second World War, where he got a Bronze Star. I felt that if our troops were fighting someplace, then we were on the side of the angels. So it was very hard for me to believe what I was hearing. Free-fire zones, torture, internment camps where people were rounded up and put into prison. The way we treated the Vietnamese belied everything I thought about my country. When I was having a hard time believing what they were telling me, they said, "Here, read this." And they gave me a book called *The Village of Ben Suc,* by Jonathan Schell.* I was one person before I read it, and I was another person after I finished. And that was when I decided I'm going to leave France and move back to the States. That was the beginning of my outrage. The more staunchly patriotic you are, when you realize that your country has betrayed your belief in it, you become angrier than most other people who don't care one way or the other. I was beside myself.

MICHAEL UHL

As soon as I arrived in Manhattan, I started looking for the movement. I was looking for the vets. I was reading the radical underground papers. I was looking for the opposition. So, by the time I walked into the NYU Law School auditorium to attend an antiwar teach-in calling for a Citi-

---

*   Published in 1967, *The Village of Ben Suc,* a classic of Vietnam War literature and journalism, describes in close, chilling detail the American military's forced removal of Ben Suc's 3,500 residents into a refugee camp and the physical annihilation of the village. Written by twenty-four-year-old Jonathan Schell, *The Village of Ben Suc* was first published by *The New Yorker* on July 15, 1967, taking up the entire magazine.

zens' Commission of Inquiry [CCI] to document the truth about war crimes in Vietnam, I had already become politicized. I was just looking for a structure in which I could become active.

By '69 and '70 the counterculture and the New Left had come together to create this mass youth rebellion. For example, the Gray Line bus service used to come down to the East Village as part of the tour of New York City. All of these straight people were sitting in the Gray Line bus driving down to St. Mark's Place and the tour guide would be giving his spiel about what folks were seeing—it was like being on safari. They were pointing out all the hippies on the street, and if I was walking down St. Mark's that day, I would not have been distinguishable from any apolitical hippie. I wore the same uniform: yellow and blue striped bell-bottom jeans and a tie-dye long underwear shirt. My hair was very long and I had a bushy mustache. I looked like any hippie.

But we were also political zealots, and I don't regret that for a moment. We were passionately opposed not only to the war, but to the entire system. We had all become instant revolutionaries, instant socialists. We studied the literature, we had study and discussion groups, we had meetings where people who were extraordinarily articulate and intelligent would debate the different positions on the nature of the Soviet state—very esoteric stuff.

So in January, at the Citizens' Commission of Inquiry teach-in at NYU Law School, Jan Barry and another activist got up and made their pitch to try to identify any Vietnam veterans in the audience, and they used the term *war crimes*. That was the moment that clicked for me. I had formed this strong consciousness in Vietnam that this war was a war waged against a civilian population, not against combatants, and I had witnessed atrocities. I went up afterwards and introduced myself to Jan. That was the beginning of my association with CCI.

JAN BARRY

I was speaking at NYU Law School and Michael Uhl comes over to me. I remember because he was very intense. He was studying linguistics, and he mentioned studying Noam Chomsky and I didn't even know who

Chomsky was.* But we got into this conversation, which, I guess, convinced him that this is something he should look further into. This really resonated with him, and shortly afterwards he decided he wanted to get involved with CCI.

At any rate, I was impressed by the fact that very quickly there was this professional network taking this extremely seriously. They were people who could speak from direct experience. Part of my initial speaking was to try to convince other veterans who had more direct experiences than I did to talk about something they had probably never talked about before. Previously, we couldn't get an audience. Nobody wanted to hear about this, but now everybody wanted to hear the latest atrocity story. It wasn't that I could one-up you with an atrocity story, but the message was this is what we are doing as a pattern.

MICHAEL UHL

The next morning Jeremy Rifkin showed up in my apartment to take my testimony with his reel-to-reel tape recorder, his Samsonite briefcase, and his safari hat. Those were his trademarks at the time. I was living on Waverly Place, and we went around the corner to a coffee shop. He set up this huge tape recorder on the table and I told him my stories.

I was a team leader of an intelligence team that was assigned to the Eleventh Infantry, was part of that Americal Division. It was located in Duc Pho, which is in the southern part of I Corps. This was an army brigade made up of several infantry battalions on the coast of the South China Sea and on the periphery of a district capital, in the province of Quang Ngai. This was a province that had been historically very militant during the period of French colonialism. Quang Ngai was still considered to be a place where the Viet Cong controlled the local hamlets, which in some ways explains the My Lai massacre. In other words, there was this sense among the commanders that they were in a very, very dangerous

---

* Noam Chomsky, a professor of linguistics at the Massachusetts Institute of Technology and left-wing political activist, is one of America's most prominent public intellectuals. The author of forty books, Chomsky is a constant critic of American foreign policy and was an early voice of protest against the Vietnam War.

area, where the enemy operated extensively if not freely. So, I think in that context there was this sense that we were at war with the entire Vietnamese population. So our infantry units operating in the field would round up all of these civilians and we treated them as guilty until proven innocent. In intelligence language we sought to classify them as civil defendants, so first they would have to be filtered through our interrogation unit.

They would be taken in and sat at desks with American GI interrogators and Vietnamese interpreters. To have called these individuals interpreters was really stretching the point, because none of them spoke very good English. So right from the start, you've got a substantial lack of communication going on. But interrogation is not about communication; it's about intimidation. So each one of these suspects would be abused to one degree or another.

I told Jeremy of this one incident the first day I arrived, when I was brought down and introduced to John Patton, who was the interrogation officer. He was showing me around and I'm watching these dinks, as we called them, being interrogated—being rapped on the head with pencils, and sort of jostled and screamed at by the Americans using their pidgin Vietnamese. So it's already an atmosphere that's tinged with a kind of racial shading.

Anyway, Patton is showing me around, and there's a trailer attached to this small building and inside there's a table with an army blanket on the table and a field telephone, and the wires are extending from the telephone because it's not hooked up to a telephone system; the wires are attached to the fingers of these victims. There was a young woman that was hooked up to this device and they're turning the crank and after a while, of course this woman is screaming and she immediately begins to menstruate—Patton and everybody was just shocked.

So there was the systematic use of torture in this unit and there were several individuals who would take this to the most extreme levels. Not the majority. But there were incidents where people were genuinely tortured, and there was this general atmosphere of constant abuse toward the Vietnamese.

JANE FONDA

One night at the home of Mike Nichols in Los Angeles, there was a screening party for Michelangelo Antonioni and his movie *Zabriskie Point*. I met Fred Gardner there, who was an antiwar activist, and he and I got to talking about the GIs. It was the first time that anyone told me that there was a movement of active-duty soldiers and veterans here in the United States called the GI movement and that people, including Fred Gardner, were creating these GI coffeehouses around the country where antiwar civilian activists would run them, and would have educational forums, conversations, libraries, where the soldiers could read literature about the war.

TOD ENSIGN

At this stage, the GI movement was gathering steam at the same time as the veterans' movement and they fed off each other. They also brought a new attitude to the antiwar movement about soldiers that was less critical and less judgmental. At the March on the Pentagon in 1967 there were signs calling vets "killers." We were against all that, of course. So we picked the right time. That's when it began to shift, as the vets came into the movement.

Jan Barry was a Vietnam vet who had struggled for years to get the VVAW off the ground and he gave me the name of this guy. We went together to see him in Brooklyn. He was disturbed but he was not changed by the war. He wasn't an antiwar-nik. He wasn't ashamed to show us the pictures of Vietnamese civilian heads lined up on the grass, with him standing over them with a rifle. I saw pictures like this many times. Often vets would be ashamed to show it to you. They wore heads—they wore pieces of eyes. They cut off a thumb, wore it around their neck on a lanyard. That's what happens. War dehumanizes people. He gave me a set of photos and I remember coming back and showing them to Jeremy and Michael, and they said, "Whoa, we can't use those!"

Word spread quickly about the Citizens' Commissions and within weeks a Veterans for Peace group in Baltimore agreed to cosponsor the first commission in Annapolis, Maryland, on March 11 and 12, 1970. This guy named Bob Johnson wanted to have his hearing. He'd been in Vietnam as a first lieutenant right out of West Point, and he saw a lot of shit.

JAN BARRY

There was a West Point graduate, Robert Johnson, who lived in the Annapolis area, and he organized the first hearing in Annapolis. It was a big deal because it was on the record in the American news media. It was a big deal because it's being treated with respect by institutions like a law school and a church.

MICHAEL UHL

A story in the Annapolis paper reported, "Photographs, motion pictures and slides of dead and maimed children were used last night to convey the horror of the Vietnamese War to an audience of 100 persons at the . . . Unitarian Church."

The *Baltimore Afro-American* quoted Peter Martinsen, a former U.S. Army prisoner of war interrogator: "One technique I saw used to get prisoners to talk was to wire them around the ears with field phones and 'ring' them up. Sometimes they would have burn marks on their ears from the electric shock."[*]

JANE FONDA

I was getting ready to drive across the country. I'd been living outside of the country for ten years, and I had to end up in New York to make a movie called *Klute*. I thought, Well, I'm just going to drive, because I don't know what this country is anymore. It was very clear to me that everything had changed. Fred Gardner suggested that I visit the GI coffeehouses.

---

[*]   Quoted from Michael Uhl's memoir, *Vietnam Awakening: My Journey from Combat to the Citizens' Commission of Inquiry on U.S. War Crimes in Vietnam* (Jefferson, NC: McFarland, 2007), p. 132.

The first one I visited was Fort Ord, in Monterey, California. I hadn't started on my trip yet, but I could just drive there and back from L.A. My friend Elisabeth Vailland came with me, and we drove to Fort Ord, and I mostly just listened. I'll never forget meeting this young kid—I mean he looked thirteen. When the conversation was winding down, he came over to me, and he got very close to my ear, because he couldn't speak above a whisper. It sounded like he was trying to tell me something that he had done to a child, and he was having a hard time getting the words out. I realized that he was totally traumatized. He wanted me to know, but he was having a hard time saying it. Some of the other guys were also talking about killing civilians. Some of them wanted to talk, and some of them had a hard time talking.

Before I left on the trip I was introduced to Donald Duncan, who had been a Green Beret in Vietnam. To be a Green Beret and become part of the GI movement meant that there were threats against his life all the time. It was very heavy being around him, because he was being followed. You could feel danger. It was weird feeling there's danger, and it's coming from my government. He was a dangerous voice for them, this Special Forces guy, who was talking about what was happening over there. Donald introduced me to Ken Cloke, who taught military law at Occidental College, and Ken gave me a crash course in the Uniform Code of Military Justice, and he would bring me piles of newspapers written by GIs that were part of the GI movement. Each coffeehouse had its own newspaper, and in these newspapers they talked about fragging, they talked about all the things that were being done to soldiers who in any way raised their voices.

TOD ENSIGN

I picked Springfield, Massachusetts, next, of all places. I just got on a bus and went up there and I found a guy right away who was one of our best witnesses ever. First I went to the local college. It wasn't hard to find people there—you could identify the vets immediately by what they looked like—long hair, incense, amulets, patchouli oil. It was a broad, cultural movement of women, blacks, Hispanics, whites, any sort mixed together. That's where I met David Bressam, but at first I didn't know how much he'd talk. I had to win his trust. His battalion was involved in a helicopter "turkey shoot" where they shot more than thirty people from their helicopter—mowed them down on orders from the commander. In the hearing, Bressam really spilled his guts. We organized a morning hearing with veterans, April 6.

This was the first commission that received national attention and both *The New York Times* and the Associated Press gave the allegations prominent coverage, and it taught us how the Pentagon would respond when unwanted publicity became too pervasive. Within hours the Pentagon sent criminal investigators to Bressam's home. They wanted to question him about the identities of those involved in the incident so, they claimed, they could prosecute any who might still be on active duty. Bressam also received a phone call from his former commander, who expressed fear that his army career might be ruined.

The Pentagon's tactic of seeking the identities of wrongdoers for possible prosecution presented us with a difficult problem. By taking the position that witnesses should not cooperate with military investigators whose goal was to prosecute low-ranking GIs, we came across as being indifferent to criminal conduct. Even though we continually explained that we wanted a thorough, independent investigation of policies conceived by our military and civilian leaders, I'm afraid that we were often viewed as moral agnostics, even by some in the peace movement.

During the next few months, we held successful Citizens' Commissions of Inquiries in Richmond, Virginia; New York City; Buffalo; Boston; Minneapolis; Los Angeles; and Portland, Oregon.

MICHAEL UHL

Whether we were in Duluth or Richmond or Philadelphia or Los Angeles, we were always with veterans who were pissed enough about the war that they were willing to go before TV cameras and reporters and tell them about what they had witnessed and experienced in Vietnam, and it always had to do with an atrocity—they were narrating their atrocities.

I gave my own testimony publicly on my twenty-sixth birthday. It was

April 14, 1970, and we had a joint press conference in New York and Los Angeles. I was nervous, but I just told my stories. My testimony appeared in articles in the New York papers. There was an article in *The New York Times, Daily News,* and *New York Post.* At CCI we were constantly having our success recognized by the fourth estate as legitimate news, and we just got tons and tons of publicity, adding to whatever else was going on in the antiwar movement. So right from the start, I could see that my two comrades, Jeremy [Rifkin] and Tod [Ensign], were natural publicists. Our primary technique in organizing these commissions all over the country was having guys step forward, and always making sure that to the best of our ability we were dealing with real veterans. We always had people verify their bona fides by showing us their discharge papers and by interviewing them first. So we went around and organized these events where vets could tell their stories directly in their own words to the American people, through the good offices of the media.

JAN BARRY

To some degree, it was therapy for those people who participated in speaking out. When you finally get mad and they speak out, you're doing something about it rather than just stewing in your anger.*

JANE FONDA

For me, the activism started in Paris with American soldiers I met who had deserted and fled to Europe. It's so ironic, given what people feel about me, vis-à-vis soldiers, like I'm against soldiers. It started with soldiers, and it was military bases that led me across country.

I remember going to Fort Lewis in Seattle and passing out copies of the Uniform Code of Military Justice. We were arrested and taken to the

---

* After the CCI hearings, the VVAW convened the Winter Soldier Investigation hearings, for which Jane Fonda helped raise funds, in January 1971. For three days in Detroit, Vietnam veterans gave testimony about war crimes. Graham Nash also helped fund the hearings. Soon after attending the hearings he wrote "Oh! Camil (The Winter Soldier)."

provost's office, and then released and barred from coming back on the base. By the time I had traveled across the country, I'd been arrested about a dozen times.

I organized my cross-country trip so that I arrived at Denver during the big national MOBE [Mobilization to End the War] demonstration in April 1970. This was my first public act against the war, a two-day fast in United Nations Square in the center of downtown Denver. About a thousand people fasted and spent the night. It was very beautiful. I'd been with Indians, I'd been with Panthers, I'd been with GIs. I hadn't spent much time with mothers and others. You know, the white, middle-class peace movement, and it felt good.

Actor Jane Fonda's first act of public peace activism was to drive across country in the spring of 1970, visiting military bases and meeting with members of the GI antiwar movement. Here she is photographed in Denver, Colorado, on April 24 participating in a two-day fast to protest the "war tax."

The next day, I went from there to Fort Carson, near Colorado Springs, which is a very conservative city. Mark Lane and Donald Duncan suggested that whenever I went to a base or a GI coffeehouse, that I bring as much literature as I could, including *The Village of Ben Suc*, the Jonathan Schell book. I smuggled boxes and boxes of books and GI coffeehouse newspapers onto the base in the trunk of my car. Leaflets were passed out that there was going to be a meeting in this place, on base. The books did get distributed, but the meeting didn't happen.

Later, the commander of the base offered to give me a tour of the base. Recently, a hundred soldiers had lined up in front of the medical dispensary flashing peace signs and saying they were sick—sick of the war. As a result, all of them had been put into the stockade. We hoped that my meeting with the commander would lead to the release of the soldier-protesters, and surprisingly, the general took us on a tour of the stockade and let us talk to prisoners. His tour backfired because we saw prisoners who seemed catatonic. Some, who identified themselves as Black Panthers, said they had been beaten, and it appeared to be so. The visit was abruptly called to an end and we were ushered out before I could determine which prisoners were protesters.* It was a very heavy experience.

I began to notice, during the drive across country, if I went over the speed limit at all I would be stopped. I was obviously being followed. Sometimes I would have to take an airplane someplace, to speak at a campus, and there would be men standing at the gate when I got off, in suits, with black glasses. It was very clear that they were agents. It was an attempt to intimidate me.

According to my FBI documents, Nixon was more obsessed with me than with the president of Russia. He was obsessed with this movie star that was working with the GIs. That I was going to be letting people know what the soldiers were saying really disturbed Nixon.†

---

* This paragraph is taken from my interview with Jane Fonda in New York City on June 14, 2014. At her suggestion, I included some details from her autobiography. See Jane Fonda, *My Life So Far* (New York: Random House, 2005), pp. 237–38.

† Fonda, along with scores of other antiwar activists, was on Nixon's enemies list. John Dean described the purpose of the list in a 1971 memo: "This memorandum addresses the matter of how we can maximize the fact of our incumbency in dealing with persons known to be active in

WAYNE SMITH (Vietnam vet)

I was in Vietnam for just over seventeen months, and then I extended for an extra six months. Remember, I volunteered and I hated the military. I was a good medic, but I was a terrible soldier, in many ways. Anyway, I extended. And it was a big, big mistake. It was the winter of 1970 and they gave me thirty days' leave. I came home, and I was totally emotionally numb. It was like I was going through the motions, but I really wasn't at home. It sounds strange, but it's true. And when I was with my family, my mom was so very proud. I had gotten a couple of medals, and she wanted me to go to my family church, the Church of God and Saints of Christ, in my uniform. And there was just no fucking way because I felt so ashamed.

Before I went to Vietnam, I went to the church and let them fawn over me and say prayers for my safety. But when I came home, it was like, "Fuck them." You know, "Fuck you, Mom," in effect. I'm not doing that. I couldn't talk to my friends. I would speak pidgin Vietnamese. There was a girl that I had a little thing for—we weren't in a relationship, fortunately, because I was going to 'Nam. I still had feelings for her but I couldn't relate to her. She grabbed me at one point and said, "Wayne, when are you going to stop destroying yourself?" I didn't even know what she was talking about. My mom said, "Where's your smile? You used to smile all the time."

I did go to the VA. I was having a lot of nightmares and just couldn't sleep. I couldn't even explain it. So I went to—I think she was a psychiatrist, or maybe a psychologist, or a social worker, for all I know—and I couldn't even explain it to her. But she said, "Because you're on active duty, we can't help you." That just closed an incredible door. I remember drinking more than I ever did, just trying to quiet those voices and echoes. It was just awful. As twisted as it sounds, I wished I'd had a flesh wound. I wished I had had some kind of injury that would manifest my pain, because I had incredible psychic pain. I mean I was the guy who wanted to

their opposition to our Administration; stated a bit more bluntly—how we can use the available federal machinery to screw our political enemies."

do good. I wanted to make a difference. Well, in my alone moments, I knew it was just all shit. It was just all for nothing.

When I came home, America was completely divided over the war. I mean everything was about the war. But my attitude was "I have friends over there dying for you motherfuckers. And you don't give a shit. And you want to talk rhetoric." Even those who were supposedly in the antiwar movement—I thought they were either cops, cowards, or people who were just pimping the game. They were not sincere. It didn't seem genuine. It didn't seem like pulling the American soldiers out would have been the answer. That would be okay for us. We would be saved. But what about all of the Vietnamese people who were still divided over their allegiance to the South or to the North? We had blood on our hands. We had a responsibility, in some ways, to make it better than it was. And it didn't seem to me that just ending America's involvement was the answer. It was too complicated for me, in some ways, to understand. So I sunk deeper into just my own abyss of avoidance and of a lot of self-loathing, contempt for the military, contempt for this country—a vicious cycle.

CHAPTER 16

TOWNHOUSE

(January–April 1970)

The revolutionary mood had been fueled by the blindingly bright illusion that human history was beginning afresh because a graced generation had willed it so. Now there wasn't enough life left to mobilize against all the death raining down.

—TODD GITLIN, *The Sixties*

FROM JANUARY TO MARCH 1970, THE WEATHERMEN PURGED nonmilitants from their membership, closed down collectives, and established cells or "tribes" in key cities like New York, San Francisco, Chicago, and Detroit to wage war on the government and bomb symbols of establishment power like banks, police stations, and government buildings. Meanwhile, the defense in the Panther 21 trial in New York City had begun to unearth evidence of judicial and police crimes aimed at destroying the Panthers. The courtroom revelations only encouraged the Weathermen's militancy.

MARK RUDD (Weather Underground leader)

By early 1970, I wound up in one of two main collectives in New York that were not linked to each other. Mine was the deeper underground collective, and Terry Robbins* and J.J.'s [John Jacobs's] was the regional collective.

---

* Terry Robbins was twenty-one years old, and a Kenyon College dropout.

The general idea was that there would be two levels of underground. One in which people would pass from aboveground to underground and back. We were modeling ourselves after the Vietnamese. There were people who lived in villages by day and at night took up arms against the Americans. It was a militia, guerrilla kind of thing. We had a part-time clandestine operation, in which some people would retain their own identities but assume other papers for some operations, and then go back to their old identity, whereas other people would just become fully underground.

BRIAN FLANAGAN (Weather Underground member)

Basically, J.J. talked the Weather Bureau into giving Terry Robbins full rein to do his thing at Cathy Wilkerson's father's townhouse, at 18 Eleventh Street in Greenwich Village.*

MARK RUDD

Terry was a feisty little guy. Incidentally, his uncle was the choreographer Jerome Robbins. I hate to use the word *Napoleonic*, but he was sort of a small guy who wanted to be tough, and he wanted to be strong, and there was a lot of anger in him. I wrote at one point about how he beat up his girlfriend and the rest of us didn't do anything about it. I mean really, if you look at it, you're not going to put a guy who beats up his girlfriend in charge of anything. At best, you'd help him get some help. At the worst, you might get rid of the guy. But here he was the leader, and he was really angry. I later found out that his father was a traumatized World War II vet who was troubled by anger, too. But he never mentioned that.

Terry had a view that leadership was kind of like *Triumph of the Will*. We want it more, and that's why we're leadership. In retrospect, it was a fascist view of leadership. And he had convinced himself that the only nonracist thing to do now was to raise the level of armed struggle. We'd

---

*   Cathy Wilkerson's father, James Platt Wilkerson, was a wealthy advertising executive who was on vacation in the Caribbean in March 1970. Cathy, the second of three Wilkerson daughters, grew up in Stamford, Connecticut, attended an all-girls boarding school in Massachusetts, and graduated from Swarthmore College in 1966.

have arguments constantly about it, and he'd always win. Any time anyone showed any wavering, he'd hit you with the arguments. "We have to do this, we have to do that. The Panthers are dying. The people in Vietnam are dying, and we're safe. But we've got to take some of the risk."

GERALD LEFCOURT (lead lawyer for the Panther 21)

On every street corner you could see signs that said, "Free the 21." You'd turn on the radio, a black station in particular, and the deejay would say, "Hey, it's Tuesday. Let's free the Twenty-One." It was everywhere.*

We were arguing for the ability to have a fair trial. We were fighting for very typical civil liberties issues. We [the lawyers] couldn't prepare for trial because the Panther defendants had been separated in seven different jails. They had no opportunity for bail because it was set at $100,000. Their mail was taken from them; many were in solitary with lights in their cells twenty-four hours a day.

I brought a civil lawsuit to get the [Panther 21 defendants] together. Judge Patterson, a federal judge, took all of our claims and said, "You can't do this to people. They need access to lawyers, and documents, and discovery." As a result of that, they were all put together in Queens.

JOHN MURTAGH, JR. (son of Judge Murtagh)

My mother told me years later that when my father, New York Supreme Court justice John M. Murtagh, found out that he was the judge handling the Panther 21 trial, the first thing he did was have his law secretary, Tom Hughes, go out and research everything that Julius Hoffman did wrong,

---

* In February 1970 thirteen members of the Black Panther Party (there were twenty-one defendants originally) sat trial in New York State Supreme Court for conspiring to bomb department stores, police stations, the New York Botanical Garden (located in the Bronx), subway switching stations, and a district school office in Queens. Very little physical evidence of the outlandish alleged crimes was produced by the prosecution, and the trial was viewed by many on the left as a sham aimed at destroying the New York chapter of the Black Panther Party. The seventeen-month trial was the longest and most expensive in New York State history. Although the jury acquitted the Panthers of all 156 charges on May 12, 1971, the New York Panther chapter was crippled by the trial and the two-year-long incarcerations.

**"Free the Panther 21" became a common rallying cry all over the country, in-
cluding New York City, where Youth Against War and Fascism held a demonstration for the Panthers on December 1, 1970.**

because the Chicago Seven trial had become such a circus. He didn't
want to be Julius Hoffman. He wanted to avoid the kind of circus that the
Chicago Seven trial became.

On the one hand, he came from a very traditional immigrant, American, law-and-order, "America-is-a-great-country" mindset, but at the same
time—informed by his Catholicism and Christianity—he had a dedication
to social justice that was somewhat ahead of its time. I think my father was
completely sympathetic, and then some, to the plight of the poor, to suffering; and at the same time would be equally offended by anyone who
was disrespectful to the legal system, disrespectful to those traditional institutions. It's an interesting combination.

GERALD LEFCOURT

The Panthers were part of the movement for social change, and they had
supporters, some of whom were famous people. On January 14, Felicia

and Leonard Bernstein hosted a fundraiser for us. We were just about to start pretrial hearings. Martin Kenner and I had set up a Panthers defense fund to help us fund the trial and support the families of the defendants who were in jail. It was really Felicia's party. She and Gail Lumet were friendly, and Gail had thrown us a party earlier. I would guess Leonard didn't have much to do with it at all. He came in late.

There were about ninety people at their Park Avenue apartment, including Barbara Walters, Otto Preminger, Sidney and Gail Lumet, and Julie Belafonte. I came with three Black Panther members, Donald Cox, Robert Bay, and Henry Miller, and several wives of the defendants.*

The New York Times, as a result of that party, wrote an editorial calling it "elegant slumming." The editorial was disgusting.

FALSE NOTE ON BLACK PANTHERS
(*New York Times* editorial, January 16, 1970)

Emergence of the Black Panthers as the romanticized darlings of the politico-cultural jet set is an affront to the majority of black Americans. . . . The group therapy plus fund-raising soiree at the home of Leonard Bernstein . . . represents the sort of elegant slumming that degrades patrons and patronized alike.†

---

* The Panther Defense Fund raised $10,000 at the Bernsteins' that night, and a total of $100,000 just in the month of January. It was a time when public sympathy for the Panthers ran high in the wake of Bobby Seale being gagged in the Chicago courtroom, Fred Hampton's assassination on December 4, 1969, and the December 8, 1969, violent police raid of the Los Angeles Panther office. The Panthers peaked in popularity in 1970 with offices in 68 cities, an annual budget of $1.2 million, and circulation of the *Black Panther* newspaper reaching 150,000. That year, *The New York Times* published 1,217 articles about the Panthers. Bloom and Martin, *Black Against Empire,* pp. 355, 392.

† After the party and *New York Times* editorial, the Bernsteins were inundated with hate mail, and the Jewish Defense League picketing outside their apartment building protesting their support of the anti-Zionist Panthers. Years later, documents proved that the FBI's COINTEL-PRO agents generated the hate mail and provoked the picketing in a deliberate attempt to dry up liberal Jewish support for the Black Panther Party. Churchill, *The COINTELPRO Papers,* p. 159. Tom Wolfe immortalized the party in his *New York* magazine article titled "Radical Chic: That Party at Lenny's" (June 2, 1970), in which he intricately dissected the social and cultural contrast between the rich donors at the party and the Panthers, and coined the phrase "radical chic."

GERALD LEFCOURT

We attacked the government and our defense was that the charges [against the Panther 21] were untrue, and that this was an attempt to destroy the Black Panther Party because they were fighting for the freedom of their people. This is a racist society: The government is racist, the FBI is racist, the police are racist, and that's what our defense was about.

CATHY WILKERSON (*Flying Close to the Sun*) *

Judge Murtagh seemed to be following in the belligerent steps of Chicago's Judge Hoffman. . . . In the New York Panther 21 Case, Murtagh seemed to take pleasure in summarily dismissing the normal rules of evidence to allow the police to introduce anything they wanted, while repeatedly denying defense motions. He had set up the courtroom with armed police, implying to the jury that he expected an armed attack at any moment. It was, Terry [Robbins] said, a way to prejudice jurors and make them frightened of the defendants, none of whom had ever engaged in armed political action.

JOHN MURTAGH, JR.

I was nine years old in February 1970, so I clearly didn't appreciate the significance of any of this. My father was a judge, he went off to work every day, and I guess I dimly understood what a judge did. We lived on 217th Street, between Park Terrace East and Park Terrace West in Manhattan, and I have this very distinct memory of dreaming that my bed was being lifted and dropped, lifted and dropped. "Boom! Boom! Boom!" The next thing I remember is my mother coming into my room in the dark.

It was February 21, Washington's Birthday weekend. It was a neighborhood of probably 90 percent either prewar or immediately postwar eight-, nine-story apartment buildings—sort of a traditional Washington Heights–y kind of neighborhood. Except the north side of 219th Street,

---

* Wilkerson, *Flying Close to the Sun,* pp. 324–25.

which runs east–west, and is only one block long, had a dozen semide-tached brownstones, which we lived in.

I remember my mother grabbing me out of bed. It was about two in the morning. The next thing I remember is standing in our kitchen in the dark—my parents were smart enough to not turn on any lights. There were very big windows in the back of our kitchen with translucent white sheer curtains. I can remember standing in the kitchen and seeing an or-ange glow. What they had done is they had set off three of these things that ultimately turned out to be nothing more than big Molotov cocktails. They were basically glass Tropicana orange juice bottles full of gasoline and rags; these guys were not sophisticated, at least not at that point.

At the front of the house there was a set of steps up to an enclosed porch. So they had put the bottles on the windowsill of the porch. Then they went down the driveway to the garage and shoved one of these things under the gas tank of my parents' car. So when we came downstairs, that's what we were seeing. I remember my parents' immediate reaction was "We're in a burning house."

I remember firemen coming into the house—it was crazy with activity. I have no idea what time it was by now: three, four in the morning. My parents took me to a friend's apartment across the street to spend the rest of the night. I must have fallen asleep—hard to believe, but I remember getting up the next morning, at my friends the Marcuses'. Their apart-ment was on the eighth floor. I looked out the window at my house, which was completely surrounded by New York City police. On the old blue-stone sidewalk in front of our house, I could see written in red spray paint, "FREE THE PANTHER 21—VIET CONG HAVE WON."

GERALD LEFCOURT

Not only did the Weathermen bomb Judge Murtagh's house, they also blew up police headquarters [June 10, 1970] and released a statement about the Panther 21. They said it was in retaliation for the assault of Joan Bird. Joan Bird was one of the Panther 21 and when she was arrested, she was beaten mercilessly. They called ahead and said that there was an ex-plosive device and that building should be evacuated. The so-called bomb was on the sidewalk in front of Murtagh's house. Murtagh's house wasn't really bombed. All of these were political statements.

The Panther 21 were the Weathermen's leaders in their minds because they were at the forefront. Their lives were on the line, and that's the way the Weathermen looked at it.

MARK RUDD

I remember that after the Murtagh bombing the reaction among Terry's collective, which was known as the New York collective, was shame that it hadn't worked. Terry Robbins and his collective had planted a bomb at the home of Judge Murtagh, who was in charge of the Panther 21 case, which was this crazy phony case where all the charges were eventually thrown out. But it was the longest-running trial in New York history at the time. And the bomb had gone off, I think it was a firebomb, and very little damage was done, and that had gotten Terry really upset. "We've got to up the ante." Which actually was true of the whole trajectory of the thing.

Todd Gitlin[*] pointed out that the media does not recognize organizing. It recognizes events. So just having a demonstration is not enough—if you had a demonstration, then you have another demonstration, it's not enough to really get the coverage. So you have to up the ante. There always has to be something more. Eventually what happens is the media becomes your base. You're playing to the media, rather than to the real base, which from '65 to '68, for example, was students. They were our base.

GERALD LEFCOURT

The trial was New York's way of destroying the Panthers through the courts. They took the entire leadership of the New York area off the streets. The FBI had no black agents because J. Edgar Hoover was totally racist. He didn't think blacks could be agents of the FBI, so instead they

[*]   Todd Gitlin, president of SDS in 1963 and 1964, is a Columbia University professor, sociologist, and prolific public intellectual who wrote, among many books, *The Whole World Is Watching: Mass Media in the Making and Unmaking of the New Left* (1980).

used informants. The Central Intelligence Agency trained what they call "Red Squads." In New York, we had the king of all Red Squads. This was a group that was so sophisticated that they had long-term intelligence operatives.

In the trial, we argued that the police were some of the founding members of the Black Panther Party. For example, Gene Roberts was a key witness in the Panther 21 case. He had been an intelligence operative for four or five years. He was Malcolm X's bodyguard when he was shot. How's that for street cred? So when the Panthers were formed, Gene Roberts came along and joined. There was another one named Ralph White. He was the head of a poverty program called the Ellesmere Tenants Council, supposedly organizing tenant strikes for bad housing. He was a cop, and he was also a section leader of the Black Panther Party. Those are just two out of five of them.

Here's one shocking example: Jamal Joseph was only sixteen and his grandmother asked him to stop going to the Panther office because she didn't want him to be in harm's way. So she told Jamal, "You can't go there anymore." But he went back one last time to tell everybody that he wasn't going to be coming back, and when he went there, Ralph White said, "Let me talk to your grandmother." So he goes with Jamal to his grandmother and says, "Don't worry, I'll take care of him." He took care of him all right. Jamal was in jail as a member of the Panther 21 a few days later and his life became one of serious struggle. And it was all because of a cop.

JOHN MURTAGH, JR.

My mother was a schoolteacher; she taught at a Catholic high school over on Pelham Parkway in the Bronx. It's not there anymore. I went to a private Catholic school down near Yankee Stadium, run by the Christian Brothers. My brother was at Fordham Prep in the Bronx. The routine was, my mother would drive me to school, down on 164th Street in the Bronx, with an unmarked police car following her; drop me off; then they'd follow her across the Bronx and sit in the faculty lounge all day while she taught. Then at the end of the school day she got back in her car, and they followed her back, and she picked me up, and home we went. That was the routine for a year and a half after the bombing.

I remember one night two or three detectives were sitting in the living room with my parents because they had gotten a call that there was a group from Baltimore coming to shoot up Judge Murtagh's house. It wasn't too long after the actual bombing. The cops wanted us to leave, but my parents' feeling was if we start doing that, we could be going out of here every night. So they increased security at the house for a period. We had a marked police car in the front, a policeman stationed in the back, and undercover cops sitting in an unmarked car, and obviously my father was protected 24/7.

I can remember looking out the kitchen window, and they had put one of those little police booths in the backyard. So the routine was, you had the cops out front, and then they had this little booth in the back that had a telephone in it, and there was always a guy stationed inside that. These guys were there full-time; and it was usually the same guys, so they used to play stickball on the street with me and my friends, and they would sit and eat their lunch at our little barbecue picnic table in the backyard. I remember noticing one day a cop was sitting at the table eating, and nobody was sitting with him. Even as a kid this was noticeable enough that I said something to my mother, who then explained who Frank Serpico[*] was—because he was sitting in the backyard and no one was talking to him. I have this dim memory of Frank Serpico in the backyard.

MARK RUDD

Terry was saying, "We've got to up the ante. The bomb at Judge Murtagh's house didn't do anything. Now we've got to do something." So, he came up with—or somebody came up with—the idea to plant three anti-personnel bombs, meaning dynamite pipe bombs with nails in them, to go off at a noncommissioned officers' dance at Fort Dix, in New Jersey. And so they were making those bombs, and had they gone off as they had

[*]   Frank Serpico was a former NYPD officer and well-known whistle-blower. His testimony was central to Mayor John Lindsay's 1970 Knapp Commission hearings on police corruption, which, at the time, caused the biggest shake-up in the history of the NYPD.

hoped, they probably would have killed officers—the sergeants, corporals, and their dates, which would have been a disaster for the antiwar movement.

I went along with Terry's plan. I didn't even question it. I was so caught up in the groupthink of the time. It was really a cult. Partially it was a cult because we had engaged in so many faction fights. Faction fights, in the left, are organic, they're natural, they're endemic. But when you're engaged in a faction fight, it's your group against this other group and that ultimately makes for a cult mentality.

JOHN MURTAGH, JR.

There were strange moments, but it became the normal routine. My father adjourned the trial [February 25, 1970], and he made a somewhat famous utterance when he said, "I've been called a pig one too many times," and he basically cleared the court and said, "You're not coming back. We're not resuming until I get a formal apology." And that would have been very much my father.

I think as an adult now looking back, I somewhat sarcastically would say that my view is that people like Bill Ayers and Bernardine Dohrn and Cathy Wilkerson were spoiled rich kids. They were extremely naïve. I obviously don't in any way condone what the Eldridge Cleavers, the Michael Tabors, and the Panthers were doing, but you certainly can sympathize with the injustice that they experienced. But a bunch of rich college kids who played pseudo-Marxist—it's all really cute until it starts destroying lives.

CATHY WILKERSON (*Flying Close to the Sun*)[*]

Teddy Gold[†] came up from the unfinished subbasement, which held only the furnace, other house vitals, and a primitive work-

---

[*]   When I interviewed Cathy Wilkerson at a diner in Park Slope, Brooklyn, on October 25, 2012, while her infant grandson slept in a stroller, she refused to discuss the townhouse explosion. This account of the explosion comes from her memoir, *Flying Close to the Sun* (pp. 345–55).

[†]   Ted Gold graduated from Columbia in 1969.

bench. Terry had decided that that was the safest place to work on the devices. Teddy said he needed to go to the drugstore to buy some cotton balls and he'd be right back. I nodded and kept ironing.

A few minutes later, I was bearing down on the wrinkles on the white sheet covering the ironing board when a shock wave shot through the house. A loud rumble followed, growing in intensity. Under the thin burnt orange carpeting, my bare feet felt the old, wood floor vibrating with escalating intensity. The ironing board, too, started to tremble and then tilt as the integrity of the house was compromised somewhere deep below. I began to sink down, my feet still planted on the thin carpet as it stretched and slid across widening, disjointed gaps. I was still standing, still holding the hot iron in my right hand, my arm still obeying the signal my mind had sent fractions of a second before to press down on the crisp, white cotton. A blast reverberated through the house and in place of the ironing board, a mountain of splintered wood and brick rose up all around me. Plaster dust and little bits of debris blew out from everywhere, instantly filling the air. Even as I tried desperately to process what was happening, I noted with resignation that this was one mess I was not going to be able to clean up.

A sharper, louder explosion then shot out from the subbasement, and as I dropped two or three feet more, I wondered if I would continue to fall down into the subbasement. I needed to put the iron down to free up my hand, but there were no surfaces anymore, just a noisy, moving, three-dimensional swirl of disintegrating house giving way to the shuddering blast waves of force that had passed through it. For a fraction of a second I worried that, with all the splinters of wood and debris flying around, the hot iron might start a fire. As the muffled noise from the second explosion persisted, I knew it didn't matter. Besides, I couldn't see anything; the light was gone, unable to penetrate the thick cloud of dust that now filled every space and crevice which crowded into my eyes, forcing them shut. . . .

In the same moment, the idea that Terry [Robbins] and Diana*
[Oughton] were both in the subbasement overwhelmed everything
else. As I forced my attention there and to them, my lungs expanded instantaneously to draw in air and dust so I could call out.
As I blinked in their direction to see if maybe— I saw the glow, like
an engorged sun rising up from a huge gaping hole between me
and the front of the house. That lungful of dust emerged as an anguished cry, as if that was the only way to connect in the last second
with the spirits as they drifted upward into some limbo that hangs
around after the body is gone but before absolute death. I cried
out, "Adam," Terry's nom de guerre, and scrambled to the edge of
the crater, only to be blinded now by the brightness. Then, I heard
the flames take up the silence left by the blast.

By then I was in the middle of the house, and Kathy Boudin,†
who had been taking a shower, heard my voice and cried out for
help. She had to be nearby, I thought, because the bathroom where
she was showering was also in the middle of the house. I called to
her, "Are you okay?" I knew that in ten or fifteen seconds we would
no longer be able to get out. "I can't see," she said, and I knew it
was because of the dust. I moved left along the edge of the crater
through the gritty haze toward her voice until I could grab her
hand. For a fraction of a second I thought to turn toward the front
door, until I realized the absurdity of looking for a door when there
was no longer any distinction between floor and ceiling or space in
between. Instead, we headed toward an opening where, dimly, it
looked like daylight was trying to fight its way into the dust. I
groped blindly, with each bare foot seeking something solid enough
to hold my weight for at least a second or two.

The first sound of the fire sucking air in from all directions

---

*   Diana Oughton, age twenty-eight, graduated from the Madeira School in 1959 and Bryn
Mawr in 1963, then worked for two years with a Quaker group in Guatemala. The experience of
working closely with indigenous poor people in Guatemala radicalized her. She eventually rejected her family's Republican political values and became a revolutionary.

†   Kathy Boudin, Bryn Mawr class of 1965, is the daughter of the late New York radical attorney Leonard Boudin.

grew louder behind us, reaching out to us. As we stumbled out of the opening in the front, it was only feet behind us. I was barely able to notice another explosion as I concentrated on climbing, still holding on to Kathy and both of us barefoot, out through the hole and over more debris onto the sidewalk. Helping hands reached out to us. Kathy was in shock. Someone wrapped a coat around her, even as she protested, as she was still wet and naked from the shower. Someone else directed us down the street. "Is there anyone else in there that we should go in for?" "No," I said, "there is no one now." Teddy had left the house, I thought, and I knew that Terry and Diana were gone. I was overwhelmed with grief. But I knew that I was not prepared to answer anyone's questions about what had happened, not then. "Was it a gas explosion?" someone asked. "Yes," I said. "It must have been." I could not think about anything but getting away to let the grief take over.

Susan Wagner [Henry Fonda's ex-wife], a longtime resident of the block, offered us her home, and we followed her to another set of brownstone stairs leading up to her front door. We were covered with dust and must have tracked the dirt in with us onto the light-colored carpet as we climbed another set of stairs to a second floor bedroom with an attached bath. She showed us the shower and hurriedly pulled out some of her own clothes, which she left on the bed for us. She left us in the care of a middle-aged black woman working as her maid, while she returned to the burning house to watch in fascinated horror.

I knew that in only a few minutes, when the police arrived and ascertained that we were down the block, they would come to question us. They would know fairly quickly that this was not a freak gas explosion. We showered as quickly as possible to get the worst of the grime off, before diving, still only half-dry, into our hostess's clothes. . . . My first thought was to get money for a subway token so we could get out of the neighborhood as fast as possible. . . . [With one subway token in hand] we walked [out of the building] as fast as we could without attracting attention, despite the pink patent-leather boots now on my feet, but by then, all eyes looked past us as people rushed toward the fire streaming out of the front of the building behind us. . . . A block away, we scrambled down the stairs into the subway . . . the two of us went through the turnstile together. . . . A minute later the train came and we were truly underground.

The house of Judge John Murtagh, who presided over the Panther 21 trial, was firebombed by the Weathermen the night of February 21, 1970. The bomb didn't cause any injuries, and the Weathermen spray-painted a declaration on the sidewalk: "FREE THE PANTHER 21—VIET CONG HAVE WON."

JANE FONDA (actor, peace activist)

Oddly enough, Susan Wagner, my ex-stepmother—who had come to Paris, and introduced me to the [American deserter] soldiers—had an apartment in Greenwich Village that was next door to the townhouse where the bomb went off in the basement. Two of the Weather Underground girls fled to Susan's apartment. Susan loaned them some clothes. Dustin Hoffman and his wife, Anne Byrne, also lived on that block.*

---

*   Actor Dustin Hoffman lived next door to the Wilkersons' townhouse and the blast blew a hole through the wall of his apartment. Hoffman and his then-wife, Anne Byrne, helped Wilkerson and Boudin escape from the rubble. Hoffman's star role in the 1967 classic *The Graduate* had made him an overnight icon of youthful discontent.

On March 6, 1970, three members of the Weathermen, Diana Oughton, Terry Robbins, and Ted Gold, were killed when a bomb they were making in the basement of a Greenwich Village townhouse accidentally exploded. The house was owned by Weatherman Cathy Wilkerson's father. Wilkerson and Kathy Boudin were also in the house during the explosion, but they survived the blast and ran away.

MARK RUDD

I had spent most of March 6 in New Jersey, visiting some people I knew there and establishing an alibi in case anything went wrong with the Fort Dix action. Then I came back, and to keep my alibi going I met my old friend from the Columbia *Daily Spectator,* Robert Friedman, and we went to see *Zabriskie Point,* Michelangelo Antonioni's latest movie. At the end of *Zabriskie Point* they blow up an upper-class modern house, out in the desert, and all this crap goes up in the air, slow-mo, and then it falls to the ground. It was symbolic of the end of this culture.

We saw *Zabriskie Point* together, and then I went back to the apartment that we had on Henry Street, on the Lower East Side, and other people in the collective said, "Mark, where have you been? Have you heard about the explosion?" There was a copy of *The New York Times* from the next day, and on the front was a picture of the townhouse, and that's how I heard about it. We had no cellphones in those days. Nobody could get in touch with me. I just felt that I had to do something. I didn't know what had happened at that point. But I had a backup arrangement with Kathy Boudin, and I managed to get in touch with her, and I immediately went to where she was, it was at somebody's apartment.

I heard the whole story. And then I set about finding the survivors, and bringing them back together again, and finding a safe place for them to stay. I was in shock, but I just kept going. At that point, I had convinced myself I was a soldier in a war, and when you're a soldier in a war, you do things and you don't even stop and think about them at the moment.

BRIAN FLANAGAN

I was in New York City when the townhouse exploded. Yeah, can't get too deep into that period. Immediately after that, I wound up in California. So, I was in the Weather Underground in California.

BERNARDINE DOHRN (Weather Underground leader)

For us, the combination of the townhouse explosion and the murder of Fred Hampton was shocking, tragic, and terrible. Of course we knew them very, very well. Both Diana Oughton and Teddy Gold had been on the trip with me to Cuba. Basically what happened was that everybody in the inner circle went underground; we disappeared without any kind of orders, plan, or design.

BRIAN FLANAGAN

Teddy Gold was a New York working-class Jew who was very smart. He was short, stubby, wore thick glasses, and had gone to Columbia. He and I did some things. He was a year older than me. He was in a thing called "Teachers for a Democratic Society." I guess he got a job at the Board of Education teaching somewhere, and he was a professional organizer. I can't organize breakfast for two. I get angry at the people I'm organizing. I soldier on, but I can't sit and convince people to agree with my point of view.

Teddy wrote a song about me, "Lay Elrod Lay."

Lay Elrod lay, lay on your back a while.
Play Elrod play, play with your toes a while.
You thought that you could stop the Weathermen.
But people knocked you on your can.

MARK RUDD

Ted wasn't one of my closer friends, but we had been together at Columbia, and he was the vice chairman of the SDS chapter the year before I was the chairman. He was just a wonderful guy. Very smart, very energetic, loved to play playground basketball, and he became a teacher to get a draft deferment. As a teacher, he founded an organization called Teachers for a Democratic Society. His father was a liberal leftist of some sort who was involved in one of the first HMOs. Ted grew up in New York City, on the Upper West Side. He was a very creative, very humane kind of person, but he was caught up in this.

BILL AYERS (Weather Underground leader)

We lost Diana, Terry, and Teddy. Teddy was a friend of ours, but I was particularly close to Terry. We'd had our ups and downs, but we were joined at the hip in some ways. Terry thought we were Butch Cassidy and the Sundance Kid. And Diana was the love of my life at that point—and also the object of a lot of jealousy with Terry. It was a complicated triangle.

What the townhouse collective was planning to do was unconscionable. Had it happened, it would have been a catastrophe of major proportions. But, it didn't happen. They killed themselves: That was a tragedy and it shouldn't have happened. In part, it was what we called this militaristic mistake. They had jacked themselves into thinking, as Terry did explicitly think, that the bigger the mess, the better. Chaos in the mother country—I don't agree with that.

It was a horrible mistake. And I'm sorry they went down that track, and I'm sorry I didn't have the wisdom or the ability to pull back, either.

Did we consider it terrorism? We did. And the townhouse collective is the clear example. Did we ever pull off a terrorist act? We never did. So, it's hard to say.

BRIAN FLANAGAN

Diana had been Bill Ayers's girlfriend, and they founded the Children's School, which was in the Midwest—it was sort of a new-age daycare center. They were both very much into children's education. She and Billy both came out of bourgeois backgrounds. His father was chairman of Commonwealth Edison in Chicago. I think her father had even more money than Billy's father, and she went to the best schools, Madeira and Bryn Mawr. She went to Guatemala for two years with a Quaker group. She was always into making her life one of service to people. She was a wonderful person.

I think that Terry Robbins was crazy. At Fort Dix, the band at the dance that they wanted to bomb was a black band. It was black musicians getting working-class pay. These poor teenage girls that had big eyes for officers were going to be blown up with the band. The whole thing was just going to go. When you feel that you have right on your side, you can do some horrific things. You can take planes and fly them into buildings, and you can kill a lot of people. And then you become God. It's unconscionable. There were other things that were going to go on that day, too, that were going to get a lot of people killed. It was going to be this bloodbath. It was like the Days of Rage. What happens the day after the Days of Rage? How do you follow? Nobody has a plan for that. What happens the day after Fort Dix? What happens the day after all this Armageddon?

The whole organization wasn't involved in the townhouse. There were various collectives throughout the country. There was one in Denver that wanted to sink an aircraft carrier. There was one in San Francisco and Seattle—there were collectives around the country. Nobody knew what the other collectives were doing, except the national leadership presumably knew most of what was going on, and J.J. had convinced them to let Terry run his show in New York in this collective. I don't think anybody in Denver knew what was going on in New York. Nobody in New York knew what was going on in Denver. So that's what it was. It was, "What do we do? Now we're underground. What do we do now? Well, let's blow up Fort Dix. Let's organize street kids in Seattle." It was different approaches. And that one was wrong. Historically wrong. Things like Moncada* and the Easter Rising† or the Harpers Ferry raid.‡ They were things that the people who did them knew there was no chance of success. [James] Connolly knew that there was no chance of success with the Easter Rising, but that it would set a tone for the future, that it was a noble effort. It's very hard to make that claim for any of the things that the early Weathermen did.

TOM HAYDEN (founder of SDS)

The townhouse explosion was pretty stunning. I knew everybody who died. I think there are too many people who view it as the end of the sixties, because you can only have so many "ends of the sixties." There are about ten of them. Altamont was the "end of the sixties." The end of the sixties was really in 1975 when it came to its natural end. I didn't think that the townhouse signified the end of the sixties, but I just felt immense sorrow and depression. I had questions of a technical nature, like, "What went wrong?" "What were they doing?" Because for a period of time, the blast was all we knew about, that people had been blasted to oblivion; there were only fingernails left.

I just thought that they were beyond logic and sense. It confirmed what I feared. Nobody ever came to me and said, "We're going to kill

---

*   On July 26, 1953, Fidel Castro led a small group of sparsely armed revolutionaries to attack the Moncada Barracks in Santiago de Cuba in what is widely seen as the start of the Cuban Revolution. Though Castro's troops were quickly defeated, he later recast the event as a success.

†   On April 24, 1916, during World War I, a group of Irish republicans mounted an armed insurrection in an attempt to end British rule in Ireland and establish an independent Irish Republic. Over the six days of the Easter Rising battle, 450 people were killed, more than half of whom were civilians, and the rebels were defeated.

‡   From October 16 to 19, 1859, abolitionist John Brown and his cadre of freed slaves and white abolitionists raided a federal armory in Harpers Ferry, Virginia. The assault was meant to be the first step in establishing a stronghold of freed slaves in the mountains of Maryland and Virginia. But Brown and his followers were defeated; those who weren't killed in battle were hanged soon after. The raid was one of the precipitating events of the Civil War.

soldiers." It was J.J.'s logic which said, "If our government is killing innocent Vietnamese, our job is to kill innocent American soldiers." I looked at the practical morality. Like, "What the fuck are you doing? You're carrying out an act which will reflect on everybody in the peace movement. Bring down the FBI and maybe the CIA on us. It has no rationale that can be voiced." You might as well say that you're organizing for Satan. It would be the political equivalent. "Hey everybody, stand on street corners, we're Satan, join us." Yes, there are some people that you'll reach, but what the fuck are you doing? It's only possible that they were doing it because they really didn't care anymore about influencing American public opinion.

MARK RUDD

We decided it was too hot for me in New York, so I went and stayed with some friends of friends and hid out in Philadelphia. Which is actually a very easy place to hide out. I had a disguise, which was very short, dark-dyed hair, and I had grown some facial hair. I had gotten some ID. I hung out in Philadelphia for about three weeks, which was when the thirty-four indictments for the Days of Rage came down against me and sixty-four other Weather members, which made us all officially federal fugitives.

BILL DYSON

I was a case agent on the Weather Underground. My job was to run that operation. I wasn't the original case agent; Bob Glendon was. But when they really became fugitives I ran the case. I was also a bomb technician. I started getting into bomb factories. One of the first bomb factories was the Weathermen bomb factory on Kenmore Street in Chicago. It was discovered by an exterminator on March 30, 1970. It was a rental apartment, and the exterminator was doing extermination work for the whole building. He went into that apartment, and found all of these chemicals and explosives, and called the police department. The police department called me. The bomb squad went out there, and I'm wandering around this bomb factory, and I really didn't know very much about it. I mean, there were some dangerous chemicals there, and I'm trying to process them for evidence.

There were big headlines in the newspaper. It was the Kenmore Street bomb factory. And so I'm wandering around with all these things, and finally, I went to my bosses and I said, "I'm going to get myself killed. I don't know anything about this." So ultimately, I learned everything I could about bombs.

RICK AYERS (Bill Ayers's brother, GI organizer)

[My girlfriend] Melody and I were driving across the country in early April, '70. We were having a regular phone call with the leadership, and they told us about Diana, because it was going to come out in the newspapers. Melody was very close to her, too. I remember she was on the pay phone, and she just bent over like she'd been kicked in the stomach. It was very hard.

It just meant it was very real. There were some people, like Terry, who you might think, Yeah, that guy might die, because he was a helluva militant and daring guy. But Diana was a real gentle soul. She had gone to Guatemala with the Quakers. I don't like the way she gets painted sometimes in the media as the innocent who got sucked in by these bad SDS men. She was very militant, and she was definitely committed to the work they were doing there. But she was someone you just wouldn't picture dying. It's the price of love. We were young, so it was a big shock for us.

MARK RUDD

On April 15, I was meeting Linda Evans, a new Weather Bureau member, at a coffee shop on Twenty-third Street. I was a little early for our 9 A.M. meeting, and I was waiting, and I noticed a bunch of guys in brand-new tie-dye jeans, and I said to myself, "Guys in *new* tie-dye jeans? I think I'll get the fuck out of here!" I threw a dollar down and raced out the door, and these guys raced after me. I'm running down Twenty-third Street, and I go down into the subway on the east side of the street, and there was no train. So I went out another exit, and there was a bus. I hopped onto the bus—I had a bunch of coins, I threw them in the collector, and then I looked back and they were right there by the bus, looking around for me, and they were holding walkie-talkies. So I threw myself on the floor of the bus—I guess nobody particularly thought it was that odd. The bus left. And I'm gone. Then I made my way to California.*

BILL DYSON

J. Edgar Hoover was opposed to undercover operations. I was undercover to a certain extent, if you can believe that. I was a terrible undercover agent, in the sense that I could not give my false name, Ralph Floyd, without putting my hand up. I mean, it was just automatic. I guess because I was brought up too honest, and I'm not a good actor. I am what I am. I could do it to a certain extent, but I didn't feel comfortable. You have to be a good actor, to look somebody right in the eye and lie to them. Most FBI agents, and most police officers, cannot be good undercover agents for any length of time. Anybody can do it for one shot. Anybody can make a drug pickup, or something like that. But if you have to get with these people, it becomes difficult. Hoover was opposed to it, but we did it anyway, especially after Hoover passed on, there were undercover operations.

The beards were the people who would do surveillance and look like they were undercover. They didn't look like FBI agents, because they would grow beards. Hoover was very big on how you looked. You had to wear a suit. He liked white shirts, as opposed to colored shirts. He wanted you to wear a fedora. He wanted you to dress respectfully. He wanted you to look, I guess, like a lawyer. But of course, when you're doing surveillance that becomes a problem. So you dress in smart clothes. Well, when you're talking about the 1960s where everybody's got long hair and all that sort of stuff, that don't work. So we did have the beards. And that name ["beards"] was given just because the agents didn't look like agents.

There were undercover FBI agents who were trying to penetrate the

---

* The FBI sting that Rudd narrowly escaped was set up by FBI informant Larry Grathwohl, who was the only undercover FBI agent to successfully infiltrate the Weathermen. After the townhouse bombing, Nixon insisted that the FBI make a Weatherman arrest. Grathwohl was forced to blow his cover in order to arrest Linda Evans, who was one of twelve Weathermen indicted on April 2, 1970, for conspiracy and inciting riots in connection with the Days of Rage. Evans served a short prison term.

Weather Underground. It just didn't work because it's not that easy. It wasn't because the guys didn't look the role; it wasn't because they were out of place age-wise. Maybe they were a little bit older than some of the others—you have to be a minimum of twenty-three to join the FBI. But most of the agents were twenty-six or twenty-seven, so it wasn't as though they were college students. Undercover operations are very, very difficult, especially if you don't have an entrée. The only thing you can do is start attending meetings, and hope somebody will come up to you, or tap you. Keep in mind that by the time we're doing this, these people are clandestine. We were trying to cast ourselves out into the local neighborhoods and hope we could find these individuals.

There was one time, it would have been around 1970, when I was sent to Canada. And that was extraordinary, sending somebody out of the country. It was to try to see if I could find the Weathermen, because I was one of the few people that could recognize them by sight. A lot of these undercover agents had never worked the Weathermen. They didn't know who they were. So I went up through Seattle, to get into Canada, and I couldn't find anybody. I knew some of the people were up there, but I just couldn't find them. I was not a good undercover agent. I was uncomfortable. And I was also nervous. My hair is naturally curly, so when I grew it out I couldn't have an Afro, because I'm not black, so it was called an Anglo. I had a beard, and it was miserable, because my hair is curly, and it would ingrow, and there'd be blood all over the pillow when I slept at night. It was horrible. I didn't feel comfortable, and I didn't succeed.

BERNARDINE DOHRN

I said goodbye to my parents, who lived in Florida, who had just turned sixty-five and retired. I didn't literally say "goodbye," I just did a visit. But I knew I wasn't going to see them again, and it was pretty terrible. There was no way to explain it to them. I don't even know if they'd ever met anybody who was against the war. They wanted me to teach for two years, get married, and have a good life. That wasn't my plan. But I did go say goodbye to them, and I also went with Jeff Jones down to see his parents in L.A., to say goodbye to them. This was in January, February. We disappeared maybe a week after the townhouse. By then we had dates to show up in Chicago for court appearances [after the Days of Rage indictments]. And so when that happened, the warrants were put out for our arrest in Chicago. I dyed my hair blond, the dream of every girl growing up in the Midwest.

We had endless meetings. We made a couple of rules at the beginning, which was to recognize the strengths that the police and the FBI had. We almost never used the telephone—never to family members, never to friends or old roommates. We saw the phone as one of their strengths, and our weaknesses. And we saw automobiles as one of their strengths, because there was a national registry system for auto thefts. They were good at that. We agreed that we would not go near old neighborhoods that were political centers. We wouldn't go to Berkeley; we wouldn't go to Madison; we wouldn't go to the parts of every city that were known as centers of youth and students and activism and hippies; we would be very disciplined about those matters. We would try to rebuild our connections to people who went underground. And then of course we spent the next six months having an internal debate about what the meaning of the townhouse was, who we were going to be, and whether we were going to be a military force or a political force.

CATHY WILKERSON (*Flying Close to the Sun*) *

My picture was on a wanted poster, posted in post offices around the country; I was wanted for murder. The FBI was busy, contacting everyone in my family, I had heard, and putting pressure on those they considered to be weak links.

TOM HAYDEN

The bombing as an act of defiance was totally isolated. The revolutionary black movement had fallen apart. There were revolutionaries in prison, but for the most part there was a mass movement of an eclectic sensibility,

* Wilkerson, *Flying Close to the Sun*, p. 355.

around ending the war in Vietnam. Earth Day. Feminism. Flower power. And the Weather Underground was in it invisibly. What's surprising to me was that my premise turned out to be accurate—public opinion can be turned around. But there was no SDS to lead it. And it didn't seem to need any leadership. What had happened was after the disintegration of SDS in 1969, the millions of people that identified with SDS just went their own way into other movements. Like the McCarthy campaign, they were in the Earth Day celebrations [April 22, 1970], the back-to-the-land movement, the commune movement in Colorado, in Oregon, in Northern California—it was massive. I don't know the numbers, but there were thousands of people that went back to the land. And they were interchangeable with the old SDS. They were just another decade's version. The ecology movement really captured a lot of their energy.

CHAPTER 17

WOMEN'S LIBERATION

(January–September 1970)

There's something contagious about demanding freedom, especially where women, who comprise the oldest oppressed group
on the face of the planet, are concerned.

—ROBIN MORGAN,
Sisterhood Is Powerful

FIFTY YEARS AFTER AMERICAN WOMEN WON THE RIGHT TO VOTE IN
1920 came a second wave of feminism. After years of feeling exploited
by the male-dominated New Left, civil rights, and peace movements,
women began to blaze their own path to freedom and power. The movement had begun in 1963 with the publication of Betty Friedan's *The Feminine Mystique* and the passage of the Equal Pay Act, followed by Title
VII of the 1964 Civil Rights Act, which prohibited employment discrimination based on race or sex. Founded in 1966, the National Organization
for Women sought to gain equal access for women to work, education,
and political participation.

By the late sixties, new and more radical women's liberation organizations formed all over the country, with names like New York Radical
Women, Redstockings, Women's International Terrorist Conspiracy from
Hell (W.I.T.C.H.), Radical Mothers, BITCH, Bread and Roses, and the
Chicago Women's Liberation Union. These groups tackled issues like
abortion, rape, domestic violence, gay rights, women's health, and workplace equality. At the same time, thousands of women were being radi-

calized by the experience of sharing their frustrations and life stories in consciousness-raising groups. "The feeling was that we were like Columbus, sailing at the edge of the world. Everything was new and intense," said one feminist.

Achieving equality in the workplace would require a steep climb. In 1970, women comprised only 9 percent of all professions, 7 percent of doctors, and 3 percent of lawyers. Women held 9 out of every 10 elementary school teacher jobs, but only 2 out of every 10 school principal positions. Banks routinely denied women credit cards, and "head and master" laws, on the books in many states, gave husbands legal rights over their wives' property. Declaring that "the personal is political," second-wave feminism redefined the meaning of equality and challenged the way sexism had shaped relationships and every element of American life from the bedroom to the boardroom.

———

ROBIN MORGAN (peace activist, poet, feminist)

There I was one day in January 1970, a young mother, in my office at Grove Press, where I was an editor. Jane Alpert called me and said, "We've all been complaining about *Rat,* and I think we're going to seize it. Will you come with us and give it feminist legitimacy?" It was the first time women had seized a male-run newspaper. I was slightly older by two or three years than most of the women I hung with. I was never in SDS. I was in MDS, Movement for a Democratic Society, which was for people who were not campus based. But I was quite delighted by this call, because I'd had run-ins with Jeff Shero, who was the editor of *Rat Subterranean News,** and they had become this porn-infested boy thing, a lot of very crude kind of rock and roll, a lot of R. Crumb cartoons, less politics, profoundly sexist. So we took it over. We marched in and said, "Out, get out!"

Three or four guys were there and we threw them out. They thought it was amusing, and that it was for one issue only. They didn't understand

---

* *Rat Subterranean News* was one of New York's most popular underground newspapers, along with *The East Village Other* and *The Rag.* A colorful, tabloid-size paper, *Rat* began publishing in March 1968 and gained early notoriety for its coverage of the Columbia student uprising.

that they were never coming back. I'm not completely sure that we understood it, either.

So we did the women's issue, which became quite famous. Jeff used to joke that it would sell better than any other issue. He thought, What's the problem, after that we'll take it back. But we changed the locks. We were radicals, after all—we knew how to do this kind of thing. We seized the bank account. We seized the whole damned paper. And then Jeff *was* very angry and the men came back and tried to get in and there were, ah— altercations. But we took the position that they had been counterrevolutionary. Once you lobbed that at somebody in those days, or called them bourgeois, they were dead in the water.

Second-wave feminism grew out of the civil rights and antiwar movements and profoundly changed the role of women both at home and in the workplace.
PHOTOGRAPH BY STEPHEN SHAMES.

BERNARDINE DOHRN

Every Weatherwoman thought of herself as a feminist, and we felt that we were part of the feminist movement. I remember when I moved to New York to work for the National Lawyers Guild, twelve other women and I formed a women's consciousness-raising group, and we didn't really know that in thousands of other apartments around the country the same thing was happening. I think we felt very much that we had been transformed by talking to other women, telling secrets about how we were raised, how we really felt about boyfriends; about the women who didn't have boyfriends but had girlfriends; about sexuality; about dreams of work, where we were told by fathers and brothers that it couldn't happen because we were girls. All of that, and the sense that all the movements, the civil rights movement, the black movement, the antiwar movement, were stifling women.

At one of the SDS conventions in 1966, a group of women took over the stage and there was practically a riot; there was just pandemonium. I was sitting on the steps up high when this happened, and there was just chaos. People were shouting and freaking out, and the more the men shouted and freaked out, the more the women freaked out; and we left that effort determined to not let our demands be shot down again.*

TOM HAYDEN (founder, SDS)

Everybody had to learn the hard way about feminism. I remember I was living in this commune called the Red Family in Berkeley with several people. There were a bunch of women, and they started meeting at our house, and I was excluded. It was my house. You had to go in the front door to go into the house, and I had to sit outside. I didn't know what they were talking about, and they said, "We're talking about you." What was interesting was that this was happening thousands of times at once. There was no steering committee; it just happened.

I couldn't convert emotionally or attitudinally from chauvinism, since I had just been introduced to feminism. But I was very supportive of the idea and somewhat awestruck at how these things kept erupting. Everybody gives us credit for organizing this phenomenon called "the sixties" but in every occasion it was more spontaneous than anything else. If you

---

* At the 1966 SDS national convention in Chicago, a group of women presented a position paper on the role of women in SDS arguing that there was a gender disparity in leadership roles. The women were booed off the stage. This led many SDS women to leave the organization and join women's liberation groups.

had been organized in 1960 as a Friend of SNCC, or you went to Mississippi, you learned some organizing techniques and then you took it with you. So there were thousands of people that had rudimentary organizing skills, and we placed a very high value on organizing. We had organizing schools, organizer training. But when these movements happened, they weren't organized. It was like an anarchist's dream: self-organization; no need for hierarchy; no need for vanguards; no need for bureaucracy.

ROBIN MORGAN

Knowing what I know today about how deeply the word *feminist* threatens the existing social compact, to say *radical* feminist now seems to me almost redundant. But it was very important then because there were radical feminists and there were reformist feminists and there were socialist feminists and there were socialist radicals, and radical socialists. I mean it was a lot about compartmentalization and identity politics—how you dressed, who you hung with. I've written about the conformity of the period, but I've never really heard anybody else address it. I think it's important.

We were all writing stuff for the first women's issue of *Rat*. I wanted the left to be pure and to be feminist and to be good for women. I felt women were the real left and I felt that if we could transform the consciousness of the left we could change this country. "Goodbye to All That" came out very fast, in one whole night. I cried while writing it. I mean I sobbed.

FROM "GOODBYE TO ALL THAT," BY ROBIN MORGAN

So, *Rat* has been liberated, for this week, at least. Next week? If the men return to reinstate the porny photos, the sexist comic strips, the "nude-chickie" covers (along with their patronizing rhetoric about being in favor of women's liberation)—if this happens, our alternatives are clear. *Rat* must be taken over permanently by women—or *Rat* must be destroyed. . . .

And that's what I wanted to write about—the friends, brothers, lovers in the counterfeit male-dominated Left. The good guys who think they know what "Women's Lib," as they so chummily call it, is all about—who then proceed to degrade and destroy women by almost everything they say and do: The cover on the last issue of *Rat* (front and back). The token "pussy power" or "clit militancy" articles. The snide descriptions of women staffers on the masthead. The little jokes, the personal ads, the smile, the snarl. No more, brothers. No more well-meaning ignorance, no more cooptation, no more assuming that this thing we're all fighting for is the same; one revolution under man, with liberty and justice for all. No more. . . .

This literally nauseated me to write, and my palms would sweat with fear and I'd go throw up, and then go back to the typewriter and get it down. I'd lie to myself and say, "You don't have to publish it, just get it written down." And then once it was down I knew I'd let it be published. The lack of ethics by the men of the New Left was like breathing in ammonia to me. It was foul, it severed any longing I had for that connection.

Let's run it down. White males are most responsible for the destruction of human life and environment on the planet today. Yet who is controlling the supposed revolution to change all that? White males (yes, yes, even with their pasty fingers back in black and brown pies again). It could just make one a bit uneasy. It seems obvious that a legitimate revolution must be led by, made by those who have been most oppressed: black, brown, yellow, red, and white *women*—with men relating to that the best they can. A genuine Left doesn't consider anyone's suffering irrelevant or titillating; nor does it function as a microcosm of capitalist economy, with men competing for power and status at the top, and women doing all the work at the bottom (and functioning as objectified prizes or "coin" as well). *Goodbye to all that.*

CATHY WILKERSON (SDS and Weather Underground member)

The women's movement at that early stage was very embedded in middle-class concerns. It wasn't against other concerns, but the women who were in the process of defining the women's movement used their own experiences, which was good and honest. But it wasn't my experience at that point.

Our women's group would talk about dividing up the housework between a husband and wife. But many in SDS lived in communes; we had no housework because we had no furniture. Everybody shared the cooking. We had different concerns than the rest of the women's movement. All of us women were in this hothouse environment where we felt like you had to participate in *either* radical politics *or* feminism and we were on both sides.

VIVIAN ROTHSTEIN (SDS peace activist, feminist activist)

The men in the movement were all smart, and pretty domineering. They were dismissive, arrogant, very fast-talking, and they intellectualized everything. Very few women could hold their own in that environment. Organizing women was not considered a particularly exciting or important thing to do.

ERICKA HUGGINS (Black Panther Party leader)

We [the women] ran the Black Panther Party. Because of the male dominant society, the first to be arrested, killed, jailed were men. So what happened was that we were at first leadership by a default because we were already running all of the day-to-day operations of offices and programs. And then as time went on, particularly between 1968 and '71, when there was so much attack and harassment of Black Panther Party members by the FBI, women created a grounded and stable network between the chapters and offices. Women also were the editors and writers for *The Black Panther,* the party's newspaper, which communicated to the globe.*

---

*   *The Black Panther* was published weekly, and from 1968 to 1970 it was the number one black weekly newspaper in the country, with a circulation of over 300,000. People sold it on street corners nationwide for twenty-five cents.

Women began to take over the leadership of the Black Panther Party by 1970 because so many of the male leaders either had been shot or were incarcerated. PHOTOGRAPH BY ROBERT ALTMAN.

ROBIN MORGAN

For the record it should be said that the heartbreak I and women like me felt was because we really thought we were building the brave new world together. We came out of the civil rights movement. We came out of being threatened and beat up and busted and water-cannoned and followed in cars in Mississippi in the middle of the night. And we were so young. I remember I'd thought at one point, I'm still a virgin and I'm going to die a virgin, I'm never even going to know what it's like to have sex!

At that moment, in the summer of '64, I was in the CORE, Congress of Racial Equality,[*] office in New York. I had been in the South doing voter registration, and now I was back in New York and we were all waiting for news of these three missing CORE workers—one black, two white—in Mississippi, James Chaney, Andrew Goodman, and Michael Schwerner. They were dredging the rivers and searching everywhere, and in the process they discovered the mutilated parts of an estimated seven-

---

[*] The Congress of Racial Equality was a civil rights organization founded in Chicago in 1942. It was one of the "big four" civil rights organizations, along with the Student Nonviolent Coordinating Committee, the National Association for the Advancement of Colored People, and the Southern Christian Leadership Conference.

teen additional bodies, and all but one of them were women. One of the men said, "There's a brother who was lynched that we never even *heard* about!" And I looked around the room and all the women, black and white, were studiously studying the tips of their shoes, and finally I screwed up the courage to say, "But what about the women?" The women looked at the floor, and the guys all looked at me incredulously as if I'd landed from Mars, and said, "Those were probably *sex* murders, those weren't *political*." It's not even anything against the guys in CORE. That was just the mindset of the time.

HEATHER BOOTH (SDS member, feminist activist)

In December of '65 there was a national SDS meeting in Champaign-Urbana [Illinois], and I was already part of SDS on my campus at the University of Chicago. That conference was designed to discuss the "woman question," and I went to the meeting in order to be part of that discussion. One of my professors was Dick Flacks, who was also at Port Huron, and he encouraged me to go. At that meeting the men wouldn't let the women talk, and would finish their sentences. So women would say, "I felt no one listened to me." And someone would say, "What do you mean? Anyone would listen to you," or, "Maybe you didn't have anything to say!" So it was acting out the very reason there needed to be an independent women's movement.

In those meetings I was for continuing the conversation with men and women. A guy named Jimmie Travis, a black SNCC worker who has since died, got up with a group of friends and said, "Look, the women aren't going to make progress on this till you get a chance to talk by yourselves." He had the experience with the black movement doing that. I thought, Oh no, we can work this out. Black and white together, men and women together. Then after about another hour I realized, We do just have to talk amongst ourselves.

BERNARDINE DOHRN

In those years, from when I started traveling—'67, '68, '69—tremendous changes were happening. Women were speaking up, and there were arguments about it all the time in SDS chapters and in resistance groups around tactics. Women were starting to do separate actions, meeting together, and telling men to shut up, or get a grip, or to change themselves. All those kinds of confrontations were happening.

One of the things I've wondered since then is, Do people change without confrontation? I really don't know, because in my formative experience, people don't change because of gentle persuasion. People change because they're confronted by people they care about, or people they have been close to. I can't tell how much that's my temperament, and how much that's true. But certainly that was happening across the country and in big universities and small. It was exciting and it was conscious; it wasn't like, "Okay, women are just in the back room serving coffee." It wasn't like that, but it was shocking. Men expected privileges. Men expected sexual privileges, though it isn't exactly like the sexual revolution was imposed on women. This was the moment of the Pill, and this was the moment of the crack-up. None of us wanted to be our mothers, or to live lives in the fifties.

ROBIN MORGAN

We were idealistic young women who wanted to change the world and we really thought our brothers did as well. We didn't mind grinding the mimeograph machines and grinding the coffee and grinding our teeth because we were doing it for what we thought was a shared thing. To find then that they would say, "Give me a little of my civil rights tonight, baby," and that that's what they really wanted us for . . . or to see women get beat up or punished by rapes in Weather collectives, was brain-blowing. I mean to keep yourself from turning right-wing was not a small thing. You could feel yourself wanting to become the antithesis of this because it was so hypocritical and hurtful. So to try and keep your vision of profound societal change in the face of this was hard.

This period comes after eight to ten years of, for many of us, me certainly, intensive involvement in the civil rights and antiwar movements, where we marched and we picketed and we signed petitions. We were pacifist. We felt we were getting nowhere. So when people turned into the downward spiral of violence, on the one hand it is emotionally and historically understandable. But it is also very much classically about manhood, and women go along because either they have a man involved or they want to have a man involved or they want agency in making societal change—and the only model they see is a male model, so they want to be just as tough as a guy, they want to be an imitation guy.

FROM "GOODBYE TO ALL THAT," BY ROBIN MORGAN

Goodbye to the Weather Vain, with the Stanley Kowalski image and theory of free sexuality but practice of sex on demand for males. "Left Out!"—not Right On!—to the Weather Sisters who (and they know better—they *know*) reject their own radical feminism for that last desperate grab at male approval that we all know so well, for claiming that the machismo style and the gratuitous violence is their own style by "free choice," and for believing that this is the way for a woman to make her revolution . . . all the while, oh my sister, not meeting my eyes because Weathermen chose Charles Manson as their—and your—hero. (Honest, at least, since Manson is only the logical extreme of the normal American male's fantasy, whether he is Dick Nixon or Mark Rudd: master of a harem, women to do all the shitwork, from raising babies and cooking and hustling to killing people on command.) Goodbye to all that shit that sets women apart from women; shit that covers the face of any Weatherwoman which is the face of any Manson Slave which is the face of Sharon Tate which is the face of Mary Jo Kopechne which is the face of Beulah Saunders, which is the face of me which is the face of Pat Nixon which is the face of Pat Swinton. In the dark we are all the same—and you better believe it: we're in the dark, baby. (Remember the old joke: Know what they call a black man with a Ph.D.? A nigger. Variations: Know what they call a Weatherwoman? A heavy cunt. Know what they call a hip revolutionary woman? A groovy cunt. Know what they call a radical militant feminist? A crazy cunt. Amerika is a land of free choice—take your pick of titles.) Left Out, my sister—don't you see? Goodbye to the illusion of strength when you run hand in hand with your oppressors; goodbye to the dream that being in the leadership collective will get you anything but gonorrhea.

HEATHER BOOTH

I was a leader on campus. I was in student government; in SDS; I was the head of Friends of SNCC; I headed a tutoring project on campus, and at this meeting I was talking, and one of the SDS guys said, "Shut up." I just wasn't used to people talking to me that way, so I went around the room and tapped every woman on the shoulder, and all the women left. We went upstairs and formed a group called WRAP, Women's Radical Action Project, which was out of SDS's set of community-based projects called ERAP [Economic Research and Action Project].

ROBIN MORGAN

You have to remember the comments coming out of the male left at this point—and I refer to it as the male left even though we were in it as women. This was the period of Stokely Carmichael, who said the only position for women in SNCC is prone. Everywhere you looked there were guys saying obnoxious things. Either just ignoring women, or with the generic male pronoun, or the assumption that the draft—which I might add affected only men—was a universal issue, but childcare, which *ought* to affect everyone because it's the next generation, was a fringe issue. To talk about rape was to be a frigid hysteric. The homophobia was enormous. To raise the issue of a leftist guy hassling a woman, sexually harassing a woman, raping a woman was to invite censure on the *woman*.

The Weather collectives began to do militant actions, and their model for security was that every woman who joined the group had to sleep with every man in the group. This was "smash monogamy" from a male perspective. Whether the women wanted to be monogamous or not didn't matter. Why a woman coming into a group sleeping with every man in the group was a test of her security when every man coming into the group was not made to do the same thing is—well, what the hell does that have to do with security? Nobody asked. Despite the image of a lot of the decade, it was a time of tremendous conformity and peer pressure—and toxic sexism. Abbie Hoffman called for "revolutionaries" to "kill your mothers."

FROM "GOODBYE TO ALL THAT," BY ROBIN MORGAN

Goodbye to Hip culture and the so-called Sexual Revolution, which has functioned toward women's freedom as did the Reconstruction toward former slaves—reinstituting oppression by another name. Goodbye to the assumption that Hugh Romney [Wavy Gravy] is safe in his "cultural revolution," safe enough to refer to "our women, who make all our clothes" without somebody not forgiving that. . . .

Let it all hang out. Let it seem bitchy, catty, dykey, Solanasesque, frustrated, crazy, nutty, frigid, ridiculous, bitter, embarrassing, man-hating, libelous, pure, unfair, envious, intuitive, low-down, stupid, petty, liberating. *We are the women that men have warned us about.*

And let's put one lie to rest for all time: the lie that men are oppressed, too, by sexism—the lie that there can be such a thing as "men's liberation groups." Oppression is something that one group of people commits against another group specifically because of a "threatening" characteristic shared by the latter group—skin color or sex or age, etc. The oppressors are indeed *fucked up* by being masters (racism hurts whites, sexual stereotypes are harmful to men) but those masters are not *oppressed*. Any master has the alternative of divesting himself of sexism or racism; the oppressed have no alternative—for they have no power—but to fight. In the long run, Women's Liberation will of course free men—but in the short term it's going to cost men a lot of privilege, which no one gives up willingly or easily. Sexism is not the fault of women—kill your fathers, not your mothers.

BERNARDINE DOHRN

To me it's a later writing that says we weren't part of the women's movement. We felt very much a part of the women's movement, just like women who were teaching, and starting the first free clinics, and going to communes felt a part of it. It wasn't like there was only one place to be, and that was in New York City with a handful of women who were writers and were working there. We felt very much a part of it. We did come to feel by '71, '2, '3 that we had chosen to identify these two issues that we felt couldn't be abandoned, even with the persuasive argument that women were always putting aside our issues in favor of bigger issues. That's a very persuasive argument. And yet we felt, "Really, your country is killing thousands of people a day in Southeast Asia, and that's not what you're talking about? You're talking about these other things? And the spearhead of the black freedom movement is being shot down in front of you?" Anyway, we felt we couldn't go there, but we didn't feel that we were *not* part of the women's movement.

ROBIN MORGAN

"Goodbye to All That" was crossing a bridge *and* burning it behind me because the male left did not forgive. I didn't want it to forgive. I was done with it. It was coming also from a very deep place inside of real rage and real hope. I thought it would explode on me. I thought, None of these people will speak to me again, and I don't care. I knew other women had gone through this because we all would whisper among ourselves. He's such a sexist pig, what about that group? And did you know that he goes and he shakes a woman's breast instead of her hand? And have you heard he raped her?

FROM "GOODBYE TO ALL THAT," BY ROBIN MORGAN

Goodbye, goodbye forever, counterfeit Left, counterleft, male-dominated cracked-glass mirror reflection of the Amerikan Nightmare. Women are the real Left. We are rising, powerful in our unclean bodies; bright glowing mad in our inferior brains; wild hair flying, wild eyes staring, wild voices keening; undaunted by blood we who hemorrhage every twenty-eight days; laughing at our own beauty we who have lost our sense of humor; mourning for all each precious one of us might have been in this one living time-place had she not been born a woman; stuffing fingers into our mouths to stop the screams of fear and hate and pity for men we have loved and love still; tears in our eyes and bitterness in our mouths for children we couldn't have, or couldn't not have, or didn't want, or didn't want *yet,* or wanted and had in this place and this time of horror. We are rising with a fury older and potentially greater than any force in history, and this time we will be free or no one will survive. *Power to all the people or to none. All the way down, this time.*

Free Kathleen Cleaver!

Free Anita Hoffman!

Free Bernardine Dohrn!

Free Donna Malone!

Free Ruth Ann Miller!

Free Leni Sinclair!

Free Jane Alpert!

Free Gumbo!

Free Bonnie Cohen!

Free Judy Lampe!

Free Kim Agnew!

Free Holly Krassner!

Free Lois Hart!

Free Alice Embree!

Free Nancy Kurshan!

Free Lynn Phillips!

Free Dinky Forman!

Free Sharon Krebs!

Free Iris Luciano!

Free Robin Morgan!

Free Valerie Solanas!

Free our sisters!   *Free ourselves!*

ROBIN MORGAN

I brought it to the collective, and frankly I thought they wouldn't publish it. Sharon Krebs said, "We have to publish this. I disagree with Robin completely—although some of her points are well taken." Then Jane Alpert[*] said, "Yes, we really have to." So we published it, and within a day

[*] Alpert was the lover of and fellow bomber with Sam Melville, whose New York collective detonated ten dynamite bombs in New York City corporate and government buildings between August and November of 1969. Melville and Alpert were turned in by an FBI informant, and Melville was sentenced to thirteen years in prison, while Alpert (who later had a romantic friendship with Robin Morgan) went underground. Although Melville was not a member of the Weathermen, his method of bombing symbolic buildings with the intention of destroying property, not people, and then issuing a communiqué taking credit for the bombing, would later be-

the shit hit the fan. I mean the phone began ringing off the hook. I received anonymous death threats from quite a few so-called revolutionary brothers. Some of them are still alive and around and should be ashamed. They would call and say, "You're a fucking cunt, you're going to be dead, and if the cops don't get you we will." There were Panthers, but it was mostly the white boys.

People came by and informed me that they were reprinting it in the *Berkeley Barb* and lots of other publications. It became this odd badge of honor among male left newspapers, "We can print this, we can handle self-criticism." And some of them printed it, saying, "This is a serious criticism, and while we don't agree with it and we feel that its tone is sexist in itself, we are going to do self-criticism and examine." But since the piece named names, each movement newspaper would bowdlerize it so that whichever men or male left groups were big in their local area just "happened" to be cut out.

MICHAEL KAZIN
(Harvard SDS leader and Weathermen member)

I remember I was living in this apartment with all women in Cambridge, Mass., when "Goodbye to All That" came out. It was painful, because they were saying, "Michael, you know, I think she's talking about you."

Later, I wrote in my book *American Dreamers* that "Goodbye to All That" became as widely known as any document by a woman radical since the 1848 declaration at Seneca Falls.

MICHAEL UHL
(Vietnam veteran, Citizens' Commission of Inquiry organizer)

Reading the women who were writing about male chauvinism in *Liberation* magazine or in *The Guardian* was no more or less like reading *Das Kapital* for the first time. It was all part of the new consciousness, the new ideology.

---

come a model for the Weather Underground in the 1970s. Sam Melville was killed in the Attica prison riots in September 1971.

Robin Morgan was a heartthrob. I had a boyhood crush on her when she played Dagmar on *I Remember Mama!*[*] Her wing of feminist separatists was very much present in our circles of second-wave feminist friends and lovers. Tod [Ensign]'s girlfriend Pamela Booth knew all of them. Shulamith Firestone was briefly in her consciousness-raising group. We men stayed safely at a distance as the women fought it out among themselves. However, most New Left activist men I knew had at least read *Our Bodies, Ourselves;* many (me) had a copy on their own bookshelves. We were all "in struggle" against "male chauvinism," and, as I have written in several places (i.e., *Vietnam Awakening,* my memoir), quite happy to cede our positions in the male world of professionals and breadwinners to a woman: Good luck with that, baby!

ROBIN MORGAN

I could never have imagined that "Goodbye to All That" would have unlocked such rage of leftist women against their men, which had been boiling all this time. I had not assumed that women would step forward and it would be like "I am Spartacus!" But this was an amazing result. I mean you have to remember when we hexed the Pentagon in 1967 and Shulamith Firestone and Marilyn Webb stood up and tried to talk, the men pelted them with raw eggs. When Naomi Jaffe and other women tried to talk at an SDS convention in 1966, demanding a plank on women's liberation be inserted in the SDS resolution, they were pelted with tomatoes and eggs and were thrown out of the convention. It was absolutely unbelievable. The token women were picked by the men and they were the Motor City Nine[†] who dangled chains or the Bernardines, and there were very few of them.

---

[*]   As a child television actor, Morgan was best known for her role as Dagmar Hansen in the popular 1950s series *Mama,* a role she started playing at age seven, based on the 1948 feature film *I Remember Mama.*

[†]   The Motor City Nine were nine female members of the Weathermen who in September 1969 performed a "jailbreak" at a high school in Detroit and lectured the students about racism and imperialism.

BERNARDINE DOHRN

I wish I had been smarter about integrating women's issues into all the other issues. It's so obvious that the oppression of women and war are integrated. We knew it at the time, and we talked about it, but I could have done more, certainly in the years that I was the head of SDS, to promote young women's leadership and development. I wish I'd had that one extra late-night meeting just with women.

I was one of the first through the door, or the glass ceiling, but an awakening was happening. So it would have been easy and doable to put extra energy into promoting the women who were activists. Every SDS chapter, for sure, was half women by that period of time, but they usually weren't giving the long speeches; they didn't have the loudest voice.

ROBIN MORGAN

The Miss America Pageant protest in Atlantic City in September of 1968 was the first mass demonstration of the women's movement in this contemporary wave of feminism, and it announced our existence to the world, and is often taken as the date of birth of this feminist wave, as differentiated from the nineteenth-century feminist suffrage struggle. We had arrests and it made history.[*]

At first we believed that we were involved in the struggle to build a new society, and the depressing realization was slowly dawning on us that we were doing the same work and playing the same roles *in* the movement as out of it; typing the speeches that men delivered, making coffee but not

---

[*]   On September 7, 1968, four hundred women protesters picketed outside the Miss America pageant in Atlantic City, New Jersey. They held signs that read, "Welcome to the Cattle Auction" and "No More Beauty Standards." The demonstration received heavy media coverage, bringing national attention to the women's liberation movement for the first time. Coverage centered around the "Freedom Trash Can," a receptacle where protesters threw items such as household cleaners, cosmetics, magazines like *Ladies' Home Journal,* and bras. False rumors spread that the trash can was set on fire, inspiring the moniker *bra burners,* which reporters and others used to describe women's liberation activists for years to come. Believe it or not, bras were never burned in Atlantic City.

policy, being accessories to the men whose politics would supposedly re-place the old order. The women's suffrage movement grew out of the drive to abolish slavery, and the current women's movement was begun largely, although not completely, by women who had been active in the civil rights movement and the antiwar movement, in student movements and in the left generally. Many women's groups already existed, but the feminist revolution went public in a certain way in Atlantic City and hasn't stopped ever since.

Bras were discarded (but not burned) along with household cleaners and cosmetics in the Freedom Trash Can at the Miss America contest in Atlantic City, September 7, 1968, in one of the first acts of second-wave feminist guerrilla theater.

TOM HAYDEN

There was that Atlantic City controversy over whether the bras were burned or not in the trash can in '68. That was one of those symbolic in-cidents that serve to signal the coming of a new movement. It's kind of distorted and weird, but that's the way the media is. After that, in '69, '70, '71, women's consciousness became extremely extreme.

VIVIAN ROTHSTEIN

In 1967, right after I got back from a trip to Vietnam with Tom Hayden and a group of peace activists, a small group of women, including Heather Booth, Naomi Weisstein, and Amy Kesselman and I, started organizing the Chicago Women's Liberation Union, CWLU. It was one of the first women's organizations. There were little collectives in New York, like the Redstockings, at the time. But because we were organizers in Chicago, and we were in a much more hostile political environment, we wanted to build a mass movement. We started bringing together women from all different backgrounds—academics, organizers, antiwar people. The idea was that it was a union of a bunch of different interests, and it didn't have to adhere to one etiology. We brought in the woman who was working in women's graphics, women working in women's health, women who were interested in antiwar activism, and we had chapters and so you could federate into a women's union. It wasn't like we had one idea, one analysis, and one solution. We really wanted to be diverse, *moralistic,* that was the term we used. We were criticized by the New York people for not being feminist enough, but we felt that they were elitist intellectuals—they were in a bubble of middle-class intellectuals.

It was a pretty neat organization, because there were all these projects: We had a newspaper, we had a graphics collective, we had an action committee for decent childcare. I ran this liberation school for women where we taught everything. For example, we took women who didn't know how to drive and taught them to drive in our clunky old cars. We also taught women's history, economics, an introduction to Marxism, how to fix your VW, and *Our Bodies, Ourselves* classes. We would come up with classes, put the word out, and we would get hundreds of women. We had no idea who they were. There were hundreds of women wanting to connect with the women's movement. I've never been involved in a movement like that where you turn around and there are thousands of people wanting to get involved. It was just amazing.

JANE FONDA (actor, peace activist)

I don't remember where on the tour across country I was when I called a woman friend of mine in New York and she said, "It's so great, there are five thousand women in the streets, protesting in favor of pro-choice." And I wrote in my journal that night, "This whole women's movement thing is such a diversion from what's really important." When I read that in my journal years later, I thought, Oh my God! I had forgotten that I felt that way then.

More than twenty-five thousand women marched down New York's Fifth Avenue in the Women's Strike for Equality on August 26, 1970, to commemorate the fiftieth anniversary of women's suffrage and demand legal abortion and equal opportunity in jobs and education. Some women held signs that read, "Don't Iron While the Strike Is Hot" and "End Human Sacrifice—Don't Get Married."

HEATHER BOOTH

After the '65 SDS meeting, a friend came to me saying that his sister, who was also at the University of Chicago, was pregnant and was not ready to have a child. She was nearly suicidal, and was looking for an abortion. I hadn't really thought about it ever before. I'd never had to face the issue myself, and didn't know very much about it, but I searched through the

Medical Committee for Human Rights, which was the medical arm of the civil rights movement, and found a doctor. It turned out that the doctor was T.R.M. Howard, who's an extraordinary person. He had been a physician in Mississippi, and had been a real activist, and had to leave the state when his name showed up on a Ku Klux Klan death list.

I was such a law-abiding person—I didn't litter, I crossed at the green light, I tried to follow the rules—but in the civil rights movement I had been picked up. I had also been arrested in an anti–Vietnam War induction. There was an understanding that when there's an unjust law, you have to challenge those laws and you can break the law if it's unjust. I viewed this more as a good deed, as a charitable act, not a political one. Later I found out how illegal it was: Three people talking about performing an abortion was considered conspiracy to commit felony murder, which I didn't quite focus on at the time, but I knew it wasn't legal.

Then a few months later someone else called. At that point I realized, Oh, this is a real issue. I started to learn about abortion, and the women's movement promoted some of the stories of botched abortions. There was a famous picture of a woman who died while trying to give herself an abortion. When I started to get more and more calls I realized we really better make a system out of this, and we called it Jane.

MARGERY TABANKIN
(University of Wisconsin student activist)

Abortion was not legal. I completely believed, whether you thought it was right or wrong, that it was a woman's choice. It was always clear to me that abortion is a person's most private decision, which they make with their family, their doctor, their boyfriend or husband, etc. It should not be public policy. I felt really strongly about it. So, to the extent that the women's movement touched me on an issue, it was over abortion.

Years later I did have an abortion, but not at that time. I had just made an intellectual commitment to it and was in the movement. But I was dealing with really frightened young people at school who had gotten pregnant and either weren't really in love or didn't want the baby because they were career driven and it was going to ruin their lives. There was an underground network of people in the Midwest who helped women find real doctors who agreed to do safe abortions. The Jane underground made this happen by raising the money to help women get where they were going, for instance if they needed to take the bus from Madison to Chicago. We would send someone to the bus station to wait for you. They would take you where you needed to go to the doctor's. You were taken care of. There were tons of women having abortions outside of the network and that's where you heard all of the horror stories of back alley abortions, coat hangers, and people bleeding out and almost dying. Many, many young women were never able to have children as a result of a botched procedure. People who were not MDs, like the woman down the street, were performing abortions to make some extra bucks. It was really horrible. Since this network existed, I was determined to be in the Madison–Chicago nexus. And so I did that for several years.*

It was amazing the way that the underground functioned, such that when people needed to know about it, they'd hear about it. Enough people knew that I was the person to talk to in Madison that people who I didn't even know would come out of the blue and say, "Can you help me?" I probably worked with Jane for about a year and I would say that seven or eight women came through me in that time.

HEATHER BOOTH

By the late sixties, Jane was providing over a hundred abortions a week. So many women were coming in that the doctor who was performing the procedures couldn't just do it himself. The women were watching the procedures, seeing everything; they knew what was involved. So he trained the women in how to perform the procedure; and by the end the women were doing the procedures themselves and had set up a front operation, which was someone's house that was ready to take the women in, often with kids. They'd wait there. They'd go to another house, and that second house would always shift where that was. Between '65, when I first

---

*   Estimates of the number of illegal abortions performed in the United States during the 1950s and '60s range from 200,000 to 1.2 million per year. As many as 5,000 women died annually from botched illegal abortions.

started to do it, and when *Roe v. Wade* became the law of the land [in 1973], the women in Jane believe they performed eleven thousand abortions.

VIVIAN ROTHSTEIN

I was the first staff member for the Chicago Women's Liberation Union, and I'd say 60 percent of our calls were for Jane. So we became a big referral service. But I wasn't part of the collective. We tried not to know too many details. The whole issue of legalization of abortion was a big deal. New York legalized it in July 1970.* But on May 4, 1972, seven women in Jane were charged with murder in Chicago.† The charges against them were dropped, but they all could have gone to prison. So they took enormous risks. Enormous.

JANE FONDA

I was in Killeen, Texas, at the Oleo Strut GI coffeehouse. I was there for two or three nights, and they had various speakers, and they had a feminist talk about the women's movement. I remember her saying, "You may think that we're talking about asking men to give up a share of their pie. But that's not what it's about. We're talking about expanding the pie, so that all of us can have a share." That was the very first time that I thought, Oh, so it's not anti-men. It's about sharing power. It's not about matriarchy. That was the first time that I started paying attention, and listening differently.

Feminists had been aggressive with me, in the beginning, because of *Barbarella.* "Aren't you ashamed that you made that sexist movie?" And

---

*   On April 11, 1970, Governor Nelson Rockefeller signed a bill that legalized abortions in New York State. Rockefeller credited women's liberation groups with playing an important role in the bill's passage.

†   On May 4, 1972, in Chicago, seven women were arrested during a police raid and charged with operating an illegal abortion clinic. Jane members were charged with three counts of performing abortions and three counts of conspiracy to perform abortions. Abortion became legal nationally in 1973 with the Supreme Court's *Roe v. Wade* decision.

I would say nobody forced me. But I started to become ashamed for the first time, and I stayed ashamed for a few decades, until I saw it again recently, and I thought that it was kind of camp and charming. There's nothing wrong with it. Barbarella is running the fucking spaceship! It just barely misses being a feminist movie, for heaven's sake, and I'd love to do

Feminists considered *Barbarella* a sexist film and criticized Jane Fonda for acting in the star role as a scantily clad science fiction action character. The 1968 film was based on a French comic strip and directed by Fonda's then husband, Roger Vadim.

a remake of it, as a feminist movie. But I wasn't sophisticated enough in 1969 to be able to think in those terms, or talk in those terms.

ROBIN MORGAN

Very soon after writing "Goodbye to All That," I was still calling myself a women's liberationist, not a feminist. But the minute I got out of New York and hit Oklahoma, Kansas, California, Minnesota, Georgia, whatever, and saw all these women who didn't call themselves radicals, quietly going about their lives and working with women in prison, working with neighborhood women, creating the first battered women's shelters, just *doing*, I fell in love with them. I thought, Oh my God, *this* is feminism. It was low on rhetoric and high on action and it was not about posturing and it was less concerned with leadership than with everybody pulling an oar. It was very practical. And I came back and I quit the *Rat* collective and started calling myself a feminist.

By then I had already begun assembling *Sisterhood Is Powerful*, which I'd started back in '67 and '68 because our various CR groups would take trips to campuses, and hand out these mimeographed papers that people were writing, like "The Politics of Housework," and "Resistances to Consciousness," and other early papers. We were getting bursitis from lugging around these goddamn heavy shopping bags. I was working as an editor at Grove Press and was already a published poet, so I thought in terms of books: I thought the movement needs a cheap, easily available *book* that anybody can pick up at an airport, that can be in newsstands as well as bookstores, so that we don't have to lug around these piles of mimeographed papers. Also, books go where organizers can't. So I tromped into my little CR group and I said, "I think we need a book, and I can assemble a book, and I want your piece in it, and your piece in it, and your piece."

Doubleday assigned me a male editor, but I wouldn't work with him. So I said, "You have to find me women." So his secretary and two junior copy editors were the women that I actually worked with, although it is true that whenever we needed some clout, we had to go to John Simon. I insisted that it be published simultaneously in hard- and paperback, which you simply didn't do then. I wanted the paperback to be short and fittable in a pocket even though it was so chunky. I was also rather proud of myself that the book had "daughters"; for example, Kate Millett—who then was an academic at Columbia—was doing a dissertation, and I asked to see it and I printed a part of it. Out of that, she got a contract for what became *Sexual Politics*.*

EMILY GOODMAN (feminist lawyer, judge)

"Sisterhood is powerful" became the slogan. Everybody had pins and trappings with the logo from the cover of the book of the red fist—it was

---

* Morgan's 1970 anthology of feminist essays, *Sisterhood Is Powerful*, is credited with launching several important feminist writers, including Kate Millett, Florynce Kennedy, and Naomi Weisstein. It was the first major anthology of the second-wave feminist movement.

on posters everywhere. It really represented the movement, and the movement was the way it was really referred to. I mean nobody said "the sisterhood." It was *the movement*.

Now, to other people, the movement might mean the civil rights movement or the antiwar movement, but for me, the movement is the women's movement, and I have to say it did change my life. I was already a lawyer, so I had made that step, but almost everything that flowed after that was attributable to the women's movement.

TOM HAYDEN

At the Red Family commune, my girlfriend wanted me to leave because her emergence as a full leader was blocked by my being a famous person. I think it was nothing more complicated than that. The group fell apart after that. It had served its purpose. I think she needed to be an independent spirit, because she had been in an early conventional marriage and had missed the wildness of the early sixties and mid-sixties. There are a lot of women like that, who got married early, had a traditional marriage, had kids, and missed the sixties. Then suddenly, in a big rupture, they left their marriages and caught up with the sixties in a hurry. Then having seen it all, they settled into a more committed relationship later on. I've met a lot of women like that. You have to break up everything to put the pieces of your life back on the table.

ROBIN MORGAN

We were a whole generation that, for the first time, said No to a war that the country had declared or found itself mired in and then began saying No to other things, and did so awkwardly at times and with bombast and rhetoric and prick waving but that at least was questioning the death grip of the 1950s, which was a stultification of passion and sanity and the genius of the human spirit. It had been a clampdown on the way life was lived in this country.

I grew up in the fifties. I had a freer, in many ways, growing up because I was a working kid in the theater. But if you had a real average middle-of-the-country growing up, god help you. And this burst through all of that with Day-Glo colors like in *The Wizard of Oz* when it goes from black and white into color. That was from the fifties into the sixties and then when people say "the sixties" they really mean the late sixties into the 1970s. Everything suddenly was Technicolor and there was hope!

CHAPTER 18

CAMBODIA

(March–May 1970)

Kissinger said Nixon usually wanted to intensify the bombing. "He was in the habit of wanting more bombing . . . his instructions most often were for more bombing."

—BOB WOODWARD,
The Last of the President's Men

ON APRIL 20, 1970, PRESIDENT NIXON ANNOUNCED THE WITHDRAWAL of 150,000 American ground troops from Vietnam as part of his Vietnamization policy, designed to pacify domestic opposition to the war. The military reported fewer American war casualties in the first three months of 1970 than in any first quarter since 1965. During this same time, the administration engaged in a secret bombing campaign against North Vietnamese forces in Cambodia. In the fourteen months leading up to April 1970, Nixon authorized 3,360 flights over Cambodia, which dropped 110,000 tons of bombs.* The secret bombing campaign soon escalated into an invasion with American troops on the ground. The first voices to protest the invasion came from inside the White House walls.

---

* These statistics come from Seymour Hersh, *The Price of Power: Kissinger in the Nixon White House* (New York: Summit Books, 1984), p. 65.

ROGER MORRIS (Nixon National Security Council aide)

The briefing memos from the February and March secret negotiations with the North Vietnamese that Henry [Kissinger] carried to Paris will never be available.* All of that is in classification way beyond any FOIA [Freedom of Information Act] request. We were down to a power-sharing arrangement in the South. We called it the "leopard spot" settlement, that would divide authority [in South Vietnam] between a South Vietnamese communist–Viet Cong military political presence and the Saigon government, with a withdrawal of the North Vietnamese main force. Now, a withdrawal of main force troops across the border was a little bit like withdrawing from Manhattan across the GW Bridge. Everybody understood that they could've come back in quickly, but the whole idea of the settlement was to buy time. We're talking about appearances here.

By early spring 1970, the negotiations are looking really encouraging, but it's at that moment that the coup takes place in Cambodia, and Prince Sihanouk is overthrown.† The coup was really a tipping point, and it set off not only the Cambodian communists, who we now know, and we should've known then, were quite independent of Hanoi. The communist Cambodians and Vietnamese looked like a monolith to many in Washington, but it was anything but. It not only set them off, but it also triggered anxieties and a counter-escalation in Hanoi, so that the flow of men and matériel into Cambodia [from North Vietnam] became heavier.

What agreement we thought we were close to achieving with North

---

* Between February and April of 1970, Kissinger held clandestine meetings in a small house in the Paris suburbs with North Vietnamese Communist Party leader Le Duc Tho. Meanwhile, a public peace conference between the two countries was taking place in Paris proper. The meetings between Kissinger and Tho were so secret that Secretary of State William Rogers and Secretary of Defense Melvin Laird didn't find out about them until a year later. Stanley Karnow, *Vietnam: A History* (New York: Viking Press, 1983), pp. 623–24.

† On March 18, 1970, the Cambodian General Assembly unseated Prince Norodom Sihanouk, who was in Paris at the time, and placed Prime Minister Lon Nol, an anticommunist and U.S. sympathizer, in power. Sihanouk, who had been in power since 1955, had kept Cambodia's neutrality in the war by tolerating the North Vietnamese use of its territory along the Vietnam border and not responding to U.S. air strikes inside the country. Lon Nol tried to kick the North Vietnamese out of Cambodia and his actions ultimately led to the Cambodian Civil War and the Khmer Rouge takeover in 1975.

Vietnam by February or March of 1970 was set back enormously by the coup. When the intelligence began to come in about the other side's response to the coup, Nixon was thoroughly pissed. He thought his manhood was at stake and we were being tested and provoked.

That's the origin of the planning for the Cambodian invasion, the "incursion," as it was called. In any case, the Cambodian coup triggers the counters by the other side [North Vietnam], and triggers in turn Nixon's descent toward the madness of the incursion. It killed the seeming progress that had been made in the secret negotiations.

If there is ever this great show trial about who did what to whom, and if anybody's going to stand in the dock, it certainly needs to be two American presidents, and the people who aided and abetted them. The guys who encouraged or nodded assent to the Cambodian generals in 1970, and who had been in close touch with them for quite a while before that, deserve to be right up there. It was a catastrophic event, and not just because it leads to the Khmer Rouge and the Killing Fields* and that genocidal nightmare, but it leads to four more years of a very bloody war, and all of the bombing of North Vietnam. When you start totaling up casualties in Indochina and in the whole peninsula, that coup looms very, very large.

I remember reading cable traffic and seeing this stream-of-consciousness stuff come from Nixon—the "Butterfieldgrams" we called them—as he read the intelligence and saw the news accounts after the coup.† It was clear that the invasion of Cambodia was building, and it was going to be on the table very soon.

Tony Lake, I love him, is a very quiet, cooperative, congenial

---

* From 1970 to 1975, Cambodia devolved into a civil war, with the American-backed Lon Nol fighting the communist North Vietnam–backed Khmer Rouge, who prevailed in April 1975. Pol Pot, the Khmer general, became one of the world's most vicious dictators, engineering the massacre of two million Cambodian people, many of whom died from sickness or execution while working as forced labor on rice paddies later known as "the Killing Fields." Pol Pot and the Khmer Rouge were forced out of power in 1979.

† Alexander Butterfield, a personal aide to Nixon who would publicly reveal Nixon's secret taping system during the Watergate investigation, wrote daily memos to White House staffers of Nixon's directives and wishes, which the National Security Council staffers called "Butterfieldgrams."

personality—a thoughtful, decent man. We had adjacent offices in the Executive Office Building, those beautiful, old, ornate offices, with marble fireplaces. I remember going in and startling my dear friend, who I used to ride on the back of his motorcycle with every night to go home to Chevy Chase. I slammed my fist down on his desk to the point where most of the papers rose off the surface of the desk and said, "If there is one fucking American trooper across that line, I'm out of here." It was just a way of expressing that any American military response to what was going on in Cambodia was going to make matters worse, and would certainly kill all the work that we had done to try to develop some kind of peaceful settlement with North Vietnam.

I never had this discussion with Kissinger; in fact, I've never seen him refer to it anywhere—I'm sure that Henry would say that there wasn't really anything that promising or that serious on the negotiation table. But that's not true. I thought we were very, very close, and he did, too, to the point where there were not so frivolous jokes about a Nobel Peace Prize for Kissinger. His whole thing was about celebrity from the get-go.

But in any case, to me, it was real. Tony and I were sitting there at the summit of the American government. Now, bear in mind that you're getting up to go to work every day in the same building with Spiro Agnew. We called them the Gestapo, the Berlin Wall. Ehrlichman* and the entire Nixon staff were made up of these right-wing, quasi-Nazis. I mean, it was a terribly squalid and reprehensible political culture to be a part of, but you've got a president whose approval ratings are a hell of a lot better than Obama's are now.

TONY LAKE (National Security Council aide)

The central tension leading up to our resignation was on the one hand, working in the government gave me extraordinary access. I always argued on the margins, and argued on tactics, but I'd never argued on my growing

---

*   John Ehrlichman, the White House chief domestic advisor, and H. R. Haldeman, White House chief of staff, were part of Nixon's inner circle. The two men were called the "Berlin Wall" by other White House staffers because of their German-sounding last names, and their success in isolating Nixon from other staffers.

belief that we simply could not succeed and therefore invading Cambodia was a deeply immoral venture because it could not lead to success, and any benefits could not possibly equal the terrible costs. That sounds very abstract, but it was far more emotional then. I was determined to argue it more with Kissinger, and he welcomed that, and I did my best, often with Roger.

The problem was that while I had that access and that opportunity to argue on the inside, the people I tended to agree with were free to voice their opinions in a way that I could not. So, while my friends were outside the ring of buses,* both metaphorical and a couple of times real, ringing the White House to keep them outside, I was inside being asked to write a statement opposing what they were doing, and what I believed. You can only do that if you're arguing honestly. But if you begin to understand that you're not effective enough inside to justify doing that, then you shouldn't stay.

ROGER MORRIS

The actual decision to invade was not considered by the September Group.† If you contrast the care and the time and the information that went into the September Group planning, the invasion was a matter of the Pentagon putting forward these contingency plans, which they had on the shelf, and Nixon saying yes. It was never a full-fledged debate in the U.S. government. It's sort of Ludendorff and Hindenburg.‡ You've got Nixon and Kissinger running the show at this point, and even somehow if Rogers and Laird and [Richard] Helms at the CIA, even if these people had somehow mounted some kind of opposition to the invasion—and none of them did—it would have been unavailing, I'm sure.

---

*   Buses were placed in a ring around the White House for protection during antiwar protests.

†   The September Group was a study group Kissinger convened of ten of his NSC staffers, including Roger Morris and Tony Lake, to explore different military options for the war, including the invasion of Cambodia.

‡   Paul von Hindenburg and Erich Ludendorff were German generals in World War I who together commanded the nation's war effort. Hindenburg later became president of the Weimar Republic.

I think that Kissinger's secret Paris negotiations were doomed by their very success. I think Kissinger thought that he could get back to where he was [with the "leopard spot" agreement] in the spring of 1970 very quickly. And, of course, it took him more than two years to do that. It isn't until late in '72, when he says, "Peace is at hand," and even then it's not at hand. They still have to do the awful Christmas bombing of Hanoi in '72 and '73. So we're a long way away from getting back to anything like a leopard spot arrangement. And ironically, the South Vietnamese government is like a frail, older person. Time is not on their side. They are a weak and weakening government, and so the longer they last, the less able they are to cope on their own. When the final withdrawal takes place, it's like a house of cards.

If somebody had said to me after the November 3 [Silent Majority] speech, "You're going to be gone from here within six months, and within six months there will be an overthrow of Prince Sihanouk, and the Marines will be in Cambodia," I would've said, "You've been smoking what they brought back from Saigon." Those are two very different worlds, the world of early November 1969 and the world of April–May 1970. And that's not very long. It's a five-month period in which the world turns upside down, in many ways.

TONY LAKE

On a Saturday morning, about a week before what they called the incursion, but it looked like an invasion to me, Kissinger called in four of us— Roger and me, Larry Lynn, and Bill Watts. I remember as we walked into the office, Kissinger said to Bill, who was his duty officer that morning, "I'm meeting with my bleeding hearts." Kissinger laid out the plan and my recollection is that I did a good bit of the arguing simply because I was the one who'd been working on Vietnam the most, and had been arguing with Kissinger all along. At the end of the meeting, Kissinger said, "Tony, I knew what you were going to say." I remember thinking to myself, I can leave now because if I've become that predictable, then I obviously don't have that much influence. So Roger and I wrote a letter of resignation, gave it to Al Haig, and said, "Please deliver this on the day of the invasion," which was about a week later. Haig hesitated a day or two and then gave it to Kissinger.

ROGER MORRIS

Kissinger called us into a meeting and we told him that this was one more flawed and futile measure, and that it was not going to have any decisive effect on the war. We all knew that there was no magic capital that you had to capture across the Cambodian border. We knew that this would have a huge effect in Cambodia, and in Vietnam would invite further escalation, would not seriously or fatally wound the other side, which was the conclusion of the September Group about a massive bombing campaign. I mean, an incursion into Cambodia by a few brigades with APCs [armored personnel carriers] and some air was just picking a scab. It wasn't really going to achieve anything, and it was going to snuff out the chance for a peaceful settlement.

We didn't believe that this was going to threaten the president's base. Hell, the president's base was cheering, "It's about time we kicked their butt." But we did say that there was going to be a violent and very bitterly divisive reaction in the United States. Kissinger was not very argumentative, but was disdainful and dismissive, and thanked us for our opinions. The decision had already been made. There were various theories that Kissinger had to go along with the Cambodian invasion in order to preserve his position, because, after all, he was the only hope for sanity in a government dominated by Haldeman and Ehrlichman and all the rest. And we didn't disagree with that. Part of the decision to not make a big deal publicly about our resignation, which I think is the biggest mistake I ever made in my life, was because Kissinger was already under fire for having what the White House thought were a bunch of Harvard communists on his staff, and subversives, who were undercutting the president. The irony is that nothing could be further from the truth. I never had any political loyalty to any president. Most of us were former Foreign Service officers. We were close enough to the dreams of our boyhood that nobody was playing partisan politics. We really were trying to bring out the best in a president who was an extraordinarily mixed bag, and capable of statesmanship, and capable of madness. So the high and the low were always there, the dark and the light. But no one was undercutting anybody. And there really was a serious effort to bring about a peaceful settlement.

Our resignations were extraordinarily rare at the moment. We were utterly alone in terms of any kind of precedent. In fact, it's a very select club even since then. A few people resigned over Serbia and Kosovo. A few people resigned over Iraq. But it's a very, very small group of people exiting American foreign policy on matters of principle and policy. We were at the end of a long and continual frustration with the administration. We knew how distorted and seedy things were even though we didn't really know about the beginning of the Plumbers. We knew that there had been some phone tapping of the staff, as, indeed, there had been. I'd been warned by [former NSC member and Kissinger aide] Larry Eagleburger about that. "Don't say anything on your phone you don't want Haldeman to read over breakfast." We knew that there was a lot of paranoia and a lot of division in the government. We knew that the people around Nixon were unreconstructed know-nothings.

Should I have stayed that long? Should I have gotten out earlier? Should I have left when Johnson left? Maybe, but I don't regret the experience, and I don't regret the decision. I think that the one big mistake was not blowing the whistle as loud as we possibly could in every corner we possibly could, and we didn't.

DANIEL ELLSBERG

When the four of them resigned, they agreed that they did not want to embarrass Kissinger, because they had the impression, falsely, that Kissinger was a restraining influence on Nixon, so they didn't want to hurt Kissinger's influence. They were quite wrong. Kissinger fanned the flames for Nixon. He was fooling them. But they said, "We will not have a press conference and say why we're leaving," which was because of Cambodia.

ROGER MORRIS

There was no formal announcement. We didn't call a press conference. We should have, and been very specific about it. But I think Bill Watts went to a friend at the time, and it was buried inside *The New York Times*. This was the price we paid for trying to preserve Henry.

NEW YORK TIMES, MAY 23, 1970

FOUR MORE LEAVE KISSINGER'S STAFF

by Robert M. Smith

The National Security Council staff headed by Henry A. Kissinger is losing at least four more members and there are unverified reports that one other is also quitting. . . .

ROGER MORRIS

I didn't know I was going to cross the aisle and go to the Hill and work for a Democrat, but I knew that whatever I was going to do, I would be trying to join an effective opposition to get this guy Nixon out of office. Tony ended up working for Muskie, and I worked for Mondale. Tony and I, we were trying to build what we knew needed to be a much stronger congressional base of opposition to the war.

Everybody in Washington who was in the know understood why we left. Mary McGrory, who was this wonderful columnist for *The Washington Post*, for example, was a friend of mine, and she called up and said, "Good going," and "Where do you want to go next?" She was the one who was responsible for introducing me to Mondale. Everybody on the Hill knew it. Mondale would take me around to meetings in Minnesota and elsewhere, whether it's a high school rally or a bunch of donors in a smoky basement, and would say, "Here's my aide, Roger Morris. The night they invaded Cambodia he walked out, and thumbed his nose, and told them all to go fuck themselves." There would be cheers and applause and "Hey, good for you," and "Now let's move on to really important business. Let's see, how about that check you promised for the campaign?"

TONY LAKE

After I got out, I did start writing op-eds, and opposing the war, and after a decent interval I went to work for Muskie. I became the foreign policy coordinator in his campaign. Together we fought with Clark Clifford, Paul Warnke, Les Gelb, and others, urging Muskie* to take a strong stand on the war. By the way, the White House kept the wiretap on my phone while I was working for Muskie, and picked up advance word of his speeches, which is not my definition of democracy in action. I sued them. It was settled many years later.

ROGER MORRIS

People on the Hill knew very little about Vietnam. They knew enough to be against it. The casualty list was too high. The draft protest was huge and there were political reasons for opposing the war, but my view is that much of the opposition was simply uninformed and highly partisan, and there was a lot of sheer Nixon hatred. They didn't always know why they hated him, or for that matter, why they should. And, of course, they should've in ways they didn't even imagine.

DANIEL ELLSBERG

Roger Morris said to me—he said I could quote him—the greatest regret and shame of his life was that they had not spoken out at the time of Cambodia about where this was going, and taken documents. He said, quote, "We should've thrown open the safes and screamed bloody murder, because that's exactly what it was."

---

*   Maine senator Edmund Muskie ran for the Democratic nomination for president in the 1972 campaign but lost in the primaries to South Dakota senator George McGovern.

CHAPTER 19

KENT STATE

(April–May 1970)

Next time a mob of students waving their nonnegotiable demands starts pitching bricks and rocks at the student union, just imagine they're wearing brown shirts or white sheets and act accordingly.

—VICE PRESIDENT SPIRO AGNEW,
April 28, 1970

IN REACTION TO THE ANNOUNCEMENT BY PRESIDENT NIXON ON April 30, 1970, that American troops would move across the border to fight North Vietnamese strongholds in Cambodia, America's peace movement reacted with new levels of intensity. High school and college campuses, already tinderboxes of antiwar sentiment, ignited and the largest student strike in the nation's history followed. The political disconnect between the Silent Majority and the peace movement presented an unbreachable chasm. On two college campuses, Kent State in Ohio and Jackson State in Mississippi, violent clashes produced tragic results.

PRESIDENT RICHARD NIXON

Televised Announcement, Thursday, April 30, 1970

I have concluded that the actions of the enemy in the last ten days clearly endanger the lives of Americans who are in Vietnam now and would constitute an unacceptable risk to those who will be there after withdrawal of another 150,000. To protect our men who are in Vietnam, and to guarantee the continued success of our withdrawal and Vietnamization program, I have concluded that the time has come for action. . . . We take this action not for the purpose of expanding the war into Cambodia but for the purpose of ending the war in Vietnam and winning the just peace we all desire.

LAUREL KRAUSE
(sister of Kent State student Allison Krause)

On April 30 Nixon goes on TV—you can watch the speech on YouTube— and he's pointing to the map of Vietnam and all of Indochina. Prior to this, he told everyone that he had a secret plan to end the war in Vietnam. And, instead, he announced that they were expanding the war in Vietnam, into Cambodia, and Laos, and they had actually been bombing there for over a year.

DEAN KAHLER (Kent State student)

I saw Nixon speak in 1968 at University of Akron, and he talked about ending the war—he had a secret plan. He wasn't going to tell anybody about it because it was secret. So that was my first thought on April 30, 1970, that he had this plan to end the war, and he was going to tell us all about it.

I went to the Robin Hood, a little tavern right off the edge of the Kent State campus, and the place was packed, and quiet. There were people drinking and talking, but people were sitting at the tables with notebooks out, and there were three or four televisions. They were all on, volumes were turned up, and Nixon comes on and gives a speech, and everybody starts booing, and everybody was saying, "Shh, shh, shh, shh."

So then everybody shut up, and we started listening to it, and when it was over it was like, "That lying sack of shit! That lying son of a bitch!"

People were pissed. And I remember talking with a couple of my friends as we walked back to the dormitories, and it was like, what does this mean? Are we expanding the war? He said cut off supply lines. But hell, that could go on for three or four more years.

So it made people upset, and we found out the next morning that people all over the country were pissed about it. There were riots and student demonstrations happening all over the country. Here at Kent nothing was happening. It was Friday afternoon. Kent is a large commuter campus. Lots of people went home on the weekends because they lived close. I was going home that weekend because my twentieth birthday was Friday.

JOHN FILO

(Kent State student, photographer for *The Valley Daily News*)

By this time it's my senior year, I'm really against the war. I just felt it was unwinnable. I just felt it was the wrong thing, and what triggered the whole May 4 thing was Nixon saying, my favorite quote is "We're expanding the war to shorten it." There was this whole semantic thing going on, and everyone was saying, "No, this is an invasion of Cambodia. This is a major expansion of the war."

From my high school, within a grade or two above and below me, five people were dead. I mean, you'd be at school and you'd say "Oh, you know, Jerry Vokish died." "Geez, Jerry, wow." You get a letter from home, and Mom would say, "I was talking to so-and-so, and Robert Ringler got killed in Vietnam." The list kept mounting. And you just saw that there was no end to this. Just more meat for the grinder, I thought.

FRIDAY, MAY 1, 1970

BOB GILES

I was managing editor of the *Akron Beacon Journal* in 1970. Kent State was a local story; the campus is only twelve miles from our newsroom, and we covered the university. Leading into that weekend in early May, we knew there was going to be trouble, and it began Thursday night after President Nixon announced the U.S. was going to be bombing Cambodia. Friday afternoon there was an informal gathering and we reported that students ripped some pages out of a textbook Constitution and buried it.

Kent was a typical college town, where there were the town-gown tensions. There's a place in the city called North Water Street, where there are a lot of bars, so that night, Friday night, the kids started to gather. And because there was all this tension over the Nixon order to go into Cambodia, things got a little bit out of hand, and there were some windows broken. The police came and tried to settle it down. And the mayor, LeRoy Satrom, called the governor and said, "Can you send the National Guard to keep peace on the campus?" One of the odd things that has never been satisfactorily explained to me was that the president of the university, Robert White, had gone to Iowa to make a speech, and he never appeared during the weekend, so there was no senior leader of the university administration present when all of this started to unfold.

SATURDAY, MAY 2, 1970

JOE LEWIS (Kent State student)

I watched as the ROTC building was burned down on Saturday night. I lived in the dormitory called Johnson Hall, that was right across the commons from the ROTC building. ROTC buildings across the country had been targeted for demonstrations, because of their connection to the military, obviously.

I observed from afar as a crowd gathered around the ROTC building and attempted to set it on fire. There were some futile attempts. They burned the drapes. They threw a flare on the roof, but they weren't successful. Then someone in the midst of the crowd suggested that we go around campus and get more people to support us. I fell along behind as this crowd walked around the front part of the campus for maybe an hour, and I saw people leave the campus and walk out onto the main street. Some people were disrupting traffic with construction compressors and barricades, piling them in the middle of the road. And then, as we were walking along the street, the National Guard began to arrive from Ravenna, which was to the east on State Route 59. They came in with trucks and jeeps and half-tracks. Everyone took off and headed back towards campus. By the time we got back to the area of my dorm, the ROTC building was fully engulfed in flames.

Governor [James A.] Rhodes was running for the Republican nomination for U.S. Senate, and he was a law-and-order guy. He was talking about quashing demonstrators, and I believe there was some communication between him and the White House—Spiro Agnew. So I blame Nixon and Agnew and Rhodes for what happened later, because I think they set the tone. And because of the media manipulation, people thought antiwar demonstrators were communist inspired. I think it was a widely held belief that the demonstrators were unsavory people not worth protecting. They didn't have the right to object to what our government was doing in Vietnam. That was the general feeling of the time.

That Saturday night my parents called me, because it was all over the news that the ROTC building had been burned to the ground. They wanted to make sure that I was okay, and not doing anything that I shouldn't be. I assured them that I wasn't. But I remember a poignant moment, standing in my buddy's dorm room watching the building burn, and Buffalo Springfield's "For What It's Worth" was playing. That connection is just forever linked in my brain. I know it seems trite, but not to me. In my friend's room, while the building was burning, we heard the song on the radio.

SUNDAY, MAY 3, 1970

DEAN KAHLER

On Sunday, the governor gave a press conference and made it pretty clear that he was going to keep the school open, and that's the day that he called us the worst element that we harbor in our society. That we, as college students, were worse than the brownshirts, the night riders, and the vigilantes. Those are all quotes from Governor Rhodes. It felt terrible.

GOVERNOR RHODES

These people just move from one campus to the other and terrorize the community. They're worse than the brownshirts and the communist elements and also the night riders and vigilantes. They're the worst type of people that we harbor in America.

DEAN KAHLER

I mean, just look where Kent is—it's surrounded by Akron, Canton, Cleveland, and Youngstown. Not exactly a hotbed for liberal thought. Maybe it was a hotbed for liberal, union thought because everybody worked in the steel industry, the auto industry, or auto-related industries in those towns. And it was in Ohio. It's not Berkeley. It's not Boston. It's not New York City. It's not Los Angeles. It's not San Francisco. This is Ohio. So it really, I thought, the Rhodes comment was a slap in the face.

I looked like Opie. I had the short haircut, comb-over, a little part in the left-hand side, full of freckles, horn-rimmed glasses. So I did not look like a hippie. I had a dress shirt on most times, or a T-shirt. I was a bit of a jock. I played football. I grew up in a rural, agricultural community called East Canton, Ohio, near my family's farm.

BOB GILES

On Sunday night, tensions started to rise again. By this time, the governor had arrived on campus, and took over, without asking the board of trustees. Jim Rhodes was in charge of what was going to happen on the campus. He issued an order saying there would be no gatherings of any kind, peaceful or otherwise. The National Guard's instructions were to break them up.

DEAN KAHLER

When I got home from celebrating my twentieth birthday with my friends Saturday evening my mom told me that they burned down the ROTC building on campus. And I thought, What? Although I understood the symbolism of the whole thing, it just didn't seem proper, at all. So I went to bed. The next day my parents and I talked about it, and we decided I wasn't going to do anything stupid. I wasn't going to get close to anything that was going to be violent or destructive.

They took me back to campus, and as we were driving in, we had to stop several times for ID checks. My father, being a truck driver during World War II in the Philippines and Okinawa, and eventually in Korea, knew how to handle it. He knew everybody's stars and stripes. He knew how to address them properly.

When I got to campus I was surprised at the number of National Guard troops that were around. Everywhere you went, there they were. National Guard troops lined up in long lines, guarding buildings, carrying rifles, helmets, green uniforms, armored personnel carriers driving around with people riding in the back of the beds with canvas-top covers. Everywhere you went they were about a parking meter away from each other.

I was looking for a friend of mine who was in the National Guard, who was four or five years older than I was. I actually found somebody who knew who he was, believe it or not. He said, "Oh, his unit were just being called up today from guarding the truckers." He was on the truckers strike. He was on his way back to the armory today, and he was to come to campus the next day, on Monday.

JOE LEWIS

Sunday, when people got up, it was a spring day and the university was occupied by nine hundred Ohio National Guardsmen. They set a bivouac up on the practice soccer field, and they were positioned around the administration buildings and other major buildings on campus. There were half-tracks, and guardsmen with helmets and bayonets on their M-1 Garands. But they were visiting with students who were walking around and chatting with them, particularly the coeds.

LAUREL KRAUSE

That Sunday afternoon was a very nice day on campus. It was gorgeous, and there was a lot of interaction with the National Guard, who were the same age as a lot of the students. My sister noticed a flower in one of the

Kent State student Allison Krause (age nineteen) was a popular campus political activist. Here she is in April 1970 collecting money at a campus rally where Jerry Rubin spoke.

National Guardsmen's guns, and his superior came out and said, "Soldier, what are you doing with a flower in your rifle?" My sister said, "What's the matter with peace? Flowers are better than bullets."

BEN POST (Kent State student, reporter for the *Record-Courier*)

I was out of town on Friday and Saturday, so I was not there for the burning of the ROTC building. But I got a call from my editor, and I got back late Saturday night. That Sunday I immediately went to the office and was sent by the paper up to what's called Prentice Gate, which is the entrance to the university where a group of students sat down in the middle of the intersection, blocking traffic. They were protesting the National Guard's presence on campus and the war. And they wanted to speak to the university president, Robert White. I got there at about seven o'clock at night, and things built over the evening into the late hours—ten, eleven o'clock.

So I'm standing there as a reporter trying to take in everything that's happening. There were two groups of authorities there—the city police and the National Guard units. At one point one of the local policemen said to the students, "Just break it up and go and we'll let you go." But at that point, a National Guard officer came over and said, "No, this is an illegal assembly," or something to that effect, and "We're going to act now." I'm standing by this telephone pole right on the corner, and I can see the university in the background and the gates and all these students in the street.

DEAN KAHLER

I went up to the front campus gate because I heard there was a gathering there. So I got up there, and people were sitting in the street, even though they were told, "You're not allowed to sit in the street," with bullhorns. Then finally someone came on and said, "The president and the mayor will be here in a half an hour to speak to you." And I said, "Okay, that's cool." Within a half an hour, the only thing that was there was more National Guard troops, and there were now two helicopters flying over us, with their spotlights shining down on us.

BEN POST

Tension was high among the students and the police and guard units and it built throughout the evening. There might have been fifty to seventy-five students sitting in the intersection. As the standoff dragged on I noticed a group of guardsmen starting to move behind the students. I was standing next to a guardsman. He was holding an M-1 rifle balanced on his hip. Then he did something that should have registered with me since I had been in the army, but it didn't. I don't know if it would have made any difference if I reported on this in the paper, or if I told my editors, but it's stayed with me all this time.

In the military, when you put in a magazine, you lock and you load it. You put in your clip and then you pull back the lever and you're ready to go. I saw a guardsman put a clip of live ammunition into his M-1. It didn't register at all. Here I wanted to be a journalist, I wanted to be a great observer. On the day of the shooting I felt that if only I had written something about them loading real bullets, and published it in the paper. Events were rushing so fast, maybe it wouldn't have made a difference. But it made a difference to me, because I should have at least recognized that and reported it and I didn't.

This was Sunday night close to 9:30 or 10 P.M., and there were some other words exchanged with the group by the National Guard, and suddenly they just moved in. They had bayonets, and they moved into the crowd, and the crowd got up. Some yelled, "betrayed," and some said, "liars," because they thought they were going to be allowed to leave on their own. Suddenly tear gas started being thrown. And because the guard had semicircled them, there was only one way for them to run, and they ran up the street.

But as they ran, there were several students who were bayoneted. I had to testify at a hearing on this about four months later, because they didn't believe that we had seen these kids bayoneted, but they were. John Hayes, another reporter, and I both saw it. I mean, they were jabbed. And we saw one kid get stabbed, and he ran up the street and he ran into a house. We followed him into the house to see what was going on with him, and he was on the floor in the kitchen. These other students were yelling at us to get out. We asked how he was doing and who he was, and they said, "Get out, get out, we don't want you here."

Then we heard a commotion outside, so we left and followed the guard up the street, and the students—it was dark by then—and the students started to fade into the darkness on the campus. The guards made a left turn and moved onto the campus. There was a little knot of journalists that I had attached myself to, because there is safety in numbers—there were about six of us. So we started this trek across the campus. It's dark, and I remember this vividly: There are lines of guardsmen with their weapons held up and balanced on their hips. And they're in semidarkness with the glow of these lights outlining them. Every once in a while you would hear one of them say, "We're going to get you." Because they probably thought we were students. Well, some of us were. Or, "You're dead." Just threatening comments that came out of this darkness.

DEAN KAHLER

The next thing you know, all hell broke loose, because there was tear gas. They locked all the dorms up, and people inside were opening the doors and letting people in. Finally I got in, and it was chaos inside. People were everywhere roaming the hallways, and opening their windows, and setting their big, huge speakers, and blasting noise out of the windows, and people were filling up book bags with water, and taking them up to the top floor, and dropping them ten stories. Ten stories, it almost reaches terminal velocity, right? It makes a hell of a sound when it hits the ground. So that was going on, and the National Guard was roaming around in their armored personnel carriers and their jeeps. It just was nuts.

JOE LEWIS

Some of the most frightening memories I have of that weekend involved three helicopters circling overhead on Sunday night with searchlights, low over the campus. The guardsmen were doing a sweep of the campus to get any students who were out and about into buildings. So, while the tear gas clouds were sprayed all over the campus, and these helicopters hovered overhead with searchlights, guardsmen, shoulder to shoulder, with bayonets fixed and put down in front of them, were herding students into buildings. And my RA [residential assistant] at the time told me later that he was holding the door open and encouraging anyone out there to come in, even if you didn't live there, and as he ushered the last student in and slammed the door closed, a guardsman with a bayonet lunged, and the knife of the bayonet was closed in the door.

LAUREL KRAUSE

It was war on that campus on Sunday night. My sister ran because she had to. They were running the students on the campus, in the middle of the night, teargassing them, helicopters, and she had been running with the crowd, to a dormitory way out, Tri-Towers, that was not near her dorm. They were shutting all the doors and not allowing the students in, and the bayoneted National Guard were coming at them. Someone opened one of the back doors, and Allison managed to get in, but she didn't get in with her boyfriend Barry. So, she made them open up the door and let Barry in. They had to. She was a force. So they spent the night, her last night, on the floor of the dormitory.

MONDAY, MAY 4, 1970

DEAN KAHLER

Monday morning I woke up, shook off the cobwebs, and went downstairs, had breakfast, and looked around outside, and there were still National Guard troops everywhere. It was a beautiful day that day, and the sun was shining. I decided not to go to my morning classes.

JOE LEWIS

On Monday I attended class with a girlfriend, and some of the professors were saying, "This is what democracy looks like. This is how you participate. You get involved, and you protest, and speak your mind." And others were saying, "This is a horrible threat to your safety, and you should not be going outside." Being eighteen, I wanted to see what was going on. I wanted to know what was going to happen next. After we went to class, there was a rally scheduled at noon. The Victory Bell, which was in the commons, rang, as it often did to gather assemblies. Myself and a thousand other people gathered around the Victory Bell. Across the commons, facing us—protecting the ashes of the burned-out ROTC building, it seemed—were a hundred and fifty or so National Guardsmen in full battle gear. Some people chanted antiwar slogans: you know, "Pigs off campus," "One, two, three, four, we don't want your f-ing war." I don't go for that. I like to think for myself. I don't like to repeat slogans others are saying.

For a long time, there was a standoff. Some campus policemen in a jeep came out to literally read us the riot act. I won't forget that—another auditory memory for me is the bullhorn and I think his name was Sergeant Rice from the campus police. He said, "Students of Kent State, this is an illegal assembly. Return to your dormitories." His jeep came by three times, with the same message. And each time the message was responded to by catcalls, threats, and a lot of raised middle fingers. Finally, a rock was thrown that hit the wheel of the jeep, and then, from the line of guardsmen, some nine or so people advanced with modified grenade launchers and fired tear gas canisters at the crowd.

A point I'd like to make, though, is that in spite of this activity, it didn't feel like there was a sense of impending disaster, or doom. It was a fairly nice spring day in Ohio, and with these tear gas canisters it became, like, a bizarre tennis match, where they would fire the tear gas towards the students. It wasn't really effective because of the wind. Students would cover their faces and throw the tear gas canisters back. When the guardsmen fired the tear gas, there would be a "boo," and when the student returned the tear gas canister, there would be a cheer.

Governor James Rhodes called in eight hundred Ohio National Guard soldiers to police the Kent State campus after students burned down the ROTC building (forefront of photo) in reaction to President Nixon's announcement that American troops had invaded Cambodia.

JOHN FILO

It's noon when all the classes changed. So whether you were for the war or against the war, it didn't make any difference. You were going to go watch what was going on. Or you had to cross that way to go to the student union to get lunch, or go back to your dorm. So, the protest starts, and all of a sudden a jeep comes out, and in it is a guardsman and state police, saying this is an illegal assembly, and of course, there were answers by the antiwar group, but then there were also answers by the students like "No, this is our university—we're paying to go here, we're not the people that burnt the ROTC building."

There was a tear gas barrage, back and forth, and I've been reading my Robert Capa books, the great Magnum photographer, and remember being told by my friend the AP war photographer Eddie Adams, "If your pictures aren't good enough, you're not close enough." Here I am trying to get down, and the guardsmen are on this end, and I'm running back to the students and then the guardsmen around the burnt-out ROTC structure are arcing tear gas canisters, and the wind comes up and blows it away. And then they run out of tear gas. So someone says, "Let's mount up and chase the students." I'm going, Wow, now is my chance. There are guardsmen with sheathed bayonets and batons, and maybe forty state policemen in riot gear are just standing there watching this all transpire. This is all happening outside of a building where I work, Taylor Hall. The guardsmen divide around Taylor Hall. The larger contingent going to the right and a smaller group to the left, who appeared to be after someone. I followed the left group to no avail for a close-contact photo of students and guardsmen.

DEAN KAHLER

I went around Taylor Hall, down the hill, across the Prentice Hall parking lot, across Midway Drive, got into a gravel parking lot, and pulled out a wet handkerchief that I had in my pocket. It was in a plastic bag. Then I grabbed a handful of gravel from the ground and flung it underhand in the direction of the National Guard who were about a hundred yards away from me. I actually hit some students in front of me. They turned around and screamed at me and gave me the finger. So it was like, Okay, I'm sorry, I'm just frustrated here, and I called the National Guard to lower their weapons that they were pointing at the students who were in the parking lot area. Students continued to throw stones from there. I saw some National Guard pick up tear gas canisters to throw at the students.

BEN POST

Suddenly the guard line said, "We are going to clear this area." So the guard line started moving towards Taylor Hall and up the hill. And as they moved, they tossed tear gas. And all of the guardsmen, or most of them at the time, had gas masks on. And I know from my experience that that's very claustrophobic. And when you're tense, I'm sure they were frightened, in certain ways. There's the uncertainty and you're wearing this rubber thing on your face with these little portholes for eyes. And you're seeing a very limited vision, and so you're tense. In front of you, what you see from that little rubber mask is people throwing stuff at you, people yelling at you. So if you're a young kid and you're about the same age as the students, the emotional level heightens.

JOE LEWIS

After a few minutes of the teargassing not being very effective, the guardsmen moved out and began approaching the students with fixed bayonets. The students, of course, got out of the way, and streamed between two buildings—Taylor Hall and Johnson Hall—up to the hill between the buildings in advance of the advancing guardsmen. And most of the guardsmen followed that path. I went that way, between Taylor Hall and Johnson Hall. And then, as I went there, I veered to the right, to the Johnson Hall side, and watched the guardsmen pass between these two groups of students. They passed over the top of the hill, and then down the other side, across a little road to what was the practice football field.

When they got down there, they made the announcement, "Students of Kent State"—over the bullhorn again—"we have you surrounded." There was actually a chuckle, because they had the fence on two sides of them, and then, opposite the road, was this group of students—a thousand or twelve hundred students, looking down on them. If anyone was surrounded, they were. But it still didn't take on the tone of seriousness that it deserved until a group of them kneeled down and aimed their rifles. They aimed their rifles towards the Prentice Hall parking lot, where the most vocal students were. Among them was Alan Canfora, my friend, who held a black flag. He was protesting the death of his neighbor, who had been killed in Vietnam about ten days before that. They didn't know that. They thought he was being defiant.

JOHN FILO

I was on the parking lot, which is elevated maybe eight feet above the practice football field. I saw a student with a black flag, and I go, "Oh, this is my picture." This student waving a black flag is running onto this big practice football field. There's a squad of guardsmen on one knee point-

John Filo took this photograph of Kent State University student Alan Canfora (age twenty) boldly waving a black flag at National Guardsmen who aim their guns at him. Minutes later, seventy-six members of Troop G marched up the hill, turned around, and twenty-eight guardsmen fired between sixty-one and sixty-seven shots at the students from approximately three hundred feet away. Canfora was shot in the right wrist, eight other students were also wounded (one was paralyzed for life), and four students were killed.

ing their rifles at him, and he's waving this flag, and so I'm like, "Oh, let me get this shot, because I can frame it." This is it, this is what I set out to do today; student protest in America is being met by this helmeted, armed force. A lone student waving one flag, and seventy-five, eighty guardsmen in the background with a squad in a rifle line pointing their rifles at him. I go, "Oh man, this is the best picture I'm ever taking. This is it." I was elated. It was a good picture. The guardsmen regrouped and marched back over the ground they had just covered, walking back toward their starting point at the burnt ROTC building.

DEAN KAHLER

I started following along behind the guard when they formed up their line and started marching uphill, and I thought, Oh, they're just going to go to the top of the hill to shoot tear gas. I'll just follow along. By then it was almost twelve thirty. I looked at my watch and thought, Why don't I go get a cup of coffee? I walked up a little bit towards the student union, which was right across the street from my next class.

So that was what was in my head when I was following along behind the National Guard, and I was on the practice football field when they turned, and lowered their weapons. I thought, Oh my God, they're going to shoot. Because I'm a farm boy and I've carried a rifle and a shotgun, and when somebody makes a deliberate motion like that, and lowers their weapons, pointing directly at you, that's a sign that they're ready to shoot because I've done that many a time when I'd been rabbit hunting, or pheasant hunting as a kid, and it was very frightening. I looked around, and there was no place to hide. I jumped to the ground, and I could hear bullets hitting the ground around me. Why are they shooting at me? And then I thought, Oh my God, I hope I don't get hit. And then, at about that time, I got hit, and it felt like a bee sting. It wasn't like Hollywood. I didn't roll over five or six times, flail in the ground, and freak out. It was just like a bee sting.

JOE LEWIS

I watched the guard pass in front of me and march to the crest of the hill. There were probably seventy-five men, and most of them crested the hill and looked like they were going to keep on going. When they got to the corner of the railing in front of Taylor Hall, as if by design, about a dozen of them wheeled and leveled their rifles back at the direction of the parking lot, which happened to be behind me. They leveled their rifles in my direction, as they had leveled their rifles on the practice football field, before, when they knelt and aimed. Being eighteen and frustrated, I responded with my middle finger upraised on my right hand. They held that position for just a second, until they began firing.

I was convinced that these guns were not loaded with live ammo— I thought, How ridiculous would that be? Until I saw the ground in front of me churn up, and I realized, at that moment, that they were live bullets. I was also shot at that point, through the middle of my body, which sent me sailing like a Disney cartoon character through the air, and I landed on my back on the ground. I had been shot through my right abdomen, with the bullet exiting my left jean pocket—it was a small entry wound, and a large exit wound.

LAUREL KRAUSE

The guard all turned in unison, and they all shoot in unison. Sixty-one to sixty-seven bullets at unarmed students. My sister was three hundred and forty-three feet away from her shooters. Everyone that was killed was at least a football field away. The excuse that the guard gave was that the students were attacking them, they feared for their lives, and had to respond to sniper fire in the crowd. The part that you don't hear is that my sister bled to death, for forty-five minutes, before an ambulance came, yet ambulances were available over the hill, reserved for guard and authority injuries only.

BEN POST

I'm standing by the corner, and I watch this ragged group of guardsmen go past me up the hill. My first impulse was to follow them up the hill. But I thought because there were so many students at that point—there were a knot of students on the corner with me—I decided to turn and run through the building, because there was an exit at the very back of the building. So I ran through the back of the building, and as I ran through the door and got out on this little portico area, the guard turned and fired. They were maybe thirty yards away from me. Not real far. A student fell in front of me, and I was just flabbergasted. A group of students immediately surrounded this person who was wounded. I just don't know what to do. I'm saying—what do you do with something like this? I asked somebody, "Who is it?" He said, "What does it matter who it is?"

JOE LEWIS

Later in court, I heard testimony that after I had been shot, and was convulsing on the ground, another guardsman shot me through the lower leg.

When quizzed on the witness stand during our civil trial why he shot someone who apparently had already been shot, his defense for attempted murder was "Well, everybody else was shooting him." That's what he said.

JOHN FILO

I get the camera to my eye, and I said, Oh, there's a guy pointing a rifle at me, I've got to get a picture of this, because no one's going to believe it. This is crazy, they're shooting blanks into the crowd, and that's when I heard a bullet go by, and I went, Wait a minute. I see this guy's gun go off, and immediately in front of me is a metal sculpture and the whole sculpture just goes *clang* and there's this cloud of rust, and then on the tree right next to me a big chunk of bark goes off. It's the same bullet. *Clang, chhk.* It was that quick. And you go, Oh shit, that's live ammunition! And you just freeze, and the firing's still going on, and you're hearing whizzes, and people are wounded here, and there's people wounded in front of me, and it seemed like forever.

Then I turned, and I literally took two giant steps down the hill, and I saw the body of Jeffrey Miller, and there was no one around, it was just a body in the street. He was literally pumping his last—it was like his neck was severed. I mean not completely, but the blood was just flowing. I said to myself, Why are you running now? It's all over. I said, Yeah, but I know this person's dead, and I'm going to stay here. He was not very far at all, about thirty feet.

I started shooting [pictures], and then this girl, out of the corner of my eye, runs up and kneels down beside him. I'm like, Oh, I've got to get a better angle. I sort of had him in profile. So I kept moving around, but I also knew I was running out of film. You're sort of counting, like, Oh man, I've got maybe three or four frames left. You wanted to shoot this, because you saw this person over the body. Once again, the iconic images that you grew up with as a child, in church. Here we are, we're looking at the pietà, except Christ isn't on Mary's lap. He's fallen off her lap onto the ground. So you want to shoot this and you're having this argument with yourself: Shoot the picture, don't shoot the picture. Shoot the picture, don't shoot

Kent State student Mary Ann Vecchio screams as she kneels over the body of fellow student Jeffrey Miller (age twenty), who was shot in the head by the Ohio National Guard from 265 feet away and killed instantly. Miller, Allison Krause, Sandra Scheuer, and Bill Schroeder were killed on May 4, 1970. Kent State student photographer John Filo won the Pulitzer Prize for this photograph.

the picture. As you're having this argument, she lets out this scream. And there's no debate anymore, you just sort of react to her movement. I shot that, shot another frame, and I was out of film on that roll.

DEAN KAHLER

If you reach around with your arm, and you put it just below the center of your shoulder blade, that's where the bullet hit me. I was on the ground. They were on top of the hill, shooting down the hill. I was ninety-two yards away, I think at that point in time. I was on the practice football field. I got hit, but the bullets are still coming. The bullets are still hitting the ground around me for another two or three or four seconds, but it seemed like an eternity. Of course, during the shooting, people were screaming. You could hear bullets hitting vehicles. You can hear bullets ricocheting off the ground. It was utter chaos. But then, when the shooting stopped, it got quiet for a few seconds, and then the screaming started all over again, but this time it had a much higher pitch to it. It had much more horror in its tone. Jeffrey Miller's lying there with half his neck blown off. Sandy Scheuer's lying there, waiting for death. Allison Krause is waiting to chat with death. People are lying on the ground, bleeding.

Me, I wasn't bleeding. My bleeding was very minimal because I was bleeding internally. It hit my lung on my left side, but I didn't bleed externally. But I couldn't get up, and I was lying there, and people were gathering around me, and I asked, believe it or not, "Is there anybody here who's got their first aid merit badge in Boy Scouts?" Yeah, four, five guys raised their hand. I say, "I need six people. I'm not going to die, right here, with my face in the grass. I want to be turned over." You know, there is a way to do it. They do it today, and EMS does the exact same technique that I learned in Boy Scouts when I was in high school.

No guardsmen came to me at all. Actually, one of the students from the Black United Students came over to me. They told the black students to stay away from these big gatherings, because they knew what had happened in 1967 and '68 in Ohio, in Youngstown, in Cleveland, Toledo, and the Columbus area. So, they told them not to be where lots of white people were gathered. They might get targeted. But the leadership was there that day, and one of the guys came to me and said, "Who are you? Do you know your parents' phone numbers?" Within five minutes of the shootings, he was on a phone in Prentice Hall, calling my parents and letting them know. So they knew about it, almost instantaneously. Unlike Joe Lewis's parents, who found out about it through the news, same with Jeffrey Miller's mom.

BEN POST

Something flashed through my brain. I said, I'm one of them, and I'm supposed to be covering this, and I'm not doing my job as a journalist because I'm being overwhelmed emotionally. I gave a broad look around the area, and there were some people at a distance, grouped around objects on the ground, which turned out to be bodies. I didn't know what to do. Should I run towards the guard? Or should I run towards students?

I decided, I've got to report it to the newspaper. So I turned around and went back to the office of the director of the journalism school; his name was Murvin Perry. I knew him pretty well, and I said, "I need to call the newspaper." He said, "Sure, go ahead." So I called the newspaper and I said, "There's been a shooting on campus, and a group of students have been shot and I don't know how many or how seriously." And then somebody said, "Well, UPI is reporting that guardsmen were shot." And I said, "No, I didn't see any guardsmen shot." I said, "I don't know if that happened. But I know students have been shot." I said, "But guardsmen haven't been shot, don't go with that." And they said, "Well, UPI is saying that they were." And then the line went dead, because they cut off all the telephones on the campus.

BOB GILES

We had seven or eight journalists on the campus on Monday morning, May 4. A key reporter was Jeff Sallot, who was just graduating from Kent State. We had offered him a job, and he was stringing for us at the time. Jeff got himself positioned in a window on the top floor of Taylor Hall, the journalism school, so he could see what was happening. The students were around, some on their way to class and some protesting, and the guards started throwing tear gas. A few of the kids were throwing rocks and giving them the finger and so on. The guards came up and went past Taylor Hall, went down the hill to the athletic field, and then they turned around and they knelt down in a firing position, which is pretty scary looking. All of a sudden they started shooting. The record says twenty-eight guardsmen shot sixty-seven bullets fired in thirteen seconds. Jeff Sallot had an open line, and he dictated what he was seeing back to the city desk in Akron.

At the moment we were ready to go to press with our main home-delivered edition and we were able to report that four students had been killed and nine wounded. We had a reporter named Bob Page, at the Robinson Memorial Hospital in Ravenna, which was a nearby town, where all the victims were taken. The UPI, which was a big wire service in Ohio in those days, moved a story that said four dead, two of them were guardsmen. A lot of radio stations and a lot of newspapers ran with that for the afternoon edition, including the Kent-Ravenna *Record-Courier*. That was their lead story: Four killed and two guardsmen. So that set in the public mind, to the extent that this version of the news was heard, the idea that the students had killed two guardsmen. Jeff Sallot, who watched the shooting from a window in Taylor Hall, insisted firmly, "I'm very sure that these were all students." So we went with him, and of course it turned out to be right.

JOHN FILO

I changed film, put that roll in my pocket, marked it, scratched it, too, re-loaded the film, and started shooting more. I had all these students shout-ing in my ears: "You pig, what are you doing? Why are you shooting? You're an animal." It was almost preventing me from shooting. So you just kept shooting, and you tried to work through it. I remember there were forty, fifty people around each wounded person up on that hill. But I knew that this person was dead. He was Jeffrey Miller. There are other casual-ties further away in the parking lot. Poor Sandy Scheuer was just going into her dorm room and got hit with a stray bullet. Bill Schroeder, the ROTC guy, was on the ground with his books over his head, but the bullet entered his buttocks, went through his thoracic cavity, and came out his shoulder. All the vital organs were gone. Allison Krause was behind a car, shot through the chest. You just saw cars with windows shattered and bul-let holes in doors. I photographed that.

A group of guardsmen finally came over to the body of Jeffrey Miller, and the sergeant leading the group put his boot under him and rolled the body over. They walked away and they never took off their gas masks.

DEAN KAHLER

The students rolled me over, and they propped my head up a little bit so I could breathe a little easier, and eventually the ambulance people came to get us. Now, remember, the ambulances back then are not the same as the ambulances today. Just think of 1965, or '66, or even 1970, that tech-nology hadn't reached northeast Ohio yet. All we had were hearses that were painted red and white with gold lettering on it for fire departments, and the technique back then was "load and go like hell." That was the unofficial title of the technique, "load and go."

JOE LEWIS

A person came up to me who was an older brother of a high school class-mate of mine. He took out my wallet I guess for identification. I couldn't sit up. I asked him, "How bad is it?" He said, "I think it's just a flesh wound." I got great relief from that, even though I still couldn't sit up. Students gathered around me, and a young woman came to my right, and I squeezed and held her hand. She stayed with me and held my hand, and other students came and tried to help by putting pressure on the wound and giving me first aid. I felt like I was dying. I could feel my life leaving my body. I wasn't afraid, but just to be safe, seeing that I was raised Catho-lic, I said a good Act of Contrition, saying I was sorry for my sins, just to cover all the bases. I felt much better after that.

They loaded us on the ambulance. I was in an ambulance with another person who had been shot. Later, I found out that it was John Cleary, who also survived. He was shot through the lungs, and he was in horrible pain. His screams at every bump and turn terrified me. I thought that I was going to die. Eventually, we got to the hospital in Ravenna—Robinson Memorial Hospital. The last thing I remember was, they said to me, "We're going to cut off your clothes."

LAUREL KRAUSE

They cut all the phone lines so that no one could call in or out. This is common in military battles. We still haven't been notified about Allison's killing by Kent State University or U.S. government authorities. My uncle Jack in Cleveland heard my sister had been killed on the radio, and he called my dad; they're brothers. I came home on the school bus, and one of my neighbors ran up to me and said, "Allison's been hurt. The newspa-per reporters have been here. Call your mom." My mom worked. I called her. She got in the car and came home. She called and called and called, finally got through to Robinson Memorial Hospital, and someone told her that Allison Krause was dead on arrival. My mom collapsed and I screamed. Then we drove to Robinson Memorial to identify her body, and men with guns standing outside the hospital muttered, "They should have shot more."

JOHN FILO

It seemed like hours before the first ambulance got there. People were saying, "The radio report said there was a gun battle here—two guardsmen and two students killed in a shoot-out." And everybody was like, "Oh my God, that was the initial radio report." So everyone was like, "Cover-up, there's going to be a big cover-up." I was shocked that—why would you shoot down the hill? Why would you retreat from a position, and then reappear, and then just start shooting, without a warning like, "If you don't disperse, we're going to shoot"? There was none of that.

A group of students said, "We're going down to ask the guard why did they shoot?" I said, "Okay, I'll go with this group." It was maybe three hundred people. They went down, and they sat in front of the guard, and we're around this burned-out ROTC building. Some envoy went over and came back and said, "The guard general said if you don't disperse, they're going to shoot again." This is the first time I was really afraid. Because the other one was, who knew you were going to be shot at? No one moved. I thought, This is crazy. Finally, one of the professors, Glenn Frank, got on a bullhorn, and he was in tears asking everyone to just go away. They mean it. I think within an hour, the university was closed. Everyone went back to their dorms. Thank God for those professors.

I got really paranoid, because the radio report hadn't changed, and there was *no one* from the national media on that side; there were just student photographers, and student journalists who witnessed everything, and I said, "Well, if it's going to be a cover-up, they're going to be coming after people that have cameras." These were paranoid times. So I said, All right, I've got to get out of here, and I've got to take my film.

I was so paranoid. I took my film, and I hid it in the car. I mean, if they searched the car, you could have found it, but I didn't want it on me. I hid my cameras; I didn't want them on me. I didn't want them to know I was a photographer. As I was driving off campus, I saw the most unusual thing. I saw guardsmen on the telephone poles, literally lopping off a big old cable, and I'm thinking, That's bizarre. That made me even more paranoid—a big heavy telephone cable dropping to the ground. I got to my apartment, grabbed a few clothes, and drove. As I drove out of Kent, there was a big crossroads being patrolled by guardsmen, and I went, Oh shit. I hope this isn't a roadblock. But actually, it was just a traffic control thing, because they were moving more guardsmen in and more trucks out. I got through that, and then for some reason, I felt once I got across the state line, it was like crossing a frontier.

I called my newspaper in Pennsylvania, *The Valley Daily News,* and I remember the chief said to me, "Did you get anything?" I said, "I think so." The newspaper was two and a half hours away. Then we had a little argument. They said, oh, they want to hold it up for the next day's paper, and I said, "No, if it's what I think I have, they're saying it's a shoot-out, and that's not the way it happened. It needs to go out today on the national wire."

JOE LEWIS

For several days I struggled to stay alive with various infections in intensive care. My wounds were a small entry wound, the size of a quarter, and a large exit wound in my hip the size of a Coke can. And then, down on my leg, because the bullet went between my leg bones, the in and out holes are both pretty small, like the size of a dime.

My parents were very suspicious after I got shot, because they were of the generation that was before Watergate. This was before anyone doubted that the government told the truth. So, at first they were very concerned that I had participated in some illegal behavior. I remember, after forty-eight hours of unconsciousness, coming to in the intensive care unit, the only thing I could say was what I needed to say to my parents, who were at my bedside—that I didn't do anything wrong. That was the only thing I could get out for another day. But I wanted to assure them that what they presumed wasn't true. That this was a horrible thing that had happened, and I had done nothing to precipitate it—well, not much to precipitate it.

JOHN FILO

We found the two rolls I had scratched and developed the film.

I was a little shaken. I was nervous. I let the guys that taught me photography do the processing. I trusted them. We did the lesser roll, processing and chemistry was fine, then we did the real roll with Mary Vecchio crying over the body of Jeffrey Miller, and then we did the student waving the flag. We got to transmit that, but this is back in the analog days; you could only move about a hundred and twenty pictures a day, not like today, with digital. You had to phase a motor, and it would scan an image, and read the caption. You had to write a caption. I kept trying to schedule this picture, Mary Vecchio over the body of Jeffrey Miller, and the New York traffic guy for the AP said, "Where are you? How far are you from the scene?" You had like about thirty seconds to state your case.

I remember my picture finally went out over the wire, and I turned up the volume, and finally, the guy who I'd been fighting with for an hour said, "Wow, kid, that's a good picture. Do you have any more?" I said, "I only have a few more." He said, "All right, we'll take them."

DEAN KAHLER

They put me into a coma, and broke three ribs to get into me. They took out one of the lobes of my lung. They sewed up the holes in my diaphragm. They manhandled all my organs, looking for shrapnel that was in the organs. Fortunately, the only organs that were damaged were the lungs, the diaphragm, and the spinal cord. There was no shrapnel in my heart or my liver or those kinds of things. So I was real lucky in that sense. But this is 1970. We don't have the technology we have today. When I started becoming aware of my surroundings, Thursday, all I could hear were machines, and I could start to feel a little pain. I was in and out of consciousness. They were obviously dripping morphine into me, but they were slowly taking me off of it, and slowly taking me out of the coma. It was a very tough reawakening. There was a lot of pain, and I noticed that the bed was moving underneath me, and it was one of the early beds designed to make people who were paraplegics comfortable because it had inflatable and deflatable cells in it. You could hear the air compressor running.

When I came to, the doctor says, "You know what's going on?" I said, "Yeah, I'm probably not going to walk for the rest of my life." He goes, "I think you're right. Why are you so cavalier about it?" I said, "Well, thank God. I'm just happy to be alive. I'm opening my eyes, I'm in a lot of pain, but I can talk, and I can breathe, and what you told me is I could live a very full life for the rest of my life." He says, "Yes, you can, and yes, you will." So that's where I come from.

I'm only a paraplegic. I'm not a quadriplegic. My thoracic 9, 10, and 11 were shattered. There are twelve bones in the thoracic region. It's just below the cervical region of your neck, that run down your back, and they get increasingly larger. So, T9, 10, and 11 were shattered. My feeling stops about an inch below my navel.

I woke up, and I remember my parents bringing over my mail. You know, my name was in papers everywhere. I remember opening up the first letter; it was a card, a very lovely card that looked like a lot of thought was put into it. I opened it up, and on the left-hand side there was a whole page full of writing, and it said, "Dear Communist, hippie, radical, I hope by the time you read this you are dead."*

LAUREL KRAUSE

My father was radicalized, and he became the voice for Kent State. He became known as Crazy Krause. He would not let it go. He gave a speech in the backyard the day after Allison was killed and he said, "I'm not going to take this sitting down. My daughter's death will not be in vain. I'm going to be launching an investigation into this. I want our government to find out for what reason they used live ammunition and guns against young people?"†

---

* A Gallup poll taken soon after May 4, 1970, showed that 58 percent of Americans blamed the demonstrating students and only 11 percent blamed the National Guard for the four deaths at Kent State.

† Four Kent State students, Allison Krause (age nineteen), Jeffrey Miller (twenty), William Schroeder (nineteen), and Sandra Scheuer (twenty), were killed on May 4, 1970, and nine other

BOB GILES

Arthur Krause emerged very quickly as someone who wanted to sue the government, bring lawsuits and so on. He and Allison had been somewhat estranged; he thought she was just a radical hippie student. He started to call me at home, and we had many long conversations in the evening. He was a deeply sad man, and troubled about what had happened to his daughter and what his relationship with her had and had not been. I would listen to him, and we became frequent conversationalists on the phone.

At that time we were getting so much hate mail that the newspaper put a guard at my house for a couple days. "You're a communist, and you're communist-lovers, these students should have been shot, the newspaper has one-sided coverage," you know, that sort of stuff. There was no personal threat to me, but it was very viciously worded criticism of the paper.

DEAN KAHLER

My father lost fifty pounds. My mom gained fifty pounds. They were shocked and in terror. They couldn't believe it. They were a mixed couple, mother was a Republican, father was a member of the Democratic Party, and they believed in their government. My father fought in World War II. My mother was a housewife from the fifties, but she had already started taking a job by the time I was sixteen. They just couldn't believe that the government would shoot their kid, when he really wasn't doing anything.

STEPHEN STILLS (Crosby, Stills, Nash & Young)

When Kent State happened, it was a visceral thing. Those were our peers. It's like, "Are you out of your mind?" It became a contest, to see who

---

students were shot and wounded by the National Guard. One of those wounded students, Dean Kahler, was permanently paralyzed from the waist down.

could write the song the quickest. I was just starting to process it, and Neil Young already had a song that I thought was a verse short. Putting the word "Nixon" in it kind of put a time frame on it that wouldn't make it last—it would be hard to sing, hard to sing now.

GREIL MARCUS (*Rolling Stone* music critic)

After Kent State, Neil Young writes "Ohio." He writes it very, very quickly. They record it practically overnight. They release it within days and get it on the radio. So it's just incredibly fast, and it's a tremendously powerful song. And that's an intervention. That's pop music as, not just a story appearing in a newspaper, but actually creating a newspaper, and getting it on the streets in response to an event. The only other time I can think of when something like that happened was when Mick Jagger and Keith Richards were arrested on a drug charge in England, and the Who went into the studio, recorded two Rolling Stones songs, and released them as a single the next day as a protest against their arrest. I just thought what a remarkable thing to do, to intervene in the story—seize the narrative. And it always helps that it was a good song.

JOHN HARTMANN (Crosby, Stills & Nash manager)

So, when "Ohio" happened, we—already in a state of rebellion—were infuriated, and Neil Young, who was the Shakespeare of our time, goes out and he writes a song about this travesty, this horror, that National Guard troops shot down college kids on a campus for objecting to a war. You piss off Neil, he's gonna write something good. The more emotion he can get into a song, the better the song is. So, "Ohio" is the direct result of what was on the news that night: four dead in Ohio, that's the truth.

Crosby, Stills, Nash & Young, they wrote the songs that were the political commentaries of their day. They were describing the historical events in their music, and the public was buying it. It was hugely commercially successful, yet heavily critical of the culture that we lived in, and there was a definite schism. We interpreted their lyrics as our advice and direction on how to be and live. It changed a generation.*

JOE LEWIS

Every time the song "Ohio" came on, I'd cry. I cried every time I heard it, for fifteen years.

JULIUS LESTER (author, civil rights activist)

I was pretty horrified when I heard about what happened at Kent State. Kent State was the first time that whites had been killed. It was the first time that they'd been confronted with violence. That was it. They didn't want to take that risk anymore. In the civil rights movement, you had to ask yourself that question, "Am I willing to die?" Okay. "I don't want to die, but am I willing—if that's a consequence, am I willing to do that?" You had to answer that question, and whites hadn't been confronted with that. Not many. Some had in the summer of '64, but after that, not many. So, when the National Guard turns on white people, whoa. That's different. That's why it got the headlines, and Jackson State didn't.

DEAN KAHLER

I just couldn't believe it. I was shocked. I mean, after the shootings at Kent, I thought, What are they doing, declaring war on students? And then as I learned more about Jackson State, which happened ten days later, I found out that it was more related to race than it was related to

---

*   The band recorded the single "Ohio" in just two or three takes at the Record Plant studio in Los Angeles, and then recorded Stephen Stills's "Find the Cost of Freedom" for the B-side. Many AM stations refused to play the politically controversial cut, but it became an instant hit on FM stations and climbed to number fourteen on the charts. Neil Young wrote in the liner notes of *Decade,* his 1977 anthology, "It's still hard to believe I had to write this song. . . . My best CSNY cut. Recorded totally live in Los Angeles. David Crosby cried after this take."

On May 7, 1970, three thousand mourners gathered along New York's Amsterdam Avenue to salute slain Kent State student Jeffrey Miller's body as it made its way in a hearse to a funeral chapel on Seventy-sixth Street. PHOTOGRAPH BY STEPHEN SHAMES.

antiwar.* I made the correlation that law enforcement, if they didn't get their way, they were going to shoot you. Black people knew this, but us white people really didn't know that. This was something new for us to deal with, as white folks.

JOHN FILO

Papers all around the world ran my pictures, like *Asahi Shimbun,* you name it, all the great papers. Once again, you have no idea the power of journalism, photography, the written word, or the picture; there's no way you can learn that. But what immediately started, within forty-eight hours,

---

*   On May 15, at Jackson State College, an African American college in Jackson, Mississippi, state police shot randomly at the windows of a dorm (where they claimed a sniper was shooting at them, which was never verified), killing Phillip Gibbs and James Earl Green and wounding twelve others. The students had been protesting the invasion of Cambodia, and other issues around race, including rumors that turned out later to be false that the mayor of Fayette, Charles Evers, brother of slain civil rights leader Medgar Evers and the first African American to be elected mayor of a town in Mississippi since Reconstruction, had been shot and killed.

was the hate mail. I got tons of hate mail and tons of calls. We had to disconnect the phone.

"It never happened, you set up the photos." "You're part of the conspiracy to bring down America." I mean, just crazy—you don't realize there's a crazy element out there; it went on for almost a month. It was coming from all directions. It was even coming from the National Press Photographers Association, like someone needs to get that guy to sign an affidavit that these are true photos. You're like, What? This really happened. Are you serious?

I had to stay at Kent another year. As a matter of fact, I took a job at the AP. I am still working in that same place, Taylor Hall, when the Pulitzers are announced, the next year; it was almost to the day. I read that I had won over an AP teletype machine, maybe two hundred feet from where I shot the picture.

A day or two later I received a letter. It was from Eddie Adams, who had won the Pulitzer in 1969. The letter said: "Congratulations, kid. Let's see what you can do tomorrow."

CHAPTER 20

STRIKE

(May 1970)

The crisis on American campuses has no parallel in the history of the nation. . . . [I]t is as deep as any since the Civil War.

**—SCRANTON COMMISSION REPORT,
June 1970**

IN THE IMMEDIATE AFTERMATH OF THE KENT STATE SHOOTINGS, the largest student strike in United States history spread across the country. Two and a half million students, on seven hundred campuses, protested, rioted, and refused to go to classes or take final exams. Thirty ROTC buildings were firebombed and governors ordered the National Guard to occupy 21 campuses in 16 states. President Nixon made a surprise appearance at the Lincoln Memorial at dawn on May 9 to talk to young protesters who were pouring into Washington, D.C., to demonstrate against the invasion of Cambodia and the killings at Kent State. The next day, the Weather Underground bombed the National Guard building in Washington, D.C., and a student at the University of California, San Diego killed himself by self-immolation, emulating Buddhist priests who had done so in Vietnam. Meanwhile, tensions at Yale were high as the Black Panthers' New Haven Nine began pretrial proceedings.

Nationwide student unrest led Nixon to believe that the revolutionary youth movement was "determined to destroy our society," and he ordered the FBI and other agencies to expand counterintelligence operations. Opposition to the war also plagued Nixon from inside his administration. Two hundred State Department employees signed a petition objecting to the invasion of Cambodia, and Secretary of the Interior Walter Hickel wrote a letter to Nixon criticizing him for failing to understand the student movement. When his letter was leaked to the press, Hickel received three thousand notes of congratulation. Nixon fired Hickel in December 1970.

———————

BUD KROGH (Nixon administration aide)

On Monday, May 4, I was having lunch in Washington at the Ritz-Carlton, and one of my staff people came running over to tell me about what had happened at Kent State. One of my responsibilities at the time was to deal with demonstrations, so I ran back to the White House and went to see Pat Moynihan [counselor to the president for urban affairs]. I said, "We've got to be very careful about how we respond." Pat worked out a statement that I thought was balanced and fair, and we went up to Ron Ziegler's office. By the time we got to the press office, they had already put out a statement that I think was unfair in the way that it placed the responsibility on the demonstrators at Kent State.

NIXON STATEMENT, MAY 4, 1970

This should remind us all once again that when dissent turns to violence, it invites tragedy. It is my hope that this tragic and unfortunate incident will strengthen the determination of all the campuses, administrations, faculty, and students alike to stand firmly for the right which exists in this country of peaceful dissent and just as strongly against the resort to violence as a means of such expression.

BUD KROGH

I was saddened that it had not been a more balanced statement. Once you get past what's actually happening on the ground and into the politics, a statement out of the White House is obviously going to be informed by what the political folks feel is important to communicate. Moynihan and I believed that if you're shifting blame to people that don't feel that they're at fault, it's going to exacerbate what we are going to be dealing with in terms of demonstrations. So, to me, the politics would have been, let's really low-key this. Let's not try to place blame. This was not just Kent State. We had campuses erupting all over the country.

That was one of the saddest days that I had at the White House, because there are so many ways that you can handle demonstrations without harming people. It was just one of the great tragedies of that period of time.

HARVARD CRIMSON, MAY 6, 1970

STRIKE HITS 166 COLLEGES; ADMINISTRATORS CLOSE B.U.

By J. W. Stillman

Boston University administrators voted yesterday to cancel exams and commencement and to send all students home as the national university strike reached tremendous proportions with at least 166 colleges reported generally on strike.

The killing of four Kent State University students by National Guardsmen Monday lent a sense of crisis to student protests against the American invasion of Cambodia.

MARK RUDD (Weathermen member)

I'm sitting on a park bench on May 6 in [Philadelphia's] Rittenhouse Square, reading a *New York Times* and hearing about the shootings at Kent State and the mass demonstrations that were breaking out in colleges all over the country, and suddenly I had this realization: What a waste. I couldn't even walk over to the University of Pennsylvania. I had been a very successful student organizer, and now I was doing nothing. I was so depressed. That was the beginning of my realization. By the end of 1970 I separated myself from the Weather Underground.

On May 5, 1970, students strike at Amherst College in Massachusetts in reaction to the U.S. invasion of Cambodia and the killing of four students at Kent State. Amherst was one of seven hundred campuses to shut down during the national student strike.

TOM HAYDEN (founder, SDS)

The May Day rally with about fifteen thousand people protesting the murder trial of the New Haven Nine took place the weekend of May 1–3, 1970, on the New Haven Green.* I don't think Nixon timed the invasion of Cambodia to be the day before the Panther rally, but that's how it happened.

ERICKA HUGGINS

(leader of the New Haven Black Panther chapter)

After John [Huggins] was killed, I traveled to New Haven with my baby daughter to be with his family and at his funeral with the thought that after

---

*   The New Haven Nine was among the highest-profile Black Panther trials. Nine Panthers, including their leaders, Bobby Seale and Ericka Huggins, were tried for the murder of fellow Panther Alex Rackley (age nineteen), who was suspected of being an FBI informant. A huge, peaceful pro-Panther rally gathered at Yale on May 1, the weekend before jury selection for the trial began, and protesters were fed and housed by the sympathetic Yale administration and students. Ultimately, three of the Panthers were convicted for the murder and Bobby Seale, Ericka Huggins, and the other four were acquitted.

The Yale campus in New Haven, Connecticut, is flooded with thousands of students and activists for a May Day rally calling for a fair trial for the Black Panther New Haven Nine.   PHOTOGRAPH BY STEPHEN SHAMES.

a while, I would go back to California. That didn't happen because some of the Yale students and members of the New Haven black community invited me to stay and start a New Haven chapter of the [Black Panther] party. So with permission from the party's leadership, I did.

My daughter was three weeks old or so when I got to New Haven and three months old when I was arrested for conspiracy with the intent to commit murder on May 22, 1969. I did not murder anyone; I did not ask that anybody be murdered; I didn't conspire to do anything. However, there was an FBI informant [George Sams]—I didn't know this originally, I just knew he was twisted and sadistic. A man came into the party office bringing another man [Alex Rackley] who he held captive and eventually orchestrated his murder.

Bobby Seale was in town speaking at Yale, and because I was living in New Haven, this man, George Sams, reported back to the FBI that Bobby Seale and I had led that conspiracy. And that is why I was arrested in the middle of the night. Sometimes I wonder why I wasn't killed that night, but I think that they were trying to keep us alive so that there could be this awful trial—and it was really awful. I think they wanted to make the black community and the movement community hate us. But that isn't what happened; it was exposed in the trial that the FBI had set up the murder because the guy who they had hired to do so wasn't psychologically well, so he couldn't endure on the witness stand.

The judge was relatively kind. The DA was, like many district attorneys, not about human beings but about winning, and my lawyers, Charles Garry and Catherine Roraback, were phenomenal. Bobby Seale and I were on trial together. I didn't have anything to do with how the trials were separated out. But two men were tried separately from us. One of them was the person to whom George Sams said, "Pull the trigger," and he did.*

It took three months to pick the jury for my case, the longest voir dire in the history of the United States to that point, because of fear-based and racist thinking. I spent fourteen months in jail awaiting trial, and six months on trial. It was such a circus. The United States was on trial.†

TOM HAYDEN

So, just as we were trying to deal with all the tensions at Yale, Cambodia happens. And that adds to the total volatility of everything, the unpredictability of everything. The rally then becomes the launching pad for a call for a nationwide student strike, and in the response that was being generated, Kent State happens. Then Jackson State happens. Then there's this big, pretty spontaneous and massive demonstration where people are

---

* George Sams, a Panther field marshal with a violent history, claimed that Bobby Seale had ordered him to kill nineteen-year-old Alex Rackley, whom Sams accused of being an FBI informant. In the end, Sams pleaded guilty to second-degree murder, and two other Panthers whom Sams ordered to shoot Rackley were also convicted. Many members of the Black Panther Party (including Huggins) believe that Sams was an FBI agent provocateur, but this has not been definitively proven. Sams and the prosecution did not have solid evidence against Seale, who, with Huggins was seen by many outside the courtroom as a target of government repression. Ericka Huggins had a harder defense than Seale because her voice could be heard on an audiotape ordering Rackley's torture, which, she testified, she did under threat from Sams. The Seale-Huggins trial began in October 1970 and ended May 25, 1971, with a hung jury, and the judge dismissing all charges.

† "Free Bobby, Free Ericka" became the rallying cry by members of the left who believed the Panthers had been set up by the police and the FBI and could not get a fair trial. Even the president of Yale, Kingman Brewster, stated: ". . . I am skeptical of the ability of Black revolutionaries to achieve a fair trial anywhere in the U.S."

Black Panther leader Ericka Huggins (pictured on this banner) was on trial with cofounder Bobby Seale. They were both accused of conspiring to murder fellow Black Panther Alex Rackley. Ultimately, the charges against them would be dismissed.

PHOTOGRAPH BY STEPHEN SHAMES.

surging around the attorney general's office, the Justice Department in Washington. And then Kingman Brewster, Jr. [president of Yale], led a delegation of Yale students, a thousand of them, to lobby Congress.

Student strike graffiti on the Hall of Languages at Syracuse University, May 1970.

So now it's everything from the most revolutionary to the most mainstream, all temporarily united against Cambodia and Nixon. It was a week of escalating madness. It was one jolt after another. They seemed to just keep on coming. People predicted a breakdown or revolution. The country seemed to be literally out of control, and we were improvising whatever tactics we could in the midst of something that was much larger than any one organization could handle.

HARVARD CRIMSON, MAY 7, 1970

324 UNIVERSITIES STRIKE NATIONALLY; PROTESTS EXPAND

By Marion E. Mccollom

. . . Yesterday morning, students at N.Y.U. seized three buildings, . . . demanding $100,000 ransom for the Black Panther Defense Fund before releasing the buildings.

Governor Ronald Reagan of California yesterday afternoon asked all seven state universities to close until Sunday, so that students could consider "the grave sequence of current events."

MICHAEL KAZIN (Harvard SDS leader)

There were student strikes, there were building takeovers, there were spontaneous demonstrations, there were smoke-ins. Ultimately, the count was seven hundred campuses and 2.5 million students. A lot of high schools, too. It just felt like if the college was not on strike, it must have been a pro-Nixon college. Because anybody who was opposed to Nixon and opposed to the war at that point was going to try to do something, especially after Kent State. Who knows what would have happened without Kent State? And Jackson State, for black students, was just as important. Radicals like me tried to make Jackson State just as important as Kent State, even though the press didn't play it up. We wanted to show that the Nixon administration and their allies were willing to kill antiwar demonstrators who were peacefully demonstrating, and we couldn't abide that. That was true for liberals as well as radicals like me.

I went to New Haven first. There was this big pro-Panther demonstration in New Haven. I tried to be everywhere. Wherever the action was, I wanted to be. I went back to Cambridge, and helped organize demonstrations, including the big one with thirty-five thousand students marching from the Boston Common to Soldiers Field in Cambridge, on the Harvard campus. A few of us freelancers decided that we couldn't have this demonstration be peaceful, and we decided when we got to Harvard Square, we would basically stage a riot. I hope that the statute of limitations has passed on these things.

HARVARD CRIMSON

POLICE DISPERSE CROWDS IN SQUARE
FOLLOWING PEACEFUL DEMONSTRATION

By M. David Landau and Mark H. O'Donoghue, May 9, 1970

An estimated 650 state and city policemen dispersed a crowd of 500 demonstrators who had occupied the Square for almost two hours last night. The crowd—largely high school and non-Harvard students . . . had marched to Shannon Hall, headquarters of Harvard ROTC. . . .

The group had intended to occupy or burn down Shannon Hall. . . .

TOM HAYDEN

The strike just happened, and it was led, in a lot of cases, by student governments. It was larger than any other student strike. In the spring of '68, from Columbia to Paris, there were more countries involved with student strikes. But '70 was so big that I think it was the turning point for the establishment. They knew that if they continued the war, there would be some kind of permanent rupture in American society.

Angry protesters flock to the Boston Common after the Kent State shootings, May 5, 1970.

BUD KROGH

In one of the planning sessions at the Justice Department, the idea occurred to me that it would be better to protect the White House if we circled it with buses rather than a SWAT team or riot police. I think that proved to be true. I've always felt that if you removed the provocation—I think sometimes a line of police can almost provoke violence—and have something inert like a bus—what can you do to a bus? You can punch the tires out, break the windows, and write graffiti on it, but it's not going to be a physical interaction. So we did that the night before the May 9 demonstration. We circled the White House with buses, and we had the Eighty-second Airborne military unit guarding the Old Executive Office Building from the inside. They came in army trucks in the middle of the night, and we had an extra police and Secret Service detail. It was a siege environment.

STEPHEN BULL (Nixon personal aide)

There was a movie theater between the residence and the East Wing. It accommodates probably a dozen people, and that's where Nixon would be watching a movie. You didn't have videotape back then. You'd bring a projector up there into the White House. I think he saw the movie *Patton* about three dozen times. Some of the famous lines in the movie are "Americans have never lost a war." "Americans love a winner, and will not tolerate a loser." I think Nixon liked the no-nonsense approach that General Patton, or the actor who played Patton, George C. Scott, took. I think that's the point. He liked no-nonsense guys.*

BUD KROGH

I was the White House liaison with the Department of Justice, the Secret Service, and the Metropolitan Police, and all the preparations for being able to deal with the major demonstration that was going to occur on May 9. I had just finished my rounds, going around the White House, and checking to make sure the buses were in place. We completed the movement of the military unit [Eighty-second Airborne] that was going to be in the Old Executive Office Building as a defense of last resort.

STEPHEN BULL

I don't know how many buses there were, but they totally encircled Lafayette Park. They went completely around E Street, the south portion, where you can't drive anymore, separating the south grounds from the Ellipse. So the buses went all around. The recollection I have is that inside what now was an enclosure, it was quiet and there was no activity. You'd look out onto Pennsylvania Avenue, and there was no one there because it had been cordoned off. But on the exterior, you could hear the noise of what was going on outside. Walking through the Executive Office Building, there were troops sitting down in the hallway prepared in the event that they were needed. That was the environment. Without making a value judgment about who was right or who was wrong, that's what was going on in this country. You have to have armed troops in the Executive

---

* *Patton,* the epic biopic about General George S. Patton during World War II, won the Academy Award for best motion picture in 1970.

Office Building, potentially to deal with violent demonstrators who might try to attack, and these are Americans. It was quite a time.

If you didn't experience it back then, you would have no idea how close we were, as a country, to revolution. It was a very violent time, a very divisive time. And I think people on both sides will say that.

BUD KROGH

I got to the Secret Service command post at about four fifteen in the morning and over the loudspeaker came, "Searchlight is on the lawn." Searchlight was the president's Secret Service code name. I asked the person there, "What does that mean?" And the Secret Service agent said, "Well, it means the president is out on the lawn."

I immediately called John Ehrlichman and woke him up, and told him what was going on. He said, "Go over and render assistance as quickly as you can." So I hung up, and left the Secret Service command post, which was in the basement of the Old Executive Office Building, and rushed across West Executive Drive, and went through the West Wing, and out to the Rose Garden just in time to see the president's limousine leaving. I immediately commandeered another car and found out from the Secret Service where the president was going, and followed them up to the Lincoln Memorial. I think we got there around four thirty in the morning. It was pretty early; it was still dark when we got there. I followed him up the stairs.

RICHARD REEVES (journalist, Nixon biographer)

We know Nixon had trouble sleeping. He either drank too much, or just didn't have much of a tolerance for alcohol. I believe the latter. I don't think the guy was sitting up there downing martinis all night. But he often was up at night, walking around, like any other politician. You have to start from the beginning. Nixon thought he was right, and he thought he would go up to the Lincoln Memorial totally on his own. He didn't tell anybody—the only aide around was a guy named Bud Krogh, who was a wonderful man. He was only thirty then.

LAUREE MOSS (peace protester from Detroit)

It was early dawn and those of us who were there were people who had driven all night long. People were just milling around and waiting for the march to begin. That's when we saw a big black limousine pull up. Then we see the president walk up the stairs to the top of the Lincoln monument, and then all of a sudden people mill around him. It was quite shocking, because he looked exhausted, greasy. His face was strained. I'm curious what's going on so I walk to the top of the steps. I can't quite get into the circle but I see that people are trying to get him to answer questions. They're throwing questions at him, and he's not answering anything; I couldn't hear anything.

BUD KROGH

When we got there, there were not a lot of people around. It was dark, but you could see clusters of young people. There were people that had come from all over the eastern part of the country to join in this demonstration. You could see them along the Mall. The president was up at the top of the stairs of the Lincoln Memorial, right inside the first set of columns. I walked up and stood close so I could hear what he was saying. It was quite a long time, I think thirty or forty minutes. It wasn't so much a conversation, but more of a monologue in which he talked about lots of different issues that were surprising to me. I think he was making a really genuine effort to reach out to these young people, to explain what he was thinking and feeling. He started by saying that he understood how they felt about their opposition to the war. He went back to his own history before World War II, where he actually sympathized with [Neville] Chamberlain's view of trying to avoid World War II because he felt that war was very bad for the U.S. But he came to change his mind after a while, and concluded that Churchill was correct, and that Chamberlain was wrong, and he was trying to show the protesters that, while he understood their clear interest in trying to stop the war, he felt that the way that it was done was very important, and he was aligning himself with the Churchill view, that you had to continue to fight even when it looked like getting out of the war was better.

But I believe he was also trying to empathize with the young people that were there.

I don't remember, specifically, what he said about his Quaker background, but he was explaining that he had come out of a pacifist tradition. One young person said, "You know, we're prepared to die for what we believe in." And he said he understood that, and what he was trying to do was to make the kind of decisions so that no one would have to die for their country. He was trying to reach out, and I could tell that they could not believe that he was there. It was almost like a stunned silence. I observed a lot of young people that looked like they'd been up for a very long time, and had driven long distances. I think you saw some peace symbols, and some military-style jackets. It was just a bunch of people that really looked like they had dropped everything to come to the city to demonstrate. They looked tired and just a little bit awestruck.

RICHARD REEVES

I think that Nixon thought he had a message to tell these kids. In his own odd way, whether he had Asperger's or whatever, he thought he could connect with them. He tried, and it was a brave thing to do, too.

BUD KROGH

Listening very closely to what the president was saying, I was amazed at the scope of the things that he talked about. He talked about how important it was to see the world, and get out and understand it, and travel. He touted the importance of traveling around the world, and then he mentioned something that I thought was quite interesting. He talked about the environmental programs he had initiated. I don't know which bills he had passed at the time, but he said we can clean up the environment and take care of all of that, but it's really the matters of the spirit that are most important. He said there's a spiritual hunger in man, which is one of the most important things that we have to respond to. And I'm not sure how most of these young people responded to that, but he was speaking from his heart. He mentioned that he was a strong supporter of the American

Indian, and he really wanted to help restore their self-determination. He said that our country took these proud people and just decimated them in so many ways. You could just feel the pain that caused him. He spoke very specifically about that.

To me, what was almost stunning was that he talked about China and how it was his hope that during his administration he would be able to visit China. I think what he was articulating was a policy initiative that he had been thinking about for a long time. I think I'm hearing something here that is probably a pretty deep secret in the administration, and here he is, sharing it with this group of people that I'm not quite sure would pick up on the significance of what he was saying. I did, because I figured that if he's talking about visiting it during his term, at least something must be under way. I was really stunned by that. I was not on the national security staff. I was on the domestic policy staff. But, you know enough when you're in that place to realize that something like that being said is not just a throwaway line.

When the kids were killed at Kent State, that was devastating to so many of us because it was so unnecessary. I think that the president had to have felt some grief about that, realizing that his decision to go into Cambodia had triggered these demonstrations at the universities, and that that decision did lead to these direct confrontations. When he was out there talking to these kids—you had a sense of just needing to reach out and let them know what he was feeling.

LAUREE MOSS

I went back down to the bottom of the memorial steps and told my friend, Nothing's going on up there, it's ridiculous. We're talking, and all of a sudden, we see our friend Bob Moustakas, who has been taking pictures with his Leica the whole time, talking to the president. Nixon asked Bob, "What are you doing here?" Bob said, "Oh, we came for the demonstration." Then he asked Bob, "Well, who are you with?" And Bob points to us. So then they both walked down to us, and the president is now approaching me, introducing himself to me and my friend, and Bob is taking pictures of us. The president asked, "How old are you?" I said twenty-two. "Oh, you're the same age as my daughter, Patricia. Oh, how great is that? Are you in college?" I told him that I graduated from Michigan undergrad and went to graduate school at Wayne State in Detroit and that I'm a social worker. Then I said, "What happened? How come you invaded Cambodia? How come you allowed those kids to be killed?" And he goes, "I'm not here to talk politics. I'm here to be with you in sympathy." He was trying to avoid conversation of anything political. He said he was just joining us in our grief at what happened to the students at Kent State. I smelled alcohol on his breath. I'm very sensitive to that.

I had a button on at the top of my army jacket that said, "Crush Nixon." It had a picture of Nixon's face and it said, "Crush him." I felt bad, so I tried to put my hair over it to cover it. I couldn't believe I did that, but I felt bad that he would see a button that said, "Crush Nixon." There's my upbringing.

BUD KROGH

As time passed, the sun began to come up and there was increased concern by the Secret Service. I think we only had four agents when we were there, which was just so far below what you would need in case anything were to go south, and the agents were not happy campers. Dr. [Walter] Tkach, his doctor, was there and Manolo Sanchez, his longtime personal butler. I was the only White House staff person that was at the Lincoln Memorial portion of this morning.

He got in his car, and I had a car right behind his. It was my understanding we were going back to the White House, but he decided he wanted to go up to Capitol Hill. We drove through the city up Constitution Avenue, and by now there were a lot more people that were visible on the Mall. We drove up to the House of Representatives side of the Capitol. This was before we had all kinds of security. It was still early in the morning, maybe five thirty. We walked up the stairs and into the House chamber and the president asked Manolo to give a speech. I had gone into the House side, and was up above in the balcony, observing this. Manolo was very reluctant to speak. "No, please, go on up, give a speech," the president said. So Manolo did. I forget exactly what he said, but I think it was short.

LAUREE MOSS

After the president drove away, the Secret Service men throw my friend and me and Bob, who has been taking pictures this entire time, into the backseat of a car, and they say, "If you give us the pictures, we will pick one, and we will publicize what happened." So I thought it was either give them the film or Bob was having his camera taken away from him. We didn't think of this as being anything important in history, or anything important to the world. We just wanted to go to the demonstration. I think they took us to some basement and took the roll of film from Bob, developed one of the pictures, and gave the roll of film back to Bob. Bob got the camera back, which was most important, and he got the roll of film back, and we went to the demonstration, never thinking twice about what had just happened.

RICHARD REEVES

The president came back to his office, sat in a chair, and wrote a thirteen-page account of what happened. Not all in his favor. He thought it was history.

In reaction to the invasion of Cambodia and the killing of four Kent State students, one hundred thousand young activists hold a last-minute rally in front of the Lincoln Memorial on May 9, 1970. PHOTOGRAPH BY DAVID FENTON.

BUD KROGH

The protest demonstration, with one hundred thousand students, took place that day. It was pretty warm as I recall, and the day went by without any real confrontations. I was, frankly, so relieved that we got him back safely. That was just my overriding emotion. I also had the feeling that he'd [Nixon] really made an effort. I had never seen anything like this. This was a totally nonscripted event. It was a pretty raw experience. But we managed to get through it. Everybody was safe.

TIME, MAY 18, 1970, "A WAR WITH WAR"

Coretta King, David Dellinger, Benjamin Spock and other matriarchs and patriarchs of the movement were there, along with newer personalities like Jane Fonda. Their audience was made up primarily of the instant army of the young, the mobile children who received basic training in the late '60s, who can travel light and fast for the peace movement and for their own enjoyment. Some 100,000 of them were there on the Ellipse just south of the White House.

JANE FONDA (actor, peace activist)

It was the first national demonstration that I was asked to speak at. Donald Duncan asked me to speak on behalf of the GI movement, and they basically wrote a speech for me. It was scary to stand on that platform. As far as you could see, there were people, all kinds of people, and there were a lot of soldiers in uniform. Of course, there were a lot of guards, military people, that were armed and keeping order. My job was to say, "The soldiers are not our enemy. They are, in growing numbers, understanding that the war is wrong. We cannot treat them as the enemy." I wish that all these people who accused me of being anti-soldier knew that I'm the one that said, "They're not the enemy. They didn't start the war. Let's be real clear, the enemy are the architects of the war." So that was my inauguration to that post. I opened my speech with "Greetings, fellow bums!" because Nixon had just called demonstrators bums a few days earlier.*

BRIAN FLANAGAN (Weathermen member)

The day of the protest in D.C., May 9, we put a bomb in the bathroom of the National Guard Headquarters in Washington, D.C. That's what we did basically, and that's what became tiresome to me. We put bombs in bathrooms because that was the easiest place to blow up. After the town-house, there was no antipersonnel [bombing] done.

LAUREE MOSS

As we were driving back home to Detroit after the rally, we pick up a hitch-hiker. We ask him where was he going, and he said, "To Berkeley." And I said, "Well, we're going to Detroit." He said, "I'll go there." He and I were kind of attracted to each other. So he and I were in the backseat smoking pot, Bob and my friend are in the front seat, and we drove home. We got home, and this guy Larry ends up living with me for six months.

The next morning, I straightened my hair and went to work. I was a social worker working in a psychiatric clinic for emotionally disturbed children and the director called me into his office, and he said, "Is this you?" I replied, "What do you mean, is this me?" He shows me the *Detroit Free Press*, and about six other newspapers, and on the front page is a picture of Nixon and me. The caption said, "The picture of President Nixon on a dawn visit to the Lincoln Memorial was made by Robert Moustakas, a student from Detroit, Michigan, here for the antiwar demonstration." It didn't have my name on it. But it was next to impossible not to identify me. So my director said, "What are you going to tell the parents

---

* On May 1, 1970, Nixon called student protesters "bums . . . blowing up the campuses" in a conversation with Pentagon employees. On May 8, Nixon was asked about his "bums" comment at a press conference. This was his answer: "On university campuses the rule of reason is supposed to prevail over the rule of force. And when students on university campuses burn buildings, when they engage in violence, when they break up furniture, when they terrorize their fellow students and terrorize the faculty, then I think 'bums' is perhaps too kind a word to apply to that kind of person. Those are the kind I was referring to."

of the children that you work with?" I looked like a hippie radical in the picture, but at work I didn't.

Just before dawn on May 9, 1970, President Nixon made a surprise visit to talk to antiwar protesters at the Lincoln Memorial. Nixon said that he told the stunned protesters, "I know that probably most of you think I'm an SOB, but I want you to know that I understand just how you feel." Detroit social worker Lauree Moss is facing the camera on Nixon's right, and her friend Bob Mousta-kas took this photograph.

I said, "I quit." And he said, "What do you mean, you quit?" I said, "I'll terminate with the children, and I'll stay another month, but I'm going to quit." He asked, "Where are you going to go?" I said, "I'm going to move to Berkeley." Never in my life have I done anything like that. My life was mostly very straight and narrow, except for, of course, smoking pot, and helping street people, and believing in civil rights and the rights of other people.

The very next day, *Rolling Stone* calls me. How they found out who I am, I have no idea. They call me, and they want to know all the wonderful political things I said to President Nixon. When I said it didn't happen, he wouldn't talk politics with me, they were very mean. "How could you miss this opportunity? What a fool. I bet you were high, and you went to D.C. just to have a good time." It was pretty bad. I hung up. Then I began to feel more and more like, "Oh God, I hope this will be over soon." The very next day, the picture of the president and me was on the cover of *Time, Life,* and *Newsweek.*

Nixon changed my life. It was a turning point for me. I moved to Berkeley with Larry to become part of the movement called "Radical Psychiatry." My whole world was turned upside down. I lived in a commune. I never wanted to get married, but at that time in my life, I wanted to get my parents off my back. Larry had dropped out of rabbinical school because of the war, so he and I wrote our own marriage ceremony, and we drove back to Detroit and had a wedding in the rabbi's chamber. We got a lot of money, about fifteen thousand dollars, which we kept in the bank, and when we divorced a year later we split it. Larry bought a bread van, which he turned into a house. I started going to consciousness-raising groups and came out as a lesbian.

ALISON TEAL (New York City mayoral staffer)

I was twenty-four years old and working for John Lindsay, New York City's liberal Republican mayor. In honor of the Kent State students who had been killed, Lindsay ordered that all of the city's flags be flown at half-mast. I don't remember if the police and fire departments followed it at that time. But they probably didn't. I remember that all the police cars had on their headlights in the middle of the day to protest the lowering of the flags.*

On May eighth about one thousand students gathered at noon to hold a memorial service and protest the killing of the students at Kent State. They started on Wall Street and moved up to Federal Hall. It was lunchtime and there were a bunch of Wall Street people out, the streets were very crowded. About two hundred construction workers wearing hard hats and carrying American flags started chasing the protesters through the streets and beating them up with lead pipes and crowbars. The police were essentially going along with it, and they stood by while the hippies

---

* Mayor John Lindsay was the target of blue-collar anger because of his patrician style and liberal policies toward blacks. One sign protesting the lowering of the flags to half-mast read, "Lindsay drops the flag more times than a whore drops her pants." *Time,* May 25, 1970, p. 21.

were being attacked. About seventy people were injured, twenty were hospitalized, and they set up a sort of hospital for all of the injured people at Trinity Church. I remember even the Episcopal flag was torn down in front of the church by the rioters. A mob pushed through security at City Hall, went up to the roof, and changed the flag back from half to full mast. I think there were only six arrests. Lindsay spoke the next day about being very disappointed in the police force and saying that they were responsible for allowing the hard-hat riot to go on.

CARL BERNSTEIN (*Washington Post* reporter)

The Nixon people wanted to make the movement look worse than it was—I don't think Nixon was sitting there saying, "Let's beat the shit out of these people." I don't think that was his thing at all, but that's certainly where some of his people went with it. But they did want to show not just the Silent Majority, but that muscular forces, meaning those perceived as male, macho, hard-hat, truck-driving men, were out there on their side, and portray the demonstrators as elite, effete, and to the extent that they could, radical.

STEPHEN BULL

In Manhattan, there was some sort of a demonstration going on after Kent State and these guys were burning American flags and the like. These construction workers, the so-called hard hats, had had enough. They went down, and I guess they reprimanded the demonstrators rather severely.

I think it was Chuck Colson who thought, Let's get these guys down here, give them a pat on the head. So they trotted them in to see the president and meet with him in the Roosevelt Room. Peter Brennan was head of the building and construction trades union then, and after Nixon's reelection, he became secretary of labor. I think what endeared him to the White House was his people decided they were not going to brook such conduct from the protesters.

On May 8, 1970, two hundred construction workers waving American flags confronted one thousand students who were holding a memorial service on Wall Street for the four students killed at Kent State. Police stood back and watched as the construction workers beat up the kids in what would be called "the hard-hat riot." About twenty people were hospitalized and seventy injured.

ALISON TEAL

Lindsay was so far from working class. They called him the "Mayor from Hanoi" and "the red mayor."

MICHAEL KAZIN

As most historians of the sixties will tell you, and me included, the war was incredibly unpopular. But the antiwar movement was also unpopular, because it was perceived as being primarily privileged white kids. We did stupid things like waving Viet Cong flags and burning American flags and saying this country sucks. Most Americans were not ready to hear that, in whatever variation. And they were right not to want to hear it, because as I've realized since, there are a lot of good things about the country, and the problem was not the country. The problem was the people who ran it.

CHAPTER 21

UNDERGROUND

(May–July 1970)

If you happen to accidentally recognize a fugitive at a movie theater or rock festival, don't freak out. Stay calm. Quietly go up to the person and empty out all of your pockets and give all your belongings to him or her, especially money, food, vitamin C, credit cards, identification, checkbooks, pot, driver's license, social security card.

Give the fugitive your beads, headband, the shirt off your back and then a big hug and a kiss. Helping and hiding a fugitive is one of the best acts of a human being.

—JERRY RUBIN, *We Are Everywhere*

ONE HUNDRED AND FIFTY WEATHERMEN SHED THEIR IDENTITIES in the spring of 1970 and waded into the alternate universe of Vietnam War deserters, resisters, Black Panthers, Catholic radicals, drug dealers, and hippies who made up "the underground." The FBI began its hunt to find the Weathermen, and J. Edgar Hoover declared that their leader, Bernardine Dohrn, was "the most dangerous woman in America." Soon to rename themselves the Weather Underground, the Weathermen's numbers were small in comparison to the thousands of others in hiding. The Pentagon reported 73,000 deserters in 1969 and another 89,000 in 1970. Seventy percent headed to Canada and other countries but thousands remained in America, hiding in plain sight, wearing disguises and using false names.

BERNARDINE DOHRN (Weather Underground leader)

That spring of '70, when we were newly underground, the invasion of Laos and Cambodia was followed by the biggest student strike in the history of the United States. Even though SDS had been lost, suddenly there was a vibrant, national student movement. The killings at Kent State and Jackson State propelled both the black and white student movements to accelerate in their organization, strategies, and tactics.

It was like being reborn—especially because for us the winter had been so horrible with the assassination of Fred Hampton, and the public's seeming nonresistance to the escalation in Vietnam. Suddenly this outpouring of resistance began, and we found a lot of hope and energy in the counterculture and in the revived student movement and the growing women's movement. It was a reminder that when people look like they're asleep, they're not always asleep; and a reminder of how hateful the government was. They were willing to shoot their own children. Of course, we now know they were shooting a lot of black children; but shooting white children at Kent State was shocking to white people in America. Kent State was a validation of our antigovernment rhetoric. It proved us right.

RICK AYERS (draft deserter, Weather Underground member)

Kent State made us remember that these are our people. We were not enemies. And it really pushed us back to respecting the mass movement.

MARK RUDD (Weather Underground leader)

(aka Marc William Rudnitsky, Frank Henry Koch, Anthony Goodman)[*]

It was the beginning of May of '70. And the Weather Bureau led us to California, and back to understanding our base. When you become a terrorist, your base becomes very abstracted. You're out there, and who's the

---

[*] Rudd's underground aliases, listed in the FBI Weather Underground Summary, August 20, 1976.

base? When we were organizers at college campuses, we knew who the base was, and who we were organizing. But then when you become a guerrilla, you're way out there. I think that if you look at that moment after the townhouse, Bernardine and Billy [Ayers] and Jeff [Jones] led us to believe that we could promote the politicization of the cultural movement. I give them a lot of credit for that.

Some people give the impression that the two worlds—political radicals versus the counterculture—were not connected. But those who were out in California understood how widespread the hippie and the youth movement was. That was our natural base. Those of us on the East Coast didn't quite get it yet.

I remember arriving in California in really straight clothes that I had used as my disguise in the East, dyed-black short hair, slacks, and a dress shirt. An old comrade, a member of our San Francisco tribe, met me at the bus. He had long hair and was wearing a beaded necklace, bell-bottoms, and a bandana with a peace sign on it. He took me to an apartment in Nob Hill, where I was reunited with Weatherman friends I hadn't seen since Flint in December. I felt as if I'd come in from the cold.

BERNARDINE DOHRN

(aka Lorraine Ann Jellins, Sharon Louise Naylor, Karen Lois DeBelius,
Bernardine Rae Ohrnstein, Rose Bridges)

From my Chicago viewpoint, the counterculture seemed to be all about music and drugs; and I thought it had a lot of the trappings of selfishness. I thought caring about your well-being and peacefulness was an evasion of our responsibilities to hurl ourselves into the catastrophes of our time.

But when we went to California, we went from being working-class, west-side-of-Chicago toughs to trying to get healthy—we were very unhealthy—trying to eat well; trying to live low on the food chain; recognizing that the commune movement was on to something. Growing food, raising animals, and living on very little; acting collaboratively, owning things communally. That kind of lifestyle was a cousin of ours, and we had things to learn.

We soon came to see that there was a huge substratum that was alienated from society and that people were impelled to leave the Midwest and the East Coast to remake themselves, whether it was because they were gay and closeted, or because they were nonconformists in other ways, or because they were evading or deserting the military. We found ourselves thrust in with a lot of American life that was clandestine; people who were using other names for huge varieties of reasons; people who worked outside of the formal economy and were paid for a day's work.

BILL AYERS (Weather Underground leader)

(aka Michael Joseph Rafferty, Jr., Jules Michael Taylor,
Hank Anderson, Joe Brown)

Immediately after the townhouse explosion on March 6, we shifted and we changed back to what we were before that fateful year. Before March 6, there was a sense that you had to craft yourself as a tool of the revolution. And that means twenty-four/seven on duty and making yourself a fighter. We had contempt for everybody else, not just the hippies—but including the hippies. I had never really been to the West Coast. We bought a pickup truck and rolled down the coast to San Francisco and began picking up hitchhikers. Oh, hippie culture was magnificent! We discovered something we had known for a couple of years, which is we shared an antiestablishment instinct with the great youth culture.

It was the first time any of us had relaxed in about a year and a half. We actually breathed the air, stopped smoking, and didn't take speed. It was kind of an unwinding. After the townhouse, Bernardine and Jeff Jones had the wisdom to see that we had just walked up to a precipice, and that we ought to think hard about what we had done. But you can't think hard in a pressure cooker, so they slowed us all down.

We were in a house in Mendocino, where we unwound slowly. There were a lot of individual meetings, and a lot of walks on the beach, and a lot of conversation about what we'd lost. And for me, embracing my particular loss. Diana Oughton, Terry Robbins, and Teddy Gold were friends and comrades of all of ours. For them to die in that horrible moment meant that some grieving, decompression, reflection, and debriefing was essential.

BERNARDINE DOHRN

I was definitely arguing that what would have happened, but for the accident in the townhouse, would have been a crime, and would have had terrible consequences for the antiwar movement as a whole and that we couldn't match the military strength of the greatest military power in human history. But we could match other strengths: We were smarter, more mobile, filled with surprises for them, and stronger than they thought because of the number of people who were disaffected from the American dream—people who were not buying it, dropped out of school having learned what really motivated universities, which was not the citadel of learning, but a cover for military and corporate power.

BILL AYERS

The group in Mendocino was mostly the Weather Bureau, all of us who had written the Weatherman statement, all of us who became the central committee, and some who weren't on the central committee. It was Bernardine, Jeff, J.J. [John Jacobs], me. There was someone we called Sonia Sanchez, who signed a lot of the communiqués, another guy we called Jimmy, and five or six others who haven't revealed themselves.

We came out of that determined not to turn back from what we'd gotten ourselves into. That is, we still thought we needed a clandestine network to survive the impending American fascism. We were sure of that. We still felt that we ought to take the war to the war-makers, and we ought to disable B-52s, and we ought to issue a screaming alarm to the American people that the society was going to uncork, and that this war and the attack on the black movement was the uncorking. So, we didn't pull back from any of that.

What we pulled back from was the speed-fueled, no sleep, make yourself an instrument of war, objectifying of ourselves. And there was a determination to resubjectify ourselves: "You have a mind of your own. You don't have to think like the rest of us." There was a lot of reading going on. We were reading Native American authors, like *Crazy Horse,* by Mari Sandoz—that was hugely important for us. We read revolutionary works, but it was stuff that was more out of the humanistic tradition.

The other piece coming out of the meetings in Mendocino was that a bright line was drawn, and I have to credit Jeff and Bernardine with drawing this line. They said, "We're not about hurting anybody." We carried guns in the summer of '69. We stopped carrying guns. I carried a gun for about nine months—carried it onto airplanes, carried it everywhere I went. Whenever I spoke, I had a gun in the back of my belt. We were walking in uncharted territory.

MARK RUDD

I knew they [the leadership] knew about the townhouse plans, but a certain myth was turned. It's like organic Stalinism, where you rewrite history because it has to be rewritten that the new leadership has always been right.

BERNARDINE DOHRN

We argued to ourselves that we had a role to play from underground, but also that we were wrong to think that that was the highest form of life, and that a mass movement had to be rebuilt, an antiracist mass movement; and certainly by that time there was the women's movement. We had a role to play from underground that would give us a loud voice, but it had to be a moral voice; and we were not going to take lives, not innocent lives, and not even guilty lives.

BILL AYERS

After March 6 [the townhouse bombing] we had a big struggle about which way to go, and J.J. believed that what they were doing in the townhouse was the right thing, but nobody else went there. We were determined to go forward as an organization, united. And one of the principles was that we would try to not risk people's lives. J.J. thought we were going on what he called a "revisionist road," and we were giving up on the revolution, so we expelled him and he went out on his own. J.J. was Mark Rudd's closest confidant at Columbia, and they were both powerful in our little circle. Mark was torn, but J.J. was his close partner, and so Mark left also. But that was it. That was the limit of what we lost in that struggle.

BRIAN FLANAGAN (Weathermen member)

Basically, J.J. talked the Weather Bureau into giving Terry Robbins free rein to do his thing at Cathy Wilkerson's father's townhouse, which is the reason that J.J. was eventually expelled from the organization.

MARK RUDD

(*Underground: My Life with SDS and the Weathermen*) *

After a few days, Bernardine announced that JJ would have to leave the organization. He had to go out on his own, she said, to learn about the emerging youth culture and "to get his head straight." She also confirmed my demotion in the organization: I would be brought into the San Francisco tribe as a cadre in order to reeducate myself about the youth culture. I had been too close to JJ and was completely expelled from leadership.

That night JJ and I went out to a bar in Fort Bragg, a slightly larger working-class town up the coast from Mendocino. We drank and played pool. In the background Creedence Clearwater Revival played on the jukebox. . . .

> *Hope you got your things together.*
> *Hope you are quite prepared to die.*
> *Looks like we're in for nasty weather.*
> *One eye is taken for an eye.*

JJ agreed he had to leave the group. "I'm accepting my expulsion for the good of the organization," he told me. "Someone has to take the blame. Bernardine, Billy, and Jeff are right about the military error."

---

* Rudd, *Underground*, p. 214.

"But everyone knew what was being planned," I said. "We were all together in New York with Terry the week before the action, and nobody raised any objections."

"It doesn't matter. We have to create the fiction that they were always right so that they can lead the organization," he replied. . . .

I was sad for JJ, but I also agreed with the criticism of his "militarism." Plus, I had gotten off easy: At least I wasn't being cast out.

BILL DYSON (FBI agent)

There were a lot of them—at least a hundred—when they first went underground. Now, problem is we don't really know what happened. Some of these people like Mark Rudd—all of a sudden, they're just sort of sloughed off. I think Barry Stein was another one, just sort of sloughed off. All of a sudden they're underground, and they're not with the people anymore. I mentioned Caroline Tanner. She went underground, and as far as I know, she never did any bombings or anything. It was like if you really weren't all that strong for what they wanted, you were gone.

TOM HAYDEN (founder, SDS)

I think they went into utter shock. The reason they disappeared for a time was that they had a soul-searching process. J.J. got blamed for the townhouse bombing. But there's never a sole figure of blame. He was the scapegoat. On the other hand, there were people who didn't know what the plan was, and they were legitimately shocked. In the middle were people that sort of knew but didn't do anything about it. They couldn't deal with it, or they were in partial denial. So the townhouse bomb blows up a lot of assumptions and a lot of denial and they go into retreat.

This is where Bernardine ascended as the new leader of the Weather Underground. And it's a kinder, gentler, earth mother, hippie organization, in time. Instead of self-hating for white privilege, they've concluded that they actually love the white youth culture. They've taken the Weathermen analysis to the limit of white revolutionary youth.

MAY 21, 1970, FIRST WEATHERMEN COMMUNIQUÉ

Hello. This is Bernardine Dohrn.

I'm going to read A DECLARATION OF A STATE OF WAR.

All over the world, people fighting Amerikan imperialism look to Amerika's youth to use our strategic position behind enemy lines to join forces in the destruction of the empire.

Black people have been fighting almost alone for years. We've known that our job is to lead white kids to armed revolution. We never intended to spend the next five or twenty-five years in jail. Ever since SDS became revolutionary, we've been trying to show how it is possible to overcome the frustration and impotence that comes from trying to reform this system. Kids know that the lines are drawn; revolution is touching all of our lives. Tens of thousands have learned that protest and marches don't do it. Revolutionary violence is the only way.[*]

MARK RUDD (*Underground*) [†]

It was suitably contradictory, first extolling the mass struggle against U.S. imperialism but then claiming that our task was "to lead white kids into armed revolution," appropriating the guerilla strategy of the Vietcong and the Tupamaros of Uruguay.

The communiqué confirmed Terry as the third person killed in the townhouse, since his body had been so mangled as to have been questionably identified.

---

[*]   A tape recording of Bernardine Dohrn reading the communiqué was dropped off at 7:30 A.M. May 21 in a phone booth near KPFK in Los Angeles, and transcripts were delivered to the Chicago bureau of *The New York Times* and the Liberation News Service in plain brown envelopes. This became the model for how the Weather Underground would communicate with the outside world. See Thai Jones, *A Radical Line* (New York: Free Press, 2004), p. 210.

[†]   Rudd, *Underground*, pp. 215–16.

MAY 21, 1970, FIRST WEATHERMEN COMMUNIQUÉ

The twelve Weathermen who were indicted for leading last October's riots in Chicago have never left the country. Terry [Robbins] is dead, Linda [Evans] was captured by a pig informer, but the rest of us move freely in and out of every city and youth scene in this country. We're not in hiding, but we're invisible.

There are several hundred members of the Weatherman underground and some of us face more years in jail than the 50,000 deserters and draft dodgers now in Canada. Already many of them are coming back to join us in the underground or to return to The Man's army and tear it up from inside along with those who never left.

We fight in many ways. Dope is one of our weapons. The laws against marijuana mean that millions of us are outlaws long before we actually split. Guns and grass are united in the youth underground.

Freaks are revolutionaries and revolutionaries are freaks. If you want to find us, this is where we are. In every tribe, commune, dormitory, farmhouse, barracks, and townhouse where kids are making love, smoking dope and loading guns—fugitives from Amerikan justice are free to go. . . .

Within the next fourteen days we will attack a symbol or institution of Amerikan injustice. This is the way we celebrate the example of Eldridge Cleaver and H. Rap Brown and all black revolutionaries who first inspired us by their fight behind enemy lines for the liberation of their people.

MARK RUDD (*Underground*)*

Eighteen days later, on June 9, a bomb was set off inside the New York City police headquarters. Due to a phoned-in warning, no one was seriously injured. A statement entitled "The Second Com-

---

*   Rudd, *Underground,* p. 216.

muniqué from the Weatherman Underground" was received by the press the next day.[*]

BRIAN FLANAGAN

There's an old anarchist saying, "propaganda of the deed," and that's what we became. We weren't recruiting any new people, and our bombings became a spectator sport. The police headquarters was great. The Capitol bathroom [bombing] was even better.[†] So what are we going to do? Eventually blow up the Statue of Liberty? I mean, where does this thing go?

A really nice thing about Weather was we could respond. We had the wherewithal and the power and the ability to respond quickly to things that happened. To hit Oswald's office in Albany after the Attica massacre[‡] for example. It felt good to be able to do those things and read about them in the paper the next day. But still, it's just a symbolic attack. It was symbolic action in response to something that the other side did. The criticism was it turned the revolution into a spectator sport. But it did make you feel good. I loved those bombings. Any time Weather blew up anything, everybody was happy and we'd have a little party.

BILL DYSON

I kept the official list of the number of Weather Underground bombings between 1970 and 1974. It was thirty-eight. Well, it was amazing. And

[*]   Seven people were injured in the New York City police headquarters bombing and the damage was estimated to cost hundreds of thousands of dollars. The bomb was made with ten sticks of dynamite. New York City offered a $25,000 reward for information about the bombers, and Mayor John Lindsay vowed that the "police investigation now going forward will be relentless." New York had been riddled with bombings. There had been 121 bombs detonated in the past sixteen months, most of them by antiwar activists. Jones, *A Radical Line*, p. 212.

[†]   On March 1, 1971, the Weather Underground detonated a bomb they had placed in a bathroom in the United States Capitol and issued a communiqué saying that it was "in protest of the U.S. invasion of Laos." President Nixon denounced the bombing as a "shocking act of violence that will outrage all Americans."

[‡]   On September 17, 1971, the Weather Underground bombed the New York State Department of Corrections in Albany in retaliation for the killing of thirty-three prisoners (including radical bomber Sam Melville) in the riots at Attica State Prison on September 13, 1971.

that was part of my story I used to tell classes [of young FBI agents]. I told them that I was a case agent on the Weather Underground. My job was to run that operation. And I said, "Tell me, class, how many of these bombings or attacks do you think I solved?" And somebody would say, "Oh, ten of them, fifteen." I'd say, "Come on, come on, come on!" Eventually somebody would say, "None." I said, "You got it!" Then I'd say, "Why are you listening to me? Why would you want to listen to me in this class? I didn't solve a thing. I was a total failure." And then I'd go on, and build it from there.

Basically, the point I was trying to make is that we didn't know how to investigate terrorism then. When I say "we," I mean law enforcement in general, and the FBI specifically. We couldn't even work together. And that's a message I try to give to all these people, that this is not an FBI problem. This is not a local police problem, or a county problem, or a state. It's all of our problems.

When you have a group like the Weather Underground that's clandestine nationally, and they do a bombing in San Francisco, the person who did the bombing may be from New York. The person who wrote the communiqué may be in Florida. And it's impossible for the San Francisco Police Department to solve it, because the people who did it may have only just come there, did it and left. They may have nothing to do with San Francisco.

On the other hand, the poor FBI, they're limited. We only had about eleven thousand agents—a handful considering the population of the United States—so how are you going to solve it? We didn't know the local areas as well as the police department did.

BILL AYERS

When we went underground, we stopped going to the old neighborhood. We stopped going home. We assumed false identities. In the beginning we were improvising, because we didn't know how to make false IDs. Sometimes people carried stolen identities. They didn't think much about it; they found a wallet of somebody five foot ten and said, "What the hell, I could be that guy."

But soon we began to build up lots of sets of IDs for each one of us. There were a lot of ways to do it, but the way that proved to be the most enduring was to go to a place like South Dakota, find a cemetery, and find the tombstones of kids who were about your age. For example, in my case, somebody who died before the age of ten or so, somebody born between 1942 and 1948. I was born in '44. If I could find a kid who was born in those years and died five years later, that was a perfect identity for me. Then I'd go to the courthouse and ask for the birth certificate of Anthony Lee, born on such-and-such a date, and I would buy the birth certificate for two dollars from the county courthouse. With that birth certificate I'd get a fishing license and something else, and when I had four or five pieces of ID I might use that ID for a drop box, and get a let-ter sent to that drop box. Then I have a mailing address. I have a birth certificate. I have a fishing license. I have three or four other little things, maybe a health card. Then I'd go to get a driver's license and a Social Security card, because there's never been a Social Security card issued for Anthony Lee, because he died when he was five. I'd get a California driver's license, or an Illinois driver's license, and now I have a perfect ID set. So that's how we did it. Things have definitely changed now, but then it was not so hard.

BILL DYSON

When you did fugitive investigations, there were basic rules. You as-sumed they had contact with their family; close family, distant family, as-sociates. But the Weather Underground was very different. The family either agreed or didn't agree with what they were doing. If the family didn't support them, then you basically abandoned the support. If Mom died, you probably weren't going to show up to the funeral. But if you were looking for a criminal fugitive—I'll use the Mafia, for an example—if Mom or Dad died, we'd always cover the funeral, because there was a good chance the guy would come to it. Maybe he couldn't come to the funeral, maybe he'd stay in the outside, maybe sneak into the funeral home at night. Not with these people. So we had to learn different meth-ods for chasing fugitives.

BILL AYERS

We would all try to build multiple ID sets. It was part of our work all the time, because it wasn't something you wanted to rest on. Because we were inexperienced, we made a lot of mistakes.

The worst one was "the encirclement," when somebody had an ID and bought a car, so the car was registered in this name and linked to a house he had rented in the same name. He used this ID to do something else, and then he got a telegram from someplace, using this ID, but the police were watching the telegraph office. And then, the FBI had the house. It turned out, at that house somebody else had bought a car, and gotten a ticket in front of that house. So then that ID was gone. And that ID was tied to another house. And somebody else had done something else in that house. And so it went: We lost everything in the first year, in just a couple of weeks' span, simply by having one ID blown, and that ID linking to every other ID. That taught us that you couldn't ever link them. That you had to rent your house—your apartment—in a different name than you bought your car in. You didn't park in front of your house—you parked two blocks away. We learned a lot. But that's just spycraft, and there's not much to it. It changes all the time, and none of what we learned would be relevant to anybody else today.

BILL DYSON

They wouldn't maintain contact with their family if they didn't think the family would support them. If the family did support, then they expected the family would practice extreme security, whereas I don't think the average criminal assumes that. He may maintain contact with his family, and he doesn't expect the family to maintain extreme security. It's not just Weathermen; this is generally true with most political extremists: Security is everything. Security, security, security. Good false identification. Not just changing your name, good false identification. And it took a long while for us to learn this. They did false ID very, very well. But once we learned how to do it, we could find them. These people didn't realize how close we were.

I was the last person to try to interview Bernardine Dohrn before she went underground. She didn't talk to me, but at least I made an effort. I talked to Bill Ayers's father very frequently when he was a fugitive, so I got to know his father—not that we were close friends by any means.

BILL AYERS

We started to develop a long list of code words and phrases, and we took a lot from rock and roll. For example, "I ain't gonna work on Maggie's farm no more." "Maggie's farm" meant the Pentagon. We called ourselves the "eggplant" for a while, because there was a song called "The Eggplant That Ate Chicago." Another word for the organization was "the joke." "Does he know the joke?" Weather was "the joke"; our aboveground support group was "the forest." The FBI were "the shoes," for gumshoes.

BERNARDINE DOHRN

If you look at the FBI documents from the time, from 1970, once we were underground, you can see that they didn't understand anything. They had the words all wrong. They were translating our words, but there's no comprehension behind the words.

BILL AYERS

We had to reorganize, and that was work. We had to find ways to be in touch with the people who weren't underground, and that was work. But all of it was pretty much accomplished within the first year or two. And then we had a functioning organization that was living underground, that was in several cities, that had good links to the radical movement aboveground, and had good relationships with the most unlikely people. I won't even tell you who. The odd and interesting thing, and what makes me know that we were a legitimate American phenomenon, is people as diffuse as John Holt, who was a right-wing school reformer and an old friend of mine, supported us. People from the Quaker pacifist community gave us money. People who had no reason to think that the Weather Underground was the right way to go didn't want to see us arrested. So I was recognized on the street on an average of every month, and no one turned

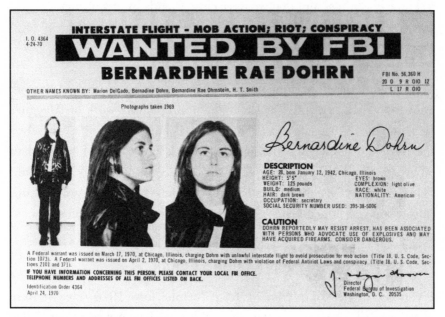

On October 14, 1970, the FBI placed Bernardine Dohrn, age twenty-eight, on the Ten Most Wanted Fugitive list, replacing Angela Davis, who had been captured the day before.

me in, ever. Why would they? What would be the point of turning me in? They weren't Weather people, but they also weren't the police. I mean, they didn't think the police were great.

BERNARDINE DOHRN

By late 1970 I took on an outlaw identity. We didn't plan it, but there is a love of the outlaw in American history. The FBI put us on the Ten Most Wanted list, and then added the students from Brandeis, and then the students from Wisconsin, and at Brown, Davis. It meant that eight or nine of the top ten most wanted were all of us. It's a very funny chapter in American life. Suddenly people had our pictures in their windows with "Welcome here!" signs.

BRIAN FLANAGAN

Most of my underground life was spent in California. A lot of times when I was traveling around California, I'd wind up staying in hippie communes. They didn't know who we were. One time somebody figured it out. "You're a Weatherman, aren't you?" And I said, "Yes, I am."

I worked for the *Berkeley Tribe* for a while, and the *San Diego Free Press, Great Speckled Bird. The East Village Other* was the one in New York, *The East Village Other* and *Rat.* Those were fertile breeding grounds for us, for people to swim in, if not to recruit them, but we didn't recruit a whole lot of people. We did get a good following of people aboveground. So, I don't know how much organizing we did underground—we took some people like Mary Moylan down that had to go under.*

BERNARDINE DOHRN

I did a lot of waiting tables, and I also spent a year cleaning women's houses; the kind of work where you get paid for at the end of the day in cash. We cut grapes. We paid our rent in cash, and we bought our cars with cash. We lived outside that economy. A lot of people were doing that as a choice, and a lot of people were doing it out of desperation.

MARK RUDD

When I was underground, I was nobody. I had no background, I had no employment or educational experience. I was a laborer in a factory. I was hired the same day as a black guy in a factory in Philadelphia. I spoke English, I read and wrote English; these were the privileges that my background gave me. Very quickly I rose in this stupid little laborer's job I had, and in a matter of a month or two I became the supervisor of the black guy I was hired with. We just looked at each other and said,

---

*   Mary Moylan, along with the Berrigan brothers, was one of the Catonsville Nine—Catholic radicals who were convicted for torching Baltimore County draft records with homemade napalm on May 17, 1968. On the day they were to go to jail, April 19, 1970, Moylan and the others became fugitives. Moylan evaded the FBI for ten years, the longest of any of the Catonsville Nine.

"Same old shit." There's no way to get rid of privilege, no matter how hard you try.

BILL AYERS

We were part of that San Francisco music scene. The Grateful Dead and Jefferson Airplane were two of the San Francisco groups that we loved. Grace Slick and Paul Kantner wrote a song about Diana [Oughton], and we had some communication with them through an intermediary.

> *Huntress of the moon and a lady of the Earth*
> *Weather woman Diana*
>
> —PAUL KANTNER AND
> GRACE SLICK, "DIANA"

BRIAN FLANAGAN

We were playacting hippies because we thought they were the base. There was a stoner part of me, but I was really a commie. The hippies seemed to be a natural group. I mean we were not going to recruit from Mormons, and Opus Dei was not a fertile field for us, either. You've got these hippies—and there were various grades of hippies, there were hippies with guns, there were stoners, there were people who went back to the earth, there was a lesbian communist community in New Mexico called Sisters of the Sun. It was every kind of weirdo you could imagine.

BILL AYERS

You could go to any rock concert or any country place and say, "Weather Underground," and they'd be like, "Hell yeah, brother!" The thing about security when you're a fugitive is that it's not so much technical as it is political: If you have the support of the people, you're okay. If the people are going to rat you out, then you're in trouble. Many times when we were in trouble, we could just hitchhike and say, "I'm a fugitive; can you help me out?" "Oh yeah, brother; what do you need?" It was very common in that time. If the FBI visited someone, even someone really square, and said, "We're looking for Bill Ayers," or "We're looking for Bernardine Dohrn," within a day or two we'd hear about it. So information would not flow their way; it would flow our way. And that's the essence of being in a guerrilla base. So we did see ourselves as fish in the sea. We wouldn't have that kind of support now. If you ran around and said, "We're bombers for Earth First," most people would say, "I don't know you." You have to understand the atmosphere at the time.

We changed our appearances a little, but not dramatically. I had very short hair and a mustache, then, I suddenly had long hair and a beard. Was that a big change? Not really. I got a new pair of glasses. We learned through experience that if you did something stupid like put on a red wig, it was garish. It was obvious. Whereas, if you just shifted slightly, some people would recognize you, if they knew you well. But nobody expects to see you there. And it wasn't like today, where everybody's image is everywhere.

RICHARD NIXON (*RN: The Memoirs of Richard Nixon*)*

On June 5, 1970, I called a meeting with Hoover, Helms of the CIA, Lieutenant General D. V. Bennett of the Defense Intelligence Agency, and Vice Admiral Noel Gayler, Director of the National Security Agency. Haldeman, Ehrlichman, Bob Finch, and Tom Huston were also present. Huston was a young lawyer and a former Defense Intelligence Agency aide whose assignments on the White House staff included the problem of violence from radicals. He was seriously concerned about the inadequacies of the U.S. intelligence apparatus, both in the face of domestic violence and in comparison to the intelligence capabilities of Communist-bloc countries.

I told the group that I wanted to know what the problems were in intelligence-gathering and what had to be done to solve them. I

*   Nixon, *RN*, p. 473.

wanted their report submitted to me jointly, and I asked Hoover to act as chairman for this purpose.

The committee formed a study group to evaluate the situation and draw up alternatives. A report was drafted that was approved by the heads of the CIA, DIA, and NSA. Then it went to Hoover, who added as footnotes to the body of the document, his personal objections to several of the sections.

The report was completed on June 25, 1970. It was officially called "Special Report Interagency Committee on Intelligence (Ad Hoc)."

The report opened with a brief analysis of the problems confronting us, ranging from the Black Panthers and the Weathermen to Communist infiltrators. It differentiated radical terrorist groups from those that merely indulged in incendiary rhetoric. It gave a summary of the available intelligence techniques, the current restrictions on them, and the advantages and disadvantages of lifting those restrictions.

There was only one technique which Hoover had no objection to seeing expanded—the National Security Agency's coverage of overseas telephone and telegraph communications. He had strong objections to the four central possibilities discussed: resumption of covert mail-opening, resumption of black bag jobs, increased electronic surveillance, and an increase in campus—therefore young—informants.*

CARL BERNSTEIN (*Washington Post* reporter)

From the first months of the Nixon presidency, they had, from the president down, decided that the antiwar movement must be undermined. . . . So, just like all his other enemies, his [Nixon's] way of dealing with the

---

* Nixon directed the FBI to prove that the Weathermen were foreign agents financed by enemies like Cuba, North Vietnam, and China, but despite years of surveillance, the FBI never could find any proof. Hoover ultimately refused to sign off on the "Huston Plan" because he feared it would give the White House too much power. But Nixon's directive continued unofficially and illegal surveillance, like wiretapping, and black-bag jobs, as well as harassment of the Weather Underground and the Panthers, increased.

antiwar movement was to regard them as subversive, not so much to the country but to his own interests. He didn't think Hoover would share all the information with him, so he decided he needed his own extralegal force to do black-bag jobs and wiretap people in the antiwar movement, and that became the Huston Plan, based on a report outlining this illegal security operation written by a young White House aide, Tom Charles Huston. The Huston Plan, and its illegal means approved by Nixon, was the first comprehensive plan of illegal actions to deal with those that Nixon thought opposed and constrained him.

BILL DYSON

There were certain people in the FBI who made the decision "we've got to do anything to get rid of these people. Anything!" Not kill them per se, but anything went. If we suspect somebody's involved in this, put a wiretap on them. Put a microphone in. Steal his mail. Do anything. There were other people who were opposed to it. I can say, in all honesty, that as the national case agent, I never violated the law. I was opposed to doing anything illegal. *But* I do not criticize those agents who said, "We've got to save our country."

BRIAN FLANAGAN

What happened was that we had an FBI group assigned to us in New York called Squad 47, and they became fond of doing black-bag jobs, which are illegal.* We also had a phone snitch in New York. We knew which phones were tapped. We found out because we had a mole in the phone company. So I knew the phone was tapped. I'm the only one that has proof from the government that my phone was tapped. I also knew from my superintendent that there was mail cover. The super was telling me that things were being intercepted. They read your mail before it comes to you. The super knew it because the FBI kept asking him, "Does he pick

---

*   The term "black-bag jobs" refers to burglars' tool bags. Black-bag jobs were illegal entry and search missions such as break-ins, phone taps, mail cover, and other forms of surveillance in search of incriminating evidence.

up his mail regularly?" And they asked him all these questions, and then told him, Don't say anything to anybody. It'll be a federal crime if you talk to them. But the super was a friend of mine, and I don't think he was a tipster. I was living on Riverside Drive, on the Upper West Side.

I had always assumed if you're in the Weather Underground, the phone conversations are unbelievable. We had code words for everything. We did pay-phone-to-pay-phone until they started recording pay-phone-to-pay-phone.

BILL DYSON

We were not so much listening in. Not too much wires in those days. Once the SDS national office found out, we didn't have wires to speak of. First of all, we had to find somebody to put a wiretap on. And you'd have to get it under the Omnibus Crime Bill of 1968.* You'd have to get probable cause. I mean, it's not like you get a wiretap just like that. So a lot of it was surveillance, development of informants, interviewing relatives, friends, and so forth. Remember, we're still learning how to catch these people.

MICHAEL KENNEDY (movement lawyer)

There were a lot of squads, Red Squads, we called them, and they were local police, or state, or federal troops who tried to tie in the antigovernment stances of the young people, particularly into communism, and try to make it clear to the world that these people were traitors, and communists, and were being funded by foreign governments. That's right, Mao was supposed to be supporting the Weather Underground. That didn't happen.

BERNARDINE DOHRN

Any suggestion that we were funded from outside the country was just invented from whole cloth. We were always very clear, even when we

---

* The Omnibus Crime Control and Safe Streets Act of 1968 was passed by Congress and signed by President Lyndon Johnson. Among other things, the bill established the Law Enforcement Assistance Administration and set rules for obtaining a wiretap.

were off the rails in the beginning, that we were not taking money from outside the country—which was offered to us and rejected—and that we were a homegrown phenomenon. We were not going to be used by somebody else. We made our own mistakes, our own way; which we did, plenty.

CHAPTER 22

CULTURE WARS

(May 1970)

I was interested in two things: overthrowing the government and fucking. They went together seamlessly.

—PETER COYOTE[*]

Can the family survive? Students in rebellion, the young people living in communes, unmarried couples living together call into question the very meaning and structure of the stable family unit as our society has known it.

—MARGARET MEAD[†]

WITH CAMPUSES IN TURMOIL, MORE AND MORE YOUNG PEOPLE disengaged from political protest and voted with their lifestyles. By 1970, the young were leaving colleges and cities in droves and up to three million people had settled in thousands of communes. The president of Columbia University reported that 50 percent of college students belonged to "an alienated culture, hostile to science and technology." One of the most popular bumper stickers at the time declared, QUESTION AUTHORITY.

Living off the economic grid was another revolutionary way to reject a racist, imperialist, capitalist government. The environmental move-

---

[*] Quoted in Sheila Weller, "Suddenly That Summer," *Vanity Fair,* July 2012.

[†] Quoted in *Time,* December 28, 1970.

ment, which was christened on April 22, 1970, when 20 million people participated in Earth Day activities, became the political arm of the back-to-the-land movement. At its core, practicing organic farming, Native American customs, and holistic health remedies required a more intimate relationship to nature. As 1970 came to a close, the euphoria of the psychedelic drug and music scene, and the idealism of the rural countercul-ture, took a sober turn. Commune poverty and squalor, heroin and cocaine abuse, and politically motivated drug busts brought King Hippie to his knees as he limped, wounded, into a new decade.

MICHAEL RANDALL (cofounder, Brotherhood of Eternal Love)

We thought the Vietnam War was a disgrace. We thought it was an unnec-essary war, and we were outraged. But we just kept to ourselves and fo-cused on what we thought we should do, which was to provide as much LSD as we could to as many people as possible. We were just certain that was what God wanted us to do. We were evangelists. We believed that we needed to show the spiritual world to as many people as possible through this magic molecule. Orange Sunshine was the color of the Buddhist robes, and we used a combination of food dyes and yellow dye number six. The most damaging thing for LSD is light, so we chose a color that we thought would protect it.*

PETER COYOTE (Digger, communard)

I've always suspected that the environmental movement was engendered, in some way, by the shootings at Kent State. When people saw that the culture was willing to shoot their own children to keep the war machine going, I think a lot of people moved their energy into the environment where they could see it as a future struggle, but it didn't engender police resistance and getting shot and killed.

We had already left confrontational politics. By that time we were deep

---

* Psychedelic chemists Tim Scully and Nick Sand first manufactured Orange Sunshine in a lab in Sonoma County, California, in 1968.

into cultural warfare. So we saw the news of the Kent and Jackson State shootings as the fulfillment of predictions that we had made.

CAROL RANDALL (Michael Randall's wife)

Sunshine was the number-one acid around. Our doses were pretty strong at that time, and it started scaring a lot of people. I used to say it "scared them into spiritual practice." Ashrams filled up. We made more of it than anybody else made of anything, and we just thought we should make it strong.

We were the ones that stood up and didn't want to fight the Vietnam War. And that's when all the protesting started, because it was all the acid heads. The college kids—God, no—don't want to do that, don't believe in that! Before Vietnam, we were all sheep, doing what our parents had lined up for us, instead of just doing our own thing—following this cord from within.

COUNTRY JOE MCDONALD (rock musician)

Things needed to be changed. But what the hippies brought with them was fun, and the lefties needed that. I'm not downplaying it, because the political stuff needed to happen. The politics needed to change. But politics tends to corrupt, because with politics comes power. Hippies don't have power; we have fun. I mean we weren't going up into Tilden Park practicing shooting guns and disciplining each other. We were having fun.

PETER COYOTE

The Diggers were cultural revolutionaries.* We began to analyze the situation more deeply and realized that the entire culture was producing the Vietnam War—this wasn't a political aberration. If you accepted the premises of profit and private property, you wound up in Vietnam.

---

* The Diggers, a hippie countercultural group that performed improv guerrilla theater, lived by a nonmaterialistic, communal standard. Between 1966 and 1969 they operated a free store, medical clinic, and soup kitchen in the Haight-Ashbury district of San Francisco.

I was in the theater called the San Francisco Mime Troupe. The Mime Troupe was kind of a traditional leftist theater. We were pretty wacky and pretty loose, but there was a definite left-wing tinge to it. We were artists and we wanted a culture in which we could be authentically who we were, and describe the world without the kind of impediments that we were seeing Marxist governments and cultures put on free expression. So the Diggers arose out of these cultural concerns. We felt that SDS and the Weathermen and all these guys were off base, and that Americans were never going to throw themselves on the battle lines to be lumpenproletariat.

A strictly class analysis was not going to play in America. The McCarthy period had already poisoned the well against communists and socialists. People were reflexively against it, as much as they are today, without even knowing what it is or anything about it. So we felt that something else was required and what that might be was to offer people the opportunity to invent their own culture; to imagine it and to make it real by acting it out, and that if they did that, they might defend it. So we set ourselves the task of imagining a culture that would be fun and compelling and cooperative and anonymous, not based on hierarchy and status.

We began this three-year social artwork called the Diggers, where we did everything anonymously and we did everything without money, feeling that if you were not getting famous and if you were not getting rich, you probably meant it. We invented provocative theater pieces, like a free store. What the fuck is a free store? Why is it a store if it's free? We collected garbage, goods, throwaways, we cleaned it up, we fixed it, and we had a beautiful, elegant storefront on Cole and Carl in the Haight, with clothes and tools and bikes and televisions and anything you need, only it was free.

We sent the women to the farmers' market, with their babies in their arms, and they charmed the Italian grocers, who gave them ripe, that-day food. We got donations. In a couple of cases we robbed a meat truck, but it was basically done by donations. We cooked these huge stews in big steel milk cans and we set it up in Golden Gate Park. The only requisite was you had to walk through a six-foot-by-six-foot yellow square, painted yellow. It was called "the Free Frame of Reference." Now, on the other side, we'd give you a little one, an inch by an inch, on a shoelace, put it around your neck, and we'd invite you to look at the world from a free frame of reference. So we weren't feeding people because they were poor, even though they were needy. The Haight-Ashbury was full of runaways. We were feeding them because we wanted to live in a world with free food.

We believed that there was no sense blaming the pigs or the Man or the system for your malaise. The deeper message was, Why put your life in thrall for a job so that you can become a consumer, when you can get stuff for free? If you're willing to bypass having the newest and the freshest and the most high status, you can have a life without being an employee, you can keep your time. So we took that on. We fed six hundred people a day for free.

JOHN PERRY BARLOW (Grateful Dead lyricist)

I was not a big fan of bombing anything. I just couldn't see how we were going to make anything better that way. I headed in that direction at one point, but eventually I became a thoroughgoing pacifist. After graduating from Wesleyan in'69, I got into Harvard Law School. Then I got a letter from a friend who was the son of a maharaja in northern India, who I had met at the London School of Economics. He said that he was going back to India and did I want to come along? So on a whim I spent the next eleven months in India. For the rest of '69 going into '70, that's where I was.

PETER COYOTE

We noticed soldiers in uniform coming into the store, leaving their uniforms, putting on old clothes, and disappearing out into the Haight, and we thought, Well, there's a kind of antiwar activity that we can get involved in. So we started an ID ring. We had a bunch of draft card blanks, and we had the codes that taught us how to put the appropriate numbers on—like if you were from Georgia, there were two numbers on there that would signify that you were from Georgia. If you had a Social Security number, a couple numbers went someplace. So it became known, and with a little bit of delicacy, a conversation could be initiated, that we could make good-looking ID that would actually hold up to the first supervisory review. So that was direct antiwar intervention.

We had a lot of arguments with the Weathermen types. I always disagreed with their strategies. The United States had an absolute hegemony over violence. I mean, when you looked at the violence that was being perpetrated in Vietnam and Cambodia and Laos, to think that you were going to whip this beast to its knees by blowing up shit was folly. I also thought that they were under the thumb of black liberation groups.

JOHN PERRY BARLOW

I came back in early '70 and set about to finish this novel that I had a contract for, which was a bit of a challenge because I had become a completely different person. It was like two different people writing it. I was hanging out some with the Grateful Dead for no particular purpose aside from the fact that my official best friend was the rhythm guitar player, Bob Weir, and it was kind of a fun scene to be around. They were on the road a lot and I'd go meet them. I just happened to be there one night when they were trying to write songs, and Robert Hunter, their A-team lyricist, turned to me and said, "Why don't you write songs with Bob? At least you *like* him." I said, "I don't know how to write songs." And he said, "I've read your poetry; you can probably do it. And besides, I'm not going to write with him anymore."

So on the strength of that, we decided to try it, and had fairly promising results right off the bat. I ended up staying there for almost twenty years, and I wrote just about everything that Jerry Garcia didn't sing, "Looks Like Rain," "Cassidy," "Estimated Prophet," "Mexicali Blues," "Picasso Moon"—about forty of them.

JOHN HARTMANN (music agent, manager)

The thing about the Grateful Dead was, their music was not as commercially successful as many of their contemporaries. Their universal love ethic made them the quintessential hippie band, and they're the only one that still survived, up until Jerry [Garcia]'s death [in 1995]. I think if you compared their sales to their popularity, there would be a ratio imbalance there, because they weren't as big in sales as they were aesthetically, spiritually, and the emotional connection with their audience was very deep. Of course, they invented what we now call the "jam band," long, drawn-out three-hour sets, with long solos by a brilliant musician, and everybody on drugs.

PETER COYOTE

The Grateful Dead felt that they were "changing consciousness." I used to hear that all the time. Changing consciousness? Like somebody's going to hear one of your songs and quit their job? But in fairness, the Grateful Dead were the most like the Diggers of all the bands. They ran their operation like a family. Until a couple of years ago, they were a collective, and I respected them for that.

JOHN PERRY BARLOW

I was much more political than the band members were. As a culture, they devoutly believed that if you changed consciousness, politics would take care of itself, and that any effort to engage in the political process directly is just going to backfire. There's a certain wisdom to that and certainly that theory was borne out repeatedly by the way in which the fiercely political became a seamless part of the problem. The brutality of the Weathermen was not so distinct from the brutality from Charlie Company.*

PETER COYOTE

The Diggers had been basically operating a soup kitchen in San Francisco. All of our efforts were going into getting food, cooking it, running the free store, getting the this, getting the that, but that's like being in a

---

* Charlie Company, or C Company, was the U.S. Army regiment in Vietnam that committed the My Lai massacre.

play for three years. It was interesting, it was compelling, but it was not exactly what I envisioned for my life, and a lot of people felt the same way. So by this time we were meeting other extended families and communal groups, and we kind of merged with them and evolved into something we called the Free Family. The Free Family was a much larger, more diverse group, and we began living communally because that was the only way we could afford to buy land or rent land. We had virtually no cash. The only cash that the Diggers had was government money that went to mothers or pregnant women. Basically, the women controlled the money because they would get food stamps and welfare checks, so that would be the cash we had to pay the rent and utilities and the stuff that we couldn't pay for by barter and trade. We were hardscrabble poor. I never made more than twenty-five hundred dollars a year, from 1965 to 1975, and our communes were hardscrabble poor.

If I could have gotten free medical care and education for my children, I'd still be living in communes. It's just a wonderful way to live—you're surrounded by friends, it's stress-free. If you get sick, somebody will watch your children. If you need a nap, somebody will watch your children. You have men and women to work with. You know each other really intimately. At night we didn't have electricity in most of these places. We'd play cards, Parcheesi, Monopoly, with the kids. We'd make stuff. It was really a self-made culture and it was very sustaining and rewarding. The problem was that it didn't exactly work with some of our ideologies about absolute freedom, because as children came along, they required certain kinds of order. When you have moms waking up at five in the morning to nurse, you can't have wino Eddie playing the tom-tom at four in the morning. So, children and their growing needs began to exert a pressure that showed us the flaws in absolute anarchy.

KARL ARMSTRONG (University of Wisconsin antiwar bomber)

I would say that half the time, you would meet people, and they would invite you over to their place and you'd smoke some weed and sit around and drink. Four times out of the week, I would spend nights with strangers in communes. They didn't call themselves that, but they were anarchist communes, eating organically, very simple meals. I was really impressed with the way they were living their lives. They were totally off the radar. I thought, I would like to live that kind of life. I thought I would rather live communally than the way I was living. But I knew that because of what I was doing, that wasn't a possibility. I was definitely living on the edge.

PETER COYOTE

I founded the Olema commune in the fall of '69, and then I went on the Grateful Dead trip to see the Beatles in London, and so I stashed my dog there and I moved there permanently in late '69. So we were there for '69, all of '70, all of '71, until the summertime, when we were evicted. So it was only a year and a half, maybe max, two years, but Jesus, it felt like five.

Peter Coyote, cofounder of the Diggers. Coyote carried a gun, rode a Harley-Davidson, and helped found the Black Bear and Olema communes in the late sixties. PHOTOGRAPH BY CHUCK GOULD.

Olema was near Point Reyes, so before all of the Diggers moved in, I went into the bar in Point Reyes one night and I said, "I live here now, so if we're going to get into the shit, let's just get into it, let's just fucking go!" Nothing happened. My hair was down to the middle of my back; I had six earrings, three in each ear. I had a little Fu Manchu mustache on the outside corners and I had a little goatee. I was wearing coveralls and a big old floppy, ruined fedora. This cowboy just slid a drink over to me; I took a shot and proceeded to get completely hammered. I guess I was scared out of my mind, but I got so hammered and he picked me up, dragged me to his truck, and delivered me home. It turned out that he was the guy that owned the grazing lease at Olema. He was running cattle there. So we became sort of friends. I had a rule that we paid every debt in that town, and when we were evicted from Olema, I paid debts that weren't mine.

If you wanted to live in a world without the law, you had to be able to deal with violent men; you had to be able to protect yourself. So we were armed. We were not kidding around about defending a life that we had created and I think that's why the Black Panthers liked us, that's why the Hells Angels liked us.

MICHAEL RANDALL

We always felt that our mission was to turn the world on to LSD. Other communes didn't define themselves that way. So, with that job description, it was hard for us to settle into a quieter lifestyle. To tell you the truth, once you start doing the things we were doing, you don't want to go into a quieter lifestyle anyway. It becomes really fun—dangerous, fun.

PETER COYOTE

One of the things we tried to study and learn were the body of skills that Native Americans had inherited, because these were people for whom the natural environment was their hardware store, their furniture store, their pharmacy, their everything, and we didn't want to see that body of information die out, and we also wanted to learn it because it was free. There was a book called *Back to Eden,* by Jethro Kloss, which was like an herbal medical book, and was the bible in every commune.* We learned the

---

*   *Back to Eden* by Jethro Kloss was first published in 1939, has sold more than five million copies, and is an important guide to herbs, natural diet, lifestyle, and holistic health. It is credited with helping create the natural foods industry. The other bible of the communards was Stewart Brand's *Whole Earth Catalog,* a magazine and catalog published between 1968 and 1972, and less frequently until 1998, that focused on self-sufficiency and do-it-yourself skills and products.

The Digger Free Family at their Forest Knolls Red House commune in Marin County, California.   PHOTOGRAPH BY CHUCK GOULD.

plants that were good for compresses and wounds and staph infections. One of the things we discovered was that hunters dumped the deerskins after their kills in the dump at Point Reyes. So we would collect those skins and we all learned to flesh them, tan them, smoke them, and turn them into buckskin, which made them trade goods—same thing for collecting acorns. We collected acorns and ground them into flour, and traded them to health food stores to get olive oil and commodities that we couldn't make. We traded elderberry wine that we made with the Indians, for salmon up at Black Bear [commune].* So we were trying to develop a sustainable economy and trying to learn those skills required to get as much of our income and livelihood off the land as we could.

A lot of women became very good beaders. The Digger women affected a kind of beautiful circular dress that was made on circular knitting needles. They were floor length and really beautiful. That became kind of a uniform for a lot of the Digger women, with silver bracelets. I collected

---

*   Peter Coyote also spent time at the Black Bear commune, which was founded in 1968 on the property of a deserted mining town in a remote part of Northern California. Black Bear's slogan is "free land for free people," and it still operates as a communal/intentional community.

fox skins from foxes that were killed on the roads. I'd skin them and tan them, and take them down to New Mexico and trade them to the Santo Domingo Indians. They needed them for the green corn dance initiation for their young men. I'd trade them for turquoise or silver, sometimes money, go to Gallup, New Mexico, and get red velvet and blue velvet Navajo cloth and bring that back to California. Women would use that to make beautiful shirts. So we were just trying to create an economy with as much found and free stuff as we possibly could.

CAROL RANDALL

By 1969 we had moved to a commune we called the Ranch, above Palm Springs, in the San Jacinto Mountains. We weren't that many people, only about twenty-five adults and a bunch of kids. Tim Leary and his wife, Rosemary, lived with us for two years. We were trying to live off the land, and working, and doing all our own cooking, baking our own bread. But we weren't like the Farm in Tennessee.[*]

The women were very feminine. We loved having babies and cooking and that whole thing. We loved it. Just being able to sit around with your girlfriends and be there with the babies, and embroider, and sew, or work in the garden together. That's what we wanted. It was our choice. We lived in a few different houses and in the summertime, the teepees went up and some people would camp out. We shared everything.[†]

PETER COYOTE

The Digger scene was very conservative and traditional, but it wasn't enforced. In other words, the Digger women were doing what they wanted to do. They could give a shit what the men wanted to do. They wanted to be with each other and take care of the babies; that's what they liked doing. There were a couple that liked to do mechanics and they did, no

---

[*]   The Farm is a commune in Tennessee that was founded in 1971 by Stephen Gaskin and 420 hippies from San Francisco. It still operates today.

[†]   Carol gave birth to one of her four children in a teepee at the Ranch with the help of her girlfriends.

The women of the "hippie mafia" at the Ranch, their commune in Idyllwild, California, in 1970 displaying various stages of pregnancy. Carol Randall, known as the Godmother of the Brotherhood of Eternal Love, stands third from the left.

one would say anything. So for us it wasn't a problem. The women had the economic power. We had to beg the women for money from their welfare checks. If we needed a fuel pump for my truck, we had to argue it out with the women. "You're not going to get the groceries unless we get a fuel pump to fix the truck." I don't remember any women ever complaining. It was like a matriarchy, and they indulged our political ideologies and our craziness, but really, this gaggle of women was together.

It wasn't until I met the Red Rockers that I began to get an idea of feminism and what those issues were about, and I had a steep learning curve. My friend lived on a commune in Colorado called Red Rockers, and they were very gender sensitive. That was the first place that I encountered feminism, and I didn't encounter it gracefully. We were visiting and my girlfriend got up and brought me a cup of coffee, and a bunch of the women jumped on her for that, and I sort of lost it. She was just being considerate, what the fuck? Who are you people? Anyway, this really smart woman named Mary got in my face, and I threatened to slap her, and I really just set myself outside that community.

CAROL RANDALL

These communities of like-minded individuals and families of communal creativity focused on family; friends; poetry; art; all kinds of music; spiritual practice like yoga and meditation; health; alternative medicine; and demanding to be free from societal restrictions, restraints, and hang-ups. The pureness of thought exploded. We were everywhere.

Carol and Michael Randall's wedding on September 27, 1970, officiated by Samu, a Chumash medicine man, at his commune in Topanga Canyon. Samu also married Timothy and Rosemary Leary. The blanket symbolizes shelter, the canes are for old age, and the vessel is a wedding vase symbolizing two becoming one.

PETER COYOTE

One of the problems was that even though we were a leaderless society, because I was the first guy out there, I was sort of the titular leader. I supplied the overarching Digger vision. But the problem with that is, if you have a leader and they stop supplying the vision, or take a day off, everything stops. So a lot of the people who came to Olema came because it was a free place to be. They would nominally accept the trip but it wasn't *their* trip. Gradually, it was not a very good emblem of the world that I hoped to see. Harmony was the perception I had when I began Olema, but more

often it was a very squalid, tumultuous, and cantankerous environment—
a lot of drugs, and a lot of anarchy, as opposed to anarchism.

If I were going to live communally today, I would do it a little differently.
Instead of having thirty people in one house or in a couple of outbuildings,
I'd have one big community kitchen with a good Wolf range and a good
refrigerator which can serve five families, six families, and then I'd have
everybody have their own house, with a little hot plate for if they didn't
want to be with people, and their library and their own roof and their own
private space, so you could come together or not. Black Bear was much
more like that. Olema was pandemonium. We were all crushed into this
tiny house and sheds and outbuildings. But it was a very rich life, and going
to a nuclear family afterwards felt extremely lonely and diminished.

MICHAEL RANDALL

Some people called us [the Brotherhood of Eternal Love] the hippie mafia.
We were making kilos of crystal acid in Europe. We had a chateau in Bel-
gium that was related to the university in Wavre. We turned it into what we
said was a research facility. We were dealing with the president of the university, and all the upper administration of the university, and scientists.

We made up fake research papers that said we had tested using THC*
in chicken feed, and it made the chickens lay 20 percent more eggs, which,
worldwide, could be billions of eggs. It was a possible way to make a lot of
money, getting these really relaxed chickens to lay eggs. I thought it
wouldn't go, but they believed it at the university. We had help from the
economic counselor at the United States Embassy in Britain. He didn't
know what we were doing, but he was helping us procure things. We had
a lot of well-known and powerful people fooled—completely fooled.

A lot of those people must have gotten into some trouble. It ruined the
career of the economic counselor at the U.S. Embassy in London. He got
tricked by the hippies.

Albert Hofmann† gave us advice, and he gave us his support. He en-

---

*   THC, or tetrahydrocannabinol, is the psychoactive chemical found in cannabis.

†   Albert Hofmann was the Swiss chemist who first discovered/invented LSD in 1943.

dorsed us 100 percent. And, man, Albert Hofmann was way hipper than he pretended to be. He took acid all the rest of his life. He was a psychedelic person. The guy was a boxer and a bodybuilder. Hofmann was not your little frail, effete Swiss chemist.

We decided to get out of the U.S. because if you get caught in the U.S., it would be the end of you, you could get three life sentences. They were getting real shitty over here with the drug laws. Plus, we could buy raw materials and chemicals easier there than you could get them here. We could get ergotamine tartrate and things like that were much easier to procure if we were a foreign company operating in a foreign country. We were pretty fucking sophisticated little shits. Before I was thirty, we had *anstalts* in Liechtenstein,* and we had Swiss bank accounts. You had to. You couldn't do what we did if you didn't have those things.

We made 120 million tabs of Sunshine there from 1968 to 1970. Nobody knows how big we were.

JOHN PERRY BARLOW

Except for the period when Owsley was in jail from 1970 to '72, any LSD that I was going to take was Owsley's.† I remember there being a lot of Orange Sunshine, but I wasn't particularly interested in it because I knew that it wasn't as pure as Owsley's stuff. I never did know who was making it.

DAVID FENTON (movement photographer)

We used to be terrified. The police were constantly trying to arrest people who were doing nothing. A lot of my friends went away [to prison] for years for marijuana possession. If you were a hippie and you had long hair, forget driving through Texas. They were out for everybody. They would even plant stuff on people.

---

*   *Anstalt*s are holding companies that foreigners can set up in Liechtenstein.

†   Augustus Owsley Stanley III, or "Bear," was often called the "King of Acid," because he was the first individual to manufacture LSD in America. Besides being the Grateful Dead's sound technician, Owsley supplied acid for Ken Kesey's famous acid tests in the mid-sixties, where the Dead often played.

LEARY GOES TO PRISON ON COAST
TO START TERM OF 1 TO 10 YEARS

By Steven V. Roberts

(SPECIAL TO *THE NEW YORK TIMES*)

. . . Superior Court Judge Byron McMillan called the former Harvard psychology professor "an insidious menace" to society. . . .

Michael Kennedy, another of Leary's lawyers, said, "the judge here is mirroring what we see going on all over the country. There is a growing fear of people in authority that their authority is being undermined and that they have to take drastic action to stop it. . . ."

MICHAEL KENNEDY (Timothy Leary's lawyer)

The half a joint Leary had one place, and the ounce or so he had in another, those were not amounts that could possibly have caused any harm or any damage, so it couldn't have been about the drugs. This was draconian. It had to be about who he was, what he was saying, and his politics. Basically what he was saying was anarchical because if you "tune in, turn on, and drop out" you're flipping the bird to the government and that was antigovernment, and they were really scared, the feds, and Nixon particularly. To imagine that all of these hippies were actually joining forces with the political antiwar people scared the devil out of the government.[*]

---

[*]   In the fall of 1966, Timothy Leary was convicted of a violation of the Marihuana Tax Act and sentenced to thirty years in prison. Released pending appeal, he took the case to the U.S. Supreme Court. On May 19, 1969, the Supreme Court concurred with Leary in *Leary v. United States* and declared the Marihuana Tax Act unconstitutional; the Court overturned his 1965 conviction in Laredo, Texas, where he was busted with three ounces of pot. Congress responded by repealing the Marihuana Tax Act and passing the federal Controlled Substances Act in 1970, under which LSD, marijuana, and other hallucinogenic drugs were classified as the most harmful of all drugs and rated Schedule I (out of five) along with heroin. Schedule I drugs were "deemed to have a high potential for abuse, and no legitimate medical use."

MICHAEL RANDALL

When Timothy was in prison, we did a benefit for him in the basement of the Village Gate, and we managed to get all the entertainment to play for free. The biggest one was Jimi Hendrix. Jimi Hendrix played a long set that night. Johnny Winter played right after Jimi Hendrix. Captain and Tennille, and the list goes on, but Jimi Hendrix was the mainstay. A friend of mine did the heavy lifting, and Rosemary [Leary] and I helped as much as we could. Abbie Hoffman was there, Allen Ginsberg was there, all kinds of people were there.

I gave Abbie a half a dose of Sunshine, and he got a little bit too stoned and started being Abbie Hoffman. He stood for his ideals, but he could be goddamn offensive. I loved him, but damn, that man wouldn't fucking shut up. He wound up getting onstage and screaming at everybody. There was a scene. There was a guy sitting on a table in a full lotus, meditating. We had passed out quite a bit of Sunshine to everybody in the crowd. So Abbie comes running out onstage and starts screaming, "Fuck you, people, and fuck the Brotherhood. You're a bunch of peace-and-love people. You're meaningless," and on and on and on. "If you want to do something meaningful, burn down the Philadelphia School of Law." I remember that's exactly what he said, and I thought, The Philadelphia School of Law? Where'd he come up with that? What good is that going to do anybody? He was out of tune with everybody. Then the guy sitting in the full lotus jumps up onstage, and *bam,* smacks Abbie Hoffman. I mean, we were in disbelief. Abbie Hoffman comes flying off the stage, lands on the roundtable, and it turns over. It was like watching a John Wayne movie here at the Village Gate. It all happened so quickly. And everybody's loaded. My God. And so Abbie gets up, and he's bleeding, and he goes, "It's all right. It's all right. Fuck you," and he runs out the door, and that was the last time I ever saw Abbie Hoffman.*

I took a dose of Sunshine myself. I'm just really, really, really stoned when Jimi Hendrix comes onstage. He came out, picked up his guitar,

---

* Abbie Hoffman was arrested after selling cocaine to an undercover police officer in 1973, jumped bail, and lived underground until he surrendered to authorities in 1980. He committed suicide in 1989.

Timothy Leary, with his wife, Rosemary (left), talks to a reporter during his campaign for governor of California in May 1969. "He ran for governor just to say 'fuck you' to the establishment," Carol Randall told me.
PHOTOGRAPH BY ROBERT ALTMAN.

right here in front of me, and there was the fallen angel. I mean, he was angelic. Here's this big, huge, beautiful black man, one of the greatest talents, and he did a wonderful show, and he played a nice, long set.

PETER COYOTE

Janis Joplin and I were friends. We were both drug users. I had a key to her house. We were both reprobates. I wouldn't say I had any privileged position in her life at all. Kris Kristofferson was in and out of there; a lot of guys were in and out of there. Janis was a homely girl from Port Arthur, Texas, that got catapulted onto the big-time stage, and her psyche never caught up with the way people saw her, and it caused her a lot of turmoil. One of the things that I think she appreciated about me and about Emmett [Grogan]* was that we always told her the truth.

---

* Emmett Grogan (1943–78), one of the founders of the Diggers, was described by *The Times* of London as a "Superman of the Underground."

We had ways of pointing out to her the difference between the machinery that was propelling her as a commodity, and what was real, and I think she trusted that, because we didn't really give a shit. We didn't want anything from her. I liked having sex. I would have sex with a dog when I was in my twenties. We used drugs together. Emmett and I spent a month in her room at the Hotel Chelsea, after the band had left, convincing the front desk that we were with the band. So we used her for things like that and she let herself be willingly used, and that was fun. Her manager, Albert Grossman, was kind of fascinated with the Diggers and gave us a base in New York and his price tag was to run around with us, and see things that he'd be afraid to see normally. But it's not like I was in love with Janis or she was in love with me. We were friends and we were fuck buddies and we were drug addicts, what can I say? I could see what was happening to her, I could just see.

GREIL MARCUS (*Rolling Stone* music critic)

Janis was really intense. When she sang "Ball and Chain" it was just so wrenching. It was such an adventure, such an epic struggle. You really felt as if you had been dragged across a battlefield; you'd been wounded, the battle is still going on, someone is dragging you to safety, and there's no real expectation you're going to be alive when you get to safety.

She had moments where she was a great, great artist. She had the sensibility of understanding what a song was, and what it meant to get everything out of it, and put everything of yourself into it. I don't think she was appreciated maybe ever, because she was also completely fucked-up. She was a junkie. She would let people take advantage of her. She let Columbia Records make her into a big star, which was not a good idea. And she died at twenty-seven. It was a horrible waste.

HOWARD WOLF (rock music promoter)

By '69, '70, the music scene was imploding. It was just imploding, period. And factions had started. It just wasn't the same. People got greedy; people were out for themselves. Let me tell you, the drugs got a little bit weird starting '69, '70, and I said to Chet Helms, "Chet, we're in trouble here. It's not the same. I think it's time we just shut down the Fillmore West." He wouldn't do it.

There were a lot of uppers, and it wasn't cool. People just got weird. I'm not a drug taker. I could see it, and they didn't notice it, because they were doing it. Then in like a six-month period Alan Wilson of Canned Heat dies [September 3, 1970], then Jimi [September 18], then Janis goes [October 4],* and Jim Morrison [July 3, 1971]. I said, "You know what? There's something wrong." I said, "I'm burned out. I just can't handle this—I have got to leave."

JOHN HARTMANN

There was a great sadness when Jimi Hendrix died, like there was when John Lennon died, or Jim Morrison, or Janis, or any of these people. They were our leaders, and our leaders were brought down by something we totally understood—abuse of dangerous drugs. Even though some of us would try it, you wouldn't necessarily do it every day; you just knew what it was. Well, some people liked it too much and stayed too long, and those people died. There were many others who were less famous who died of the same thing.

What happens is you ride up the drug scale. You try acid, well, I get what that was. You try mescaline, oh, I get what that is. Then, there are more exotic things like DMT, STP—they're very powerful drugs that are dangerous, the most significant being one called PCP, also known as angel dust. That drug stripped away your ability to discern between right and wrong, so you better be looking in the right direction or you're going to go to hell. So that drug then led to cocaine and heroin, cocaine being the most dangerous drug and the one that destroyed these people. Jim Morrison, Jimi Hendrix, Janis Joplin, many others died because of cocaine

---

*   Janis Joplin died of an accidental heroin overdose in a Hollywood hotel on October 4, 1970. She left $2,500 in her will, "so my friends can have a party after I'm gone." An all-night bash was held in her memory in San Anselmo, California, where the Grateful Dead played to two hundred friends. Four months after Joplin's death, her album *Pearl* was released and became her biggest-ever commercial success.

and its influence to take heroin to come down from the cocaine, what's called a speedball; when you get into that now you're starting to lose it, and then you get severely addicted. I mean, most rock stars either died or burned out their septum from snorting cocaine. I don't want to name some of those people, but I observed it.

What happened that destroyed so many of these great artists was drugs.* Drugs were not only the catalyst for the rise of it, but they were the catalyst for its destruction because the government lied to us about pot. "This will kill you." Well, anybody who ever smoked pot knows it ain't gonna kill you, right? Well, maybe they were lying about all the other drugs. It was part of the hippie ethic that you had to try every drug, you didn't have to continue with it, but you had to know what it was. So, every new drug that came along, everybody did it.

---

*   Nineteen seventy was called "the year of the middle-class junkie," and heroin flooded the youth market for the first time. Psychedelic movement leaders, including Michael Randall, distinguished between "death drugs" (heroin, speed, cocaine, alcohol) and "people drugs" (marijuana and LSD).

CHAPTER 23

COMING HOME

(May–August 1970)

Out on the street I couldn't tell the Vietnam veterans from the rock-and-roll veterans. The Sixties had made so many casualties, its war and its music had run power off the same circuit for so long they didn't even have to fuse. The war primed you for lame years while rock and roll turned more lurid and dangerous than bullfighting, rock stars started falling like second lieutenants; ecstasy and death and (of course and for sure) life, but it didn't seem so then. What I'd thought of as two obsessions were really only one.

—MICHAEL HERR, *Dispatches*

NIXON'S VIETNAMIZATION POLICY, WHICH REDUCED AMERICAN ground troops and increased the air war against North Vietnam, had an unintended consequence. Between 1968 and 1970, 200,000 Vietnam vets, many wounded, shell-shocked, and disillusioned with the war, came home to a country in turmoil and transition. Their war stories exposed the futility of the conflict and the grisly truth of what was really happening on the ground in Vietnam. As they began to meet, rap, and organize, the vets brought new vitality and credibility to the peace movement. Images of vets at antiwar rallies in their tattered army jackets, or in wheelchairs with long hair holding signs saying "End the War in Vietnam" and "We

Won't Fight Another Rich Man's War," terrified the Nixon administration. Realizing the power of their message, the FBI targeted the vets for infiltration, surveillance, and disruption. FBI files on the activities of Vietnam Veterans Against the War covered 19,978 pages.

———

WAYNE SMITH (Vietnam veteran)

I got orders to go home. The next day, I was going to get on the plane, and this son of a bitch in the bunker next to me, that had these thin plywood walls, played what has become one of my favorite songs about America and Vietnam: Steppenwolf's "Monster." He played it over and over all night. The song sums up, in more ways than I can ever describe, my reality near the end of Vietnam and my understanding of this country. It is that powerful.*

> *The cities have turned into jungles*
> *And corruption is stranglin' the land*
> *The police force is watching the people*
> *And the people just can't understand*
> *We don't know how to mind our own business*
> *'Cause the whole world's got to be just like us*
> *Now we are fighting a war over there*
> *No matter who's the winner we can't pay the cost*
>
> *'Cause there's a monster on the loose*
> *It's got our heads into the noose*
> *And it just sits there watchin'*
>
> *America, where are you now*
> *Don't you care about your sons and daughters*
> *Don't you know we need you now*
> *We can't fight alone against the monster*

---

* "Monster" is the title song of Steppenwolf's most political album, released in November 1969.

I had known Steppenwolf, of course, but this was the first time I had ever heard this song. At the time, I had this yearning to try to understand how I could have gotten it so wrong. How could I have believed in this country, when I swore to defend and protect the United States?

We flew out on a private carrier from Long Binh. There were American stewardesses on board who were trying to be gracious, but guys were hooting and being ugly Americans. I just zoned out. I didn't know anybody. I couldn't find words. I was aware of the Vietnamese we killed, the buddies that I had who died—these really beautiful guys.

We were broken. I had so much anger and pain. I was crushed. I felt like I had blood on my hands. I resisted calling the Vietnamese gooks and dinks, but near the end of it I found those vulgar words would come out of my mouth several times; I had contempt for myself. How could I have been so stupid and foolish to believe this country? How could I have been so foolish to think that I could really save lives as a medic? How could I really make a difference in the face of so many catastrophic injuries?

I don't think I really spoke much on that flight, at all. I had contempt for the guys I was with because they were doing stupid American shit, like, "We're number one," and slapping fives. "We're going to screw everything that moves." But I wasn't alone; there were also some other folks who just weren't in that space. It was more nods and recognition, rather than engagement.

BOBBY MULLER

(spokesman, organizer, Vietnam Veterans Against the War)

I was shot April 29, 1969. It took a while to get back to the States. I wound up at a naval hospital on Long Island, and then I got transferred from the naval hospital to the veterans hospital up in the Bronx. I spent a year there as an inpatient, and started on an outpatient basis, probably around July, August of '70. So that's where I was parked.

My first day in the veterans hospital, the chief of the service walks by. He looks at my three-by-five card and he says, "Well, son, I hope you realize you're going to be hopelessly paralyzed for the rest of your life." The fucking first words out of the chief of the service's mouth off of a three-by-five card. I didn't respond.

Later on a shrink says, "You look like you might want to talk. Come see me." I go roll in. It's a woman. The first thing out of her mouth was "What are you going to do now?" I said, "I think I'm going to become a political assassin and kill the sons of bitches responsible for this bullshit war. Okay?" We wound up with her wanting to know about my relationship with my mother, until I finally said, "Look, this is not about my mother. Okay?" They didn't know how to handle it.

WAYNE SMITH

Landing in Seattle, Washington, there was an announcement: "Anyone that was injured, or if you have problems of any kind, get in that long line over there. Anyone who doesn't have any problems, go there to get on the bus to take you to the airport, to take you home." I was really pretty bad off, but I wasn't going to get in any long line.

I went into the airport men's room and there were all of these khaki uniforms bulging out of the trash bin, where people had taken off their uniforms and thrown them away as soon as they could. It was unbelievable. When I got on the plane home, there were guys who were wearing long-hair wigs. I don't even know how they got them, but they were obviously wigs. It was absolutely amazing. The uniform thing was big, not wanting people to know you were in the military.

When I saw the uniforms in the men's room trash bin, I was like, Whoa . . . Welcome home! Walking through the airport in uniform, people didn't make a lot of eye contact. I was trying to find friendly faces, and I was just not getting any connection. I thought, Okay, America, you motherfuckers. I'm home. I'm going to deal with you. I'm going to get through this bullshit. You know, Fuck you. It was like getting my false combat face on; in some ways I was thinking I was in a different style of war. I felt like it was a hostile environment. It didn't feel friendly. It didn't feel like home. I didn't believe in America anymore. I couldn't tell if it was me that changed, or the country that had changed. I guess that was the question for a lot of us.

BOBBY MULLER

The notable thing that happened was that one of the guys on my ward at Kingsbridge VA hospital in the Bronx, a fellow by the name of Mark Dumpert, became the centerpiece of a cover story that *Life* magazine put out, May 22, 1970. It was the Walter Reed scandal of our times. The cover of *Life* had two photos. The top one was a color photo of some wounded American soldiers riding on the top of an armored personnel carrier. And below that was a black-and-white picture of this guy, Mark, who was a quadriplegic, meaning no use of his legs or his arms, sitting in the shower at the VA hospital, with a towel draped over him. The article inside had a lot more photos—again, a lot of them on my ward—depicting the overcrowding and filth. Overall, the article described the place as a medical slum. It turned out to be the second-largest-selling issue *Life* magazine ever put out. It created an uproar.

JAN BARRY (cofounder, Vietnam Veterans Against the War)

I happened to be in upstate New York when the invasion of Cambodia took place. I was on Syracuse University's campus. The invasion of Cambodia happens. This university closes down. The students refuse to go to class. I was initially looking for student veterans and trying to have the conversation about war crimes testimony, and I discovered there were something like five hundred student veterans on campus and they were outraged by what had happened at Kent State. A couple of these vets said, "Come with me," to a house they rented just off campus, and they were turning it into a center for organizing vets. They even imported a whole bunch of phones and made all kinds of phone calls, and they were going to have their own march. They needed a professional organizer, but in the end, they organized it themselves. They had vets coming in from campuses across the whole of upstate New York, and it was a big story in New York State.

They put out the word that if the police even thought about coming onto the Syracuse University campus, they were going to have to wade through a line of vets. A group of them decided they were going to have a protest at a veterans memorial in downtown Syracuse. They were mainly conservative veterans and they wanted to protest the war as veterans at this setting. There were a couple police cars in the vicinity, and all of a sudden the police cars disappear, and some other cars come roaring up, and these American Legion types jump out, and they're going to attack this group of hippies who are protesting the war and beat them up. But all of a sudden they're confronted by veterans, one of whom takes a flagpole and aims it at them. He's going to charge them with the flagpole and he says, "Get the fuck out of here! We're vets!" They didn't know what to do with that, because they had been told it was a bunch of hippies that they could beat up. They were going to do a mob scene and beat up some hippies, and that further fueled other vets hearing about this: "I'm going to come and march through the streets of Syracuse and tell these people what I think of them." And that's what they did. The police, of course, treated them with great care.

The vets wanted nothing to do with the peace movement. They wanted to speak as this group of veterans who were outraged about Kent State and the invasion of Cambodia. I was talking to vets all across the country on the phone, and the same thing was happening all across the country. They made it very clear that if any police or National Guard were going to come on campus, they were going to have to go through a line of vets.

BOBBY MULLER

I don't know if you remember who Phil Donahue was. Phil Donahue was the Oprah Winfrey of the seventies and eighties. I quickly became a spokesman for the spinal cord injury guys because I was college educated and I had the bona fides of being a combat casualty. I didn't give a shit anymore, so I would talk to anybody. I got called upon to comment on the situation at the hospital, and wound up rapidly doing a lot of media. Donahue was operating out of Orrville, Ohio, where they made Smucker's jelly, and he flew me out there to do his TV show. It was all about, "What's going on with the veterans hospital? How'd you get there? What's it like? What do you think about the war?"

We also had congressional hearings that were triggered by the *Life* magazine piece. I still remember the first time I ever did the *Today* show. I remember going into the NBC studio in New York at six thirty in the morning and I said to the producer, "You must be fucking kidding. Is anybody watching television at this hour?" He said, "Is anybody watching? This is the biggest news show." What? Are you for real? I had no fucking idea. So because I was getting media attention, I started talking to some guys that were part of Vietnam Vets Against the War.

MICHAEL UHL
(Vietnam vet, Citizens' Commission of Inquiry organizer)

Vietnam Vets Against the War was really emerging as a mass organization after the revelation of My Lai, so by the summer of 1970, VVAW was now marching primarily under its own steam. Whatever Citizens' Commission of Inquiry had done to help stimulate the growth of the organization was now pretty much in the past. Al Hubbard had emerged as the president, Jan Barry had resigned for the second time—he just really didn't like conflict and politics. This is a period where everybody was fighting; fighting against the war, fighting each other, escalating the polemic. It was hardly peace and love. So Al and others had now begun to assemble a talented core of organizers. By the end of 1970, VVAW claimed, at least on paper, to have over twenty-five thousand members but that figure certainly underestimates the size of the antiwar veteran community in the early 1970s. Consider, for example, that I never officially joined VVAW.

JAN BARRY

We were hearing about the conditions at the Bronx VA Hospital, where rats are running over people's feet who are paralyzed, and they can't chase the rats off. That's where Bobby Muller was, who also became active in VVAW. Bobby Muller and some other people would soon be leading the marches in their wheelchairs.

We called them rap groups, which got picked up from the black liberation groups, and the women's liberation groups were also using the same
terminology. It was the concept, "Let's sit down and compare notes about
something that society doesn't want to talk about. . . ." Many of these vets
couldn't keep a marriage together, couldn't keep a friendship together,
and they'd been out of the war for a while, but their life was still a mess.
They may or may not be finishing college, and they just felt like their life
really didn't hold together well, and why is that?

Robert J. Lifton had written about Hiroshima and a number of other
issues from a psychological perspective. He'd been an air force psychiatrist in the Korean War, and he was teaching at Yale. He testified before a
congressional committee in 1970 about something that he was tentatively
calling post-Vietnam syndrome. He explained that a lot of these veterans
are having a hard time readjusting to society. I sent him a letter, and I said,
"I have a group of veterans who are wrestling with this. I wonder if you
could meet with us."

He said yes and I said, "We don't want to be treated as patients. This
is peer-to-peer. We're veterans. You've been in the military. What are we
looking at here?" And in those conversations, what we initially seemed to
be hearing was there wasn't a terminology for this. In World War II it was
shell shock, or World War I, combat fatigue, various other terms that actually were more applicable if you're under constant bombardment.

BOBBY MULLER

I didn't get a chance to talk to the guys in the hospital about actually
being in the war. So when I got out of the hospital and started talking
publicly about the conditions there, it ended a sense of isolation. I had
thought that I had just had a bad experience; I just drew a bad hand. It
wasn't until talking to other guys that I started to really put it together. I
said, "Wait a second, it wasn't just me?" These guys are saying the same
thing. And there was a process of communalizing the shared experience
we'd had, one by one, and then we started to realize that, "Okay, it wasn't
just me."

WAYNE SMITH

When I got home my family was very happy to see me. But I didn't like them. They had no sense of how to ask what I did. I'm not sure I wanted to talk about it, but for them not even to ask, just to pretend, was avoiding this obvious subject. I treated them like strangers. I couldn't even fake it well. "You must be so glad you're home." I'd say, "Mm-hmm." It was really equivocating, keeping them at a distance. . . . Even one of my nephews blurted out, "Did you kill anybody?" I said, "Yeah, lots of people." That was a showstopper. That worked. No one wanted to take it to the next level of questions.

Some of my friends came by to pick me up. I told my mom to tell them I wasn't home. It was really awful. Maybe two weeks after being home, some friends threw a party for me, but I couldn't go. I was terrified. I couldn't face this party that they had. It was at a steak house, a nice restaurant in our neighborhood. It had a bar, so I went to the bar and just drank quite a bit. I'm not a drinker, but I did. I eventually made my way to the party and people clapped when I walked in. I felt so dirty, so awful. I managed to get to the bathroom, and I stayed in the bathroom for forty-five minutes to an hour. I just felt dishonest. They were celebrating that I survived and that I did my duty. They would repeatedly knock on the bathroom door, "You okay, Wayne? Come on out." Finally when I came out, almost no one was there, fortunately.

I felt completely alone even with friends of mine in Rhode Island that had gone to Vietnam and were back home, and reached out to me. I saw a few of them. We didn't talk much. It was this strange kind of co-conspiracy to avoid talking about what was troubling us. We thought, You're home. You should feel glad. That was the attitude: You're home. Thank God you're home. Everything's going to be okay now. No, it isn't going to be okay. That was what I was thinking. I had this attitude, "Fuck you, America. You're not to be trusted." If I was not in the military, I think I would have fled this country. I really felt that you can't go home again.

I increased using drugs. I went back to my next assignment, which was down in Fort Sam Houston, to train medics to go to war. I said, "Fuck this.

I'm not going to do it." I had a little bit of rank; I was an E-4 at the time. They threatened to take rank. I said, "Do your best shot."

OLIVER STONE (Vietnam veteran, filmmaker)

When I came back, I was definitely "Fuck you. Fuck the system," you know, anti-authority, smoking dope—I carried dope back with me from Vietnam. I'd just come out of the field about five days before they let me go. We were on this mission that got stuck up in the mountains with a lot of rain and we couldn't get out. So five days after I'm out of the jungle, I'm in Fort Lewis, Washington.

Anyway, I took acid in San Francisco. I was trying to get into the groove of what was going on. I just felt like this freedom is too much. I couldn't handle the freedom. No one wanted to know about Vietnam. You couldn't talk to anybody. I went to Santa Cruz and San Francisco and no one wanted to talk about that shit. I got the message pretty quick: "Shut up, just don't talk about it."

I broke up with all my friends in my platoon. They went back to small towns. These guys came from Utah, Indiana, or Kentucky and Tennessee towns. I made my way back to New York. I don't remember 1969 too well. Put it this way: It was really alienating. The whole thing in New York was alien to me. I started to take half steps, but I just couldn't get back into society. I began taking drugs, a lot of LSD, and stuff like that. My acid trips were really dark sometimes. I was taking acid in subways. I wasn't doing the peaceful shit. It was more like "Strange Days," with Jim Morrison, like strange people coming out of the rain.

Getting the GI Bill was important. I don't know if I would have done it any other way. I had to do it on my own. In September '69 I enrolled in NYU film school. I was older than the other students, which made me strange. It was hard because I didn't like some of those kids. They were all protesting. They were doing documentaries on tunnel workers, and talking the game but not living it. There was a lot of talk, talk, talk, but I was quiet. I was alienated. I would sit in the corner. I made short films that were not good. But we worked together and it brought us into a collective. Marty Scorsese was my first teacher, so that helped. Marty was one of these guys who didn't make a lot of sense to me. He had long hair, and talked a mile a minute, but he loved film.

After the Kent State shootings the protests went through the school; there were protesters all over New York. I was not joining them. I was not even talking about Vietnam. Gradually I made better and better short films, and I made a film that Marty praised, called *Last Year in Vietnam*. It was a twelve-minute film about a veteran who returns from a war, who is alienated. It's a good film, a lonely film. And that was reintegration. The kids in my class didn't know I had been in Vietnam until I made that film.

JANE FONDA (actor, peace activist)

I became friends with Al Hubbard, who was the president of the VVAW, and I was made a civilian member of the VVAW. They were planning the Valley Forge march, which I thought was a really cool idea. The idea was, we're going to do the march that the American revolutionary forces made, ending at Valley Forge, and all along the way, we are going to reenact what we are doing in Vietnam. You know, the bayoneting, pulling people out of their homes—search-and-destroy missions in civilian villages. We're going to bring the war to the streets that we pass through in Pennsylvania, on the way to Valley Forge. It was called Operation RAW, for Rapid American Withdrawal. It was a big deal. It didn't have the impact that we hoped it would. But people were pretty affected by it. I did not march with them, because I didn't want to detract attention.

We were all waiting at the staging area where the rally was going to take place, and a lot of the parents of the soldiers were there. I will never forget—whew. It was so moving when over two hundred vets who had walked a hundred miles came up over the hill, carrying these fake guns. Some of them were in wheelchairs, and on crutches. And they came down singing and chanting. I spoke, as did others, including John Kerry, on the back of a flatbed truck.

In my speech I said, "I cannot escape the belief that My Lai was not an isolated incident but rather a way of life for many of our military. . . . One thing Nixon can't ignore is the sound of his own troops marching against his policies. . . . The rest of us can be accused of being reds, hippies, unpatriotic, what-have-you, but the guys who have been there can't be ignored."*

Later, the right wing doctored the photos to make it look like Kerry and I were speaking together, which we weren't.†

WAYNE SMITH

I was on active duty in 1970 in Texas, and the VVAW was pretty big. Jane Fonda and Donald Sutherland were doing this routine, "FTA," for "Fuck the Army." They traveled the country to towns with military bases to do these political vaudeville skits. It was a spoof on Bob Hope's pro-war USO, and it also poked fun at the army's slogan, "Fun Travel and Adventure." It was mildly entertaining, and mildly educational. They had a couple of people go up onstage, and they would talk about the war and what they were trying to do was convince soldiers not to be deployed, and organize vets to oppose the war at home.

BERNARDINE DOHRN (Weather Underground leader)

When the people coming back from Vietnam became a force in the movement, organized the Vietnam Vets Against the War, organized throwing back the medals during Dewey Canyon III,‡ their stories of having been lied to about the light at the end of the tunnel were just unacceptable. And you had to believe them. They were truth tellers in a way that the antiwar movement up to then had not been able to be.

---

*   This excerpt from Jane Fonda's speech at Operation RAW comes from Gerald Nicosia, *Home to War: A History of the Vietnam Veterans' Movement* (New York: Crown, 2001).

†   Kerry and Fonda both spoke at Operation RAW (Rapid American Withdrawal), which took place over Labor Day weekend, 1970, and was a three-day march from Morristown, New Jersey, to Valley Forge, Pennsylvania, where VVAW members dramatized the inhumanity of the war with guerrilla theater reenactments. The vets were greeted at the end of their march in Valley Forge by 1,500 supporters and speakers including Senators George McGovern and Edmund Muskie, Congressman Allard "Al" Lowenstein, Jane Fonda, Donald Sutherland, and John Kerry, who at the time was a young returning vet and VVAW organizer.

‡   Dewey Canyon III was a VVAW protest, named after a military incursion into Laos, that took place in Washington, D.C., April 19–23, 1971. It was at this protest that Vietnam vets threw their war medals on the steps of the U.S. Capitol.

Vietnam veterans demonstrate against the war at the Dewey Canyon III protest outside the U.S. Capitol building in April 1971. More than eight hundred veterans threw their medals and other military-related materials over the fence in front of the Capitol building.

BOBBY MULLER

I think people came to look at Vietnam Veterans Against the War as a political entity that had the uniqueness of being the first time that veterans who had fought in an American war actively came together to say, "This war sucks." And that's how they knew us, for politically opposing the war. But for those of us who were part of VVAW, it was really just a continuous fucking rap group. It was an ability to actually talk about what you had gone through, and how you felt with others that understood what you were saying.

Out of the rap groups with Vietnam Vets Against the War, we got this whole thing of peer support, talking it through, and what essentially became the vet center program. That's what we were talking about. "Hey, we've got issues here. We've got unemployment. The GI Bill is bullshit. It's nothing compared to what it was in the Second World War. We've got issues with the chemicals that we used like Agent Orange."

I never really saw any Vietnam vets on the other side of the argument going, "Yay team, rah, rah, rah." That came later. So my experience out of

New York was, if you're a Vietnam vet, you thought the war was stupid, and those were the only guys I ever saw. And there were a lot of them. Those of us that were part of Vietnam Vets Against the War, when a group of like-minded people get together and talk to each other, they reinforce each other and they radicalize each other. So we talked to ourselves, and the anger built and the radicalization built. That happened quickly.

Vietnam Veterans Against the War grew rapidly in size in 1969 and 1970 as more and more troops came home from the war, many of them injured and demoralized. The vets brought new energy and credibility to the peace movement, and were targeted by the FBI for harassment and disruption.
PHOTOGRAPH BY STEPHEN SHAMES.

RICK AYERS (GI antiwar organizer)

The war eventually ended because these guys wouldn't fight. Everyone talks about the mean antiwar movement, and the poor GIs, and the antiwar movement spit on the GIs, and no one gave us a parade when we got home, which is crap. The heart of the antiwar movement *was* the GIs. Even on the streets it was veterans. A bunch of veterans led in all the marches. They would not fight that war. They were the ones who knew that Vietnam was a people's war. They knew that the [North] Vietnamese strategy was "We're never going to beat the Americans militarily, but we're going to wear them down, demoralize them, and psychologically make them say, 'Screw this.'" Now, Americans will say, "We didn't lose that war. We won every battle." But they don't understand that war is a holistic thing. It's moral, psychological, and physical; Americans still don't get that. The Pentagon doesn't get that.*

---

* A breakdown in military morale turned into near mutiny by 1970. There were frequent cases of fragging, combat refusals, and infantry platoons purposely avoiding enemy engagements. The military prison population increased from 4,800 in 1968 to 6,400 in 1969. Army desertion rates rose 400 percent during peak years of the war, from 14.9 incidents per 1,000 in 1966, to 73.5 per 1,000 in 1971. Army desertion and AWOL rates in 1971 were the highest in modern history. Nicosia, *Home to War*, p. 40.

CHAPTER 24

ARMY MATH

(May–September 1970)

In the illumination of that bomb [in Madison, Wisconsin] the movement knew sin. . . . The revolutionary mood had been fueled by the blindingly bright illusion that human history was beginning afresh because a graced generation had willed it so. Now there wasn't enough life left to mobilize against all the death raining down.

—TODD GITLIN,
The Sixties: Years of Hope, Days of Rage

ANGER OVER THE INVASION OF CAMBODIA AND THE KENT STATE and Jackson State shootings reverberated throughout the country. The University of Wisconsin–Madison was famous for its violent activists and aggressive police force. In May 1970, eighty-four Wisconsin students were arrested after conducting twenty firebombings, and Governor Warren Knowles deployed 2,100 National Guardsmen to quell the campus revolt. But by late August, campus unrest turned into something more deadly.

_____

KARL ARMSTRONG

(former University of Wisconsin–Madison student)

My brother Dwight and I were watching television together in the student union and there was a special announcement about the shootings at Kent

State. All of the students stopped and watched. It was really crowded in the union and we were all just aghast. My overwhelming feeling was, Now they're killing us. It had come to killing us to stop the protests. I turned around to Dwight and all I said to him was "Army Math." And that's what we resolved to bomb.

I was back and forth between Minneapolis and Madison, maybe three times after the Kent State shootings. In Minneapolis there were about two hundred thousand people out on the street marching, in a candlelight vigil. The diversity of the people protesting impressed me; maybe a quarter of the people in the march were students, and the rest were people from the community, all ages. People were just outraged.

When I came back to Madison, it was like a war zone. All of the windows on State Street were boarded up. There was so much rioting after Kent State that a hush fell over the campus, and people were super-paranoid. I felt really sad. What I saw in Minneapolis was inspiring, and what I saw in Madison wasn't. And yet I knew the people marching in Minneapolis didn't really get it. I knew these protests were going to come to naught.

I saw the movement against the war as a nascent revolutionary movement, mainly because stopping the war in a militant way basically took on the power structure. And I believed that if we were successful at stopping the war, it would just spread to all the other issues: blacks in America, women, gays, the environment. The war was the overarching glue between the different movements because our people were getting killed. The main issue, as far as I was concerned, was class. I saw myself as fighting for my class against the ruling class. I felt that my class was the cannon fodder for Vietnam.

PAUL SOGLIN (University of Wisconsin student activist)

In 1969–70, Jim Rowen was writing in the student newspaper, *The Daily Cardinal*, about the connections between the university and General Electric, and what was going on at the Army Math Research Center. I had also written a number of pieces about the connections between the university and chemical and biological warfare. The Department of Defense published technical abstracts on a monthly basis. They were books that detailed Defense Department contracts with universities and private companies. In those days you could just walk into the Engineering campus and get them, like any other reference book. So I was able to get that stuff on CBW [chemical and biological weapons].

We were doing research on antidotes. The university's response was "We're doing good research." But the reason you do research on antidotes is so that you can use CBW on your enemy without a threat to your own people. You have to have antidotes to safely handle it yourself. At one point, I went back up to the Engineering Department and all the technical abstracts were locked up; you couldn't get to them anymore. The FBI had been there.

You have to understand that in those days, when the *Cardinal* was breaking those stories, it was getting national news coverage because nobody was making the connections we were making between the university, the money, and the military. It's hard to believe that on a campus like this you had a building that said, "No students allowed."

What happened was that in May of 1970, we got the disclosure about the invasion of Cambodia, the expansion of the war, and the revelation that we weren't crackpots; that everything we were saying about the secret expansion of the war into Cambodia was true, and all hell broke loose.

TOM McCARTHY (Madison, Wisconsin, police officer)

Everyone on the Madison police force celebrated after we heard about the Kent State shootings. During the riots that followed, I would taunt the kids by putting up four fingers with one hand and make a zero with the other, like a score keeper: Kent students zero, Army four.

It's almost impossible to describe how bad it was in Madison in those days. The riots would go from eight o'clock in the morning to four o'clock the next morning. We hated everybody. One night we were ready to go home and we were going to call it a night. We'd been battling these guys all night; helicopters were flying over where the mall is now, with spotlights. We pulled up to a barricade on Mifflin Street and when we pulled up onto the sidewalk to go around it, some guys jumped off a porch, with baseball bats with spikes driven through them, and took out our tires.

KARL ARMSTRONG

The Army Math building was a military facility, located on campus. This was not right. It had no place in the university. And even if it hadn't been located on a university campus, it would have been a target. But the fact that there were demonstrations, and that the university was well aware of what this institution was all about, gave them the moral responsibility.

We started doing some surveillance of Army Math, walking around and so forth. Army Math was only about two or three floors in a wing of Sterling Hall, which housed the astronomy and physics departments. I had in mind that when we bombed Army Math, all I wanted left was a pit in the ground. Just because I thought that would send a great message to the government, to see one of their facilities burned to a pit in the ground. A crater.

So we hatched a plan. We read the *Encyclopaedia Britannica*. I believe it was under "Explosives." They made it really handy for me. That was the obvious place to look. If the *Encyclopaedia Britannica* didn't have it, it couldn't be done.

We rented a trailer and stole three barrels—fifty-five-gallon drums— from a service station. Then we ripped off a van outside the computer science building. We went to a farmers' co-op near Baraboo, asked them to scoop a couple thousand pounds of ammonium nitrate into these barrels—I think by weight it was 5 percent fuel oil in the barrels—and we hoisted the barrels into the van. We might have used a stick of dynamite for each barrel just for detonation.

We spent a little over a week surveying the building. We would note traffic, people walking around, when the security guard was going in and out of the building. We decided that Monday morning, August 24, sometime between three and four in the morning, was the optimum time for doing the bombing, because there wasn't any car or foot traffic, and it was after the security guard left the building. At about 3 A.M. we drove off.

It was a beautiful summer night—very, very quiet. David Fine was out in front of the building, surveying, and he was supposed to come back when the coast was clear, when the security guards were gone. He came back and said everything was ready to go. But unfortunately, his lookout was stationed in the wrong place, because he never checked down the alley. He was out in front, in the bushes by the chemistry building, watching from there. He had a view of the front of Sterling Hall, but if he had just gone down the alley, he would have seen that there were lights on in the building and we probably would have scotched the whole operation.

So, I drive up to Army Math, turn the corner into the alley, and see that there are lights on in the fourth floor and in a basement room. I said, "Oh shit," and just kept driving up the steep ramp. So now we're kind of half-committed. To get the van out of there we'd have to back it out, which was doable, but just psychologically, it was like, we were there. So I got out of the vehicle and checked the basement room. If I spotted anyone, I was going to break the window and warn them that we were ready to blow up the building. I walked up and down the length of the room twice, looking in the windows, making sure I didn't miss anything. There was no one in the room, so it was my conclusion that somebody had just left the lights on.

The fourth-floor windows were also lit up. I thought, Well, we didn't find anybody in the room down here, right? David didn't see anybody walk in or out of the building. It caught us totally by surprise, because we figured David would have told us about these lights on in the building. And so, my assumption was that if the janitor left the lights on down here, he could very well have left the lights on up above. But we knew that there was a chance that there might be somebody in there. That's when I turned to my confederates, who were looking at me, and I made some comment like, "The building needs to be bombed. This is basically the only time we are going to be able to do it. We've taken all the precautions that we possibly could. It's probably not going to be any better any other time."

Basically they left it up to me to decide what to do. I said, "Light the fuse." So we lit the fuse, locked the van door, and walked about fifty yards, where David could see us from a phone. He made the call to the Madison police and said something like, "Listen pigs, listen good. We have bombed the Army Math Research Center." So he made that call, and we all got back to the car at the same time and drove off. When we were two blocks away, the bomb went off.

JACK CIPPERLY (University of Wisconsin assistant dean)

The night the bomb went off, my asthma kept me up. I was awake and I heard the explosion. We lived about four miles from the campus. Kate said, "Oh, it's thunder." I said, "Boy, that sounds like it's a 155[mm] howitzer." So I jumped in the car and went right down to the campus; it was deathly quiet. There was computer paper in all the trees. There was broken glass in all the buildings. I went up to the edge of Sterling Hall and there were four black things like this on the ground, and they were flat. I knew many of the police officers there, and I asked one I knew, "What are those things down there?" It looked like the building was under construction, because it was so torn up. And he said, "Those are tires from a van." In other words, the explosion was so powerful that it flattened out the tires.

KARL ARMSTRONG

As the bomb went off, it lifted up our car, and we could hear the panes of glass falling out of storefront windows all the way down University Avenue—one after another, falling out of the windows. Apparently it blew out like three or four blocks' worth of store windows. At the very same moment, when the bomb went off, my first reaction was, "Oh shit." I knew that it had gone off two minutes before it should have, which wasn't really enough time for people to get out. I just had this feeling that something bad had happened.

We headed further south, about another mile and a half from there, and Dwight said, "Look. You've got to see this." I was in no mood to see anything, but everyone got out of the car and looked back: There was a mushroom cloud of burning debris, which was probably like four or five hundred feet high above the building, just glowing red.

JACK CIPPERLY

My neighbor was a firefighter at that time. They had to go into Sterling Hall, which was full of water. They looked down and there was a door, and inside, behind the door, was a body. They had to get the Jaws of Life and they saved that guy; he got out and lived. Everybody was so stunned that they came by and just looked. It was very quiet.

PAUL SOGLIN

I was in bed, and I felt the explosion. I picked up the phone, called the dispatcher at the Fire Department, and said, "What was that?" The dispatcher said, "The Army Math Research Center." I slipped on my jeans and drove over to University Avenue. There were one or two fire trucks and about eight people there; I was one of the first people to arrive. There weren't more than half a dozen civilians. I walked around, but I didn't walk into the area. I didn't want to be seen there. So I stayed on University Avenue, looking at the debris that had come into the street from over the chemistry building. Within a matter of minutes there were hundreds of people there. Everybody was so preoccupied with the building that I got into my car and I left. I didn't want to be seen there; I didn't want to be photographed. I knew I was going to have to answer one way or another for this, and if I was there that early, someone might try to link me to it. I drove back home.

PHIL BALL (University of Wisconsin student, Vietnam vet)

I walked down Langdon Street, still not knowing the bomb had gone off. It was seven thirty in the morning, and I didn't know. I got to the corner and I noticed something funny; something was in the air. I couldn't put my finger on it. And then I recognized the smell: It was the dust, the particulate matter in the air. There was so much of it. I walked down University Avenue, and there was chaos.

The building was a smoldering mass that stood still in form. The outline of the building was still discernible. All the windows were blown out. There was rubble everywhere. Most of the trees were gone: nothing left but a couple of stubs. I looked across the street: Windows were blown out of the church. Everything that faced Army Math was damaged, but not caved in. The inside of the chemistry and pharmacy building, which was on the corner of Charter and University, right next to Army Math, was gutted.*

Karl and Dwight Armstrong, Leo Burt, and David Fine bombed the University of Wisconsin–Madison's Sterling Hall, also known as the Army Math building, on August 24, 1970, killing a graduate student by mistake. It was considered the worst act of domestic terrorism until the Oklahoma City bombing in 1995.

KARL ARMSTRONG

We continued driving south around the city, with the radio on. The first report was that there was a bombing, but they said there didn't appear to be any injuries. So we stopped at this truck stop to celebrate with a glass of Coca-Cola—a quiet celebration to congratulate each other. I was so relieved when I heard that on the radio. It was just weighing on me.

We were driving through Waunakee when another report came over the radio. They're pulling a body out of the building. Everybody just groaned. And I remember that David Fine was in the backseat crying. It was everything we could do to just keep control of ourselves. That went

---

*   The explosion could be heard thirty miles away, and building repairs cost $6 million.

on for a while. We got on Highway 12, and no one was talking or saying anything. So I said, "Well, maybe with the passage of time, we'll feel differently about this."

PAUL SOGLIN

I was on the City Council in my second term. I had been elected in April 1968, and reelected in April of 1970. Murray Fromson, a CBS reporter, called me, because we had done previous interviews. "Paul, you must have some idea who it is." But I didn't. As the days went by, it came out that there had been the death, and the suspects were identified. I was in the kitchen with Rena Steinzor, the editor of the *Cardinal,* talking about it, and she said something so simple. She said, "I asked myself whether I had the capability of doing something like that, and when I instantly came to the answer, 'No,' I knew the bombing was morally wrong." Everybody was wrestling with the morality of it. What Rena said was really very simple, and very eloquent: "I knew I couldn't do it. I didn't have the capacity. I knew it was morally wrong."

The place was swarming with FBI, and everybody was paranoid. We were angry with the bombers. We thought that they had no right, on behalf of the rest of us in the movement, to do that.

JACK CIPPERLY

To me, the bombing was a bridge too far. In other words, it sort of put a damper on a lot of the demonstrations, because Robert Fassnacht was killed. It just looked like that was too much. It went too far.

TOM MCCARTHY

After the bomb went off, we had a meeting with the FBI, the university police, and the sheriff's department, in the conference room of the chief's office. [Wilbur] Emery, the [Madison] police chief, told the FBI right there that in this bomb case, "if you do not share information that you get with us, you can leave right now." But they never shared anything, and in a way I don't blame them, because would you want to share with Chicago police what you find out?

BILL DYSON (FBI agent)

We knew it was horrible when the first reports came in. Of course, it got national attention, worldwide attention, and the FBI and local police were there immediately. The fact that somebody was killed gave it federal jurisdiction. After the bombing, I went up there. At first, the idea was that it was the Weather Underground. But it soon became apparent that it wasn't, and these people were would-be Weathermen, if anything. When I saw the building, I had never seen that type of devastation. They called the university Plywood University for a year after, because it blew out almost every window on the campus. It took a year to try to get the windows fixed. It was horrific damage.

I thought, Oh my God, this was the worst terrorist attack we've had in the United States since the Wall Street bombing in 1920, which killed thirty people and was allegedly done by anarchists. They blew up a horse cart in downtown New York City on Wall Street. But other than that, there'd never been an attack like this in the United States. So it was the Oklahoma City of its day. They were able to trace back the truck that was used to bring in the 1,950 pounds of ammonium nitrate fertilizer that did it.*

MARGERY TABANKIN
(University of Wisconsin student activist)

At 7:30 A.M. the day after the bombing happened, I was at home in New Jersey and there was a knock on the door. It was these FBI agents, who asked me, "Do you know what happened last night?" I couldn't believe they found me so quickly. I said, "What are you talking about?" They

---

* The Sterling Hall bombing was considered the largest act of domestic terrorism until 1995, when Timothy McVeigh bombed an Oklahoma City federal building, killing 168 people.

said, "Somebody was killed in Madison in the physics building. You would call it the Army Mathematics Research Center. We're trying to figure out who did it." So they showed me a list of people with lots of names on it. I didn't recognize most of them, but some I did. I said, "There is no way these people would have ever done this." When we get to the two names that I knew pretty well—Leo Burt and David Fine—because both of them had worked at *The Daily Cardinal,* I started laughing. I said, "These are the quietest, mousiest, and really the shyest people. There's just no way. Take them off this list." I was so certain.

I did not know either Dwight or Karl Armstrong. Their names were on the list, but I had no idea who they were. I knew a lot about the people who were into throwing blood on buildings, acting in guerrilla theater, and being in intense debates about violence versus nonviolence. Leo Burt and David Fine were not visibly part of any of that. So I was completely sure that it wasn't possible. Years later, it turned out that it was them. David turned himself in and served some time, but Leo's never been found.

KARL ARMSTRONG

We picked up a paper in Chicago and there was an editorial in the *Chicago Tribune* saying that there should be the death penalty for bombers. At that point we knew we'd better stay on the run. We stopped in Ann Arbor and tried to get help from the White Panthers,* but they didn't want anything to do with us. Then we drove to Toledo, Ohio, gave each other haircuts, and that's where we split up.

Dwight and I drove from Toledo to New York and ended up on Fifth Avenue or something, a very ritzy area. We found a parking space, slept in the car, and tried to figure out some sort of game plan. I talked to my uncle on the phone and asked if he could wire us some money, because we had about twenty bucks between us. I don't even know if we even had that, because I remember Dwight going in and shoplifting some sandwich

---

* The White Panther Party was a left-wing radical collective of white antiracists based in Detroit, Michigan, and spearheaded by the poet and MC5 rock band manager John Sinclair.

meat from a market. I remember because I was so pissed-off at him, risking our lives over shoplifting lunch meat. Dwight and I split up and agreed to meet a week later in Times Square.

Finally the day came to meet Dwight. I got to Times Square at the appointed hour, and there he was. I was as happy as I had ever been in my life. We waited there for David [Fine] and Leo [Burt] to show up, but they never did. That's when we saw the huge ticker-tape marquee: "Four men wanted in Wisconsin bombing. . . . Four men put on the FBI's Most Wanted list."

Dwight and I walked to this motel in Times Square, and I called our parents, because I knew we were going to leave New York City, but we wanted them to think we were in New York City. I talked to my father, and he asked me to give myself up. I told him, "I don't think I can do that." I basically just let them know we were still alive, hung up, and we immediately jumped on the subway and got out of the city.

MARGERY TABANKIN

In the documentary *The War at Home*[*] there is a scene where I am holding a press conference. I'm wearing this red crewneck sweater, with very short hair, representing the student body, saying, "We are calling for the closure of the Army Mathematics Research Center." I was reading a big treatise written by Jim Rowen in the *Daily Cardinal*. Later Jim went on to work in the mayor's office. He was also married to Susan McGovern [daughter of Senator George McGovern]. But at the time he was one of the smart graduate students who were framing what the university was doing. I wasn't that kind of an original thinker, but I was an organizer. So I created this big student press conference and called for the university to stop being complicit with the war and to stop the secret research that was going on at the Army Mathematics Research Center.

After the bombing, literally all I could think about was, Oh my God. I had that press conference. I created all this publicity about this, and some-

---

[*]   *The War at Home* is a 1979 feature documentary, produced and directed by Barry Alexander Brown and Glenn Silber, about the student antiwar movement at the University of Wisconsin.

body died. I was devastated, just devastated. I was surprised because, while people had started to do anarchistic stuff, like lying down to try to stop jets from taking off and throwing blood on ROTC buildings, nobody had done anything like this at this level. I never thought anybody intended for anybody to die. It was clear that this happened in the middle of the night, and they never dreamed somebody would be working there. I knew that immediately. But I still felt this unbelievable sickness in my stomach, that I was somehow connected to this experience.

KARL ARMSTRONG

We stole a car that we found with keys and we drove north towards the border. As we're driving through Little Falls, New York, Dwight, with his long hair, is driving. I noticed that a local cop starts following us, and I dove for the glove compartment and read everything I could about the owner of this car. We memorized all the information in the space of a minute, and we concocted a story about why we were in this car. The cop pulled us over and asked for the registration. We gave him the registration, but it's not ours. It didn't match my brother's driver's license. We told him we'd borrowed a friend's car, that we were in college together at the University of Wisconsin, and he let us borrow the car. The cop was just about ready to buy it, and he says, "Why don't you follow me back to the police station, I want to look further into this."

We got to the station and the cop said, "My office is on the second floor, if you want to come up." Meanwhile, I'm whispering to Dwight, "We're gonna have to take him. But we won't jump him until the plates come back as being stolen." So we go up there in the office and give him our real IDs. On the wall of his office were posters of the Weather people and all of these antiwar people, like Bernardine Dohrn and Angela Davis. So, he puts in the call and we're sitting there in front of the desk. He asked us where we were going, and we said, "We're going to meet a friend of ours in Buffalo." So we're waiting as he checks the plate number. Meanwhile, Dwight asks to read the newspaper that's on his desk while we're waiting. Dwight gets the paper, and he points to the front page: There are our names on the front page of the newspaper. I'm thinking, This is really getting bad. We're sitting in this cop shop, with no money, don't know anybody, have a car out there that's running out of gas, and I'm thinking, Can it get any worse? We know we've got to jump this guy, who was actually bigger than us. It can't get any worse than this.

Then the phone rings. Dwight and I are like cats ready to spring at him. We were going to jump over the desk and pin him down. He got the phone call, but I didn't see anything on his face. Then he says, "I'm sorry, guys. Everything checks out. The car's not stolen. You're free to go."

Later we read in the newspaper that he had gotten one of the digits wrong on the license plate. When he finally got around to reading the paper, probably an hour and a half later, and discovered his mistake, he probably thought, Oh, I'll never live that down! Poor guy. He was a nice enough guy, you know? I really felt sorry for him. I thought, This just ruined his career.

PHIL BALL

The moral ambiguity took up everybody's time, especially those of us who had devoted our lives to ending the war. The reason is that we were not about to condemn the boys. We could condemn the action if we wanted to, and it was better to make sure it didn't happen again—which it didn't—but condemning the boys would be the height of hypocrisy, because we had all called for the downfall of Army Math. We were the ones marching and demanding, "Off Army Math! Smash Army Math!" We were the ones who broke up classes in Army Math. We were the ones who laid the moral foundation for the boys, Karl and Dwight Armstrong, David Fine, and Leo Burt. That was felt very powerfully. My God, we did this! It wasn't just the boys. The best we could do was support them. They needed a defense fund. They needed people to speak for them. They needed the best legal help that we could get.

KARL ARMSTRONG

My original plan was to turn ourselves in in a brief period after the bombing. But because Robert Fassnacht, a thirty-three-year-old physicist with three young children, had been killed and people had been injured, there was no longer any political support for us. I felt like we would just be thrown to the wolves. So I knew that we had to either stay free or get enough time between the bombing and being captured, in order to get anywhere close to a fair trial.

When we got to Montreal, we were totally broke and really, really hungry, because we still hadn't had anything to eat in a couple of days. I had phoned this organization. I can't tell you their name, but they didn't want to talk to me on the phone. They knew all about us, and after we'd gotten there they said, "Yeah, everybody in the left political community was waiting for you to show up." They had all been following what was happening, but they were really paranoid about helping us.

They fed us, found us this place to live, and gave us a little money for food. Then they sent our getaway car to a chop shop and disposed of it. We spent about three months in Montreal. I bought a cheap wig that I used when I went into the post office, where they had wanted posters with pictures of the four of us on the walls.

PAUL SOGLIN

Nationally, it changed the whole scope of the antiwar movement. Millions of Americans were sobered by what happened. There were still very large demonstrations, but now virtually all of them were peaceful. Yet on the Nixon side of the ledger, all the murder and mayhem that they created didn't sober them, because it was still going to be another five years before the war would come to an end.

There is no question that the bombing sucked the life out of the national antiwar movement. There is no question that it was counterproductive. If the bombing had not taken place, the movement would have been far stronger as we went into the fall of 1970 and the winter of 1971.

KARL ARMSTRONG

The argument has been made that it was counterproductive, at least in the short term. The movement in Madison was definitely stifled, because they had about three hundred FBI agents in town going through people's garbage. That's going to repress anybody's political activity. The standard mantra is that the bombing hurt the antiwar movement, and my feeling is, yes it did, for a short time around Madison, but generally it didn't seem to have a negative effect on the national movement.*

MARK RUDD (Weather Underground member)

The bombing of the Math Army Research Center at Madison was a disaster. It caused the antiwar movement to crumble for a period of a few years in Madison, in 1970, which was still the height of the war. The war didn't actually end until '75. But again, a small group of people knew that they were right, and they didn't put it up to any vote, they just went ahead and planted the bombs.

It's nice to be able to say that we [the Weather Underground] never harmed anybody, but in truth, we not only killed three of our own, but we were the intellectual authors of the Wisconsin action which did kill an antiwar graduate student named Fassnacht. I don't think the public was aware of the difference between bombing buildings and hurting people. The fundamental mistake was choosing that strategy, as compared to organizing.

PETER GREENBERG
(University of Wisconsin student, *Daily Cardinal* reporter)

Two things happened shortly after the bombing. One was a university symposium that took place a week after we got back to campus, around the eighth or ninth of September 1970. The symposium was to discuss the bombing and I was chosen to represent the *Cardinal*. It was me, a member of the Board of Regents—you couldn't get more right-wing than

---

* Karl Armstrong was arrested in Canada in 1972. In his 1973 trial, he pled guilty to second-degree murder and was sentenced to twenty-three years in prison. He was released from Waupun maximum security prison in Madison after seven years. Karl's brother Dwight was arrested in 1977 and served three years in prison. David Fine was captured in 1976, pled guilty to two felonies, and served a three-year prison term. Fine later graduated from the University of Oregon law school but was denied admission to the Oregon bar. Leo Burt is still at large.

this guy—and somebody else. I drew the short straw and had to go first. I said, "There is no way I'm going to sit here tonight and defend the bombing, but I think we need to discuss why it happened, and the history of it, to understand why it could also happen again." That's as far as I got. The member of the Board of Regents got up and said, "You have no right to talk in this room. You're the murderer. A man was killed in that building."

At that moment, this woman in the back of the room raises her hand and goes, "No, you're the murderer!" And the regent looks at her and says, "May I remind you a man was killed in that building?" She said, "I know, it was my husband." That was Stephanie Fassnacht.

CHAPTER 25

ESCAPE

(September 1970)

They [the Weather Underground] are not in hiding, but are invisible. They are in every tribe, commune, dormitory, farmhouse, barracks and townhouse where kids are making love, smoking dope, preparing for the future.

—TIMOTHY LEARY,
Confessions of a Hope Fiend

DOOM PERMEATED THE ANTIWAR MOVEMENT AFTER THE AUGUST 24 bombing of the Army Math building in Madison. Fighting fire with fire, rage with rage, locked the movement with its enemy into a dead-end battle. Two weeks later Timothy Leary escaped from a California prison with the help of the Weather Underground. The symbolic event married the two cultural and political wings of the revolution, bringing hope, as Bernardine Dohrn announced, to "the task of creating a new culture on the barren wasteland that has been imposed on this country by Democrats, Republicans, capitalists and creeps."

BILL AYERS (Weather Underground leader)

We were approached by Timothy Leary's people, who asked us to help him get out of prison and out of the country. It lit some of us up immediately. We thought it was hilarious and wonderful and funny. Others of us didn't think it was a good idea. So we had a lot of discussion, and we ended up going ahead and doing it for a couple of reasons. One was that we thought this would be good practice, and we thought we could learn how to do it. Just like with everything else we were doing then, this was all new to us. We didn't know how to break anybody out of jail. We would strike a blow against prison and practice for more to come. The other reason we decided to do it is they gave us money, which we sorely needed. The Brotherhood of Eternal Love said, "We'll fund this thing."*

TIMOTHY LEARY (note left behind when he escaped San Luis Obispo prison, September 12, 1970)

IN THE NAME OF THE FATHER . . . AND OF THE SON . . .
AND OF THE HOLY GHOST . . . AVE MARIA. PRISON GUARDS
LISTEN, TO CAGE A LIVING CREATURE IS . . .
A SIN AGAINST GOD
LISTEN GUARDS . . . TO THE ANCIENT TRUTH. . . .
HE WHO ENSLAVES . . . IS HIMSELF ENSLAVED. . . .
THE FUTURE BELONGS TO THE BLACKS AND THE BROWNS
AND THE YOUNG AND THE WILD AND THE FREE

BILL AYERS

Our code name for the operation was "juju eyeballs," from the Beatles song "Come Together." I was involved in the planning and reconnaissance, and a group of us met with Tim, once we got him out of jail. He had to do most of the work himself and he was an old man. He was almost fifty, and he had to go hand over hand on a wire, and get the fuck out of there. We left him a statue of the Buddha near a rail siding to tell him which way to go. Then he hid in the weeds, and we had a car pick him up and take him to a camper, with a family. The camper took him north and the car

---

*   Brotherhood of Eternal Love members Michael Randall and Travis Ashbrook gave the Weather Underground approximately twenty-five thousand dollars to help Leary escape.

took his clothing south, and left his clothes in a convenience store. We ditched the car and had another car pick that person up. So we led them south, and we went north. We got Tim and Rosemary [his wife] to Canada, and then we got them to Europe, and then to Algeria. All of that took money. But we did learn some things from it, and we felt much more engaged in the prison work. So, it wasn't a bad thing.

BERNARDINE DOHRN,
SEPTEMBER 15, 1970, COMMUNIQUÉ

The Weatherman Underground has had the honor and pleasure of helping Dr. Timothy Leary escape from the POW camp in San Luis Obispo, California.

Dr. Leary was being held against his will and against the will of millions of kids in this country. He was a political prisoner, captured for the work he did in helping all of us begin the task of creating a new culture on the barren wasteland that has been imposed on this country by Democrats, Republicans, Capitalists and creeps.

LSD and grass, like the herbs and cactus and mushrooms of the American Indians and countless civilizations that have existed on this planet, will help us make a future world where it will be possible to live in peace.

Now we are at war. . . .

Our organization commits itself to the task of freeing these prisoners of war.

We are outlaws, we are free!

RICK AYERS
(Weather Underground member, brother of Bill Ayers)

We had a nice farmhouse that we'd rented, outside of Seattle, and that was the second safe house we took him to. I never met him. I met his wife, Rosemary. She showed up before him. We all hugged and kissed, "This is great; here's the house, here's the dog, here's where you feed the goat, and, okay, we're leaving, and Tim will be here in three days." Melody and

I didn't even stay at the house. We just established the house. So that was our only contribution. Rosemary was lovely, much more SoCal than we were. We were sort of Northwest hippies with homemade vests, and she was more the long scarf.

Then he flew to France and Algeria. His idea was, "Oh, this is great. Let's hijack a plane and go to Cuba. Is that what we're doing?" He was partly nuts, and he was probably too drugged out. We babysat a lot of fugitives who didn't know what the hell they were doing, because we felt some responsibility. We felt like, "Okay, we're kind of going to take care of the whole illegal part of the movement."

MICHAEL KENNEDY
(Leary's lawyer, in a San Francisco press conference, September 17, 1970)

It's a merger of dope and dynamite, flower and flames. There is now a merger of Timothy and the Weathermen. This portends more destruction to the American government than anything in history. I wholeheartedly support him. . . . [While he was in jail Leary] began relating to blacks and other prisoners of war. He recognized himself as a political prisoner.

As it happens in almost every instance, in this case prison took a peace-loving man and in eight months turned him into a roaring revolutionary. Millions of kids look to Timothy for leadership and God knows how many other kids look to the Weathermen for leadership. Now the two are together . . . this merger portends thousands of prison breaks.*

RICK AYERS

The hippies were very alienated from America. They were going to be the base of the revolution on some level, and this [Leary jailbreak] was a gesture of solidarity with them. So I don't think it was a bad move. It wasn't

---

* UPI story published in the *Desert Sun,* September 18, 1970.

just that we were going to only support more privileged people; it was who we could get. But it was a stance around prisons, and it was a stance around that relationship.*

BRIAN FLANAGAN

The Weather Bureau sent Jennifer [Dohrn, Bernardine's sister] and me to Algeria to welcome Tim Leary. He was going to stay with Eldridge Cleaver, the Black Panthers' minister of information, who was running the International Section of the Black Panther Party there. At that time, Algeria was one of the main meeting places for all of these national liberation movement exiles. Probably Havana and Algiers were the two main places.

TIMOTHY LEARY
(letter to Michael and Eleanora Kennedy, October 10, 1970)

Beloved Friends,

How perfect to hear your voice! Your loving vibrations. We love you two! You are such heroes—so wise and strong and effective. . . . The whole thing was miraculous. Really statistically impossible. The escape was incredibly reckless. It was all a dream. . . . It was all automatic and perfect and unbelievably lucky.

BRIAN FLANAGAN

It was the worst mix of people ever. You had Eldridge Cleaver. He was just a total alpha male, armed to the teeth and spoke slowly, with a deep voice, and told you what to do. He had his wife, Kathleen, and his gumada [mistress], this gorgeous secular Arab woman, Malika. They were living in a

---

* The Leary jailbreak increased the Weather Underground's notoriety and they followed with a series of synchronized bombings on October 8, 1970: the statue of policemen in Chicago's Haymarket Square; the Hall of Justice in Marin County, California, where Black Panther Jonathan Jackson and two others had recently been shot; the Criminal Courthouse in Queens; and the Harvard Center for International Affairs.

Black Panther compound in the building that was the former North Korean Embassy.

Eldridge decided that he was Leary's boss. And Leary doesn't really have bosses. He's an acid head. So the relationship between Eldridge and Leary was doomed. Eldridge decided to bust Leary. He called it a revolutionary detainment, and it was clear that the whole relationship was degenerating and wasn't going to last because he had this hippie acid head who wasn't buckling under his authority. Eldridge was the lord of the manor. He was the official ambassador; he had the Vietnamese in the morning, and the North Koreans in the afternoon for tea, and he was living the life of this great Afro-American diplomat. Leary was Leary. Leary was just his own thing.

MICHAEL RANDALL

We had to provide some money to make it easy for Timothy to go to Switzerland and get out of Eldridge's clutches. It was fucked up.

CHAPTER 26

RECKONING

How is it possible in a democratic society for an official to de-
ceive the American public and many of its officials and to per-
vert the basic principles of democracy and an open society with
such egregious secret policies and actions for nearly a half-
century without constraints?

—BETTY MEDSGER,
The Burglary: The Discovery of
J. Edgar Hoover's Secret FBI

During most of my tenure as director of the FBI, I have been
compelled to devote much of my time attempting to reconstruct
and then to explain activities that occurred years ago. Some of
those activities were clearly wrong and quite indefensible. We
most certainly must never allow them to be repeated.

—CLARENCE M. KELLEY, FBI
DIRECTOR, SPEECH AT WESTMIN-
STER COLLEGE, June 15, 1976

AS THE SIXTIES GAVE WAY TO THE SEVENTIES, HANOI AND WASHINGTON,
Haiphong and New York, Bach Mai and Chicago had more in common
than meets the eye. The Nixon administration waged an overt bombing
campaign on North Vietnam while conducting a covert war of sabotage,
surveillance, and dirty tricks on the leadership of the antiwar, black
power, and counterculture movements. Nixon instituted new draconian
drug laws in 1971 and used them as a political weapon against his domes-

tic foes, while the FBI's assault on the Black Panthers succeeded in destroying the party from within. Meanwhile, the Weather Underground spent the seventies on the run from the law. The 1970s were littered with a slew of grand juries, indictments, trials, convictions, dismissals, plea bargains, fines, jail terms, and pardons of U.S. citizens opposed to the war and the government officials who tried to stop them. The legal morass was part of the collateral damage of the War at Home.

Hundreds of thousands of pages of top-secret documents would eventually show that J. Edgar Hoover's FBI and the Nixon administration's modus operandi was to use covert destabilization and misinformation against any person or group it considered to be in opposition to their goals. In their fearful battle against the movement, Hoover, Nixon, and their henchmen would prove guilty of flouting the very Constitution they were charged to protect and defend. Hoover's forty-eight-year reign over the FBI took on despotic proportions as no one inside or out of the organization—including the eight presidents he served—had the courage to challenge him.

The White House and the FBI's campaign against the Panthers and every faction of the antiwar movement kicked off a chain reaction that severely tarnished the credibility of both offices of the executive branch. FBI wiretaps of NSC official Morton Halperin's phone and the White House Plumbers' break-in at Daniel Ellsberg's psychiatrist's office became foundation stones in the mounting evidence of the Nixon administration's criminal acts, evidence that animated the Watergate investigation. Instead of serving a long prison sentence for treason, Daniel Ellsberg walked free, while U.S. attorney general John Mitchell and Nixon advisors H. R. Haldeman, John Ehrlichman, and Charles Colson all went to jail.

The iconic image of Nixon being helicoptered off the White House South Lawn on August 9, 1974, in Army One following his resignation was repeated just five months later as the last military helicopter lifted off the roof of the evacuated American Embassy in Saigon. The Vietnam War and the Nixon presidency were forever linked in history for their parallel ignominious endings.

Proof of deceit and illegal government surveillance and harassment continued to be unearthed even after Nixon's resignation and the war's end. In 1976, a cache of top-secret files revealed illegal break-ins by a special FBI squad conducted in 1972 and 1973 against friends and relatives of the Weather Underground. Forty-six FBI agents, including the three highest-ranking officials in the bureau, were indicted in one of the biggest scandals in FBI history. By 1980, the remaining Weather Underground fugitives came out of hiding and resumed normal lives after the government dropped federal charges that years earlier had landed many of them on the FBI's Most Wanted list. Also in 1980, President Ronald Reagan pardoned Mark Felt, a senior FBI agent convicted of greenlighting much of the bureau's illegal surveillance activity against the movement. No one knew at the time that Mark Felt was *Washington Post* reporter Bob Woodward's infamous source, "Deep Throat." The plot, laden with irony, thickened and so did the connection between Nixon's war against the movement and Watergate.

GERALD LEFCOURT (movement lawyer)

Here I was, in March of 1971, in the middle of one of the biggest trials that there ever was in this country [the Panther 21], with seventeen months in court—four months in pretrial hearings and a thirteen-month trial. I'm totally focused on these police and FBI Panther infiltrators and here you have the revelation that there was a burglary in the FBI office in Media, Pennsylvania, which changed the world.

Without these eight people, who were simple antiwar activists, willing to risk everything, all of us didn't know what we didn't know. They released the documents and unearthed COINTELPRO, the actions of the FBI to destroy these movements, and it was like a revelation. We learned that the FBI was out to destroy the Panthers and that out of the 295 operations [between 1968 and 1971] against what they called "black nationalist hate groups," 233 were done against the Panthers.[*]

---

[*]   Eight antiwar activists calling themselves the Citizens' Commission to Investigate the FBI broke into a small FBI office in Media, Pennsylvania, on March 8, 1971, and stole more than one thousand classified documents. They leaked the documents to the press and publicly exposed for the first time the existence of the FBI's secret counterintelligence operation (COINTEL-

MICHAEL KENNEDY (movement lawyer)

When the group of radicals who called themselves the Citizens' Commission to Investigate the FBI broke into the FBI's office in Media, Pennsylvania, in 1971 and stole hundreds of secret files, I thought that was a wonderful action. I loved those people for that, and the files that they stole were really the first concrete evidence of COINTELPRO that was made public.

COINTELPRO wasn't able to do anything to the Weather Underground because they couldn't find them. The only ones they could find were a few supporters aboveground. So because they were racists, they concentrated on the Black Panthers. COINTELPRO played devastating work on the Black Panther Party, and actually got them to start hurting one another because the FBI would claim so-and-so was an informant, and if somebody didn't like them, they'd use that as a basis to kill him. That was the mischief and the nastiness of COINTELPRO.

NEW YORK TIMES, MAY 9, 1976

F.B.I. SOUGHT DOOM OF PANTHER PARTY:
SENATE STUDY SAYS PLOT LED TO INTERNAL SPLITS,
GANG WARFARE, AND KILLINGS

By John Kifner

The Federal Bureau of Investigation carried out a secret, nation-wide effort to "destroy" the Black Panthers, including attempts to stir bloody "gang warfare" between the Panthers and other groups and to create factional splits within the party, according to the Senate Select Committee on Intelligence.

PRO) and its illegal efforts to repress, harass, and disrupt hundreds of liberal and left individuals and political groups. The Media files showed that the FBI was investigating two hundred different left-leaning political groups. The discovery led to a congressional investigation into the FBI's actions chaired by Senator Frank Church (Democrat of Idaho) in 1975. The FBI never caught the eight burglars, and some of the Citizens' Commission group went public for the first time in 2014 with the publication of Betty Medsger's book *The Burglary: The Discovery of J. Edgar Hoover's Secret FBI* (New York: Knopf, 2014).

JEFFREY HENSON SCALES (Black Panther photographer)

At the time, we on the left really felt that some sort of revolution, some major change was imminent and we were not fully grasping what it meant for the United States government to bear down without mercy on its own citizens, and the insidiousness of the methodologies of undermining the movement. To me, the undermining [by FBI informants] was almost as sad as the killings, but not quite; infiltrating and diminishing things, rotting things out from the inside deliberately.*

HOUSE COMMITTEE ON INTERNAL SECURITY, AUGUST 1971

The Black Panther Party, as a national organization, is near disintegration. . . . The Committee hearings document the steady decline in [party membership] during the last year. Furthermore, the feud between Eldridge Cleaver and Huey Newton threatens the start of a time of violence and terror within what remains of the Panther Party. Probably only remnants of the party will remain alive here and there to bedevil the police and enchant a few of the young, but its day as a national influence and influence in the black community seems over. It is hard to believe that only a little over a year ago the Panthers . . . ranked as the most celebrated ghetto militants. They fascinated the left, inflamed the police, terrified much of America, and had an extraordinary effect on the black community. . . . Liberals and idealists who once sympathized with the Panthers have . . . withdrawn their support.

STEVE WASSERMAN (student activist)

I remember when Huey [Newton] was released from prison on August 5, 1970. I had attended a few days of his 1968 trial and was convinced, like so many others, that he was being railroaded. Now, finally, he was being

---

* Through the use of fake letters, rumors spread to the press, informants, and agents provocateurs, the FBI incited a rivalry between Huey Newton and Eldridge Cleaver. The ensuing internal conflict led to a rash of brutal murders in the early seventies of Panthers by Panthers.

freed and thousands, including myself, had assembled to witness his release on the steps of the Alameda County Court House in Oakland. Few
of us could see then what he would become: a sawdust Stalin who, as we
would later learn, under the relentless persecution and murderous campaign waged by the FBI's COINTELPRO program and hostage to his
own growing cocaine-and-cognac-fueled megalomania, would preside
over the ruin of his own beloved party, which, over the next few years,
would devolve into little more than a cult and a gang.

JEFFREY HENSON SCALES

I moved on in my life and then watched from a little bit afar as Huey got
out of jail and things started to digress. There were powerful forces at
work when he was out of jail to nudge him along his demonic path. The
FBI had placed so many people in key places in the party to influence
people to do things that were wrong. That was part of their whole meth-
odology. You could just see that. It was unfortunate.

I always knew the personality cult that had built around Huey was going
to be a problem. There was also the rise of cocaine in the seventies, so there
were all those things going on.[*] It was kind of painful to watch because the
person I identified most with was Bobby Seale. I remember seeing him
move away [from the party]. But they were very violent times and there was
violence on all ends and the police were trying to kill the left, literally.

NEW YORK TIMES, OCTOBER 22, 1980

LEONARD BERNSTEIN ASSERTS F.B.I. USED "DIRTY TRICKS" AGAINST HIM

". . . F.B.I.-inspired harassment ranged from floods of hate letters
sent to me over what are now clearly fictitious signatures, thinly-

---

[*]   Panther party chairman Huey Newton became increasingly violent, his mental health de-
teriorated, and his drug problem escalated. In August 1974 he was charged with murdering
eighteen-year-old Kathleen Smith. Newton fled to Havana and Elaine Brown took over the party
chairmanship position. Newton was shot and killed in Oakland in 1989 by a drug dealer.

veiled threats couched in anonymous letters to magazines and newspapers, . . . plus innumerable other dirty tricks. . . . I should be happy to see this whole shameful F.B.I. episode exposed for what it truly was: incitement to violence."

PENTAGON PAPERS

RANDY KEHLER (draft resister)

Dan Ellsberg came to visit me at La Tuna prison in Texas in 1971. He wanted to know what prison was like. Before he left he said, "By the way, you don't have a subscription to *The New York Times,* do you?" I said, "No." He said, "Want me to send you one?" I said, "Sure, that'd be great, Dan, thanks." So, in the meantime, this whole thing is about to burst into the press, which he knew, but he couldn't talk to me about it in the prison yard. So, I'm starting to get the daily *New York Times,* and soon enough he's all over the front page.* The prison officials went berserk. They said, "That's that guy who came in here to see Kehler! Who let him in here? How come we didn't know?" They were just beside themselves. "This traitor to his country was in our prison, we let him in. He saw Kehler, oh my God." It was all very exciting. They didn't take any action against me.

STEVE WASSERMAN

Two weeks after *The New York Times* published a selection from the Papers [June 13, 1971] and after *The Washington Post,* too, began publish-

---

* *The New York Times* published the first excerpt of what became known as the Pentagon Papers on June 13, 1971. Attorney General John Mitchell forced the *Times* to stop publication with a court injunction after the paper published three articles containing classified information from the study, but *The Washington Post* followed on June 18, 1971, and published a series of articles based on the documents Daniel Ellsberg had given the newspaper. The Supreme Court lifted the administration's newspaper censorship order on June 30, and Ellsberg was eventually indicted.

ing extracts [June 18, 1971], the Nixon White House created the so-called Plumbers Unit in the basement of the Executive Office Building to plug the suspected leaks. On September 3, 1971, E. Howard Hunt, G. Gordon Liddy, and the other bagmen broke into Ellsberg's psychiatrist, Lewis Fielding's, office in Beverly Hills to try to get information to smear him and thus ineluctably launched the country on the slippery slope that would lead to Watergate, the unraveling of the administration, and Nixon's ignominious resignation on August 9, 1974. The origins of all this can be found in the hinge year of 1970.

It is instructive to remember the heresy committed by Daniel Ellsberg when he leaked what came to be known as the Pentagon Papers. This was an intolerable act for the national security state to permit. It explains why Ellsberg had to be made an example of and it is why our rulers threw the book at him, why he was going to suffer terribly if he'd been convicted on espionage charges, why he faced one hundred and fifteen years in prison, and why Anthony Russo, his co-conspirator, faced thirty-five years.

While some argue that the Pentagon Papers didn't have very much effect on the country, I remember it differently. For those of us in the antiwar movement, it emboldened us because the Pentagon Papers suggested that the radical critique of the war was the correct critique, that we'd gotten it right all along, and we now knew this from the government's own documents.

CARL BERNSTEIN (*Washington Post* reporter)

This was a criminal presidency from beginning to end, first against the antiwar movement, then the press, and then the political opposition and the Democrats, then the system of justice, and finally against history.

I believe that when Ellsberg gave the Pentagon Papers to the *Times,* he anticipated that he would be prosecuted. This was an act of civil disobedience, knowingly undertaken, knowing what the consequences might be, and therefore a really courageous act at the time. But by the time of his trial in 1973, the crazy thing that the Nixon people did was they didn't even have enough faith in the system of justice to be satisfied with putting Ellsberg on trial. So as with almost all of the wretched excess of Nixonian retributive and illegal actions against those who opposed him, instead of simply putting Ellsberg on trial, they decided to keep him from becoming a hero, both to the antiwar movement and to the country. They decided they would get the records of Ellsberg's psychiatrist and put them out there, before Ellsberg went on trial.

By that time, the criminality of Nixon and those under him was already full-blown. Go to the tapes and listen to June 17 of 1971 to get an idea of the mentality, and Nixon's obsession with the antiwar movement. Nixon orders Kissinger and Haldeman [his chief of staff] to break into the Brookings Institution, where they think Ellsberg has kept classified NSC documents, that they called the Bombing Halt file. Nixon says, "Goddamn it, get in [to Brookings] and get those files. Blow the safe and get it!" He keeps coming back to it, day after day, on the tapes. "Have you gotten into Brookings yet?"*

Nixon, on earlier tapes, has already said to Kissinger that the war was unwinnable, yet he stayed in for three more years and twenty-seven thousand more American deaths, not to mention a couple hundred thousand "yellow people," as they regarded them. But Nixon saw Vietnam as part of a much larger chess game. He was playing China and the Soviet Union against each other and Vietnam was just a pawn. Not on any of Nixon's tapes is there a discussion about what would be right for the country, not once. There is not a word on the tapes about the human lives involved. [Bob] Woodward calls it "the dog that never barks."

STEVE WASSERMAN

I remember attending the 1973 Ellsberg-Russo trial in Los Angeles. I went only one day. It was a startling day because there, testifying for the defense, was McGeorge Bundy, one of the architects of the war. I'll never forget Lenny Weinglass, who was Russo's attorney, asking him: "Mr. Bundy, if you were a spy working for a foreign power, engaged in espionage, how would you go about your business?" Bundy replied: "Well,

---

*   The break-in at Brookings was never attempted.

first I would take out a subscription to *The New York Times,* and second I would take out a subscription to the *Congressional Quarterly,* and third I would make sure that my library card was up-to-date. Doing these three things would give me 98 percent of everything I would need to know."

The Pentagon Papers confirmed the remaining 2 percent and made legitimate everything else we knew or had long suspected.

MORT HALPERIN (former Nixon national security aide)

When John Dean went to the Justice Department and spilled everything he knew, one of the things he told them was there was an illegal wiretap program. Twenty-one people were wiretapped. One of them was Halperin. Judge [William] Byrne was told that Ellsberg had been overheard on my wiretap. I had been wiretapped for twenty-one months, and the files were missing from the Justice Department. He announced that at the trial in the morning, and that afternoon he dismissed the case, based on governmental misconduct, in part, we think, because the wiretaps were missing, and therefore there was no way to tell whether they had learned anything relevant to the trial. The next day, Ehrlichman [the White House counsel], who Nixon had just fired, announced the wiretap files weren't missing. They had removed them from the Justice Department because they didn't want Hoover to get his hands on them, and they were in the White House, in his old safe. So, I think the judge might not have dismissed the case, because he could have looked at the wiretaps and saw that there was nothing remotely related to the trial in the wiretap.

DANIEL ELLSBERG (defense expert)

We had been in court for four and a half months at that point. One morning, an announcement came in from the judge in the courtroom, a memo from Earl Silbert, the Watergate prosecutor, saying that on the orders of the White House, burglars had broken into my former psychiatrist's office to get information on me. Well, this came from John Dean. When that announcement was read in court, it was quite electrifying. Reporters who had been stuck in Los Angeles while their colleagues were doing exciting things on Watergate in Washington envisioned headlines, "Watergate Meets the Pentagon Papers Trial." That was the headline they all wanted. They dashed from their seats in court for the pay phones in the hall. It was just like the movie *Front Page* for the first time in the trial, and not the last time.

CARL BERNSTEIN

It was a huge surprise to everybody. I remember Woodward and I were in the newsroom when Judge Byrne in Los Angeles declared a mistrial on May 11 of '73.* It was as shocking as anything that happened during Watergate. It was, at the time, almost incomprehensible, but it fit the pattern. It fit because it was the same Plumbers, the same people.†

RICHARD NIXON, OVAL OFFICE TAPE, MAY 11, 1973

The sonofabitch thief is made a national hero and is going to get off on a mistrial, and the New York Times gets a Pulitzer Prize for stealing documents. . . . They're trying to get at us with thieves. What in the name of God have we come to?

DANIEL ELLSBERG

If they hadn't had to commit those crimes against me, Nixon would've stayed in office. Did I do this by myself? No. I wouldn't have released the

---

*   The mistrial was called because of both the break-in to Dr. Fielding's office and the illegal wiretaps of Morton Halperin's phone. On May 11, 1973, Judge Byrne ruled: "The totality of the circumstances of this case . . . offend a sense of justice. The bizarre events have incurably infected the prosecution of this case."

†   H. R. Haldeman, Richard Kleindienst, and John Dean were forced to resign after revelations that the White House ordered the burglary of Fielding's office.

Daniel Ellsberg and his wife, Patricia Marx, celebrate outside the courthouse in Los Angeles the day his Pentagon Papers case was dismissed, May 11, 1973. The conspiracy charges against Ellsberg, which carried a maximum penalty of 115 years in jail, were dismissed because of government misconduct and illegal evidence gathering.

Pentagon Papers in the first place if it hadn't been for the antiwar movement, and people like Randy Kehler going to prison.

Meanwhile, in the political atmosphere accompanying these revelations of White House crimes and cover-up in the spring of 1973, Congress finally cut off funding for further combat operations in Vietnam: initially, in the House with respect to Cambodia, on May 10, the day before our trial was dismissed, and totally on August 15, 1973. Together, these developments were crucial to ending the war in Indochina in 1975.*

---

* The unwinding of the war took place in stages in 1973 starting with the signing of the Paris Peace Accords in January, in which the United States agreed to withdraw its troops in sixty days in exchange for a cease-fire, the return of American prisoners of war, and a promise by North Vietnam to recognize the legitimacy of South Vietnam's government. In June 1973 Congress passed the Case-Church Amendment, by a solid majority (325–86 in the House, 73–16 in the Senate), prohibiting funding for U.S. military activity in Vietnam, Laos, and Cambodia. This ended direct U.S. military involvement in the war. The last induction of draftees took place on July 1, 1973, and draft registration ended in March 1975. In April 1975, North Vietnam invaded South Vietnam. Saigon fell April 29, helicopters carried the last employees out of the American Embassy, and U.S. Navy ships secreted thousands of South Vietnamese out of the country.

WEATHER UNDERGROUND

BILL DYSON (FBI agent)

The list that I maintained was the official list used by the FBI. It was thirty-eight bombings. I had that list memorized at one time. The Weather Underground was extremely sophisticated with their devices—more so than many people realize. None of the Weathermen bombings have been solved. They put one in the Pentagon in May 1972. So with that in mind, we'd still like to find out who did them. However, the statute of limitations is over for all of them, except for the Golden Gate police department in California, where a police officer was killed.* And nobody has ever been named. We closed the Weather Underground investigation in '77, which is when I wrote the closing report, because the group had become defunct.[†]

MICHAEL KENNEDY

There was a special prosecutor out of Washington, D.C., named Guy Goodwin. Goodwin's job was to try to interdict the aboveground support people who were helping the Weather Underground. So when anybody would ever speak about Weather—and a lot of people did—he would subpoena them. He was very angry and paranoid, and he became the guy who organized the grand jury in California, Chicago, and New York, in order

---

*   On February 19, 1970, a bomb was detonated at the Golden Gate Park branch of the San Francisco Police Department. One officer was killed and several were seriously wounded. No one took responsibility and the case is still open.

†   The search for the Weather Underground fugitives was one of the largest manhunts in U.S. history. Bryan Burrough, in his book *Days of Rage: America's Radical Underground, the FBI, and the Forgotten Age of Revolutionary Violence* (New York: Penguin Press, 2015), was the first to publish the name of the Weather Underground's expert bomb maker, or "bomb guru," Ron Fliegelman. Fliegelman, who worked closely with Cathy Wilkerson in New York, studied bomb making and designed almost all of the Weathermen's bombs. Remarkably, Fliegelman's story and name had been kept a secret, despite the publication of six memoirs and three books about the Weathermen.

to subpoena people. There were a lot of people subpoenaed to grand juries. Several of them were clients of mine. We only knew a little bit about the COINTELPRO illegal break-ins and illegal gathering of evidence then. We didn't have a clue as to how deep it really went, until later. But we fought those grand juries. We fought Guy Goodwin, mostly to a standstill, because the defense primarily was that these were political people, and they were not going to testify against anybody. They were not going to bear witness against their comrades.

BRIAN FLANAGAN (Weather Underground member)

When Jimmy Carter took over the White House, it became in his interest to clear the FBI of the people that were loyal to Hoover because it was this rogue organization. It was uncontrollable and would defy anybody in the government. So he did a housecleaning. One of the things he did was jack up this guy John Kearney in New York who ran the FBI's Squad 47, and had approved of all these black-bag jobs—these illegal break-ins, wiretaps, mail covers, etc. Kearney was charged with five felonies. One of the things that they charged him with was wiretap and mail cover of me after I surfaced.

BILL DYSON

In 1976 information came out that some of the FBI agents were doing break-ins and so forth in connection with the Weather Underground, and fifty-six FBI agents were charged with crimes.* That became a national

---

*   On August 19, 1976, the FBI raided its own headquarters and found Hoover's black-bag jobs file and discovered a series of burglaries in the New York apartments of relatives and friends of the fugitive members of the Weather Underground. The break-ins had been conducted in 1972 and 1973 by the FBI's Squad 47, led by John Kearney in New York. In April 1978, a thirty-two-count indictment was brought against three of the FBI's most senior retired leaders, Ed Miller, Mark Felt, and L. Patrick Gray. Charges were for "conspiracy to injure and oppress citizens" with warrantless searches. Felt and Gray were both convicted in 1980, but neither served jail time. Ronald Reagan pardoned Mark Felt for his actions involving the Weather Underground investigation, not knowing that he had just pardoned Deep Throat, *Washington Post* reporter Bob Woodward's key source in the Watergate scandal. Felt would reveal himself publicly as "Deep Throat" twenty-five years later, in 2005. See Tim Weiner, *Enemies: A History of the FBI* (New York: Random House, 2012), p. 349.

scandal. It was one of the worst scandals ever to hit the FBI. And it affected me tremendously because I was the national case agent [for the Weather Underground]. Dick Held, senior assistant director at that time, contacted me and said, "Bill, what do you think of this?" And I said, "I'm opposed to these break-ins, but I don't think the agents should be criticized for what they did." You had the [acting] director of the FBI, L. Patrick Gray, and [Deputy Assistant Director of Inspections] Ed Miller and [Associate Director] Mark Felt basically saying, "Yeah, we did it." And you had a lot in the middle management saying, "Don't know nothing about it." Bull, they all knew about it. I knew about it, but I wouldn't do it.

Today we realize that the Weather Underground made a decision not to kill people, but we didn't know it at the time. And I'm not so sure they're telling us the truth today. They may have been lying. There may have been some people willing to kill people. In other words, these people could bring down our government. Maybe they couldn't overthrow the United States government but, if you kill the president, if you kill key congressmen, key senators, you kill Supreme Court justices. They were telling us they had the ability to do it.

BRIAN FLANAGAN

What happened with President Carter clearing house at the FBI, Kearney said, "They're not getting me, because this was okayed from the top." He gave up Mark Felt. Now, Mark Felt is a felon, and one of his felonies is wiretapping and mail-covering me without a court order. He was convicted of those charges, and Reagan pardoned him. So that's a lot of the reason why hardly any Weathermen went to jail—all of those charges against them were thrown out. COINTELPRO's activities were all illegal under the letter of the law.[*]

In addition, they did break-ins to Bernardine's sister Jennifer Dohrn's

---

[*]   The 1975 Church Committee hearings unearthed COINTELPRO files that showed that the FBI went so far as to infiltrate the women's liberation movement in dozens of cities and towns across the country. The committee's chief counsel, Frederick A. O. Schwarz, Jr., concluded, "The FBI abuses were much more dangerous" than those of the people they were pursuing. "They undermined American democracy, violated the law and subverted the Constitution." Medsger, *The Burglary,* p. 344.

place. They were really after Jennifer because they knew she was the nexus between the above- and underground organization. So they did black-bag break-ins into her place, put listening devices in, and stole her underwear. That was a big thing.*

MICHAEL KENNEDY

When the federal government tried to prosecute a number of my clients and clearly Daniel Ellsberg, the defense attorneys, including myself, would raise issues of ill-gotten evidence. Evidence gotten mostly by the COINTELPRO people, by break-ins and illegal wiretaps and other forms of surveillance, and when you raise that as an issue to dismiss the case, the government would be in a position where it had to disclose what it considered to be matters of national security. All their peccadilloes, almost everything they did that they knew was wrong, they claimed to do in order to protect national security. That was all bullshit. That's what they claimed, but we were allowed to bring it forth, and frequently the government would dismiss cases rather than let us reveal the fact that they had acted illegally, because they didn't want the publicity. So for example, when Bill [Ayers] and Bernardine [Dohrn] surfaced in 1980, there were no charges against Bill, and Bernardine's charges were minor misdemeanors, potential felonies, involving the Days of Rage and the 1968 Democratic National Convention.†

The FBI was all over us for so many years. I assumed that our phones were tapped, but I never had proof of it until I saw the documents years later. We knew we were under surveillance from '69 to '73, almost perpetually. We'd see them all the time. They would even occasionally come bang on our front door. God, it was awful, and they were mean, nasty sons

---

* Files retrieved under the Freedom of Information Act showed that Mark Felt told his FBI subordinates that one way they could convince Jennifer Dohrn to reveal her sister's location would be to kidnap her baby boy. Medsger, *The Burglary,* p. 493.

† Bernardine Dohrn got three years of probation and a $1,500 fine. She and Ayers settled in Chicago, where Ayers became a professor at the College of Education at the University of Illinois in Chicago, and Dohrn founded the Children and Family Justice Center at Northwestern University School of Law, which she ran for twenty years.

of bitches. I got my FBI files through the Freedom of Information Act a few years ago, and when we got the first tranche of documents, it made me so sick to see all of that, I just couldn't keep on reading. Whereas, when Emile de Antonio, the radical filmmaker, got his FBI files, he made a movie out of his, *Mr. Hoover and I*. God bless "De."

MARK RUDD (Weather Underground member)

I stayed a fugitive until '77, with the help of my then wife, Sue LeGrand. I stayed in touch with the organization, and I knew what was going on. I increasingly became cynical. I had a sense that the information I was getting was not real. You know, "Oh, we have such a big impact on this part of the movement, or that part of the movement."[*]

BILL AYERS (Weather Underground member)

J.J. [John Jacobs] died in 1997. He's one person who never came aboveground. His ashes were taken to Cuba and put on Che Guevara's memorial. J.J. was the main author of the Weathermen document. He left the Weather Underground after the townhouse explosion. He was a revolutionary until the end.

COUNTERCULTURE

MICHAEL KENNEDY

In October of 1971, Nixon signed the Controlled Substance Act and decided that he was going to put marijuana in Schedule One. Well, mari-

---

[*]   When Mark Rudd surrendered to authorities in 1977, all charges against him were dropped because of FBI illegalities. He taught math for twenty-six years at Central New Mexico Community College in Albuquerque.

juana didn't belong in Schedule One, because it's not dangerous, and it *does* have medical properties, as we all now know and the vast majority of the country now recognizes. But Nixon said, "I'm going to give it the worst classification possible," meaning that those who were dealing marijuana could face twenty years in prison because of that classification. There was an uproar. People were saying, "Why are you putting marijuana in Schedule One? I mean, it's nothing!"

Nixon said, "All right, what I'm going to do is appoint a blue-ribbon commission," and it was called the Shafer Commission. [Raymond] Shafer was then the governor of Pennsylvania, and a great number of very intelligent, sophisticated people, mostly Republicans, were appointed to that commission. They spent about a year studying marijuana. In 1972, the Shafer Commission voted unanimously to recommend decriminalization. Not only did marijuana not belong in Schedule One, said the commission, but the possession and distribution of marijuana for personal use should be decriminalized. That's exactly what the Shafer Commission said. Nixon ignored them. He said, "They don't know what the hell they're talking about," even though there were medical doctors and all sorts of people testifying during that commission. That's when Nixon declared the war on drugs. He used the phrase first in '71 but he really declared the war after the Shafer Commission had sent him their report in 1972.

Nixon thought that if he could empower his federal agents to go after marijuana, it would be a very good excuse, politically, to get inside the left, because he considered them all "dopers," and lot of us were. That wasn't our common denominator. Our common denominator was antiracism and anti-imperialism. So the thing about drug laws is, they really are not about the drugs; they were about politics.

NEW YORK TIMES, SUNDAY, AUGUST 6, 1972

Fifty-seven persons connected with Timothy Leary's sex and drug sect, the Brotherhood of Eternal Love, were arrested or indicted and large quantities of LSD, hashish, hashish oil, cocaine, mescaline and marijuana were seized in dawn raids in California, Oregon and Hawaii today, the Bureau of Narcotics and Dangerous Drugs announced. . . .

MICHAEL KENNEDY

They charged Michael Randall in the '72 conspiracy involving over fifty members of the Brotherhood of Eternal Love for manufacturing massive quantities of LSD and distributing them around the world and dosing everybody. That was basically the charge.

With reference to the Brotherhood of Eternal Love, they were not after them because they made the best acid in the world. They were after them because of their politics. These guys were total screaming libertarian, anarchist, crazy motherfuckers, and they were determined to dose the entire world if they could, and they took a real shot at it. They spread "Orange Sunshine" all over Southern California. I can't tell you how many judges ended up getting dosed because it had gotten into their water up on their desk, up on their dais, or they would put it on the doorknobs, so when the judge grabbed the doorknob, they would take it dermally through the skin. That's the Brotherhood of Eternal Love.

MICHAEL RANDALL

There was a federal case against me for passport violation. The grand jury was convening in San Francisco, and it didn't look good. It was just unwinnable. So I got the hell out of there before I was indicted. I was on the run from the Brotherhood conspiracy, from a passport charge, and from the conspiracy in Northern California to manufacture LSD. The best thing I ever did was run.

MICHAEL KENNEDY

Michael Randall was out on bail and within literally hours of being free, he and Carol and the kids were in the wind. They went to Mexico and stayed there for a long time, and then moved up to New Mexico and Arizona and stayed around those places. Michael became a master jeweler. It took them twelve years to find him, and he did the five years for a bail-jumping violation.[*]

RALPH METZNER (psychedelic psychiatrist)

Albert Hofmann recognized right from the beginning, LSD is more than just another drug. When he was a hundred and one years old, he said, "I don't think we have yet found the best way for these substances to be employed in society for human betterment."

That's the way I feel. I think research needs to continue. Basically for the entire seventies and eighties and nineties, research for LSD's therapeutic uses came to a standstill. It's very limited now.

DAVID FENTON (movement photographer)

Culturally, it was a revolution. And it was instant. It was as fast as it took a tab of LSD to dissolve. People were never the same again. And that's part of why, to me, shutting down all the clinical, psychopharmacological research on those drugs was a terrible mistake, and something I blame Tim Leary for. He flaunted it too much. He caused too much of a counterreaction.

BILL AYERS

When they captured Tim Leary [in Afghanistan in 1972] he did some time, and he told [the FBI] everything he could remember about us. That's why we kept him at arm's length. He never went to any of our houses, and he never really knew the names of anybody except me, Jeff,

---

[*]   By 1972, the secretive group of hippie drug dealers from Laguna had become America's largest international hashish smuggling and LSD distribution network, with more than 750 worldwide operatives. The Brotherhood laundered money in foreign bank accounts and forged passports so accurately that the government studied the group's techniques for its own use. All told, the Brotherhood reportedly moved twenty-four tons of hashish to America in surfboards, VW buses, and Land Rovers from countries as far-flung as Afghanistan, India, and Nepal.

and Bernardine. But he did rat us out to the authorities, and that was bad.[*]

BRIAN FLANAGAN

The problem is Tim snitched on a lot of us. When he came back to the United States and stood trial, he named names and told tales after we saved his ass.

VIETNAM VETERANS

RICK AYERS (army deserter, Weather Underground member)

I stayed underground until 1977—seven years. The Weather Underground pretty much broke up around '76 and I said, "I'm out of here." I came back to the Bay Area. It was just before the Carter amnesty.[†] I had Dennis Cunningham for my lawyer, and all I had to do was fly into New York and turn myself in.

They put me on a bus to Fort Dix, and there were probably two hundred deserters who came in that week. In other words, there were thousands coming in. A lot of them were just working-class people who stayed at their uncle's farm. But the point is, the numbers were so high—that's

---

[*]   Leary, whom Richard Nixon called "the most dangerous man in America," was put in solitary confinement in California's Folsom Prison, with bail set at $5 million. In return for a shortened sentence, he agreed to cooperate with the FBI's Weather Underground investigation. Leary would later claim that his attorney Michael Kennedy masterminded his jailbreak, which Kennedy denies, and a federal investigation into Kennedy's involvement came up empty. Leary's wife, Rosemary Woodruff, refused to cooperate with the FBI, and to avoid being subpoenaed she lived in hiding for twenty-three years, surfacing in 1994. Leary was released from prison in April 1976 by Governor Jerry Brown.

[†]   On his first full day in office, January 21, 1977, President Carter pardoned hundreds of thousands of men who had evaded the Vietnam War draft, many of whom were living in Canada. But the pardon did not clear civilian war protesters who were convicted of violent acts, nor did it clear an estimated 500,000 to 1,000,000 active-duty personnel who went AWOL (absent without leave) or deserted when they were serving during the war.

why Jimmy Carter did an amnesty. I got a less-than-honorable discharge. But if I'd been arrested in '72, I would probably have gotten two years for desertion.*

MICHAEL UHL (Vietnam veterans organizer)

The turnabout began with Reagan. The Vietnam debacle, the enormity of the war's unpopularity and active resistance to it, was a real setback for managers of U.S. military policy and a threat for the militarized sector of the economy. Addressing the alienation of the veterans was an important vehicle to refashion the narrative of the Vietnam War.

Reagan went against the grain of the conventional wisdom, which had already concluded that the war was a mistake, if not worse, and recast the war as a "noble cause." This is around the time the "spat-upon vet" urban myth also took hold. I guess Reagan's message resonated strongly among those who don't study the background of historical events, and who simply wanted to feel good about themselves again, feel good about America. It could become cool to defend what in a prior state of mind a vet would have viewed as indefensible. So, in my view, Reagan exploited veterans' ignorance and damaged psyches by promoting the empty gesture of belatedly welcoming us home. I say empty because he didn't really want to back that up with services and benefits. Keep in mind that this was the same Reagan who vigorously opposed the creation of vet centers because he claimed they would "mollycoddle" the vets. When in fact, given the controversy of the war, and the numbers of postwar problems this generation of vets was facing, the vet centers were critical as a kind of halfway house for reintegrating 'Nam vets into society, and as a buffer to the VA, which was run then by World War II vets who had contempt for us, for "losing" our war.

Today the campaign to commemorate Vietnam and honor its veterans serves a similar service, to further remove the onus of having participated in a bad war by abstracting the veterans from the bad history of the war,

---

* Rick Ayers moved to Oakland and became a professor of education at the University of San Francisco.

and honoring them for just showing up (thank you for your service), and for which the word *valor* serves as a convenient euphemism. Thankfully, there are still many of us who refuse to buy into that historical falsification, and who wish to see an honest portrayal of the Vietnam War passed down to future generations.

JANE FONDA (actor, peace activist)

My mail was opened, my house was broken into and ransacked by the FBI. I remember when we were filming *Steelyard Blues* in Berkeley, I put my daughter into a playschool called the Blue Fairyland, which was part of the Red Family collective. They followed my daughter to the Blue Fairyland. Everything was so misunderstood.

In 1973 I filed a lawsuit against the Nixon administration to compel the various government agencies to admit they had been carrying on a campaign of harassment and intimidation in an attempt to silence and impugn me. When my case was settled in 1979, the FBI admitted that I had been under surveillance from 1970 to 1973 and that they had used counterintelligence techniques, in violation of my constitutional rights, to "neutralize" me and "impair my personal and professional standing." The CIA admitted that they had read my mail, and the FBI had seized without subpoena my bank records.[*] They tried to get [Armand] "Army" Archerd, the *Variety* columnist, to plant what they called "black propaganda," which was rumors they knew weren't true. Archerd didn't do it, but he did write about it later, and he told me that they were trying to get him to say that I had threatened Nixon's life. I also found out that I was on Nixon's enemies list.

When I came back from Hanoi in 1972,[†] the write-up about my trip

---

[*]   Most of this quote is from my interview with Jane Fonda in New York on June 14, 2014, but in some cases she suggested that I cross-reference her autobiography, *My Life So Far,* for factual and historical details, which I have done here (pp. 353–54).

[†]   Fonda traveled alone to Hanoi for two weeks in July 1972 at the invitation of the North Vietnamese, who wanted a celebrity to bring attention to the aggressive new U.S. bombing campaign, which had begun in April and would conclude over Christmas of 1972. The Haiphong

was an inch in *The New York Times*. Nothing. What was going on behind the scenes at the White House was completely different. Nixon was freaking out. He instructed the Justice Department to get me for treason. It's funny, because the lawyers for the Justice Department who were asked to do this ended up coming back and saying, "She really hasn't done anything treasonous. There's nothing here."

No big deal was made about my trip to Hanoi until Reagan was elected. Three hundred Americans had already gone [to North Vietnam], including Ramsey Clark [LBJ's attorney general]. Then, during the Reagan administration, it was decided to use me as a way to discredit the antiwar movement, and to build a case against me as a traitor, even though I wasn't legally a traitor, and they used state legislators. In Maryland, a state legislator refused to allow me to enter the state to give a speech, and another one refused to have any of my movies shown in his state. The term "Hanoi Jane" was coined and raised to an art form. It was very cleverly orchestrated.

The photograph was taken in 1972, but it never really surfaced until Reagan. I have explained how the picture was taken and publicly apologized:

> ... Here is my best, honest recollection of what happened: someone (I don't remember who) led me towards the [anti-aircraft] gun, and I sat down. . . . I hardly even thought about where I was sitting. The cameras flashed. . . . It is possible that it was a setup, that the Vietnamese had it all planned. I will never know. But if they did I can't blame them. The buck stops here. If I was used, I allowed it to happen . . . a two-minute lapse of sanity that will haunt me forever. . . . But the photo exists, delivering its message regardless of what I was doing or feeling. I carry this heavy in my heart. I

Harbor was mined, and dikes, bridges, railroads, and the city of Hanoi were bombed by a barrage of B-52s. It was the first time the United States had bombed North Vietnam since 1968. Fonda made several radio broadcasts, delivered letters to POWs from their families (in a visit that would later become very controversial), and brought the POWs' letters back to their families. On the last day of her trip, her photograph was hastily taken in front of an anti-aircraft gun.

In a photograph that would haunt her for decades, Jane Fonda is in Hanoi on July 1, 1972, sitting on an anti-aircraft gun that was used to shoot down American planes during the intensive 1972 bombing raids on North Vietnam.

have apologized numerous times for any pain I may have caused servicemen and their families because of this photograph. It was never my intention to cause harm.[*]

Between what I actually did and what they said I did, I became a pariah. It was a little hard for me to get work for a while. There were threats of boycotts of my films. I did make movies that were very successful, but there was always this threat hanging in the air. A couple of years ago, I was going to go on the QVC channel to promote my book, and QVC got bombarded with threats and they canceled me. That became a big story.

The only thing that I would do differently is that I would have not sat on that anti-aircraft gun. I just didn't even think what I was doing. I was about to leave. I had been there for two weeks, by myself. I never should have gone for that long and gone alone. Tom Hayden, who I was dating at the time, didn't come with me. Although I was a grown-up, that was a big

[*]   Quoted from "The Truth About My Trip to Hanoi," http://www.janefonda.com/the-truth-about-my-trip-to-hanoi/.

mistake, because no matter what reality was, that image says something. I will go to my grave regretting that.

KENT STATE

JOE LEWIS (injured Kent State student)

While I was in the hospital, my sister got some phone calls saying that I deserved what I got, and I should die. I also got some hate mail. I was pretty cowed into keeping a low profile, because it seemed like not only was I shot, but public opinion considered me to be the evildoer. It's a classic case of blaming the victim. It got even worse that fall, when the Portage County grand jury indicted twenty-five students and professors, including myself. I got charged with a misdemeanor of fourth-degree riot.

BOB GILES (*Akron Beacon Journal* managing editor)

The FBI investigated the shootings and issued a report in July 1970 saying that the National Guard was not in danger, and there was no need to shoot the students. In the months following, President Nixon empaneled the Scranton Commission, which basically said that there was no reason for the guards to shoot.* Then there was the Portage County grand jury, which was made up of about fifteen citizens, and they indicted twenty-five people, most of them students, some faculty—and it was critical of everybody but the Guard, and the Guard was totally exonerated. In 1974, a federal grand jury indicted eight guardsmen. Federal judge Frank Battisti dismissed the charges and acquitted the guardsmen.

---

* In September 1970, the Scranton Commission report concluded: "Even if the guardsmen faced danger, it was not a danger that called for lethal force. The 61 [to 67] shots by 28 guardsmen certainly cannot be justified. Apparently, no order to fire was given, and there was inadequate fire control discipline on Blanket Hill. The Kent State tragedy must mark the last time that, as a matter of course, loaded rifles are issued to guardsmen confronting student demonstrators."

JOE LEWIS

We couldn't get into the courtroom and prosecute these guys [the national guardsmen], because these people, as agents of the state, were protected by the divine right of kings. They had something called sovereign immunity.*

The only legal avenue we had was to pursue a civil lawsuit, and we looked like a greedy bunch of people when we sued for $48 million. But that was our effort to get the truth out. We spent the whole summer of '75 in the Cleveland courthouse. Across the aisle from us were the men who had shot us, and they were laughing and flirting with the court reporters. The judge was making all these pronouncements, introducing the governor when he came to testify as "Your Excellency," and not allowing some of the photographic evidence to be seen by the jury, or showing the wounds of the students who were murdered, or shot, because it would be prejudicial. It was just a nightmare. It was a horrible, horrible experience. In some ways, it was worse than being shot.

DEAN KAHLER (paralyzed Kent State student)

The jury came back after six, seven days of deliberations, found in favor of the defendants, and against the plaintiffs in the civil trial. Then we had an appeal that worked its way all the way up to the U.S. Supreme Court, and if you read the Supreme Court's decision, you'll see that they were thoroughly disgusted with the way that it was handled in the original court, and remanded it back to trial to start all over again. They threw out that original verdict.

When the second trial started, they heard a couple of witnesses, and Judge [William K.] Thomas, who was the new judge, a real judge, in Cleveland in 1979, looked over all the evidence. In the seventh week, we said we won't settle unless we get an apology from the Guard. The judge said, "Well, how about if they take responsibility, and say that they

* Sovereign immunity is a legal doctrine that protects the state from civil or criminal prosecution.

shouldn't have shot you?" None of us were happy with that, but everybody kept saying maybe we should accept it. We'll get them on record saying they were wrong for shooting us, and taking responsibility for shooting us. We decided to settle at that point in time.

LAUREL KRAUSE
(sister of slain Kent State student Allison Krause)

In the 1979 Kent State civil settlement, all we got was a statement of regret, and fifteen thousand dollars that we received for Allison.

DEAN KAHLER

The grand total for everything was $675,000. It was the era prior to large jury settlements. I didn't particularly care for this, but all the people who weren't as injured as I was said that they were only going to take a certain amount of money, and they wanted the most of it to go to me. So I ended up with $350,000. It helped me with medical bills. It's still helping with medical bills.

My view is we don't have truth and justice yet on Kent State. But we got as much as we're going to get for quite a while, because I don't see the government wanting to open up an old wound.

JOHN FILO (Kent State student photojournalist)

I was a student that not only survived being shot at, but I was now a famous student over the death of other students. It was very hard for me. Back then you never went to a psychiatrist. You never went and sought help, because that meant you were crazy. You learned how to deal with it. And it screwed me up for a very, very long time.

JOE LEWIS

I think I had post-traumatic stress disorder, but about fifteen years after I was shot, I found that speaking about it was healing. Prior to that, I just cried. Then I realized that by speaking to students in colleges and high schools about the Kent State shootings, I was sharing the burden of sadness and truth with students, and I realized that it was a healing experience to talk about it. I've actually tried to share what I consider to be the truth about what happened, which is a government conspiracy and cover-up.

I ask students to seek the truth of this case, because some of the testimony was locked away for seventy-five years. In 2050 that testimony should become available, and I encourage students who I'm speaking to now, that in 2050, to please pay attention and think of me.

MADISON

PAUL SOGLIN (mayor of Madison, Wisconsin)

There was a spontaneous reunion of the left in the summer of 1989. On the last night, there was a dinner at a restaurant called the Second Story. Karl Armstrong got up and said, "I've apologized to the Fassnacht family. I've apologized to the university. I've apologized to the people of the state of Wisconsin. I want to apologize to you. We did something very wrong and you paid the consequences. We had no right to act on your behalf." He was absolutely correct in saying that.

PETER GREENBERG (student, *Daily Cardinal* reporter)

One day, about thirty years ago, a letter came, addressed to me at *Newsweek,* with no return address. It was a single-spaced, typewritten diatribe against me. It said that because I worked at *Newsweek,* I had sold out. The postmark on it was Jackson, Mississippi. The handwriting reminded me of Leo's [Burt], and I just figured that he was probably hiding in plain sight in the most unpredictable place you'd ever imagine: Jackson, Mississippi. He's probably married, a Little League coach. I have no idea. That was as close as I got to thinking I might know where he was. The interesting thing about all of that is, I think if you ask anybody from the *Cardinal* who knew where Leo was, "Would you tell anybody?," to this day they'd say, "No."

BILL DYSON

Leo Burt is a fugitive, and they would prosecute him, because a person died. Last heard, he was in Canada, allegedly crossed over the Niagara Falls. But for forty-four years Burt has remained at large, the last phantom of the 1960s.

TRANSFORMATION

America is moving out of Vietnam. . . . But Vietnam is not moving out of America. . . .

There was no cease-fire on this front. . . . [F]ew Americans challenge the proposition that for good or bad, something has happened to American life—something not yet understood or agreed upon, something that is different, important and probably enduring.

—JAMES RESTON, *New York Times,*
January 24, 1973

IN THE SPACE OF JUST ONE WEEK IN JANUARY 1973, RICHARD NIXON took the oath of office for his second, short-lived presidential term; Lyndon Baines Johnson died at his ranch in Stonewall, Texas; North Vietnam and the United States signed a cease-fire agreement in Paris; and Secretary of Defense Melvin Laird announced an end to the draft. That same week, in his second inaugural address, Nixon outlined a new, more cautious American foreign policy: "The time has passed when America will make every other nation's conflict our own . . . or presume to tell other nations how to manage their own affairs."

The war was over, and however the Nixon administration tried to dress it up, North Vietnam, though crippled, had prevailed. Vietnam, in the words of veteran war correspondent Neil Sheehan, was "a bad war, an unnecessary war, a mistake by American politicians and statesmen." America was indeed close to looking like what Nixon said he feared most, "a pitiful helpless giant." While America's superpower role was diminished in the thaw of post–Cold War global politics, its domestic identity had transformed. The political, cultural, and spiritual fallout from the Vietnam War and the War at Home would profoundly and permanently change the nation.

———

ROGER MORRIS

There is a kind of trauma involved in the moral, emotional implications of what went on in Vietnam. It was a great American tragedy. Nineteen seventy was a climactic moment in American life, and we're still living with the consequences, and just getting rid of the Vietnam syndrome. Vietnam, as a factor in the mentality of American foreign affairs, the way we see the world, and the lessons that we draw from it, is terribly important. We never really came to grips with the reasons for the mistake to begin with, which was our hubris and our ignorance of another people.

JOHN PERRY BARLOW

I think everybody, whether they went to 'Nam or not, everybody had a life that was profoundly altered. There's no way in the world that I would have gone to college in four years straight if it hadn't been fear of matriculating to the University of Vietnam. It affected everybody and in ways that people still don't quite know how to discuss. The people who went to Vietnam and came back with stories that they couldn't tell because nobody wanted to hear; the people who didn't go to Vietnam and felt guilty because they hadn't supported their brethren who did. I think it is a terrible scar.

TOM HAYDEN (April 27, 2015, speech)

One can only guess at why many in the elites hope to forget the Vietnam peace movement, why public memories have atrophied, and why there are few if any memorials to peace. The denial of our very impact, the caricatures of who we really were, the questioning of our patriotism, the snide suggestions that we offered no alternative but surrender to the external threat, has cast a pall of illegitimacy over our memory and a chilling effect among many peace dissenters. One reason for this forgetting is that the Vietnam War was lost, a historical fact which representatives of a self-proclaimed superpower can hardly acknowledge. Rather than admit that their war was a failure, it is more convenient to lay blame on the peace movement, the mainstream media, the dovish politicians at home, and the so-called enemies within.

HOW THE PEACE MOVEMENT WILL BE REMEMBERED—HONORED, or reviled—is still a moving target. What will remain indisputable, however, is that the draft played a central role in politicizing a generation. Forced conscription in an unpopular war propelled millions of men and women who were born anywhere near the years 1944 to 1950 to engage in American public policy. Whether they reacted to the draft out of self-interest, or based on moral principles, the draft played a critical role in turning the youth of the late sixties into an acutely politically engaged and awakened generation.

The activism of the time created, as Ralph Nader called it, "a new form of citizenship." Rebelling against conformity, promoting American values of self-determination, and owning a sense of responsibility to be agents for change are all hallmarks of the movement. Even though the movement opposed the U.S. government at almost every turn, it did so out of its own flavor of patriotism and drive to hold the government accountable for what it considered unjust conduct at home and abroad. As *Time* managing editor Henry Grunwald wrote in June 1970 after touring the country, "The radicals—always excepting the most violent fringe—insist that America must be great. That is why, within reason, we must cherish them."

Yet, the question remains, who won the war at home? Cultural and political extremism both produced their own lasting backlash, but history's verdict generally holds that the cultural revolutionaries won and the political revolutionaries lost. Marxist rhetoric never found a broad base in a country founded on democracy and free markets. The political revolutionaries reacted to a brief moment in time, in a political vortex, and ultimately they lost sight of their audience. But in the end, hippies, feminists, and black power, environmental, and gay rights advocates permanently changed the DNA of American freedom.

DANIEL ELLSBERG

I think what neither the antiwar movement nor scholars nor journalists have come to understand after all these years about the Vietnam War is that the war could've been very much bigger than it ever got. The antiwar movement always assumed that the war was being fought ferociously at the highest possible level. But right from the beginning, the Joint Chiefs had been urging strongly that it be much bigger. They had a litany—it was like a catechism—of escalations that they wanted to be done simultaneously and it involved moving toward at least 500,000 troops in Vietnam, and possibly up to a million. A million was mentioned to the president by the chairman as early as 1965. We eventually got to 550,000.

The antiwar movement, which was extremely admirable, and conscientious, and dedicated, and right, was doing what they should have been doing, except for the violence of the Weathermen, which helped Nixon. But I would say their efforts didn't change Nixon's plans and didn't shorten the war, but it did something that they weren't even focused on: It put a ceiling on the war, not just at one point but at many points along the way. They kept that war from getting enormously larger and more lethal than it would've been—as many as three to four million Vietnamese may have died during the war. Horrible. But it could easily have been ten million. When I say easily, it wasn't just a future possibility; it's what the Joint Chiefs were asking for.

ROGER MORRIS

I think the antiwar movement was very real for a time, but it didn't take long to dissipate. There was real fatigue. My own view of the antiwar movement was that it was largely a draft protest, beyond the few principal people who knew what they were talking about, and the people who really did have a moral objection. Don't forget what happened—as the troops come home and casualty lists begin to go down in 1971 and '72, and we begin to savage the Vietnamese people from thirty thousand feet with computers [from B-52 bombers], the opposition became less and less vocal. The war ends not because of the people in the streets. The war ends because the North Vietnamese finally relent on some of the negotiation points, and the Congress of the United States finally pulls the plug.

JULIUS LESTER

One of the legacies of the antiwar movement was to end the draft. That was a huge mistake, because now we have a mercenary army. Therefore, if your son or brother is not in the army, then you're not affected by what the United States does abroad. Whereas with Vietnam, everybody was liable to the draft. That was democracy. And so getting rid of the draft was a huge, huge mistake. I don't consider that a political victory.

MARK RUDD

The draft forced people to pay attention, and that's why they eliminated the draft. But the cultural revolution was critical, too, because the cultural revolution brought people in. It was like an entry drug. For so many years you had a fixed system that had no brakes in it. In the Eisenhower fifties it was seamless. The only thing happening then was the labor movement, and the growing civil rights movement, that was mostly confined to the black population in the South and a handful of white liberals. But the sixties showed the major shake-up of the culture, which then led people into looking at the whole thing.

PETER COYOTE

I think it's fair to say that we lost all our political struggles in the sixties. We didn't end capitalism, we didn't end imperialism, we didn't end racism, we didn't actually end the war in Vietnam. However, we did win all the cultural battles. There's no place in the United States you can go today where there's not a women's movement, an environmental movement, alternative health movements, alternative spiritual practices, yoga, Buddhism, Hinduism, Jainism, organic food, alternative ways of eating and nutrition, gay rights. These things are locked in the culture and these things are exerting long-term pressures that are deeply and subtly transformative, and it is the Diggers' assertion that they were more powerful than politics, and I still hold to that.

When I returned to Olema in 1992, it was a little mournful. The place had been leveled, the park service had taken over the land. There was nothing there. I thought, How could such a people so visible in the present, so colorful, so inventive, so imaginative, how could they have disappeared without a trace? But I decided that they didn't disappear without a trace. It's kind of like seasoning a stew; you can't see the salt and the pepper anymore once you've put it in the stew. You can't distinguish the turnips from the potatoes, but they're all in the stew. But the stew tastes differently because of those ingredients. We're not so recognizable as individuals, but we all have contributed to making these cultural changes.

MARK RUDD

I think the hippies have gotten no credit for having accomplished a lot. In fact, you say the word *hippie* and people laugh. It's like *hippie* and *train wreck* are somehow related. But actually, the New Left was a train wreck because we lost bad. In essence, the New Left forgot power, or we thought that power was going to fall into place somehow automatically. We thought the liberals would take power and we would be to the left of them. But that's not what happened. What happened was a far-right reaction took place. The right-wing reaction, both within the Republican Party and within the Democratic Party, moved everything to the right. It was a closing of the New Deal chapter. And those of us who were self-consciously political, we were the tail end of the entire socialist movement of one hundred and more years. Now there's no more socialism.

MARGERY TABANKIN

I know an enormous number of people who really did wake up and say, "This is a fight for the soul of our country. What kind of country do we want it to be? Do we want to accept that some things are not possible? Or do we want to fight for the possible?" I agree that a civil war happened, that we had to fight for our country, and that everything changed. Yet I can't help but think that our generation lost with the money. Today I sit in conversations with people my age recounting all that we accomplished: We created a women's movement and lives were changed; we put the environmental movement on the map; and we ultimately ended a war and made it harder for the U.S. to choose to go to war. But in the end, the forces of corporate capital essentially beat our generation in terms of the power we wield in this country. We were so focused on all these other things that we didn't really understand that they were taking control of the country.

MARK RUDD

Essentially what we need is a new cultural revolution which will repoliticize young people. The problem is the depoliticization of society as a whole, and the very low number of people who are paying attention to politics, especially young people.

THE 1969-70 SCHOOL YEAR MARKED A BRIEF MOMENT IN THE modern era when rebels believed that revolution was possible, and radical political rhetoric had a rare, nearly mainstream place in American political discourse. Now, with historical hindsight, we see that the movement did not bring permanent political change. If anything, its militant, ideological fringe, like the Weathermen and the Black Panthers, hurt the movement's popularity and certainly helped ignite a conservative backlash that is alive and well today. Committing violence in the name of peace and justice proved to be politically self-destructive—a form of revolutionary suicide. "Every time they burn another building," said one Nixon administration official in 1970, "Republican registration goes up."

MICHAEL KAZIN

You've got to be really mad and organize other mad people if you're going to get change. People in history who've been called extremist often achieve some important things. Sometimes good, sometimes not so good. I recently wrote, "Extremism is the coin of conviction, whether virtuous or malign. It forces middle-roaders to crush the disrupter or adapt." Abolitionists were called extremists at the time; so were suffragettes. You're no longer an extremist when you win.

MARK RUDD

The errors that were made on the basis of our moral engagement were so enormous that even last night, I dreamt I was in an argument with Bernardine [Dohrn] and Jeff [Jones] and Bill [Ayers] in which we were arguing about their position that our *motivation* was right, and *that's* what should be retained by history.

They haven't apologized because in their heads, they haven't realized the extent of the errors that were made. I realized at some point that good motivations are extremely common. Bernardine and Billy believe that we were morally engaged, and so we made some mistakes.

Myself, I believe that results are where it counts, and that had we not been so enamored of our own heroic morality, we might have been able to judge the fact that our theories were not working. For example, nobody came to the Days of Rage. Nobody came. We had many fewer people there in Chicago in October than when we started organizing it. We went from about 500 down to about 350. But we were so deeply involved in our rightness. So, I'm for accountability, I'm for democracy.

The Weather leadership adopted the bombing-light position, which was, we're not going to kill anybody. And somehow, luckily, we never did, after the first three [in the townhouse]. But I think that the bombing-light business is just a continuation of the same strategy, which is armed struggle, which is a mistake.

JOHN MURTAGH, JR.

When they say today, as Bill Ayers has, that they were scrupulous and were targeting government buildings, they were never targeting people, well, wait a second, Bill, you didn't think that Judge Murtagh and his family were asleep in his house? Let's not sugarcoat it: We're all sitting here today, and my mother is about to celebrate her eighty-eighth birthday, not because the Weathermen didn't try, but because they were incompetent. They set off four firebombs at a house where a husband, wife, and three children were sound asleep in their beds. If they had been any good at what they were doing, they would have killed some or all of us. What was your goal, and what was your endgame? They did such harm, and they accomplished very little.

BILL AYERS

What do people want me to apologize for? I would say I was sorry about our political sectarianism and dogma. I'm sorry about the arrogance. I'm sorry about the male chauvinism and sexism and supremacy. I'm sorry that I was mean. I'm sorry that I betrayed a friend. I could go on. And you could, too. So, I'm sorry. But a blanket apology is just too much. And it's insincere. The Days of Rage? Not sorry. The Pentagon?* Not sorry.

As I've said for years, I think we're badly in need of a truth and reconciliation process. Put me and Bernardine on a stage, please, with John McCain, John Kerry, Bob Kerrey, George Bush, Dick Cheney, Donald Rumsfeld, Henry Kissinger—and have every one of us say what we did—what our bad work was—and ask forgiveness. I want to be on that stage. I want to say what I did that was wrong. I want to ask forgiveness. But I want Kissinger to say what *he* did that was wrong, because he killed three million people, and I killed no one. John McCain bombed civilians in an act of terror. I killed no one. Bob Kerrey slit the throats of two elderly people on the outskirts of a village, because he was leading a group of Navy SEALs into a Viet Cong–held village and he had to quiet them. That's a war crime. He did it. Is he sorry? Why doesn't he say so publicly? And in that company, I'll tell you exactly

---

*   On May 19, 1972, Ho Chi Minh's birthday, the Weather Underground exploded a bomb in a bathroom on the fourth floor of the Pentagon, causing serious damage and flooding.

what I'm sorry for, and I'll even tell you the names and places of the things I did. But, without that, I don't feel like I have a unique responsibility to apologize.

I'm saying it's ludicrous to single me or us out, as if we're the representatives of going off the tracks. The country was off the tracks. How do you act in an insane time? How does love answer genocide? How do you organize a sane response? We're not heroes. But, frankly, everybody our age can measure their own commitment against our commitment, and ask themselves, Did I do enough? And when I say we didn't do enough, that's not a statement of tactics. That's a statement of fact. We didn't stop the war. So, people like to pretend that "the wonderful antiwar movement—look at all the great it did." You know what? We convinced the American people to oppose the war in three years, and the war went on for seven more years. And every week that the war went on, six thousand people were murdered in our names. Every week. We couldn't stop it.

CATHY WILKERSON

On some level I don't have any regrets. I don't see how it could have been done differently. I feel like I tried my best at every step of the way, and failed miserably on many occasions, particularly in joining Weathermen. The forces aligned against us were enormous in terms of seeing these dead Vietnamese children on the front page of the newspaper every day and knowing what was happening to the black movement and feeling like the police were out of control. It was very hard to maintain your equilibrium. So, to look back at the movement, there's huge amounts to learn from it, both good and bad.

MICHAEL KAZIN

One of the things that makes the sixties somewhat different from other periods of rebellion in American history—and there have been a lot, going back to the American Revolution—is that *everything seemed to be up for grabs.* All received authority was suspect for people who were rebelling.

That meant that authorities representing gender and race, media, politics, and business were all seen as being on the wrong side of morality and history by people who saw themselves as rebels. There was general agreement that the whole system was at fault.

JOHN PERRY BARLOW

I think in terms of consciousness in general, there are a lot of fundamental, almost invisible, things that are different now that we can take responsibility for having made different. The biggest of these is that I can really remember living in a world where just about everybody believed in God-given authority. William Burroughs believed in God-given authority. Jack Kerouac certainly did. Whether you were the president, or the general, or the CEO, there was this assumption that you had been ordained in the holy hierarchy to be there. But after about 1972, you really had to earn it in most people's minds. You were no longer automatically worthy of respect just because you had power. That's a pretty big shift.

JULIUS LESTER

There was a set of values by which America knew itself that the sixties challenged vigorously. The set of values was the way democracy had been defined, and the way democracy had been defined was white men on top. Well, the black power movement comes along and says, "No, we will define ourselves." Black studies comes along and says, "No, black studies is not the study of black people. Black studies is the study of Western civilization from another point of view, from the point of view of those who have suffered under Western civilization." That's a huge value change.*

So who's going to have power? Then the women's movement comes along, and that really challenges white men at their core. Who controls the home? Who defines what women do? Well, men have always in American history been in charge of that. Women were saying what the black move-

---

* In 1967, less than 5 percent of research universities offered black studies courses, and by 1971 the number had increased to 35 percent. Bloom and Martin, *Black Against Empire*, p. 349.

ment was saying, which was, "No, we define for ourselves who we are. We define for ourselves what our history is, and we're going to look at history differently than you look at history."

ROBIN MORGAN

For some of us it was transformational and there was no going back. There were moments when you could not but be incredibly proud to be part of anything that showed the human spirit in the way that some of these movements did. Primarily the civil rights movement, where you had children scrubbed with their little pigtails standing and singing while fire hoses were trained on them, or the peace movement, where you had people linking arms and being pepper sprayed or beaten for calling for an end to the war. You were part of moments where the human spirit was really at its best.

I wouldn't go back to 1970 for anything in the world. But I wouldn't have *not* been in that year for anything in the world, either—in that time, in that place, doing what I did with the people I was doing it with. It was a real gift. People who get misty-eyed about that period drive me nuts because then I trot out all the things that were wrong with that period. But it was also a visionary period in the life of this country, and I'm glad I was a part of it.

WHETHER REBELLING AGAINST THE DRAFT, THE ATROCITIES of the war, police and FBI repression, the conformity of the 1950s, the sexist, racist establishment, or all of the above, the movement in the final years of the sixties threatened the entire power structure of American society and transformed the country.

VOICES

Karl Armstrong (born 1948) was the leader of four University of Wisconsin–Madison students who, on August 24, 1970, bombed Sterling Hall, home of the Army Mathematics Research Center, accidentally killing a thirty-three-year-old postdoctoral physics researcher, Robert Fassnacht. Armstrong went into hiding following the bombing and was caught on February 16, 1972, in Toronto. Sentenced to twenty-three years in prison, Armstrong was released after seven. Upon his release, he returned to Madison, where he operated a juice cart called Loose Juice on the university campus in Madison. He became friendly with Robert Fassnacht's widow, Stephanie, and daughter, Heidi, who also live in Madison.

Rick Ayers (1946), an antiwar and anti-draft activist during the 1960s and 1970s, is the brother of Bill Ayers. After dropping out of the University of Michigan and fleeing to Canada to avoid the draft, Ayers returned to America in 1969 and joined the army with the intention of organizing fellow soldiers to go AWOL. Ayers briefly joined the Weather Underground after deserting the army in 1970. Today he is a professor of education at the University of San Francisco, as well as the author of five books, including *Teaching the Taboo* (2010), which he coauthored with his brother Bill.

William "Bill" Ayers (born 1944) was a founding member of the radical Weathermen group. Ayers is married to Bernardine Dohrn and the two were fugitives from 1970 to 1980. They had two sons while living underground. When they surfaced, the charges against Ayers—and most of the other members of the Weather Underground—were dropped, because the FBI had been illegally spying on the group. Ayers is now an elementary school theorist, author, and retired professor in the College of Education at the University of Illinois at Chicago. He is a prolific blogger and lecturer, has published dozens of articles about education policy, and has written thirteen books (including two memoirs). Barack Obama, as a presidential candidate in 2008, was attacked for serving on the same charity board with Ayers in Chicago.

Phil Ball (born 1949) served as a marine in Vietnam in 1968. Afterward he enrolled as a student at the University of Wisconsin–Madison and became an antiwar activist. He published a book of combat diaries, *Ghosts and Shadows: A Marine in Vietnam, 1968–1969* (2012).

John Perry Barlow (born 1947) is a poet, writer, lyricist, cyber-rights activist, and former cattle rancher. Barlow wrote many of the Grateful Dead's best songs with his high school friend Bob Weir. We have Barlow to thank for "Cassidy," "Mexicali Blues," "Looks Like Rain," "Estimated Prophet," "Let It Grow," and many others. He is the cofounder of the Electronic Frontier Foundation and has been a fellow with the Berkman Center for Internet and Society at Harvard Law School since 1998. Barlow travels the globe as a consultant and lecturer on civil rights, freedom of speech, and cyber civil liberties. He is a friend and supporter of Edward Snowden.

Jan Barry (born 1943) is a poet, author, journalist, and educator. Barry served in the army in Vietnam and is cofounder of Vietnam Veterans Against the War. He carried the first VVAW banner during a New York antiwar demonstration in 1967. Barry's poems on the war have appeared in the *Chicago Tribune* and *The New York Times* and anthologies such as *From Both Sides Now: The Poetry of the Vietnam War and Its Aftermath* (1998).

Carl Bernstein (born 1944) is a Pulitzer Prize–winning author and investigative journalist who has written books on Richard Nixon, Hillary Clinton, and Pope John Paul II. In 1972, Bernstein and Bob Woodward, young reporters at *The Washington Post,* broke the Watergate story. Together they wrote *All the President's Men* (1974) and *The Final Days* (1977). Bernstein has written for *Vanity Fair, Time, USA Today, Rolling Stone,* and *The New Republic,* and was a Washington bureau chief and correspondent for ABC News.

Heather Booth (born 1945) is a civil rights, peace, and feminist organizer and one of the country's leading strategists for progressive issue campaigns. Booth is the president of Midwest Academy, which trains social change leaders and organizers. As a student at the University of Chicago, Booth initiated one of the first campus women's consciousness-raising groups, Women's Radical Action Program. She is a founding member of the Jane Collective, a Chicago women's health group that performed about twelve thousand safe, illegal abortions between 1969 and 1973.

Sam Brown (born 1943) is a political organizer and an antiwar activist. Brown was the head of ACTION under President Jimmy Carter, and ambassador to the Organization for Security and Co-operation in Europe. He was an antiwar activist and the youth coordinator of "Get Clean for Gene," an effort by antiwar students to cut their hair and shave their beards to campaign door-to-door for Senator Eugene McCarthy's 1968 presidential run. Brown was also a founding member of the Vietnam Moratorium Committee, which organized the largest U.S. antiwar demonstration of all time, on October 15, 1969.

Wesley Brown (born 1945) is a playwright, novelist, and emeritus professor at Rutgers University, where he taught creative writing and literature for twenty-six years. His most recent novel, *Push Comes to Shove* (2011), focuses on an African American activist group in the late 1960s that is targeted by the U.S. government. Briefly a member of the Black Panther Party, Brown went to federal prison for eighteen months for resisting the draft.

Stephen Bull (born 1941) was special assistant to the president and appointments secretary under President Nixon. Bull later worked for the Commission on the Review of the National Policy toward Gambling, Philip Morris Company, and the United States Olympic Committee, and was a member of the Salvation Army's board of advisors.

Jack Cipperly (born 1927) is emeritus assistant dean in the College of Letters at the University of Wisconsin–Madison, where he worked from 1967 to 1997. Cipperly served in the Marine Corps and then enrolled at the University of Wisconsin on the GI Bill. He stayed on for his master's and PhD degrees.

Peter Coyote (born 1941) (né Robert Peter Cohon) is an award-winning actor, author, film director, screenwriter, and film narrator. Coyote has appeared in more than one hundred films, including *E.T. the Extra-Terrestrial, Patch Adams,* and *Erin Brockovich,* and he has narrated 165 documentaries. He was a prominent member of the San Francisco counterculture community from 1967 to 1975, during which he and others started the Diggers, an anarchist improv group that supplied free food, housing, and medical aid to hippies living in Haight-Ashbury. The Diggers evolved into the "Free Family," which founded chains of communes around the Pacific Northwest and Southwest. Coyote describes his sixties exploits in his memoir, *Sleeping Where I Fall* (1998).

Bernardine Dohrn (born 1942) is a founding member, leader, and chief spokesperson of the radical Weathermen group. Dohrn lived underground as a fugitive from 1970 to 1980, where she raised two sons with her husband, Weather Underground member Bill Ayers. Dohrn and Ayers turned themselves in to authorities in Chicago in 1980. Although she was one of the most wanted fugitives of the sixties, a judge gave Dohrn three years of probation and a $1,500 fine because FBI evidence against her was illegally obtained. Dohrn, who graduated from the University of Chicago Law School in 1967, is a retired clinical associate professor of law at Northwestern University School of Law's Children and Family Justice Center. The founder and former director of the center, Dohrn worked for twenty years as an advocate for fair sentencing for children, and ending over-incarceration of children of color.

William "Bill" Dyson, Jr. (born 1941), served as an FBI special agent in the Chicago bureau from 1967 to 1998. Two years after joining the bureau, Dyson was assigned to surveillance of the Students for a Democratic Society. He watched as the student group evolved into the militant Weathermen in June 1969. Dyson became a bomb expert and chief case agent investigating the Weather Underground until the group disbanded in 1976. He was a senior counterterrorism specialist and supervisor of Chicago's Terrorism Task Force for fourteen years.

Daniel Ellsberg (born 1931) is an antiwar activist and a former marine, academic, strategic analyst for the RAND Corporation, and consultant to the White House and Defense Department. The Harvard-educated Ellsberg joined the Defense Department in 1964 and worked on plans to escalate the war in Vietnam. While stationed in Saigon from 1965 to 1967, he began to understand that the war was unwinnable. In 1967 Ellsberg contributed to a top-secret study on the United States military's conduct in Vietnam from 1945 to 1967. The study later became known as the Pentagon Papers, which Ellsberg leaked to *The New York Times, The Washington Post,* and seventeen other newspapers in 1971. Ellsberg was charged with twelve federal felony counts, which could have meant a 115-year prison sentence. The charges were dropped in 1973 because of criminal misconduct by the White House Plumbers against Ellsberg. Ellsberg is now an outspoken activist on the dangers of nuclear war and the importance of whistle-blowers. He is author of three books, including *Secrets: A Memoir of Vietnam and the Pentagon Papers* (2002).

Tod Ensign (1940–2014) was an author, veterans' rights lawyer, and director of Citizen Soldier, a nonprofit GI and veterans rights advocacy organization. Ensign cofounded in 1970 the Citizens' Commission of Inquiry, which publicized war crimes and other atrocities in Vietnam. In 1970, CCI held Citizens' Commissions in cities all over the country where Vietnam vets described the atrocities they either witnessed or committed themselves during battle. In later years Ensign worked on a wide range of legal cases, and was the first public advocate for veterans exposed to toxic levels of Agent Orange herbicide.

David Fenton (born 1953) is a public relations executive, political activist, and photojournalist. At age seventeen Fenton dropped out of high school to photograph the antiwar and counterculture movements for Liberation News Service. He photographed most of the major demonstrations, trials, and concerts of the late 1960s and early 1970s. He developed a reputation as one of the movement's principal and most trusted photographers. In 1972 Fenton published a book of his photographs, *Shots: Photographs from the Underground Press.* He is the founder and CEO of Fenton Communications, a progressive public relations firm focused on the environment, public health, and human rights.

John Filo (born 1948) is a photojournalist whose iconic photo of Mary Ann Vecchio kneeling over the body of twenty-year-old student Jeffrey Miller at Kent State University on May 4, 1970, won the Pulitzer Prize. At the time Filo was a photojournalism student at the university. Since then he has worked for an array of news organizations, including the Associated Press, *Philadelphia Inquirer,* Baltimore *Evening Sun,* and *Newsweek.* Filo is currently director of photography at CBS.

Brian Flanagan (born 1946) is a pool shark, former bar owner, and *Jeopardy!* champion. As a student at Columbia University he was one of the leaders in the

1968 student revolt and later became a prominent member of the Weathermen. Flanagan was arrested during the Days of Rage protest in October 1965 and accused of breaking the neck of Richard Elrod, a Chicago prosecutor who was paralyzed after a scuffle with Flanagan. Flanagan was acquitted in 1970 and eventually joined the Prairie Fire Organizing Committee, the aboveground wing of the Weather Underground. He now runs a wine consulting business in New York City.

Jane Fonda (born 1937), a celebrated actor, antiwar activist, and feminist, was an early supporter of GIs and Vietnam vets, and worked for the antiwar movement as an organizer, spokeswoman, and fundraiser. She was vilified for allowing herself to be photographed on an anti-aircraft gun while visiting Hanoi in 1972. Fonda was followed and harassed by the FBI for years and her file was twenty-two thousand pages long. Fonda won an Academy Award for best actress in *Klute* (1971) and *Coming Home* (1978), and was nominated for five others.

Robert "Bob" Giles (born 1933) is a journalist, editor, and author. Giles spent more than forty years in the newspaper business. He was managing editor of the *Akron Beacon Journal* at the time of the Kent State University shootings in 1970. The paper won a Pulitzer Prize for its coverage of the shootings. While he was editor of *The Detroit News,* Giles directed Pulitzer Prize–winning coverage of a 1994 scandal in the Michigan House Fiscal Agency. He served as curator of the Nieman Foundation for Journalism at Harvard University from 2000 to 2011.

Emily Goodman (born 1941) is a retired New York Supreme Court justice. She rose to prominence as an activist feminist lawyer, working for abortion rights and representing only women in divorce cases.

Peter Greenberg (born 1950) is an author, editor, producer, and a multiple-Emmy-winning broadcast journalist. He is also the travel editor for CBS News. As a student at the University of Wisconsin–Madison, Greenberg covered campus unrest in 1969 and 1970 for the student newspaper, *The Daily Cardinal,* and for *Newsweek.* His most recent book is *The Best Places for Everything: The Ultimate Insider's Guide to the Greatest Experiences Around the World* (2012).

Morton Halperin (born 1938) is an expert on foreign policy and civil liberties. Halperin served as the deputy assistant secretary of defense under President Lyndon B. Johnson, and senior staff member of the National Security Council under President Richard Nixon. He became disillusioned with the war and resigned in September 1969. Halperin's phone was wiretapped by the FBI from May 1969 to February 1971. He later served in the Clinton administration as director of the Policy Planning Staff at the Department of State (1998–2001), special assistant to the president, and senior director for democracy at the National Security Council (1994–96). Halperin also served as consultant to the secretary of defense and the undersecretary of defense for policy (1993). He is a senior advisor at the Open Society Foundation.

David Harris (born 1946) is a journalist and author. As a student at Stanford in the mid-1960s, Harris became involved with the civil rights movement, and later the antiwar movement. In 1967 he founded the Resistance, an organization and widespread movement that promoted draft resistance. Harris was arrested in July 1969 for draft evasion and served fifteen months in prison. At the time, he was married to the folksinger and civil rights and peace activist Joan Baez, who told the story of his arrest during her Woodstock festival performance. He is a former contributing editor at *The New York Times Magazine* and *Rolling Stone* as well as the author of ten nonfiction books and one novel.

John Hartmann (born 1940) is a veteran music agent, manager, and record executive who represented some of the greatest artists and bands of the 1960s and '70s, including Buffalo Springfield, Neil Young, Joni Mitchell, the Eagles, Peter, Paul & Mary, Crosby, Stills & Nash, and Jackson Browne. Hartmann teaches music management at UCLA Extension and a weekly yoga class.

David Hawk (born 1943) is an international human rights expert. As a Cornell student in the 1960s, he worked on voter registration campaigns, community organizing, and civil rights efforts in Mississippi and Georgia. Hawk worked as an advance man on Eugene McCarthy's presidential campaign in 1968, and was a cofounder of the Vietnam Moratorium Committee. Hawk served as executive director of Amnesty International from 1974 to 1978 and director of the Cambodia office of the UN High Commissioner for Human Rights. He has documented the genocides in Cambodia and Rwanda, worked to eradicate land mines in Vietnam, and written about political prison camps in North Korea.

Tom Hayden (born 1939) was a leading organizer, spokesman, and visionary of the sixties peace movement. While a student at the University of Michigan and civil rights activist, Hayden cofounded Students for a Democratic Society (SDS) in 1960 and wrote the first draft of its manifesto, the Port Huron Statement, in 1962, which became the blueprint for the New Left. During the rest of the decade, he visited North Vietnam, organized teach-ins against the war, and spoke at antiwar protests, including the one at the Chicago Democratic convention in 1968 for which he was later tried with seven others on conspiracy charges and acquitted. In 1982, Hayden was elected to the California state assembly. He represented Santa Monica for eighteen years in the California State Assembly and Senate. A prolific writer, lecturer, blogger, and social justice and peace activist, Hayden has written twenty books, most recently *Inspiring Participatory Democracy: Student Movements from Port Huron to Today* (2012). Hayden was married to Jane Fonda from 1973 to 1990. His FBI file is twenty thousand pages long.

Gray Henry (born 1943) is a writer, film producer, and professor of world religions and art history. Henry's company Fons Vitae publishes the work of Catholic mystic and pacifist Thomas Merton. She graduated from Sarah Lawrence College in 1965 and afterward worked as a filmmaker in New York City, where she became friends with Timothy Leary. Henry lives in Louisville, Kentucky, and devotes her life to promoting interfaith peace and fellowship.

Jeffrey Henson Scales (born 1954) is a photographer and photo editor at *The New York Times*. Born in San Francisco, Henson Scales at the age of thirteen began taking pictures of the Black Panthers with a 35mm Leica his father had given him. His photographs of Stokely Carmichael, Eldridge Cleaver, Bobby Seale, and other activists appeared regularly in *The Black Panther* newspaper. Scales's photos can be found in the permanent collections of the Museum of Modern Art in New York, the Baltimore Museum of Art, the Museum of the City of New York, and many other institutions.

Seymour Hersh (born 1937) is considered by many to be the dean of American investigative journalism. He is a regular contributor to *The New Yorker* on military and security issues. In November 1969, as a young freelancer, Hersh broke the My Lai massacre story, which earned him a Pulitzer Prize for International Reporting. Hersh has also won two National Magazine Awards, five Polk Awards, and a National Book Critics Circle Award, among others. He is author of nine books, most recently *Chain of Command: The Road from 9/11 to Abu Ghraib* (2004).

Ericka Huggins (born 1951) is an African American activist, educator, writer, poet, and former member of the Black Panther Party. In 1969, at age eighteen, Huggins joined the party with her husband, John, in Los Angeles. John was murdered in January 1969 by members of the rival black nationalist organization United Slaves on the campus of the University of California, Los Angeles. Ericka Huggins returned east with her three-month-old daughter, where she founded the New Haven, Connecticut, chapter of the Black Panther Party. She was arrested in New Haven in May 1969, along with other party members, and charged with conspiracy to murder Alex Rackley, who was suspected by the Panthers of disloyalty. Huggins went on trial alongside party founder Bobby Seale, and the judge dismissed the charges after the jury deadlocked. Huggins moved back to California, where she worked as the director of the Oakland Community School and became the first woman and African American to serve on the Alameda County board of education. She's introduced the practice of yoga and meditation to hundreds of prisoners over the years, and currently is a lecturer in women's studies at California State University, East Bay.

Dean Kahler (born 1950) was a freshman at Kent State University when he was shot by the Ohio National Guard on May 4, 1970. Of the nine students wounded that day, Kahler sustained the most severe injuries and was permanently paralyzed from the waist down. After the shooting, he returned to Kent State and earned a degree in education in 1977. Kahler has taught history and worked in several government jobs, including for the Ohio secretary of state, where he helped the state conform to the Americans with Disabilities Act. Kahler served two terms as the Athens County commissioner and is a frequent participant in competitive road races.

Michael Kazin (born 1948) is a professor of history at Georgetown University and co-editor of *Dissent* magazine. He is an expert in nineteenth- and twentieth-century U.S. politics and social movements. As a student at Harvard University in the late 1960s Kazin was a prominent antiwar activist and became cochair of the campus chapter of Students for a Democratic Society. He and others led an occupation of University Hall, nonviolently expelling university administrators on April 9, 1969. Kazin was briefly a member of the radical antiwar group the Weathermen. He is author of five books, most recently *American Dreamers: How the Left Changed a Nation* (2011).

Randy Kehler (born 1944) is a social justice, peace, and environmental advocate. During the Vietnam War he served a twenty-two-month prison sentence for resisting the draft. As a member of the Resistance and an outspoken advocate against the war, Kehler inspired Daniel Ellsberg to leak the Pentagon Papers to the press. Kehler was coordinator of the successful Safe & Green Campaign to shut down the Vermont Yankee nuclear power plant.

Michael Kennedy (1938–2016) was one of a handful of "radical" criminal defense lawyers who roamed the country representing their clients in court, trying to keep them out of jail, and serving as the behind-the-scenes backbone of the movement. Kennedy represented Timothy Leary, members of the Brotherhood of Eternal Love, members of the Weather Underground, Huey Newton and other Black Panthers, many draft dodgers and resisters, and a slew of other sixties activists who ran into trouble with the law. For the rest of his life, Kennedy remained a prominent New York trial lawyer with a colorful and often famous list of clients. He also served as general counsel and co-owner of *High Times* magazine for forty-one years and was an outspoken advocate for marijuana legalization.

Laurel Krause (born 1955) is a writer, environmental activist, and cofounder of the Kent State Truth Tribunal. She is currently forming the Allison Center for Peace. Her sister, Allison Krause, age nineteen, was killed in the May 4, 1970, shootings at Kent State University.

Egil "Bud" Krogh (born 1939) is a lawyer, a former Nixon administration official, and one of the most prominent defendants in the Watergate scandal. From 1970 to 1972, Krogh was White House deputy for domestic affairs, and his duties included codirecting the Special Investigations Unit, eventually known as the "Plumbers." Krogh approved a covert operation to burglarize Daniel Ellsberg's psychiatrist's office. He later pleaded guilty to conspiracy and served four and a half months in prison. Krogh is currently a senior fellow on Ethics and Leadership at the Center for the Study of the Presidency and Congress, and counselor to the director at the School for Ethics and Global Leadership.

Anthony "Tony" Lake (born 1939) is a foreign policy expert who served as a Foreign Service officer in the U.S. State Department from 1962 to 1970. Lake resigned from his position as special assistant to National Security Advisor Henry Kissinger in May 1970 because of his opposition to the invasion of Cambodia. He served as national security advisor for President Clinton from 1993 to 1997 and is currently the executive director of the United Nations Children's Fund (UNICEF). Lake has written and edited eight books, including *Legacy of Vietnam: The War, American Society, and the Future of U.S. Foreign Policy* (1976, contributing editor).

Gerald Lefcourt (born 1941) is a prominent New York–based criminal defense lawyer with a long history of representing activists. Soon after graduating from Brooklyn Law School, Lefcourt represented Mark Rudd, the Black Panthers' New York chapter, and Abbie Hoffman. He was lead defense lawyer for the Panther 21 during their 1969 conspiracy trial. Hoffman, who remained a lifelong client, inscribed his 1971 manual for revolutionary living, *Steal This Book*, to Lefcourt, with these words: "Dedicated to Jerry Lefcourt Lawyer and Brother."

Julius Lester (born 1939) is a professor, writer of fiction and nonfiction, poet, political commentator, musician, folklorist, photographer, and former civil rights activist. He is a professor emeritus at the University of Massachusetts, Amherst, where he taught for thirty-three years. Lester joined the Student Nonviolent Coordinating Committee in the mid-1960s as the head of the committee's photography department. In 1968 he published his first book, *Look Out, Whitey! Black Power's Gon' Get Your Mama!*, which was followed in 1969 by *Revolutionary Notes* and *Search for the New Land: History as Subjective Experience*. All three books chronicle the events, emotions, and hopes of the 1960s with grace and rage. Lester went on to write more than forty books, many for children, and win dozens of awards, including the Newbery Medal.

Joe Lewis (born 1951) was shot twice as a student at Kent State—once in the abdomen and once in the lower left leg—by members of the Ohio National Guard on May 4, 1970. Today Lewis is a public employee in Scappoose, Oregon. He travels to high schools, colleges, and universities around the country to speak about the shootings at Kent State and the Vietnam peace movement.

Greil Marcus (born 1945) is one of the country's most respected and prolific music and cultural critics. A San Francisco native and graduate of the University of California, Berkeley, Marcus got his start writing music reviews for *Rolling Stone* in the 1960s. His insightful, highbrow writing can be found in innumerable articles and reviews and more than twenty books, including *Mystery Train* (1975) and his most recent, *The History of Rock 'n' Roll in Ten Songs* (2014).

Tom McCarthy (born 1930) was detective supervisor for the city of Madison, Wisconsin, police force, where he worked from 1953 to 1986. McCarthy is not shy about admitting his animosity for the student protesters in Madison: "They hated me and I hated them."

Country Joe McDonald (born 1942) (né Joseph Allen McDonald) is a rock musician who was the lead singer of the Berkeley-based Country Joe and the Fish. The band's most popular song, "I-Feel-Like-I'm-Fixin'-to-Die Rag" (1965), became an anthem of the antiwar movement. McDonald has recorded thirty-three albums, most recently *Time Flies By* (2012).

Phyllis Menken (born 1951) is a lawyer who lives in Boston. She lived in political asylum for American draft resisters and military deserters in Sweden with her boyfriend from 1970 to 1972.

Ralph Metzner (born 1936) is an academic, psychologist, and writer. In the early 1960s, as a graduate student at Harvard University, Metzner conducted research on LSD with Timothy Leary and Richard Alpert (later Ram Dass). Their research is widely credited with introducing psychedelic drugs to the American counterculture. Metzner is cofounder and president of the Green Earth Foundation, an educational nonprofit "dedicated to the healing and harmonizing of the relationships between humanity and the Earth."

David Mixner (born 1946) is a civil rights activist, political strategist, and author. In 1969 he founded the Vietnam Moratorium Committee with Sam Brown, David Hawk, and Marge Sklencar, and the group successfully organized the largest antiwar protest in American history on October 15, 1969. Later in his career as an LGBT and human rights activist, *Newsweek* named Mixner "the most powerful gay man in America." He has worked as a strategist and fundraiser on seventy-five Democratic political campaigns, is an active writer and blogger, and wrote the acclaimed memoir *Stranger Among Friends* (1997).

Richard Moose (1932–2015) was a military and foreign policy expert who worked on the National Security Council as staff secretary under Presidents Johnson and Nixon. From 1970 to 1975, as a staff member on the Senate Foreign Relations Committee chaired by J. William Fulbright, Moose specialized in the war in Southeast Asia. Moose later served as assistant secretary of state for African affairs under President Jimmy Carter and undersecretary of state for management under President Bill Clinton.

Robin Morgan (born 1941) is a poet, author, academic, feminist activist, and journalist. She is recognized as a founder of contemporary "second wave" feminism. Morgan helped start New York Radical Women and Women's International Terrorist Conspiracy from Hell (W.I.T.C.H.) in the late 1960s. From 1990 to 1994 Morgan was editor in chief of *Ms.* magazine. She has published more than twenty books, including the acclaimed anthologies *Sisterhood Is Powerful* (1970), *Sisterhood Is Global* (1984), and *Sisterhood Is Forever: The Women's Anthology for a New Millennium* (2003). She is founder and president of the Sisterhood Is Global Institute, and cofounder (with Gloria Steinem and Jane Fonda) of the Women's Media Center.

Roger Morris (born 1937) is a foreign policy expert, investigative journalist, and author. Morris served on the National Security Council under Presidents Johnson and Nixon. In 1970 he resigned from the NSC because he opposed the U.S. invasion of Cambodia. Morris went on to work as a legislative advisor to Senator George McGovern and a director of policy studies at the Carnegie Endowment for International Peace. He has written books about Richard Nixon, Henry Kissinger, Alexander Haig, and the Clintons. His 1990 biography, *Richard Milhous Nixon: The Rise of an American Politician* (1989), won the National Book Award Silver Medal.

Lauree Moss (born 1946) is a life coach, teacher of body psychotherapy, and former professor of psychology and somatic therapy at Antioch University in San Francisco. On May 9, 1970, she attended a pre-demonstration gathering at the Lincoln Memorial in Washington, D.C., when President Nixon made an unexpected visit at dawn. A photograph of Nixon talking with Moss that morning was widely published and has gained iconic status.

Bobby Muller (born 1946) is one of America's most well-known advocates for Vietnam veterans. Muller enlisted in 1967 and served as a lieutenant in Vietnam. He was wounded in combat in April 1969 and paralyzed from the chest down. The neglect and inadequate care that Muller experienced at a veterans hospital when he came home motivated him to spend the rest of his career fighting for veterans' rights. Muller is former president of the Vietnam Veterans of America Foundation, which he founded in 1980. In 1981 he led the first American delegation of veterans back to Vietnam and successfully lobbied Congress for legislation compensating vets for Vietnam-related illnesses such as PTSD and Agent Orange poisoning. Muller also cofounded the International Campaign to Ban Landmines, which won a Nobel Peace Prize in 1997 for its work in Cambodia.

John Murtagh, Jr. (born 1960), is a litigation and government affairs attorney and former Yonkers, New York, council member. In February 1970, when Murtagh was nine years old, the Weathermen bombed his family's home because his father, Judge John Murtagh, Sr., was presiding over the Black Panther 21 trial.

Ben Post (born 1945) was a journalism student at Kent State University and a reporter for the *Record-Courier* when he witnessed and wrote about the May 4, 1970, shootings. Post arrived at Kent State as a student after serving three years in the army, stationed in Germany. After the shootings, he worked as a researcher for James A. Michener on his book *Kent State: What Happened and Why* (1971). He is the former managing editor of the Louisville *Courier-Journal*.

Raymond "Ray" Price, Jr. (born 1930), was the chief speechwriter for President Richard Nixon. He later wrote a memoir *With Nixon* (1977) and assisted Nixon in writing several of his books. From 1957 to 1964 Price served on the editorial staff of the *New York Herald Tribune* and was editorial page editor from 1964 to 1966.

Carol Griggs Randall (born 1945) was a charismatic fixture in mid-to-late-1960s California counterculture. Active in the effort to turn on the world and achieve universal peace, Randall joined her husband, John Griggs, and his friend Michael Randall and others in forming the Brotherhood of Eternal Love. Griggs died in 1969 from a psilocybin overdose, and Carol married Randall in 1970. A poet, Carol founded Mystic Artists, a loosely organized group of visionaries who gathered and exhibited at Mystic Arts World, the Laguna Beach shop that served as the hub of psychedelic culture from 1967 to 1970. Today the woman known as the Godmother of the Brotherhood of Eternal Love works with her husband, Michael, at their custom jewelry store in Marin County, California.

Michael Randall (born 1943) was a founding member of the Brotherhood of Eternal Love, a secretive group of surfer drug dealers from Laguna, California, who have been called the "hippie mafia." They started out importing marijuana from Mexico inside surfboards, and grew into an international drug cartel that imported thousands of pounds of hashish to America from Afghanistan, India, and other countries and manufactured, sold, and gave away its own potent brand of LSD, Orange Sunshine. The late-sixties effort was part of a master plan to "turn on the world" and start a "psychedelic revolution." After living as a fugitive for twelve years and serving a five-year prison sentence, Randall is now a jeweler and lives with his wife, Carol, in Marin County, California.

Richard Reeves (born 1936) is a veteran political journalist, author, and syndicated columnist. His long and varied career spanned from chief political correspondent for *The New York Times,* to chief correspondent for PBS *Frontline,* to national editor and columnist for *Esquire.* He wrote a syndicated column for thirty-five years and published fifteen books, including an acclaimed biography of Nixon, *President Nixon: Alone in the White House* (2001). He is currently a senior lecturer at the Annenberg School for Communication at the University of Southern California.

Steven Reiner (born 1949) was editor in chief of the University of Wisconsin–Madison campus newspaper, *The Daily Cardinal,* in the late 1960s. Reiner is director of broadcast and digital journalism at Stony Brook University in New York. He is a multiple-Emmy-winning journalist, editor, and producer. He has worked at NBC, ABC, NPR, and as a producer for CBS's *60 Minutes.*

Barry Romo (born 1947) is a Vietnam veteran and peace activist. Romo enlisted in the army and served as a platoon leader at the age of nineteen in the 196th Light Infantry Brigade and American Division in 1967–68. He was awarded a Bronze Star for saving wounded men under his command during an attack by enemy fire. In 1968 he was discharged from the army, and in 1970 he became the national coordinator for Vietnam Veterans Against the War. Currently Romo is the leader of the Chicago chapter of VVAW.

Vivian Rothstein (born 1946), a feminist and social justice and peace activist, started out as a community organizer in the Mississippi Freedom Summer project of 1965. An active member of SDS, Rothstein traveled to North Vietnam in 1967 with six other peace activists and in 1968 helped organize the Jeannette Rankin Brigade—the first national women's march against the war. She is currently the director of special projects at LAANE, a social and economic justice advocacy nonprofit in Los Angeles.

Mark Rudd (born 1947) was chairman of the Columbia University SDS chapter in 1968, during the student rebellion, and the organization's national secretary in 1969. Rudd is one of the founders of the Weathermen, the militant faction of SDS. Wanted on federal charges for bombing and conspiracy, he lived as a fugitive from 1970 to 1977. When he surrendered to authorities, all charges against him were dropped because of FBI illegalities. Rudd taught mathematics at Central New Mexico Community College in Albuquerque for twenty-six years. He has published two memoirs, *Truth and Consequences: The Education of Mark Rudd* (1990) and *Underground: My Life with the SDS and the Weathermen* (2009). Rudd remains a political organizer and an environmental and peace activist.

Thelma Schoonmaker (born 1940) is a three-time Oscar-winning film editor who has worked with director Martin Scorsese on all of his films for more than forty years. Her work as editor and assistant director on Michael Wadleigh's *Woodstock* documentary is credited with helping popularize documentary film, and solidified the legacy of the storied festival.

Wayne Smith (born 1951) is a Vietnam veteran who joined the army in 1968 and became a combat medic. Wayne earned a BA in psychology after returning from Vietnam and has spent the rest of his career helping veterans heal the wounds caused by war. Smith worked with Bobby Muller at the Vietnam Veterans of America Foundation and is a co-recipient of the 1997 Nobel Peace Prize for the organization's work to ban land mines. In 1998, Smith bicycled 1,200 miles across Vietnam with twenty American veterans to promote peace and reconciliation.

Paul Soglin (born 1945) was active in the civil rights and antiwar movements as a student at the University of Wisconsin–Madison. In 1962 Soglin was elected treasurer of the university's chapter of the Student Nonviolent Coordinating Committee, SNCC. He has been mayor of Madison three times. He was first elected at the age of twenty-eight, in 1973, and served until 1979. He was then reelected and served from 1989 to 1997. Soglin loved the job so much that he ran again for mayor in 2011 and won.

Rena Steinzor (born 1949) was the first female editor in chief of University of Wisconsin–Madison's *Daily Cardinal* in 1970–71. Steinzor is a professor at the University of Maryland School of Law, specializing in environmental law, and she is the president of the Center for Progressive Reform. Her most recent book, *Why Not Jail?* (2014), argues for tougher treatment for corporate crime.

Stephen Stills (born 1945) was a member of the Reserve Officer Training Corps during his high school years, but feigned insanity to avoid the Vietnam War draft. The singer, songwriter, and virtuoso guitar player is probably best known for his work with the bands Buffalo Springfield and Crosby, Stills & Nash. His songs "For What It's Worth" and "Love the One You're With" are both iconic sixties anthems.

Oliver Stone (born 1946) is an Oscar-winning filmmaker and Vietnam veteran. Stone served in the army in Vietnam from 1967 to 1968; he was wounded twice and earned a Bronze Star and a Purple Heart. Soon after coming home, Stone studied film under Martin Scorsese at New York University. Stone is credited with writing or directing more than twenty feature-length films. He is known for portraying critical or alternative narratives of recent American history, including *Platoon* (1986), the first of the Vietnam trilogy; *Born on the Fourth of July* (1989); *JFK* (1991); *Natural Born Killers* (1994); *Heaven and Earth* (1993); *Nixon* (1995); and *Snowden* (2015).

Margery Tabankin (born 1948) was deeply involved in antiwar and civil rights activities as a student at the University of Wisconsin–Madison from 1965 to 1969. She joined SDS and later became the first woman president of the National Student Association. Tabankin is a peace and social justice activist who has spent most of her career helping wealthy individuals implement their philanthropic and political giving. She is the former executive director of the Hollywood Women's Political Committee and serves on the board of the Streisand Foundation and People for the American Way.

Alison Teal (born 1945), after graduating from Smith College, worked for antiwar causes, among them Eugene McCarthy's 1968 presidential campaign (where she met her husband Sam Brown) and the Moratorium Committee. Teal is a journalist, blogger, photojournalist, and political activist. In 1970 she worked as a young aide to New York City mayor John Lindsay. During the Carter administration, she served as a special assistant to health, education, and welfare secretary Patricia Harris, and to health and human services secretary Donna Shalala during the Clinton administration.

Michael Uhl (born 1944) is a Vietnam veteran, peace activist, and independent scholar. He served as a first lieutenant in Vietnam in 1968–69. When he came home, he entered New York University as a PhD candidate in linguistics. As a member of the Citizens' Commission of Inquiry on U.S. War Crimes in Vietnam (CCI), Uhl played a key role in organizing the National Veterans Inquiry and the Winter Soldier Investigations. In 1970 he testified at the International Enquiry on U.S. War Crimes, held in Stockholm, Sweden. Uhl currently serves on the board of directors of Veterans for Peace. His writing has appeared in *The Nation,* the *Boston Sunday Globe, Forbes,* and *In These Times.* He wrote a memoir about his experience during and after the war: *Vietnam Awakening: My Journey from Combat to the Citizens' Commission of Inquiry on U.S. War Crimes in Vietnam* (2007).

Steve Wasserman (born 1952) was a peace activist in high school and college in Berkeley, California. He is the publisher and executive editor of Heyday, and the former executive editor at large for Yale University Press and editor of the *Los Angeles Times Book Review* and New Republic Books. Wasserman writes about literature and politics for a variety of publications; he has served as editorial director of Times Books and publisher of Hill & Wang, and is a past partner at the Kneerim & Williams Literary Agency.

Susan Werbe (born 1946) became involved in antiwar activism in college at the University of California, Berkeley. In 1969 Werbe joined the Moratorium Committee and ran its speakers bureau for the October 15 and November 15, 1969, moratoriums. She is an award-winning television producer and has received two Primetime Emmy Awards. Werbe also won a Peabody Award in 2005 for *Voices of Civil Rights*. Currently, she is executive producer, programming, for the History Channel.

Cathy Wilkerson (born 1945) was active in the civil rights movement, SDS, and the Weathermen. After graduating from Swarthmore College in 1966, Wilkerson worked for SDS in Chicago and Washington, D.C. She was editor of *New Left Notes* and elected to the SDS National Interim Council. Wilkerson's father, James, was an advertising executive who owned the Greenwich Village townhouse where Weathermen members accidentally exploded a bomb, killing three Weathermen members and destroying the house, on March 6, 1970. After the explosion, Wilkerson, who was in the house at the time and survived the blast, became a fugitive and studied how to make explosives, working closely with the Weather Underground's chief bomb maker, Ron Fliegelman (the father of her child).* In 1980 Wilkerson turned herself in to authorities and pled guilty to charges of unlawful possession of dynamite; she served eleven months in the Bedford Hills Correctional Center. She later earned a master's degree in mathematics education and spent twenty years teaching math to high school and adult education students in Brooklyn, New York.

Howard Wolf (born 1938) is a concert producer, promoter, and talent buyer. During the 1960s and 1970s, Wolf worked with prominent artists such as the Grateful Dead, Jefferson Airplane, the Doors, Cream, and Jimi Hendrix, and produced up to forty concerts a year. He teaches courses about the concert touring business at UCLA Extension.

---

* Burrough, *Days of Rage*, p. 126.

ACKNOWLEDGMENTS

Born in 1946, a birth year that thrust her into the cultural and political crosshairs of change and rebellion, the youngest of my father's four siblings, Eleanor Bingham, embraced her baby boomer birthright to the fullest. A hippie extraordinaire, Eleanor was, among other things, a seamstress on Carnaby Street, where she tailored Mick Jagger's pants, and a videographer for the Grateful Dead and TVTV. She counted among her friends legends like Bear Owsley and Abbie Hoffman. As a child, I worshipped Eleanor for her charisma, far-out clothing, and big-hearted free spirit. I still do. In many ways, she is the reason why I decided to embark on this book project.

If Eleanor is the godmother of *Witness to the Revolution,* Hamilton Fish V is its godfather. In June 2011, when *Witness* was just a germ of an idea, we had our first meeting to discuss the book, and Ham continued to give me regular advice over the next four years. Ham, who knows everyone and everything about the sixties, picked up the phone many times on my behalf, and guided me through the thickets of sixties culture and politics.

Jon Meacham and I conceived of this book together over several lunches at various Manhattan diners. He is a font of original ideas, an editing wizard with an encyclopedic knowledge of history, and an invaluable resource. I couldn't have asked for a more brilliant editor and friend. My agent, Esther Newberg, who was Congresswoman Bella Abzug's chief of staff in 1971, knows this era cold. I am so lucky to have her by my side as the book's protector and champion.

Terry McDonald, Jennifer Maguire, Ham Fish, Ellen McGrath, and Tao Ruspoli took the time to read an early draft of *Witness,* and their astute suggestions helped to greatly improve the final product. I relied on

Timothy Rockwood's eagle eye for detail, as he became the book's unofficial copy editor.

To the one hundred people who gave me many hours of their precious time and trusted me with their life stories, I am very grateful. Even though, in the end, not everyone I interviewed appeared in the book, they all played an important role in informing *Witness*.

Finding the right people in the movement to interview required leaning on a lot of friends for help. I owe so much to the generosity of the late Michael Kennedy and his wife, Eleanora, the high priest and priestess of the radical sixties, who introduced me to some of their media-shy friends and former legal clients in the Weather Underground and the Brotherhood of Eternal Love.

Many friends opened doors and made introductions on my behalf. I am in debt to Tao Ruspoli, Peter Greenberg, Sallie Bingham, Peter Emerson, Evan Thomas, Elsa and Bob Woodward, Mark Danner, Steve Wasserman, the late Peter Kaplan, Patricia Bosworth, Gray Henry, Jean Stein, Courtenay Valenti, Steve Atlas, Keith Runyon, Julie Anderson, Stanley Nelson, Jeffrey Eugenides, Molly Bingham, Steve Connors, Charles Kaiser, Sam Brumbaugh, Holly Dando, Michael Uhl, Jonathan Alter, and I'm sure I'm forgetting many more. Tad Flynn and Annie Stackhouse Browning kindly acted as my personal music consultants.

I relied heavily on the moral support and advice of a group of people I am lucky enough to call my close friends: Jennifer Maguire, Cary Netchvolodoff, Stephanie Cabot, Emily Bingham, Natalie Williams, Mary Zients, Courtenay Valenti, Carolyn Strauss, Claudia Silver, Electra Toub, Virginia Moseley, Martha Sherrill, Perri Peltz, Ariadne Calvo-Platero, Aleksandra Crapanzano, John Burnham Schwartz, Mary Beth Harvey, Bill Haney, Keith Meacham, Bill O'Farrell, Laura and Bob Peabody, Katty Kay, Tom Carver, Libby Cameron, Nan Hudson, Matt Arnold, Chris Isham, Jeffrey Zients, Hugo Williams, Tom Nides, Marcus Lovell Smith, Nadia Sopher, Eugenie Voorhees, Liz Massie, Karin Day, Laura Yorke, Michael Kafka, Sarah Slusser, George and Leslie Biddle, Margaret and Tom Rietano, Mahnaz Ispahani Bartos, Josh Steiner, Jacob Weisberg, Jake Siewart, Paula Zakaria, Stephen Warnke, Helen Ward, Wally Obermeyer, Donna Wick, Peter Soros, Jessica Guff, Beth and Ron Dozoretz,

Bill Powers, Chris Harvey, Jeffrey Leeds, Adam and Kate Platt, Mario Calvo-Platero, Sarah Chace, Holly Peterson, Stephen and Cathy Graham, and Tony and Shelly Malkin.

I am immensely grateful to Tracy Kolker for her friendship and for keeping my life on track, and to Ellen McGrath for keeping me sane.

I regularly relied on the technical expertise of Elba Furlonge, Freddie Isozaki, Jamie Michaelis, and Emily Dietrich. Patrick Emond, Benjamin Hilton, Lauren Hinkle and their colleagues at the Audio Transcription Center in Boston provided accurate and swift transcripts of hundreds of hours of interviews, as did Anna Wainwright and Yoshi Salaverry.

Several able researchers helped me over the years, beginning with Sam Dresser, Matthew Teti, Jonah Furman, and Robert Nedelkoff, an expert on all things Nixon. The talented and tenacious Maura Ewing gave more than a year of hard and thoughtful work to the book. Alexandra Styron and Gabriel Packard at the Hunter College MFA Creative Writing program sent me a Hertog research fellow who helped me bring *Witness* over the finish line. I am in debt to Peter Schmader (born 1951) for his big-hearted support, dedication, and remarkable ability to track down every answer to the barrage of questions I sent his way. A hearty thanks to Jack Bales for his meticulous work on the reading and watch lists.

I couldn't have asked for a better publishing team at Random House, guided by the gifted Susan Kamil. The precociously capable Molly Turpin expertly line edited three drafts of the manuscript. Born in 1990, Molly helped make *Witness* not just a better book, but also one that is relevant to her generation. Many thanks to Tom Perry, Melanie DeNardo, Steve Messina, Leigh Marchant, Katie Rice, and Sophie Vershbow for putting their formidable creativity and muscle behind the publication of *Witness*. Expert publicist Emi Battaglia was also a welcome addition to the team.

The archives at the University of Wisconsin, directed by David Null, were particularly helpful for fact checking and photo resources, and I often relied on the collections at the New York Society Library. The library's quiet Hornblower Room became a much-appreciated and productive outpost where I wrote most of *Witness*.

I owe everything to my family, who have patiently cheered me on for so many years. My mother, Joan Bingham (a Eugene McCarthy delegate in '68), is my constant companion, advisor, and role model. I relied heavily and often on my loving cousins Emily Bingham and Stephen Reily and my aunt Eleanor. David Michaelis and Nancy Steiner rewrote the definition of ex-husband and stepmother, as we co-parented our three children together during the crucible of their teenage years. I am so fortunate to be able to rely on them as part of my extended nuclear family.

Joe Finnerty miraculously came into my life in April 2012. We were married two years later, and ever since I have experienced a kind of happiness that I never knew existed. Joe's mother, five siblings, and three amazing children, Katherine, Alice, and Sam, have brought much joy to my family life. I relied on Joe as my first reader and quickly became dependent on his keen editing skills.

My children, Jamie (twenty), Henry (eighteen), and Diana (fifteen), reside deeply at my heart's center. Their humor, adventurousness, curiosity, and charm make me proud to be their mother. Jamie, Henry, and Diana essentially grew up while I wrote this book, and although it was sometimes against their best interest, they gave me the time and space I needed to explore and work. They are the very best of what life has to offer me, and my love for them and Joe has no limits.

PLAYLIST

CHAPTER 14: DECEMBER

"You Can't Always Get What You Want," the Rolling Stones

"Gimme Shelter," the Rolling Stones

"Sympathy for the Devil," the Rolling Stones

"Stand!," Sly and the Family Stone

CHAPTER 15: WAR CRIMES

"Oh! Camil (The Winter Soldier)," Graham Nash

CHAPTER 19: KENT STATE

"For What It's Worth," Buffalo Springfield

"Ohio," Crosby, Stills, Nash & Young

CHAPTER 20: STRIKE

"Jackson-Kent Blues," the Steve Miller Band

CHAPTER 21: UNDERGROUND

"Bad Moon Rising," Creedence Clearwater Revival

"Estimated Prophet," the Grateful Dead

"California," Joni Mitchell

"Maggie's Farm," Bob Dylan

"The Eggplant That Ate Chicago," Dr. West's Medicine Show and
    Junk Band

"Diana," Paul Kantner and Grace Slick

CHAPTER 22: CULTURE WARS

"Going Up the Country," Canned Heat

"Cassidy," "Looks Like Rain," "Mexicali Blues," the Grateful Dead

"Come Together," the Beatles

"Ball and Chain," Janis Joplin

Surrealistic Pillow, Jefferson Airplane

CHAPTER 23: COMING HOME

"Monster," Steppenwolf

"Strange Days," the Doors

WATCH LIST

DOCUMENTARIES

Berkeley in the Sixties. Produced and directed by Mark Kitchell, 1990.

The Black Panthers: Vanguard of the Revolution. Produced by Sam Aleshinloye, Laurens Grant, and Nicole London; directed by Stanley Nelson, 2015.

Carry It On. Produced and directed by James Coyne, Robert C. Jones, and Christopher Knight, 1970.

Chicago 10. Produced by Brett Morgen and Graydon Carter; directed by Brett Morgen, 2008.

Citizen Stan: A Documentary. Produced and directed by Patty Sharaf, 2004.

Commune. Produced and directed by Jonathan Berman, 2005.

Earth Days. Produced and directed by Robert Stone, 2009.

Festival Express. Produced by Gavin Poolman and John Trapman; directed by Bob Smeaton, 2003.

Final 24: Janis Joplin, Her Final Hours. Produced by Katherine Buck and John Vandervelde; directed by Paul Kilback, 2007.

Fog of War: Eleven Lessons from the Life of Robert S. McNamara. Produced and directed by Errol Morris, 2003.

Free Angela and All Political Prisoners. Produced by Carole Lambert, Shola Lynch, Carine Ruszniewski, and Sidra Smith; directed by Shola Lynch, 2012.

Gimme Shelter. Produced by Porter Bibb and Ronald Schneider; directed by David Maysles, Albert Maysles, and Charlotte Zwerin, 1970.

Going Upriver: The Long War of John Kerry. Produced and directed by George Butler, 2004.

Hearts and Minds. Produced by Bert Schneider and Peter Davis; directed by Peter Davis, 1974.

The History of Rock 'n' Roll (ten episodes). Series creator and producer, Jeffrey Peisch; executive producers, Quincy Jones, Robert B. Meyrowitz, David Salzman, and Andrew Solt, 1995.

In the Year of the Pig. Produced by John Attlee, Emile de Antonio, Terry Morrone, and Orville Schell; directed by Emile de Antonio, 1968.

Kissinger. Produced by Melanie Fall; directed by Adrian Pennink, 2011.

Making Sense of the Sixties. A six-hour PBS series directed by David Hoffman, 1991.

The Memory of Justice. Produced by Ana Carrigan, Hamilton Fish, Sanford Lieberson, Max Palevsky, and David Putnam; directed by Marcel Ophüls, 1976.

Millhouse: A White Comedy. Produced by Emile de Antonio and Vincent Hanlon; directed by Emile de Antonio, 1971.

Monterey Pop. Produced by John Phillips and Lou Adler; directed by D. A. Pennebaker, 1968.

The Most Dangerous Man in America: Daniel Ellsberg and the Pentagon Papers. Produced and directed by Judith Ehrlich and Rick Goldsmith, 2009.

Mr. Hoover and I. Produced and directed by Emile de Antonio, 1989.

The Murder of Fred Hampton. Produced by Mike Gray; directed by Howard Alk, 1971.

Ram Dass, Fierce Grace. Produced and directed by Mickey Lemle, 2001.

Rebel with a Cause: Death of a Man, Birth of a Legend. Produced by J. Mervyn Williams and Amanda Rees; edited by John Gillanders, 1999.

Sir! No Sir! Produced, directed, and written by David Zeiger; produced by Evangeline Griego and Aaron Zarrow, 2005.

Stonewall Uprising. Produced by Kate Davis and Mark Samels; directed by Kate Davis and David Heilbroner, 2010.

Tell Them Who You Are. Produced and directed by Mark S. Wexler, 2004.

Two Days in October. Produced and directed by Robert Kenner, 2005.

Underground. Produced by Emile de Antonio and Mary Lampson; directed by Emile de Antonio, Haskell Wexler, and Mary Lampson, 1976.

The U.S. vs. John Lennon. Produced and directed by David Leaf and John Scheinfeld, 2006.

The War at Home. Produced and directed by Barry Alexander Brown and Glenn Silber, 1979.

The Weather Underground. Produced by Sam Green, Carrie Lozano, Bill Siegel, and Marc Smolowitz; directed by Sam Green and Bill Siegel, 2003.

William Kunstler: Disturbing the Universe. Produced by Emily Kunstler, Sarah Kunstler, Jesse Moss, Susan Korda, and Vanessa Hope; directed by Emily Kunstler and Sarah Kunstler, 2009.

Winter Soldier. Produced and directed by Winterfilm, in association with Vietnam Veterans Against the War, 1972.

Woodstock. Produced by Bob Maurice; directed by Michael Wadleigh, 1970.

FEATURE FILMS

Alice's Restaurant. Directed by Arthur Penn, 1969.

Apocalypse Now. Directed by Francis Ford Coppola, 1979.

Bananas. Directed by Woody Allen, 1971.

Bob & Carol & Ted & Alice. Directed by Paul Mazursky, 1969.

Born on the Fourth of July. Directed by Oliver Stone, 1989.

Butch Cassidy and the Sundance Kid. Directed by George Roy Hill, 1969.

Che. Directed by Steven Soderbergh, 2008.

Coming Home. Directed by Hal Ashby, 1978.

Easy Rider. Directed by Dennis Hopper, 1969.

Forrest Gump. Directed by Robert Zemeckis, 1994.

Getting Straight. Directed by Richard Rush, 1970.

The Graduate. Directed by Mike Nichols, 1967.

Heaven and Earth. Directed by Oliver Stone, 1993.

Joe. Directed by John G. Avildsen, 1970.

Klute. Directed by Alan J. Pakula, 1971.

Medium Cool. Directed by Haskell Wexler, 1969.

Nixon. Directed by Oliver Stone, 1995.

The Pentagon Papers. Directed by Rod Holcomb, 2003.

Platoon. Directed by Oliver Stone, 1986.

Psych-Out. Directed by Richard Rush, 1968.

A Small Circle of Friends. Directed by Rob Cohen, 1980.

Sometimes a Great Notion. Directed by Paul Newman, 1971.

Steal This Movie. Directed by Robert Greenwald, 2000.

The Trip. Directed by Roger Corman, 1967.

Wild in the Streets. Directed by Barry Shear, 1968.

Zabriskie Point. Directed by Michelangelo Antonioni, 1970.

READING LIST

Albert, Judith Clavir, and Stewart Edward Albert, eds. *The Sixties Papers: Documents of a Rebellious Decade*. New York: Praeger, 1984.

Alpert, Jane. *Growing Up Underground*. New York: William Morrow, 1981.

Andersen, Kurt. *True Believers: A Novel*. New York: Random House, 2012.

Anderson, Terry H. *The Movement and the Sixties*. New York: Oxford University Press, 1996.

———. *The Sixties*. New York: Longman, 1999.

Appy, Christian G. *Working-Class War: American Combat Soldiers and Vietnam*. Chapel Hill: University of North Carolina Press, 1993.

Ayers, Bill. *Fugitive Days: A Memoir*. New York: Beacon Press, 2001.

———. *Public Enemy: Confessions of an American Dissident*. Boston: Beacon Press, 2013.

Baker, Mark. *Nam: The Vietnam War in the Words of the Men and Women Who Fought There*. New York: William Morrow, 1981.

Barbato, Carole A., Laura L. Davis, and Mark F. Seeman. *This We Know: A Chronology of the Shootings at Kent State, May 1970*. Kent, OH: Kent State University Press, 2012.

Bass, Paul, and Douglas W. Rae. *Murder in the Model City: The Black Panthers, Yale, and the Redemption of a Killer*. New York: Basic Books, 2006.

Bates, Milton J., Lawrence Lichty, and others, comps. *Reporting Vietnam*. Vol. 1, *American Journalism, 1959–1969*. Vol. 2, *American Journalism, 1969–1975*. New York: Literary Classics of the United States, 1998.

Bates, Tom. *Rads: The 1970 Bombing of the Army Math Research Center at the University of Wisconsin and Its Aftermath*. New York: HarperCollins, 1992.

Berger, Dan. *Outlaws of America: The Weather Underground and the Politics of Solidarity*. Oakland, CA: AK Press, 2006.

Berrigan, Daniel. *Night Flight to Hanoi: War Diary with 11 Poems*. New York: Macmillan, 1968.

Biondi, Martha. *The Black Revolution on Campus.* Berkeley: University of California Press, 2012.

Black, Jonathan. *Radical Lawyers: Their Role in the Movement and in the Courts.* [New York]: Avon, 1971.

Bloom, Alexander, ed. *Long Time Gone: Sixties America Then and Now.* New York: Oxford University Press, 2001.

———, and Wini Breines, eds. *"Takin' It to the Streets": A Sixties Reader.* New York: Oxford University Press, 1995.

Bloom, Joshua, and Waldo E. Martin, Jr. *Black Against Empire: The History and Politics of the Black Panther Party.* Berkeley: University of California Press, 2013.

Booth, Stanley. *The True Adventures of the Rolling Stones.* Cambridge: Granta, 1984.

Bosworth, Patricia. *Jane Fonda: The Private Life of a Public Woman.* Boston: Houghton Mifflin Harcourt, 2011.

Brightman, Carol. *Sweet Chaos: The Grateful Dead's American Adventure.* New York: Clarkson Potter, 1998.

Brinkley, Douglas. *Tour of Duty: John Kerry and the Vietnam War.* New York: William Morrow, 2004.

———, and Luke Nichter, eds. *The Nixon Tapes, 1971–1972.* Boston: Houghton Mifflin Harcourt, 2014.

Brown, Elaine. *A Taste of Power: A Black Woman's Story.* New York: Pantheon Books, 1992.

Brown, Wesley. *Push Comes to Shove: A Novel.* Concord, MA: Concord Free Press, 2009.

Browne, David. *Fire and Rain: The Beatles, Simon and Garfunkel, James Taylor, CSNY, and the Lost Story of 1970.* Cambridge, MA: Da Capo Press, 2011.

Brownmiller, Susan. *In Our Time: Memoir of a Revolution.* New York: Dial Press, 1999.

Bugliosi, Vincent, with Curt Gentry. *Helter Skelter: The True Story of the Manson Murders.* New York: Norton, 1974.

Buhle, Mari Jo, Paul Buhle, and Harvey J. Kaye, eds. *The American Radical.* New York: Routledge, 1994.

Burrough, Bryan. *Days of Rage: America's Radical Underground, the FBI, and the Forgotten Age of Revolutionary Violence.* New York: Penguin Press, 2015.

Capps, Walter, ed. *The Vietnam Reader.* New York: Routledge, 1991.

Caputo, Philip. *13 Seconds: A Look Back at the Kent State Shootings.* New York: Chamberlain Brothers, 2005.

Carlsson, Chris, with Lisa Ruth Elliott, eds. *Ten Years That Shook the City: San Francisco, 1968–1978; A Reclaiming San Francisco Book*. San Francisco: City Lights Foundation Books, 2011.

Chafe, William H. *The Unfinished Journey: America Since World War II*. New York: Oxford University Press, 1986.

Choi, Susan. *American Woman: A Novel*. New York: Perennial, 2004.

Churchill, Ward, and Jim Vander Wall. *Agents of Repression: The FBI's Secret Wars Against the Black Panther Party and the American Indian Movement*. Cambridge, MA: South End Press, 1988.

———. *The COINTELPRO Papers: Documents from the FBI's Secret Wars Against Domestic Dissent*. Cambridge, MA: South End Press, 1990.

Cleaver, Eldridge. *Soul on Ice*. New York: Dell, 1968.

Collier, Peter, and David Horowitz. *Destructive Generation: Second Thoughts About the Sixties*. New York: Summit Books, 1989.

———, eds. *Second Thoughts: Former Radicals Look Back at the Sixties*. Lanham, MD: Madison Books, 1989.

Collins, Gail. *When Everything Changed: The Amazing Journey of American Women from 1960 to the Present*. New York: Little, Brown, 2009.

Conners, Peter. *White Hand Society: The Psychedelic Partnership of Timothy Leary and Allen Ginsberg*. San Francisco: City Lights Books, 2010.

Coontz, Stephanie. *A Strange Stirring:* The Feminine Mystique *and American Women at the Dawn of the 1960s*. New York: Basic Books, 2012.

Cortright, David. *Soldiers in Revolt: The American Military Today*. New York: Anchor Press, 1975.

Coyote, Peter. *The Rainman's Third Cure: An Irregular Education*. Berkeley: Counterpoint, 2015.

———. *Sleeping Where I Fall: A Chronicle*. Washington, DC: Counterpoint, 1998.

Currey, Cecil Barr. *Long Binh Jail: An Oral History of Vietnam's Notorious U.S. Military Prison*. Washington, DC: Brassey's, 1999.

Dang Thuy Tram. *Last Night I Dreamed of Peace: The Diary of Dang Thuy Tram*. Translated by Andrew X. Pham. London: Rider, 2007.

Dass, Ram, and Ralph Metzner, with Gary Bravo and commentaries by other contributors. *Birth of a Psychedelic Culture: Conversations About Leary, the Harvard Experiments, Millbrook and the Sixties*. Santa Fe, NM: Synergetic Press, 2010.

Davies, Peter, and the Board of Church and Society of the United Methodist Church. *The Truth About Kent State: A Challenge to the American Conscience*. New York: Farrar, Straus & Giroux, 1973.

Davis, Stephen. *More Room in a Broken Heart: The True Adventures of Carly Simon*. Photographs by Peter Simon. New York: Gotham Books, 2012.

Dean, John W. *The Nixon Defense: What He Knew and When He Knew It*. New York: Penguin Books, 2015.

DeBenedetti, Charles, and Charles Chatfield, assisting author. *An American Ordeal: The Antiwar Movement of the Vietnam Era*. Syracuse, NY: Syracuse University Press, 1990.

Didion, Joan. *The White Album*. New York: Simon & Schuster, 1979.

Dohrn, Bernardine, Bill Ayers, and Jeff Jones, eds. *Sing a Battle Song: The Revolutionary Poetry, Statements, and Communiqués of the Weather Underground, 1970–1974*. New York: Seven Stories Press, 2006.

Ellsberg, Daniel. *Secrets: A Memoir of Vietnam and the Pentagon Papers*. New York: Viking Press, 2002.

Ephron, Nora. *Wallflower at the Orgy*. New York: Viking Press, 1970.

Epstein, Jason. *The Great Conspiracy Trial: An Essay on Law, Liberty, and the Constitution*. New York: Random House, 1970.

Farber, David, ed. *The Sixties: From Memory to History*. Chapel Hill: University of North Carolina Press, 1994.

Felt, Mark, and John O'Connor. *A G-Man's Life: The FBI, Being "Deep Throat," and the Struggle for Honor in Washington*. New York: PublicAffairs, 2006.

Fonda, Jane. *My Life So Far*. New York: Random House, 2005.

Forbes, Flores A. *Will You Die with Me? My Life and the Black Panther Party*. New York: Atria Books, 2006.

Freed, Donald. *Agony in New Haven: The Trial of Bobby Seale, Ericka Huggins, and the Black Panther Party*. New York: Simon & Schuster, 1973.

Friedan, Betty. *The Feminine Mystique*. New York: Norton, 1963.

Garvy, Helen. *Rebels with a Cause: A Collective Memoir of the Hopes, Rebellions, and Repression of the 1960s*. Los Gatos, CA: Shire Press, 2007.

Gitlin, Todd. *The Sixties: Years of Hope, Days of Rage*. New York: Bantam Books, 1987.

——. *The Whole World Is Watching: Mass Media in the Making and Unmaking of the New Left*. Berkeley: University of California Press, 1980.

Glick, Brian. *War at Home: Covert Action Against U.S. Activists and What We Can Do About It*. Boston: South End Press, 1989.

Goodale, James C. *Fighting for the Press: The Inside Story of the Pentagon Papers and Other Battles*. New York: CUNY Journalism Press, 2013.

Gordon, Neil. *The Company You Keep*. New York: Penguin Books, 2013.

Gordon, William A. *Four Dead in Ohio: Was There a Conspiracy at Kent State?*

Laguna Hills, CA: North Ridge Books, 1995. Originally published in 1990 as *The Fourth of May: Killings and Coverups at Kent State,* by Prometheus Books.

Gore, Dayo F., Jeanne Theoharis, and Komozi Woodard, eds. *Want to Start a Revolution? Radical Women in the Black Freedom Struggle.* New York: New York University Press, 2009.

Gottlieb, Annie. *Do You Believe in Magic? The Second Coming of the Sixties Generation.* New York: Times Books, 1987.

Grathwohl, Larry, as told to Frank Reagan. *Bringing Down America: An FBI Informer with the Weathermen.* New Rochelle, NY: Arlington House, 1976.

Green, Jonathon. *Days in the Life: Voices from the English Underground, 1961–71.* London: William Heinemann, 1988.

Greenfield, Robert. *Timothy Leary: A Biography.* Orlando, FL: Harcourt, 2006.

Grof, Stanislav. *LSD: Doorway to the Numinous: The Groundbreaking Psychedelic Research into Realms of the Human Unconscious.* Rochester, VT: Park Street Press, 2009. Originally published in 1975 as *Realms of the Human Unconscious: Observations from LSD Research,* by Viking Press.

Groff, Lauren. *Arcadia.* New York: Voice/Hyperion, 2012.

Guinn, Jeff. *Manson: The Life and Times of Charles Manson.* New York: Simon & Schuster, 2013.

Haas, Jeffrey. *The Assassination of Fred Hampton: How the FBI and the Chicago Police Murdered a Black Panther.* Chicago: Lawrence Hill Books/Chicago Review Press, 2010.

Halberstam, David. *The Making of a Quagmire.* New York: Random House, 1965.

Haldeman, H. R. *The Haldeman Diaries: Inside the Nixon White House.* New York: G. P. Putnam's Sons, 1994.

Halpert, Stephen, and Tom Murray, eds. *Witness of the Berrigans.* Garden City, NY: Doubleday, 1972.

Halstead, Fred. *Out Now! A Participant's Account of the American Movement Against the Vietnam War.* New York: Monad Press, 1978.

Hampton, Henry, and Steve Fayer, comps., with Sarah Flynn. *Voices of Freedom: An Oral History of the Civil Rights Movement from the 1950s Through the 1980s.* New York: Bantam Books, 1990.

Hantschel, Allison. *It Doesn't End with Us: The Story of the* Daily Cardinal: *How a College Newspaper's Fight for Freedom Changed Its University, Challenged Journalism, and Influenced Hundreds of Lives.* Westminster, MD: Heritage Books, 2007.

Harris, David. *Dreams Die Hard.* New York: St. Martin's/Marek, 1982.

———. *Our War: What We Did in Vietnam and What It Did to Us*. New York: Times Books, 1996.

Harris, Mark. *Pictures at a Revolution: Five Movies and the Birth of the New Hollywood*. New York: Penguin Press, 2008.

Hayden, Tom. *The Long Sixties: From 1960 to Barack Obama*. Boulder, CO: Paradigm, 2010.

Hayes, Harold, comp. *Smiling Through the Apocalypse:* Esquire's *History of the Sixties*. New York: McCall, 1969.

Hensley, Thomas R., and Jerry M. Lewis. *Kent State and May 4th: A Social Science Perspective*. Dubuque, IA: Kendall/Hunt, 1978.

Herr, Michael. *Dispatches*. New York: Knopf, 1977.

Hersh, Seymour. *The Price of Power: Kissinger in the Nixon White House*. New York: Summit Books/Simon & Schuster, 1983.

Hershberger, Mary. *Jane Fonda's War: A Political Biography of an Antiwar Icon*. New York: New Press, 2005.

Hilliard, David, and Lewis Cole. *This Side of Glory: The Autobiography of David Hilliard and the Story of the Black Panther Party*. Boston: Little, Brown, 1993.

Hoffman, Abbie. *The Autobiography of Abbie Hoffman*. With an introduction by Norman Mailer. New York: Four Walls Eight Windows, 2000. Originally published in 1980 as *Soon to Be a Major Motion Picture,* by G. P. Putnam's Sons.

———. *The Best of Abbie Hoffman*. Edited by Daniel Simon with the author. With a foreword by Norman Mailer. New York: Four Walls Eight Windows, 1989.

———. *Steal This Book*. New York: Pirate Editions, 1971.

———. *Woodstock Nation: A Talk-Rock Album*. New York: Random House, 1969.

Hoffman, Paul. *Moratorium: An American Protest*. New York: Tower, 1970.

Holland, Max. *Leak: Why Mark Felt Became Deep Throat*. Lawrence: University Press of Kansas, 2012.

Horn, Miriam. *Rebels in White Gloves: Coming of Age with Hillary's Class, Wellesley '69*. New York: Times Books, 1999.

Hunt, Andrew E. *The Turning: A History of Vietnam Veterans Against the War*. New York: New York University Press, 1999.

Isserman, Maurice, and Michael Kazin. *America Divided: The Civil War of the 1960s*. New York: Oxford University Press, 2000.

Jacobs, Harold. *Weatherman*. Berkeley: Ramparts Press, 1970.

Jacobs, Ron. *The Way the Wind Blew: A History of the Weather Underground*. London: Verso, 1997.

Jones, Thai. *A Radical Line: From the Labor Movement to the Weather Underground, One Family's Century of Conscience*. New York: Free Press, 2004.

Joseph, Jamal. *Panther Baby: A Life of Rebellion and Reinvention*. Chapel Hill, NC: Algonquin Books of Chapel Hill, 2012.

Kaiser, Charles. *The Gay Metropolis, 1940–1996*. Boston: Houghton Mifflin, 1997.

———. *1968 in America: Music, Politics, Chaos, Counterculture, and the Shaping of a Generation*. New York: Weidenfeld & Nicolson, 1988.

Karlin, Wayne. *Wandering Souls: Journeys with the Dead and the Living in Viet Nam*. New York: Nation Books, 2009.

Karnow, Stanley. *Vietnam: A History*. New York: Viking Press, 1983.

Kaufman, Michael T. *1968*. New York: Roaring Brook Press, 2008.

Kazin, Michael. *The Populist Persuasion: An American History*. New York: Basic Books, 1995.

Kelman, Steven. *Push Comes to Shove: The Escalation of Student Protest*. Boston: Houghton Mifflin, 1970.

Kelner, Joseph, and James Munves. *The Kent State Coverup*. New York: Harper & Row, 1980.

Kempton, Murray. *The Briar Patch: The People of the State of New York v. Lumumba Shakur et al*. New York: Dutton, 1973.

Kerrey, Bob. *When I Was a Young Man: A Memoir*. New York: Harcourt, 2002.

Kesey, Ken. *Sometimes a Great Notion: A Novel*. New York: Viking Press, 1964.

Kidder, Tracy. *My Detachment: A Memoir*. New York: Random House, 2006.

Kimball, Roger. *The Long March: How the Cultural Revolution of the 1960s Changed America*. San Francisco: Encounter Books, 2001.

Kirkpatrick, Rob. *1969: The Year Everything Changed*. New York: Skyhorse, 2009.

Kisseloff, Jeff. *Generation on Fire: Voices of Protest from the 1960s: An Oral History*. Lexington: University Press of Kentucky, 2007.

Kissinger, Henry. *Ending the Vietnam War: A History of America's Involvement in and Extrication from the Vietnam War*. New York: Simon & Schuster, 2003.

Kloss, Jethro. *Back to Eden: A Human Interest Story of Health and Restoration to Be Found in Herb, Root, and Bark*. Coalmont, TN: Longview, 1939.

Kreutzmann, Bill, with Benjy Eisen. *Deal: My Three Decades of Drumming, Dreams, and Drugs with the Grateful Dead*. New York: St. Martin's Press, 2015.

Krogh, Egil "Bud," with Matthew Krogh. *Integrity: Good People, Bad Choices, and Life Lessons from the White House*. New York: PublicAffairs, 2007.

Kurlansky, Mark. *1968: The Year That Rocked the World*. New York: Ballantine, 2004.

Lang, Michael, with Holly George-Warren. *The Road to Woodstock*. New York, Ecco, 2010.

Lattin, Don. *The Harvard Psychedelic Club: How Timothy Leary, Ram Dass, Huston Smith, and Andrew Weil Killed the Fifties and Ushered in a New Age for America*. New York: HarperOne, 2010.

Leary, Timothy, Ralph Metzner, and Richard Alpert. *The Psychedelic Experience: A Manual Based on the Tibetan Book of the Dead*. New York: University Books, 1964.

Lee, Martin A., and Bruce Shlain. *Acid Dreams: The CIA, LSD, and the Sixties Rebellion*. New York: Grove Press, 1985.

Lembcke, Jerry. *The Spitting Image: Myth, Memory, and the Legacy of Vietnam*. New York: New York University Press, 1998.

Lester, Julius. *Look Out, Whitey! Black Power's Gon' Get Your Mama!* New York: Dial Press, 1968.

———. *Revolutionary Notes*. New York: R. W. Baron, 1969.

———. *Search for the New Land: History as Subjective Experience*. New York: Dial Press, 1969.

Lewis, John, with Michael D'Orso. *Walking with the Wind: A Memoir of the Movement*. New York: Simon & Schuster, 1998.

Lewis, Penny. *Hardhats, Hippies, and Hawks: The Vietnam Antiwar Movement as Myth and Memory*. Ithaca, NY: ILR Press, 2013.

Lifton, Robert Jay. *Home from the War: Vietnam Veterans: Neither Victims Nor Executioners*. New York: Simon & Schuster, 1973.

Lipset, Seymour Martin. *Rebellion in the University*. Boston: Little, Brown, 1971.

Magruder, Jeb Stuart. *An American Life: One Man's Road to Watergate*. New York: Atheneum, 1974.

Mailer, Norman. *The Armies of the Night: History as a Novel, the Novel as History*. New York: New American Library, 1968.

Makower, Joel. *Woodstock: The Oral History*. New York: Doubleday, 1989.

Mao Zedong. *Quotations from Chairman Mao Tse-Tung*. Translation of *Mao Chu Hsi Yü Lu*. Edited by Stuart R. Schram. New York: Praeger, 1967.

Maraniss, David. *They Marched into Sunlight: War and Peace, Vietnam and America, October 1967*. New York: Simon & Schuster, 2003.

Marcus, Greil. *Mystery Train: Images of America in Rock 'n' Roll Music*. New York: Dutton, 1975.

Maroon, Fred J., and Tom Wicker. *The Nixon Years, 1969–1974: White House to Watergate*. New York: Abbeville Press, 1999.

Massa, Mark S. *The American Catholic Revolution: How the Sixties Changed the Church Forever*. New York: Oxford University Press, 2010.

McCarthy, Timothy Patrick, and John McMillian, eds. *Protest Nation: Words That Inspired a Century of American Radicalism*. New York: New Press, 2010.

McMillian, John. *Smoking Typewriters: The Sixties Underground Press and the Rise of Alternative Media in America*. New York: Oxford University Press, 2011.

McNally, Dennis. *A Long Strange Trip: The Inside History of the Grateful Dead*. New York: Broadway Books, 2002.

Medsger, Betty. *The Burglary: The Discovery of J. Edgar Hoover's Secret FBI*. New York: Knopf, 2014.

Michener, James A. *Kent State: What Happened and Why*. New York: Random House, 1971.

Milam, Ron. *Not a Gentleman's War: An Inside View of Junior Officers in the Vietnam War*. Chapel Hill: University of North Carolina Press, 2009.

Miles, Barry. *In the Seventies: Adventures in the Counter-Culture*. London: Serpent's Tail, 2011.

Miller, Timothy. *The 60s Communes: Hippies and Beyond*. Syracuse, NY: Syracuse University Press, 1999.

Millett, Kate. *Sexual Politics*. Garden City, NY: Doubleday, 1970.

Miraldi, Robert. *Seymour Hersh: Scoop Artist*. Lincoln, NE: Potomac Books, 2013.

Mixner, David. *Stranger Among Friends*. New York: Bantam Books, 1996.

Morgan, Robin. *The Demon Lover: On the Sexuality of Terrorism*. New York: Norton, 1989.

———. *Going Too Far: The Personal Chronicle of a Feminist*. New York: Random House, 1977.

———, ed. *Sisterhood Is Powerful: An Anthology of Writings from the Women's Liberation Movement*. New York: Random House, 1970.

———. *The Word of a Woman: Feminist Dispatches, 1968–1992*. New York: Norton, 1992.

Morris, Roger. *Uncertain Greatness: Henry Kissinger and American Foreign Policy*. New York: Harper & Row, 1977.

Morrison, Joan, and Robert K. Morrison. *From Camelot to Kent State: The Sixties Experience in the Words of Those Who Lived It*. New York: Times Books, 1987.

Mungo, Raymond. *Famous Long Ago: My Life and Hard Times with Liberation News Service*. Boston: Beacon Press, 1970.

Neale, Jonathan. *A People's History of the Vietnam War*. New York: New Press, 2003. Originally published in 2001 as *The American War: Vietnam, 1960–1975*, by Bookmarks.

Newton, Huey P. *The Huey P. Newton Reader*. Edited by David Hilliard and Donald Weise. New York: Seven Stories Press, 2002.

Nicosia, Gerald. *Home to War: A History of the Vietnam Veterans' Movement*. New York: Crown, 2001.

Nixon, Richard M. *RN: The Memoirs of Richard Nixon*. New York: Grosset & Dunlap, 1978.

O'Brien, Tim. *The Things They Carried: A Work of Fiction*. Boston: Houghton Mifflin, 1990.

O'Rourke, P. J. *The Baby Boom: How It Got That Way and It Wasn't My Fault and I'll Never Do It Again*. New York: Atlantic Monthly Press, 2014.

Oudes, Bruce, ed. *From the President: Richard Nixon's Secret Files*. New York: Harper & Row, 1989.

Payne, Charles M. *I've Got the Light of Freedom: The Organizing Tradition and the Mississippi Freedom Struggle*. Berkeley: University of California Press, 1995.

Payne, Cril. *Deep Cover: An FBI Agent Infiltrates the Radical Underground*. New York: Newsweek Books, 1979.

Perlstein, Rick. *Nixonland: The Rise of a President and the Fracturing of America*. New York: Scribner, 2008.

Pickering, Leslie James. *Mad Bomber Melville*. Portland, OR: Arissa Media Group, 2007.

Povich, Lynn. *The Good Girls Revolt: How the Women of* Newsweek *Sued Their Bosses and Changed the Workplace*. New York: PublicAffairs, 2012.

Powers, Thomas. *Vietnam, the War at Home: Vietnam and the American People, 1964–1968*. Boston: G. K. Hall, 1984. Originally published in 1973 as *The War at Home: Vietnam and the American People, 1964–1968* by Grossman.

Price, Raymond. *With Nixon*. New York: Viking Press, 1977.

Raskin, Jonah. *For the Hell of It: The Life and Times of Abbie Hoffman*. Berkeley: University of California Press, 1996.

———, ed. *The Weather Eye: Communiques from the Weather Underground, May 1970–May 1974*. San Francisco: Union Square Press, 1974.

Reeves, Richard. *President Nixon: Alone in the White House*. New York: Simon & Schuster, 2001.

Reich, Charles. *The Greening of America*. New York: Random House, 1970.

Richardson, Peter. *A Bomb in Every Issue: How the Short, Unruly Life of* Ramparts *Magazine Changed America*. New York: New Press, 2009.

Riesman, David, in collaboration with Reuel Denney and Nathan Glazer. *The Lonely Crowd: A Study of the Changing American Character*. New Haven, CT: Yale University Press, 1950.

Riordan, James. *Stone: The Controversies, Excesses, and Exploits of a Radical Filmmaker*. New York: Hyperion, 1995.

Rome, Adam. *The Genius of Earth Day: How a 1970 Teach-In Unexpectedly Made the First Green Generation*. New York: Hill & Wang, 2013.

Rosen, Ruth. *The World Split Open: How the Modern Women's Movement Changed America*. New York: Viking Press, 2000.

Roszak, Theodore. *The Making of a Counter Culture: Reflections on the Technocratic Society and Its Youthful Opposition*. Garden City, NY: Doubleday, 1969.

Rubin, Jerry. *We Are Everywhere*. New York: Harper & Row, 1971.

Sale, Kirkpatrick. *SDS*. New York: Random House, 1973.

Sanders, Ed. *The Family: The Story of Charles Manson's Dune Buggy Attack Battalion*. New York: Dutton, 1971.

———. *Fug You: An Informal History of the Peace Eye Bookstore, the Fuck You Press, the Fugs, and Counterculture in the Lower East Side*. Cambridge, MA: Da Capo Press, 2011.

Schell, Jonathan. *The Village of Ben Suc*. New York: Knopf, 1967.

Schou, Nicholas. *Orange Sunshine: The Brotherhood of Eternal Love and Its Quest to Spread Peace, Love, and Acid to the World*. New York: Thomas Dunne Books, 2010.

Smith, Richard Norton. *The Harvard Century: The Making of a University to a Nation*. New York: Simon & Schuster, 1986.

Spiotta, Dana. *Eat the Document: A Novel*. New York: Scribner, 2006.

Stein, Jean, edited with George Plimpton. *Edie: An American Biography*. New York: Knopf, 1982.

Steinem, Gloria. *Outrageous Acts and Everyday Rebellions*. New York: Holt, Rinehart, & Winston, 1983.

Stern, Susan. *With the Weathermen: The Personal Journal of a Revolutionary Woman*. New York: Doubleday, 1975.

Stone, Robert. *Dog Soldiers: A Novel*. Boston: Houghton Mifflin, 1974.

Strausbaugh, John. *The Village: 400 Years of Beats and Bohemians, Radicals and Rogues: A History of Greenwich Village*. New York: Ecco, 2013.

Terry, Wallace, ed. *Bloods: An Oral History of the Vietnam War*. New York: Random House, 1984.

Thomas, Evan. *Being Nixon: A Man Divided*. New York: Random House, 2015.

Uhl, Michael. *Vietnam Awakening: My Journey from Combat to the Citizens' Commission of Inquiry on U.S. War Crimes in Vietnam*. Jefferson, NC: McFarland, 2007.

Von Hoffman, Nicholas. *We Are the People Our Parents Warned Us Against*. Chicago: Quadrangle Books, 1968.

Wasserstein, Wendy. *The Heidi Chronicles*. Garden City, NY: Fireside Theatre, 1989.

Weiner, Tim. *Enemies: A History of the FBI*. New York: Random House, 2012.

Weller, Sheila. *Girls Like Us: Carole King, Joni Mitchell, Carly Simon—and the Journey of a Generation*. New York: Atria Books, 2008.

Wells, Tom. *The War Within: America's Battle over Vietnam*. Berkeley: University of California Press, 1994.

Wiener, Jon, ed. *Conspiracy in the Streets: The Extraordinary Trial of the Chicago Eight*. New York: New Press, 2006.

———. *Gimme Some Truth: The John Lennon FBI Files*. Berkeley: University of California Press, 1999.

Wilentz, Sean. *Bob Dylan in America*. New York: Doubleday, 2010.

Wilkerson, Cathy. *Flying Close to the Sun: My Life and Times as a Weatherman*. New York: Seven Stories Press, 2007.

Williams, Reese, ed. *Unwinding the Vietnam War: From War into Peace*. Seattle: Real Comet Press, 1987.

Wolfe, Tom. *The Electric Kool-Aid Acid Test*. New York: Farrar, Straus & Giroux, 1968.

Wolff, Tobias. *In Pharaoh's Army: Memories of the Lost War*. New York: Knopf, 1994.

Woodward, Bob. *The Last of the President's Men*. New York: Simon & Schuster, 2015.

———. *The Secret Man: The Story of Watergate's Deep Throat*. With a reporter's assessment by Carl Bernstein. New York: Simon & Schuster, 2005.

Yablonsky, Lewis. *The Hippie Trip*. New York: Pegasus, 1968.

Young, Neil. *Waging Heavy Peace: A Hippie Dream*. New York: Blue Rider Press, 2012.

Zimroth, Peter L. *Perversions of Justice: The Prosecution and Acquittal of the Panther 21*. New York: Viking Press, 1974.

Zinn, Howard. *A People's History of the United States*. New York: Harper & Row, 1980.

PERMISSION CREDITS

ILLUSTRATION CREDITS

Page 193: The Richard Nixon Presidential Library and Museum (National Archives and Records Administration)

Page 198: Fred W. McDarrah/Getty Images

Page 200: © Bettmann/Corbis

Page 201: AP Photo

Page 213: Courtesy of Oliver Stone

Page 223: AP Photo

Page 227: Cleveland *Plain Dealer* Archives

Page 228: *Time* Magazine Archives

Page 232: © Jim Marshall Photography LLC

Page 244: Keystone-France/Gamma-Keystone via Getty Images

Page 246: Paul Sequeira/Getty Images

Page 247: Paul Sequeira/Getty Images

Page 249: Paul Sequeira/Getty Images

Page 254: © Robert Altman

Page 255: © Robert Altman

Page 284: AP Photo

Page 291: Jean-Pierre Laffont/Sygma/Corbis

Page 302: Jack Clarity/New York *Daily News* Archive via Getty Images

Page 303: Fred W. McDarrah/Getty Images

Page 316: © Stephen Shames/Polaris Images

Page 321: © Robert Altman

Page 332: Alix Kates Shulman

Page 334: Fred W. McDarrah/Getty Images

Page 338: ullstein bild via Getty Images

Page 359: Courtesy of Laurel Krause

Page 365: © Bettmann/Corbis

Page 368: John Filo/Getty Images

Page 372: John Filo/Getty Images

Page 384: © Stephen Shames/Polaris Images

Page 389: Amherst College Archives and Special Collections

Page 390: © Stephen Shames/Polaris Images

Page 392 (top): © Stephen Shames/Polaris Images

Page 392 (bottom): Syracuse University Archives

Page 395: Spencer Grant/Boston Public Library

Page 402: David Fenton/Getty Images

Page 405: © Bettmann/Corbis, photo by Bob Moustakas

Page 408: © Bettmann/Corbis

Page 424: © Bettmann/Corbis

Page 440: Chuck Gould Photography

Page 442: Chuck Gould Photography

Page 444: Courtesy of Carol and Michael Randall

Page 445: Courtesy of Carol and Michael Randall

Page 450: © Robert Altman

Page 466: Fred W. McDarrah/Getty Images

Page 467: © Stephen Shames/Polaris Images

Page 476: Wisconsin Historical Society

Page 503: © Bettmann/Corbis

Page 516: AP Photo/ Nihon Denpa News

INDEX

Page numbers in *italics* refer to illustrations.

ABOUT THE AUTHOR

CLARA BINGHAM is the author of *Class Action: The Landmark Case That Changed Sexual Harassment Law* (with Laura Leedy Gansler) and *Women on the Hill: Challenging the Culture of Congress*. She is a former *Newsweek* White House correspondent, and her writing has appeared in *Vanity Fair*, *Vogue*, *Harper's Bazaar*, *Talk*, *The Washington Monthly*, *Ms.*, and other publications. Bingham produced the 2011 documentary *The Last Mountain*. She lives in Manhattan and Brooklyn with her husband, three children, and three stepchildren.